# ELDER LAW:
## SELECTED STATUTES
## AND REGULATIONS

### 2007 Edition

# LexisNexis Law School Publishing Advisory Board

# ELDER LAW:
## SELECTED STATUTES AND REGULATIONS

### 2007 Edition

**Lawrence A. Frolik**
*Professor of Law*
*University of Pittsburgh*
*School of Law*

**Alison McChrystal Barnes**
*Professor of Law*
*Marquette University*
*Law School*

---

**NOTE TO USERS**

To ensure that you are using the latest materials available in this area, please be sure to periodically check the LexisNexis Law School web site for downloadable updates and supplements at www.lexisnexis.com/lawschool

---

Editorial Offices
744 Broad Street, Newark, NJ 07102 (973) 820-2000
201 Mission St., San Francisco, CA 94105-1831 (415) 908-3200
701 East Water Street, Charlottesville, VA 22902-7587 (434) 972-7600
www.lexis.com

(Pub.03039)

# Table of Contents

# National Housing Act

12 U.S.C. § 1701 et seq.

## § 1701q. Supportive housing for the elderly

### (a) *Purpose*

The purpose of this section is to enable elderly persons to live with dignity and independence by expanding the supply of supportive housing that —

(1) is designed to accommodate the special needs of elderly persons; and

(2) provides a range of services that are tailored to the needs of elderly persons occupying such housing.

. . . .

### (c) *Forms of assistance*

#### (1) Capital advances

A capital advance provided under this section shall bear no interest and its repayment shall not be required so long as the housing remains available for very low-income elderly in accordance with this section. Such advance shall be in an amount calculated in accordance with the development cost limitation established in subsection (h).

#### (2) Project rental assistance

Contracts for project rental assistance shall obligate the Secretary to make monthly payments to cover any part of the costs attributed to units occupied (or, as approved by the Secretary, held for occupancy) by very low-income elderly persons that is not met from project income. The annual contract amount for any project shall not exceed the sum of the initial annual project rentals for all units so occupied and any initial utility allowances for such units, as approved by the Secretary. Any contract amounts not used by a project in any year shall remain available to the project until the expiration of the contract. The Secretary may adjust the annual contract amount if the sum of the project income and the amount of assistance payments available under this paragraph are inadequate to provide for reasonable project costs.

#### (3) Tenant rent contribution

A very low-income person shall pay as rent for a dwelling unit assisted under this section the highest of the following amounts, rounded to the nearest dollar:  (A) 30 percent of the person's adjusted monthly income, (B) 10 percent of the person's monthly income, or (C) if the person is receiving payments for welfare assistance from a public agency and a part of such payments, adjusted in accordance with the person's actual housing costs, is specifically designated agency to meet the person's housing costs, the portion of such payments which is so designated.

(d) *Term of commitment*

(1)  Use limitations

All units in housing assisted under this section shall be made available for occupancy by very low-income elderly persons for not less than 40 years.

(2)  Contract terms

The initial term of a contract entered into under subsection (c)(2) shall be 240 months. The Secretary shall, to the extent approved in appropriation Acts, extend any expiring contract for a term of not less than 60 months. In order to facilitate the orderly extension of expiring contracts, the Secretary is authorized to make commitments to extend expiring contracts during the year prior to the date of expiration.

(e) *Applications*

Funds made available under this section shall be allocated by the Secretary among approvable applications submitted by private nonprofit organizations. Applications for assistance under this section shall be submitted by an applicant in such form and in accordance with such procedures as the Secretary shall establish. Such applications shall contain —

(1) a description of the proposed housing;

(2) a description of the assistance the applicant seeks under this section;

(3) a description of the resources that are expected to be made available in compliance with subsection (h);

(4) a description of (A) the category or categories of elderly persons the housing is intended to serve; (B) the supportive services, if any, to be provided to the persons occupying such housing; (C) the manner in which such services will be provided to such persons, including, in the case of frail elderly persons, evidence of such residential supervision as the Secretary determines is necessary to facilitate the adequate provision of such services; and (D) the public

or private sources of assistance that can reasonably be expected to fund or provide such services;

(5) a certification from the public official responsible for submitting a housing strategy for the jurisdiction to be served in accordance with section 105 of the Cranston-Gonzalez National Affordable Housing Act that the proposed project is consistent with the housing strategy; and

(6) such other information or certifications that the Secretary determines to be necessary or appropriate to achieve the purposes of this section.

The Secretary shall not reject an application on technical grounds without giving notice of that rejection and the basis therefor to the applicant and affording the applicant an opportunity to respond.

(f) *Selection criteria*

The Secretary shall establish selection criteria for assistance under this section, which shall include —

(1) the ability of the applicant to develop and operate the proposed housing;

(2) the need for supportive housing for the elderly in the area to be served, taking into consideration the availability of public housing for the elderly and vacancy rates in such facilities;

(3) the extent to which the proposed size and unit mix of the housing will enable the applicant to manage and operate the housing efficiently and ensure that the provision of supportive services will be accomplished in an economical fashion;

(4) the extent to which the proposed design of the housing will meet the special physical needs of elderly persons;

(5) the extent to which the applicant has demonstrated that the supportive services identified in subsection (e)(4) will be provided on a consistent, long-term basis;

(6) the extent to which the proposed design of the housing will accommodate the provision of supportive services that are expected to be needed, either initially or over the useful life of the housing, by the category or categories of elderly persons the housing is intended to serve; and

(7) such other factors as the Secretary determines to be appropriate to ensure that funds made available under this section are used effectively.

(g) *Provisions of services*

### (1) In general

In carrying out the provisions of this section, the Secretary shall ensure that housing assisted under this section provides a range of services tailored to the needs of the category or categories of elderly persons (including frail elderly persons) occupying such housing. Such services may include (A) meal service adequate to meet nutritional need; (B) housekeeping aid; (C) personal assistance; (D) transportation services; (E) health-related services; (F) providing education and outreach regarding telemarketing fraud, in accordance with the standards issued under section 671(f) of the Housing and Community Development Act of 1992 (f)); and (G) such other services as the Secretary deems essential for maintaining independent living. The Secretary may permit the provision of services to elderly persons who are not residents if the participation of such persons will not adversely affect the cost-effectiveness or operation of the program or add significantly to the need for assistance under this Act.

### (2) Local coordination of services

The Secretary shall ensure that owners have the managerial capacity to —

(A) assess on an ongoing basis the service needs of residents;

(B) coordinate the provision of supportive services and tailor such services to the individual needs of residents; and

(C) seek on a continuous basis new sources of assistance to ensure the long-term provision of supportive services.

Any cost associated with this subsection shall be an eligible cost under subsection (c)(2).

### (3) Service coordinators

Any cost associated with employing or otherwise retaining a service coordinator in housing assisted under this section shall be considered an eligible cost under subsection (c)(2). If a project is receiving congregate housing services assistance under section 802 of the Cranston-Gonzalez National Affordable Housing Act, the amount of costs provided under subsection (c)(2) for the project service coordinator may not exceed the additional amount necessary to cover the costs of providing for the coordination of services for residents of the project who are not eligible residents under such section 802. To the extent that amounts are available pursuant to subsection (c)(2) for the costs of carrying out this paragraph within a project, an owner of housing assisted under this section shall provide a service coordinator for the housing to coordinate the provision of services under this subsection within the housing.

. . . .

(k) *Definitions*

(1) The term "elderly person" means a household composed of one or more persons at least one of whom is 62 years of age or more at the time of initial occupancy.

(2) The term "frail elderly" means an elderly person who is unable to perform at least 3 activities of daily living adopted by the Secretary for purposes of this program. Owners may establish additional eligibility requirements (acceptable to the Secretary) based on the standards in local supportive services programs.

(3) The term "owner" means a private nonprofit organization that receives assistance under this section to develop and operate supportive housing for the elderly.

(4) The term "private nonprofit organization" means any incorporated private institution or foundation —

(A) no part of the net earnings of which inures to the benefit of any member, founder, contributor, or individual;

(B) which has a governing board (i) the membership of which is selected in a manner to assure that there is significant representation of the views of the community in which such housing is located, and (ii) which is responsible for the operation of the housing assisted under this section; and

(C) which is approved by the Secretary as to financial responsibility.

Such term includes a for-profit limited partnership the sole general partner of which is an organization meeting the requirements under subparagraphs (A), (B), and (C), or a corporation wholly owned and controlled by an organization meeting the requirements under subparagraphs (A), (B), and (C).

(5) The term "State" includes the several States, the District of Columbia, the Commonwealth of Puerto Rico, and the possessions of the United States.

(6) The term "Secretary" means the Secretary of Housing and Urban Development.

(7) The term "supportive housing for the elderly" means housing that is designed (A) to meet the special physical needs of elderly persons and

(B) to accommodate the provision of supportive services that are expected to be needed, either initially or over the useful life of the housing, by the category or categories of elderly persons that the housing is intended to serve.

(8) The term "very low-income" has the same meaning as given the term "very low-income families" under section 3(b)(2) of the United States Housing Act of 1937.

# Age Discrimination in Employment Act (Excerpts)

29 U.S.C. § 621 et seq.

## § 621. Congressional statement of findings and purpose

(a) The Congress hereby finds and declares that —

(1) in the face of rising productivity and affluence, older workers find themselves disadvantaged in their efforts to retain employment, and especially to regain employment when displaced from jobs;

(2) the setting of arbitrary age limits regardless of potential for job performance has become a common practice, and certain otherwise desirable practices may work to the disadvantage of older persons;

(3) the incidence of unemployment, especially long-term unemployment with resultant deterioration of skill, morale, and employer acceptability is, relative to the younger ages, high among older workers; their numbers are great and growing; and their employment problems grave;

(4) the existence in industries affecting commerce, of arbitrary discrimination in employment because of age, burdens commerce and the free flow of goods in commerce.

(b) It is therefore the purpose of this Act to promote employment of older persons based on their ability rather than age; to prohibit arbitrary age discrimination in employment; to help employers and workers find ways of meeting problems arising from the impact of age on employment.

## § 622.   Education and research program; recommendation to Congress

(a) The Secretary of Labor shall undertake studies and provide information to labor unions, management, and the general public concerning the needs and abilities of older workers, and their potentials for continued employment and contribution to the economy. In order to achieve the purposes of this Act, the Secretary of Labor shall carry on a continuing program of education and information, under which he may, among other measures —

(1) undertake research, and promote research, with a view to reducing barriers to the employment of older persons, and the promotion of measures for utilizing their skills;

(2) publish and otherwise make available to employers, professional societies, the various media of communication, and other interested persons the findings of studies and other materials for the promotion of employment;

(3) foster through the public employment service system and through cooperative effort the development of facilities of public and private agencies for expanding the opportunities and potentials of older persons;

(4) sponsor and assist State and community informational and educational programs.

(b) Not later than six months after the effective date of this Act, the Secretary shall recommend to the Congress any measures he may deem desirable to change the lower or upper age limits set forth in section 12.

## § 623. Prohibition of age discrimination

(a) *Employer practices*

It shall be unlawful for an employer —

(1) to fail or refuse to hire or to discharge any individual or otherwise discriminate against any individual with respect to his compensation, terms, conditions, or privileges of employment, because of such individual's age;

(2) to limit, segregate, or classify his employees in any way which would deprive or tend to deprive any individual of employment opportunities or otherwise adversely affect his status as an employee, because of such individual's age; or

(3) to reduce the wage rate of any employee in order to comply with this Act.

(b) *Employment agency practices*

It shall be unlawful for an employment agency to fail or refuse to refer for employment, or otherwise to discriminate against, any individual because of such individual's age, or to classify or refer for employment any individual on the basis of such individual's age.

(c) *Labor organization practices*

It shall be unlawful for a labor organization —

(1) to exclude or to expel from its membership, or otherwise to discriminate against, any individual because of his age;

(2) to limit, segregate, or classify its membership, or to classify or fail or refuse to refer for employment any individual, in any way which would deprive or tend to deprive any individual of employment opportunities, or would limit such employment opportunities or otherwise adversely affect his status as an employee or as an applicant for employment, because of such individual's age;

(3) to cause or attempt to cause an employer to discriminate against an individual in violation of this section.

(d) *Opposition to unlawful practices; participation in investigations, proceedings, or litigation*

It shall be unlawful for an employer to discriminate against any of his employees or applicants for employment, for an employment agency to discriminate against any individual, or for a labor organization to discriminate against any member thereof or applicant for membership, because such individual, member or applicant for membership has opposed any practice made unlawful by this section, or because such individual, member or applicant for membership has made a charge, testified, assisted, or participated in any manner in an investigation, proceeding, or litigation under this Act.

(e) *Printing or publication of notice or advertisement indicating preference, limitation, etc.*

It shall be unlawful for an employer, labor organization, or employment agency to print or publish, or cause to be printed or published, any notice or advertisement relating to employment by such an employer or membership in or any classification or referral for employment by such a labor organization, or relating to any classification or referral for employment by such an employment agency, indicating any preference, limitation, specification, or discrimination, based on age.

*(f) Lawful practices; age an occupational qualification; other reasonable factors; seniority system; employee benefit plans; discharge or discipline for good cause*

It shall not be unlawful for an employer, employment agency, or labor organization —

(1) to take any action otherwise prohibited under subsections (a), (b), (c), or (e) of this section where age is a bona fide occupational qualification reasonably necessary to the normal operation of the particular business, or where the differentiation is based on reasonable factors other than age, or where such practices involve an employee in a workplace in a foreign country, and compliance with such subsections would cause such employer, or a corporation controlled by such employer, to violate the laws of the country in which such workplace is located;

(2) to take any action otherwise prohibited under subsection (a), (b), (c), or (e) of this section —

(A) to observe the terms of a bona fide seniority system that is not intended to evade the purposes of this Act, except that no such seniority system shall require or permit the involuntary retirement of any individual specified by section 12(a) because of the age of such individual; or

(B) to observe the terms of a bona fide employee benefit plan —

(i) where, for each benefit or benefit package, the actual amount of payment made or cost incurred on behalf of an older worker is no less than that made or incurred on behalf of a younger worker, as permissible under section 1625.10, title 29, Code of Federal Regulations (as in effect on June 22, 1989); or

(ii) that is a voluntary early retirement incentive plan consistent with the relevant purpose or purposes of this Act.

Notwithstanding clause (i) or (ii) of subparagraph (B), no such employee benefit plan or voluntary early retirement incentive plan shall excuse the failure to hire any individual, and no such employee benefit plan shall require or permit the involuntary retirement of any individual specified by section 12(a), because of the age of such individual. An employer, employment agency, or labor organization acting under subparagraph (A), or under clause (i) or (ii) of subparagraph (B), shall have the burden of proving that such actions are lawful in any civil enforcement proceeding brought under this Act; or

(3) to discharge or otherwise discipline an individual for good cause.

. . . .

(h) *Foreign practices*

(1) If an employer controls a corporation whose place of incorporation is in a foreign country, any practice by such corporation prohibited under this section shall be presumed to be such practice by such employer.

(2) The prohibitions of this section shall not apply where the employer is a foreign person not controlled by an American employer.

(3) For the purpose of this subsection the determination of whether an employer controls a corporation shall be based upon the —

    (A) interrelation of operations,

    (B) common management,

    (C) centralized control of labor relations, and

    (D) common ownership or financial control, of the employer and the corporation.

(i) *Employee pension benefit plans; cessation or reduction of benefit accrual or of allocation to employee account; distribution of benefits after attainment of normal retirement age; compliance; highly compensated employees*

(1) Except as otherwise provided in this subsection, it shall be unlawful for an employer, an employment agency, a labor organization, or any combination thereof to establish or maintain an employee pension benefit plan which requires or permits —

    (A) in the case of a defined benefit plan, the cessation of an employee's benefit accrual, or the reduction of the rate of an employee's benefit accrual, because of age, or

    (B) in the case of a defined contribution plan, the cessation of allocations to an employee's account, or the reduction of the rate at which amounts are allocated to an employee's account, because of age.

(2) Nothing in this section shall be construed to prohibit an employer, employment agency, or labor organization from observing any provision of an employee pension benefit plan to the extent that such provision imposes (without regard to age) a limitation on the amount of benefits that the plan provides or a limitation on the number of years of service or years

or participation which are taken into account for purposes of determining benefit accrual under the plan.

(3) In the case of any employee who, as of the end of any plan year under a defined benefit plan, has attained normal retirement age under such plan —

(A) if distribution of benefits under such plan with respect to such employee has commenced as of the end of such plan year, then any requirement of this subsection for continued accrual of benefits under such plan with respect to such employee during such plan year shall be treated as satisfied to the extent of the actuarial equivalent of in-service distribution of benefits, and

(B) if distribution of benefits under such plan with respect to such employee has not commenced as of the end of such year in accordance with section 206(a)(3) of the Employee Retirement Income Security Act of 1974 and section 401(a)(14)(C) of the Internal Revenue Code of 1986, and the payment of benefits under such plan with respect to such employee is not suspended during such plan year pursuant to section 203(a)(3)(B) of the Employee Retirement Income Security Act of 1974 or section 411(a)(3)(B) of the Internal Revenue Code of 1986, then any requirement of this subsection for continued accrual of benefits under such plan with respect to such employee during such plan year shall be treated as satisfied to the extent of any adjustment in the benefit payable under the plan during such plan year attributable to the delay in the distribution of benefits after the attainment of normal retirement age. The provisions of this paragraph shall apply in accordance with regulations of the Secretary of the Treasury. Such regulations shall provide for the application of the preceding provisions of this paragraph to all employee pension benefit plans subject to this subsection and may provide for the application of such provisions, in the case of any such employee, with respect to any period of time within a plan year.

(4) Compliance with the requirements of this subsection with respect to an employee pension benefit plan shall constitute compliance with the requirements of this section relating to benefit accrual under such plan.

(5) Paragraph (1) shall not apply with respect to any employee who is a highly compensated employee (within the meaning of section 414(q) of the Internal Revenue Code of 1986) to the extent provided in regulations prescribed by the Secretary of the Treasury for purposes of precluding discrimination in favor of highly compensated employees

within the meaning of subchapter D of chapter 1 of the Internal Revenue Code of 1986.

(6) A plan shall not be treated as failing to meet the requirements of paragraph (1) solely because the subsidized portion of any early retirement benefit is disregarded in determining benefit accruals or it is a plan permitted by subsection (m).[.]

(7) Any regulations prescribed by the Secretary of the Treasury pursuant to clause (v) of section 411(b)(1)(h) of the Internal Revenue Code of 1986 and subparagraphs (C) and (D) of section 411(b)(2) of such Code shall apply with respect to the requirements of this subsection in the same manner and to the same extent as such regulations apply with respect to the requirements of such sections 411(b)(1)(H) and 411(b)(2).

(8) A plan shall not be treated as failing to meet the requirements of this section solely because such plan provides a normal retirement age described in section 3(24)(B) of the Employee Retirement Income Security Act of 1974 and section 411(a)(8)(B) of the Internal Revenue Code of 1986.

(9) For purposes of this subsection —

(A) The terms "employee pension benefit plan", "defined benefit plan", "defined contribution plan", and "normal retirement age" have the meanings provided such terms in section 3 of the Employee Retirement Income Security Act of 1974.

(B) The term "compensation" has the meaning provided by section 414(s) of the Internal Revenue Code of 1986.

(j) *Employment as firefighter or law enforcement officer*

It shall not be unlawful for an employer which is a State, a political subdivision of a State, an agency or instrumentality of a State or a political subdivision of a State, or an interstate agency to fail or refuse to hire or to discharge any individual because of such individual's age if such action is taken —

(1) with respect to the employment of an individual as a firefighter or as a law enforcement officer, the employer has complied with section 3(d)(2) of the Age Discrimination in Employment Amendments of 1996 if the individual was discharged after the date described in such section, and the individual has attained —

(A) the age of hiring or retirement, respectively, in effect under applicable State or local law on March 3, 1983; or

(B) (i) if the individual was not hired, the age of hiring in effect on the date of such failure or refusal to hire under applicable State or local law enacted after the date of enactment of the Age Discrimination in Employment Amendments of 1996 [enacted Sept. 30, 1996]; or

(ii) if applicable State or local law was enacted after the date of enactment of the Age Discrimination in Employment Amendments of 1996 [enacted Sept. 30, 1996] and the individual was discharged, the higher of —

(I) the age of retirement in effect on the date of such discharge under such law; and

(II) age 55; and

(2) pursuant to a bona fide hiring or retirement plan that is not a subterfuge to evade the purposes of this Act.

(k) *Seniority system or employee benefit plan; compliance*

A seniority system or employee benefit plan shall comply with this Act regardless of the date of adoption of such system or plan.

(l) *Lawful practices; minimum age as condition of eligibility for retirement benefits; deduction from severance pay; reduction of long-term disability benefits*

Notwithstanding clause (i) or (ii) of subsection (f)(2)(B) —

(1) It shall not be a violation of subsection (a), (b), (c), or (e) solely because —

(A) an employee pension benefit plan (as defined in section 3(2) of the Employee Retirement Income Security Act of 1974 provides for the attainment of a minimum age as a condition of eligibility for normal or early retirement benefits; or

(B) a defined benefit plan (as defined in section 3(35) of such Act provides for —

(i) payments that constitute the subsidized portion of an early retirement benefit; or

(ii) social security supplements for plan participants that commence before the age and terminate at the age (specified by the plan) when participants are eligible to receive reduced or unreduced old-age insurance benefits under title II of the Social Security Act, and that do not exceed such old-age insurance benefits.

(2)  (A) It shall not be a violation of subsection (a), (b), (c), or (e) solely because following a contingent event unrelated to age —

(i) the value of any retiree health benefits received by an individual eligible for an immediate pension;

(ii) the value of any additional pension benefits that are made available solely as a result of the contingent event unrelated to age and following which the individual is eligible for not less than an immediate and unreduced pension; or

(iii) the values described in both clauses (i) and (ii);

are deducted from severance pay made available as a result of the contingent event unrelated to age.

(B) For an individual who receives immediate pension benefits that are actuarially reduced under subparagraph (A)(i), the amount of the deduction available pursuant to subparagraph (A)(i) shall be reduced by the same percentage as the reduction in the pension benefits.

(C) For purposes of this paragraph, severance pay shall include that portion of supplemental unemployment compensation benefits (as described in section 501(c)(17) of the Internal Revenue Code of 1986) that —

(i) constitutes additional benefits of up to 52 weeks;

(ii) has the primary purpose and effect of continuing benefits until an individual becomes eligible for an immediate and unreduced pension; and

(iii) is discontinued once the individual becomes eligible for an immediate and unreduced pension.

(D) For purposes of this paragraph and solely in order to make the deduction authorized under this paragraph, the term "retiree health benefits" means benefits provided pursuant to a group health plan covering retirees, for which (determined as of the contingent event unrelated to age) —

(i) the package of benefits provided by the employer for the retirees who are below age 65 is at least comparable to benefits provided under title XVIII of the Social Security Act;

(ii) the package of benefits provided by the employer for the retirees who are age 65 and above is at least comparable to that offered under a plan that provides a benefit package with one-fourth the value of benefits provided under title XVIII of such Act; or

(iii) the package of benefits provided by the employer is as described in clauses (i) and (ii).

(E) (i) If the obligation of the employer to provide retiree health benefits is of limited duration, the value for each individual shall be calculated at a rate of $3,000 per year for benefit years before age 65, and $750 per year for benefit years beginning at age 65 and above.

(ii) If the obligation of the employer to provide retiree health benefits is of unlimited duration, the value for each individual shall be calculated at a rate of $48,000 for individuals below age 65, and $24,000 for individuals age 65 and above.

(iii) The values described in clauses (i) and (ii) shall be calculated based on the age of the individual as of the date of the contingent event unrelated to age. The values are effective on the date of enactment of this subsection [enacted Oct. 16, 1990], and shall be adjusted on an annual basis, with respect to a contingent event that occurs subsequent to the first year after the date of enactment of this subsection [enacted Oct. 16, 1990], based on the medical component of the Consumer Price Index for all-urban consumers published by the Department of Labor.

(iv) If an individual is required to pay a premium for retiree health benefits, the value calculated pursuant to this subparagraph shall be reduced by whatever percentage of the overall premium the individual is required to pay.

(F) If an employer that has implemented a deduction pursuant to subparagraph (A) fails to fulfill the obligation described in subparagraph (E), any aggrieved individual may bring an action for specific performance of the obligation described in subparagraph (E). The relief shall be in addition to any other remedies provided under Federal or State law.

(3) It shall not be a violation of subsection (a), (b), (c), or (e) solely because an employer provides a bona fide employee benefit plan or plans under which long-term disability benefits received by an individual are reduced by any pension benefits (other than those attributable to employee contributions) —

(A) paid to the individual that the individual voluntarily elects to receive; or

(B) for which an individual who has attained the later of age 62 or normal retirement age is eligible.

## § 626. Recordkeeping, investigation, and enforcement

(a) *Attendance of witnesses; investigations, inspections, records, and homework regulations*

The Secretary shall have the power to make investigations and require the keeping of records necessary or appropriate for the administration of this Act in accordance with the powers and procedures provided in sections 9 and 11 of the Fair Labor Standards Act of 1938, as amended.

(b) *Enforcement; prohibition of age discrimination under fair labor standards; unpaid minimum wages and unpaid overtime compensation; liquidated damages; judicial relief; conciliation, conference, and persuasion*

The provisions of this Act shall be enforced in accordance with the powers, remedies, and procedures provided in sections 11(b), 16 (except for subsection (a) thereof), and 17 of the Fair Labor Standards Act of 1938, as amended, and subsection (c) of this section. Any act prohibited under section 4 of this Act shall be deemed to be a prohibited act under section 15 of the Fair Labor Standards Act of 1938, as amended. Amounts owing to a person as a result of a violation of this Act shall be deemed to be unpaid minimum wages or unpaid overtime compensation for purposes of sections 16 and 17 of the Fair Labor Standards Act of 1938, as amended: Provided, That liquidated damages shall be payable only in cases of willful violations of this Act. In any action brought to enforce this Act the court shall have jurisdiction to grant such legal or equitable relief as may be appropriate to effectuate the purposes of this Act, including without limitation judgments compelling employment, reinstatement or promotion, or enforcing the liability for amounts deemed to be unpaid minimum wages or unpaid overtime compensation under this section. Before instituting any action under this section, the Secretary shall attempt to eliminate the discriminatory practice or practices alleged, and to effect voluntary compliance with the requirements of this Act through informal methods of conciliation, conference, and persuasion.

(c) *Civil actions; persons aggrieved; jurisdiction; judicial relief; termination of individual action upon commencement of action by Secretary; jury trial*

(1) Any person aggrieved may bring a civil action in any court of competent jurisdiction for such legal or equitable relief as will effectuate the purposes of this Act: Provided, That the right of any person to bring such action shall terminate upon the commencement of an action by the Secretary to enforce the right of such employee under this Act.

(2) In an action brought under paragraph (1), a person shall be entitled to a trial by jury of any issue of fact in any such action for recovery of amounts owing as a result of a violation of this Act, regardless of whether equitable relief is sought by any party in such action.

(d) *Filing of charge with Secretary; timeliness; conciliation, conference, and persuasion*

No civil action may be commenced by an individual under this section until 60 days after a charge alleging unlawful discrimination has been filed with the Secretary. Such a charge shall be filed —

(1) within 180 days after the alleged unlawful practice occurred; or

(2) in a case to which section 14(b) applies, within 300 days after the alleged unlawful practice occurred, or within 30 days after receipt by the individual of notice of termination of proceedings under State law, whichever is earlier.

Upon receiving such a charge, the Secretary shall promptly notify all persons named in such charge as prospective defendants in the action and shall promptly seek to eliminate any alleged unlawful practice by informal methods of conciliation, conference, and persuasion.

(e) *Reliance on administrative rulings; notice of dismissal or termination; civil action after receipt of notice*

Section 10 of the Portal-to-Portal Act of 1947 shall apply to actions under this Act. If a charge filed with the Commission under this Act is dismissed or the proceedings of the Commission are otherwise terminated by the Commission, the Commission shall notify the person aggrieved. A civil action may be brought under this section by a person defined in section 11(a) against the respondent named in the charge within 90 days after the date of the receipt of such notice.

(f) *Waiver*

(1) An individual may not waive any right or claim under this Act unless the waiver is knowing and voluntary. Except as provided in paragraph (2), a waiver may not be considered knowing and voluntary unless at a minimum —

(A) the waiver is part of an agreement between the individual and the employer that is written in a manner calculated to be understood by such individual, or by the average individual eligible to participate;

(B) the waiver specifically refers to rights or claims arising under this Act;

(C) the individual does not waive rights or claims that may arise after the date the waiver is executed;

(D) the individual waives rights or claims only in exchange for consideration in addition to anything of value to which the individual already is entitled;

(E) the individual is advised in writing to consult with an attorney prior to executing the agreement;

(F) (i) the individual is given a period of at least 21 days within which to consider the agreement; or

(ii) if a waiver is requested in connection with an exit incentive or other employment termination program offered to a group or class of employees, the individual is given a period of at least 45 days within which to consider the agreement;

(G) the agreement provides that for a period of at least 7 days following the execution of such agreement, the individual may revoke the agreement, and the agreement shall not become effective or enforceable until the revocation period has expired;

(H) if a waiver is requested in connection with an exit incentive or other employment termination program offered to a group or class of employees, the employer (at the commencement of the period specified in subparagraph (F)) informs the individual in writing in a manner calculated to be understood by the average individual eligible to participate, as to —

(i) any class, unit, or group of individuals covered by such program, any eligibility factors for such program, and any time limits applicable to such program; and

(ii) the job titles and ages of all individuals eligible or selected for the program, and the ages of all individuals in the same job classification or organizational unit who are not eligible or selected for the program.

(2) A waiver in settlement of a charge filed with the Equal Employment Opportunity Commission, or an action filed in court by the individual or the individual's representative, alleging age discrimination of a kind prohibited under section 4 or 15 may not be considered knowing and voluntary unless at a minimum —

(A) subparagraphs (A) through (E) of paragraph (1) have been met; and

(B) the individual is given a reasonable period of time within which to consider the settlement agreement.

(3) In any dispute that may arise over whether any of the requirements, conditions, and circumstances set forth in subparagraph (A), (B), (C), (D), (E), (F), (G), or (H) of paragraph (1), or subparagraph (A) or (B) of paragraph (2), have been met, the party asserting the validity of a waiver shall have the burden of proving in a court of competent jurisdiction that a waiver was knowing and voluntary pursuant to paragraph (1) or (2).

(4) No waiver agreement may affect the Commission's rights and responsibilities to enforce this Act. No waiver may be used to justify interfering with the protected right of an employee to file a charge or participate in an investigation or proceeding conducted by the Commission.

## § 627. Notices to be posted

Every employer, employment agency, and labor organization shall post and keep posted in conspicuous places upon its premises a notice to be prepared or approved by the Secretary setting forth information as the Secretary deems appropriate to effectuate the purposes of this Act.

## § 628. Rules and regulations; exemptions

In accordance with the provisions of subchapter II of chapter 5 of title 5, United States Code, the Secretary of Labor may issue such rules and regulations as he may consider necessary or appropriate for carrying out this Act, and may establish such reasonable exemptions to and from any or all provisions of this Act as he may find necessary and proper in the public interest.

## § 629. Criminal penalties

Whoever shall forcibly resist, oppose, impede, intimidate or interfere with a duly authorized representative of the Secretary while he is engaged in the performance of duties under this Act shall be punished by a fine of not more than $500 or by imprisonment for not more than one year, or by both: Provided, however, That no person shall be imprisoned under this section except when there has been a prior conviction hereunder.

## § 630. Definitions

For the purposes of this Act —

(a) The term "person" means one or more individuals, partnerships, associations, labor organizations, corporations, business trusts, legal representatives, or any organized groups of persons.

(b) The term "employer" means a person engaged in an industry affecting commerce who has twenty or more employees for each working day in each of twenty or more calendar weeks in the current or preceding calendar year: Provided, That prior to June 30, 1968, employers having fewer than fifty employees shall not be considered employers. The term also means (1) any agent of such a person, and (2) a State or political subdivision of a State and any agency or instrumentality of a State or a political subdivision of a State, and any interstate agency, but such term does not include the United States, or a corporation wholly owned by the Government of the United States.

(c) The term "employment agency" means any person regularly undertaking with or without compensation to procure employees for an employer and includes an agent of such a person; but shall not include an agency of the United States.

(d) The term "labor organization" means a labor organization engaged in an industry affecting commerce, and any agent of such an organization, and includes any organization of any kind, any agency, or employee representation committee, group, association, or plan so engaged in which employees participate and which exists for the purpose, in whole or in part, of dealing with employers concerning grievances, labor disputes, wages, rates of pay, hours, or other terms or conditions of employment, and any conference, general committee, joint or system board, or joint council so engaged which is subordinate to a national or international labor organization.

(e) A labor organization shall be deemed to be engaged in an industry affecting commerce if (1) it maintains or operates a hiring hall or hiring office which procures employees for an employer or procures for employees opportunities to work for an employer, or (2) the number of its members (or, where it is a labor organization composed of other labor organizations or their representatives, if the aggregate number of the members of such other labor organization) is fifty or more prior to July 1, 1968, or twenty-five or more on or after July 1, 1968, and such labor organization —

(1) is the certified representative of employees under the provisions of the National Labor Relations Act, as amended, or the Railway Labor Act, as amended; or

(2) although not certified, is a national or international labor organization or a local labor organization recognized or acting as the representative of employees of an employer or employers engaged in an industry affecting commerce; or

(3) has chartered a local labor organization or subsidiary body which is representing or actively seeking to represent employees of employers within the meaning of paragraph (1) or (2); or

(4) has been chartered by a labor organization representing or actively seeking to represent employees within the meaning of paragraph (1) or (2) as the local or subordinate body through which such employees may enjoy membership or become affiliated with such labor organization; or

(5) is a conference, general committee, joint or system board, or joint council subordinate to a national or international labor organization, which includes a labor organization engaged in an industry affecting commerce within the meaning of any of the preceding paragraphs of this subsection.

(f) The term "employee" means an individual employed by any employer except that the term "employee" shall not include any person elected to public office in any State or political subdivision of any State by the qualified voters thereof, or any person chosen by such officer to be on such officer's personal staff, or an appointee on the policymaking level or an immediate adviser with respect to the exercise of the constitutional or legal powers of the office. The exemption set forth in the preceding sentence shall not include employees subject to the civil service laws of a State government, governmental agency, or political subdivision. The term "employee" includes any individual who is a citizen of the United States employed by an employer in a workplace in a foreign country.

(g) The term "commerce" means trade, traffic, commerce, transportation, transmission, or communication among the several States; or between a State and any place outside thereof; or within the District of Columbia, or a possession of the United States; or between points in the same State but through a point outside thereof.

(h) The term "industry affecting commerce" means any activity, business, or industry in commerce or in which a labor dispute would hinder or obstruct commerce or the free flow of commerce and includes any activity or industry "affecting commerce" within the meaning of the Labor-Management Reporting and Disclosure Act of 1959.

(i) The term "State" includes a State of the United States, the District of Columbia, Puerto Rico, the Virgin Islands, American Samoa, Guam, Wake Island, the Canal Zone, and Outer Continental Shelf lands defined in the Outer Continental Shelf Lands Act.

(j) The term "firefighter" means an employee, the duties of whose position are primarily to perform work directly connected with the control and extinguishment of fires or the maintenance and use of firefighting apparatus and equipment, including an employee engaged in this activity who is transferred to a supervisory or administrative position.

(k) The term "law enforcement officer" means an employee, the duties of whose position are primarily the investigation, apprehension, or detention of individuals suspected or convicted of offenses against the criminal laws of a State, including an employee engaged in this activity who is transferred to a supervisory or administrative position. For the purpose of this subsection, "detention" includes the duties of employees assigned to guard individuals incarcerated in any penal institution.

(l) The term "compensation, terms, conditions, or privileges of employment" encompasses all employee benefits, including such benefits provided pursuant to a bona fide employee benefit plan.

## § 631. Age limits

(a) *Individuals at least 40 years of age*

The prohibitions in this Act shall be limited to individuals who are at least 40 years of age.

(b) *Employees or applicants for employment in Federal Government*

In the case of any personnel action affecting employees or applicants for employment which is subject to the provisions of section 15 of this Act, the prohibitions established in section 15 of this Act shall be limited to individuals who are at least 40 years of age.

(c) *Bona fide executives or high policymakers*

(1) Nothing in this Act shall be construed to prohibit compulsory retirement of any employee who has attained 65 years of age and who, for the 2-year period immediately before retirement, is employed in a bona fide executive or a high policymaking position, if such employee is entitled to an immediate nonforfeitable annual retirement benefit from a pension, profit-sharing savings, or deferred compensation plan, or any combination of such plans, of the employer of such employee, which equals, in the aggregate, at least $44,000.

(2) In applying the retirement benefit test of paragraph (1) of this subsection, if any such retirement benefit is in a form other than a straight life annuity (with no ancillary benefits), or if employees contribute to any such plan or make rollover contributions, such benefit shall be adjusted in accordance with regulations prescribed by the Secretary, after consultation with the Secretary of the Treasury, so that the benefit is the equivalent of a straight life annuity (with no ancillary benefits) under a plan to which employees do not contribute and under which no rollover contributions are made.

## § 633. Federal-State relationship

(a) *Federal action superseding State action*

Nothing in this Act shall affect the jurisdiction of any agency of any State performing like functions with regard to discriminatory employment practices on account of age except that upon commencement of action under this Act such action shall supersede any State action.

(b) *Limitation of Federal action upon commencement of State proceedings*

In the case of an alleged unlawful practice occurring in a State which has a law prohibiting discrimination in employment because of age and establishing or authorizing a State authority to grant or seek relief from such discriminatory practice, no suit may be brought under section 7 of this Act before the expiration of sixty days after proceedings have been commenced under the State law, unless such proceedings have been earlier terminated: Provided, That such sixty-day period shall be extended to one hundred and twenty days during the first year after the effective date of such State law. If any requirement for the commencement of such proceedings is imposed by a State authority other than a requirement of the filing of a written and signed statement of the facts upon which the proceeding is based, the proceeding shall be deemed to have been commenced for the purposes of this subsection at the time such statement is sent by registered mail to the appropriate State authority.

## § 633a. Nondiscrimination on account of age in Federal Government employment

(a) *Federal agencies affected*

All personnel actions affecting employees or applicants for employment who are at least 40 years of age (except personnel actions with regard to aliens employed outside the limits of the United States) in military departments as defined in section 102 of title 5, United States Code, in executive agencies as defined in section 105 of title 5, United States Code (including employees and applicants for employment who are paid from nonappropriated funds), in the United States Postal Service and the Postal Rate Commission, in those units in the government of the District of Columbia having positions in the competitive service, and in those units of the judicial branch of the Federal Government having positions in the competitive service, in the Smithsonian Institution, and in the Government Printing Office, the General Accounting Office, and the Library of Congress shall be made free from any discrimination based on age.

(b) *Enforcement by Civil Service Commission and by Librarian of Congress in the Library of Congress; remedies; rules, regulations, orders, and instructions of Commission: compliance by Federal agencies; powers and duties of Commission; notification of final action on complaint of discrimination; exemptions: bona fide occupational qualification*

Except as otherwise provided in this subsection, the Civil Service Commission is authorized to enforce the provisions of subsection (a) through appropriate remedies, including reinstatement or hiring of employees with or without backpay, as will effectuate the policies of this section. The Civil Service Commission shall issue such rules, regulations, orders, and instructions as it deems necessary and appropriate to carry out its responsibilities under this section. The Civil Service Commission shall —

(1) be responsible for the review and evaluation of the operation of all agency programs designed to carry out the policy of this section, periodically obtaining and publishing (on at least a semiannual basis) progress reports from each department, agency, or unit referred to in subsection (a);

(2) consult with and solicit the recommendations of interested individuals, groups, and organizations relating to nondiscrimination in employment on account of age; and

(3) provide for the acceptance and processing of complaints of discrimination in Federal employment on account of age.

The head of each such department, agency, or unit shall comply with such rules, regulations, orders, and instructions of the Civil Service Commission which shall include a provision that an employee or applicant for employment shall be notified of any final action taken on any complaint of discrimination filed by him thereunder. Reasonable exemptions to the provisions of this section may be established by the Commission but only when the Commission has established a maximum age requirement on the basis of a determination that age is a bona fide occupational qualification necessary to the performance of the duties of the position. With respect to employment in the Library of Congress, authorities granted in this subsection to the Civil Service Commission shall be exercised by the Librarian of Congress.

(c) *Civil actions; jurisdiction; relief*

Any person aggrieved may bring a civil action in any Federal district court of competent jurisdiction for such legal or equitable relief as will effectuate the purposes of this Act.

(d) *Notice to Commission; time of notice; Commission notification of prospective defendants; Commission elimination of unlawful practices*

When the individual has not filed a complaint concerning age discrimination with the Commission, no civil action may be commenced by any individual under this section until the individual has given the Commission not less than thirty days' notice of an intent to file such action. Such notice shall be filed within one hundred and eighty days after the alleged unlawful practice occurred. Upon receiving a notice of intent to sue, the Commission shall promptly notify all persons named therein as prospective defendants in the action and take any appropriate action to assure the elimination of any unlawful practice.

(e) *Duty of Government agency or official*

Nothing contained in this section shall relieve any Government agency or official of the responsibility to assure nondiscrimination on account of age in employment as required under any provision of Federal law.

(f) *Applicability of statutory provisions to personnel action of Federal departments, etc.*

Any personnel action of any department, agency, or other entity referred to in subsection (a) of this section shall not be subject to, or affected by, any provision of this Act, other than the provisions of section 12(b) of this Act and the provisions of this section.

(g) *Study and report to President and Congress by Civil Service Commission; scope*

(1) The Civil Service Commission shall undertake a study relating to the effects of the amendments made to this section by the Age Discrimination in Employment Act Amendments of 1978, and the effects of section 12(b) of this Act, as added by the Age Discrimination in Employment Act Amendments of 1978.

(2) The Civil Service Commission shall transmit a report to the President and to the Congress containing the findings of the Commission

resulting from the study of the Commission under paragraph (1) of this subsection.  Such report shall be transmitted no later than January 1, 1980.

# Old Age, Survivors, and Disability Insurance Act, as amended
## (Excerpts)
### 42 U.S.C. § 401 et seq.

## § 401. Trust Funds

(a) *Federal Old-Age and Survivors Insurance Trust Fund*

There is hereby created on the books of the Treasury of the United States a trust fund to be known as the "Federal Old-Age and Survivors Insurance Trust Fund." The Federal Old-Age and Survivors Insurance Trust Fund shall consist of the securities held by the Secretary of the Treasury for the Old-Age Reserve Account and the amount standing to the credit of the Old-Age Reserve Account on the books of the Treasury on January 1, 1940, which securities and amount the Secretary of the Treasury is authorized and directed to transfer to the Federal Old-Age and Survivors Insurance Trust Fund, and, in addition, such gifts and bequests as may be made as provided in subsection (i)(1), and such amounts as may be appropriated to, or deposited in, the Federal Old-Age and Survivors Insurance Trust Fund as hereinafter provided. There is hereby appropriated to the Federal Old-Age and Survivors Insurance Trust Fund for the fiscal year ending June 30, 1941, and for each fiscal year thereafter, out of any moneys in the Treasury not otherwise appropriated, amounts equivalent to 100 per centum of —

(1) the taxes (including interest, penalties, and additions to the taxes) received under subchapter A of chapter 9 of the Internal

Revenue Code of 1939 (and covered into the Treasury) which are deposited into the Treasury by collectors of internal revenue before January 1, 1951; and

(2) the taxes certified each month by the Commissioner of Internal Revenue as taxes received under subchapter A of chapter 9 of the Internal Revenue Code of 1939 which are deposited into the Treasury by collectors of internal revenue after December 31, 1950, and before January 1, 1953, with respect to assessments of such taxes made before January 1, 1951; and

(3) the taxes imposed by subchapter A of chapter 9 of the Internal Revenue Code of 1939 with respect to wages (as defined in section 1426 of such Code), and by chapter 21 (other than sections 3101(b) and 3111(b)) of the Internal Revenue Code of 1954 with respect to wages (as defined in section 3121 of such Code) reported to the Commissioner of Internal Revenue pursuant to section 1420(c) of the Internal Revenue Code of 1939 after December 31, 1950, or to the Secretary of the Treasury or his delegates pursuant to subtitle F of the Internal Revenue Code of 1954 after December 31, 1954, as determined by the Secretary of the Treasury by applying the applicable rates of tax under such subchapter or chapter 21 (other than sections 3101(b) and 3111(b)) to such wages, which wages shall be certified by the Commissioner of Social Security on the basis of the records of wages established and maintained by such Commissioner in accordance with such reports, less the amounts specified in clause (1) of subsection (b) of this section; and

(4) the taxes imposed by subchapter E of chapter 1 of the Internal Revenue Code of 1939, with respect to self-employment income (as defined in section 481 of such Code), and by chapter 2 (other than section 1401(b)) of the Internal Revenue Code of 1954 with respect to self-employment income (as defined in section 1402 of such Code) reported to the Commissioner of Internal Revenue on tax returns under such subchapter or to the Secretary of the Treasury or his delegate on tax returns under subtitle F of such Code, as determined by the Secretary of the Treasury by applying the applicable rate of tax under such subchapter or chapter (other than section 1401(b)) to such self-employment income, which self-employment income shall be certified by the Commissioner of Social Security on the basis of the records of self-employment income established and maintained by the Commissioner of Social Security

in accordance with such returns, less the amounts specified in clause (2) of subsection (b) of this section.

The amounts appropriated by clauses (3) and (4) of this subsection shall be transferred from time to time from the general fund in the Treasury to the Federal Old-Age and Survivors Insurance Trust Fund, and the amounts appropriated by clauses (1) and (2) of subsection (b) shall be transferred from time to time from the general fund in the Treasury to the Federal Disability Insurance Trust Fund, such amounts to be determined on the basis of estimates by the Secretary of the Treasury of the taxes, specified in clauses (3) and (4) of this subsection, paid to or deposited into the Treasury; and proper adjustments shall be made in amounts subsequently transferred to the extent prior estimates were in excess of or were less than the taxes specified in such clauses (3) and (4) of this subsection. All amounts transferred to either Trust Fund under the preceding sentence shall be invested by the Managing Trustee in the same manner and to the same extent as the other assets of such Trust Fund. Notwithstanding the preceding sentence, in any case in which the Secretary of the Treasury determines that the assets of either such Trust Fund would otherwise be inadequate to meet such Fund's obligations for any month, the Secretary of the Treasury shall transfer to such Trust Fund on the first day of such month the amount which would have been transferred to such Fund under this section as in effect on October 1, 1990; and such Trust Fund shall pay interest to the general fund on the amount so transferred on the first day of any month at a rate (calculated on a daily basis, and applied against the difference between the amount so transferred on such first day and the amount which would have been transferred to the Trust Fund up to that day under the procedures in effect on January 1, 1983) equal to the rate earned by the investments of such Fund in the same month under subsection (d) of this section.

(b) *Federal Disability Insurance Trust Fund*

There is hereby created on the books of the Treasury of the United States a trust fund to be known as the "Federal Disability Insurance Trust Fund." The Federal Disability Insurance Trust Fund shall consist of such gifts and bequests as may be made as provided in subsection (i)(1) of this section, and such amounts as may be appropriated to, or deposited in, such fund as provided in this section. There is hereby appropriated to the Federal Disability Insurance Trust Fund for the fiscal year ending June 30, 1957, and for each fiscal year thereafter, out of any moneys in the Treasury not otherwise appropriated, amounts equivalent to 100 per centum of —

(1)   (A) 1/2 of 1 per centum of the wages (as defined in section 3121 of the Internal Revenue Code of 1954 paid after December 31, 1956, and before January 1, 1966, and reported to the Secretary of the Treasury or his delegate pursuant to subtitle F of the Internal Revenue Code of 1954, (B) 0.70 of 1 per centum of the wages (as so defined) paid after December 31, 1965, and before January 1, 1968, and so reported, (C) 0.95 of 1 per centum of the wages (as so defined) paid after December 31, 1967, and before January 1, 1970, and so reported, (D) 1.10 per centum of the wages (as so defined) paid after December 31, 1969, and before January 1, 1973, and so reported, (E) 1.1 per centum of the wages (as so defined) paid after December 31, 1972, and before January 1, 1974, and so reported, (F) 1.15 per centum of the wages (as so defined) paid after December 31, 1973, and before January 1, 1978, and so reported, (G) 1.55 per centum of the wages (as so defined) paid after December 31, 1977, and before January 1, 1979, and so reported, (H) 1.50 per centum of the wages (as so defined) paid after December 31, 1978, and before January 1, 1980, and so reported, (I) 1.12 per centum of the wages (as so defined) paid after December 31, 1979, and before January 1, 1981, and so reported, (J) 1.30 per centum of the wages (as so defined) paid after December 31, 1980, and before January 1, 1982, and so reported, (K) 1.65 per centum of the wages (as so defined) paid after December 31, 1981, and before January 1, 1983, and so reported, (L) 1.25 per centum of the wages (as so defined) paid after December 31, 1982, and before January 1, 1984, and so reported, (M) 1.00 per centum of the wages (as so defined) paid after December 31, 1983, and before January 1, 1988, and so reported, (N) 1.06 per centum of the wages (as so defined) paid after December 31, 1987, and before January 1, 1990, and so reported, (O) 1.20 per centum of the wages (as so defined) paid after December 31, 1989, and before January 1, 1994, and so reported, (P) 1.88 per centum of the wages (as so defined) paid after December 31, 1993, and before January 1, 1997, and so reported, (Q) 1.70 per centum of the wages (as so defined) paid after December 31, 1996, and before January 1, 2000, and so reported, and (R) 1.80 per centum of the wages (as so defined) paid after December 31, 1999, and so reported, which wages shall be certified by the Commissioner of Social Security on the basis of the records of wages established and maintained by such Commissioner in accordance with such reports; and

(2) (A) 3/8 of 1 per centum of the amount of self-employment income (as defined in section 1402 of the Internal Revenue Code of 1954) reported to the Secretary of the Treasury or his delegate on tax returns under subtitle F of the Internal Revenue Code of 1954 for any taxable year beginning after December 31, 1956, and before January 1, 1966, (B) 0.525 of 1 per centum of the amount of self-employment income (as so defined) so reported for any taxable year beginning after December 31, 1965, and before January 1, 1968, (C) 0.7125 of 1 per centum of the amount of self-employment income (as so defined) so reported for any taxable year beginning after December 31, 1967, and before January 1, 1970, (D) 0.825 of 1 per centum of the amount of self-employment income (as so defined) so reported for any taxable year beginning after December 31, 1969, and before January 1, 1973, (E) 0.795 of 1 per centum of the amount of self-employment income (as so defined) so reported for any taxable year beginning after December 31, 1972, and before January 1, 1974, (F) 0.815 of 1 per centum of the amount of self-employment income (as so defined) as reported for any taxable year beginning after December 31, 1973, and before January 1, 1978, (G) 1.090 per centum of the amount of self-employment income (as so defined) so reported for any taxable year beginning after December 31, 1977, and before January 1, 1979 (H) 1.0400 per centum of the amount of self-employment income (as so defined) so reported for any taxable year beginning after December 31, 1978, and before January 1, 1980, (I) 0.7775 per centum of the amount of self-employment income (as so defined) so reported for any taxable year beginning after December 31, 1979, and before January 1, 1981, (J) 0.9750 per centum of the amount of self-employment income (as so defined) so reported for any taxable year beginning after December 31, 1980, and before January 1, 1982, (K) 1.2375 per centum of the amount of self-employment income (as so defined) so reported for any taxable year beginning after December 31, 1981, and before January 1, 1983, (L) 0.9375 per centum of the amount of self-employment income (as so defined) so reported for any taxable year beginning after December 31, 1982, and before January 1, 1984, (M) 1.00 per centum of the amount of self-employment income (as so defined) so reported for any taxable year beginning after December 31, 1983, and before January 1, 1988, (N) 1.06 per centum of the self-employment income (as so defined) so reported for any taxable year beginning after December 31, 1987, and before

January 1, 1990, (O) 1.20 per centum of the amount of self-employment income (as so defined) so reported for any taxable year beginning after December 31, 1989, and before January 1, 1994, (P) 1.88 per centum of the amount of self-employment income (as so defined) so reported for any taxable year beginning after December 31, 1993, and before January 1, 1997, (Q) 1.70 per centum of the amount of self-employment income (as so defined) so reported for any taxable year beginning after December 31, 1996, and before January 1, 2000, and (R) 1.80 per centum of the amount of self-employment income (as so defined) so reported for any taxable year beginning after December 31, 1999, which self-employment income shall be certified by the Commissioner of Social Security on the basis of the records of self-employment income established and maintained by the Commissioner of Social Security in accordance with such returns.

(c) *Board of Trustees; duties; reports to Congress*

With respect to the Federal Old-Age and Survivors Insurance Trust Fund and the Federal Disability Insurance Trust Fund (hereinafter in this title called the "Trust Funds") there is hereby created a body to be known as the Board of Trustees of the Trust Funds (hereinafter in this title called the "Board of Trustees") which Board of Trustees shall be composed of the Commissioner of Social Security, the Secretary of the Treasury, the Secretary of Labor, and the Secretary of Health and Human Services, all ex officio, and of two members of the public (both of whom may not be from the same political party), who shall be nominated by the President for a term of four years and subject to confirmation by the Senate. A member of the Board of Trustees serving as a member of the public and nominated and confirmed to fill a vacancy occurring during a term shall be nominated and confirmed only for the remainder of such term. An individual nominated and confirmed as a member of the public may serve in such position after the expiration of such member's term until the earlier of the time at which the member's successor takes office or the time at which a report of the Board is first issued under paragraph (2) after the expiration of the member's term. The Secretary of the Treasury shall be the Managing Trustee of the Board of Trustees (hereinafter in this title called the "Managing Trustee"). The Deputy Commissioner of Social Security shall serve as Secretary of the Board of Trustees. The Board of Trustees shall meet not less frequently than once each calendar year. It shall be the duty of the Board of Trustees to —

(1) Hold the Trust Funds;

(2) Report to the Congress not later than the first day of April of each year on the operation and status of the Trust Funds during the preceding fiscal year and on their expected operation and status during the next ensuing five fiscal years;

(3) Report immediately to the Congress whenever the Board of Trustees is of the opinion that the amount of either of the Trust Funds is unduly small;

(4) Recommend improvements in administrative procedures and policies designed to effectuate the proper coordination of the old-age and survivors insurance and Federal-State unemployment compensation program; and

(5) Review the general policies followed in managing the Trust Funds, and recommend changes in such policies, including necessary changes in the provisions of the law which govern the way in which the Trust Funds are to be managed.

The report provided for in paragraph (2) above shall include a statement of the assets of, and the disbursements made from, the Trust Funds during the preceding fiscal year, an estimate of the expected future income to, and disbursements to be made from, the Trust Funds during each of the next ensuing five fiscal years, and a statement of the actuarial status of the Trust Funds. Such statement shall include a finding by the Board of Trustees as to whether the Federal Old-Age and Survivors Insurance Trust Fund and the Federal Disability Insurance Trust Fund, individually and collectively, are in close actuarial balance (as defined by the Board of Trustees). Such report shall include an actuarial opinion by the Chief Actuary of the Social Security Administration certifying that the techniques and methodologies used are generally accepted within the actuarial profession and that the assumptions and cost estimates used are reasonable. Such report shall also include an actuarial analysis of the benefit disbursements made from the Federal Old-Age and Survivors Insurance Trust Fund with respect to disabled beneficiaries. Such report shall be printed as a House document of the session of the Congress to which the report is made. A person serving on the Board of Trustees shall not be considered to be a fiduciary and shall not be personally liable for actions taken in such capacity with respect to the Trust Funds.

(d) *Investments*

It shall be the duty of the Managing Trustee to invest such portion of the Trust Funds as is not, in his judgment, required to meet current withdrawals.  Such investments may be made only in interest-bearing obligations of the United States or in obligations guaranteed as to both principal and interest by the United States.  For such purpose such obligations may be acquired (1) on original issue at the issue price, or (2) by purchase of outstanding obligations at the market price.  The purposes for which obligations of the United States may be issued under chapter 31 of title 31, United States Code, are hereby extended to authorize the issuance at par of public-debt obligations for purchase by the Trust Funds.  Such obligations issued for purchase by the Trust Funds shall have maturities fixed with due regard for the needs of the Trust Funds and shall bear interest at a rate equal to the average market yield (computed by the Managing Trustee on the basis of market quotations as of the end of the calendar month next preceding the date of such issue) on all marketable interest-bearing obligations of the United States then forming a part of the public debt which are not due or callable until after the expiration of four years from the end of such calendar month; except that where such average market yield is not a multiple of one-eighth of 1 per centum, the rate of interest of such obligations shall be the multiple of one-eighth of 1 per centum nearest such market yield.  Each obligation issued for purchase by the Trust Funds under this subsection shall be evidenced by a paper instrument in the form of a bond, note, or certificate of indebtedness issued by the Secretary of the Treasury setting forth the principal amount, date of maturity, and interest rate of the obligation, and stating on its face that the obligation shall be incontestable in the hands of the Trust Fund to which it is issued, that the obligation is supported by the full faith and credit of the United States, and that the United States is pledged to the payment of the obligation with respect to both principal and interest.  The Managing Trustee may purchase other interest-bearing obligations of the United States or obligations guaranteed as to both principal and interest by the United States, on original issue or at the market price, only where he determines that the purchase of such other obligations is in the public interest.

## § 402. Old-age and survivors insurance benefit payments

(a) *Old-age insurance benefits*

Every individual who —

(1) is a fully insured individual (as defined in section 214(a)).

(2) has attained age 62, and

(3) has filed application for old-age insurance benefits or was entitled to disability insurance benefits for the month preceding the month in which he attained retirement age (as defined in section 216(l)), shall be entitled to an old-age insurance benefit for each month, beginning with —

(A) in the case of an individual who has attained retirement age (as defined in section 216(l)), the first month in which such individual meets the criteria specified in paragraphs (1), (2), and (3), or

(B) in the case of an individual who has attained age 62, but has not attained retirement age (as defined in section 216(l)), the first month throughout which such individual meets the criteria specified in paragraphs (1) and (2) (if in that month he meets the criterion specified in paragraph (3)),

and ending with the month preceding the month in which he dies. Except as provided in subsection (q) and subsection (w), such individual's old-age insurance benefit for any month shall be equal to his primary insurance amount (as defined in section 215(a)) for such month.

(b) *Wife's insurance benefits*

(1) The wife (as defined in section 216(b)) and every divorced wife (as defined in section 216(d)) of an individual entitled to old-age or disability insurance benefits, if such wife or such divorced wife —

(A) has filed application for wife's insurance benefits,

(B) has attained age 62 or (in the case of a wife) has in her care (individually or jointly with such individual) at the time of filing such application a child entitled to a child's insurance benefit on the basis of the wages and self-employment income of such individual,

(C) in the case of a divorced wife, is not married, and

(D) is not entitled to old-age or disability insurance benefits, or is entitled to old-age or disability insurance benefits based on a primary insurance amount which is less than one-half of the primary insurance amount of such individual, shall (subject to subsection(s)) be entitled to a wife's insurance benefit for each month, beginning with —

(i) in the case of a wife or divorced wife (as so defined) of an individual entitled to old-age benefits, if such wife or divorced wife has attained retirement age (as defined in section 216(l)), the first month in which she meets the criteria specified in subparagraphs (A), (B), (C), and (D), or

(ii) in the case of a wife or divorced wife (as so defined) of —

(I) an individual entitled to old-age insurance benefits, if such wife or divorced wife has not attained retirement age (as defined in section 216(l)), or

(II) an individual entitled to disability insurance benefits, the first month throughout which she is such a wife or divorced wife and meets the criteria specified in subparagraphs (B), (C), and (D) (if in such month she meets the criterion specified in subparagraph (A)), whichever is earlier, and ending with the month preceding the month in which any of the following occurs —

(E) she dies,

(F) such individual dies,

(G) in the case of a wife, they are divorced and either (i) she has not attained age 62, or (ii) she has attained age 62 but has not been married to such individual for a period of 10 years immediately before the date the divorce became effective,

(H) in the case of a divorced wife, she marries a person other than such individual,

(I) in the case of a wife who has not attained age 62, no child of such individual is entitled to a child's insurance benefit,

(J) she becomes entitled to an old-age or disability insurance benefit based on a primary insurance amount which is equal to or exceeds one-half of the primary insurance amount of such individual, or

(K) such individual is not entitled to disability insurance benefits and is not entitled to old-age insurance benefits.

(2) Except as provided in subsection (q) and paragraph (4) of this subsection, such wife's insurance benefit for each month shall be equal to one-half of the primary insurance amount of her husband (or, in the case of a divorced wife, her former husband) for such month.

(3) In the case of any divorced wife who marries —

    (A) an individual entitled to benefits under subsection (c), (f), (g), or (h) of this section, or

    (B) an individual who has attained the age of 18 and is entitled to benefits under subsection (d),

such divorced wife's entitlement to benefits under this subsection shall, notwithstanding the provisions of paragraph (1) (but subject to subsection(s)), not be terminated by reason of such marriage.

    (4)  (A) The amount of a wife's insurance benefit for each month (as determined after application of the provisions of subsections (q) and (k)) shall be reduced (but not below zero) by an amount equal to two-thirds of the amount of any monthly periodic benefit payable to the wife (or divorced wife) for such month which is based upon her earnings while in the service of the Federal Government or any State (or political subdivision thereof, as defined in section 218(b)(2)) if, on the last day she was employed by such entity —

    (i) such service did not constitute "employment" as defined in section 210, or

    (ii) such service was being performed while in the service of the Federal Government, and constituted "employment" as so defined solely by reason of —

        (I) clause (ii) or (iii) of subparagraph (G) of section 210(a)(5), where the lump-sum payment described in such clause (ii) or the cessation of coverage described in such clause (iii) (whichever is applicable) was received or occurred on or after January 1, 1988, or

        (II) an election to become subject to the Federal Employees' Retirement System provided in chapter 84 of title 5, United States Code, or the Foreign Service Pension System provided in subchapter II of chapter 8 of title I of the Foreign Service Act of 1980 made pursuant to law after December 31, 1987,

unless subparagraph (B) applies. The amount of the reduction in any benefit under this subparagraph, if not a multiple of $0.10, shall be rounded to the next higher multiple of $0.10.

    (B)  (i) Subparagraph (A)(i) shall not apply with respect to monthly periodic benefits based wholly on service as a member of a uniformed service (as defined in section 210(m)).

    (ii) Subparagraph (A)(ii) shall not apply with respect to monthly periodic benefits based in whole or in part on service which constituted "employment" as defined in section 210 if such service was performed for at least 60 months in the aggregate during the period beginning January 1, 1988, and ending with the close of the first calendar month as of the end of which the wife (or divorced wife) is eligible for benefits under this subsection and has made a valid application for such benefits.

(C) For purposes of this paragraph, any periodic benefit which otherwise meets the requirements of subparagraph (A), but which is paid on other than a monthly basis, shall be allocated on a basis equivalent to a monthly benefit (as determined by the Commissioner of Social Security) and such equivalent monthly benefit shall constitute a monthly periodic benefit for purposes of subparagraph (A). For purposes of this subparagraph, the term "periodic benefit" includes a benefit payable in a lump sum if it is a commutation of, or a substitute for, periodic payments.

(5) (A) Notwithstanding the preceding provisions of this subsection, except as provided in subparagraph (B), the divorced wife of an individual who is not entitled to old-age or disability insurance benefits, but who has attained age 62 and is a fully insured individual (as defined in section 214), if such divorced wife —

(i) meets the requirements of subparagraphs (A) through (D) of paragraph (1), and

(ii) has been divorced from such insured individual for not less than 2 years,

shall be entitled to a wife's insurance benefit under this subsection for each month, in such amount, and beginning and ending with such months, as determined (under regulations of the Commissioner of Social Security) in the manner otherwise provided for wife's insurance benefits under this subsection, as if such insured individual had become entitled to old-age insurance benefits on the date on which the divorced wife first meets the criteria for entitlement set forth in clauses (i) and (ii).

(B) A wife's insurance benefit provided under this paragraph which has not otherwise terminated in accordance with subparagraph (E), (F), (H), or (J) of paragraph (1) shall terminate with the month preceding the first month in which the insured individual is no longer a fully insured individual.

(c) *Husband's insurance benefits*

(1) The husband (as defined in section 216(f)) and every divorced husband (as defined in section 216(d)) of an individual entitled to old-age or disability insurance benefits, if such husband or such divorced husband —

(A) has filed application for husband's insurance benefits,

(B) has attained age 62 or (in the case of a husband) has in his care (individually or jointly with such individual) at the time of filing such application a child entitled to child's insurance benefits on the basis of the wages and self-employment income of such individual,

(C) in the case of a divorced husband, is not married, and

(D) is not entitled to old-age or disability insurance benefits, or is entitled to old-age or disability insurance benefits based on a primary insurance amount which is less than one-half of the primary insurance amount of such individual,

shall (subject to subsection(s)) be entitled to a husband's insurance benefit for each month, beginning with —

(i) in the case of a husband or divorced husband (as so defined) of an individual who is entitled to an old-age insurance benefit, if such husband or divorced husband has attained retirement age (as defined in section 216(l)), the first month in which he meets the criteria specified in subparagraphs (A), (B), (C), and (D), or

(ii) in the case of a husband or divorced husband (as so defined) of —

(I) an individual entitled to old-age insurance benefits, if such husband or divorced husband has not attained retirement age (as defined in section 216(l)), or

(II) an individual entitled to disability insurance benefits, the first month throughout which he is such a husband or divorced husband and meets the criteria specified in subparagraphs (B), (C), and (D) (if in such month he meets the criterion specified in subparagraph (A)), whichever is earlier, and ending with the month preceding the month in which any of the following occurs:

(E) he dies,

(F) such individual dies,

(G) in the case of a husband, they are divorced and either (i) he has not attained age 62, or (ii) he has attained age 62 but has not been married to such individual for a period of 10 years immediately before the divorce became effective,

(H) in the case of a divorced husband, he marries a person other than such individual,

(I) in the case of a husband who has not attained age 62, no child of such individual is entitled to a child's insurance benefit,

(J) he becomes entitled to an old-age or disability insurance benefit based on a primary insurance amount which is equal to or exceeds one-half of the primary insurance amount of such individual, or

(K) such individual is not entitled to disability insurance benefits and is not entitled to old-age insurance benefits.

(2)   (A) The amount of a husband's insurance benefit for each month (as determined after application of the provisions of subsections (q) and (k)) shall be reduced (but not below zero) by an amount equal to two-thirds of the amount of any monthly periodic benefit payable to the husband (or divorced husband) for such month which is based upon his earnings while in the service of the Federal Government or any State (or political subdivision thereof, as defined in section 218(b)(2)) if, on the last day he was employed by such entity —

(i) such service did not constitute "employment" as defined in section 210, or

(ii) such service was being performed while in the service of the Federal Government, and constituted "employment" as so defined solely by reason of —

(I) clause (ii) or (iii) of subparagraph (G) of section 210(a)(5), where the lump-sum payment described in such clause (ii) or the cessation of coverage described in such clause (iii) (whichever is applicable) was received or occurred on or after January 1, 1988, or

(II) an election to become subject to the Federal Employees' Retirement System provided in chapter 84 of title 5, United States Code, or the Foreign Service Pension System provided in subchapter II of chapter 8 of title I of the Foreign Service Act of 1980 made pursuant to law after December 31, 1987, unless subparagraph (B) applies. The amount of the reduction in any benefit under this subparagraph, if not a multiple of $0.10, shall be rounded to the next higher multiple of $0.10.

(B) (i) Subparagraph (A)(i) shall not apply with respect to monthly periodic benefits based wholly on service as a member of a uniformed service (as defined in section 210(m)).

(ii) Subparagraph (A)(ii) shall not apply with respect to monthly periodic benefits based in whole or in part on service which constituted "employment" as defined in section 210 if such service was performed for at least 60 months in the aggregate during the period beginning January 1, 1988, and ending with the close of the first calendar month as of the end of which the husband (or divorced husband) is eligible for benefits under this subsection and has made a valid application for such benefits.

(C) For purposes of this paragraph, any periodic benefit which otherwise meets the requirements of subparagraph (A), but which is paid on other than a monthly basis, shall be allocated on a basis equivalent to a monthly benefit (as determined by the Commissioner of Social Security) and such equivalent monthly benefit shall constitute a monthly periodic benefit for purposes of subparagraph (A). For purposes of this subparagraph, the term "periodic benefit" includes a benefit payable in a lump sum if it is a commutation of, or a substitute for, periodic payments.

(3) Except as provided in subsection (q) and paragraph (2) of this subsection, such husband's insurance benefit for each month shall be equal to one-half of the primary insurance amount of his wife (or, in the case of a divorced husband, his former wife) for such month.

(4) In the case of any divorced husband who marries —

(A) an individual entitled to benefits under subsection (b), (e), (g), or (h) of this section, or

(B) an individual who has attained the age of 18 and is entitled to benefits under subsection (d), by reason of paragraph (1)(B)(ii) thereof, such divorced husband's entitlement to benefits under this subsection, notwithstanding the provisions of paragraph (1) (but subject to subsection(s)), shall not be terminated by reason of such marriage.

(5) (A) Notwithstanding the preceding provisions of this subsection, except as provided in subparagraph (B), the divorced husband of an individual who is not entitled to old-age or disability insurance benefits, but who has attained age 62 and is a fully insured individual (as defined in section 214), if such divorced husband —

(i) meets the requirements of subparagraphs (A) through (D) of paragraph (1), and

(ii) has been divorced from such insured individual for not less than 2 years,

shall be entitled to a husband's insurance benefit under this subsection for each month, in such amount, and beginning and ending with such months, as determined (under regulations of the Commissioner of Social Security) in the manner otherwise provided for husband's insurance benefits under this subsection, as if such insured individual had become entitled to old-age insurance benefits on the date on which the divorced husband first meets the criteria for entitlement set forth in clauses (i) and (ii).

(B) A husband's insurance benefit provided under this paragraph which has not otherwise terminated in accordance with subparagraph (E), (F), (H), or (J) of paragraph (1) shall terminate with the month preceding the first month in which the insured individual is no longer a fully insured individual.

. . . .

(e) *Widow's insurance benefits*

(1) The widow (as defined in section 216(c)) and every surviving divorced wife (as defined in section 216(d)) of an individual who died a fully insured individual, if such widow or such surviving divorced wife —

(A) is not married,

(B)   (i) has attained age 60, or (ii) has attained age 50 but has not attained age 60 and is under a disability (as defined in section 223(d)) which began before the end of the period specified in paragraph (4).

(C)   (i) has filed application for widow's insurance benefits,

(ii) was entitled to wife's insurance benefits, on the basis of the wages and self-employment income of such individual, for the month preceding the month in which such individual died, and —

(I) has attained retirement age (as defined in section 216(l)),

(II) is not entitled to benefits under subsection (a) or section 223, or

(III) has in effect a certificate (described in paragraph (8)) filed by her with the Commissioner of Social Security, in accordance with regulations prescribed by the Commissioner of Social Security, in which she elects to receive widow's insurance benefits (subject to reduction as provided in subsection (q)), or

(iii) was entitled, on the basis of such wages and self-employment income, to mother's insurance benefits for the month preceding the month in which she attained retirement age (as defined in section 216(l)), and

(D) is not entitled to old-age insurance benefits or is entitled to old-age insurance benefits each of which is less than the primary insurance amount (as determined after application of subparagraphs (B) and (C) of paragraph (2)) of such deceased individual,

shall be entitled to a widow's insurance benefit for each month, beginning with —

(E) if she satisfies subparagraph (B) by reason of clause (i) thereof, the first month in which she becomes so entitled to such insurance benefits, or

(F) if she satisfies subparagraph (B) by reason of clause (ii) thereof —

(i) the first month after her waiting period (as defined in paragraph (5)) in which she becomes so entitled to such insurance benefits, or

(ii) the first month during all of which she is under a disability and in which she becomes so entitled to such insurance benefits, but only if she was previously entitled to insurance benefits under this subsection on the basis of being under a disability and such first month occurs (I) in the period specified in paragraph (4) and (II) after the month in which a previous entitlement to such benefits on such basis terminated,

and ending with the month preceding the first month in which any of the following occurs: she remarries, dies, becomes entitled to an old-age insurance benefit equal to or exceeding the primary insurance amount (as determined after application of subparagraphs (B) and (C) of paragraph (2)) of such deceased individual, or, if she became entitled to such benefits before she attained age 60, subject to section 223(e), the termination month (unless she attains retirement age (as defined in § 216(l)) on or before the last day of such termination month). For purposes of the preceding sentence, the termination month for any individual shall be the third month following the month in which her disability ceases; except that, in the case of an individual who has a period of trial work which ends as determined by application of section 222(c)(4)(A), the termination month shall be the earlier of (I) the third month following the earliest month after the end of such period of trial work with respect to which such individual is determined to no longer be suffering from a disabling physical or mental impairment, or (II) the third month following the earliest month in which such individual engages or is determined able to engage in substantial gainful activity, but in no event earlier than the first month occurring after the 36 months following such period of trial work in which she engages or is determined able to engage in substantial gainful activity.

(2) (A) Except as provided in subsection (q), paragraph (7) of this subsection, and subparagraph (D) of this paragraph, such widow's insurance benefit for each month shall be equal to the primary insurance amount (as determined for purposes of this subsection after application of subparagraphs (B) and (C) of such deceased individual.

(B) (i) For purposes of this subsection, in any case in which such deceased individual dies before attaining age 62 and section 215(a)(1) (as in effect after December 1978) is applicable in determining such individual's primary insurance amount —

(I) such primary insurance amount shall be determined under the formula set forth in section 215(a)(1)(B)(i) and (ii) which is applicable to individuals who initially become eligible for old-age insurance benefits in the second year after the year specified in clause (ii),

(II) the year specified in clause (ii) shall be substituted for the second calendar year specified in section 215(b)(3)(A)(ii)(I), and

(III) such primary insurance amount shall be increased under section 215(i) as if it were the primary insurance amount referred to in section 215(i)(2)(A)(ii)(II), except that it shall be increased only for years beginning after the first year after the year specified in clause (ii).

(ii) The year specified in this clause is the earlier of —

(I) the year in which the deceased individual attained age 60, or would have attained age 60 had he lived to that age, or

(II) the second year preceding the year in which the widow or surviving divorced wife first meets the requirements of paragraph (1)(B) or the second year preceding the year in which the deceased individual died, whichever is later.

(iii) This subparagraph shall apply with respect to any benefit under this subsection only to the extent its application does not result in a primary insurance amount for purposes of this subsection which is less than the primary insurance amount otherwise determined for such deceased individual under section 215.

(C) If such deceased individual was (or upon application would have been) entitled to an old-age insurance benefit which was increased (or subject to being increased) on account of delayed retirement under the provisions of subsection (w), then, for purposes of this subsection, such individual's primary insurance amount, if less than the old-age insurance benefit (increased, where applicable, under section 215(f)(5) or (6) and under section 215(i) as if such individual were still alive in the case of an individual who has died) which he was receiving (or would upon application have received) for the month prior to the month in which he died, shall be deemed to be equal to such old-age insurance benefit, and (notwithstanding the provisions of paragraph (3) of such subsection (w)) the number of increment months shall include any month in the months of the calendar year in which he died, prior to the month in which he died, which satisfy the conditions in paragraph (2) of such subsection (w).

(D) If the deceased individual (on the basis of whose wages and self-employment income a widow or surviving divorced wife is entitled to widow's insurance benefits under this subsection) was, at any time, entitled to an old-age insurance benefit which was reduced by reason of the application of subsection (q), the widow's insurance benefit of such widow or surviving divorced wife for any month shall, if the amount of the widow's insurance benefit of such widow or surviving divorced wife (as determined under subparagraph (A) and after application of subsection (q)) is greater than —

(i) the amount of the old-age insurance benefit to which such deceased individual would have been entitled (after application of subsection (q)) for such month if such individual were still living and section 215(f)(5), 215(f)(6), or 215(f)(9)(B) were applied, where applicable, and

(ii) 82 1/2 percent of the primary insurance amount (as determined without regard to subparagraph (C)) of such deceased individual, be reduced to the amount referred to in clause (i), or (if greater) the amount referred to in clause (ii).

(3) For purposes of paragraph (1), if —

(A) a widow or surviving divorced wife marries after attaining age 60 (or after attaining age 50 if she was entitled before such marriage occurred to benefits based on disability under this subsection), or

(B) a disabled widow or disabled surviving divorced wife described in paragraph (1)(B)(ii) marries after attaining age 50, such marriage shall be deemed not to have occurred.

(4) The period referred to in paragraph (1)(B)(ii), in the case of any widow or surviving divorced wife, is the period beginning with whichever of the following is the latest:

(A) the month in which occurred the death of the fully insured individual referred to in paragraph (1) on whose wages and self-employment income her benefits are or would be based, or

(B) the last month for which she was entitled to mother's insurance benefits on the basis of the wages and self-employment income of such individual, or

(C) the month in which a previous entitlement to widow's insurance benefits on the basis of such wages and self-employment income terminated because her disability had ceased,

and ending with the month before the month in which she attains age 60, or, if earlier, with the close of the eighty-fourth month following the month with which such period began.

(5) (A) The waiting period referred to in paragraph (1)(F), in the case of any widow or surviving divorced wife, is the earliest period of five consecutive calendar months —

(i) throughout which she has been under a disability, and

(ii) which begins not earlier than with whichever of the following is the later: (I) the first day of the seventeenth month before the month in which her application is filed, or (II) the first day of the fifth month before the month in which the period specified in paragraph (4) begins.

(B) For purposes of paragraph (1)(F)(i), each month in the period commencing with the first month for which such widow or surviving divorced wife is first eligible for supplemental security income benefits under title XVI, or State supplementary payments of the type referred to in section 1616(a) (or payments of the type described in section 212(a) of Public Law 93-66) which are paid by the Commissioner of Social Security under an agreement referred to in section 1616(a) (or in section 212(b) of Public Law 93-66), shall be included as one of the months of such waiting period for which the requirements of subparagraph (A) have been met.

(6) In the case of an individual entitled to monthly insurance benefits payable under this section for any month prior to January 1973 whose benefits were not redetermined under section 102(g) of the Social Security Amendments of 1972 [note to this section], such benefits shall not be redetermined pursuant to such section, but shall be increased pursuant to any general benefit increase (as defined in section 215(i)(3)) or any increase in benefits made under or pursuant to section 215(i), including for this purpose the increase provided effective for March 1974, as though such redetermination had been made.

(7) (A) The amount of a widow's insurance benefit for each month (as determined after application of the provisions of subsections (q) and (k), paragraph (2)(D), and paragraph (3)) shall be reduced (but not below zero) by an amount equal to two-thirds of the amount of any monthly periodic benefit payable to the widow (or surviving divorced wife) for such month which is based upon her earnings while in the service of the Federal Government or any State (or political subdivision thereof, as defined in section 218(b)(2)) if, on the last day she was employed by such entity —

> (i) such service did not constitute "employment" as defined in section 210, or
>
> (ii) such service was being performed while in the service of the Federal Government, and constituted "employment" as so defined solely by reason of —
>
> > (I) clause (ii) or (iii) of subparagraph (G) of section 210(a)(5); where the lump-sum payment described in such clause (ii) or the cessation of coverage described in such clause (iii) (whichever is applicable) was received or occurred on or after January 1, 1988, or
> >
> > (II) an election to become subject to the Federal Employees' Retirement System provided in chapter 84 of title 5, United States Code, or the Foreign Service Pension System provided in subchapter II of chapter 8 of title I of the Foreign Service Act of 1980 made pursuant to law after December 31, 1987,

unless subparagraph (B) applies.  The amount of the reduction in any benefit under this subparagraph, if not a multiple of $0.10, shall be rounded to the next higher multiple of $0.10.

(B)  (i) Subparagraph (A)(i) shall not apply with respect to monthly periodic benefits based wholly on service as a member of a uniformed service (as defined in section 210(m)).

(ii) Subparagraph (A)(ii) shall not apply with respect to monthly periodic benefits based in whole or in part on service which constituted "employment" as defined in section 210 if such service was performed for at least 60 months in the aggregate during the period beginning January 1, 1988, and ending with the close of the first calendar month as of the end of which the widow (or surviving divorced wife) is eligible for benefits under this subsection and has made a valid application for such benefits.

(C) For purposes of this paragraph, any periodic benefit which otherwise meets the requirements of subparagraph (A), but which is paid on other than a monthly basis, shall be allocated on a basis equivalent to a monthly benefit (as determined by the Commissioner of Social Security) and such equivalent monthly benefit shall constitute a monthly periodic benefit for purposes of subparagraph (A).  For purposes of this subparagraph, the term "periodic benefit" includes a benefit payable in a lump sum if it is a commutation of, or a substitute for, periodic payments.

(8) Any certificate filed pursuant to paragraph (1)(C)(ii)(III) shall be effective for purposes of this subsection —

(A) for the month in which it is filed and for any month thereafter, and

(B) for months, in the period designated by the individual filing such certificate, of one or more consecutive months (not exceeding 12) immediately preceding the month in which such certificate is filed;

except that such certificate shall not be effective for any month before the month in which she attains age 62.

(9) An individual shall be deemed to be under a disability for purposes of paragraph (1)(B)(ii) if such individual is eligible for supplemental security income benefits under title XVI, or State supplementary payments of the type referred to in section 1616(a) (or payments of the type described in section 212(a) of Public Law 93-66) which are paid by the Commissioner of Social Security under an

agreement referred to in section 1616(a) (or in section 212(b) of Public Law 93-66), for the month for which all requirements of paragraph (1) for entitlement to benefits under this subsection (other than being under a disability) are met.

(f) *Widower's insurance benefits*

(1) The widower (as defined in section 216(g)) and every surviving divorced husband (as defined in section 216(d)) of an individual who died a fully insured individual, if such widower or such surviving divorced husband —

(A) is not married,

(B) (i) has attained age 60, or (ii) has attained age 50 but has not attained age 60 and is under a disability (as defined in section 223(d)) which began before the end of the period specified in paragraph (5),

(C) (i) has filed application for widower's insurance benefits,

(ii) was entitled to husband's insurance benefits, on the basis of the wages and self-employment income of such individual, for the month preceding the month in which such individual died, and —

(I) has attained retirement age (as defined in section 216(l)),

(II) is not entitled to benefits under subsection (a) or section 223, or

(III) has in effect a certificate (described in paragraph (8)) filed by him with the Commissioner of Social Security, in accordance with regulations prescribed by the Commissioner of Social Security, in which he elects to receive widower's insurance benefits (subject to reduction as provided in subsection (q)), or

(iii) was entitled, on the basis of such wages and self-employment income, to father's insurance benefits for the month preceding the month in which he attained retirement age (as defined in section 216(l)), and

(D) is not entitled to old-age insurance benefits, or is entitled to old-age insurance benefits each of which is less than the primary insurance amount (as determined after application of subparagraphs (B) and (C) of paragraph (3)) of such deceased individual,

shall be entitled to a widower's insurance benefit for each month, beginning with —

(E) if he satisfies subparagraph (B) by reason of clause (i) thereof, the first month in which he becomes so entitled to such insurance benefits, or

(F) if he satisfies subparagraph (B) by reason of clause (ii) thereof —

(i) the first month after his waiting period (as defined in paragraph (6)) in which he becomes so entitled to such insurance benefits, or

(ii) the first month during all of which he is under a disability and in which he becomes so entitled to such insurance benefits, but only if he was previously entitled to insurance benefits under this subsection on the basis of being under a disability and such first month occurs (I) in the period specified in paragraph (5) and (II) after the month in which a previous entitlement to such benefits on such basis terminated,

and ending with the month preceding the first month in which any of the following occurs:  he remarries, dies, or becomes entitled to an old-age insurance benefit equal to or exceeding the primary insurance amount (as determined after application of subparagraphs (B) and (C) of paragraph (3)) of such deceased individual, or, if he became entitled to such benefits before he attained age 60, subject to section 223(e), the termination month (unless he attains retirement age (as defined in section 216(l)) on or before the last day of such termination month).  For purposes of the preceding sentence, the termination month for any individual shall be the third month following the month in which his disability ceases; except that, in the case of an individual who has a period of trial work which ends as determined by application of section 222(c)(4)(A), the termination month shall be the earlier of (I) the third month following the earliest month after the end of such period of trial work with respect to which such individual is determined to no longer be suffering from a disabling physical or mental impairment, or (II) the third month following the earliest month in which such individual engages or is determined able to engage in substantial gainful activity, but in no event earlier than the first month occurring after the 36 months following such period of trial work in which he engages or is determined able to engage in substantial gainful activity.

(2)  (A) The amount of a widower's insurance benefit for each month (as determined after application of the provisions of subsections (q) and (k), paragraph (3)(D), and paragraph (4)) shall be reduced (but not below zero) by an amount equal to two-thirds of the amount of any monthly periodic benefit payable to the widower (or surviving divorced

husband) for such month which is based upon his earnings while in the service of the Federal Government or any State (or political subdivision thereof, as defined in section 218(b)(2)) if, on the last day he was employed by such entity —

    (i) such service did not constitute "employment" as defined in section 210, or

    (ii) such service was being performed while in the service of the Federal Government, and constituted "employment" as so defined solely by reason of —

        (I) clause (ii) or (iii) of subparagraph (G) of section 210(a)(5), where the lump-sum payment described in such clause (ii) or the cessation of coverage described in such clause (iii) (whichever is applicable) was received or occurred on or after January 1, 1988, or

        (II) an election to become subject to the Federal Employees' Retirement System provided in chapter 84 of title 5, United States Code, or the Foreign Service Pension System provided in subchapter II of chapter 8 of title I of the Foreign Service Act of 1980 made pursuant to law after December 31, 1987,

unless subparagraph (B) applies. The amount of the reduction in any benefit under this subparagraph, if not a multiple of $0.10, shall be rounded to the next higher multiple of $0.10.

    (B) (i) Subparagraph (A)(i) shall not apply with respect to monthly periodic benefits based wholly on service as a member of a uniformed service (as defined in section 210(m)).

    (ii) Subparagraph (A)(ii) shall not apply with respect to monthly periodic benefits based in whole or in part on service which constituted "employment" as defined in section 210 if such service was performed for at least 60 months in the aggregate during the period beginning January 1, 1988, and ending with the close of the first calendar month as of the end of which the widower (or surviving divorced husband) is eligible for benefits under this subsection and has made a valid application for such benefits.

    (C) For purposes of this paragraph, any periodic benefit which otherwise meets the requirements of subparagraph (A), but which is paid on other than a monthly basis, shall be allocated on a basis equivalent to a monthly benefit (as determined by the Commissioner of Social Security) and such equivalent monthly benefit shall constitute a monthly periodic benefit for purposes of subparagraph (A). For purposes of this subparagraph, the term "periodic benefit" includes a benefit payable in a lump sum if it is a commutation of, or a substitute for, periodic payments.

(3)   (A) Except as provided in subsection (q), paragraph (2) of this subsection, and subparagraph (D) of this paragraph, such widower's insurance benefit for each month shall be equal to the primary insurance amount (as determined for purposes of this subsection after application of subparagraphs (B) and (C)) of such deceased individual.

(B)   (i) For purposes of this subsection, in any case in which such deceased individual dies before attaining age 62 and section 215(a)(1) (as in effect after December 1978) is applicable in determining such individual's primary insurance amount —

(I) such primary insurance amount shall be determined under the formula set forth in section 215(a)(1)(B)(i) and (ii) which is applicable to individuals who initially become eligible for old-age insurance benefits in the second year after the year specified in clause (ii),

(II) the year specified in clause (ii) shall be substituted for the second calendar year specified in section 215(b)(3)(A)(ii)(I), and

(III) such primary insurance amount shall be increased under section 215(i) as if it were the primary insurance amount referred to in section 215(i)(2)(A)(ii)(II), except that it shall be increased only for years beginning after the first year after the year specified in clause (ii).

(ii) The year specified in this clause is the earlier of —

(I) the year in which the deceased individual attained age 60, or would have attained age 60 had she lived to that age, or

(II) the second year preceding the year in which the widower or surviving divorced husband first meets the requirements of paragraph (1)(B) or the second year preceding the year in which the deceased individual died, whichever is later.

(iii) This subparagraph shall apply with respect to any benefit under this subsection only to the extent its application does not result in a primary insurance amount for purposes of this subsection which is less than the primary insurance amount otherwise determined for such deceased individual under section 215.

(C) If such deceased individual was (or upon application would have been) entitled to an old-age insurance benefit which was increased (or subject to being increased) on account of delayed retirement under the provisions of subsection (w), then, for purposes of this subsection, such individual's primary insurance amount, if less than the old-age insurance benefit (increased, where applicable, under section 215(f)(5), 215(f)(6), or 215(f)(9)(B) and under section 215(i) as if such individual were still alive in the case of an individual who has died) which she was receiving (or would upon application have received) for the month prior to the month in which she died, shall be deemed to be equal to such old-age insurance benefit, and (notwithstanding the provisions of paragraph (3) of such subsection (w)) the number of increment months shall include any month in the months of the calendar year in which she died, prior to the month in which she died, which satisfy the conditions in paragraph (2) of such subsection (w).

(D) If the deceased individual (on the basis of whose wages and self-employment income a widower or surviving divorced husband is entitled to widower's [or surviving divorced husband's] insurance benefits under this subsection) was, at any time, entitled to an old-age insurance benefit which was reduced by reason of the application of subsection (q), the widower's [or surviving divorced husband's] insurance benefit of such widower or surviving divorced husband for any month shall, if the amount of the widower's insurance benefit of such widower or surviving divorced husband (as determined under subparagraph (A) and after application of subsection (q)) is greater than —

(i) the amount of the old-age insurance benefit to which such deceased individual would have been entitled (after application of subsection (q)) for such month if such individual were still living and section 215(f)(5), 215(f)(6), or 215(f)(9)(B) were applied, where applicable, and

(ii) 82 1/2 percent of the primary insurance amount (as determined without regard to subparagraph (C)) of such deceased individual;

be reduced to the amount referred to in clause (i), or (if greater) the amount referred to in clause (ii).

(4) For purposes of paragraph (1), if —

(A) a widower or surviving divorced husband marries after attaining age 60 (or after attaining age 50 if he was entitled before such marriage occurred to benefits based on disability under this subsection), or

(B) a disabled widower or surviving divorced husband described in paragraph (1)(B)(ii) marries after attaining age 50,

such marriage shall be deemed not to have occurred.

(5) The period referred to in paragraph (1)(B)(ii), in the case of any widower or surviving divorced husband, is the period beginning with whichever of the following is the latest:

(A) the month in which occurred the death of the fully insured individual referred to in paragraph (1) on whose wages and self-employment income his benefits are or would be based,

(B) the last month for which he was entitled to father's insurance benefits on the basis of the wages and self-employment income of such individual, or

(C) the month in which a previous entitlement to widower's insurance benefits on the basis of such wages and self-employment income terminated because his disability had ceased,

and ending with the month before the month in which he attains age 60, or, if earlier, with the close of the eighty-fourth month following the month with which such period began.

(6)   (A) The waiting period referred to in paragraph (1)(F), in the case of any widower or surviving divorced husband, is the earliest period of five consecutive calendar months —

(i) throughout which he has been under a disability, and

(ii) which begins not earlier than with whichever of the following is the later:  (I) the first day of the seventeenth month before the month in which his application is filed, or (II) the first day of the fifth month before the month in which the period specified in paragraph (5) begins.

(B) For purposes of paragraph (1)(F)(i), each month in the period commencing with the first month for which such widower or surviving divorced husband is first eligible for supplemental security income benefits; under title XVI, or State supplementary payments of the type referred to in section 1616(a) (or payments of the type described in section 212(a) of Public Law 93-66), which are paid by the Commissioner of Social Security under an agreement referred to in section 1616(a) (or in section 212(b) of Public Law 93-66, shall be included as one of the months of such waiting period for which the requirements of subparagraph (A) have been met.

(7) In the case of an individual entitled to monthly insurance benefits payable under this section for any month prior to January 1973 whose benefits were not redetermined under section 102(g) of the Social Security Amendments of 1972 note to this section], such benefits shall not be redetermined pursuant to such section, but shall be increased pursuant to any general benefit increase (as defined in section 215(i)(3) or any increase in benefits made under or pursuant to section 215(i), including for this purpose the increase provided effective for March 1974, as though such redetermination had been made.

(8) Any certificate filed pursuant to paragraph (1)(C)(ii)(III) shall be effective for purposes of this subsection —

    (A) for the month in which it is filed and for any month thereafter, and

    (B) for months, in the period designated by the individual filing such certificate, of one or more consecutive months (not exceeding 12) immediately preceding the month in which such certificate is filed;

except that such certificate shall not be effective for any month before the month in which he attains age 62.

(9) An individual shall be deemed to be under a disability for purposes of paragraph (1)(B)(ii) if such individual is eligible for supplemental security income benefits under title XVI, or State supplementary payments or the type referred to in section 1616(a) (or payments of the type described in section 212(a) of Public Law 93-66) which are paid by the Commissioner of Social Security under an agreement referred to in such section 1616(a) (or in section 212(b) of Public Law 93-66), for the month for which all requirements of paragraph (1) for entitlement to benefits under this subsection (other than being under a disability) are met.

(g) *Mother's and father's insurance benefits*

(1) The surviving spouse and every surviving divorced parent (as defined in section 216(d)) of an individual who died a fully or currently insured individual, if such surviving spouse or surviving divorced parent —

    (A) is not married,

    (B) is not entitled to a surviving spouse's insurance benefit,

(C) is not entitled to old-age insurance benefits, or is entitled to old-age insurance benefits each of which is less than three-fourths of the primary insurance amount of such individual,

(D) has filed application for mother's or father's insurance benefits, or was entitled to a spouse's insurance benefit on the basis of the wages and self-employment income of such individual for the month preceding the month in which such individual died,

(E) at the time of filing such application has in his or her care a child of such individual entitled to a child's insurance benefit, and

(F) in the case of a surviving divorced parent —

(i) the child referred to in subparagraph (E) is his or her son, daughter, or legally adopted child, and

(ii) the benefits referred to in such subparagraph are payable on the basis of such individual's wages and self-employment income,

shall (subject to subsection(s)) be entitled to a mother's or father's insurance benefit for each month, beginning with the first month in which he or she becomes so entitled to such insurance benefits and ending with the month preceding the first month in which any of the following occurs: no child of such deceased individual is entitled to a child's insurance benefit, such surviving spouse or surviving divorced parent becomes entitled to an old-age insurance benefit equal to or exceeding three-fourths of the primary insurance amount of such deceased individual, he or she becomes entitled to a surviving spouse's insurance benefit, he or she remarries, or he or she dies. Entitlement to such benefits shall also end, in the case of a surviving divorced parent, with the month immediately preceding the first month in which no son, daughter, or legally adopted child of such surviving divorced parent is entitled to a child's insurance benefit on the basis of the wages and self-employment income of such deceased individual.

(2) Except as provided in paragraph (4) of this subsection, such mother's or father's insurance benefit for each month shall be equal to three-fourths of the primary insurance amount of such deceased individual.

(3) In the case of a surviving spouse or surviving divorced parent who marries —

(A) an individual entitled to benefits under this subsection or subsection (a), (b), (c), (e), (f), or (h), or under section 223(a), or

(B) an individual who has attained the age of eighteen and is entitled to benefits under subsection (d), the entitlement of such surviving spouse or surviving divorced parent to benefits under this subsection shall, notwithstanding the provisions of paragraph (1) but subject to subsection(s), not be terminated by reason of such marriage.

(4) (A) The amount of a mother's or father's insurance benefit for each month (as determined after application of the provisions of subsection (k)) shall be reduced (but not below zero) by an amount equal to two-thirds of the amount of any monthly periodic benefit payable to the individual for such month which is based upon the individual's earnings while in the service of the Federal Government or any State (or political subdivision thereof, as defined in section 218(b)(2)) if, on the last day the individual was employed by such entity —

(i) such service did not constitute "employment" as defined in section 210, or

(ii) such service was being performed while in the service of the Federal Government, and constituted "employment" as so defined solely by reason of —

(I) clause (ii) or (iii) of subparagraph (G) of section 210(a)(5), where the lump-sum payment described in such clause (ii) or the cessation of coverage described in such clause (iii) (whichever is applicable) was received or occurred on or after January 1, 1988, or

(II) an election to become subject to the Federal Employees' Retirement System provided in chapter 84 of title 5, United States Code, or the Foreign Service Pension System provided in subchapter II of chapter 8 of title I of the Foreign Service Act of 1980 made pursuant to law after December 31, 1987,

unless subparagraph (B) applies. The amount of the reduction in any benefit under this subparagraph, if not a multiple of $0.10, shall be rounded to the next higher multiple of $0.10.

(B) (i) Subparagraph (A)(i) shall not apply with respect to monthly periodic benefits based wholly on service as a member of a uniformed service (as defined in section 210(m).

(ii) Subparagraph (A)(ii) shall not apply with respect to monthly periodic benefits based in whole or in part on service which constituted "employment" as defined in section 210 if such service was performed for at least 60 months in the aggregate during the period beginning January 1, 1988, and ending with the close of the first calendar month as of the end of which the individual is eligible for benefits under this subsection and has made a valid application for such benefits.

(C) For purposes of this paragraph, any periodic benefit which otherwise meets the requirements of subparagraph (A), but which is paid on other than a monthly basis, shall be allocated on a basis equivalent to a monthly benefit (as determined by the Commissioner of Social Security) and such equivalent monthly benefit shall constitute a monthly periodic benefit for purposes of subparagraph (A). For purposes of this subparagraph, the term "periodic benefit" includes a benefit payable in a lump sum if it is a commutation of, or a substitute for, periodic payments.

(h) *Parent's insurance benefits*

(1) Every parent (as defined in this subsection) of an individual who died a fully insured individual, if such parent —

(A) has attained age 62,

(B) (i) was receiving at least one-half of his support from such individual at the time of such individual's death or, if such individual had a period of disability which did not end prior to the month in which he died, at the time such period began or at the time of such death, and

(ii) filed proof of such support within two years after the date of such death, or, if such individual had such a period of disability, within two years after the month in which such individual filed application with respect to such period of disability or two years after the date of such death, as the case may be,

(C) has not married since such individual's death,

(D) is not entitled to old-age insurance benefits, or is entitled to old-age insurance benefits each of which is less than 82 1/2 percent of the primary insurance amount of such deceased individual if the amount of the parent's insurance benefit for such month is determinable under paragraph (2)(A) (or 75 percent of such primary insurance amount in any other case), and

(E) has filed application for parent's insurance benefits,

shall be entitled to a parent's insurance benefit for each month beginning with the first month after August 1950 in which such parent becomes so entitled to such parent's insurance benefits and ending with the month preceding the first month in which any of the following occurs: such parent dies, marries, or becomes entitled to an old-age insurance benefit equal to or exceeding 82 1/2 percent of the primary insurance amount of such deceased individual if the amount of the parent's insurance benefit for such month is determinable under paragraph (2)(A) (or 75 percent of such primary insurance amount in any other case).

(2)   (A) Except as provided in subparagraphs (B) and (C), such parent's insurance benefit for each month shall be equal to 82 1/2 percent of the primary insurance amount of such deceased individual.

(B) For any month for which more than one parent is entitled to parent's insurance benefits on the basis of such deceased individual's wages and self-employment income, such benefit for each such parent for such month shall (except as provided in subparagraph (C)) be equal to 75 percent of the primary insurance amount of such deceased individual.

(C) In any case in which —

(i) any parent is entitled to a parent's insurance benefit for a month on the basis of a deceased individual's wages and self-employment income, and

(ii) another parent of such deceased individual is entitled to a parent's insurance benefit for such month on the basis of such wages and self-employment income, and on the basis of an application filed after such month and after the month in which the application for the parent's benefits referred to in clause (i) was filed,

the amount of the parent's insurance benefit of the parent referred to in clause (i) for the month referred to in such clause shall be determined under subparagraph (A) instead of subparagraph (B) and the amount of the parent's insurance benefit of a parent referred to in clause (ii) for such month shall be equal to 150 percent of the primary insurance amount of the deceased individual minus the amount (before the application of section 203(a)) of the benefit for such month of the parent referred to in clause (i).

(3) As used in this subsection, the term "parent" means the mother or father of an individual, a stepparent of an individual by a marriage contracted before such individual attained the age of sixteen, or an adopting parent by whom an individual was adopted before he attained the age of sixteen.

(4) In the case of a parent who marries —

(A) an individual entitled to benefits under this subsection or subsection (b), (c), (e), (f), or (g), or

(B) an individual who has attained the age of eighteen and is entitled to benefits under subsection (d),

such parent's entitlement to benefits under this subsection shall, notwithstanding the provisions of paragraph (1) but subject to subsection(s), not be terminated by reason of such marriage.

(i) *Lump-sum death payments*

Upon the death, after August 1950, of an individual who died a fully or currently insured individual, an amount equal to three times such individual's primary insurance amount (as determined without regard to the amendments made by section 2201 of the Omnibus Budget Reconciliation Act of 1981, relating to the repeal of the minimum benefit provisions), or an amount equal to $255, whichever is the smaller, shall be paid in a lump sum to the person, if any, determined by the Commissioner of Social Security to be the widow or widower of the deceased and to have been living in the same household with the deceased at the time of death. If there is no such person, or if such person dies before receiving payment, then such amount shall be paid —

(1) to a widow (as defined in section 216(c)) or widower (as defined in section 216(g)) who is entitled (or would have been so entitled had a timely application been filed), on the basis of the wages and self-employment income of such insured individual, to benefits under subsection (e), (f), or (g) of this section for the month in which occurred such individual's death; or

(2) if no person qualifies for payment under paragraph (1), or if such person dies before receiving payment, in equal shares to each person who is entitled (or would have been so entitled had a timely application been filed), on the basis of the wages and self-employment income of such insured individual, to benefits under subsection (d) of this section for the month in which occurred such individual's death.

No payment shall be made to any person under this subsection unless application therefor shall have been filed, by or on behalf of such person (whether or not legally competent), prior to the expiration of two years after the date of death of such insured individual, or unless such person was entitled to wife's or husband's insurance benefits, on the basis of the wages and self-employment income of such insured individual, for the month preceding the month in which such individual died. In the case of any individual who died outside the forty-eight States and the District of Columbia after December 1953 and before January 1, 1957, whose death occurred while he was in the active military or naval service of the United States, and who is returned to any of such States, the District of Columbia, Alaska, Hawaii, the Commonwealth of Puerto Rico, the Virgin Islands, Guam, or American Samoa, for interment or reinterment, the provisions of the preceding sentence shall not prevent payment to any person under the second sentence of this subsection if application for a lump-sum death payment with respect to such deceased individual is filed by or on behalf of such person (whether or not legally competent) prior to the expiration of two years after the date of such interment or reinterment. In the case of any individual who died outside the fifty States and the District of Columbia after December 1956 while he was performing service, as a member of a uniformed service, to which the provision of section 210(1)(1) are applicable, and who is returned to any State, or to any Territory or possession of the United States, for interment or reinterment, the provisions of the third sentence of this subsection shall not prevent payment to any person under the second sentence of this subsection if application for a lump-sum death payment with respect to such deceased individual is filed by or on behalf of such person (whether or not legally competent) prior to the expiration of two years after the date of such interment or reinterment.

(j) *Application for monthly insurance benefits*

(1) Subject to the limitations contained in paragraph (4), an individual who would have been entitled to a benefit under subsection (a), (b), (c), (d), (e), (f), (g), or (h) for any month after August 1950 had he filed application therefor prior to the end of such month shall be entitled to such benefit for such month if he files application therefor prior to —

(A) the end of the twelfth month immediately succeeding such month in any case where the individual (i) is filing application for a benefit under subsection (e) or (f), and satisfies paragraph (1)(B) of such subsection by reason of clause (ii) thereof, or (ii) is filing application for a benefit under subsection (b), (c), or (d) on the basis of the wages and self-employment income of a person entitled to disability insurance benefits, or

(B) the end of the sixth month immediately succeeding such month in any case where subparagraph (A) does not apply.

Any benefit under this title for a month prior to the month in which application is filed shall be reduced, to any extent that may be necessary, so that it will not render erroneous any benefit which, before the filing of such application, the Commissioner of Social Security has certified for payment for such prior month.

(2) An application for any monthly benefits under this section filed before the first month in which the applicant satisfies the requirements for such benefits shall be deemed a valid application (and shall be deemed to have been filed in such first month) only if the applicant satisfies the requirements for such benefits before the Commissioner of Social Security makes a final decision on the application and no request under section 205(b) for notice and opportunity for a hearing thereon is made or, if such a request is made, before a decision based upon the evidence adduced at the hearing is made (regardless of whether such decision becomes the final decision of the Commissioner of Social Security).

(3) Notwithstanding the provisions of paragraph (1), an individual may, at his option, waive entitlement to any benefit referred to in paragraph (1) for any one or more consecutive months (beginning with the earliest month for which such individual would otherwise be entitled to such benefit) which occur before the month in which such individual files application for such benefit; and, in such case, such individual shall not be considered as entitled to such benefits for any such month or months before such individual filed such application. An individual shall be deemed to have waived such entitlement for any such month for which such benefit would, under the second sentence of paragraph (1), be reduced to zero.

(4) (A) Except as provided in subparagraph (B), no individual shall be entitled to a monthly benefit under subsection (a), (b), (c), (e), or (f) for any month prior to the month in which he or she files an application for benefits under that subsection if the amount of the monthly benefit to which such individual would otherwise be entitled for any such month would be subject to reduction pursuant to subsection (q).

(B) (i) If the individual applying for retroactive benefits is a widow, surviving divorced wife, or widower and is under a disability (as defined in section 223(d)), and such individual would, except for subparagraph (A), be entitled to retroactive benefits as a disabled widow or widower or disabled surviving divorced wife for any month before attaining the age of 60, then subparagraph (A) shall not apply with respect to such month or any subsequent month.

(ii) Subparagraph (A) does not apply to a benefit under subsection (e) or (f) for the month immediately preceding the month of application, if the insured individual died in that preceding month.

(iii) As used in this subparagraph, the term "retroactive benefits" means benefits to which an individual becomes entitled for a month prior to the month in which application for such benefits is filed.

(5) In any case in which it is determined to the satisfaction of the Commissioner of Social Security that an individual failed as of any date to apply for monthly insurance benefits under this title by reason of misinformation provided to such individual by any officer or employee of the Social Security Administration relating to such individual's eligibility for benefits under this title, such individual shall be deemed to have applied for such benefits on the later of —

(A) the date on which such misinformation was provided to such individual, or

(B) the date on which such individual met all requirements for entitlement to such benefits (other than application therefor).

(k) *Simultaneous entitlement to benefits*

(1) A child, entitled to child's insurance benefits on the basis of the wages and self-employment income of an insured individual, who would be entitled, on filing application, to child's insurance benefits on the basis of the wages and self-employment income of some other insured individual, shall be deemed entitled, subject to the provisions of paragraph (2) hereof, to child's insurance benefits on the basis of the wages and self-employment income of such other individual if an application for child's insurance benefits on the basis of the wages and self-employment income of such other individual has been filed by any other child who would, on filing application, be entitled to child's insurance benefits on the basis of the wages and self-employment income of both such insured individuals.

(2) (A) Any child who under the preceding provisions of this section is entitled for any month to child's insurance benefits on the wages and self-employment income of more than one insured individual shall, notwithstanding such provisions, be entitled to only one of such child's insurance benefits for such month. Such child's insurance benefits for such month shall be the benefit based on the wages and self-employment income of the insured individual who has the greatest primary insurance amount, except that such child's insurance benefits for such month shall be the largest benefit to which such child could be entitled under subsection (d) (without the application of section 203(a)) or subsection (m) if entitlement to such benefit would not, with respect to any person, result in a benefit lower (after the application of section 203(a)) than the

benefit which would be applicable if such child were entitled on the wages and self-employment income of the individual with the greatest primary insurance amount. Where more than one child is entitled to child's insurance benefits pursuant to the preceding provisions of this paragraph, each such child who is entitled on the wages and self-employment income of the same insured individuals shall be entitled on the wages and self-employment income of the same such insured individual.

(B) Any individual[(]other than an individual to whom subsection (e)(3) or (f)(4) applies) who, under the preceding provisions of this section and under the provisions of section 223, is entitled for any month to more than one monthly insurance benefit (other than an old-age or disability insurance benefit) under this title shall be entitled to only one such monthly benefit for such month, such benefit to be the largest of the monthly benefits to which he (but for this subparagraph (B)) would otherwise be entitled for such month. Any individual who is entitled for any month to more than one widow's or widower's insurance benefit to which subsection (e)(3) or (f)(4) applies shall be entitled to only one such benefit for such month, such benefit to be the largest of such benefits.

(3) (A) If an individual is entitled to an old-age or disability insurance benefit for any month and to any other monthly insurance benefit for such month, such other insurance benefit for such month, after any reduction under subsection (q), subsection (e)(2) or (f)(3), and any reduction under section 203(a), shall be reduced, but not below zero, by an amount equal to such old-age or disability insurance benefit (after reduction under such subsection (q)).

(B) If an individual is entitled for any month to a widow's or widower's insurance benefit to which subsection (e)(3) or (f)(4) applies and to any other monthly insurance benefit under section 202 [this section] (other than an old-age insurance benefit), such other insurance benefit for such month, after any reduction under subparagraph (A), any reduction under subsection (q), and any reduction under section 203(a), shall be reduced, but not below zero, by an amount equal to such widow's or widower's insurance benefit after any reduction or reductions under such subparagraph (A) and such section 203(a).

(4) Any individual who, under this section and section 223, is entitled for any month to both an old-age insurance benefit and a disability insurance benefit under this title shall be entitled to only the larger of such

benefits for such month, except that, if such individual so elects, he shall instead be entitled to only the smaller of such benefits for such month.

(l) *Entitlement to survivor benefits under railroad retirement provisions*

If any person would be entitled, upon filing application therefor to an annuity under section 2 of the Railroad Retirement Act of 1974 or to a lump-sum payment under section 6(b) of such Act with respect to the death of an employee (as defined in such Act) no lump-sum death payment, and no monthly benefit for the month in which such employee died or for any month thereafter, shall be paid under this section to any person on the basis of the wages and self-employment income of such employee.

(m) *[Repealed]*

(n) *Termination of benefits upon deportation of primary beneficiary*

(1) If any individual is (after the date of enactment of this subsection [enacted Sept. 1, 1954]) deported under section 241(a) [237(a)] (other than under paragraph (1)(C) or (1)(E) thereof) of the Immigration and Nationality Act, then, notwithstanding any other provisions of this title —

(A) no monthly benefit under this section or section 223 shall be paid to such individual, on the basis of his wages and self-employment income, for any month occurring (i) after the month in which the Commissioner of Social Security is notified by the Attorney General that such individual has been so deported, and (ii) before the month in which such individual is thereafter lawfully admitted to the United States for permanent residence.

(B) if no benefit could be paid to such individual (or if no benefit could be paid to him if he were alive) for any month by reason of subparagraph (A), no monthly benefit under this section shall be paid, on the basis of his wages and self-employment income, for such month to any other person who is not a citizen of the United States and is outside the United States for any part of such month, and

(C) no lump-sum death payment shall be made on the basis of such individual's wages and self-employment income if he dies (i) in or after the month in which such notice is received, and (ii) before the month in which he is thereafter lawfully admitted to the United States for permanent residence.

Section 203(b), (c), and (d) of this Act shall not apply with respect to any such individual for any month for which no monthly benefit may be paid to him by reason of this paragraph.

(2) As soon as practicable after the deportation of any individual under any of the paragraphs of section 241(a) [237(a)] of the Immigration and Nationality Act(other than under paragraph (1)(C) or (1)(E) thereof) the Attorney General shall notify the Commissioner of Social Security of such deportation.

(3) For purposes of paragraphs (1) and (2) of this subsection, an individual against whom a final order of deportation has been issued under paragraph (19) of section 241(a) [237(a)] of the Immigration and Nationality Act (relating to persecution of others on account of race, religion, national origin, or political opinion, under the direction of or in association with the Nazi government of Germany or its allies) shall be considered to have been deported under such paragraph (19) as of the date on which such order became final.

(o) *Application for benefits by survivors of members and former members of the uniformed services*

In the case of any individual who would be entitled to benefits under subsection (d), (e), (g), or (h) upon filing proper application therefor, the filing with the Administrator of Veterans' Affairs by or on behalf of such individual of an application for such benefits, on the form described in section 3005 [5105] of title 38, United States Code, shall satisfy the requirement of such subsection (d), (e), (g), or (h) that an application for such benefits be filed.

(p) *Extension of period for filing proof of support and applications for lump-sum death payment*

In any case in which there is a failure —

(1) to file proof of support under subparagraph (B) of subsection (h)(1), or under clause (B) of subsection (f)(1) of this section as in effect prior to the Social Security Act Amendments of 1950, within the period prescribed by such subparagraph or clause, or

(2) to file, in the case of a death after 1946, application for a lump-sum death payment under subsection (i), or under subsection (g) of this section as in effect prior to the Social Security Act Amendments of 1950, within the period prescribed by such subsection,

any such proof or application, as the case may be, which is filed after the expiration of such period shall be deemed to have been filed within such period if it is shown to the satisfaction of the Commissioner of Social Security that there was good cause for failure to file such proof or application within such period. The determination of what constitutes good cause for purposes of this subsection shall be made in accordance with regulations of the Commissioner of Social Security.

(q) *Reduction of benefit amounts for certain beneficiaries*

(1) Subject to paragraph (9), if the first month for which an individual is entitled to an old-age, wife's, husband's, widow's, or widower's insurance benefit is a month before the month in which such individual attains retirement age, the amount of such benefit for such month and for any subsequent month shall, subject to the succeeding paragraphs of this subsection, be reduced by —

(A) 5/9 of 1 percent of such amount if such benefit is an old-age insurance benefit, 25/36 of 1 percent of such amount if such benefit is a wife's or husband's insurance benefit, or 19/40 of 1 percent of such amount if such benefit is a widow's or widower's insurance benefit, multiplied by

(B) (i) the number of months in the reduction period for such benefit (determined under paragraph (6)), if such benefit is for a month before the month in which such individual attains retirement age, or

(ii) if less, the number of such months in the adjusted reduction period for such benefit (determined under paragraph (7)), if such benefit is (I) for the month in which such individual attains age 62, or (II) for the month in which such individual attains retirement age.

(2) If an individual is entitled to a disability insurance benefit for a month after a month for which such individual was entitled to an old-age insurance benefit, such disability insurance benefit for each month shall be reduced by the amount such old-age insurance benefit would be reduced under paragraphs (1) and (4) for such month had such individual attained retirement age (as defined in section 216(l)) in the first month for which he most recently became entitled to a disability insurance benefit.

(3) (A) If the first month for which an individual both is entitled to a wife's, husband's, widow's, or widower's insurance benefit and has attained age 62 (in the case of a wife's or husband's insurance benefit) or

age 50 (in the case of a widow's or widower's insurance benefit) is a month for which such individual is also entitled to —

  (i) an old-age insurance benefit (to which such individual was first entitled for a month before he attains retirement age (as defined in section 216(l))), or

  (ii) a disability insurance benefit,

then in lieu of any reduction under paragraph (1) (but subject to the succeeding paragraphs of this subsection) such wife's, husband's, widow's, or widower's insurance benefit for each month shall be reduced as provided in subparagraph (B), (C), or (D).

(B) For any month for which such individual is entitled to an old-age insurance benefit and is not entitled to a disability insurance benefit, such individual's wife's or husband's insurance benefit shall be reduced by the sum of —

  (i) the amount by which such old-age insurance benefit is reduced under paragraph (1) for such month, and

  (ii) the amount by which such wife's or husband's insurance benefit would be reduced under paragraph (1) for such month if it were equal to the excess of such wife's or husband's insurance benefit (before reduction under this subsection) over such old-age insurance benefit (before reduction under this subsection).

(C) For any month for which such individual is entitled to a disability insurance benefit, such individual's wife's, husband's, widow's, or widower's insurance benefit shall be reduced by the sum of —

  (i) the amount by which such disability insurance benefit is reduced under paragraph (3) for such month (if such paragraph applied to such benefit), and

  (ii) the amount by which such wife's, husband's, widow's, or widower's insurance benefit would be reduced under paragraph (1) for such month if it were equal to the excess of such wife's, husband's, widow's, or widower's insurance benefit (before reduction under this subsection) over such disability insurance benefit (before reduction under this subsection).

(D) For any month for which such individual is entitled neither to an old-age insurance benefit nor to a disability insurance benefit, such individual's wife's, husband's, widow's, or widower's insurance benefit shall be reduced by the amount by which it would be reduced under paragraph (1).

(E) Notwithstanding subparagraph (A) of this paragraph, if the first month for which an individual is entitled to a widow's or widower's insurance benefit is a month for which such individual is also entitled to an old-age insurance benefit to which such individual was first entitled for that month or for a month before she or he became entitled to a widow's or widower's benefit, the reduction in such widow's or widower's insurance benefit shall be determined under paragraph (1).

(4) If —

(A) an individual is or was entitled to a benefit subject to reduction under paragraph (1) or (3) of this subsection, and

(B) such benefit is increased by reason of an increase in the primary insurance amount of the individual on whose wages and self-employment income such benefit is based,

then the amount of the reduction of such benefit (after the application of any adjustment under paragraph (7)) for each month beginning with the month of such increase in the primary insurance amount shall be computed under paragraph (1) or (3), whichever applies, as though the increased primary insurance amount had been in effect for and after the month for which the individual first became entitled to such monthly benefit reduced under such paragraph (1) or (3).

(5) (A) No wife's or husband's insurance benefit shall be reduced under this subsection —

(i) for any month before the first month for which there is in effect a certificate filed by him or her with the Commissioner of Social Security, in accordance with regulations prescribed by the Commissioner of Social Security, in which he or she elects to receive wife's or husband's insurance benefits reduced as provided in this subsection, or

(ii) for any month in which he or she has in his or her care (individually or jointly with the person on whose wages and self-employment income the wife's or husband's insurance benefit is based) a child of such person entitled to child's insurance benefits.

(B) Any certificate described in subparagraph (A) (i) shall be effective for purposes of this subsection (and for purposes of preventing deductions under section 203(c)(2)) —

(i) for the month in which it is filed and for any month thereafter, and

(ii) for months, in the period designated by the individual filing such certificate, of one or more consecutive months (not exceeding 12) immediately preceding the month in which such certificate is filed;

except that such certificate shall not be effective for any month before the month in which he or she attains age 62, nor shall it be effective for any month to which subparagraph (A)(ii) applies.

(C) If an individual does not have in his or her care a child described in subparagraph (A)(ii) in the first month for which he or she is entitled to a wife's or husband's insurance benefit, and if such first month is a month before the month in which he or she attains retirement age (as defined in section 216(l)), he or she shall be deemed to have filed in such first month the certificate described in subparagraph (A)(i).

(D) No widow's or widower's insurance benefit for a month in which he or she has in his or her care a child of his or her deceased spouse (or deceased former spouse) entitled to child's insurance benefits shall be reduced under this subsection below the amount to which he or she would have been entitled had he or she been entitled for such month to mother's or father's insurance benefits on the basis of his or her deceased spouse's (or deceased former spouse's) wages and self-employment income.

(6) For purposes of this subsection, the "reduction period" for an individual's old-age, wife's, husband's, widow's, or widower's insurance benefit is the period —

(A) beginning —

(i) in the case of an old-age insurance benefit, with the first day of the first month for which such individual is entitled to such benefit,

(ii) in the case of a wife's or husband's insurance benefit, with the first day of the first month for which a certificate described in paragraph (5)(A)(i) is effective, or

(iii) in the case of a widow's or widower's insurance benefit, with the first day of the first month for which such individual is entitled to such benefit or the first day of the month in which such individual attains age 60, whichever is the later, and

(B) ending with the last day of the month before the month in which such individual attains retirement age.

(7) For purposes of this subsection, the "adjusted reduction period" for an individual's old-age, wife's, husband's, widow's, or widower's insurance benefit is the reduction period prescribed in paragraph (6) for such benefit, excluding —

(A) any month in which such benefit was subject to deductions under section 203(b), 203(c)(1), 203(d)(1), or 222(b),

(B) in the case of wife's or husband's insurance benefits, any month in which such individual had in his or her care individually or jointly with the person on whose wages and self-employment income such benefit is based a child of such person entitled to child's insurance benefits.

(C) in the case of wife's or husband's insurance benefits, any month for which such individual was not entitled to such benefits because of the occurrence of an event that terminated her or his entitlement to such benefits,

(D) in the case of widow's or widower's insurance benefits, any month in which the reduction in the amount of such benefit was determined under paragraph (5)(D),

(E) in the case of widow's or widower's insurance benefits, any month before the month in which she or he attained age 62, and also for any later month before the month in which she or he attained retirement age, for which she or he was not entitled to such benefit because of the occurrence of an event that terminated her or his entitlement to such benefits, and

(F) in the case of old-age insurance benefits, any month for which such individual was entitled to a disability insurance benefit.

(8) This subsection shall be applied after reduction under section 203(a) and before application of section 215(g). If the amount of any reduction computed under paragraph (1), (2) or (3) is not a multiple of $0.10, it shall be increased to the next higher multiple of $0.10.

(9) The amount of the reduction for early retirement specified in paragraph (1) —

(A) for old-age insurance benefits, wife's insurance benefits, and husband's insurance benefits, shall be the amount specified in such paragraph for the first 36 months of the reduction period (as defined in paragraph (6)) or adjusted reduction period (as defined in paragraph (7)), and five-twelfths of 1 percent for any additional months included in such periods; and

(B) for widow's insurance benefits and widower's insurance benefits, shall be periodically revised by the Commissioner of Social Security such that —

(i) the amount of the reduction at early retirement age as defined in section 216(l) shall be 28.5 percent of the full benefit; and

(ii) the amount of the reduction for each month in the reduction period (specified in paragraph (6)) or the adjusted reduction period (specified in paragraph (7)) shall be established by linear interpolation between 28.5 percent at the month of attainment of early retirement age and 0 percent at the month of attainment of retirement age.

(10) For purposes of applying paragraph (4), with respect to monthly benefits payable for any month after December 1977 to an individual who was entitled to a monthly benefit as reduced under paragraph (1) or (3) prior to January 1978, the amount of reduction in such benefit for the first month for which such benefit is increased by reason of an increase in the primary insurance amount of the individual on whose wages and self-employment income such benefit is based and for all subsequent months (and similarly for all subsequent increases) shall be increased by a percentage equal to the percentage increase in such primary insurance amount (such increase being made in accordance with the provisions of paragraph (8)). In the case of an individual whose reduced benefit under this section is increased as a result of the use of an adjusted reduction period (in accordance with paragraphs (1) and (3) of this subsection), then for the first month for which such increase is effective, and for all subsequent months, the amount of such reduction (after the application of the previous sentence, if applicable) shall be determined —

(A) in the case of old-age, wife's, and husband's insurance benefits, by multiplying such amount by the ratio of (i) the number of months in the adjusted reduction period to (ii) the number of months in the reduction period,

(B) in the case of widow's and widower's insurance benefits for the month in which such individual attains age 62, by multiplying such amount by the ratio of (i) the number of months in the reduction period beginning with age 62 multiplied by 19/40 of 1 percent, plus the number of months in the adjusted reduction period prior to age 62 multiplied by 19/40 of 1 percent to (ii) the number of months in the reduction period multiplied by 19/40 of 1 percent, and

(C) in the case of widow's and widower's insurance benefits for the month in which such individual attains retirement age (as defined in section 216(l)) by multiplying such amount by the ratio of (i) the number of months in the adjusted reduction period multiplied by 19/40 of 1 percent to (ii) the number of months in the reduction period beginning with age 62 multiplied by 19/40 of 1 percent, plus the number of months in the adjusted reduction period prior to age 62 multiplied by 19/40 of 1 percent,

such determination being made in accordance with the provisions of paragraph (8).

(11) When an individual is entitled to more than one monthly benefit under this title and one or more of such benefits are reduced under this subsection, paragraph (10) shall apply separately to each such benefit reduced under this subsection before the application of subsection (k) (pertaining to the method by which monthly benefits are offset when an individual is entitled to more than one kind of benefit) and the application of this paragraph shall operate in conjunction with paragraph (3).

(r) *Presumed filing of application by individuals eligible for old-age insurance benefits and for wife's or husband's insurance benefits*

(1) If the first month for which an individual is entitled to an old-age insurance benefit is a month before the month in which such individual attains retirement age (as defined in section 216(l)), and if such individual is eligible for a wife's or husband's insurance benefit for such first month, such individual shall be deemed to have filed an application in such month for wife's or husband's insurance benefits.

(2) If the first month for which an individual is entitled to a wife's or husband's insurance benefit reduced under subsection (q) is a month before the month in which such individual attains retirement age (as defined in section 216(l)), and if such individual is eligible (but for section 202(k)(4) [subsec. (k)(4) of this section]) for an old-age insurance benefit for such first month, such individual shall be deemed to have filed an application for old-age insurance benefits —

(A) in such month, or

(B) if such individual is also entitled to a disability insurance benefit for such month, in the first subsequent month for which such individual is not entitled to a disability insurance benefit.

(3) For purposes of this subsection, an individual shall be deemed eligible for a benefit for a month if, upon filing application therefor in such month, he would be entitled to such benefit for such month.

. . . .

(w) *Increase in old-age insurance benefit amounts on account of delayed retirement*

(1) The amount of an old-age insurance benefit (other than a benefit based on a primary insurance amount determined under section 215(a)(3) as in effect in December 1978 or section 215(a)(1)(C)(i)(i) as in effect thereafter), which is payable without regard to this subsection to an individual shall be increased by —

(A) the applicable percentage (as determined under paragraph (6)) of such amount, multiplied by

(B) the number (if any) of the increment months for such individual.

(2) For purposes of this subsection, the number of increment months for any individual shall be a number equal to the total number of the months —

(A) which have elapsed after the month before the month in which such individual attained retirement age (as defined in section 216(l)) or (if later) December 1970 and prior to the month in which such individual attained age 70, and

(B) with respect to which —

(i) such individual was a fully insured individual (as defined in section 214(a)),

(ii) such individual either was not entitled to an old-age insurance benefit or, if so entitled, did not receive benefits pursuant to a request by such individual that benefits not be paid, and

(iii) such individual was not subject to a penalty imposed under section 1129A.

(3) For purposes of applying the provisions of paragraph (1), a determination shall be made under paragraph (2) for each year, beginning with 1972, of the total number of an individual's increment months through the year for which the determination is made and the total so determined shall be applicable to such individual's old-age insurance benefits beginning with benefits for January of the year following the year for which such determination is made; except that the total number applicable in the case of an individual who attains age 70 after 1972 shall be determined through the month before the month in which he attains such age and shall be applicable to his old-age insurance benefit beginning with the month in which he attains such age.

(4) This subsection shall be applied after reduction under section 203(a).

(5) If an individual's primary insurance amount is determined under paragraph (3) of section 215(a) as in effect in December 1978, or section 215(a)(1)(C)(i)(i) as in effect thereafter, and, as a result of this subsection, he would be entitled to a higher old-age insurance benefit if his primary insurance amount were determined under section 215(a) (whether before, in, or after December 1978) without regard to such paragraph, such individual's old-age insurance benefit based upon his primary insurance amount determined under such paragraph shall be increased by an amount equal to the difference between such benefit and the benefit to which he would be entitled if his primary insurance amount were determined under such section without regard to such paragraph.

(6) For purposes of paragraph (1)(A), the "applicable percentage" is —

(A) 1/12 of 1 percent in the case of an individual who first becomes eligible for an old-age insurance benefit in any calendar year before 1979;

(B) 1/4 of 1 percent in the case of an individual who first becomes eligible for an old-age insurance benefit in any calendar year after 1978 and before 1987;

(C) in the case of an individual who first becomes eligible for an old-age insurance benefit in a calendar year after 1986 and before 2005, a percentage equal to the applicable percentage in effect under this paragraph for persons who first became eligible for an old-age insurance benefit in the preceding calendar year (as increased pursuant to this subparagraph), plus 1/24 of 1 percent if the calendar year in which that particular individual first becomes eligible for such benefit is not evenly divisible by 2; and

(D) 2/3 of 1 percent in the case of an individual who first becomes eligible for an old-age insurance benefit in a calendar year after 2004.

. . . .

## § 403.  Reduction of insurance benefits

. . . .

(b)  *Deductions on account of work*

(1) Deductions, in such amounts and at such time or times as the Commissioner of Social Security shall determine, shall be made from any payment or payments under this title to which an individual is entitled, and from any payment or payments to which any other persons are entitled on the basis of such individual's wages and self-employment income, until the total of such deductions equals —

    (A) such individual's benefit or benefits under section 202 for any month, and

    (B) if such individual was entitled to old-age insurance benefits under section 202(a) for such month, the benefit or benefits of all other persons for such month under section 202 based on such individual's wages and self-employment income,

if for such month he is charged with excess earnings, under the provisions of subsection (f) of this section, equal to the total of benefits referred to in clauses (A) and (B). If the excess earnings so charged are less than such total of benefits, such deductions with respect to such month shall be equal only to the amount of such excess earnings. If a child who has attained the age of 18 and is entitled to child's insurance benefits, or a person who is entitled to mother's or father's insurance benefits, is married to an individual entitled to old-age insurance benefits under section 202(a), such child or such person, as the case may be, shall, for the purposes of this subsection and subsection (f), be deemed to be entitled to such benefits on the basis of the wages and self-employment income of such individual entitled to old-age insurance benefits. If a deduction has already been made under this subsection with respect to a person's benefit or benefits under section 202 for a month, he shall be deemed entitled to payments under such section for such month for purposes of further deductions under this subsection, and for purposes of charging of each person's excess earnings under subsection (f), only to the extent of the total of his benefits remaining after such earlier deductions have been made. For purposes of this subsection and subsection (f) —

    (i) an individual shall be deemed to be entitled to payments under section 202 equal to the amount of the benefit or benefits to which he is entitled under such section after the application of subsection (a) of this section, but without the application of the first sentence of paragraph (4) thereof; and

(ii) if a deduction is made with respect to an individual's benefit or benefits under section 202 because of the occurrence in any month of an event specified in subsection (c) or (d) of this section or in section 222(b), such individual shall not be considered to be entitled to any benefits under such section 202 for such month.

(2) (A) Except as provided in subparagraph (B), in any case in which —

(i) any of the other persons referred to in paragraph (1)(B) is entitled to monthly benefits as a divorced spouse under section 202(b) or (c) for any month, and

(ii) such person has been divorced for not less than 2 years,

the benefit to which he or she is entitled on the basis of the wages and self-employment income of the individual referred to in paragraph (1) for such month shall be determined without regard to deductions under this subsection as a result of excess earnings of such individual, and the benefits of all other individuals who are entitled for such month to monthly benefits under section 202 on the basis of the wages and self-employment income of such individual referred to in paragraph (1) shall be determined as if no such divorced spouse were entitled to benefits for such month.

(B) Clause (ii) of subparagraph (A) shall not apply with respect to any divorced spouse in any case in which the individual referred to in paragraph (1) became entitled to old-age insurance benefits under section 202(a) before the date of the divorce.

. . . .

(j) *Attainment of retirement age*

For the purposes of this section, an individual shall be considered as having attained retirement age (as defined in section 216(l)) during the entire month in which he attains such age.

. . . .

## § 404. Overpayments and underpayments

(a) *Procedure for adjustment or recovery*

(1) Whenever the Commissioner of Social Security finds that more or less than the correct amount of payment has been made to any person under this title, proper adjustment or recovery shall be made, under regulations prescribed by the Commissioner of Social Security, as follows:

(A) With respect to payment to a person of more than the correct amount, the Commissioner of Social Security shall decrease any payment under this title to which such overpaid person is entitled, or shall require such overpaid person or his estate to refund the amount in excess of the correct amount, or shall decrease any payment under this title payable to his estate or to any other person on the basis of the wages and self-employment income which were the basis of the payments to such overpaid person, or shall obtain recovery by means of reduction in tax refunds based on notice to the Secretary of the Treasury as permitted under section 3720A of title 31, United States Code, or shall apply any combination of the foregoing. A payment made under this title on the basis of an erroneous report of death by the Department of Defense of an individual in the line of duty while he is a member of the uniformed services (as defined in section 210(m)) on active duty (as defined in section 210(l)) shall not be considered an incorrect payment for any month prior to the month such Department notifies the Commissioner of Social Security that such individual is alive.

(B) With respect to payment to a person of less than the correct amount, the Commissioner of Social Security shall make payment of the balance of the amount due such underpaid person, or, if such person dies before payments are completed or before negotiating one or more checks representing correct payments, disposition of the amount due shall be made in accordance with subsection (d).

(2) Notwithstanding any other provision of this section, when any payment of more than the correct amount is made to or on behalf of an individual who has died, and such payment —

(A) is made by direct deposit to a financial institution;

(B) is credited by the financial institution to a joint account of the deceased individual and another person; and

(C) such other person was entitled to a monthly benefit on the basis of the same wages and self-employment income as the deceased individual for the month preceding the month in which the deceased individual died, the amount of such payment in excess of the correct amount shall be treated as a payment of more than the correct amount to such other person. If any payment of more than the correct amount is made to a representative payee on behalf of an individual after the individual's death, the representative payee shall be liable for the repayment of the overpayment, and the Commissioner of Social Security shall establish an overpayment control record under the social security account number of the representative payee.

(b) *No recovery from persons without fault*

In any case in which more than the correct amount of payment has been made, there shall be no adjustment of payments to, or recovery by the United States from, any person who is without fault if such adjustment or recovery would defeat the purpose of this title or would be against equity and good conscience. In making for purposes of this subsection any determination of whether any individual is without fault, the Commissioner of Social Security shall specifically take into account any physical, mental, educational, or linguistic limitation such individual may have (including any lack of facility with the English language).

. . . .

(d) *Payment to survivors or heirs when eligible person is deceased*

If an individual dies before any payment due him under this title is completed, payment of the amount due (including the amount of any unnegotiated checks) shall be made —

(1) to the person, if any, who is determined by the Commissioner of Social Security to be the surviving spouse of the deceased individual and who either (i) was living in the same household with the deceased at the time of his death or (ii) was, for the month in which the deceased individual died, entitled to a monthly benefit on the basis of the same wages and self-employment income as was the deceased individual;

(2) if there is no person who meets the requirements of paragraph (1), or if the person who meets such requirements dies before the payment due him under this title is completed, to the child or children, if any, of the deceased individual who were, for the month in which the deceased individual died, entitled to monthly benefits on the basis of the same wages and self-employment income

as was the deceased individual (and, in case there is more than one such child, in equal parts to each such child);

(3) if there is no person who meets the requirements of paragraph (1) or (2), or if each person who meets such requirements dies before the payment due him under this title is completed, to the parent or parents, if any, of the deceased individual who were, for the month in which the deceased individual died, entitled to monthly benefits on the basis of the same wages and self-employment income as was the deceased individual (and, in case there is more than one such parent, in equal parts to each such parent);

(4) if there is no person who meets the requirements of paragraph (1), (2), or (3), or if each person who meets such requirements dies before the payment due him under this title is completed, to the person, if any, determined by the Commissioner of Social Security to be the surviving spouse of the deceased individual;

(5) if there is no person who meets the requirements of paragraph (1), (2), (3), or (4), or if each person who meets such requirements dies before the payment due him under this title is completed, to the person or persons, if any, determined by the Commissioner of Social Security to be the child or children of the deceased individual (and, in case there is more than one such child, in equal parts to each such child);

(6) if there is no person who meets the requirements of paragraph (1), (2), (3), (4), or (5), or if each person who meets such requirements dies before the payment due him under this title is completed, to the parent or parents, if any, of the deceased individual (and, in case there is more than one such parent, in equal parts to each such parent); or

(7) if there is no person who meets the requirements of paragraph (1), (2), (3), (4), (5), or (6), or if each person who meets such requirements dies before the payment due him under this title is completed, to the legal representative of the estate of the deceased individual, if any.

. . . .

## § 405. Evidence and procedure for establishment of benefits

(a) *Rules and regulations; procedures*

The Commissioner of Social Security shall have full power and authority to make rules and regulations and to establish procedures, not inconsistent with the provisions of this title, which are necessary or appropriate to carry out such provisions, and shall adopt reasonable and proper rules and regulations to regulate and provide for the nature and extent of the proofs and evidence and the method of taking and furnishing the same in order to establish the right to benefits hereunder.

(b) *Administrative determination of entitlement to benefits; findings of fact; hearings; investigations; evidentiary hearings in reconsiderations of disability benefit terminations*

(1) The Commissioner of Social Security is directed to make findings of fact, and decisions as to the rights of any individual applying for a payment under this title. Any such decision by the Commissioner of Social Security which involves a determination of disability and which is in whole or in part unfavorable to such individual shall contain a statement of the case, in understandable language, setting forth a discussion of the evidence, and stating the Commissioner's determination and the reason or reasons upon which it is based. Upon request by any such individual or upon request by a wife, divorced wife, surviving divorced mother, surviving divorced father husband, divorced husband, widower, surviving divorced husband, child, or parent who makes a showing in writing that his or her rights may be prejudiced by any decision the Commissioner of Social Security has rendered, the Commissioner shall give such applicant and such other individual reasonable notice and opportunity for a hearing with respect to such decision, and, if a hearing is held, shall, on the basis of evidence adduced at the hearing, affirm, modify, or reverse the Commissioner's findings of fact and such decision. Any such request with respect to such a decision must be filed within sixty days after notice of such decision is received by the individual making such request. The Commissioner of Social Security is further authorized, on the Commissioner's own motion, to hold such hearings and to conduct such investigations and other proceedings as the Commissioner may deem necessary or proper for the administration of this title. In the course of any hearing, investigation or other proceeding, the Commissioner may administer oaths and affirmations, examine witnesses and receive evidence. Evidence may be received at any hearing before the

Commissioner of Social Security even though inadmissible under rules of evidence applicable to court procedure.

(2) In any case where —

(A) an individual is a recipient of disability insurance benefits, or of child's, widow's, or widower's insurance benefits based on disability,

(B) the physical or mental impairment on the basis of which such benefits are payable is found to have ceased, not to have existed, or to no longer be disabling, and

(C) as a consequence of the finding described in subparagraph (B), such individual is determined by the Commissioner of Social Security not to be entitled to such benefits,

any reconsideration of the finding described in subparagraph (B), in connection with a reconsideration by the Commissioner of Social Security (before any hearing under paragraph (1) on the issue of such entitlement) of the Commissioner's determination described in subparagraph (C), shall be made only after opportunity for an evidentiary hearing, with regard to the finding described in subparagraph (B), which is reasonably accessible to such individual.  Any reconsideration of a finding described in subparagraph (B) may be made either by the State agency or the Commissioner of Social Security where the finding was originally made by the State agency, and shall be made by the Commissioner of Social Security where the finding was originally made by the Commissioner of Social Security.  In the case of a reconsideration by a State agency of a finding described in subparagraph (B) which was originally made by such State agency, the evidentiary hearing shall be held by an adjudicatory unit of the State agency other than the unit that made the finding described in subparagraph (B).  In the case of a reconsideration by the Commissioner of Social Security of a finding described in subparagraph (B) which was originally made by the Commissioner of Social Security, the evidentiary hearing shall be held by a person other than the person or persons who made the finding described in subparagraph (B).

(3)  (A) A failure to timely request review of an initial adverse determination with respect to an application for any benefit under this title or an adverse determination on reconsideration of such an initial determination shall not serve as a basis for denial of a subsequent application for any benefit under this title if the applicant demonstrates that the applicant, or any other individual referred to in paragraph (1), failed to so request such a review acting in good faith reliance upon incorrect, incomplete, or misleading information, relating to the

consequences of reapplying for benefits in lieu of seeking review of an adverse determination, provided by any officer or employee of the Social Security Administration or any State agency acting under section 221.

(B) In any notice of an adverse determination with respect to which a review may be requested under paragraph (1), the Commissioner of Social Security shall describe in clear and specific language the effect on possible entitlement to benefits under this title of choosing to reapply in lieu of requesting review of the determination.

. . . .

(g) *Judicial review*

Any individual, after any final decision of the Commissioner of Social Security made after a hearing to which he was a party, irrespective of the amount in controversy, may obtain a review of such decision by a civil action commenced within sixty days after the mailing to him of notice of such decision or within such further time as the Commissioner of Social Security may allow. Such action shall be brought in the district court of the United States for the judicial district in which the plaintiff resides, or has his principal place of business, or, if he does not reside or have his principal place of business within any such judicial district, in the District Court of the United States for the District of Columbia [United States District Court for the District of Columbia]. As part of the Commissioner's answer the Commissioner of Social Security shall file a certified copy of the transcript of the record including the evidence upon which the findings and decision complained of are based. The court shall have power to enter, upon the pleadings and transcript of the record, a judgment affirming, modifying, or reversing the decision of the Commissioner of Social Security, with or without remanding the cause for a rehearing. The findings of the Commissioner of Social Security as to any fact, if supported by substantial evidence, shall be conclusive, and where a claim has been denied by the Commissioner of Social Security or a decision is rendered under subsection (b) hereof which is adverse to an individual who was a party to the hearing before the Commissioner of Social Security, because of failure of the claimant or such individual to submit proof in conformity with any regulation prescribed under subsection (a) hereof, the court shall review only the question of conformity with such regulations and the validity of such regulations. The court may, on motion of the Commissioner of Social Security made for good cause shown before the Commissioner files the Commissioner's

answer, remand the case to the Commissioner of Social Security for further action by the Commissioner of Social Security, and it may at any time order additional evidence to be taken before the Commissioner of Social Security, but only upon a showing that there is new evidence which is material and that there is good cause for the failure to incorporate such evidence into the record in a prior proceeding; and the Commissioner of Social Security shall, after the case is remanded, and after hearing such additional evidence if so ordered, modify or affirm the Commissioner's findings of fact or the Commissioner's decision, or both, and shall file with the court any such additional and modified findings of fact and decision, and a transcript of the additional record and testimony upon which the Commissioner's action in modifying or affirming was based. Such additional or modified findings of fact and decision shall be reviewable only to the extent provided for review of the original findings of fact and decision. The judgment of the court shall be final except that it shall be subject to review in the same manner as a judgment in other civil actions. Any action instituted in accordance with this subsection shall survive notwithstanding any change in the person occupying the office of Commissioner of Social Security or any vacancy in such office.
. . . .

(j) *Representative payees*

(1) (A) If the Commissioner of Social Security determines that the interest of any individual under this title would be served thereby, certification of payment of such individual's benefit under this title may be made, regardless of the legal competency or incompetency of the individual, either for direct payment to the individual, or for his or her use and benefit, to another individual, or an organization, with respect to whom the requirements of paragraph (2) have been met (hereinafter in this subsection referred to as the individual's "representative payee"). If the Commissioner of Social Security or a court of competent jurisdiction determines that a representative payee has misused any individual's benefit paid to such representative payee pursuant to this subsection or section 807 or 1631(a)(2), the Commissioner of Social Security shall promptly revoke certification for payment of benefits to such representative payee pursuant to this subsection and certify payment to an alternative representative payee or, if the interest of the individual under this title would be served thereby, to the individual.

(B) In the case of an individual entitled to benefits based on disability, the payment of such benefits shall be made to a representative payee if the Commissioner of Social Security determines that such payment would serve the interest of the individual because the individual also has an alcoholism or drug addiction condition (as determined by the Commissioner) and the individual is incapable of managing such benefits.

(2) (A) Any certification made under paragraph (1) for payment of benefits to an individual's representative payee shall be made on the basis of —

(i) an investigation by the Commissioner of Social Security of the person to serve as representative payee, which shall be conducted in advance of such certification and shall, to the extent practicable, include a face-to-face interview with such person, and

(ii) adequate evidence that such certification is in the interest of such individual (as determined by the Commissioner of Social Security in regulations).

(B) (i) As part of the investigation referred to in subparagraph (A)(i), the Commissioner of Social Security shall —

(I) require the person being investigated to submit documented proof of the identity of such person, unless information establishing such identity has been submitted with an application for benefits under this title, title VIII, or title XVI,

(II) verify such person's social security account number (or employer identification number),

(III) determine whether such person has been convicted of a violation of section 208, 811, or 1632, and

(IV) determine whether certification of payment of benefits to such person has been revoked pursuant to this subsection, the designation of such person as a representative payee has been revoked pursuant to section 807(a), or payment of benefits to such person has been terminated pursuant to section 1631(a)(2)(A)(iii) by reason of misuse of funds paid as benefits under this title, title VIII, or title XVI.

(ii) The Commissioner of Social Security shall establish and maintain a centralized file, which shall be updated periodically and which shall be in a form which renders it readily retrievable by each servicing office of the Social Security Administration. Such file shall consist of —

(I) a list of the names and social security account numbers (or employer identification numbers) of all persons with respect to whom certification of payment of benefits has been revoked on or after January 1, 1991, pursuant to this subsection, whose designation as a representative payee has been revoked pursuant to section 807(a), or with respect to whom payment of benefits has been terminated on or after such date pursuant to section 1631(a)(2)(A)(iii), by reason of misuse of funds paid as benefits under this title, title VIII, or title XVI, and

(II) a list of the names and social security account numbers (or employer identification numbers) of all persons who have been convicted of a violation of section 208, 811, or 1632.

(C) (i) Benefits of an individual may not be certified for payment to any other person pursuant to this subsection if —

(I) such person has previously been convicted as described in subparagraph (B)(i)(III),

(II) except as provided in clause (ii), certification of payment of benefits to such person under this subsection has previously been revoked as described in subparagraph (B)(i)(IV),[,] the designation of such person as a representative payee has been revoked pursuant to section 807(a), or payment of benefits to such person pursuant to section 1631(a)(2)(A)(ii) has previously been terminated as described in section 1631(a)(2)(B)(ii)(IV), or

(III) except as provided in clause (iii), such person is a creditor of such individual who provides such individual with goods or services for consideration.

(ii) The Commissioner of Social Security shall prescribe regulations under which the Commissioner of Social Security may grant exemptions to any person from the provisions of clause (i)(II) on a case-by-case basis if such exemption is in the best interest of the individual whose benefits would be paid to such person pursuant to this subsection.

(iii) Clause (i)(III) shall not apply with respect to any person who is a creditor referred to therein if such creditor is —

(I) a relative of such individual if such relative resides in the same household as such individual,

(II) a legal guardian or legal representative of such individual,

(III) a facility that is licensed or certified as a care facility under the law of a State or a political subdivision of a State,

(IV) a person who is an administrator, owner, or employee of a facility referred to in subclause (III) if such individual resides in such facility, and the certification of payment to such facility or such person is made only after good faith efforts have been made by the local servicing office of the Social Security Administration to locate an alternative representative payee to whom such certification of payment would serve the best interests of such individual, or

(V) an individual who is determined by the Commissioner of Social Security, on the basis of written findings and under procedures which the Commissioner of Social Security shall prescribe by regulation, to be acceptable to serve as a representative payee.

(iv) The procedures referred to in clause (iii)(V) shall require the individual who will serve as representative payee to establish, to the satisfaction of the Commissioner of Social Security, that —

(I) such individual poses no risk to the beneficiary,

(II) the financial relationship of such individual to the beneficiary poses no substantial conflict of interest, and

(III) no other more suitable representative payee can be found.

(v) In the case of an individual described in paragraph (1)(B), when selecting such individual's representative payee, preference shall be given to —

(I) a community-based nonprofit social service agency licensed or bonded by the State,

(II) a Federal, State, or local government agency whose mission is to carry out income maintenance, social service, or health care-related activities,

(III) a State or local government agency with fiduciary responsibilities, or

(IV) a designee of an agency (other than of a Federal agency) referred to in the preceding subclauses of this clause, if the Commissioner of Social Security deems it appropriate,

unless the Commissioner of Social Security determines that selection of a family member would be appropriate.

(D) (i) Subject to clause (ii), if the Commissioner of Social Security makes a determination described in the first sentence of paragraph (1) with respect to any individual's benefit and determines that direct payment of the benefit to the individual would cause substantial harm to the individual, the Commissioner of Social Security may defer (in the case of initial entitlement) or suspend (in the case of existing entitlement) direct payment of such benefit to the individual, until such time as the selection of a representative payee is made pursuant to this subsection.

(ii) (I) Except as provided in subclause (II), any deferral or suspension of direct payment of a benefit pursuant to clause (i) shall be for a period of not more than 1 month.

(II) Subclause (I) shall not apply in any case in which the individual is, as of the date of the Commissioner's determination, legally incompetent, under the age of 15 years, or described in paragraph (1)(B).

(iii) Payment pursuant to this subsection of any benefits which are deferred or suspended pending the selection of a representative payee shall be made to the individual or the representative payee as a single sum or over such period of time as the Commissioner of Social Security determines is in the best interest of the individual entitled to such benefits.

(E) (i) Any individual who is dissatisfied with a determination by the Commissioner of Social Security to certify payment of such individual's benefit to a representative payee under paragraph (1) or with the designation of a particular person to serve as representative payee shall be entitled to a hearing by the Commissioner of Social Security to the same extent as is provided in subsection (b), and to judicial review of the Commissioner's final decision as is provided in subsection (g).

(ii) In advance of the certification of payment of an individual's benefit to a representative payee under paragraph (1), the Commissioner of Social Security shall provide written notice of the Commissioner's initial determination to certify such payment. Such notice shall be provided to such individual, except that, if such individual —

(I) is under the age of 15,

(II) is an unemancipated minor under the age of 18, or

(III) is legally incompetent,

then such notice shall be provided solely to the legal guardian or legal representative of such individual.

(iii) Any notice described in clause (ii) shall be clearly written in language that is easily understandable to the reader, shall identify the person to be designated as such individual's representative payee, and shall explain to the reader the right under clause (i) of such individual or of such individual's legal guardian or legal representative —

(I) to appeal a determination that a representative payee is necessary for such individual,

(II) to appeal the designation of a particular person to serve as the representative payee of such individual, and

(III) to review the evidence upon which such designation is based and submit additional evidence.

(3) (A) In any case where payment under this title is made to a person other than the individual entitled to such payment, the Commissioner of Social Security shall establish a system of accountability monitoring whereby such person shall report not less often than annually with respect to the use of such payments. The Commissioner of Social Security shall establish and implement statistically valid procedures for reviewing such reports in order to identify instances in which such persons are not properly using such payments.

(B) Subparagraph (A) shall not apply in any case where the other person to whom such payment is made is a State institution. In such cases, the Commissioner of Social Security shall establish a system of accountability monitoring for institutions in each State.

(C) Subparagraph (A) shall not apply in any case where the individual entitled to such payment is a resident of a Federal institution and the other person to whom such payment is made is the institution.

(D) Notwithstanding subparagraphs (A), (B), and (C), the Commissioner of Social Security may require a report at any time from any person receiving payments on behalf of another, if the

Commissioner of Social Security has reason to believe that the person receiving such payments is misusing such payments.

(E) The Commissioner of Social Security shall maintain a centralized file, which shall be updated periodically and which shall be in a form which will be readily retrievable by each servicing office of the Social Security Administration, of —

(i) the address and the social security account number (or employer identification number) of each representative payee who is receiving benefit payments pursuant to this subsection, section 807, or section 1631(a)(2), and

(ii) the address and social security account number of each individual for whom each representative payee is reported to be providing services as representative payee pursuant to this subsection, section 807, or section 1631(a)(2).

(F) Each servicing office of the Administration shall maintain a list, which shall be updated periodically, of public agencies and community-based nonprofit social service agencies which are qualified to serve as representative payees pursuant to this subsection or section 807 or 1631(a)(2) and which are located in the area served by such servicing office.

(4) (A) (i) A qualified organization may collect from an individual a monthly fee for expenses (including overhead) incurred by such organization in providing services performed as such individual's representative payee pursuant to this subsection if such fee does not exceed the lesser of —

(I) 10 percent of the monthly benefit involved, or

(II) $25.00 per month ($50.00 per month in any case in which the individual is described in paragraph (1)(B)).

The Commissioner of Social Security shall adjust annually (after 1995) each dollar amount set forth in subclause (II) under procedures providing for adjustments in the same manner and to the same extent as adjustments are provided for under the procedures used to adjust benefit amounts under section 215(i)(2)(A), except that any amount so adjusted that is not a multiple of $1.00 shall be rounded to the nearest multiple of $1.00.

(ii) In the case of an individual who is no longer currently entitled to monthly insurance benefits under this title but to whom all past-due benefits have not been paid, for purposes of clause (i), any amount of such past-due benefits payable in any month shall be treated as a monthly benefit referred to in clause (i)(I).

Any agreement providing for a fee in excess of the amount permitted under this subparagraph shall be void and shall be treated as misuse by such organization of such individual's benefits.

(B) For purposes of this paragraph, the term "qualified organization" means any State or local government agency whose mission is to carry out income maintenance, social service, or health care-related activities, any State or local government agency with fiduciary responsibilities, or any community-based nonprofit social service agency which is bonded or licensed in each State in which it serves as a representative payee, if such agency, in accordance with any applicable regulations of the Commissioner of Social Security —

(i) regularly provides services as the representative payee, pursuant to this subsection or section 807 or 1631(a)(2), concurrently to 5 or more individuals, [and]

(ii) demonstrates to the satisfaction of the Commissioner of Social Security that such agency is not otherwise a creditor of any such individual.

The Commissioner of Social Security shall prescribe regulations under which the Commissioner of Social Security may grant an exception from clause (ii) for any individual on a case-by-case basis if such exception is in the best interests of such individual.

(C) Any qualified organization which knowingly charges or collects, directly or indirectly, any fee in excess of the maximum fee prescribed under subparagraph (A) or makes any agreement, directly or indirectly, to charge or collect any fee in excess of such maximum fee, shall be fined in accordance with title 18, United States Code, or imprisoned not more than 6 months, or both.

(5) In cases where the negligent failure of the Commissioner of Social Security to investigate or monitor a representative payee results in misuse of benefits by the representative payee, the Commissioner of Social Security shall certify for payment to the beneficiary or the beneficiary's alternative representative payee an amount equal to such misused benefits. The Commissioner of Social Security shall make a good faith effort to obtain restitution from the terminated representative payee.

(6) The Commissioner of Social Security shall include as a part of the annual report required under section 704 information with respect to the implementation of the preceding provisions of this subsection, including the number of cases in which the representative payee was changed, the number of cases discovered where there has been a misuse of funds, how any such cases were dealt with by the Commissioner of Social Security,

the final disposition of such cases, including any criminal penalties imposed, and such other information as the Commissioner of Social Security determines to be appropriate.

(7) For purposes of this subsection, the term "benefit based on disability" of an individual means a disability insurance benefit of such individual under section 223 or a child's, widow's, or widower's insurance benefit of such individual under section 202 based on such individual's disability.

(k) *Payments to incompetents*

Any payment made after December 31, 1939, under conditions set forth in subsection (j) any payment made before January 1, 1940, to, or on behalf of, a legally incompetent individual, and any payment made after December 31, 1939, to a legally incompetent individual without knowledge by the Commissioner of Social Security of incompetency prior to certification of payment, if otherwise valid under this title, shall be a complete settlement and satisfaction of any claim, right, or interest in and to such payment.

. . . .

## § 406. Representation of claimants before Commissioner of Social Security

(a)  *Recognition of representatives; fees for representation before Commissioner*

(1) The Commissioner of Social Security may prescribe rules and regulations governing the recognition of agents or other persons, other than attorneys as hereinafter provided, representing claimants before the Commissioner of Social Security, and may require of such agents or other persons, before being recognized as representatives of claimants that they shall show that they are of good character and in good repute, possessed of the necessary qualifications to enable them to render such claimants valuable service, and otherwise competent to advise and assist such claimants in the presentation of their cases. An attorney in good standing who is admitted to practice before the highest court of the State, Territory, District, or insular possession of his residence or before the Supreme Court of the United States or the inferior Federal courts, shall be entitled to represent claimants before the Commissioner of Social Security. The Commissioner of Social Security may, after due notice and opportunity for hearing, suspend or prohibit from further practice before the Commissioner any such person, agent, or attorney who refuses to comply

with the Commissioner's rules and regulations or who violates any provision of this section for which a penalty is prescribed. The Commissioner of Social Security may, by rule and regulation, prescribe the maximum fees which may be charged for services performed in connection with any claim before the Commissioner of Social Security under this title, and any agreement in violation of such rules and regulations shall be void. Except as provided in paragraph (2)(A), whenever the Commissioner of Social Security, in any claim before the Commissioner for benefits under this title, makes a determination favorable to the claimant, the Commissioner shall, if the claimant was represented by an attorney in connection with such claim, fix (in accordance with the regulations prescribed pursuant to the preceding sentence) a reasonable fee to compensate such attorney for the services performed by him in connection with such claim.

(2) (A) In the case of a claim of entitlement to past-due benefits under this title, if —

(i) an agreement between the claimant and another person regarding any fee to be recovered by such person to compensate such person for services with respect to the claim is presented in writing to the Commissioner of Social Security prior to the time of the Commissioner's determination regarding the claim,

(ii) the fee specified in the agreement does not exceed the lesser of —

(I) 25 percent of the total amount of such past-due benefits (as determined before any applicable reduction under section 1127(a)), or

(II) $4,000, and

(iii) the determination is favorable to the claimant,

then the Commissioner of Social Security shall approve that agreement at the time of the favorable determination, and (subject to paragraph (3)) the fee specified in the agreement shall be the maximum fee. The Commissioner of Social Security may from time to time increase the dollar amount under clause (ii)(II) to the extent that the rate of increase in such amount, as determined over the period since January 1, 1991, does not at any time exceed the rate of increase in primary insurance amounts under section 215(i) since such date. The Commissioner of Social Security shall publish any such increased amount in the Federal Register.

(B) For purposes of this subsection, the term "past-due benefits" excludes any benefits with respect to which payment has been continued pursuant to subsection (g) or (h) of section 223.

(C) In any case involving —

(i) an agreement described in subparagraph (A) with any person relating to both a claim of entitlement to past-due benefits under this title and a claim of entitlement to past-due benefits under title XVI, and

(ii) a favorable determination made by the Commissioner of Social Security with respect to both such claims, the Commissioner of Social Security may approve such agreement only if the total fee or fees specified in such agreement does not exceed, in the aggregate, the dollar amount in effect under subparagraph (A)(ii)(II).

(D) In the case of a claim with respect to which the Commissioner of Social Security has approved an agreement pursuant to subparagraph (A), the Commissioner of Social Security shall provide the claimant and the person representing the claimant a written notice of —

(i) the dollar amount of the past-due benefits (as determined before any applicable reduction under section 1127(a)) and the dollar amount of the past-due benefits payable to the claimant,

(ii) the dollar amount of the maximum fee which may be charged or recovered as determined under this paragraph, and

(iii) a description of the procedures for review under paragraph (3).

(3) (A) The Commissioner of Social Security shall provide by regulation for review of the amount which would otherwise be the maximum fee as determined under paragraph (2) if, within 15 days after receipt of the notice provided pursuant to paragraph (2)(D) —

(i) the claimant, or the administrative law judge or other adjudicator who made the favorable determination, submits a written request to the Commissioner of Social Security to reduce the maximum fee, or

(ii) the person representing the claimant submits a written request to the Commissioner of Social Security to increase the maximum fee.

Any such review shall be conducted after providing the claimant, the person representing the claimant, and the adjudicator with reasonable notice of such request and an opportunity to submit written information in favor of or in opposition to such request. The adjudicator may request the Commissioner of Social Security to reduce the maximum fee only on the basis of evidence of the failure of the person representing the claimant to represent adequately the claimant's interest or on the basis of evidence that the fee is clearly excessive for services rendered.

(B) (i) In the case of a request for review under subparagraph (A) by the claimant or by the person representing the claimant, such review shall be conducted by the administrative law judge who made the favorable determination or, if the Commissioner of Social Security determines that such administrative law judge is unavailable or if the determination was not made by an administrative law judge, such review shall be conducted by another person designated by the Commissioner of Social Security for such purpose.

(ii) In the case of a request by the adjudicator for review under subparagraph (A), the review shall be conducted by the Commissioner of Social Security or by an administrative law judge or other person (other than such adjudicator) who is designated by the Commissioner of Social Security.

(C) Upon completion of the review, the administrative law judge or other person conducting the review shall affirm or modify the amount which would otherwise be the maximum fee. Any such amount so affirmed or modified shall be considered the amount of the maximum fee which may be recovered under paragraph (2). The decision of the administrative law judge or other person conducting the review shall not be subject to further review.

(4) Subject to subsection (d), if the claimant is determined to be entitled to past-due benefits under this title and the person representing the claimant is an attorney, the Commissioner of Social Security shall, notwithstanding section 205(i), certify for payment out of such past-due benefits (as determined before any applicable reduction under section 1127(a)) to such attorney an amount equal to so much of the maximum fee as does not exceed 25 percent of such past-due benefits (as determined before any applicable reduction under section 1127(a)).

(5) Any person who shall, with intent to defraud, in any manner willfully and knowingly deceive, mislead, or threaten any claimant or prospective claimant or beneficiary under this title by word, circular, letter or advertisement, or who shall knowingly charge or collect directly or indirectly any fee in excess of the maximum fee, or make any agreement directly or indirectly to charge or collect any fee in excess of the maximum fee, prescribed by the Commissioner of Social Security shall be deemed guilty of a misdemeanor and, upon conviction thereof, shall for each offense be punished by a fine not exceeding $500 or by imprisonment not exceeding one year, or both. The Commissioner of Social Security shall

maintain in the electronic information retrieval system used by the Social Security Administration a current record, with respect to any claimant before the Commissioner of Social Security, of the identity of any person representing such claimant in accordance with this subsection.

(b)  *Fees for representation before court*

(1)  (A) Whenever a court renders a judgment favorable to a claimant under this title who was represented before the court by an attorney, the court may determine and allow as part of its judgment a reasonable fee for such representation, not in excess of 25 percent of the total of the past-due benefits to which the claimant is entitled by reason of such judgment, and the Commissioner of Social Security may, notwithstanding the provisions of section 205(i), but subject to subsection (d) of this section, certify the amount of such fee for payment to such attorney out of, and not in addition to, the amount of such past-due benefits.  In case of any such judgment, no other fee may be payable or certified for payment for such representation except as provided in this paragraph.

(B) For purposes of this paragraph —

(i) the term "past-due benefits" excludes any benefits with respect to which payment has been continued pursuant to subsection (g) or (h) of section 223, and

(ii) amounts of past-due benefits shall be determined before any applicable reduction under section 1127(a).

(2) Any attorney who charges, demands, receives, or collects for services rendered in connection with proceedings before a court to which paragraph (1) is applicable any amount in excess of that allowed by the court thereunder shall be guilty of a misdemeanor and upon conviction thereof shall be subject to a fine of not more than $500, or imprisonment for not more than one year, or both.

(c)  *Notification of options for obtaining attorneys*

The Commissioner of Social Security shall notify each claimant in writing, together with the notice to such claimant of an adverse determination, of the options for obtaining attorneys to represent individuals in presenting their cases before the Commissioner of Social Security.  Such notification shall also advise the claimant of the availability to qualifying claimants of legal services organizations which provide legal services free of charge.

(d) *Assessment on attorneys*

(1) In general.  Whenever a fee for services is required to be certified for payment to an attorney from a claimant's past-due benefits pursuant to subsection (a)(4) or (b)(1), the Commissioner shall impose on the attorney an assessment calculated in accordance with paragraph (2).

(2) Amount.

(A) The amount of an assessment under paragraph (1) shall be equal to the product obtained by multiplying the amount of the representative's fee that would be required to be so certified by subsection (a)(4) or (b)(1) before the application of this subsection, by the percentage specified in subparagraph (B).

(B) The percentage specified in this subparagraph is —

(i) for calendar years before 2001, 6.3 percent, and

(ii) for calendar years after 2000, such percentage rate as the Commissioner determines is necessary in order to achieve full recovery of the costs of determining and certifying fees to attorneys from the past-due benefits of claimants, but not in excess of 6.3 percent.

(3) Collection.  The Commissioner may collect the assessment imposed on an attorney under paragraph (1) by offset from the amount of the fee otherwise required by subsection (a)(4) or (b)(1) to be certified for payment to the attorney from a claimant's past-due benefits.

(4) Prohibition on claimant reimbursement.  An attorney subject to an assessment under paragraph (1) may not, directly or indirectly, request or otherwise obtain reimbursement for such assessment from the claimant whose claim gave rise to the assessment.

(5) Disposition of assessments.  Assessments on attorneys collected under this subsection shall be credited to the Federal Old-Age and Survivors Insurance Trust Fund and the Federal Disability Insurance Trust Fund, as appropriate.

(6) Authorization of appropriations.  The assessments authorized under this section shall be collected and available for obligation only to the extent and in the amount provided in advance in appropriations Acts. Amounts so appropriated are authorized to remain available until expended, for administrative expenses in carrying out this title and related laws.

## § 407. Assignment; amendment of section

(a) The right of any person to any future payment under this title shall not be transferable or assignable, at law or in equity, and none of the moneys paid or payable or rights existing under this title shall be subject to execution, levy, attachment, garnishment, or other legal process, or to the operation of any bankruptcy or insolvency law.

. . . .

## § 408. Penalties

(a) *In general*

Whoever —

(1) for the purpose of causing an increase in any payment authorized to be made under this title, or for the purpose of causing any payment to be made where no payment is authorized under this title, shall make or cause to be made any false statement or representation (including any false statement or representation in connection with any matter arising under subchapter E of chapter 1, or subchapter A or E of chapter 9 of the Internal Revenue Code of 1939 or chapter 2 or 21 or subtitle F of the Internal Revenue Code of 1954) as to —

(A) whether wages were paid or received for employment (as said terms are defined in this title and the Internal Revenue Code), or the amount of wages or the period during which paid or the person to whom paid; or

(B) whether net earnings from self-employment (as such term is defined in this title and in the Internal Revenue Code) were derived, or as to the amount of such net earnings or the period during which or the person by whom derived; or

(C) whether a person entitled to benefits under this title had earnings in or for a particular period (as determined under section 203(f) of this title for purposes of deductions from benefits), or as to the amount thereof; or

(2) makes or causes to be made any false statement or representation of a material fact in any application for any payment or for a disability determination under this title; or

(3) at any time makes or causes to be made any false statement or representation of a material fact for use in determining rights to payment under this title; or

(4) having knowledge of the occurrence of any event affecting (1) his initial or continued right to any payment under this title, or (2) the initial or continued right to any payment of any other individual in 'whose behalf he has applied for or is receiving such payment, conceals or fails to disclose such event with an intent fraudulently to secure payment either in a greater amount than is due or when no payment is authorized; or

(5) having made application to receive payment under this title for the use and benefit of another and having received such a payment, knowingly and willfully converts such a payment, or any part thereof, to a use other than for the use and benefit of such other person; or

(6) willfully, knowingly, and with intent to deceive the Commissioner of Social Security as to his true identity (or the true identity of any other person) furnishes or causes to be furnished false information to the Commissioner of Social Security with respect to any information required by the Commissioner of Social Security in connection with the establishment and maintenance of the records provided for in section 205(c)(2); or

(7) for the purpose of causing an increase in any payment authorized under this title (or any other program financed in whole or in part from Federal funds), or for the purpose of causing a payment under this title (or any such other program) to be made when no payment is authorized thereunder, or for the purpose of obtaining (for himself or any other person) any payment or any other benefit to which he (or such other person) is not entitled, or for the purpose of obtaining anything of value from any person, or for any other purpose —

(A) willfully, knowingly, and with intent to deceive, uses a social security account number, assigned by the Commissioner of Social Security (in the exercise of the Commissioner's authority under section 205(c)(2) to establish and maintain records) on the basis of false information furnished to the Commissioner of Social Security by him or by any other person: or

(B) with intent to deceive, falsely represents a number to be the social security account number assigned by the Commissioner of Social Security to him or to another person, when in fact such number is not the social security account number assigned by the Commissioner of Social Security to him or to such other person; or

(C) knowingly alters a social security card issued by the Commissioner of Social Security, buys or sells a card that is, or purports to be, a card so issued, counterfeits a social security card, or possesses a social security card or counterfeit social security card with intent to sell or alter it; or

(8) discloses, uses, or compels the disclosure of the social security number of any person in violation of the laws of the United States; shall be guilty of a felony and upon conviction thereof shall be fined under title 18, United States Code, or imprisoned for not more than five years, or both.

(b) *Violations by certified payees*

Any person or other entity who is convicted of a violation of any of the provisions of this section, if such violation is committed by such person or entity in his role as, or in applying to become, a certified payee under section 205(j) on behalf of another individual (other than such person's spouse), upon his second or any subsequent such conviction shall, in lieu of the penalty set forth in the preceding provisions of this section, be guilty of a felony and shall be fined under title 18, United States Code, or imprisoned for not more than five years, or both. In the case of any violation described in the preceding sentence, including a first such violation, if the court determines that such violation includes a willful misuse of funds by such person or entity, the court may also require that full or partial restitution of such funds be made to the individual for whom such person or entity was the certified payee.

(c) *Effect upon certification as payee; definitions*

Any individual or entity convicted of a felony under this section or under section 1632(b) may not be certified as a payee under section 205(j). For the purpose of subsection (a)(7), the terms "social security number" and "social security account number" mean such numbers as are assigned by the Commissioner of Social Security under section 205(c)(2) whether or not, in actual use, such numbers are called social security numbers.

(d) *Application of subsection (a)(6) and (7) to certain aliens*

(1) Except as provided in paragraph (2), an alien —

(A) whose status is adjusted to that of lawful temporary resident under section 210 or 245A of the Immigration and Nationality Act or under section 902 of the Foreign Relations Authorization Act, Fiscal Years 1988 and 1989,

    (B) whose status is adjusted to that of permanent resident —

        (i) under section 202 of the Immigration Reform and Control Act of 1986, or

        (ii) pursuant to section 249 of the Immigration and Nationality Act, or

    (C) who is granted special immigrant status under section 101(a)(27)(I) of the Immigration and Nationality Act,

shall not be subject to prosecution for any alleged conduct described in paragraph (6) or (7) of subsection (a) if such conduct is alleged to have occurred prior to 60 days after the date of the enactment of the Omnibus Budget Reconciliation Act of 1990 [enacted Nov. 5, 1990].

    (2) Paragraph (1) shall not apply with respect to conduct (described in subsection (a)(7)(C)) consisting of —

    (A) selling a card that is, or purports to be, a social security card issued by the Commissioner of Social Security,

    (B) possessing a social security card with intent to sell it, or

    (C) counterfeiting a social security card with intent to sell it.

    (3) Paragraph (1) shall not apply with respect to any criminal conduct involving both the conduct described in subsection (a)(7) to which paragraph (1) applies and any other criminal conduct if such other conduct would be criminal conduct if the conduct described in subsection (a)(7) were not committed.

## § 413. Quarter and quarter of coverage

(a) *Definitions*

    For the purposes of this title —

    (1) The term "quarter," and the term "calendar quarter," mean a period of three calendar months ending on March 31, June 30, September 30, or December 31.

    (2) (A) The term "quarter of coverage" means —

        (i) for calendar years before 1978, and subject to the provisions of subparagraph (B), a quarter in which an individual has been paid $50 or more in wages (except wages for agricultural labor paid after 1954) or for which he has been credited (as determined under section 212 with $100 or more of self-employment income; and

(ii) for calendar years after 1977, and subject to the provisions of subparagraph (B), each portion of the total of the wages paid and the self-employment income credited (pursuant to section 212) to an individual in a calendar year which equals the amount required for a quarter of coverage in that calendar year (as determined under subsection (d)), with such quarter of coverage being assigned to a specific calendar quarter in such calendar year only if necessary in the case of any individual who has attained age 62 or died or is under a disability and the requirements for insured status in subsection (a) or (b) of section 214, the requirements for entitlement to a computation or recomputation of his primary insurance amount, or the requirements of paragraph (3) of section 216(i) would not otherwise be met.

(B) Notwithstanding the provisions of subparagraph (A) —

(i) no quarter after the quarter in which an individual dies shall be a quarter of coverage, and no quarter any part of which is included in a period of disability (other than the initial quarter and the last quarter of such period) shall be a quarter of coverage;

(ii) if the wages paid to an individual in any calendar year equal $3,000 in the case of a calendar year before 1951, or $3,600 in the case of a calendar year after 1950 and before 1955, or $4,200 in the case of a calendar year after 1954 and before 1959, or $4,800 in the case of a calendar year after 1958 and before 1966, or $6,600 in the case of a calendar year after 1965 and before 1968, or $7,800 in the case of a calendar year after 1967 and before 1972, or $9,000 in the case of the calendar year 1972, or $10,800 in the case of the calendar year 1973, or $13,200 in the case of the calendar year 1974, or an amount equal to the contribution and benefit base (as determined under section 230) in the case of any calendar year after 1974 and before 1978 with respect to which such contribution and benefit base is effective, each quarter of such year shall (subject to clauses (i) and (v)) be a quarter of coverage;

(iii) if an individual has self-employment income for a taxable year, and if the sum of such income and the wages paid to him during such year equals $3,600 in the case of a taxable year beginning after 1950 and ending before 1955, or $4,200 in the case of a taxable year ending after 1954 and before 1959, or $4,800 in the case of a taxable year ending after 1958 and before 1966, or $6,600 in the case of a taxable year ending after 1965 and before 1968, or $7,800 in the case of a taxable year ending after 1967 and before 1972, or $9,000 in the case of a taxable year beginning after 1971 and before 1973, or $10,800 in the case of a taxable year beginning after 1972 and before 1974, or $13,200 in the case of a taxable year beginning after 1973 and before 1975, or an amount equal to the contribution and benefit base (as determined under section 230) which is effective for the calendar year in the case of any taxable year beginning in any calendar year after 1974 and before 1978, each quarter any part of which falls in such year shall (subject to clauses (i) and (v)) be a quarter of coverage;

(iv) if an individual is paid wages for agricultural labor in a calendar year after 1954 and before 1978, the, subject to clauses (i) and (v), (I) the last quarter of such year which can be but is not otherwise a quarter of coverage shall be a quarter of coverage if such wages equal or exceed $100 but are less than $200; (II) the last two quarters of such year which can be but are not otherwise quarters of coverage shall be quarters of coverage if such wages equal or exceed $200 but are less than $300; (III) the last three quarters of such year which can be but are not otherwise quarters of coverage shall be quarters of coverage if such wages equal or exceed $300 but are less than $400; and (IV) each quarter of such year which is not otherwise a quarter of coverage shall be a quarter of coverage if such wages are $400 or more;

(v) no quarter shall be counted as a quarter of coverage prior to the beginning of such quarter;

(vi) not more than one quarter of coverage may be credited to a calendar quarter; and

(vii) no more than four quarters of coverage may be credited to any calendar year after 1977.

If in the case of an individual who has attained age 62 or died or is under a disability and who has been paid wages for agricultural labor in a calendar year after 1954 and before 1978, the requirements for insured status in subsection (a) or (b) of section 214, the requirements for entitlement to a computation or recomputation of his primary insurance amount, or the requirements of paragraph (3) of section 216(i) are not met after assignment of quarters of coverage to quarters in such year as provided in clause (iv) of the preceding sentence, but would be met if such quarters of coverage were assigned to different quarters in such year, then such quarters of coverage shall instead be assigned, for purposes only of determining compliance with such requirements, to such different quarters. If, in the case of an individual who did not die prior to January 1, 1955, and who attained age 62 (if a woman) or age 65 (if a man) or died before July 1, 1957, the requirements for insured status in section 214(a)(3) are not met because of his having too few quarters of coverage but would be met if his quarters of coverage in the first calendar year in which he had any covered employment had been determined on the basis of the period during which wages were earned rather than on the basis of the period during which wages were paid (any such wages paid that are reallocated on an earned basis shall not be used in determining quarters of coverage for subsequent calendar years), then upon application filed by the individual or his survivors and satisfactory proof of his record of wages earned being furnished by such individual or his survivors, the quarters of coverage in such calendar year may be determined on the basis of the periods during which wages were earned.

(b) *Crediting of wages paid in 1937*

With respect to wages paid to an individual in the six-month periods commencing either January 1, 1937, or July 1, 1937; (A) if wages of not less than $100 were paid in any such period, one-half of the total amount thereof shall be deemed to have been paid in each of the calendar quarters in such period; and (B) if wages of less than $100 were paid in any such period, the total amount thereof shall be deemed to have been paid in the latter quarter of such period, except that if in any such period, the individual attained age sixty-five, all of the wages paid in such period shall be deemed to have been paid before such age was attained.

(c) *Alternative method for determining quarters of coverage with respect to wages in the period from 1937 to 1950*

For purposes of sections 214(a) and 215(d), an individual shall be deemed to have one quarter of coverage for each $400 of his total wages prior to 1951 (as defined in section 215(d)(1)(C)), except where such individual is not a fully insured individual on the basis of the number of quarters of coverage so derived plus the number of quarters of coverage derived from the wages and self-employment income credited to such individual for periods after 1950.

(d) *Amount required for a quarter of coverage*

(1) The amount of wages and self-employment income which an individual must have in order to be credited with a quarter of coverage in any year under subsection (a)(2)(A)(ii) shall be $250 in the calendar year 1978 and the amount determined under paragraph (2) of this subsection for years after 1978.

(2) The Commissioner of Social Security shall, on or before November 1 of 1978 and of every year thereafter, determine and publish in the Federal Register the amount of wages and self-employment income which an individual must have in order to be credited with a quarter of coverage in the succeeding calendar year. The amount required for a quarter of coverage shall be the larger of —

(A) the amount in effect in the calendar year in which the determination under this subsection is made, or

(B) the product of the amount prescribed in paragraph (1) which is required for a quarter of coverage in 1978 and the ratio of the national average wage index (as defined in section 209(k)(1)) for the calendar year before the year in which the determination under this paragraph is made to the national average wage index (as so defined) for 1976,

with such product, if not a multiple of $10, being rounded to the next higher multiple of $10 where such amount is a multiple of $5 but not of $10 and to the nearest multiple of $10 in any other case.

## § 414. Insured status for purposes of old-age and survivors insurance benefits

For the purposes of this title —

(a) *"Fully insured individual" defined*

The term "fully insured individual" means any individual who had not less than —

(1) one quarter of coverage (whenever acquired) for each calendar year elapsing after 1950 (or, if later, the year in which he attained age 21) and before the year in which he died or (if earlier) the year in which he attained age 62, except that in no case shall an individual be a fully insured individual unless he has at least 6 quarters of coverage; or

(2) 40 quarters of coverage; or

(3) in the case of an individual who died prior to 1951, 6 quarters of coverage;

not counting as an elapsed year for purposes of paragraph (1) any year any part of which was included in a period of disability (as defined in section 216(i)).

(b) *"Currently insured individual" defined*

The term "currently insured individual" means any individual who had not less than six quarters of coverage during the thirteen-quarter period ending with (1) the quarter in which he died, (2) the quarter in which he became entitled to old-age insurance benefits, (3) the quarter in which he became entitled to primary insurance benefits under this title as in effect prior to the enactment of this section [enacted Aug. 28, 1950], or (4) in the case of any individual entitled to disability insurance benefits, the quarter in which he most recently became entitled to disability insurance benefits, not counting as part of such thirteen-quarter period any quarter any part of which was included in a period of disability unless such quarter was a quarter of coverage.

## § 416. Additional definitions

For the purposes of this title —

(a) *Spouse; surviving spouse*

(1) The term "spouse" means a wife as defined in subsection (b) or a husband as defined in subsection (f).

(2) The term "surviving spouse" means a widow as defined in subsection (c) or a widower as defined in subsection (g).

(b) *Wife*

The term "wife" means the wife of an individual, but only if she (1) is the mother of his son or daughter, (2) was married to him for a period of not less than one year immediately preceding the day on which her application is filed, or (3) in the month prior to the month of her marriage to him (A) was entitled to, or on application therefor and attainment of age 62 in such prior month would have been entitled to, benefits under subsection (b), (e), or (h) of section 202, (B) had attained age eighteen and was entitled to, or on application therefor would have been entitled to, benefits under subsection (d) of such section (subject, however, to section 202(s)), or (C) was entitled to, or upon application therefor and attainment of the required age (if any) would have been entitled to, a widow's, child's (after attainment of age 18), or parent's insurance annuity under section 2 of the Railroad Retirement Act of 1974. For purposes of clause (2), a wife shall be deemed to have been married to an individual for a period of one year throughout the month in which occurs the first anniversary of her marriage to such individual. For purposes of subparagraph (C) of section 202(b)(1), a divorced wife shall be deemed not to be married throughout the month in which she becomes divorced.

(c) *Widow*

The term "widow" (except when used in the first sentence of section 202(i)) means the surviving wife of an individual, but only if (1) she is the mother of his son or daughter, (2) she legally adopted his son or daughter while she was married to him and while such son or daughter was under the age of eighteen, (3) he legally adopted her son or daughter while she was married to him and while such son or daughter was under the age of eighteen, (4) she was married to him at the time both of them legally adopted a child under the age of eighteen, (5) she was married to him for a period of not less than nine months immediately prior to the day on which he died, or (6) in the month prior to the month of her marriage to him (A) she was entitled to, or on application therefor and attainment of age 62 in such prior month would have been entitled to, benefits under subsection (b), (e), or (h) of section 202, (B) she had attained age eighteen and was entitled to, or on application therefor would have been entitled to, benefits under subsection (d) of such section (subject, however, to section

202(s)), or (C) she was entitled to, or upon application therefor and attainment of the required age (if any) would have been entitled to, a widow's, child's (after attainment of age 18), or parent's insurance annuity under section 2 of the Railroad Retirement Act of 1974.

(d)  *Divorced spouses; divorce*

(1) The term "divorced wife" means a woman divorced from an individual, but only if she had been married to such individual for a period of 10 years immediately before the date the divorce became effective.

(2) The term "surviving divorced wife" means a woman divorced from an individual who has died, but only if she had been married to the individual for a period of 10 years immediately before the date the divorce became effective.

(3) The term "surviving divorced mother" means a woman divorced from an individual who has died, but only if (A) she is the mother of his son or daughter, (B) she legally adopted his son or daughter while she was married to him and while such son or daughter was under the age of 18, (C) he legally adopted her son or daughter while she was married to him and while such son or daughter was under the age of 18, or (D) she was married to him at the time both of them legally adopted a child under the age of 18.

(4) The term "divorced husband" means a man divorced from an individual, but only if he had been married to such individual for a period of 10 years immediately before the date the divorce became effective.

(5) The term "surviving divorced husband" means a man divorced from an individual who has died, but only if he had been married to the individual for a period of 10 years immediately before the divorce became effective.

(6) The term "surviving divorced father" means a man divorced from an individual who has died, but only if (A) he is the father of her son or daughter, (B) he legally adopted her son or daughter while he was married to her and while such son or daughter was under the age of 18, (C) she legally adopted his son or daughter while he was married to her and while such son or daughter was under the age of 18, or (D) he was married to her at the time both of them legally adopted a child under the age of 18.

(7) The term "surviving divorced parent" means a surviving divorced mother as defined in paragraph (3) of this subsection or a surviving divorced father as defined in paragraph (6).

(8) The terms "divorce" and "divorced" refer to a divorce a vinculo matrimonii.

(e) *Child*

The term "child" means (1) the child or legally adopted child of an individual, (2) a stepchild who has been such stepchild for not less than one year immediately preceding the day on which application for child's insurance benefits is filed or (if the insured individual is deceased) not less than nine months immediately preceding the day on which such individual died, and (3) a person who is the grandchild or stepgrandchild of an individual or his spouse, but only if (A) there was no natural or adoptive parent (other than such a parent who was under a disability, as defined in section 223(d)) of such person living at the time (i) such individual became entitled to old-age insurance benefits or disability insurance benefits or died, or (ii) if such individual had a period of disability which continued until such individual became entitled to old-age insurance benefits or disability insurance benefits, or died, at the time such period of disability began, or (B) such person was legally adopted after the death of such individual by such individual's surviving spouse in an adoption that was decreed by a court of competent jurisdiction within the United States and such person's natural or adopting parent or stepparent was not living in such individual's household and making regular contributions toward such person's support at the time such individual died. For purposes of clause (1), a person shall be deemed, as of the date of death of an individual, to be the legally adopted child of such individual if such person was either living with or receiving at least one-half of his support from such individual at the time of such individual's death and was legally adopted by such individual's surviving spouse after such individual's death but only if (A) proceedings for the adoption of the child had been instituted by such individual before his death, or (B) such child was adopted by such individual's surviving spouse before the end of two years after (i) the day on which such individual died or (ii) the date of enactment of the Social Security Amendments of 1958 [enacted Aug. 28, 1958]. For purposes of clause (2), a person who is not the stepchild of an individual shall be deemed the stepchild of such individual if such individual was not the mother or adopting mother or the father or adopting father of such person and such individual and the mother or adopting mother, or the father or adopting father, as the case may be, of such person went through a marriage ceremony resulting in a purported marriage between them which, but for a legal impediment described in the last sentence of subsection (h)(1)(B), would have been a valid marriage. For purposes of clause (2), a child shall be deemed to have been the stepchild of an individual for a period of one year throughout the month in which occurs the expiration of such one year. For purposes of clause (3), a person shall be deemed to have no natural or adoptive parent living (other than a parent who was under a disability) throughout the most recent month in which a natural or adoptive parent (not under a disability) dies.

(f) *Husband*

The term "husband" means the husband of an individual, but only if (1) he is the father of her son or daughter, (2) he was married to her for a period of not less than one year immediately preceding the day on which his application is filed, or (3) in the month prior to the month of his marriage to her (A) he was entitled to, or on application therefor and attainment of age 62 in such prior month would have been entitled to, benefits under subsection (c), (f) or (h) of section 202, (B) he had attained age eighteen and was entitled to, or on application therefor would have been entitled to, benefits under subsection (d) of such section (subject, however, to section 202(s)), or (C) he was entitled to, or upon application therefor and attainment of the required age (if any) he would have been entitled to, a widower's, child's (after attainment of age 18), or parent's insurance annuity under section 2 of the Railroad Retirement Act of 1974. For purposes of clause (2), a husband shall be deemed to have been married to an individual for a period of one year throughout the month in which occurs the first anniversary of his marriage to her. For purposes of subparagraph (C) of section 202(c)(1), a divorced husband shall be deemed not to be married throughout the month which he becomes divorced.

(g) *Widower*

The term "widower" (except when used in the first sentence of section 202(i)) means the surviving husband of an individual, but only if (1) he is the father of her son or daughter, (2) he legally adopted her son or daughter while he was married to her and while such son or daughter was under the age of eighteen, (3) she legally adopted his son or daughter while he was married to her and while such son or daughter was under the age of eighteen, (4) he was married to her at the time both of them legally adopted a child under the age of eighteen, (5) he was married to her for a period of not less than nine months immediately prior to the day on which she died, or (6) in the month before the month of his marriage to her (A) he was entitled to, or on application therefor and attainment of age 62 in such prior month would have been entitled to, benefits under subsection (c), (f) or (h) of section 202, (B) he had attained age eighteen and was entitled to, or on application therefor would have been entitled to, benefits under subsection (d) of such section (subject, however, to section 202(s)), or (C) he was entitled to, or on application therefor and attainment of the required age (if any) he would have been entitled to, a widower's, child's (after attainment of age 18), or parent's insurance annuity under section 2 of the Railroad Retirement Act of 1974.

(h) *Determination of family status*

(1) (A) (i) An applicant is the wife, husband, widow, or widower of a fully or currently insured individual for purposes of this title if the courts of the State in which such insured individual is domiciled at the time such applicant files an application, or, if such insured individual is dead, the courts of the State in which he was domiciled at the time of death, or, if such insured individual is or was not so domiciled in any State, the courts of the District of Columbia, would find that such applicant and such insured individual were validly married at the time such applicant files such application or, if such insured individual is dead, at the time he died.

(ii) If such courts would not find that such applicant and such insured individual were validly married at such time, such applicant shall, nevertheless be deemed to be the wife, husband, widow, or widower, as the case may be, of such insured individual if such applicant would, under the laws applied by such courts in determining the devolution of intestate personal property, have the same status with respect to the taking of such property as a wife, husband, widow, or widower of such insured individual.

(B) (i) In any case where under subparagraph (A) an applicant is not (and is not deemed to be) the wife, widow, husband, or widower of a fully or currently insured individual, or where under subsection (b), (c), (d), (f), or (g) such applicant is not the wife, divorced wife, widow, surviving divorced wife, husband, divorced husband, widower, or surviving divorced husband of such individual, but it is established to the satisfaction of the Commissioner of Social Security that such applicant in good faith went through a marriage ceremony with such individual resulting in a purported marriage between them which, but for a legal impediment not known to the applicant at the time of such ceremony, would have been a valid marriage, then, for purposes of subparagraph (A) and subsections (b), (c), (d), (f), and (g), such purported marriage shall be deemed to be a valid marriage. Notwithstanding the preceding sentence, in the case of any person who would be deemed under the preceding sentence a wife, widow, husband, or widower of the insured individual, such marriage shall not be deemed to be a valid marriage unless the applicant and the insured individual were living in the same household at the time of the death of the insured individual or (if the insured individual is living) at the time the applicant files the application. A marriage that is deemed to be a valid marriage by reason of the preceding sentence shall continue to be deemed a valid marriage if the insured individual and the person entitled to benefits as the wife or husband of the insured individual are no longer living in the same household at the time of the death of such insured individual.

(ii) The provisions of clause (i) shall not apply if the Commissioner of Social Security determines, on the basis of information brought to the Commissioner's attention, that such applicant entered into such purported marriage with such insured individual with knowledge that it would not be a valid marriage.

(iii) The entitlement to a monthly benefit under subsection (b) or (c) of section 202, based on the wages and self-employment income of such insured individual, of a person who would not be deemed to be a wife or husband, or widower of such insured individual but for this subparagraph, shall end with the month before the month in which such person enters into a marriage, valid without regard to this subparagraph, with a person other than such insured individual.

(iv) For purposes of this subparagraph, a legal impediment to the validity of a purported marriage includes only an impediment (I) resulting from the lack of dissolution of a previous marriage or otherwise arising out of such previous marriage or its dissolution, or (II) resulting from a defect in the procedure followed in connection with such purported marriage.

(2)    (A) In determining whether an applicant is the child or parent of a fully or currently insured individual for purposes of this title, the Commissioner of Social Security shall apply such law as would be applied in determining the devolution of intestate personal property by the courts of the State in which such insured individual is domiciled at the time such

applicant files application, or, if such insured individual is dead, by the courts of the State in which he was domiciled at the time of his death, or, if such insured individual is or was not so domiciled in any State, by the courts of the District of Columbia. Applicants who according to such law would have the same status relative to taking intestate personal property as a child or parent shall be deemed such.

(B) If an applicant is a son or daughter of a fully or currently insured individual but is not (and is not deemed to be) the child of such insured individual under subparagraph (A), such applicant shall nevertheless be deemed to be the child of such insured individual if such insured individual and the mother or father, as the case may be, of such applicant went through a marriage ceremony resulting in a purported marriage between them which, but for a legal impediment described in the last sentence of paragraph (1)(B), would have been a valid marriage.

(3) An applicant who is the son or daughter of a fully or currently insured individual, but who is not (and is not deemed to be) the child of such insured individual under paragraph (2), shall nevertheless be deemed to be the child of such insured individual if:

(A) in the case of an insured individual entitled to old-age insurance benefits (who was not, in the month preceding such entitlement, entitled to disability insurance benefits) —

(i) such insured individual —

(I) has acknowledged in writing that the applicant is his or her son or daughter,

(II) has been decreed by a court to be the mother or father of the applicant, or

(III) has been ordered by a court to contribute to the support of the applicant because the applicant is his or her son or daughter,

and such acknowledgment, court decree, or court order was made not less than one year before such insured individual became entitled to old-age insurance benefits or attained retirement age (as defined in subsection (l)),whichever is earlier; or

(ii) such insured individual is shown by evidence satisfactory to the Commissioner of Social Security to be the mother or father of the applicant and was living with or contributing to the support of the applicant at the time such applicant's application for benefits was filed;

(B) in the case of an insured individual entitled to disability insurance benefits, or who was entitled to such benefits in the month preceding the first month for which he or she was entitled to old-age insurance benefits —

(i) such insured individual —

(I) has acknowledged in writing that the applicant is his or her son or daughter,

(II) has been decreed by a court to be the mother or father of the applicant, or

(III) has been ordered by a court to contribute to the support of the applicant because the applicant is his or her son or daughter,

and such acknowledgment, court decree, or court order was made before such insured individual's most recent period of disability began; or

(ii) such insured individual is shown by evidence satisfactory to the Commissioner of Social Security to be the mother or father of the applicant and was living with or contributing to the support of that applicant at the time such applicant's application for benefits was filed;

(C) in the case of a deceased individual —

(i) such insured individual —

(I) had acknowledged in writing that the applicant is his or her son or daughter,

(II) had been decreed by a court to be the mother or father of the applicant, or

(III) had been ordered by a court to contribute to the support of the applicant because the applicant was his or her son or daughter,

and such acknowledgment, court decree, or court order was made before the death of such insured individual, or

(ii) such insured individual is shown by evidence satisfactory to the Commissioner of Social Security to have been the mother or father of the applicant, and such insured individual was living with or contributing to the support of the applicant at the time such insured individual died.

For purposes of subparagraph (A)(i) and (B)(i), an acknowledgment, court decree, or court order shall be deemed to have occurred on the first day of the month in which it actually occurred.

(i) *Disability; period of disability*

(1) Except for purposes of sections 202(d), 202(e), 202(f), 223, and 225, the term "disability" means (A) inability to engage in any substantial gainful activity by reason of any medically determinable physical or mental impairment which can be expected to result in death or has lasted or can be expected to last for a continuous period of not less than 12 months, or (B) blindness; and the term "blindness" means central visual acuity of 20/200 or less in the better eye with the use of a correcting lens. An eye which is accompanied by a limitation in the fields of vision such that the widest diameter of the visual field subtends an angle no greater than 20 degrees shall be considered for purposes of this paragraph as having a central visual acuity of 20/200 or less. The provisions of paragraphs (2)(A), (2)(B), (3), (4), (5), and (6) of section 223(d) shall be applied for purposes of determining whether an individual is under a disability within the meaning of the first sentence of this paragraph in the same manner as they are applied for purposes of paragraph (1) of such section. Nothing in this title shall be construed as authorizing the Commissioner of Social Security or any other officer or employee of the United States to interfere in any way with the practice of medicine or with relationships between practitioners of medicine and their patients, or to exercise any supervision or control over the administration or operation of any hospital.

(2) (A) The term "period of disability" means a continuous period (beginning and ending as hereinafter provided in this subsection) during which an individual was under a disability (as defined in paragraph (1)), but only if such period is of not less than five full calendar months' duration or such individual was entitled to benefits under section 223 for one or more months in such period.

(B) No period of disability shall begin as to any individual unless such individual files an application for a disability determination with respect to such period; and no such period shall begin as to any individual after such individual attains retirement age (as defined in subsection (l)). In the case of a deceased individual, the requirement of an application under the preceding sentence may be satisfied by an application for a disability determination filed with respect to such individual within 3 months after the month in which he died.

(C) A period of disability shall begin —

(i) on the day the disability began, but only if the individual satisfies the requirements of paragraph (3) on such day; or

(ii) if such individual does not satisfy the requirements of paragraph (3) on such day, then on the first day of the first quarter thereafter in which he satisfies such requirements.

(D) A period of disability shall end with the close of whichever of the following months is the earlier; (i) the month preceding the month in which the individual attains retirement age (as defined in subsection (1)), or (ii) the month preceding (I) the termination month (as defined in section 223(a)(1)), or, if earlier (II) the first month for which no benefit is payable by reason of section 223(e), where no benefit is payable for any of the succeeding months during the 36-month period referred to in such section. The provisions set forth in section 223(f) with respect to determinations of whether entitlement to benefits under this title or title XVIII based on the disability of any individual is terminated (on the basis of a finding that the physical or mental impairment on the basis of which such benefits are provided has ceased, does not exist, or is not disabling) shall apply in the same manner and to the same extent with respect to determinations of whether a period of disability has ended (on the basis of a finding that the physical or mental impairment on the basis of which the finding of disability was made has ceased, does not exist, or is not disabling).

(E) Except as is otherwise provided in subparagraph (F), no application for a disability determination which is filed more than 12 months after the month prescribed by subparagraph (D) as the month in which the period of disability ends (determined without regard to subparagraph (B) and this subparagraph) shall be accepted as an application for purposes of this paragraph.

(F) An application for a disability determination which is filed more than 12 months after the month prescribed by subparagraph (D) as the month in which the period of disability ends (determined without regard to subparagraphs (B) and (E)) shall be accepted as an application for purposes of this paragraph if —

(i) in the case of an application filed by or on behalf of an individual with respect to a disability which ends after the month in which the Social Security Amendments of 1967 is enacted [enacted Jan. 1968], such application is filed not more than 36 months after the month in which such disability ended, such individual is alive at the time the application is filed, and the Commissioner of Social Security finds in accordance with regulations prescribed by the Commissioner that the failure of such individual to file an application for a disability determination within the time specified in subparagraph (E) was attributable to a physical or mental condition of such individual which rendered him incapable of executing such an application, and

(ii) in the case of an application filed by or on behalf of an individual with respect to a period of disability which ends in or before the month in which the Social Security Amendments of 1967 is enacted [enacted Jan. 1968] —

(I) such application is filed not more than 12 months after the month in which the Social Security Amendments of 1967 is enacted [enacted Jan. 1968],

(II) a previous application for a disability determination has been filed by or on behalf of such individual (1) in or before the month in which the Social Security Amendments of 1967 is enacted [enacted Jan. 1968], and (2) not more than 36 months after the month in which his disability ended, and

(III) the Commissioner of Social Security finds in accordance with regulations prescribed by him, that the failure of such individual to file an application within the then specified time period was attributable to a physical or mental condition of such individual which rendered him incapable of executing such an application.

In making a determination under this subsection, with respect to the disability or period of disability of any individual whose application for a determination thereof is accepted solely by reason of the provisions of this subparagraph (F), the provisions of this subsection (other than the provisions of this subparagraph) shall be applied as such provisions are in effect at the time such determination is made.

(G) An application for a disability determination filed before the first day on which the applicant satisfies the requirements for a period of disability under this subsection shall be deemed a valid application (and shall be deemed to have been filed on such first day) only if the applicant satisfies the requirements for a period of disability before the Commissioner of Social Security makes a final decision on the application and no request under section 205(b) for notice and opportunity for a hearing thereon is made or, if such a request is made, before a decision based upon the evidence adduced at the hearing is made (regardless of whether such decision becomes the final decision of the Commissioner of Social Security).

(3) The requirements referred to in clauses (i) and (ii) of paragraph (2)(C) are satisfied by an individual with respect to any quarter only if—

(A) he would have been a fully insured individual (as defined in section 214) had he attained age 62 and filed application for benefits under section 202(a) on the first day of such quarter; and

(B)   (i) he had not less than 20 quarters of coverage during the 40-quarter period which ends with such quarter, or

(ii) if such quarter ends before he attains (or would attain) age 31, not less than one-half (and not less than 6) of the quarters during the period ending with such quarter and beginning after he attained the age of 21 were quarters of coverage, or (if the number of quarters in such period is less than 12) not less than 6 of the quarters in the 12-quarter period ending with such quarter were quarters of coverage, or

(iii) in the case of an individual (not otherwise insured under clause (i)) who, by reason of clause (ii), had a prior period of disability that began during a period before the quarter in which he or she attained age 31, not less than one-half of the quarters beginning after such individual attained age 21 and ending with such quarter are quarters of coverage, or (if the number of quarters in such period is less than 12) not less than 6 of the quarters in the 12-quarter period ending with such quarter are quarters of coverage;

except that the provisions of subparagraph (B) of this paragraph shall not apply in the case of an individual who is blind (within the meaning of 'blindness' as defined in paragraph (1)). For purposes of subparagraph (B) of this paragraph, when the number of quarters in any period is an odd number, such number shall be reduced by one, and a quarter shall not be counted as part of any period if any part of such quarter was included in a prior period of disability unless such quarter was a quarter of coverage.

(j)  *Periods of limitation ending on nonwork days*

Where this title, any provision of another law of the United States (other than the Internal Revenue Code of 1986) relating to or changing the effect of this title, or any regulation issued by the Commissioner of Social

Security pursuant thereto provides for a period within which an act is required to be done which affects eligibility for or the amount of any benefit or payment under this title or is necessary to establish or protect any rights under this title, and such period ends on a Saturday, Sunday, or legal holiday, or on any other day all or part of which is declared to be a nonwork day for Federal employees by statute or Executive order, then such act shall be considered as done within such period if it is done on the first day thereafter which is not a Saturday, Sunday, or legal holiday or any other day all or part of which is declared to be a nonwork day for Federal employees by statute or Executive order. For purposes of this subsection, the day on which a period ends shall include the day on which an extension of such period, as authorized by law or by the Commissioner of Social Security pursuant to law, ends. The provisions of this subsection shall not extend the period during which benefits under this title may (pursuant to section 202(j)(1) or 223(b)) be paid for months prior to the day application for such benefits is filed, or during which an application for benefits under this title may (pursuant to section 202(j)(2) or 223(b)) be accepted as such.

(k) *Waiver of nine-month requirement for widow, stepchild, or widower in case of accidental death or in case of serviceman dying in line of duty, or in case of remarriage to the same individual*

The requirements in clause (5) of subsection (c) or clause (5) of subsection (g) that the surviving spouse of an individual have been married to such individual for a period of not less than nine months immediately prior to the day on which such individual died in order to qualify as such individual's widow or widower, and the requirement in subsection (e) that the stepchild of a deceased individual have been such stepchild for not less than nine months immediately preceding the day on which such individual died in order to qualify as such individual's child, shall be deemed to be satisfied, where such individual dies within the applicable nine-month period, if —

    (1) his death —

        (A) is accidental, or

        (B) occurs in line of duty while he is a member of a uniformed service serving on active duty (as defined in section 210(1)(2),

unless the Commissioner of Social Security determines that at the time of the marriage involved the individual could not have reasonably been expected to live for nine months, or

(2)  (A) the widow or widower of such individual had been previously married to such individual and subsequently divorced and such requirement would have been satisfied at the time of such divorce if such previous marriage had been terminated by the death of such individual at such time instead of by divorce; or

(B) the stepchild of such individual had been the stepchild of such individual during a previous marriage of such stepchild's parent to such individual which ended in divorce and such requirement would have been satisfied at the time of such divorce if such previous marriage had been terminated by the death of such individual at such time instead of by divorce;

except that paragraph (2) of this subsection shall not apply if the Commissioner of Social Security determines that at the time of the marriage involved the individual could not have reasonably been expected to live for nine months.  For purposes of paragraph (1)(A) of this subsection, the death of an individual is accidental if he receives bodily injuries solely through violent, external, and accidental means and, as a direct result of the bodily injuries and independently of all other causes, loses his life not later than three months after the day on which he receives such bodily injuries.

(l)  *Retirement age*

(1) The term "retirement age" means —

(A) with respect to an individual who attains early retirement age (as defined in paragraph (2)) before January 1, 2000, 65 years of age;

(B) with respect to an individual who attains early retirement age after December 31, 1999, and before January 1, 2005, 65 years of age plus the number of months in the age increase factor (as determined under paragraph (3)) for the calendar year in which such individual attains early retirement age;

(C) with respect to an individual who attains early retirement age after December 31, 2004, and before January 1, 2017, 66 years of age;

(D) with respect to an individual who attains early retirement age after December 31, 2016, and before January 1, 2022, 66 years of age plus the number of months in the age increase factor (as determined under paragraph (3)) for the calendar year in which such individual attains early retirement age; and

(E) with respect to an individual who attains early retirement age after December 31, 2021, 67 years of age.

(2) The term "early retirement age" means age 62 in the case of an old-age, wife's, or husband's insurance benefit, and age 60 in the case of a widow's or widower's insurance benefit.

(3) The age increase factor for any individual who attains early retirement age in a calendar year within the period to which subparagraph (B) or (D) of paragraph (1) applies shall be determined as follows:

(A) With respect to an individual who attains early retirement age in the 5-year period consisting of the calendar years 2000 through 2004, the age increase factor shall be equal to two-twelfths of the number of months in the period beginning with January 2000 and ending with December of the year in which the individual attains early retirement age.

(B) With respect to an individual who attains early retirement age in the 5-year period consisting of the calendar years 2017 through 2021, the age increase factor shall be equal to two-twelfths of the number of months in the period beginning with January 2017 and ending with December of the year in which the individual attains early retirement age.

## § 420.  Disability provisions inapplicable if benefit rights impaired

None of the provisions of this title relating to periods of disability shall apply in any case in which their application would result in the denial of monthly benefits or a lump-sum death payment which would otherwise be payable under this title; nor shall they apply in the case of any monthly benefit or lump-sum death payment under this title if such benefit or payment would be greater without their application.

## § 421.  Disability determinations

(a) *State agencies*

(1) In the case of any individual, the determination of whether or not he is under a disability (as defined in section 216(i) or 223(d)) and of the day such disability began, and the determination of the day on which such disability ceases, shall be made by a State agency, notwithstanding any other provision of law, in any State that notifies the Commissioner of Social Security in writing that it wishes to make such disability determinations commencing with such month as the Commissioner of Social Security and the State agree upon, but only if (A) the Commissioner of Social Security has not found, under subsection (b)(1), that the State

agency has substantially failed to make disability determinations in accordance with the applicable provisions of this section or rules issued thereunder, and (B) the State has not notified the Commissioner of Social Security, under subsection (b)(2), that it does not wish to make such determinations. If the Commissioner of Social Security once makes the finding described in clause (A) of the preceding sentence, or the State gives the notice referred to in clause (B) of such sentence, the Commissioner of Social Security may thereafter determine whether (and, if so, beginning with which month and under what conditions) the State may again make disability determinations under this paragraph.

(2) The disability determinations described in paragraph (1) made by a State agency shall be made in accordance with the pertinent provisions of this title and the standards and criteria contained in regulations or other written guidelines of the Commissioner of Social Security pertaining to matters such as disability determinations, the class or classes of individuals with respect to which a State may make disability determinations (if it does not wish to do so with respect to all individuals in the State), and the conditions under which it may choose not to make all such determinations. In addition, the Commissioner of Social Security shall promulgate regulations specifying, in such detail as the Commissioner deems appropriate, performance standards and administrative requirements and procedures to be followed in performing the disability determination function in order to assure effective and uniform administration of the disability insurance program throughout the United States. The regulations may, for example, specify matters such as —

(A) the administrative structure and the relationship between various units of the State agency responsible for disability determinations,

(B) the physical location of and relationship among agency staff units, and other individuals or organizations performing tasks for the State agency, and standards for the availability to applicants and beneficiaries of facilities for making disability determinations,

(C) State agency performance criteria, including the rate of accuracy of decisions, the time periods within which determinations must be made, the procedures for and the scope of review by the Commissioner of Social Security, and, as the Commissioner finds appropriate, by the State, of its performance in individual cases and in classes of cases, and rules governing access of appropriate Federal officials to State offices and to State records relating to its administration of the disability determination function,

(D) fiscal control procedures that the State agency may be required to adopt, and

(E) the submission of reports and other data, in such form and at such time as the Commissioner of Social Security may require, concerning the State agency's activities relating to the disability determination.

Nothing in this section shall be construed to authorize the Commissioner of Social Security to take any action except pursuant to law or to regulations promulgated pursuant to law.

(b) *Determinations by Commissioner of Social Security*

(1) If the Commissioner of Social Security finds, after notice and opportunity for a hearing, that a State agency is substantially failing to make disability determinations in a manner consistent with the Commissioner's regulations and other written guidelines, the Commissioner of Social Security shall, not earlier than 180 days following the Commissioner's finding, and after the Commissioner has complied with the requirements of paragraph (3), make the disability determinations referred to in subsection (a)(1).

(2) If a State, having notified the Commissioner of Social Security of its intent to make disability determinations under subsection (a)(1), no longer wishes to make such determinations, it shall notify the Commissioner of Social Security in writing of that fact, and, if an agency of the State is making disability determinations at the time such notice is given, it shall continue to do so for not less than 180 days, or (if later) until the Commissioner of Social Security has complied with the requirements of paragraph (3). Thereafter, the Commissioner of Social Security shall make the disability determinations referred to in subsection (a)(1).

(3) (A) The Commissioner of Social Security shall develop and initiate all appropriate procedures to implement a plan with respect to any partial or complete assumption by the Commissioner of Social Security of the disability determination function from a State agency, as provided in this section, under which employees of the affected State agency who are capable of performing duties in the disability determination process for the Commissioner of Social Security shall, notwithstanding any other provision of law, have a preference over any other individual in filling an appropriate employment position with the Commissioner of Social Security (subject to any system established by the Commissioner of Social

Security for determining hiring priority among such employees of the State agency) unless any such employee is the administrator, the deputy administrator, or assistant administrator (or his equivalent) of the State agency, in which case the Commissioner of Social Security may accord such priority to such employee.

(B) The Commissioner of Social Security shall not make such assumption of the disability determination function until such time as the Secretary of Labor determines that, with respect to employees of such State agency who will be displaced from their employment on account of such assumption by the Commissioner of Social Security and who will not be hired by the Commissioner of Social Security to perform duties in the disability determination process, the State has made fair and equitable arrangements to protect the interests of employees so displaced. Such protective arrangements shall include only those provisions which are provided under all applicable Federal, State and local statutes including, but not limited to, (i) the preservation of rights, privileges, and benefits (including continuation of pension rights and benefits) under existing collective-bargaining agreements; (ii) the continuation of collective-bargaining rights; (iii) the assignment of affected employees to other jobs or to retraining programs; (iv) the protection of individual employees against a worsening of their positions with respect to their employment; (v) the protection of health benefits and other fringe benefits; and (vi) the provision of severance pay, as may be necessary.

(c) *Review of determinations by Commissioner of Social Security*

(1) The Commissioner of Social Security may on the Commissioner's own motion or as required under paragraphs (2) and (3) review a determination, made by a State agency under this section, that an individual is or is not under a disability (as defined in section 216(i) or 223(d) and, as a result of such review, may modify such agency's determination and determine that such individual either is or is not under a disability (as so defined) or that such individual's disability began on a day earlier or later than that determined by such agency, or that such disability ceased on a day earlier or later than that determined by such agency. A review by the Commissioner of Social Security on the Commissioner's own motion of a State agency determination under this paragraph may be made before or after any action is taken to implement such determination.

(2) The Commissioner of Social Security (in accordance with paragraph (3)) shall review determinations, made by State agencies pursuant to this section, that individuals are under disabilities (as defined in section 216(i) or 223(d). Any review by the Commissioner of Social Security of a State agency determination under this paragraph shall be made before any action is taken to implement such determination.

(3)   (A) In carrying out the provisions of paragraph (2) with respect to the review of determinations made by State agencies pursuant to this section that individuals are under disabilities (as defined in section 216(i) or 223(d)), the Commissioner of Social Security shall review —

(i) at least 50 percent of all such determinations made by State agencies on applications for benefits under this title, and

(ii) other determinations made by State agencies pursuant to this section to the extent necessary to assure a high level of accuracy in such other determinations.

(B) In conducting reviews pursuant to subparagraph (A), the Commissioner of Social Security shall, to the extent feasible, select for review those determinations which the Commissioner of Social Security identifies as being the most likely to be incorrect.

(C) Not later than April 1, 1992, and annually thereafter, the Commissioner of Social Security shall submit to the Committee on Ways and Means of the House of Representatives and the Committee on Finance of the Senate a written report setting forth the number of reviews conducted under subparagraph (A)(ii) during the preceding fiscal year and the findings of the Commissioner of Social Security based on such reviews of the accuracy of the determinations made by State agencies pursuant to this section.

(d) *Hearings and judicial review*

Any individual dissatisfied with any determination under subsection (a), (b), (c), or (g) shall be entitled to a hearing thereon by the Commissioner of Social Security to the same extent as is provided in section 205(b) with respect to decisions of the Commissioner of Social Security, and to judicial review of the Commissioner's final decision after such hearing as is provided in section 205(g).

(e) *State's right to cost from Trust Funds*

Each State which is making disability determinations under subsection (a)(1) shall be entitled to receive from the Trust Funds, in advance or by way of reimbursement, as determined by the Commissioner of Social Security, the cost to the State of making disability determinations under subsection (a)(1). The Commissioner of Social Security shall from time to time certify such amount as is necessary for this purpose to the Managing Trustee, reduced or increased, as the case may be, by any sum (for which adjustment hereunder has not previously been made) by which the amount certified for any prior period was greater or less than the amount which should have been paid to the State under this subsection for such period; and the Managing Trustee, prior to audit or settlement by the General Accounting Office, shall make payment from the Trust Funds at the time or times fixed by the Commissioner of Social Security, in accordance with such certification. Appropriate adjustments between the Federal Old-Age and Survivors Insurance Trust Fund and the Federal Disability Insurance Trust Fund with respect to the payments made under this subsection shall be made in accordance with paragraph (1) of subsection (g) of section 201 (but taking into account any refunds under subsection (f) of this section) to insure that the Federal Disability Trust Fund is charged with all expenses incurred which are attributable to the administration of section 223 and the Federal Old-Age and Survivors Insurance Trust Fund is charged with all other expenses.

(f)  *Use of funds by State*

All money paid to a State under this section shall be used solely for the purposes for which it is paid; and any money so paid which is not used for such purposes shall be returned to the Treasury of the United States for deposit in the Trust Funds.

(g)  *Regulations governing determinations in certain cases*

In the case of individuals in a State which does not undertake to perform disability determinations under subsection (a)(1), or which has been found by the Commissioner of Social Security to have substantially failed to make disability determinations in a manner consistent with the Commissioner's regulations and guidelines, in the case of individuals outside the United States, and in the case of any class or classes of individuals for whom no State undertakes to make disability determinations, the determinations referred to in subsection (a) shall be made by the Commissioner of Social Security in accordance with regulations prescribed by the Commissioner.

(h) *Evaluation of mental impairments by qualified medical professionals*

An initial determination under subsection (a), (c), (g), or (i) that an individual is not under a disability, in any case where there is evidence which indicates the existence of a mental impairment, shall be made only if the Commissioner of Social Security has made every reasonable effort to ensure that a qualified psychiatrist or psychologist has completed the medical portion of the case review and any applicable residual functional capacity assessment.

(i) *Review of disability cases to determine continuing eligibility; permanent disability cases; appropriate number of cases reviewed; reporting requirements*

(1) In any case where an individual is or has been determined to be under a disability, the case shall be reviewed by the applicable State agency or the Commissioner of Social Security (as may be appropriate), for purposes of continuing eligibility, at least once every 3 years, subject to paragraph (2); except that where a finding has been made that such disability is permanent, such reviews shall be made at such times as the Commissioner of Social Security determines to be appropriate. Reviews of cases under the preceding sentence shall be in addition to, and shall not be considered as a substitute for, any other reviews which are required or provided for under or in the administration of this title.

(2) The requirement of paragraph (1) that cases be reviewed at least every 3 years shall not apply to the extent that the Commissioner of Social Security determines, on a State-by-State basis, that such requirement should be waived to insure that only the appropriate number of such cases are reviewed. The Commissioner of Social Security shall determine the appropriate number of cases to be reviewed in each State after consultation with the State agency performing such reviews, based upon the backlog of pending reviews, the projected number of new applications for disability insurance benefits, and the current and projected staffing levels of the State agency, but the Commissioner of Social Security shall provide for a waiver of such requirement only in the case of a State which makes a good faith effort to meet proper staffing requirements for the State agency and to process case reviews in a timely fashion. The Commissioner of Social Security shall report annually to the Committee on Finance of the Senate and the Committee on Ways and Means of the House of Representatives with respect to the determinations made by the Commissioner of Social Security under the preceding sentence.

(3) The Commissioner of Social Security shall report annually to the Committee on Finance of the Senate and the Committee on Ways and Means of the House of Representatives with respect to the number of reviews of continuing disability carried out under paragraph (1), the number of such reviews which result in an initial termination of benefits, the number of requests for reconsideration of such initial termination or for a hearing with respect to such termination under subsection (d), or both, and the number of such initial terminations which are overturned as the result of a reconsideration or hearing.

(4) In any case in which the Commissioner of Social Security initiates a review under this subsection of the case of an individual who has been determined to be under a disability, the Commissioner of Social Security shall notify such individual of the nature of the review to be carried out, the possibility that such review could result in the termination of benefits, and the right of the individual to provide medical evidence with respect to such review.

(5) For suspension of reviews under this subsection in the case of an individual using a ticket to work and self-sufficiency, see section 1148(i).

(j) *Rules and regulations; consultative examinations*

The Commissioner of Social Security shall prescribe regulations which set forth, in detail —

(1) the standards to be utilized by State disability determination services and Federal personnel in determining when a consultative examination should be obtained in connection with disability determinations;

(2) standards for the type of referral to be made; and

(3) procedures by which the Commissioner of Social Security will monitor both the referral processes used and the product of professionals to whom cases are referred.

Nothing in this subsection shall be construed to preclude the issuance, in accordance with section 553(b)(A) of title 5, United States Code, of interpretive rules, general statements of policy, and rules of agency organization relating to consultative examinations if such rules and statements are consistent with such regulations.

(k) *Establishment of uniform standards for determination of disability*

(1) The Commissioner of Social Security shall establish by regulation uniform standards which shall be applied at all levels of determination,

review, and adjudication in determining whether individuals are under disabilities as defined in section 216(i) or 223(d).

(2) Regulations promulgated under paragraph (1) shall be subject to the rulemaking procedures established under section 553 of title 5, United States Code.

(l) *Applicability to blind beneficiaries under 42 USCS §§ 401 et seq. of notice standards currently applicable to blind beneficiaries under 42 USCS §§ 1381 et seq.*

(1) In any case where an individual who is applying for or receiving benefits under this title on the basis of disability by reason of blindness is entitled to receive notice from the Commissioner of Social Security of any decision or determination made or other action taken or proposed to be taken with respect to his or her rights under this title, such individual shall at his or her election be entitled either (A) to receive a supplementary notice of such decision, determination, or action, by telephone, within 5 working days after the initial notice is mailed, (B) to receive the initial notice in the form of a certified letter, or (C) to receive notification by some alternative procedure established by the Commissioner of Social Security and agreed to by the individual.

(2) The election under paragraph (1) may be made at any time, but an opportunity to make such an election shall in any event be given, to every individual who is an applicant for benefits under this title on the basis of disability by reason of blindness, at the time of his or her application. Such an election, once made by an individual, shall apply with respect to all notices of decisions, determinations, and actions which such individual may thereafter be entitled to receive under this title until such time as it is revoked or changed.

(m) *Work activity as basis for review*

(1) In any case where an individual entitled to disability insurance benefits under section 223 or to monthly insurance benefits under section 202 based on such individual's disability (as defined in section 223(d)) has received such benefits for at least 24 months —

(A) no continuing disability review conducted by the Commissioner may be scheduled for the individual solely as a result of the individual's work activity;

(B) no work activity engaged in by the individual may be used as evidence that the individual is no longer disabled; and

(C) no cessation of work activity by the individual may give rise to a presumption that the individual is unable to engage in work.

(2) An individual to which paragraph (1) applies shall continue to be subject to —

(A) continuing disability reviews on a regularly scheduled basis that is not triggered by work; and

(B) termination of benefits under this title in the event that the individual has earnings that exceed the level of earnings established by the Commissioner to represent substantial gainful activity.

## § 428. Benefits at age 72 for certain uninsured individuals

(a) *Eligibility*

Every individual who —

(1) has attained the age of 72,

(2) (A) attained such age before 1968, or (B)(i) attained such age after 1967 and before 1972, and (ii) has not less than 3 quarters of coverage, whenever acquired, for each calendar year elapsing after 1966 and before the year in which he or she attained such age,

(3) is a resident of the United States (as defined in subsection (e)), and is (A) a citizen of the United States or (B) an alien lawfully admitted for permanent residence who has resided in the United States (as defined in section 210(i)) continuously during the 5 years immediately preceding the month in which he or she files application under this section, and

(4) has filed application for benefits under this section,

shall (subject to the limitations in this section) be entitled to a benefit under this section for each month beginning with the first month after September 1966 in which he or she becomes so entitled to such benefits and ending with the month preceding the month in which he or she dies. No application under this section which is filed by an individual more than 3 months before the first month in which he or she meets the requirements of paragraphs (1), (2), and (3) shall be accepted as an application for purposes of this section.

(b) *Amount of benefits*

The benefit amount to which an individual is entitled under this section for any month shall be the larger of $64.40 or the amount most recently established in lieu thereof under section 215(i).

. . . .

# Older Americans Act of 1965, as amended (Excerpts)

## 42 U.S.C. § 3001 et seq.

## § 3001. Congressional declaration of objectives

The Congress hereby finds and declares that, in keeping with the traditional American concept of the inherent dignity of the individual in our democratic society, the older people of our Nation are entitled to, and it is the joint and several duty and responsibility of the governments of the United States, of the several States and their political subdivisions, and of Indian tribes to assist our older people to secure equal opportunity to the full and free enjoyment of the following objectives:

(1) An adequate income in retirement in accordance with the American standard of living.

(2) The best possible physical and mental health which science can make available and without regard to economic status.

(3) Obtaining and maintaining suitable housing, independently selected, designed and located with reference to special needs and available at costs which older citizens can afford.

(4) Full restorative services for those who require institutional care, and a comprehensive array of community-based, long-term care services adequate to appropriately sustain older people in their communities and in their homes, including support to family members and other persons providing voluntary care to older individuals needing long-term care services.

(5) Opportunity for employment with no discriminatory personnel practices because of age.

(6) Retirement in health, honor, dignity — after years of contribution to the economy.

(7) Participating in and contributing to meaningful activity within the widest range of civic, cultural, education and training and recreational opportunities.

(8) Efficient community services, including access to low-cost transportation, which provide a choice in supported living arrangements and social assistance in a coordinated manner and which are readily available when needed, with emphasis on maintaining a continuum of care for vulnerable older individuals.

(9) Immediate benefit from proven research knowledge which can sustain and improve health and happiness.

(10) Freedom, independence, and the free exercise of individual initiative in planning and managing their own lives, full participation in the planning and operation of community-based services and programs provided for their benefit, and protection against abuse, neglect, and exploitation.

## § 3002. Definitions

For the purposes of this Act —

(1) The term "Secretary" means the Secretary of Health and Human Services, except that for purposes of title V such term means the Secretary of Labor.

(2) The term "Assistant Secretary" means the Assistant Secretary for Aging.

(3) The term "State" means any of the several States, the District of Columbia, the United States Virgin Islands of the United States, the Commonwealth of Puerto Rico, Guam, American Samoa, and the Commonwealth of the Northern Mariana Islands.

(4) The term "nonprofit" as applied to any agency, institution, or organization means an agency, institution, or organization which is, or is owned and operated by, one or more corporations or associations no part of the net earnings of which inures, or may lawfully inure, to the benefit of any private shareholder or individual.

. . . .

## § 3003. Congressional declaration of additional objectives

The Congress finds that millions of older citizens in this Nation are suffering unnecessary harm from the lack of adequate services. It is therefore the purpose of this Act, in support of the objectives of the Older Americans Act of 1965, to —

(1) make available comprehensive programs which include a full range of health, education, and supportive services to our older citizens who need them,

(2) give full and special consideration to older citizens with special needs in planning such programs, and, pending the availability of such programs for all older citizens, give priority to the elderly with the greatest economic and social need,

(3) provide comprehensive programs which will assure the coordinated delivery of a full range of essential services to our older citizens, and, where applicable, also furnish meaningful employment opportunities for many individuals, including older persons, young persons, and volunteers from the community, and

(4) insure that the planning and operation of such programs will be undertaken as a partnership of older citizens, community agencies, and State and local governments, with appropriate assistance from the Federal Government.

## SUBCHAPTER II – ADMINISTRATION ON AGING

## § 3011.  Establishment of Administration; Assistant Secretary for Aging

(a) *Function and operation*

There is established in the Office of the Secretary an Administration on Aging which shall be headed by an Assistant Secretary for Aging. Except for title V, the Administration shall be the agency for carrying out this Act. In the performance of the functions of the Assistant Secretary, the Assistant Secretary shall be directly responsible to the Secretary. There shall be a direct reporting relationship between the Assistant Secretary and the Secretary. The Secretary shall not approve or require any delegation of the functions of the Assistant Secretary (including the functions of the Assistant Secretary carried out through regional offices) to any other officer not directly responsible to the Assistant Secretary.

(b) *Appointment of Assistant Secretary*

The Assistant Secretary shall be appointed by the President by and with the advice and consent of the Senate.

(c)  *Office for American Indian, Alaskan Native, and Native Hawaiian Programs; Director*

(1) There is established in the Administration an Office for American Indian, Alaskan Native, and Native Hawaiian Programs.

(2) The Office shall be headed by a Director of the Office for American Indian, Alaskan Native, and Native Hawaiian Aging appointed by the Assistant Secretary.

(3) The Director of the Office for American Indian, Alaskan Native, and Native Hawaiian Aging shall —

(A)  (i) evaluate the adequacy of outreach under title III and title VI for older individuals who are Native Americans and recommend to the Assistant Secretary necessary action to improve service delivery, outreach, coordination between title III and title VI services, and particular problems faced by older Indians and Native Hawaiians; and

(ii) include a description of the results of such evaluation and recommendations in the annual report required by section 207(a) to be submitted by the Assistant Secretary;

(B) serve as the effective and visible advocate in behalf of older individuals who are Native Americans within the Department of Health and Human Services and with other departments and agencies of the Federal Government regarding all Federal policies affecting such individuals, with particular attention to services provided to Native Americans by the Indian Health Service;

(C) coordinate activities between other Federal departments and agencies to assure a continuum of improved services through memoranda of agreements or through other appropriate means of coordination;

(D) administer and evaluate the grants provided under this Act to Indian tribes, public agencies and nonprofit private organizations serving Native Hawaiians;

(E) recommend to the Assistant Secretary policies and priorities with respect to the development and operation of programs and activities conducted under this Act relating to older individuals who are Native Americans;

(F) collect and disseminate information related to problems experienced by older Native Americans, including information (compiled with assistance from public or nonprofit private entities, including institutions of higher education, with experience in assessing the characteristics and health status of older individuals who are Native Americans) on elder abuse, in-home care, health problems, and other problems unique to Native Americans;

(G) develop research plans, and conduct and arrange for research, in the field of American Native aging with a special emphasis on the gathering of statistics on the status of older individuals who are Native Americans;

(H) develop and provide technical assistance and training programs to grantees under title VI;

(I) promote coordination —

(i) between the administration of title III and the administration of title VI; and

(ii) between programs established under title III by the Assistant Secretary and programs established under title VI by the Assistant Secretary;

including sharing among grantees information on programs funded, and on training and technical assistance provided, under such titles; and

(J) serve as the effective and visible advocate on behalf of older individuals who are Indians, Alaskan Natives, and Native Hawaiians, in the States to promote the enhanced delivery of services and implementation of programs, under this Act and other Federal Acts, for the benefit of such individuals.

(d) *Office of Long-Term Care Ombudsman Programs*

(1) There is established in the Administration the Office of Long-Term Care Ombudsman Programs (in this subsection referred to as the "Office").

(2) (A) The Office shall be headed by a Director of the Office of Long-Term Care Ombudsman Programs (in this subsection referred to as the " Director") who shall be appointed by the Assistant Secretary from among individuals who have expertise and background in the fields of long-term care advocacy and management. The Director shall report directly to the Assistant Secretary.

(B) No individual shall be appointed Director if —

(i) the individual has been employed within the previous 2 years by —

(I) a long-term care facility;

(II) a corporation that then owned or operated a long-term care facility; or

(III) an association of long-term care facilities;

(ii) the individual —

(I) has an ownership or investment interest (represented by equity, debt, or other financial relationship) in a long-term care facility or long-term care service; or

(II) receives, or has the right to receive, directly or indirectly remuneration (in cash or in kind) under a compensation arrangement with an owner or operator of a long-term care facility; or

(iii) the individual, or any member of the immediate family of the individual, is subject to a conflict of interest.

(3) The Director shall —

(A) serve as an effective and visible advocate on behalf of older individuals who reside in long-term care facilities, within the Department of Health and Human Services and with other departments, agencies, and instrumentalities of the Federal Government regarding all Federal policies affecting such individuals;

(B) review and make recommendations to the Assistant Secretary regarding —

(i) the approval of the provisions in State plans submitted under section 307(a) that relate to State Long-Term Care Ombudsman programs; and

(ii) the adequacy of State budgets and policies relating to the programs;

(C) after consultation with State Long-Term Care Ombudsmen and the State agencies, make recommendations to the Assistant Secretary regarding —

(i) policies designed to assist State Long-Term Care Ombudsmen; and

(ii) methods to periodically monitor and evaluate the operation of State Long-Term Care Ombudsman programs, to ensure that the programs satisfy the requirements of section 307(a)(9) and section 712, including provision of service to residents of board and care facilities and of similar adult care facilities;

(D) keep the Assistant Secretary and the Secretary fully and currently informed about —

(i) problems relating to State Long-Term Care Ombudsman programs; and

(ii) the necessity for, and the progress toward, solving the problems;

(E) review, and make recommendations to the Secretary and the Assistant Secretary regarding, existing and proposed Federal legislation, regulations, and policies regarding the operation of State Long-Term Care Ombudsman programs;

(F) make recommendations to the Assistant Secretary and the Secretary regarding the policies of the Administration, and coordinate the activities of the Administration with the activities of other Federal entities, State and local entities, and nongovernmental entities, relating to State Long-Term Care Ombudsman programs;

(G) supervise the activities carried out under the authority of the Administration that relate to State Long-Term Care Ombudsman programs;

(H) administer the National Ombudsman Resource Center established under section 202(a)(21) and make recommendations to the Assistant Secretary regarding the operation of the National Ombudsman Resource Center;

(I) advocate, monitor, and coordinate Federal and State activities of Long-Term Care Ombudsmen under this Act;

(J) submit to the Speaker of the House of Representatives and the President pro tempore of the Senate an annual report on the effectiveness of services provided under section 307(a)(9) and section 712;

(K) have authority to investigate the operation or violation of any Federal law administered by the Department of Health and Human Services that may adversely affect the health, safety, welfare, or rights of older individuals; and

(L) not later than 180 days after the date of the enactment of the Older Americans Act Amendments of 1992 [enacted Sept. 30, 1992], establish standards applicable to the training required by section 712(h)(4).

## § 3012.  Administrative provisions

(a) *Duties and functions of Administration*

It shall be the duty and function of the Administration to —

(1) serve as the effective and visible advocate for older individuals within the Department of Health and Human Services and with other departments, agencies, and instrumentalities of the

Federal Government by maintaining active review and commenting responsibilities over all Federal policies affecting older individuals;

(2) collect and disseminate information related to problems of the aged and aging;

(3) directly assist the Secretary in all matters pertaining to problems of the aged and aging;

(4) administer the grants provided by this Act;

(5) develop plans, conduct and arrange for research in the field of aging, and assist in the establishment and implementation of programs designed to meet the needs of older individuals for supportive services, including nutrition, hospitalization, education and training (including preretirement training, and continuing education), low-cost transportation and housing, and health (including mental health) services;

(6) provide technical assistance and consultation to States and political subdivisions thereof with respect to programs for the aged and aging;

(7) prepare, publish, and disseminate educational materials dealing with the welfare of older individuals;

(8) gather statistics in the field of aging which other Federal agencies are not collecting, and take whatever action is necessary to achieve coordination of activities carried out or assisted by all departments, agencies, and instrumentalities of the Federal Government with respect to the collection, preparation, and dissemination of information relevant to older individuals;

(9) develop basic policies and set priorities with respect to the development and operation of programs and activities conducted under authority of this Act;

(10) coordinate Federal programs and activities related to such purposes;

(11) coordinate, and assist in, the planning and development by public (including Federal, State, and local agencies) and private organizations of programs for older individuals, with a view to the establishment of a nationwide network of comprehensive, coordinated services and opportunities for such individuals;

(12) carry on a continuing evaluation of the programs and activities related to the objectives of this Act, with particular attention to the impact of medicare and medicaid, the Age Discrimination in Employment Act of 1967, and the programs of the National Housing Act relating to housing for older individuals and

the setting of standards for the licensing of nursing homes, intermediate care homes, and other facilities providing care for such individuals;

(13) provide information and assistance to private organizations for the establishment and operation by them of programs and activities related to the objectives of this Act;

(14) develop, in coordination with other agencies, a national plan for meeting the needs for trained personnel in the field of aging, and for training persons for carrying out programs related to the objectives of this Act, and conduct and provide for the conducting of such training;

(15) consult with national organizations representing minority individuals to develop and disseminate training packages and to provide technical assistance efforts designed to assist State and area agencies on aging, and service providers, in providing services to older individuals with the greatest economic need or individuals with greatest social need, with particular attention to and specific objectives for providing services to low-income minority individuals and older individuals residing in rural areas;

(16) collect for each fiscal year, for fiscal years beginning after September 30, 1988, directly or by contract, statistical data regarding programs and activities carried out with funds provided under this Act, including —

(A) with respect to each type of service or activity provided with such funds —

(i) the aggregate amount of such funds expended to provide such service or activity;

(ii) the number of individuals who received such service or activity; and

(iii) the number of units of such service or activity provided;

(B) the number of senior centers which received such funds; and

(C) the extent to which each area agency on aging designated under section 305(a) satisfied the requirements of paragraphs (2) and (4)(A) of section 306(a);

(17) obtain from —

(A) the Department of Agriculture information explaining the requirements for eligibility to receive benefits under the Food Stamp Act of 1977; and

(B) the Social Security Administration information explaining the requirements for eligibility to receive supplemental security income benefits under title XVI of the Social Security Act;

and distribute such information, in written form, to State agencies, for redistribution to area agencies on aging, to carry out outreach activities and application assistance;

(18) (A) establish and operate the National Ombudsman Resource Center (in this paragraph referred to as the "Center"), under the administration of the Director of the Office of Long-Term Care Ombudsman Programs, that will —

(i) by grant or contract —

(I) conduct research;

(II) provide training, technical assistance, and information to State Long-Term Care Ombudsmen;

(III) analyze laws, regulations, programs, and practices; and

(IV) provide assistance in recruiting and retaining volunteers for State Long-Term Care Ombudsman programs by establishing a national program for recruitment efforts that utilizes the organizations that have established a successful record in recruiting and retaining volunteers for ombudsman or other programs;

relating to Federal, State, and local long-term care ombudsman policies; and

(ii) assist State Long-Term Care Ombudsmen in the implementation of State Long-Term Care Ombudsman programs; and

(B) make available to the Center not less than the amount of resources made available to the Long-Term Care Ombudsman National Resource Center for fiscal year 2000;

(19) conduct strict monitoring of State compliance with the requirements in effect, under this Act to prohibit conflicts of interest and to maintain the integrity and public purpose of services provided and service providers, under this Act in all contractual and commercial relationships;

(20) encourage, and provide technical assistance to, States and area agencies on aging to carry out outreach to inform older individuals with greatest economic need who may be eligible to

receive, but are not receiving, supplemental security income benefits under title XVI of the Social Security Act (or assistance under a State plan program under such title), medical assistance under title XIX of such Act, and benefits under the Food Stamp Act of 1977, of the requirements for eligibility to receive such benefits and such assistance;

(21) establish information and assistance services as priority services for older individuals, and develop and operate, either directly or through contracts, grants, or cooperative agreements, a National Eldercare Locator Service, providing information and assistance services through a nationwide toll-free number to identify community resources for older individuals;

(22) develop guidelines for area agencies on aging to follow in choosing and evaluating providers of legal assistance;

(23) develop guidelines and a model job description for choosing and evaluating legal assistance developers referred to in sections 307(a)(13) and section 731;

(24) establish and carry out pension counseling and information programs described in section 215;

(25) provide technical assistance, training, and other means of assistance to State agencies, area agencies on aging, and service providers regarding State and local data collection and analysis;

(26) design and implement, for purposes of compliance with paragraph (19), uniform data collection procedures for use by State agencies, including —

(A) uniform definitions and nomenclature;

(B) standardized data collection procedures;

(C) a participant identification and description system;

(D) procedures for collecting information on gaps in services needed by older individuals, as identified by service providers in assisting clients through the provision of the supportive services; and

(E) procedures for the assessment of unmet needs for services under this Act; and

(27) improve the delivery of services to older individuals living in rural areas through —

(A) synthesizing results of research on how best to meet the service needs of older individuals in rural areas;

(B) developing a resource guide on best practices for States, area agencies on aging, and service providers;

(C) providing training and technical assistance to States to implement these best practices of service delivery; and

(D) submitting a report on the States' experiences in implementing these best practices and the effect these innovations are having on improving service delivery in rural areas to the relevant committees not later than 36 months after enactment.

(28) — (30) [Redesignated]

(b) *Policy alternatives in long-term care*

In order to strengthen the involvement of the Administration in the development of policy alternatives in long-term care and to insure that the development of community alternatives is given priority attention, the Assistant Secretary shall —

(1) develop planning linkages with utilization and quality control peer review organizations under title XI of the Social Security Act, with the Substance Abuse and Mental Health Services Administration and the Administration on Developmental Disabilities;

(2) participate in all departmental and interdepartmental activities which concern issues of institutional and noninstitutional long-term health care services development;

(3) review and comment on all departmental regulations and policies regarding community health and social service development for older individuals; and

(4) participate in all departmental and interdepartmental activities to provide a leadership role for the Administration, State agencies, and area agencies on aging in the development and implementation of a national community-based long-term care program for older individuals.

(c) *Encouragement by Assistant Secretary of program and activity by voluntary social services group; establishment of and technical assistance to State and area volunteer coordinators*

In executing the duties and functions of the Administration under this Act and carrying out the programs and activities provided for by this Act, the Assistant Secretary, in consultation with the Corporation for National and Community Service, shall take all possible steps to encourage and permit voluntary groups active in supportive services, including youth organizations active at the high school or college levels, to participate and be involved individually or through representative groups in such programs or activities to the maximum extent feasible, through the performance of advisory or consultative functions, and in other appropriate ways.

(d) *National Center on Elder Abuse*

(1) The Assistant Secretary shall establish and operate the National Center on Elder Abuse (in this subsection referred to as the "Center").

(2) In operating the Center, the Assistant Secretary shall —

(A) annually compile, publish, and disseminate a summary of recently conducted research on elder abuse, neglect, and exploitation;

(B) develop and maintain an information clearinghouse on all programs (including private programs) showing promise of success, for the prevention, identification, and treatment of elder abuse, neglect, and exploitation;

(C) compile, publish, and disseminate training materials for personnel who are engaged or intend to engage in the prevention, identification, and treatment of elder abuse, neglect, and exploitation;

(D) provide technical assistance to State agencies and to other public and nonprofit private agencies and organizations to assist the agencies and organizations in planning, improving, developing, and carrying out programs and activities relating to the special problems of elder abuse, neglect, and exploitation; and

(E) conduct research and demonstration projects regarding the causes, prevention, identification, and treatment of elder abuse, neglect, and exploitation.

(3) (A) The Assistant Secretary shall carry out paragraph (2) through grants or contracts.

(B) The Assistant Secretary shall issue criteria applicable to the recipients of funds under this subsection. To be eligible to receive a grant or enter into a contract under subparagraph (A), an entity shall submit an application to the Assistant Secretary at such time, in such manner, and containing such information as the Assistant Secretary may require.

(C) The Assistant Secretary shall —

(i) establish research priorities for making grants or contracts to carry out paragraph (2)(E); and

(ii) not later than 60 days before the date on which the Assistant Secretary establishes such priorities, publish in the

Federal Register for public comment a statement of such proposed priorities.

(4) The Assistant Secretary shall make available to the Center such resources as are necessary for the Center to carry out effectively the functions of the Center under this Act and not less than the amount of resources made available to the Resource Center on Elder Abuse for fiscal year 2000.

(e) *National Aging Information Center*

(1)   (A) The Assistant Secretary shall make grants or enter into contracts with eligible entities to establish the National Aging Information Center (in this subsection referred to as the "Center") to —

(i) provide information about grants and projects under title IV;

(ii) annually compile, analyze, publish, and disseminate —

(I) statistical data collected under subsection (a)(19);

(II) census data on aging demographics; and

(III) data from other Federal agencies on the health, social, and economic status of older individuals and on the services provided to older individuals;

(iii) biennially compile, analyze, publish, and disseminate statistical data collected on the functions, staffing patterns, and funding sources of State agencies and area agencies on aging;

(iv) analyze the information collected under section 201(c)(3)(F) by the Director of the Office for American Indian, Alaskan Native, and Native Hawaiian Aging;

(v) provide technical assistance, training, and other means of assistance to State agencies, area agencies on aging, and service providers, regarding State and local data collection and analysis; and

(vi) be a national resource on statistical data regarding aging;[.]

(B) To be eligible to receive a grant or enter into a contract under subparagraph (A), an entity shall submit an application to the Assistant Secretary at such time, in such manner, and containing such information as the Assistant Secretary may require.

(C) Entities eligible to receive a grant or enter into a contract under subparagraph (A) shall be organizations with a demonstrated record of experience in education and information dissemination.

(2) (A) The Assistant Secretary shall establish procedures specifying the length of time that the Center shall provide the information described in paragraph (1) with respect to a particular project or activity. The procedures shall require the Center to maintain the information beyond the term of the grant awarded, or contract entered into, to carry out the project or activity.

(B) The Assistant Secretary shall establish the procedures described in subparagraph (A) after consultation with —
   (i) practitioners in the field of aging;
   (ii) older individuals;
   (iii) representatives of institutions of higher education;
   (iv) national aging organizations;
   (v) State agencies;
   (vi) area agencies on aging;
   (vii) legal assistance providers;
   (viii) service providers; and
   (ix) other persons with an interest in the field of aging.

(f) *Development of performance outcome measures*

(1) The Assistant Secretary, in accordance with the process described in paragraph (2), and in collaboration with a representative group of State agencies, tribal organizations, area agencies on aging, and providers of services involved in the performance outcome measures shall develop and publish by December 31, 2001, a set of performance outcome measures for planning, managing, and evaluating activities performed and services provided under this Act. To the maximum extent possible, the Assistant Secretary shall use data currently collected (as of the date of development of the measures) by State agencies, area agencies on aging, and service providers through the National Aging Program Information System and other applicable sources of information in developing such measures.

(2) The process for developing the performance outcome measures described in paragraph (1) shall include —
   (A) a review of such measures currently in use by State agencies and area agencies on aging (as of the date of the review);
   (B) development of a proposed set of such measures that provides information about the major activities performed and services provided under this Act;
   (C) pilot testing of the proposed set of such measures, including an identification of resource, infrastructure, and data collection issues at the State and local levels; and

(D) evaluation of the pilot test and recommendations for modification of the proposed set of such measures.

## SUBCHAPTER III – GRANTS FOR STATE AND COMMUNITY PROGRAMS ON AGING

### PART A — GENERAL PROVISIONS

### § 3021.  Purpose and program

(a)  *Congressional declaration of purpose*

(1) It is the purpose of this title to encourage and assist State agencies and area agencies on aging to concentrate resources in order to develop greater capacity and foster the development and implementation of comprehensive and coordinated systems to serve older individuals by entering into new cooperative arrangements in each State with the persons described in paragraph (2), for the planning, and for the provision of, supportive services, and multipurpose senior centers, in order to —

(A) secure and maintain maximum independence and dignity in a home environment for older individuals capable of self care with appropriate supportive services;

(B) remove individual and social barriers to economic and personal independence for older individuals;

(C) provide a continuum of care for vulnerable older individuals; and

(D) secure the opportunity for older individuals to receive managed in-home and community-based long-term care services.

. . . .

### § 3025.  Designation of State agencies

(a)  *Duties of designated agency*

In order for a State to be eligible to participate in programs of grants to States from allotments under this title —

(1) the State shall, in accordance with regulations of the Assistant Secretary, designate a State agency as the sole State agency to —

(A) develop a State plan to be submitted to the Assistant Secretary for approval under section 307;

(B) administer the State plan within such State;

(C) be primarily responsible for the planning, policy development, administration, coordination, priority setting, and evaluation of all State activities related to the objectives of this Act;

(D) serve as an effective and visible advocate for older individuals by reviewing and commenting upon all State plans, budgets, and policies which affect older individuals and providing technical assistance to any agency, organization, association, or individual representing the needs of older individuals; and

(E) divide the State into distinct planning and service areas (or in the case of a State specified in subsection (b)(5)(A), designate the entire State as a single planning and service area), in accordance with guidelines issued by the Assistant Secretary, after considering the geographical distribution of older individuals in the State, the incidence of the need for supportive services, nutrition services, multipurpose senior centers, and legal assistance, the distribution of older individuals who have greatest economic need (with particular attention to low-income minority individuals and older individuals residing in rural areas) residing in such areas, the distribution of older individuals who have greatest social need (with particular attention to low-income minority individuals and older individuals residing in rural areas) residing in such areas, the distribution of older individuals who are Indians residing in such areas, the distribution of resources available to provide such services or centers, the boundaries of existing areas within the State which were drawn for the planning or administration of supportive services programs, the location of units of general purpose local government within the State, and any other relevant factors;

(2) the State agency shall —

(A) except as provided in subsection (b)(5), designate for each such area after consideration of the views offered by the unit or units of general purpose local government in such area, a public or private nonprofit agency or organization as the area agency on aging for such area;

(B) provide assurances, satisfactory to the Assistant Secretary, that the State agency will take into account, in connection with matters of general policy arising in the development and administration of the State plan for any fiscal year, the views of recipients of supportive services or nutrition services, or individuals using multipurpose senior centers provided under such plan;

(C) in consultation with area agencies, in accordance with guidelines issued by the Assistant Secretary, and using the best available data, develop and publish for review and comment a formula for distribution within the State of funds received under this title that takes into account —

(i) the geographical distribution of older individuals in the State; and

(ii) the distribution among planning and service areas of older individuals with greatest economic need and older individuals with greatest social need, with particular attention to low-income minority older individuals;

(D) submit its formula developed under subparagraph (C) to the Assistant Secretary for approval;

(E) provide assurances that preference will be given to providing services to older individuals with greatest economic need and older individuals with greatest social need, with particular attention to low-income minority individuals and older individuals residing in rural areas, and include proposed methods of carrying out the preference in the State plan;

(F) provide assurances that the State agency will require use of outreach efforts described in section 307(a)(16); and

(G) (i) set specific objectives, in consultation with area agencies on aging, for each planning and service area for providing services funded under this title to low-income minority older individuals and older individuals residing in rural areas;

(ii) provide an assurance that the State agency will undertake specific program development, advocacy, and outreach efforts focused on the needs of low-income minority older individuals and older individuals residing in rural areas; and

(iii) provide a description of the efforts described in clause (ii) that will be undertaken by the State agency.

(b)  *Planning and service area designated; Indian reservations; redesignation; adjustment of State allotment; review by Assistant Secretary; additional planning and service areas; right to first refusal to units of local government; procedures and review of boundaries*

(1) In carrying out the requirement of subsection (a)(1), the State may designate as a planning and service area any unit of general purpose local government which has a population of 100,000 or more. In any case in which a unit of general purpose local government makes application to the State agency under the preceding sentence to be designated as a planning and service area, the State agency shall, upon request, provide an opportunity for a hearing to such unit of general purpose local government. A State may designate as a planning and service area under subsection (a)(1), any region within the State recognized for purposes of areawide planning which includes one or more such units of general purpose local government when the State determines that the designation of such a regional planning and service area is necessary for, and will enhance, the effective administration of the programs authorized by this title. The State may include in any planning and service area designated under subsection (a)(1) such additional areas adjacent to the unit of general purpose local government or regions so designated as the State determines to be necessary for, and will enhance the effective administration of the programs authorized by this title.

(2) The State is encouraged in carrying out the requirement of subsection (a)(1) to include the area covered by the appropriate economic development district involved in any planning and service area designated under subsection (a)(1), and to include all portions of an Indian reservation within a single planning and service area, if feasible.

(3) The chief executive officer of each State in which a planning and service area crosses State boundaries, or in which an interstate Indian reservation is located, may apply to the Assistant Secretary to request redesignation as an interstate planning and service area comprising the entire metropolitan area or Indian reservation. If the Assistant Secretary approves such an application, the Assistant Secretary shall adjust the State allotments of the areas within the planning and service area in which the interstate planning and service area is established to reflect the number of older individuals within the area who will be served by an interstate planning and service area not within the State.

(4) Whenever a unit of general purpose local government, a region, a metropolitan area or an Indian reservation is denied designation under

the provisions of subsection (a)(1), such unit of general purpose local government, region, metropolitan area, or Indian reservation may appeal the decision of the State agency to the Assistant Secretary. The Assistant Secretary shall afford such unit, region, metropolitan area, or Indian reservation an opportunity for a hearing. In carrying out the provisions of this paragraph, the Assistant Secretary may approve the decision of the State agency, disapprove the decision of the State agency and require the State agency to designate the unit, region, area, or Indian reservation appealing the decision as a planning and service area, or take such other action as the Assistant Secretary deems appropriate.

(5) (A) A State which on or before October 1, 1980, had designated, with the approval of the Assistant Secretary, a single planning and service area covering all of the older individuals in the State, in which the State agency was administering the area plan, may after that date designate one or more additional planning and service areas within the State to be administered by public or private nonprofit agencies or organizations as area agencies on aging, after considering the factors specified in subsection (a)(1)(E). The State agency shall continue to perform the functions of an area agency on aging for any area of the State not included in a planning and service area for which an area agency on aging has been designated.

(B) Whenever a State agency designates a new area agency on aging after the date of enactment of the Older Americans Act Amendments of 1984 [enacted Oct. 9, 1984], the State agency shall give the right to first refusal to a unit of general purpose local government if (i) such unit can meet the requirements of subsection (c), and (ii) the boundaries of such a unit and the boundaries of the area are reasonably contiguous.

(C) (i) A State agency shall establish and follow appropriate procedures to provide due process to affected parties, if the State agency initiates an action or proceeding to —

(I) revoke the designation of the area agency on aging under subsection (a);

(II) designate an additional planning and service area in a State;

(III) divide the State into different planning and services [service] areas; or

(IV) otherwise affect the boundaries of the planning and service areas in the State.

(ii) The procedures described in clause (i) shall include procedures for —

(I) providing notice of an action or proceeding described in clause (i);

(II) documenting the need for the action or proceeding;

(III) conducting a public hearing for the action or proceeding;

(IV) involving area agencies on aging, service providers, and older individuals in the action or proceeding; and

(V) allowing an appeal of the decision of the State agency in the action or proceeding to the Assistant Secretary.

(iii) An adversely affected party involved in an action or proceeding described in clause (i) may bring an appeal described in clause (ii)(V) on the basis of —

(I) the facts and merits of the matter that is the subject of the action or proceeding; or

(II) procedural grounds.

(iv) In deciding an appeal described in clause (ii)(V), the Assistant Secretary may affirm or set aside the decision of the State agency. If the Assistant Secretary sets aside the decision, and the State agency has taken an action described in subclauses (I) through (III) of clause (i), the State agency shall nullify the action.

(c) *Eligible State area agencies; development of area; preferred area agency designees*

An area agency on aging designated under subsection (a) shall be —

(1) an established office of aging which is operating within a planning and service area designated under subsection (a);

(2) any office or agency of a unit of general purpose local government, which is designated to function only for the purpose of serving as an area agency on aging by the chief elected official of such unit;

(3) any office or agency designated by the appropriate chief elected officials of any combination of units of general purpose local government to act only on behalf of such combination for such purpose;

(4) any public or nonprofit private agency in a planning and service area or any separate organizational unit within such agency, which is under the supervision or direction for this purpose of the designated State agency and which can and will engage only in the planning or provision of a broad range of supportive services, or nutrition services within such planning and service area; or

(5) in the case of a State specified in subsection (b)(5), the State agency;

and shall provide assurance, determined adequate by the State agency, that the area agency on aging will have the ability to develop an area plan and to carry out, directly or through contractual or other arrangements, a program in accordance with the plan within the planning and service area. In designating an area agency on aging within the planning and service area or within any unit of general purpose local government designated as a planning and service area the State shall give preference to an established office on aging, unless the State agency finds that no such office within the planning and service area will have the capacity to carry out the area plan.

(d) *Publication for review and comment; contents*

The publication for review and comment required by paragraph (2)(C) of subsection (a) shall include —

(1) a descriptive statement of the formula's assumptions and goals, and the application of the definitions of greatest economic or social need,

(2) a numerical statement of the actual funding formula to be used,

(3) a listing of the population, economic, and social data to be used for each planning and service area in the State, and

(4) a demonstration of the allocation of funds, pursuant to the funding formula, to each planning and service area in the State.

## § 3026. Area plans

(a) *Preparation and development by area agency on aging; requirements*

Each area agency on aging designated under section 305(a)(2)(A) shall, in order to be approved by the State agency, prepare and develop an area plan for a planning and service area for a two-, three-, or four-year period determined by the State agency, with such annual adjustments as may be necessary. Each such plan shall be based upon a uniform format for area plans within the State prepared in accordance with section 307(a)(1). Each such plan shall —

(1) provide, through a comprehensive and coordinated system, for supportive services, nutrition services, and, where appropriate, for the establishment, maintenance, or construction of multipurpose senior centers, within the planning and service area covered by the plan, including determining the extent of need for supportive services, nutrition services, and multipurpose senior centers in such area (taking into consideration, among other things, the number of older individuals with low incomes residing in such area, the number of older individuals who have greatest economic need (with particular attention to low-income minority individuals and older individuals residing in rural areas) residing in such area, the number of older individuals who have greatest social need (with particular attention to low-income minority individuals and older individuals residing in rural areas) residing in such area, and the number of older individuals who are Indians residing in such area, and the efforts of voluntary organizations in the community), evaluating the effectiveness of the use of resources in meeting such need, and entering into agreements with providers of supportive services, nutrition services, or multipurpose senior centers in such area, for the provision of such services or centers to meet such need;

(2) provide assurances that an adequate proportion, as required under section 307(a)(2), of the amount allotted for part B to the planning and service area will be expended for the delivery of each of the following categories of services —

(A) services associated with access to services (transportation, outreach, information and assistance, and case management services);

(B) in-home services, including supportive services for families of older individuals who are victims of Alzheimer's disease and for related disorders with neurological and organic brain dysfunction); and

(C) legal assistance;

and assurances that the area agency on aging will report annually to the State agency in detail the amount of funds expended for each such category during the fiscal year most recently concluded;

(3) (A) designate, where feasible, a focal point for comprehensive service delivery in each community, giving special consideration to designating multipurpose senior centers (including

multipurpose senior centers operated by organizations referred to in paragraph (6)(C) as such focal point; and

(B) specify, in grants, contracts, and agreements implementing the plan, the identity of each focal point so designated;

(4) (A) (i) provide assurances that the area agency on aging will set specific objectives for providing services to older individuals with greatest economic need and older individuals with greatest social need, include specific objectives for providing services to low-income minority individuals and older individuals residing in rural areas, and include proposed methods of carrying out the preference in the area plan;

(ii) provide assurances that the area agency on aging will include in each agreement made with a provider of any service under this title, a requirement that such provider will —

(I) specify how the provider intends to satisfy the service needs of low-income minority individuals and older individuals residing in rural areas in the area served by the provider;

(II) to the maximum extent feasible, provide services to low-income minority individuals and older individuals residing in rural areas in accordance with their need for such services; and

(III) meet specific objectives established by the area agency on aging, for providing services to low-income minority individuals and older individuals residing in rural areas within the planning and service area; and

(iii) with respect to the fiscal year preceding the fiscal year for which such plan is prepared —

(I) identify the number of low-income minority older individuals in the planning and service area;

(II) describe the methods used to satisfy the service needs of such minority older individuals; and

(III) provide information on the extent to which the area agency on aging met the objectives described in clause (i);

(B) provide assurances that the area agency on aging will use outreach efforts that will —

(i) identify individuals eligible for assistance under this Act, with special emphasis on —

(I) older individuals residing in rural areas;

(II) older individuals with greatest economic need (with particular attention to low-income minority individuals and older individuals residing in rural areas);

(III) older individuals with greatest social need (with particular attention to low-income minority individuals and older individuals residing in rural areas);

(IV) older individuals with severe disabilities;

(V) older individuals with limited English-speaking ability; and

(VI) older individuals with Alzheimer's disease or related disorders with neurological and organic brain dysfunction (and the caretakers of such individuals); and

(ii) inform the older individuals referred to in subclauses (I) through (VI) of clause (i), and the caretakers of such individuals, of the availability of such assistance; and

(C) contain an assurance that the area agency on aging will ensure that each activity undertaken by the agency, including planning, advocacy, and systems development, will include a focus on the needs of low-income minority older individuals and older individuals residing in rural areas;

(5) provide assurances that the area agency on aging will coordinate planning, identification, assessment of needs, and provision of services for older individuals with disabilities, with particular attention to individuals with severe disabilities, with agencies that develop or provide services for individuals with disabilities;

(6) provide that the area agency on aging will —

(A) take into account in connection with matters of general policy arising in the development and administration of the area plan, the views of recipients of services under such plan;

(B) serve as the advocate and focal point for older individuals within the community by (in cooperation with agencies, organizations, and individuals participating in activities under the plan) monitoring, evaluating, and commenting upon all policies, programs, hearings, levies, and community actions which will affect older individuals;

(C) (i) where possible, enter into arrangements with organizations providing day care services for children, assistance to older individuals caring for relatives who are children, and respite for families, so as to provide opportunities for older individuals to aid or assist on a voluntary basis in the delivery of such services to children, adults, and families; and

(ii) if possible regarding the provision of services under this title, enter into arrangements and coordinate with organizations that have a proven record of providing services to older individuals, that —

(I) were officially designated as community action agencies or community action programs under section 210 of the Economic Opportunity Act of 1964 (42 U.S.C. 2790) for fiscal year 1981, and did not lose the designation as a result of failure to comply with such Act; or

(II) came into existence during fiscal year 1982 as direct successors in interest to such community action agencies or community action programs;

and that meet the requirements under section 676B of the Community Services Block Grant Act;

(D) establish an advisory council consisting of older individuals (including minority individuals and older individuals residing in rural areas) who are participants or who are eligible to participate in programs assisted under this Act, representatives of older individuals, local elected officials, providers of veterans' health care (if appropriate), and the general public, to advise continuously the area agency on aging on all matters relating to the development of the area plan, the administration of the plan and operations conducted under the plan;

(E) establish effective and efficient procedures for coordination of —

(i) entities conducting programs that receive assistance under this Act within the planning and service area served by the agency; and

(ii) entities conducting other Federal programs for older individuals at the local level, with particular emphasis on entities conducting programs described in section 203(b), within the area;

(F) coordinate any mental health services provided with funds expended by the area agency on aging for part B with the mental health services provided by community health centers and by other public agencies and nonprofit private organizations; and

(G) if there is a significant population of older individuals who are Indians in the planning and service area of the area agency on aging, the area agency on aging shall conduct outreach activities to identify such individuals in such area and shall inform such individuals of the availability of assistance under this Act;

(7) provide that the area agency on aging will facilitate the coordination of community-based, long-term care services designed to enable older individuals to remain in their homes, by means including —

(A) development of case management services as a component of the long-term care services, consistent with the requirements of paragraph (8);

(B) involvement of long-term care providers in the coordination of such services; and

(C) increasing community awareness of and involvement in addressing the needs of residents of long-term care facilities;

(8) provide that case management services provided under this title through the area agency on aging will —

(A) not duplicate case management services provided through other Federal and State programs;

(B) be coordinated with services described in subparagraph (A); and

(C) be provided by a public agency or a nonprofit private agency that —

(i) gives each older individual seeking services under this title a list of agencies that provide similar services within the jurisdiction of the area agency on aging;

(ii) gives each individual described in clause (i) a statement specifying that the individual has a right to make an independent choice of service providers and documents receipt by such individual of such statement;

(iii) has case managers acting as agents for the individuals receiving the services and not as promoters for the agency providing such services; or

(iv) is located in a rural area and obtains a waiver of the requirements described in clauses (i) through (iii);

(9) provide assurances that the area agency on aging, in carrying out the State Long-Term Care Ombudsman program under section 307(a)(9), will expend not less than the total amount of funds appropriated under this Act and expended by the agency in fiscal year 2000 in carrying out such a program under this title;

(10) provide a grievance procedure for older individuals who are dissatisfied with or denied services under this title;

(11) provide information and assurances concerning services to older individuals who are Native Americans (referred to in this paragraph as "older Native Americans"), including —

(A) information concerning whether there is a significant population of older Native Americans in the planning and service area and if so, an assurance that the area agency on aging will pursue activities, including outreach, to increase access of those older Native Americans to programs and benefits provided under this title;

(B) an assurance that the area agency on aging will, to the maximum extent practicable, coordinate the services the agency provides under this title with services provided under title VI; and

(C) an assurance that the area agency on aging will make services under the area plan available, to the same extent as such services are available to older individuals within the planning and service area, to older Native Americans; and

(12) provide that the area agency on aging will establish procedures for coordination of services with entities conducting other Federal or federally assisted programs for older individuals at the local level, with particular emphasis on entities conducting programs described in section 203(b) within the planning and service area.

(13) provide assurances that the area agency on aging will —

(A) maintain the integrity and public purpose of services provided, and service providers, under this title in all contractual and commercial relationships;

(B) disclose to the Assistant Secretary and the State agency —

(i) the identity of each nongovernmental entity with which such agency has a contract or commercial relationship relating to providing any service to older individuals; and

(ii) the nature of such contract or such relationship;

(C) demonstrate that a loss or diminution in the quantity or quality of the services provided, or to be provided, under this title by such agency has not resulted and will not result from such contract or such relationship;

(D) demonstrate that the quantity or quality of the services to be provided under this title by such agency will be enhanced as a result of such contract or such relationship; and

(E) on the request of the Assistant Secretary or the State, for the purpose of monitoring compliance with this Act (including conducting an audit), disclose all sources and expenditures of funds such agency receives or expends to provide services to older individuals;

(14) provide assurances that funds received under this title will not be used to pay any part of a cost (including an administrative cost) incurred by the area agency on aging to carry out a contract or commercial relationship that is not carried out to implement this title; and

(15) provide assurances that preference in receiving services under this title will not be given by the area agency on aging to particular older individuals as a result of a contract or commercial relationship that is not carried out to implement this title.

[(16)](15) provide assurances that funds received under this title will not be used to pay any part of a cost (including an administrative cost) incurred by the area agency on aging to carry out a contract or commercial relationship that is not carried out to implement this title;

[(17)](16) provide assurances that preference in receiving services under this title will not be given by the area agency on aging to particular older individuals as a result of a contract or commercial relationship that is not carried out to implement this title;

(b)  *Waiver of requirements; notice and hearing; opportunity to testify; record*

Each State, in approving area agency on aging plans under this section, shall waive the requirement described in paragraph (2) of subsection (a) for any category of services described in such paragraph if the area agency on aging demonstrates to the State agency that services being furnished for such category in the area are sufficient to meet the need for such services in such area and had conducted a timely public hearing upon request.

(c)  *Transportation services; funds*

(1) Subject to regulations prescribed by the Assistant Secretary, an area agency on aging designated under section 305(a)(2)(A) or, in areas of a State where no such agency has been designated, the State agency, may enter into agreements with agencies administering programs under the Rehabilitation Act of 1973, and title XIX and XX of the Social Security Act for the purpose of developing and implementing plans for meeting the common need for transportation services of individuals receiving benefits under such Acts and older individuals participating in programs authorized by this title.

(2) In accordance with an agreement entered into under paragraph (1), funds appropriated under this title may be used to purchase transportation services for older individuals and may be pooled with funds made available for the provision of transportation services under the Rehabilitation Act of 1973, and title XIX and XX of the Social Security Act.

(d)  *Confidentiality of information relating to legal assistance*

An area agency on aging may not require any provider of legal assistance under this title to reveal any information that is protected by the attorney-client privilege.

(e)  *Withholding of area funds*

(1) If the head of a State agency finds that an area agency on aging has failed to comply with Federal or State laws, including the area plan requirements of this section, regulations, or policies, the State may withhold a portion of the funds to the area agency on aging available under this title.

(2)  (A) The head of a State agency shall not make a final determination withholding funds under paragraph (1) without first

affording the area agency on aging due process in accordance with procedures established by the State agency.

(B) At a minimum, such procedures shall include procedures for —

(i) providing notice of an action to withhold funds;

(ii) providing documentation of the need for such action; and

(iii) at the request of the area agency on aging, conducting a public hearing concerning the action.

(3)    (A) If a State agency withholds the funds, the State agency may use the funds withheld to directly administer programs under this title in the planning and service area served by the area agency on aging for a period not to exceed 180 days, except as provided in subparagraph (B).

(B) If the State agency determines that the area agency on aging has not taken corrective action, or if the State agency does not approve the corrective action, during the 180-day period described in subparagraph (A), the State agency may extend the period for not more than 90 days.

## PART B – SUPPORTIVE SERVICES

### § 3030d.  Grants for supportive services

(a) The Assistant Secretary shall carry out a program for making grants to States under State plans approved under section 307 for any of the following supportive services:

(1) health (including mental health), education and training, welfare, informational, recreational, homemaker, counseling, or referral services;

(2) transportation services to facilitate access to supportive services or nutrition services, and services provided by an area agency on aging, in conjunction with local transportation service providers, public transportation agencies, and other local government agencies, that result in increased provision of such transportation services for older individuals;

(3) services, designed to encourage and assist older individuals to use the facilities and services (including information and assistance services) available to them, including language translation services to assist older individuals with limited-English speaking ability to obtain services under this title;

(4) services designed (A) to assist older individuals to obtain adequate housing, including residential repair and renovation projects designed to enable older individuals to maintain their homes in conformity

with minimum housing standards; (B) to adapt homes to meet the needs of older individuals who have physical disabilities; (C) to prevent unlawful entry into residences of older individuals, through the installation of security devices and through structural modifications or alterations of such residences; or (D) to assist older individuals in obtaining housing for which assistance is provided under programs of the Department of Housing and Urban Development;

(5) services designed to assist older individuals in avoiding institutionalization and to assist individuals in long-term care institutions who are able to return to their communities, including —

(A) client assessment, case management services, and development and coordination of community services;

(B) supportive activities to meet the special needs of caregivers, including caretakers who provide in-home services to frail older individuals; and

(C) in-home services and other community services, including home health, homemaker, shopping, escort, reader, and letter writing services, to assist older individuals to live independently in a home environment;

(6) services designed to provide to older individuals legal assistance and other counseling services and assistance, including —

(A) tax counseling and assistance, financial counseling, and counseling regarding appropriate health and life insurance coverage;

(B) representation —

(i) of individuals who are wards (or are allegedly incapacitated); and

(ii) in guardianship proceedings of older individuals who seek to become guardians, if other adequate representation is unavailable in the proceedings; and

(C) provision, to older individuals who provide uncompensated care to their adult children with disabilities, of counseling to assist such older individuals with permanency planning for such children;

(7) services designed to enable older individuals to attain and maintain physical and mental well-being through programs of regular physical activity, exercise, music therapy, art therapy, and dance-movement therapy;

(8) services designed to provide health screening to detect or prevent illnesses, or both, that occur most frequently in older individuals;

(9) services designed to provide, for older individuals, preretirement counseling and assistance in planning for and assessing future post-

retirement needs with regard to public and private insurance, public benefits, lifestyle changes, relocation, legal matters, leisure time, and other appropriate matters;

(10) services of an ombudsman at the State level to receive, investigate, and act on complaints by older individuals who are residents of long-term care facilities and to advocate for the well-being of such individuals;

(11) services which are designed to meet the unique needs of older individuals who are disabled, and of older individuals who provide uncompensated care to their adult children with disabilities;

(12) services to encourage the employment of older workers, including job and second career counseling and, where appropriate, job development, referral, and placement, and including the coordination of the services with programs administered by or receiving assistance from the Department of Labor, including programs carried out under the Workforce Investment Act of 1998 (29 U.S.C. 2801 et seq.);

(13) crime prevention services and victim assistance programs for older individuals;

(14) a program, to be known as "Senior Opportunities and Services", designed to identify and meet the needs of low-income older individuals in one or more of the following areas: (A) development and provision of new volunteer services; (B) effective referral to existing health, employment, housing, legal, consumer, transportation, and other services; (C) stimulation and creation of additional services and programs to remedy gaps and deficiencies in presently existing services and programs; and (D) such other services as the Assistant Secretary may determine are necessary or especially appropriate to meet the needs of low income older individuals and to assure them greater self-sufficiency;

(15) services for the prevention of abuse of older individuals in accordance with chapter 3 of subtitle A of title VII and section 307(a)(12);

(16) inservice training and State leadership for legal assistance activities;

(17) health and nutrition education services, including information concerning prevention, diagnosis, treatment, and rehabilitation of age-related diseases and chronic disabling conditions;

(18) services designed to enable mentally impaired older individuals to attain and maintain emotional well-being and independent living through a coordinated system of support services;

(19) services designed to support family members and other persons providing voluntary care to older individuals that need long-term care services;

(20) services designed to provide information and training for individuals who are or may become guardians or representative payees of older individuals, including information on the powers and duties of guardians and representative payees and on alternatives to guardianships;

(21) services to encourage and facilitate regular interaction between school-age children and older individuals, including visits in long-term care facilities, multipurpose senior centers, and other settings;

(22) in-home services for frail older individuals, including individuals with Alzheimer's disease and related disorders with neurological and organic brain dysfunction, and their families, including in-home services defined by a State agency in the State plan submitted under section 307, taking into consideration the age, economic need, and noneconomic and nonhealth factors contributing to the frail condition and need for services of the individuals described in this paragraph, and in-home services defined by an area agency on aging in the area plan submitted under section 306.[; or]

(23) any other services necessary for the general welfare of older individuals;

if such services meet standards prescribed by the Assistant Secretary and are necessary for the general welfare of older individuals. For purposes of paragraph (5), the term "client assessment through case management" includes providing information relating to assistive technology.

(b) (1) The Assistant Secretary shall carry out a program for making grants to States under State plans approved under section 307 for the acquisition, alteration, or renovation of existing facilities, including mobile units, and, where appropriate, construction of facilities to serve as multipurpose senior centers.

(2) Funds made available to State under this part [this section] may be used for the purpose of assisting in the operation of multipurpose senior centers and meeting all or part of the costs of compensating professional and technical personnel required for the operation of multipurpose senior centers.

(c) In carrying out the provisions of this part [this section], to more efficiently and effectively deliver services to older individuals, each area agency on aging shall coordinate services described in subsection (a) with other community agencies and voluntary organizations providing the same services. In coordinating the services, the area agency on aging shall make efforts to coordinate the services with agencies and organizations carrying out intergenerational programs or projects.

(d) Funds made available under this part [this section] shall supplement, and not supplant, any Federal, State, or local funds expended by a State or unit of general purpose local government (including an area agency on aging) to provide services described in subsection (a).

PART C – NUTRITION SERVICES

Subpart I — Congregate Nutrition Services

## § 3030e. Grants for establishment and operation of nutrition projects

The Assistant Secretary shall carry out a program for making grants to States under State plans approved under section 307　for the establishment and operation of nutrition projects —

(1) which, 5 or more days a week (except in a rural area where such frequency is not feasible (as defined by the Assistant Secretary by regulation) and a lesser frequency is approved by the State agency), provide at least one hot or other appropriate meal per day and any additional meals which the recipient of a grant or contract under this subpart [this section] may elect to provide;

(2) which shall be provided in congregate settings, including adult day care facilities and multigenerational meal sites; and

(3) which may include nutrition education services and other appropriate nutrition services for older individuals.

Subpart II — Home Delivered Nutrition Services

## § 3030f. Grants for establishment and operation of nutrition projects for older individuals

The Assistant Secretary shall carry out a program for making grants to States under State plans approved under section 307 for the establishment and operation of nutrition projects for older individuals which, 5 or more days a week (except in a rural area where such frequency is not feasible (as defined by the Assistant Secretary by regulation) and a lesser frequency is approved by the State agency), provide at least one home delivered hot, cold, frozen, dried, canned, or supplemental foods (with a satisfactory storage life) meal per day and any additional meals which the recipient of a grant or contract under this subpart may elect to provide.

# Supplemental Security Income for the Aged, Blind, and Disabled (Excerpts)

## 42 U.S.C. § 1381 et seq.

## SUBCHAPTER XVI — SUPPLEMENTAL SECURITY INCOME FOR THE AGED, BLIND, AND DISABLED

### § 1381. Statement of purpose; authorization of appropriations

For the purpose of establishing a national program to provide supplemental security income to individuals who have attained age 65 or are blind or disabled, there are authorized to be appropriated sums sufficient to carry out this title.

## PART A — DETERMINATION OF BENEFITS

### § 1382. Eligibility for benefits

(a) *"Eligible individual" defined*

(1) Each aged, blind, or disabled individual who does not have an eligible spouse and —

(A) whose income, other than income excluded pursuant to section 1612(b), is at a rate of not more than $1,752 (or, if greater, the amount determined under section 1617) for the calendar year 1974 or any calendar year thereafter, and

(B) whose resources, other than resources excluded pursuant to section 1613(a), are not more than (i) in case such individual has a spouse with whom he is living, the applicable amount determined under paragraph (3)(A), or (ii) in case such individual has no spouse with whom he is living, the applicable amount determined under paragraph (3)(B),

shall be an eligible individual for purposes of this title

    (2) Each aged, blind, or disabled individual who has an eligible spouse and —

        (A) whose income (together with the income of such spouse), other than income excluded pursuant to section 1612(b), is at a rate of not more than $2,628 (or, if greater, the amount determined under section 1617) for the calendar year 1974, or any calendar year thereafter, and

        (B) whose resources (together with the resources of such spouse), other than resources excluded pursuant to section 1613(a), are not more than the applicable amount determined under paragraph (3)(A),

shall be an eligible individual for purposes of this title.

    (3)  (A) The dollar amount referred to in clause (i) of paragraph (1)(B), and in paragraph (2)(B), shall be $2,250 prior to January 1, 1985, and shall be increased to $2,400 on January 1, 1985, to $2,550 on January 1, 1986, to $2,700 on January 1, 1987, to $2,850 on January 1, 1988, and to $3,000 on January 1, 1989.

        (B) The dollar amount referred to in clause (ii) of paragraph (1)(B), shall be $1,500 prior to January 1, 1985, and shall be increased to $1,600 on January 1, 1985, to $1,700 on January 1, 1986, to $1,800 on January 1, 1987, to $1,900 on January 1, 1988, and to $2,000 on January 1, 1989.

(b) *Amount of benefits*

    (1) The benefit under this title for an individual who does not have an eligible spouse shall be payable at the rate of $1,752 (or, if greater, the amount determined under section 1617) for the calendar year 1974 and any calendar year thereafter, reduced by the amount of income, not excluded pursuant to section 1612(b), of such individual.

    (2) The benefit under this title for an individual who has an eligible spouse shall be payable at the rate of $2,628 (or, if greater, the amount determined under section 1617) for the calendar year 1974 and any calendar year thereafter, reduced by the amount of income, not excluded pursuant to section 1612(b), of such individual and spouse.

(c) *Period for determination of benefits*

(1) An individual's eligibility for a benefit under this title for a month shall be determined on the basis of the individual's (and eligible spouse's, if any) income, resources, and other relevant characteristics in such month, and, except as provided in paragraphs (2), (3), (4), (5), and (6) the amount of such benefit shall be determined for such month on the basis of income and other characteristics in the first or, if the Commissioner of Social Security so determines, second month preceding such month. Eligibility for and the amount of such benefits shall be redetermined at such time or times as may be provided by the Commissioner of Social Security.

(2) The amount of such benefit for the month in which an application for benefits becomes effective (or, if the Commissioner of Social Security so determines, for such month and the following month) and for any month immediately following a month of ineligibility for such benefits (or, if the Commissioner of Social Security so determines, for such month and the following month) shall —

(A) be determined on the basis of the income of the individual and the eligible spouse, if any, of such individual and other relevant circumstances in such month; and

(B) in the case of the month in which an application becomes effective or the first month following a period of ineligibility, if such application becomes effective, or eligibility is restored, after the first day of such month, bear the same ratio to the amount of the benefit which would have been payable to such individual if such application had become effective, or eligibility had been restored, on the first day of such month as the number of days in such month including and following the effective date of such application or restoration of eligibility bears to the total number of days in such month.

(3) For purposes of this subsection, an increase in the benefit amount payable under title II (over the amount payable in the preceding month, or, at the election of the Commissioner of Social Security, the second preceding month) to an individual receiving benefits under this title shall be included in the income used to determine the benefit under this title of such individual for any month which is —

(A) the first month in which the benefit amount payable to such individual under this title is increased pursuant to section 1617, or

(B) at the election of the Commissioner of Social Security, the month immediately following such month.

(4)   (A) Notwithstanding paragraph (3), if the Commissioner of Social Security determines that reliable information is currently available with respect to the income and other circumstances of an individual for a month (including information with respect to a class of which such individual is a member and information with respect to scheduled cost-of-living adjustments under other benefit programs), the benefit amount of such individual under this title for such month may be determined on the basis of such information.

(B) The Commissioner of Social Security shall prescribe by regulation the circumstances in which information with respect to an event may be taken into account pursuant to subparagraph (A) in determining benefit amounts under this title.

(5) Notwithstanding paragraphs (1) and (2), any income which is paid to or on behalf of an individual in any month pursuant to (A) a State program funded under part A of title IV, (B) section 472 of this Act (relating to foster care assistance), (C) section 412(e) of the Immigration and Nationality Act (relating to assistance for refugees), (D) section 501(a) of Public Law 96-422 (relating to assistance for Cuban and Haitian entrants), or (E) the Act of November 2, 1921 (42 Stat. 208), as amended (relating to assistance furnished by the Bureau of Indian Affairs), shall be taken into account in determining the amount of the benefit under this title of such individual (and his eligible spouse, if any) only for that month, and shall not be taken into account in determining the amount of the benefit for any other month.

(6) The dollar amount in effect under subsection (b) as a result of any increase in benefits under this title by reason of section 1617 determine the value of any in-kind support and maintenance required to be taken into account in determining the benefit payable under this title to an individual (and the eligible spouse, if any, of the individual) for the 1st 2 months for which the increase in benefits applies.

(7) For purposes of this subsection, an application of an individual for benefits under this title shall be effective on the later of —

(A) the first day of the month following the date such application is filed, or

(B) the first day of the month following the date such individual becomes eligible for such benefits with respect to such application.

(8) The Commissioner of Social Security may waive the limitations specified in subparagraphs (A) and (B) of subsection (e)(1) on an individual's eligibility and benefit amount for a month (to the extent either such limitation is applicable by reason of such individual's presence

throughout such month in a hospital, extended care facility, nursing home, or intermediate care facility) if such waiver would promote the individual's removal from such institution or facility. Upon waiver of such limitations, the Commissioner of Social Security shall apply, to the month preceding the month of removal, or, if the Commissioner of Social Security so determines, the two months preceding the month of removal, the benefit rate that is appropriate to such individual's living arrangement subsequent to his removal from such institution or facility.

(d) *Limitation on amount of gross income earned; "gross income" defined*

The Commissioner of Social Security may prescribe the circumstances under which, consistently with the purposes of this title, the gross income from a trade or business (including farming) will be considered sufficiently large to make an individual ineligible for benefits under this title. For purposes of this subsection, the term "gross income" has the same meaning as when used in chapter 1 of the Internal Revenue Code of 1954.

(e) *Limitation on eligibility of certain individuals*

(1)  (A) Except as provided in subparagraphs (B), (C), (D), (E), and (G) no person shall be an eligible individual or eligible spouse for purposes of this title with respect to any month if throughout such month he is an inmate of a public institution.

(B) In any case where an eligible individual or his eligible spouse (if any) is subject to subparagraph (G)), throughout any month subject to subparagraph (G)), in a medical treatment facility receiving payments (with respect to such individual or spouse) under a State plan approved under title XIX, or an eligible individual is a child described in section 1614(f)(2)(B), or, in the case of an eligible individual who is a child under the age of 18, receiving payments (with respect to such individual) under any health insurance policy issued by a private provider of such insurance the benefit under this title for such individual for such month shall be payable (subject to subparagraph (E)) —

(i) at a rate not in excess of $360 per year (reduced by the amount of any income not excluded pursuant to section 1612(b)) in the case of an individual who does not have an eligible spouse;

(ii) in the case of an individual who has an eligible spouse, if only one of them is in such a facility throughout such month, at a rate not in excess of the sum of —

(I) the rate of $360 per year (reduced by the amount of any income, not excluded pursuant to section 1612(b), of the one who is in such facility), and

(II) the applicable rate specified in subsection (b)(1) (reduced by the amount of any income, not excluded pursuant to section 1612(b), of the other); and

(iii) at a rate not in excess of $720 per year (reduced by the amount of any income not excluded pursuant to section 1612(b)) in the case of an individual who has an eligible spouse, if both of them are in such a facility throughout such month.

For purposes of this subsection, a medical treatment facility that provides services described in section 1917(c)(1)(C) shall be considered to be receiving payments with respect to an individual under a State plan approved under title XIX during any period of ineligibility of such individual provided for under the State plan pursuant to section 1917(c).

(C) As used in subparagraph (A), the term "public institution" does not include a publicly operated community residence which serves no more than 16 residents.

(D) A person may be an eligible individual or eligible spouse for purposes of this title with respect to any month throughout which he is a resident of a public emergency shelter for the homeless (as defined in regulations which shall be prescribed by the Commissioner of Social Security); except that no person shall be an eligible individual or eligible spouse by reason of this subparagraph more than 6 months in any 9-month period.

(E) Notwithstanding subparagraphs (A) and (B), any individual who —

(i)    (I) is an inmate of a public institution, the primary purpose of which is the provision of medical or psychiatric care, throughout any month as described in subparagraph (A), or

(II) is in a medical treatment facility throughout any month as described in subparagraph (B),

(ii) was eligible under section 1619 (a) or (b) for the month preceding such month, and

(iii) under an agreement of the public institution or the medical treatment facility is permitted to retain any benefit payable by reason of this subparagraph,

may be an eligible individual or eligible spouse for purposes of this title (and entitled to a benefit determined on the basis of the rate applicable under subsection (b)) for the month referred to in subclause (I) or (II) of clause (i) and, if such subclause still applies, for the succeeding month.

(F) An individual who is an eligible individual or an eligible spouse for a month by reason of subparagraph (E) shall not be treated as being eligible under section 1619 (a) or (b) for such month for purposes of clause (ii) of such subparagraph.

(G) A person may be an eligible individual or eligible spouse for purposes of this title, and subparagraphs (A) and (B) shall not apply, with respect to any particular month throughout which he or she is an inmate of a public institution the primary purpose of which is the provision of medical or psychiatric care, or is in a medical treatment facility receiving payments (with respect to such individual or spouse) under a State plan approved under title XIX or, in the case of an individual who is a child under the age of 18, under any health insurance policy issued by a private provider of such insurance, if it is determined in accordance with subparagraph (H) or (J) that —

(i) such person's stay in that institution or facility (or in that institution or facility and one or more other such institutions or facilities during a continuous period of institutionalization) is likely (as certified by a physician) not to exceed 3 months, and the particular month involved is one of the first 3 months throughout which such person is in such an institution or facility during a continuous period of institutionalization; and

(ii) such person needs to continue to maintain and provide for the expenses of the home or living arrangement to which he or she may return upon leaving the institution or facility.

The benefit of any person under this title (including State supplementation if any) for each month to which this subparagraph applies shall be payable, without interruption of benefit payments and on the date the benefit involved is regularly due, at the rate that was applicable to such person in the month prior to the first month throughout which he or she is in the institution or facility.

(H) The Commissioner of Social Security shall establish procedures for the determinations required by clauses (i) and (ii) of subparagraph (G), and may enter into agreements for making such determinations (or for providing information or assistance in connection with the making of such determinations) with appropriate State and local public and private agencies and organizations. Such procedures and agreements shall include the provision of appropriate assistance to individuals who, because of their physical or mental condition, are limited in their ability to furnish the information needed in connection with the making of such determinations.

(I)    (i) The Commissioner shall enter into an agreement, with any interested State or local institution comprising a jail, prison, penal institution, or correctional facility, or with any other interested State or local institution a purpose of which is to confine individuals as described in section 202(x)(1)(A)(ii), under which —

(I) the institution shall provide to the Commissioner, on a monthly basis and in a manner specified by the Commissioner, the names, social security account numbers, dates of birth, confinement commencement dates, and, to the extent available to the institution, such other identifying information concerning the inmates of the institution as the Commissioner may require for the purpose of carrying out this paragraph and the other provisions of this title; and

(II) the Commissioner shall pay to any such institution, with respect to each individual who receives in the month preceding the first month throughout which such individual is an inmate of the jail, prison, penal institution, or correctional facility that furnishes information respecting such individual pursuant to subclause (I), or is confined in the institution (that so furnishes such information) as described in section 202(x)(1)(A)(ii), a benefit under this title for such preceding month, and who is determined by the Commissioner to be ineligible for benefits under this title by reason of confinement based on the information provided by such institution, $400 (subject to reduction under clause (ii)) if the institution furnishes the information described in subclause (I) to the Commissioner within 30 days after the date such individual becomes an inmate of such institution, or $200 (subject to reduction under clause (ii)) if the institution furnishes such information after 30 days after such date but within 90 days after such date.

(ii) The dollar amounts specified in clause (i)(II) shall be reduced by 50 percent if the Commissioner is also required to make a payment to the institution with respect to the same individual under an agreement entered into under section 202(x)(3)(B).

(iii) The Commissioner shall maintain, and shall provide on a reimbursable basis, information obtained pursuant to agreements entered into under clause (i) to any Federal or federally-assisted cash, food, or medical assistance program for eligibility and other administrative purposes under such program.

(iv) Payments to institutions required by clause (i)(II) shall be made from funds otherwise available for the payment of benefits under this title and shall be treated as direct spending for purposes of the Balanced Budget and Emergency Deficit Control Act of 1985.

(J) For the purpose of carrying out this paragraph, the Commissioner of Social Security shall conduct periodic computer matches with data maintained by the Secretary of Health and Human Services under title XVIII or XIX. The Secretary shall furnish to the Commissioner, in such form and manner and under such terms as the Commissioner and the Secretary shall mutually agree, such information as the Commissioner may request for this purpose. Information obtained pursuant to such a match may be substituted for the physician's certification otherwise required under subparagraph (G)(i).

(2) No person shall be an eligible individual or eligible spouse for purposes of this title if, after notice to such person by the Commissioner of Social Security that it is likely that such person is eligible for any payments of the type enumerated in section 1612(a)(2)(B), such person fails within 30 days to take all appropriate steps to apply for and (if eligible) obtain any such payments.

(3) Notwithstanding anything to the contrary in the criteria being used by the Commissioner of Social Security in determining when a husband and wife are to be considered two eligible individuals for purposes of this title and when they are to be considered an eligible individual with an eligible spouse, the State agency administering or supervising the administration of a State plan under any other program

under this Act may (in the administration of such plan) treat a husband and wife living in the same medical treatment facility described in paragraph (1)(B) as though they were an eligible individual with his or her eligible spouse for purposes of this title (rather than two eligible individuals), after they have continuously lived in the same such facility for 6 months, if treating such husband and wife as two eligible individuals would prevent either of them from receiving benefits or assistance under such plan or reduce the amount thereof.

(4) No person shall be considered an eligible individual or eligible spouse for purposes of this title with respect to any month if during such month the person is —

(A) fleeing to avoid prosecution, or custody or confinement after conviction, under the laws of the place from which the person flees, for a crime, or an attempt to commit a crime, which is a felony under the laws of the place from which the person flees, or which, in the case of the State of New Jersey, is a high misdemeanor under the laws of such State; or

(B) violating a condition of probation or parole imposed under Federal or State law.

(5) Notwithstanding any other provision of law (other than section 6103 of the Internal Revenue Code of 1986 and section 1106(c) of this Act), the Commissioner shall furnish any Federal, State, or local law enforcement officer, upon the written request of the officer, with the current address, Social Security number, and photograph (if applicable) of any recipient of benefits under this title, if the officer furnishes the Commissioner with the name of the recipient, and other identifying information as reasonably required by the Commissioner to establish the unique identity of the recipient, and notifies the Commissioner that —

(A) the recipient —

(i) is described in subparagraph (A) or (B) of paragraph (4); and

(ii) has information that is necessary for the officer to conduct the officer's official duties; and

(B) the location or apprehension of the recipient is within the officer's official duties.

(f) *Individuals outside the United States; determination of status*

(1) Notwithstanding any other provision of this title, no individual (other than a child described in section 1614(a)(1)(B)(ii)) shall be considered an eligible individual for purposes of this title for any month

during all of which such individual is outside the United States (and no person shall be considered the eligible spouse of an individual for purposes of this title with respect to any month during all of which such person is outside the United States). For purposes of the preceding sentence, after an individual has been outside the United States for any period of 30 consecutive days, he shall be treated as remaining outside the United States until he has been in the United States for a period of 30 consecutive days.

(2) For a period of not more than 1 year, the first sentence of paragraph (1) shall not apply to any individual who —

(A) was eligible to receive a benefit under this title for the month immediately preceding the first month during all of which the individual was outside the United States; and

(B) demonstrates to the satisfaction of the Commissioner of Social Security that the absence of the individual from the United States will be —

(i) for not more than 1 year; and

(ii) for the purpose of conducting studies as part of an educational program that is —

(I) designed to substantially enhance the ability of the individual to engage in gainful employment;

(II) sponsored by a school, college, or university in the United States; and

(III) not available to the individual in the United States.

(g) *Individuals deemed to meet resources test. In the case of any individual or any individual and his spouse (as the case may be) who —*

(1) received aid or assistance for December 1973 under a plan of a State approved under title I, X, XIV, or XVI,

(2) has, since December 31, 1973, continuously resided in the State under the plan of which he or they received such aid or assistance for December 1973, and

(3) has, since December 31, 1973, continuously been (except for periods not in excess of six consecutive months) an eligible individual or eligible spouse with respect to whom supplemental security income benefits are payable,

the resources of such individual or such individual and his spouse (as the case may be) shall be deemed not to exceed the amount specified in sections 1611(a)(1)(B) and 1611(a)(2)(B) [subsecs. (a)(1)(B) and (a)(2)(B) of this section] during any period that the resources of such individual or such individual and his spouse (as the case may be) does not exceed the maximum amount of resources specified in the State plan, as in effect for October 1972, under which he or they received such aid or assistance for December 1973.

(h) *Individuals deemed to meet income test. In determining eligibility for, and the amount of, benefits payable under this section in the case of any individual or any individual and his spouse (as the case may be) who* —

(1) received aid or assistance for December 1973 under a plan of a State approved under title X or XVI,

(2) is blind under the definition of that term in the plan, as in effect for October 1972, under which he or they received such aid or assistance for December 1973,

(3) has, since December 31, 1973, continuously resided in the State under the plan of which he or they received such aid or assistance for December 1973, and

(4) has, since December 31, 1973, continuously been (except for periods not in excess of six consecutive months) an eligible individual or an eligible spouse with respect to whom supplemental security income benefits are payable,

there shall be disregarded an amount equal to the greater of (A) the maximum amount of any earned or unearned income which could have been disregarded under the State plan, as in effect for October 1972, under which he or they received such aid or assistance for December 1973, and

(B) the amount which would be required to be disregarded under section 1612 without application of this subsection.

(i) Application and review requirements for certain individuals. For application and review requirements affecting the eligibility of certain individuals, see section 1631(j).

## § 1382a. Income; earned and unearned income defined; exclusions from income

(a) For purposes of this title, income means both earned income and unearned income; and —

(1) earned income means only —

(A) wages as determined under section 203(f)(5)(C) but without the application of section 210(j)(3);

(B) net earnings from self-employment, as defined in section 211 (without the application of the second and third sentences following subsection (a)(11), the last paragraph of subsection (a), and section 210(j)(3)), including earnings for services described in paragraphs (4), (5), and (6) of subsection (c);

(C) remuneration received for services performed in a sheltered workshop or work activities center; and

(D) any royalty earned by an individual in connection with any publication of the work of the individual, and that portion of any honorarium which is received for services rendered; and

(2) unearned income means all other income, including —

(A) support and maintenance furnished in cash or kind; except that

(i) in the case of any individual (and his eligible spouse, if any) living in another person's household and receiving support and maintenance in kind from such person, the dollar amounts otherwise applicable to such individual (and spouse) as specified in subsections (a) and (b) of section 1611 shall be reduced by 33 1/3 percent in lieu of including such support and maintenance in the unearned income of such individual (and spouse) as otherwise required by this subparagraph and

(ii) in the case of any individual or his eligible spouse who resides in a nonprofit retirement home or similar nonprofit institution, support and maintenance shall not be included to the extent that it is furnished to such individual or such spouse without such institution receiving payment therefor (unless such institution has expressly undertaken an obligation to furnish full support and maintenance to such individual or spouse without any current or future payment therefor) or payment therefor is made by another nonprofit organization, and

(iii) support and maintenance shall not be included and the provisions of clause (i) shall not be applicable in the case of any individual (and his eligible spouse, if any) for the period which begins with the month in which such individual (or such individual and his eligible spouse) began to receive support and maintenance while living in a residential facility (including a private household) maintained by another person and ends with the close of the month in which such individual (or such individual and his eligible spouse) ceases to receive support and maintenance while living in such a residential facility (or, if earlier, with the close of the seventeenth month following the month in which such period began), if, not more than 30 days prior to the date on which such individual (or such individual and his eligible spouse) began to receive support and maintenance while living in such a residential facility,

> (I) such individual (or such individual and his eligible spouse) were residing in a household maintained by such individual (or by such individual and others) as his or their own home,

> (II) there occurred within the area in which such household is located (and while such individual, or such individual and his spouse, were residing in the household referred to in subclause (I) a catastrophe on account of which the President declared a major disaster to exist therein for purposes of the Disaster Relief and Emergency Assistance Act, and

> (III) such individual declares that he (or he and his eligible spouse) ceased to continue living in the household referred to in subclause (II) because of such catastrophe;

(B) any payments received as an annuity, pension, retirement, or disability benefit, including veterans' compensation and pensions, workmen's compensation payments, old-age, survivors, and disability insurance benefits, railroad retirement annuities and pensions, and unemployment insurance benefits;

(C) prizes and awards;

(D) payments to the individual occasioned by the death of another person, to the extent that the total of such payments exceeds the amount expended by such individual for purposes of the deceased person's last illness and burial;

(E) support and alimony payments, and (subject to the provisions of subparagraph (D) excluding certain amounts expended for purposes of a last illness and burial) gifts (cash or otherwise) and inheritances;

(F) rents, dividends, interest, and royalties not described in paragraph (1)(E); and

(G) any earnings of, and additions to, the corpus of a trust established by an individual (within the meaning of section 1613(e)), of which the individual is a beneficiary, to which section 1613(e) applies, and, in the case of an irrevocable trust, with respect to which circumstances exist under which a payment from the earnings or additions could be made to or for the benefit of the individual.

(b) In determining the income of an individual (and his eligible spouse) there shall be excluded —

(1) subject to limitations (as to amount or otherwise) prescribed by the Commissioner of Social Security, if such individual is a child who is, as determined by the Commissioner of Social Security, a student regularly attending a school, college, or university, or a course of vocational or technical training designed to prepare him for gainful employment, the earned income of such individual;

(2) (A) the first $240 per year (or proportionately smaller amounts for shorter periods) of income (whether earned or unearned) other than income which is paid on the basis of the need of the eligible individual, and

(B) monthly (or other periodic) payments received by any individual, under a program established prior to July 1, 1973 (or any program established prior to such date but subsequently amended so as to conform to State or Federal constitutional standards), if

(i) such payments are made by the State of which the individual receiving such payments is a resident,

(ii) eligibility of any individual for such payments is not based on need and is based solely on attainment of age 65 or any other age set by the State and residency in such State by such individual, and

(iii) on or before September 30, 1985, such individual

(I) first becomes an eligible individual or an eligible spouse under this title, and

(II) satisfies the twenty-five-year residency requirement of such program as such program was in effect prior to January 1, 1983;

(3) (A) the total unearned income of such individual (and such spouse, if any) in a month which, as determined in accordance with criteria prescribed by the Commissioner of Social Security, is received too infrequently or irregularly to be included, if such income so received does not exceed $20 in such month, and

(B) the total earned income of such individual (and such spouse, if any) in a month which, as determined in accordance with such criteria, is received too infrequently or irregularly to be included, if such income so received does not exceed $10 in such month;

(4) (A) if such individual (or such spouse) is blind (and has not attained age 65, or received benefits under this title (or aid under a State plan approved under section 1002 or 1602) for the month before the month in which he attained age 65),

(i) the first $780 per year (or proportionately smaller amounts for shorter periods) of earned income not excluded by the preceding paragraphs of this subsection, plus one-half of the remainder thereof,

(ii) an amount equal to any expenses reasonably attributable to the earning of any income, and

(iii) such additional amounts of other income, where such individual has a plan for achieving self-support approved by the Commissioner of Social Security, as may be necessary for the fulfillment of such plan,

(B) if such individual (or such spouse) is disabled but not blind (and has not attained age 65, or received benefits under this title (or aid under a State plan approved under section 1402 or 1602) for the month before the month in which he attained age 65),

(i) the first $780 per year (or proportionately smaller amounts for shorter periods) of earned income not excluded by the preceding paragraphs of this subsection,

(ii) such additional amounts of earned income of such individual, if such individual's disability is sufficiently severe to result in a functional limitation requiring assistance in order for him to work, as may be necessary to pay the costs (to such individual) of attendant care services, medical devices, equipment, prostheses, and similar items and services (not including routine drugs or routine medical services unless such drugs or services are necessary for the control of the disabling condition) which are necessary (as determined by the Commissioner of Social Security in regulations) for that purpose, whether or not such assistance is also needed to enable him to carry out his normal daily functions, except that the amounts to be excluded shall be subject to such reasonable limits as the Commissioner of Social Security may prescribe,

(iii) one-half of the amount of earned income not excluded after the application of the preceding provisions of this subparagraph, and

(iv) such additional amounts of other income, where such individual has a plan for achieving self-support approved by the Commissioner of Social Security, as may be necessary for the fulfillment of such plan, or

(C) if such individual (or such spouse) has attained age 65 and is not included under subparagraph (A) or (B), the first $780 per year (or proportionately smaller amounts for shorter periods) of earned income not excluded by the preceding paragraphs of this subsection, plus one-half of the remainder thereof;

(5) any amount received from any public agency as a return or refund of taxes paid on real property or on food purchased by such individual (or such spouse);

(6) assistance, furnished to or on behalf of such individual (and spouse), which is based on need and furnished by any State or political subdivision of a State;

(7) any portion of any grant, scholarship, or fellowship received for use in paying the cost of tuition and fees at any educational (including technical or vocational education) institution;

(8) home produce of such individual (or spouse) utilized by the household for its own consumption;

(9) if such individual is a child, one-third of any payment for his support received from an absent parent;

(10) any amounts received for the foster care of a child who is not an eligible individual but who is living in the same home as such

individual and was placed in such home by a public or nonprofit private child-placement or child-care agency;

(11) assistance received under the Disaster Relief Act of 1974 or other assistance provided pursuant to a Federal statute on account of a catastrophe which is declared to be a major disaster by the President;

(12) interest income received on assistance funds referred to in paragraph (11) within the 9-month period beginning on the date such funds are received (or such longer periods as the Commissioner of Social Security shall by regulations prescribe in cases where good cause is shown by the individual concerned for extending such period);

(13) any assistance received to assist in meeting the costs of home energy, including both heating and cooling, which (as determined under regulations of the Commissioner of Social Security by such State agency as the chief executive officer of the State may designate)

(A) is based on need for such assistance, and

(B) is (i) assistance furnished in kind by a private nonprofit agency, or (ii) assistance furnished by a supplier of home heating oil or gas, by an entity providing home energy whose revenues are primarily derived on a rate-of-return basis regulated by a State or Federal governmental entity, or by a municipal utility providing home energy;

(14) assistance paid, with respect to the dwelling unit occupied by such individual (or such individual and spouse), under the United States Housing Act of 1937, the National Housing Act, section 101 of the Housing and Urban Development Act of 1965, title V of the Housing Act of 1949, or section 202(h) of the Housing Act of 1959;

(15) the value of any commercial transportation ticket, for travel by such individual (or spouse) among the 50 States, the District of Columbia, the Commonwealth of Puerto Rico, the Virgin Islands, Guam, American Samoa, and the Northern Mariana Islands, which is received as a gift by such individual (or such spouse) and is not converted to cash;

(16) interest accrued on the value of an agreement entered into by such individual (or such spouse) representing the purchase of a burial space excluded under section 1613(a)(2)(B), and left to accumulate;

(17) any amount received by such individual (or such spouse) from a fund established by a State to aid victims of crime; and

(18) relocation assistance provided by a State or local government to such individual (or such spouse), comparable to assistance provided under title II of the Uniform Relocation Assistance and Real Property Acquisitions Policies Act of 1970 which is subject to the treatment required by section 216 of such Act;

(19) any refund of Federal income taxes made to such individual (or such spouse) by reason of section 32 of the Internal Revenue Code of 1986 (relating to earned income tax credit), and any payment made to such individual (or such spouse) by an employer under section 3507 of such Code (relating to advance payment of earned income credit);

(20) special pay received pursuant to section 310 of title 37, United States Code;

(21) the interest or other earnings on any account established and maintained in accordance with section 1631(a)(2)(F); and

(22) any gift to, or for the benefit of, an individual who has not attained 18 years of age and who has a life-threatening condition, from an organization described in section 501(c)(3) of the Internal Revenue Code of 1986 which is exempt from taxation under section 501(a) of such Code —

(A) in the case of an in-kind gift, if the gift is not converted to cash; or

(B) in the case of a cash gift, only to the extent that the total amount excluded from the income of the individual pursuant to this paragraph in the calendar year in which the gift is made does not exceed $2,000.

## § 1382b. Resources

(a) *Exclusions from resources*

In determining the resources of an individual (and his eligible spouse, if any) there shall be excluded —

(1) the home (including the land that appertains thereto);

(2) (A) household goods, personal effects, and an automobile, to the extent that their total value does not exceed such amount as the Commissioner of Social Security determines to be reasonable; and

(B) the value of any burial space or agreement (including any interest accumulated thereon) representing the purchase of a burial space (subject to such limits as to size or value as the Commissioner of Social Security may by regulation prescribe) held for the purpose of providing a place for the burial of the individual, his spouse, or any other member of his immediate family;

(3) other property which is so essential to the means of self-support of such individual (and such spouse) as to warrant its exclusion, as determined in accordance with and subject to limitations prescribed by the Commissioner of Social Security, except that the Commissioner of Social Security shall not establish a limitation on property (including the tools of a tradesperson and the machinery and livestock of a farmer) that is used in a trade or business or by such individual as an employee;

(4) such resources of an individual who is blind or disabled and who has a plan for achieving self-support approved by the Commissioner of Social Security, as may be necessary for the fulfillment of such plan;

(5) in the case of Natives of Alaska, shares of stock held in a Regional or a Village Corporation, during the period of twenty years in which such stock is inalienable, as provided in section 7(h) and section 8(c) of the Alaska Native Claims Settlement Act;

(6) assistance referred to in section 1612(b)(11) for the 9-month period beginning on the date such funds are received (or for such longer period as the Commissioner of Social Security shall by regulations prescribe in cases where good cause is shown by the individual concerned for extending such period); and, for purposes of this paragraph, the term "assistance" includes interest thereon which is excluded from income under section 1612(b)(12);

(7) any amount received from the United States which is attributable to under payments of benefits due for one or more prior months, under this title or title II to such individual (or spouse) or to any other person whose income is deemed to be included in such individual's (or spouse's) income for purposes of this title but the application of this paragraph in the case of any such individual (and eligible spouse if any), with respect to any amount so received from the United States, shall be limited to the first 6 months following the month in which such amount is received (or to the first 9 months following such month with respect to any amount so received during the period beginning October 1, 1987, and ending September 30,

1989), and written notice of this limitation shall be given to the recipient concurrently with the payment of such amount;

(8) the value of assistance referred to in section 1612(b)(14), paid with respect to the dwelling unit occupied by such individual (or such individual and spouse);

(9) for the 9-month period beginning after the month in which received, any amount received by such individual (or such spouse) from a fund established by a State to aid victims of crime, to the extent that such individual (or such spouse) demonstrates that such amount was paid as compensation for expenses incurred or losses suffered as a result of a crime;

(10) for the 9-month period beginning after the month in which received, relocation assistance provided by a State or local government to such individual (or such spouse), comparable to assistance provided under title II of the Uniform Relocation Assistance and Real Property Acquisitions Policies Act of 1970 which is subject to the treatment required by section 216 of such Act;

(11) for the month of receipt and the following month, any refund of Federal income taxes made to such individual (or such spouse) by reason of section 32 of the Internal Revenue Code of 1986 (relating to earned income tax credit), and any payment made to such individual (or such spouse) by an employer under section 3507 of such Code (relating to advance payment of earned income credit);

(12) any account, including accrued interest or other earnings thereon, established and maintained in accordance with section 1631(a)(2)(F); and

(13) any gift to, or for the benefit of, an individual who has not attained 18 years of age and who has a life-threatening condition, from an organization described in section 501(c)(3) of the Internal Revenue Code of 1986 which is exempt from taxation under section 501(a) of such Code —

(A) in the case of an in-kind gift, if the gift is not converted to cash; or

(B) in the case of a cash gift, only to the extent that the total amount excluded from the resources of the individual pursuant to this paragraph in the calendar year in which the gift is made does not exceed $2,000.

In determining the resources of an individual (or eligible spouse) an insurance policy shall be taken into account only to the extent of its cash surrender value; except that if the total face value of all life insurance policies on any person is $1,500 or less, no part of the value of any such policy shall be taken into account.

(b) *Disposition of resources; grounds for exemption from disposition requirements*

(1) The Commissioner of Social Security shall prescribe the period or periods of time within which, and the manner in which, various kinds of property must be disposed of in order not to be included in determining an individual's eligibility for benefits. Any portion of the individual's benefits paid for any such period shall be conditioned upon such disposal; and any benefits so paid shall (at the time of the disposal) be considered overpayments to the extent they would not have been paid had the disposal occurred at the beginning of the period for which such benefits were paid.

(2) Notwithstanding the provisions of paragraph (1), the Commissioner of Social Security shall not require the disposition of any real property for so long as it cannot be sold because

(A) it is jointly owned (and its sale would cause undue hardship, due to loss of housing, for the other owner or owners),

(B) its sale is barred by a legal impediment, or

(C) as determined under regulations issued by the Commissioner of Social Security, the owner's reasonable efforts to sell it have been unsuccessful.

(c) *Disposal of resources for less than fair market value*

(1) (A) (i) If an individual or the spouse of an individual disposes of resources for less than fair market value on or after the look-back date described in clause (ii)(I), the individual is ineligible for benefits under this title for months during the period beginning on the date described in clause (iii) and equal to the number of months calculated as provided in clause (iv).

(ii) (I) The look-back date described in this subclause is a date that is 36 months before the date described in subclause (II).

(II) The date described in this subclause is the date on which the individual applies for benefits under this title or, if later, the date on which the individual (or the spouse of the individual) disposes of resources for less than fair market value.

(iii) The date described in this clause is the first day of the first month in or after which resources were disposed of for less than fair market value and which does not occur in any other period of ineligibility under this paragraph.

(iv) The number of months calculated under this clause shall be equal to —

(I) the total, cumulative uncompensated value of all resources so disposed of by the individual (or the spouse of the individual) on or after the look-back date described in clause (ii)(I); divided by

(II) the amount of the maximum monthly benefit payable under section 1611(b), plus the amount (if any) of the maximum State supplementary payment corresponding to the State's payment level applicable to the individual's living arrangement and eligibility category that would otherwise be payable to the individual by the Commissioner pursuant to an agreement under section 1616(a) of this Act or section 212(b) of Public Law 93-66, for the month in which occurs the date described in clause (ii)(II),

rounded, in the case of any fraction, to the nearest whole number, but shall not in any case exceed 36 months.

(B) (i) Notwithstanding subparagraph (A), this subsection shall not apply to a transfer of a resource to a trust if the portion of the trust attributable to the resource is considered a resource available to the individual pursuant to subsection (e)(3) (or would be so considered but for the application of subsection (e)(4)).

(ii) In the case of a trust established by an individual or an individual's spouse (within the meaning of subsection (e)), if from such portion of the trust, if any, that is considered a resource available to the individual pursuant to subsection (e)(3) (or would be so considered but for the application of subsection (e)(4)) or the residue of the portion on the termination of the trust —

(I) there is made a payment other than to or for the benefit of the individual; or

(II) no payment could under any circumstance be made to the individual,

then, for purposes of this subsection, the payment described in clause (I) or the foreclosure of payment described in clause (II) shall be considered a transfer of resources by the individual or the individual's spouse as of the date of the payment or foreclosure, as the case may be.

(C) An individual shall not be ineligible for benefits under this title by reason of the application of this paragraph to a disposal of resources by the individual or the spouse of the individual, to the extent that —

(i) the resources are a home and title to the home was transferred to —

(I) the spouse of the transferor;

(II) a child of the transferor who has not attained 21 years of age, or is blind or disabled;

(III) a sibling of the transferor who has an equity interest in such home and who was residing in the transferor's home for a period of at least 1 year immediately before the date the transferor becomes an institutionalized individual; or

(IV) a son or daughter of the transferor (other than a child described in subclause (II)) who was residing in the transferor's home for a period of at least 2 years immediately before the date the transferor becomes an institutionalized individual, and who provided care to the transferor which permitted the transferor to reside at home rather than in such an institution or facility;

(ii) the resources —

(I) were transferred to the transferor's spouse or to another for the sole benefit of the transferor's spouse;

(II) were transferred from the transferor's spouse to another for the sole benefit of the transferor's spouse;

(III) were transferred to, or to a trust (including a trust described in section 1917(d)(4)) established solely for the benefit of, the transferor's child who is blind or disabled; or

(IV) were transferred to a trust (including a trust described in section 1917(d)(4)) established solely for the benefit of an individual who has not attained 65 years of age and who is disabled;

(iii) a satisfactory showing is made to the Commissioner of Social Security (in accordance with regulations promulgated by the Commissioner) that —

(I) the individual who disposed of the resources intended to dispose of the resources either at fair market value, or for other valuable consideration;

(II) the resources were transferred exclusively for a purpose other than to qualify for benefits under this title; or

(III) all resources transferred for less than fair market value have been returned to the transferor; or

(iv) the Commissioner determines, under procedures established by the Commissioner, that the denial of eligibility would work an undue hardship as determined on the basis of criteria established by the Commissioner.

(D) For purposes of this subsection, in the case of a resource held by an individual in common with another person or persons in a joint tenancy, tenancy in common, or similar arrangement, the resource (or the affected portion of such resource) shall be considered to be disposed of by the individual when any action is taken, either by the individual or by any other person, that reduces or eliminates the individual's ownership or control of such resource.

(E) In the case of a transfer by the spouse of an individual that results in a period of ineligibility for the individual under this subsection, the Commissioner shall apportion the period (or any portion of the period) among the individual and the individual's spouse if the spouse becomes eligible for benefits under this title.

(F) For purposes of this paragraph —

(i) the term "benefits under this title" includes payments of the type described in section 1616(a) of this Act and of the type described in section 212(b) of Public Law 93-66;

(ii) the term "institutionalized individual" has the meaning given such term in section 1917(e)(3); and

(iii) the term "trust" has the meaning given such term in subsection (e)(6)(A) of this section.

(2) (A) At the time an individual (and the individual's eligible spouse, if any) applies for benefits under this title, and at the time the eligibility of an individual (and such spouse, if any) for such benefits is redetermined, the Commissioner of Social Security shall —

(i) inform such individual of the provisions of paragraph (1) and section 1917(c) providing for a period of ineligibility for benefits under this title and title XIX, respectively, for individuals who make certain dispositions of resources for less than fair market value, and inform such individual that information obtained pursuant to clause (ii) will be made available to the State agency administering a State plan under title XIX (as provided in subparagraph (B)); and

(ii) obtain from such individual information which may be used in determining whether or not a period of ineligibility for such benefits would be required by reason of paragraph (1) or section 1917(c).

(B) The Commissioner of Social Security shall make the information obtained under subparagraph (A)(ii) available, on request, to any State agency administering a State plan approved under title XIX.

(d) *Funds set aside for burial expenses*

(1) In determining the resources of an individual, there shall be excluded an amount, not in excess of $1,500 each with respect to such individual and his spouse (if any), that is separately identifiable and has been set aside to meet the burial and related expenses of such individual or spouse.

(2) The amount of $1,500, referred to in paragraph (1), with respect to an individual shall be reduced by an amount equal to

(A) the total face value of all insurance policies on his life which are owned by him or his spouse and the cash surrender value of which has been excluded in determining the resources of such individual or of such individual and his spouse, and

(B) the total of any amounts in an irrevocable trust (or other irrevocable arrangement) available to meet the burial and related expenses of such individual or his spouse.

(3) If the Commissioner of Social Security finds that any part of the amount excluded under paragraph (1) was used for purposes other than those for which it was set aside in cases where the inclusion of any portion of the amount would cause the resources of such individual, or of such individual and spouse, to exceed the limits specified in paragraph (1) or (2) (whichever may be applicable) of section 1611(a), the Commissioner shall reduce any future benefits payable to the eligible individual (or to such individual and his spouse) by an amount equal to such part.

(4) The Commissioner of Social Security may provide by regulations that whenever an amount set aside to meet burial and related expenses is excluded under paragraph (1) in determining the resources of an individual, any interest earned or accrued on such amount (and left to

accumulate), and any appreciation in the value of prepaid burial arrangements for which such amount was set aside, shall also be excluded (to such extent and subject to such conditions or limitations as such regulations may prescribe) in determining the resources (and the income) of such individual.

(e) *Trusts*

(1) In determining the resources of an individual, paragraph (3) shall apply to a trust (other than a trust described in paragraph (5)) established by the individual.

(2) (A) For purposes of this subsection, an individual shall be considered to have established a trust if any assets of the individual (or of the individual's spouse) are transferred to the trust other than by will.

(B) In the case of an irrevocable trust to which are transferred the assets of an individual (or of the individual's spouse) and the assets of any other person, this subsection shall apply to the portion of the trust attributable to the assets of the individual (or of the individual's spouse).

(C) This subsection shall apply to a trust without regard to —
(i) the purposes for which the trust is established;
(ii) whether the trustees have or exercise any discretion under the trust;
(iii) any restrictions on when or whether distributions may be made from the trust; or
(iv) any restrictions on the use of distributions from the trust.

(3) (A) In the case of a revocable trust established by an individual, the corpus of the trust shall be considered a resource available to the individual.

(B) In the case of an irrevocable trust established by an individual, if there are any circumstances under which payment from the trust could be made to or for the benefit of the individual (or of the individual's spouse), the portion of the corpus from which payment to or for the benefit of the individual (or of the individual's spouse) could be made shall be considered a resource available to the individual.

(4) The Commissioner of Social Security may waive the application of this subsection with respect to an individual if the Commissioner determines that such application would work an undue hardship (as

determined on the basis of criteria established by the Commissioner) on the individual.

(5) This subsection shall not apply to a trust described in subparagraph (A) or (C) of section 1917(d)(4).

(6) For purposes of this subsection —

(A) the term "trust" includes any legal instrument or device that is similar to a trust;

(B) the term "corpus" means, with respect to a trust, all property and other interests held by the trust, including accumulated earnings and any other addition to the trust after its establishment (except that such term does not include any such earnings or addition in the month in which the earnings or addition is credited or otherwise transferred to the trust); and

(C) the term "asset" includes any income or resource of the individual (or of the individual's spouse), including —

(i) any income excluded by section 1612(b);

(ii) any resource otherwise excluded by this section; and

(iii) any other payment or property to which the individual (or of the individual's spouse) is entitled but does not receive or have access to because of action by —

(I) the individual or spouse;

(II) a person or entity (including a court) with legal authority to act in place of, or on behalf of, the individual or spouse; or

(III) a person or entity (including a court) acting at the direction of, or on the request of, the individual or spouse.

## § 1382c. Definitions

(a)    (1) For purposes of this title, the term "aged, blind, or disabled individual" means an individual who —

(A) is 65 years of age or older, is blind (as determined under paragraph (2)), or is disabled (as determined under paragraph (3)), and

(B)    (i) is a resident of the United States, and is either

(I) a citizen or

(II) an alien lawfully admitted for permanent residence or otherwise permanently residing in the United States under color of law (including any alien who is lawfully present in the United States as a result of the application of the provisions of section 212(d)(5) of the Immigration and Nationality Act), or

(ii) is a child who is a citizen of the United States, who is living with a parent of the child who is a member of the Armed Forces of the United States assigned to permanent duty ashore outside the United States, and who, for the month before the parent reported for such assignment, received a benefit under this title.

(2) An individual shall be considered to be blind for purposes of this title if he has central visual acuity of 20/200 or less in the better eye with the use of a correcting lens. An eye which is accompanied by a limitation in the fields of vision such that the widest diameter of the visual field subtends an angle no greater than 20 degrees shall be considered for purposes of the first sentence of this subsection as having a central visual acuity of 20/200 or less. An individual shall also be considered to be blind for purposes of this title if he is blind as defined under a State plan approved under title X or XVI as in effect for October 1972 and received aid under such plan (on the basis of blindness) for December 1973, so long as he is continuously blind as so defined.

(3)  (A) Except as provided in subparagraph (C), an individual shall be considered to be disabled for purposes of this title if he is unable to engage in any substantial gainful activity by reason of any medically determinable physical or mental impairment which can be expected to result in death or which has lasted or can be expected to last for a continuous period of not less than twelve months.

(B) For purposes of subparagraph (A), an individual shall be determined to be under a disability only if his physical or mental impairment or impairments are of such severity that he is not only unable to do his previous work but cannot, considering his age, education, and work experience, engage in any other kind of substantial gainful work which exists in the national economy, regardless of whether such work exists in the immediate area in which he lives, or whether a specific job vacancy exists for him, or whether he would be hired if he applied for work. For purposes of the preceding sentence (with respect to any individual), "work which exists in the national economy" means work which exists in significant numbers either in the region where such individual lives or in several regions of the country.

(C)  (i) An individual under the age of 18 shall be considered disabled for the purposes of this title if that individual has a medically determinable physical or mental impairment, which results in marked and severe functional limitations, and which can be expected to result in death or which has lasted or can be expected to last for a continuous period of not less than 12 months.

(ii) Notwithstanding clause (i), no individual under the age of 18 who engages in substantial gainful activity (determined in accordance with regulations prescribed pursuant to subparagraph (E)) may be considered to be disabled.

(D) For purposes of this paragraph, a physical or mental impairment is an impairment that results from anatomical, physiological, or psychological abnormalities which are demonstrable by medically acceptable clinical and laboratory diagnostic techniques.

(E) The Commissioner of Social Security shall by regulations prescribe the criteria for determining when services performed or earnings derived from services demonstrate an individual's ability to engage in substantial gainful activity. In determining whether an individual is able to engage in substantial gainful activity by reason of his earnings, where his disability is sufficiently severe to result in a functional limitation requiring assistance in order for him to work, there shall be excluded from such earnings an amount equal to the cost (to such individual) of any attendant care services, medical devices, equipment, prostheses, and similar items and services (not including routine drugs or routine medical services unless such drugs or services are necessary for the control of the disabling condition) which are necessary (as determined by the Commissioner of Social Security in regulations) for that purpose, whether or not such assistance is also needed to enable him to carry out his normal daily functions; except that the amounts to be excluded shall be subject to such reasonable limits as the Commissioner of Social Security may prescribe. Notwithstanding the provisions of subparagraph (B), an individual whose services or earnings meet such criteria shall be found not to be disabled. The Commissioner of Social Security shall make determinations under this title with respect to substantial gainful activity, without regard to the legality of the activity.

(F) Notwithstanding the provisions of subparagraphs (A) through (E), an individual shall also be considered to be disabled for purposes of this title if he is permanently and totally disabled as defined under a State plan approved under title XIV or XVI as in effect for October 1972 and received aid under such plan (on the basis of disability) for December 1973 (and for at least one month prior to July 1973), so long as he is continuously disabled as so defined.

(G) In determining whether an individual's physical or mental impairment or impairments are of a sufficient medical severity that such impairment or impairments could be the basis of eligibility under this section, the Commissioner of Social Security shall consider the combined effect of all of the individual's impairments without regard to whether any such impairment, if considered separately, would be of such severity. If the Commissioner of Social Security does find a medically severe combination of impairments, the combined impact of the impairments shall be considered throughout the disability determination process.

(H) (i) In making determinations with respect to disability under this title, the provisions of sections 221(h), 221(k), and 223(d)(5) shall apply in the same manner as they apply to determinations of disability under title II

(ii) (I) Not less frequently than once every 3 years, the Commissioner shall review in accordance with paragraph (4) the continued eligibility for benefits under this title of each individual who has not attained 18 years of age and is eligible for such benefits by reason of an impairment (or combination of impairments) which is likely to improve (or, at the option of the Commissioner, which is unlikely to improve).

(II) A representative payee of a recipient whose case is reviewed under this clause shall present, at the time of review, evidence demonstrating that the recipient is, and has been, receiving treatment, to the extent considered medically necessary and available, of the condition which was the basis for providing benefits under this title.

(III) If the representative payee refuses to comply without good cause with the requirements of subclause (II), the Commissioner of Social Security shall, if the Commissioner determines it is in the best interest of the individual, promptly suspend payment of benefits to the representative payee, and provide for payment of benefits to an alternative representative payee of the individual or, if the interest of the individual under this title would be served thereby, to the individual.

(IV) Subclause (II) shall not apply to the representative payee of any individual with respect to whom the Commissioner determines such application would be inappropriate or unnecessary. In making such determination, the Commissioner shall take into consideration the nature of the individual's impairment (or combination of impairments). Section 1631(c) shall not apply to a finding by the Commissioner that the requirements of subclause (II) should not apply to an individual's representative payee.

(iii) If an individual is eligible for benefits under this title by reason of disability for the month preceding the month in which the individual attains the age of 18 years, the Commissioner shall redetermine such eligibility —

(I) by applying the criteria used in determining initial eligibility for individuals who are age 18 or older; and

(II) either during the 1-year period beginning on the individual's 18th birthday or, in lieu of a continuing disability review, whenever the Commissioner determines that an individual's case is subject to a redetermination under this clause.

With respect to any redetermination under this clause, paragraph (4) shall not apply.

(iv) (I) Except as provided in subclause (VI), not later than 12 months after the birth of an individual, the Commissioner shall review in accordance with paragraph (4) the continuing eligibility for benefits under this title by reason of disability of such individual whose low birth weight is a contributing factor material to the Commissioner's determination that the individual is disabled.

(II) A review under subclause (I) shall be considered a substitute for a review otherwise required under any other provision of this subparagraph during that 12-month period.

(III) A representative payee of a recipient whose case is reviewed under this clause shall present, at the time of review, evidence demonstrating that the recipient is, and has been, receiving treatment, to the extent considered medically necessary and available, of the condition which was the basis for providing benefits under this title.

(IV) If the representative payee refuses to comply without good cause with the requirements of subclause (III), the Commissioner of Social Security shall, if the Commissioner determines it is in the best interest of the individual, promptly suspend payment of benefits to the representative payee, and provide for payment of benefits to an alternative representative payee of the individual or, if the interest of the individual under this title would be served thereby, to the individual.

(V) Subclause (III) shall not apply to the representative payee of any individual with respect to whom the Commissioner determines such application would be inappropriate or unnecessary. In making such determination, the Commissioner shall take into consideration the nature of the individual's impairment (or combination of impairments). Section 1631(c) shall not apply to a finding by the Commissioner that the requirements of subclause (III) should not apply to an individual's representative payee.

(VI) Subclause (I) shall not apply in the case of an individual described in that subclause who, at the time of the individual's initial disability determination, the Commissioner determines has an impairment that is not expected to improve within 12 months after the birth of that individual, and who the Commissioner schedules for a continuing disability review at a date that is after the individual attains 1 year of age.

(I) In making any determination under this title with respect to the disability of an individual who has not attained the age of 18 years and to whom section 221(h) does not apply, the Commissioner of Social Security shall make reasonable efforts to ensure that a qualified pediatrician or other individual who specializes in a field of medicine appropriate to the disability of the individual (as determined by the Commissioner of Social Security) evaluates the case of such individual.

(J) Notwithstanding subparagraph (A), an individual shall not be considered to be disabled for purposes of this title if alcoholism or drug addiction would (but for this subparagraph) be a contributing factor material to the Commissioner's determination that the individual is disabled.

(4) A recipient of benefits based on disability under this title may be determined not to be entitled to such benefits on the basis of a finding that the physical or mental impairment on the basis of which such benefits are provided has ceased, does not exist, or is not disabling only if such finding is supported by —

(A) in the case of an individual who is age 18 or older —

(i) substantial evidence which demonstrates that —

(I) there has been any medical improvement in the individual's impairment or combination of impairments (other than medical improvement which is not related to the individual's ability to work), and

(II) the individual is now able to engage in substantial gainful activity; or

(ii) substantial evidence (except in the case of an individual eligible to receive benefits under section 1619 which —

(I) consists of new medical evidence and a new assessment of the individual's residual function capacity, and demonstrates that —

(aa) although the individual has not improved medically, he or she is nonetheless a beneficiary of advances in medical or vocational therapy or technology (related to the individual's ability to work), and

(bb) the individual is now able to engage in substantial gainful activity, or

(II) demonstrates that —

(aa) although the individual has not improved medically, he or she has undergone vocational therapy (related to the individual's ability to work), and

(bb) the individual is now able to engage in substantial gainful activity; or

(iii) substantial evidence which demonstrates that, as determined on the basis of new or improved diagnostic techniques or evaluations, the individual's impairment or combination of impairments is not as disabling as it was considered to be at the time of the most recent prior decision that he or she was under a disability or continued to be under a disability, and that therefore the individual is able to engage in substantial gainful activity; or

(B) in the case of an individual who is under the age of 18 —

(i) substantial evidence which demonstrates that there has been medical improvement in the individual's impairment or combination of impairments, and that such impairment or combination of impairments no longer results in marked and severe functional limitations; or

(ii) substantial evidence which demonstrates that, as determined on the basis of new or improved diagnostic techniques or evaluations, the individual's impairment or combination of impairments, is not as disabling as it was considered to be at the time of the most recent prior decision that the individual was under a disability or continued to be under a disability, and such impairment or combination of impairments does not result in marked and severe functional limitations; or

(C) in the case of any individual, substantial evidence (which may be evidence on the record at the time any prior determination of the entitlement to benefits based on disability was made, or newly obtained evidence which relates to that determination) which demonstrates that a prior determination was in error.

Nothing in this paragraph shall be construed to require a determination that an individual receiving benefits based on disability under this title is entitled to such benefits if the prior determination was fraudulently obtained or if the individual is engaged in substantial gainful activity, cannot be located, or fails, without good cause, to cooperate in a review of his or her entitlement or to follow prescribed treatment which would be expected (i) to restore his or her ability to engage in substantial gainful activity, or (ii) in the case of an individual under the age of 18, to eliminate or improve the individual's impairment or combination of impairments so that it no longer results in marked and severe functional limitations. Any determination under this paragraph shall be made on the basis of all the evidence available in the individual's case file, including new evidence concerning the individual's prior or current condition which is presented by the individual or secured by the Commissioner of Social Security. Any determination made under this paragraph shall be made on the basis of the weight of the evidence and on a neutral basis with regard to the individual's condition, without any initial inference as to the presence or absence of disability being drawn from the fact that the individual has previously been determined to be disabled.

(b) For purposes of this title, the term "eligible spouse" means an aged, blind, or disabled individual who is the husband or wife of another aged, blind, or disabled individual, and who, in a month, is living with such aged, blind, or disabled individual on the first day of the month or, in any case in which either spouse files an application for benefits, on the first day of the month following the date the application is filed, or, in any case in which either spouse requests restoration of eligibility under this title during the month, at the time the application or request is filed. If two aged, blind, or disabled individuals are husband and wife as described in the preceding sentence, only one of them may be an "eligible individual" within the meaning of section 1611(a).

(c) For purposes of this title, the term "child" means an individual who is neither married nor (as determined by the Commissioner of Social Security) the head of a household, and who is (1) under the age of eighteen, or (2) under the age of twenty-two and (as determined by the Commissioner of Social Security) a student regularly attending a school, college, or university, or a course of vocational or technical training designed to prepare him for gainful employment.

(d) In determining whether two individuals are husband and wife for purposes of this title, appropriate State law shall be applied; except that —

(1) if a man and woman have been determined to be husband and wife under section 216(h)(1) for purposes of title II et seq.], they shall be considered (from and after the date of such determination or the date of their application for benefits under this title, whichever is later) to be husband and wife for purposes of this title, or

(2) if a man and woman are found to be holding themselves out to the community in which they reside as husband and wife, they shall be so considered for purposes of this title notwithstanding any other provision of this section.

(e) For purposes of this title, the term "United States", when used in a geographical sense, means the 50 States and the District of Columbia

(f) (1) For purposes of determining eligibility for and the amount of benefits for any individual who is married and whose spouse is living with him in the same household but is not an eligible spouse, such individual's income and resources shall be deemed to include any income and resources of such spouse, whether or not available to such individual, except to the extent determined by the Commissioner of Social Security to be inequitable under the circumstances.

(2)  (A) For purposes of determining eligibility for and the amount of benefits for any individual who is a child under age 18, such individual's income and resources shall be deemed to include any income and resources of a parent of such individual (or the spouse of such a parent) who is living in the same household as such individual, whether or not available to such individual, except to the extent determined by the Commissioner of Social Security to be inequitable under the circumstances.

(B) Subparagraph (A) shall not apply in the case of any child who has not attained the age of 18 years who —

(i) is disabled;

(ii) received benefits under this title, pursuant to section 1611(e)(1)(B), while in an institution described in section 1611(e)(1)(B);

(iii) is eligible for medical assistance under a State home care plan approved by the Commissioner of Social Security under the provisions of section 1915(c) relating to waivers, or authorized under section 1902(e)(3); and

(iv) but for this subparagraph, would not be eligible for benefits under this title.

(3) For purposes of determining eligibility for and the amount of benefits for any individual who is an alien, such individual's income and resources shall be deemed to include the income and resources of his sponsor and such sponsor's spouse (if such alien has a sponsor) as provided in section 1621. Any such income deemed to be income of such individual shall be treated as unearned income of such individual.

(4) For purposes of paragraphs (1) and (2), a spouse or parent (or spouse of such a parent) who is absent from the household in which the individual lives due solely to a duty assignment as a member of the Armed Forces on active duty shall, in the absence of evidence to the contrary, be deemed to be living in the same household as the individual.

## § 1382e. Supplementary assistance by State or subdivision to needy individuals

(a) *Exclusion of cash payments in determination of income of individuals for purposes of eligibility for benefits; agreement by Commissioner of Social Security and State for Commissioner of Social Security to make supplementary payments on behalf of State or subdivision*

Any cash payments which are made by a State (or political subdivision thereof) on a regular basis to individuals who are receiving benefits under this title or who would but for their income be eligible to receive benefits under this title, as assistance based on need in supplementation of such benefits (as determined by the Commissioner of Social Security), shall be excluded under section 1612(b)(6) in determining the income of such individuals for purposes of this title and the Commissioner of Social Security and such State may enter into an agreement which satisfies subsection (b) under which the Commissioner of Social Security will, on behalf of such State (or subdivision) make such supplementary payments to all such individuals.

(b) *Agreement between Commissioner of Social Security and State; contents*

Any agreement between the Commissioner of Social Security and a State entered into under subsection (a) shall provide —

(1) that such payments will be made (subject to subsection (c)) to all individuals residing in such State (or subdivision) who are receiving benefits under this title, and

(2) such other rules with respect to eligibility for or amount of the supplementary payments, and such procedural or other general administrative provisions, as the Commissioner of Social Security finds necessary (subject to subsection (c)) to achieve efficient and effective administration of both the program which the Commissioner conducts under this title and the optional State supplementation.

At the option of the State (but subject to paragraph (2) of this subsection), the agreement between the Commissioner of Social Security and such State entered into under subsection (a) shall be modified to provide that the Commissioner of Social Security will make supplementary payments, on and after an effective date to be specified in the agreement as so modified, to individuals receiving benefits determined under section 1611(e)(1)(B).

(c) *Residence requirement by State or subdivision for supplementary payments; disregarding amounts of certain income by State or subdivision in determining eligibility for supplementary payments*

(1) Any State (or political subdivision) making supplementary payments described in subsection (a) may at its option impose as a condition of eligibility for such payments, and include in the State's agreement with the Commissioner of Social Security under such subsection, a residence requirement which excludes individuals who have resided in the State (or political subdivision) for less than a minimum period prior to application for such payments.

(2) Any State (or political subdivision), in determining the eligibility of any individual for supplementary payments described in subsection (a), may disregard amounts of earned and unearned income in addition to other amounts which it is required or permitted to disregard under this section in determining such eligibility, and shall include a provision specifying the amount of any such income that will be disregarded, if any.

(d) *Payment to Commissioner of Social Security by State of amount equal to expenditure by Commissioner of Social Security as supplementary payments; time and manner of payment by State*

(1) Any State which has entered into an agreement with the Commissioner of Social Security under this section which provides that the Commissioner of Social Security will, on behalf of the State (or political subdivision), make the supplementary payments to individuals who are receiving benefits under this title (or who would but for their income be eligible to receive such benefits), shall, in accordance with paragraph (5), pay to the Commissioner of Social Security an amount equal to the expenditures made by the Commissioner of Social Security as such supplementary payments, plus an administration fee assessed in accordance with paragraph (2) and any additional services fee charged in accordance with paragraph (3).

(2)   (A) The Commissioner of Social Security shall assess each State an administration fee in an amount equal to —

(i) the number of supplementary payments made by the Commissioner of Social Security on behalf of the State under this section for any month in a fiscal year; multiplied by

(ii) the applicable rate for the fiscal year.

(B) As used in subparagraph (A), the term "applicable rate" means —

(i) for fiscal year 1994, $1.67;

(ii) for fiscal year 1995, $3.33;

(iii) for fiscal year 1996, $5.00;

(iv) for fiscal year 1997, $5.00;

(v) for fiscal year 1998, $6.20;

(vi) for fiscal year 1999, $7.60;

(vii) for fiscal year 2000, $7.80;

(viii) for fiscal year 2001, $8.10;

(ix) for fiscal year 2002, $8.50; and

(x) for fiscal year 2003 and each succeeding fiscal year —

(I) the applicable rate in the preceding fiscal year, increased by the percentage, if any, by which the Consumer Price Index for the month of June of the calendar year of the increase exceeds the Consumer Price Index for the month of June of the calendar year preceding the calendar year of the increase, and rounded to the nearest whole cent; or

(II) such different rate as the Commissioner determines is appropriate for the State.

(C) Upon making a determination under subparagraph (B)(x)(II), the Commissioner of Social Security shall promulgate the determination in regulations, which may take into account the complexity of administering the State's supplementary payment program.

(D) All fees assessed pursuant to this paragraph shall be transferred to the Commissioner of Social Security at the same time that amounts for such supplementary payments are required to be so transferred.

(3)   (A) The Commissioner of Social Security may charge a State an additional services fee if, at the request of the State, the Commissioner of Social Security provides additional services beyond the level customarily provided, in the administration of State supplementary payments pursuant to this section.

(B) The additional services fee shall be in an amount that the Commissioner of Social Security determines is necessary to cover all costs (including indirect costs) incurred by the Federal Government in furnishing the additional services referred to in subparagraph (A).

(4)   (A) The first $5 of each administration fee assessed pursuant to paragraph (2), upon collection, shall be deposited in the general fund of the Treasury of the United States as miscellaneous receipts.

(B) That portion of each administration fee in excess of $5, and 100 percent of each additional services fee charged pursuant to paragraph (3), upon collection for fiscal year 1998 and each subsequent fiscal year, shall be credited to a special fund established in the Treasury of the United States for State supplementary payment fees. The amounts so credited, to the extent and in the amounts provided in advance in appropriations Acts, shall be available to defray expenses incurred in carrying out this title and related laws.

(5) [Caution: See § 410(b) of Act Dec. 17, 1999, P.L. 106-170 (note to this section), for provisions relating to applicability of this paragraph.]

(A)   (i) Any State which has entered into an agreement with the Commissioner of Social Security under this section shall remit the payments and fees required under this subsection with respect to monthly benefits paid to individuals under this title no later than —

(I) the business day preceding the date that the Commissioner pays such monthly benefits; or

(II) with respect to such monthly benefits paid for the month that is the last month of the State's fiscal year, the fifth business day following such date.

(ii) The Commissioner may charge States a penalty in an amount equal to 5 percent of the payment and the fees due if the remittance is received after the date required by clause (i).

(B) The Cash Management Improvement Act of 1990 shall not apply to any payments or fees required under this subsection that are paid by a State before the date required by subparagraph (A)(i).

(C) Notwithstanding subparagraph (A)(i), the Commissioner may make supplementary payments on behalf of a State with funds appropriated for payment of benefits under this title, and subsequently to be reimbursed for such payments by the State at such times as the Commissioner and State may agree. Such authority may be exercised only if extraordinary circumstances affecting a State's ability to make payment when required by subparagraph (A)(i) are determined by the Commissioner to exist.

(e)   *State standards; establishment; annual public review; annual certification; payments to individuals*

(1) Each State shall establish or designate one or more State or local authorities which shall establish, maintain, and insure the enforcement of standards for any category of institutions, foster homes, or group living arrangements in which (as determined by the State) a significant number

of recipients of supplemental security income benefits is residing or is likely to reside. Such standards shall be appropriate to the needs of such recipients and the character of the facilities involved, and shall govern such matters as admission policies, safety, sanitation, and protection of civil rights.

(2) Each State shall annually make available for public review a summary of the standards established pursuant to paragraph (1), and shall make available to any interested individual a copy of such standards, along with the procedures available in the State to insure the enforcement of such standards and a list of any waivers of such standards and any violations of such standards which have come to the attention of the authority responsible for their enforcement.

(3) Each State shall certify annually to the Commissioner of Social Security that it is in compliance with the requirements of this subsection.

(4) Payments made under this title with respect to an individual shall be reduced by an amount equal to the amount of any supplementary payment (as described in subsection (a)) or other payment made by a State (or political subdivision thereof) which is made for or on account of any medical or any other type of remedial care provided by an institution of the type described in paragraph (1) to such individual as a resident or an inpatient of such institution if such institution is not approved as meeting the standards described in such paragraph by the appropriate State or local authorities.

## § 1382f.  Cost-of-living adjustments in benefits

(a)  *Increase of dollar amounts*

Whenever benefit amounts under title II are increased by any percentage effective with any month as a result of a determination made under section 215(i) —

(1) each of the dollar amounts in effect for such month under subsections (a)(1)(A), (a)(2)(A), (b)(1), and (b)(2) of section 1611, and subsection (a)(1)(A) of section 211 of Public Law 93-66, as specified in such subsections or as previously increased under this section, shall be increased by the amount (if any) by which —

(A) the amount which would have been in effect for such month under such subsection but for the rounding of such amount pursuant to paragraph (2), exceeds

(B) the amount in effect for such month under such subsection; and

(2) the amount obtained under paragraph (1) with respect to each subsection shall be further increased by the same percentage by which benefit amounts under title II are increased for such month, or, if greater (in any case where the increase under title II was determined on the basis of the wage increase percentage rather than the CPI increase percentage), the percentage by which benefit amounts under title II would be increased for such month if the increase had been determined on the basis of the CPI increase percentage, (and rounded, when not a multiple of $12, to the next lower multiple of $12), effective with respect to benefits for months after such month.

(b) *Publication in Federal Register of new dollar amounts*

The new dollar amounts to be in effect under section 1611 of this title and under section 211 of Public Law 93-66 by reason of subsection (a) of this section shall be published in the Federal Register together with, and at the same time as, the material required by section 215(i)(2)(D) to be published therein by reason of the determination involved.

. . . .

## PART B — PROCEDURAL AND GENERAL PROVISIONS

## § 1383. Procedure for payment of benefits

(a) *Time, manner, form, and duration of payments; representative payees; promulgation of regulations*

(1) Benefits under this title shall be paid at such time or times and (subject to paragraph (10)) in such installments as will best effectuate the purposes of this title, as determined under regulations (and may in any case be paid less frequently than monthly where the amount of the monthly benefit would not exceed $10).

(2) (A) (i) Payments of the benefit of any individual may be made to any such individual or to the eligible spouse (if any) of such individual or partly to each.

(ii) (I) Upon a determination by the Commissioner of Social Security that the interest of such individual would be served thereby, such payments shall be made, regardless of the legal competency or incompetency of the individual or eligible spouse, to another individual, or an organization, with respect to whom the requirements of subparagraph (B) have been met (in this paragraph referred to as such individual's "representative payee") for the use and benefit of the individual or eligible spouse.

(II) In the case of an individual eligible for benefits under this title by reason of disability, the payment of such benefits shall be made to a representative payee if the Commissioner of Social Security determines that such payment would serve the interest of the individual because the individual also has an alcoholism or drug addiction condition (as determined by the Commissioner) and the individual is incapable of managing such benefits.

(iii) If the Commissioner of Social Security or a court of competent jurisdiction determines that the representative payee of an individual or eligible spouse has misused any benefits which have been paid to the representative payee pursuant to clause (ii) or section 205(j)(1) or 807. The Commissioner of Social Security shall promptly terminate payment of benefits to the representative payee pursuant to this subparagraph, and provide for payment of benefits to an alternative representative payee of the individual or eligible spouse or, if the interest of the individual under this title would be served thereby, to the individual or eligible spouse.

(B)  (i) Any determination made under subparagraph (A) for payment of benefits to the representative payee of an individual or eligible spouse shall be made on the basis of —

(I) an investigation by the Commissioner of Social Security of the person to serve as representative payee, which shall be conducted in advance of such payment, and shall, to the extent practicable, include a face-to-face interview with such person; and

(II) adequate evidence that such payment is in the interest of the individual or eligible spouse (as determined by the Commissioner of Social Security in regulations).

(ii) As part of the investigation referred to in clause (i)(I), the Commissioner of Social Security shall —

(I) require the person being investigated to submit documented proof of the identity of such person, unless information establishing such identity was submitted with an application for benefits under title II, title VIII, or this title;

(II) verify the social security account number (or employer identification number) of such person;

(III) determine whether such person has been convicted of a violation of section 208, 811, or 1632; and

(IV) determine whether payment of benefits to such person has been terminated pursuant to subparagraph (A)(iii), whether the designation of such person as a representative payee has been revoked pursuant to section 807(a), and whether certification of payment of benefits to such person has been revoked pursuant to section 205(j), by reason of misuse of funds paid as benefits under title II, title VIII, or this title.

(iii) Benefits of an individual may not be paid to any other person pursuant to subparagraph (A)(ii) if —

(I) such person has previously been convicted as described in clause (ii)(III);

(II) except as provided in clause (iv), payment of benefits to such person pursuant to subparagraph (A)(ii) has previously been terminated as described in clause (ii)(IV), the designation of such person as a representative payee has been revoked pursuant to section 807(a), or certification of payment of benefits to such person under section 205(j) has previously been revoked as described in section 205(j)(2)(B)(i)(IV); or

(III) except as provided in clause (v), such person is a creditor of such individual who provides such individual with goods or services for consideration.

(iv) The Commissioner of Social Security shall prescribe regulations under which the Commissioner of Social Security may grant an exemption from clause (iii)(II) to any person on a case-by-case basis if such exemption would be in the best interest of the individual or eligible spouse whose benefits under this title would be paid to such person pursuant to subparagraph (A)(ii).

(v) Clause (iii)(III) shall not apply with respect to any person who is a creditor referred to therein if such creditor is —

(I) a relative of such individual if such relative resides in the same household as such individual;

(II) a legal guardian or legal representative of such individual;

(III) a facility that is licensed or certified as a care facility under the law of a State or a political subdivision of a State;

(IV) a person who is an administrator, owner, or employee of a facility referred to in subclause (III) if such individual resides in such facility, and the payment of benefits under this title to such facility or such person is made only after good faith efforts have been made by the local servicing office of the Social Security Administration to locate an alternative representative payee to whom the payment of such benefits would serve the best interests of such individual; or

(V) an individual who is determined by the Commissioner of Social Security, on the basis of written findings and under procedures which the Commissioner of Social Security shall prescribe by regulation, to be acceptable to serve as a representative payee.

(vi) The procedures referred to in clause (v)(V) shall require the individual who will serve as representative payee to establish, to the satisfaction of the Commissioner of Social Security, that —

(I) such individual poses no risk to the beneficiary;

(II) the financial relationship of such individual to the beneficiary poses no substantial conflict of interest; and

(III) no other more suitable representative payee can be found.

(vii) In the case of an individual described in subparagraph (A)(ii)(II), when selecting such individual's representative payee, preference shall be given to —

(I) a community-based nonprofit social service agency licensed or bonded by the State;

(II) a Federal, State, or local government agency whose mission is to carry out income maintenance, social service, or health care-related activities;

(III) a State or local government agency with fiduciary responsibilities; or

(IV) a designee of an agency (other than of a Federal agency) referred to in the preceding subclauses of this

clause, if the Commissioner of Social Security deems it
appropriate,

unless the Commissioner of Social Security determines that selection of
a family member would be appropriate.

(viii) Subject to clause (ix), if the Commissioner of Social
Security makes a determination described in subparagraph
(A)(ii) with respect to any individual's benefit and determines
that direct payment of the benefit to the individual would cause
substantial harm to the individual, the Commissioner of Social
Security may defer (in the case of initial entitlement) or suspend
(in the case of existing entitlement) direct payment of such
benefit to the individual, until such time as the selection of a
representative payee is made pursuant to this subparagraph.

(ix) (I) Except as provided in subclause (II), any deferral
or suspension of direct payment of a benefit pursuant to clause
(viii) shall be for a period of not more than 1 month.

(II) Subclause (I) shall not apply in any case in which
the individual or eligible spouse is, as of the date of the
Commissioner's determination, legally incompetent,
under the age of 15 years, or described in subparagraph
(A)(ii)(II).

(x) Payment pursuant to this subparagraph of any benefits
which are deferred or suspended pending the selection of a
representative payee shall be made to the individual, or to the
representative payee upon such selection, as a single sum or
over such period of time as the Commissioner of Social
Security determines is in the best interests of the individual
entitled to such benefits.

(xi) Any individual who is dissatisfied with a
determination by the Commissioner of Social Security to pay
such individual's benefits to a representative payee under this
title, or with the designation of a particular person to serve as
representative payee, shall be entitled to a hearing by the
Commissioner of Social Security, and to judicial review of the
Commissioner's final decision, to the same extent as is
provided in subsection (c).

(xii) In advance of the first payment of an individual's
benefit to a representative payee under subparagraph (A)(ii), the
Commissioner of Social Security shall provide written notice
of the Commissioner's initial determination to make any such

payment. Such notice shall be provided to such individual, except that, if such individual —

> (I) is under the age of 15,
> (II) is an unemancipated minor under the age of 18,

or

> (III) is legally incompetent,

then such notice shall be provided solely to the legal guardian or legal representative of such individual.

(xiii) Any notice described in clause (xii) shall be clearly written in language that is easily understandable to the reader, shall identify the person to be designated as such individual's representative payee, and shall explain to the reader the right under clause (xi) of such individual or of such individual's legal guardian or legal representative —

> (I) to appeal a determination that a representative payee is necessary for such individual,
> (II) to appeal the designation of a particular person to serve as the representative payee of such individual, and
> (III) to review the evidence upon which such designation is based and submit additional evidence.

(C) (i) In any case where payment is made under this title to a representative payee of an individual or spouse, the Commissioner of Social Security shall establish a system of accountability monitoring whereby such person shall report not less often than annually with respect to the use of such payments. The Commissioner of Social Security shall establish and implement statistically valid procedures for reviewing such reports in order to identify instances in which such persons are not properly using such payments.

(ii) Clause (i) shall not apply in any case where the representative payee is a State institution. In such cases, the Commissioner of Social Security shall establish a system of accountability monitoring for institutions in each State.

(iii) Clause (i) shall not apply in any case where the individual entitled to such payment is a resident of a Federal institution and the representative payee is the institution.

(iv) Notwithstanding clauses (i), (ii), and (iii), the Commissioner of Social Security may require a report at any time from any representative payee, if the Commissioner of

Social Security has reason to believe that the representative payee is misusing such payments.

(D)   (i) A qualified organization may collect from an individual a monthly fee for expenses (including overhead) incurred by such organization in providing services performed as such individual's representative payee pursuant to subparagraph (A)(ii) if the fee does not exceed the lesser of —

(I) 10 percent of the monthly benefit involved, or

(II) $25.00 per month ($50.00 per month in any case in which an individual is described in subparagraph (A)(ii)(II)).

The Commissioner of Social Security shall adjust annually (after 1995) each dollar amount set forth in subclause (II) of this clause under procedures providing for adjustments in the same manner and to the same extent as adjustments are provided for under the procedures used to adjust benefit amounts under section 215(i)(2)(A), except that any amount so adjusted that is not a multiple of $1.00 shall be rounded to the nearest multiple of $1.00.  Any agreement providing for a fee in excess of the amount permitted under this clause shall be void and shall be treated as misuse by the organization of such individual's benefits.

(ii) For purposes of this subparagraph, the term "qualified organization" means any State or local government agency whose mission is to carry out income maintenance, social service, or health care-related activities, any State or local government agency with fiduciary responsibilities, or any community-based nonprofit social service agency, which —

(I) is bonded or licensed in each State in which the agency serves as a representative payee; and

(II) in accordance with any applicable regulations of the Commissioner of Social Security —

(aa)   regularly   provides   services   as   a representative   payee   pursuant   to   subparagraph (A)(ii) or section 205(j)(4) or 807 concurrently to 5 or more individuals; and

(bb) demonstrates to the satisfaction of the Commissioner of Social Security that such agency is not otherwise a creditor of any such individual.

The Commissioner of Social Security shall prescribe regulations under which the Commissioner of Social Security may grant an exception from subclause (II)(bb) for any individual on a case-by-case basis if such exception is in the best interests of such individual.

(iii) Any qualified organization which knowingly charges or collects, directly or indirectly, any fee in excess of the maximum fee prescribed under clause (i) or makes any agreement, directly or indirectly, to charge or collect any fee in excess of such maximum fee, shall be fined in accordance with title 18, United States Code, or imprisoned not more than 6 months, or both.

(iv) In the case of an individual who is no longer eligible for benefits under this title but to whom any amount of past-due benefits under this title has not been paid, for purposes of clause (i), any amount of such past-due benefits payable in any month shall be treated as a monthly benefit referred to in clause (i)(I).

(E) Restitution.  In cases where the negligent failure of the Commissioner of Social Security to investigate or monitor a representative payee results in misuse of benefits by the representative payee, the Commissioner of Social Security shall make payment to the beneficiary or the beneficiary's representative payee of an amount equal to such misused benefits.  The Commissioner of Social Security shall make a good faith effort to obtain restitution from the terminated representative payee.

(F)    (i)    (I) Each representative payee of an eligible individual under the age of 18 who is eligible for the payment of benefits described in subclause (II) shall establish on behalf of such individual an account in a financial institution into which such benefits shall be paid, and shall thereafter maintain such account for use in accordance with clause (ii).

(II) Benefits described in this subclause are past-due monthly benefits under this title (which, for purposes of this subclause, include State supplementary payments made by the Commissioner pursuant to an agreement under section 1616 or section 212(b) of Public Law 93-66) in an amount (after any withholding by the Commissioner for reimbursement to a State for interim assistance under subsection (g)) that exceeds the product of —

(aa) 6, and

(bb) the maximum monthly benefit payable under this title to an eligible individual.

(ii) (I) A representative payee shall use funds in the account established under clause (i) to pay for allowable expenses described in subclause (II).

(II) An allowable expense described in this subclause is an expense for —

(aa) education or job skills training;

(bb) personal needs assistance;

(cc) special equipment;

(dd) housing modification;

(ee) medical treatment;

(ff) therapy or rehabilitation; or

(gg) any other item or service that the Commissioner determines to be appropriate;

provided that such expense benefits such individual and, in the case of an expense described in item (bb), (cc), (dd), (ff), or (gg), is related to the impairment (or combination of impairments) of such individual.

(III) The use of funds from an account established under clause (i) in any manner not authorized by this clause —

(aa) by a representative payee shall be considered a misapplication of benefits for all purposes of this paragraph, and any representative payee who knowingly misapplies benefits from such an account shall be liable to the Commissioner in an amount equal to the total amount of such benefits; and

(bb) by an eligible individual who is his or her own payee shall be considered a misapplication of benefits for all purposes of this paragraph and in any case in which the individual knowingly misapplies benefits from such an account, the Commissioner shall reduce future benefits payable to such individual (or to such individual and his spouse) by an amount equal to the total amount of such benefits so misapplied.

(IV) This clause shall continue to apply to funds in the account after the child has reached age 18, regardless of whether benefits are paid directly to the beneficiary or through a representative payee.

(iii) The representative payee may deposit into the account established under clause (i) any other funds representing past due benefits under this title to the eligible individual, provided that the amount of such past due benefits is equal to or exceeds the maximum monthly benefit payable under this title to an eligible individual (including State supplementary payments made by the Commissioner pursuant to an agreement under section 1616 or section 212(b) of Public Law 93-66).

(iv) The Commissioner of Social Security shall establish a system for accountability monitoring whereby such representative payee shall report, at such time and in such manner as the Commissioner shall require, on activity respecting funds in the account established pursuant to clause (i).

(G) Restitution. In cases where the negligent failure of the Commissioner of Social Security to investigate or monitor a representative payee results in misuse of benefits by the representative payee, the Commissioner of Social Security shall make payment to the beneficiary or the beneficiary's representative payee of an amount equal to such misused benefits. The Commissioner of Social Security shall make a good faith effort to obtain restitution from the terminated representative payee.

(H) The Commissioner of Social Security shall include as a part of the annual report required under section 704 information with respect to the implementation of the preceding provisions of this paragraph, including —

(i) the number of cases in which the representative payee was changed;

(ii) the number of cases discovered where there has been a misuse of funds;

(iii) how any such cases were dealt with by the Commissioner of Social Security;

(iv) the final disposition of such cases (including any criminal penalties imposed); and

(v) such other information as the Commissioner of Social Security determines to be appropriate.

(3) The Commissioner of Social Security may by regulation establish ranges of incomes within which a single amount of benefits under this title shall apply.

(4) The Commissioner of Social Security —

(A) may make to any individual initially applying for benefits under this title who is presumptively eligible for such benefits for the month following the date the application is filed and who is faced with financial emergency a cash advance against such benefits, including any federally-administered State supplementary payments, in an amount not exceeding the monthly amount that would be payable to an eligible individual with no other income for the first month of such presumptive eligibility, which shall be repaid through proportionate reductions in such benefits over a period of not more than 6 months; and

(B) may pay benefits under this title to an individual applying for such benefits on the basis of disability or blindness for a period not exceeding 6 months prior to the determination of such individual's disability or blindness, if such individual is presumptively disabled or blind and is determined to be otherwise eligible for such benefits, and any benefits so paid prior to such determination shall in no event be considered overpayments for purposes of subsection (b) solely because such individual is determined not to be disabled or blind.

(5) Payment of the benefit of any individual who is an aged, blind, or disabled individual solely by reason of blindness (as determined under section 1614(a)(2)) or disability (as determined under section 1614(a)(3)), and who ceases to be blind or to be under such disability, shall continue (so long as such individual is otherwise eligible) through the second month following the month in which such blindness or disability ceases.

(6) Notwithstanding any other provision of this title, payment of the benefit of any individual who is an aged, blind, or disabled individual solely by reason of blindness (as determined under section 1614(a)(2)) or disability (as determined under section 1614(a)(3)) shall not be terminated or suspended because the blindness or other physical or mental impairment, on which the individual's eligibility for such benefit is based, has or may have ceased, if —

(A) such individual is participating in a program consisting of the Ticket to Work and Self-Sufficiency Program under section 1148 or another program of vocational rehabilitation services, employment services, or other support services approved by the Commissioner of Social Security, and

(B) the Commissioner of Social Security determines that the completion of such program, or its continuation for a specified period of time, will increase the likelihood that such individual may (following his participation in such program) be permanently removed from the blindness and disability benefit rolls.

(7)    (A) In any case where —

(i) an individual is a recipient of benefits based on disability or blindness under this title,

(ii) the physical or mental impairment on the basis of which such benefits are payable is found to have ceased, not to have existed, or to no longer be disabling, and as a consequence such individual is determined not to be entitled to such benefits, and

(iii) a timely request for review or for a hearing is pending with respect to the determination that he is not so entitled, such individual may elect (in such manner and form and within such time as the Commissioner of Social Security shall by regulations prescribe) to have the payment of such benefits continued for an additional period beginning with the first month beginning after the date of the enactment of this paragraph [enacted Oct. 9, 1984] for which (under such determination) such benefits are no longer otherwise payable, and ending with the earlier of

(I) the month preceding the month in which a decision is made after such a hearing, or

(II) the month preceding the month in which no such request for review or a hearing is pending.

(B)    (i) If an individual elects to have the payment of his benefits continued for an additional period under subparagraph (A), and the final decision of the Commissioner of Social Security affirms the determination that he is not entitled to such benefits, any benefits paid under this title pursuant to such election (for months in such additional period) shall be considered overpayments for all purposes of this title, except as otherwise provided in clause (ii).

(ii) If the Commissioner of Social Security determines that the individual's appeal of his termination of benefits was made in good faith, all of the benefits paid pursuant to such individual's election under subparagraph (A) shall be subject to waiver consideration under the provisions of subsection (b)(1).

(C) The provisions of subparagraphs (A) and (B) shall apply with respect to determinations (that individuals are not entitled to benefits) which are made on or after the date of the enactment of this paragraph [enacted Oct. 9, 1984], or prior to such date but only on the basis of a timely request for review or for a hearing.

(8) (A) In any case in which an administrative law judge has determined after a hearing as provided in subsection (c) that an individual is entitled to benefits based on disability or blindness under this title and the Commissioner of Social Security has not issued the Commissioner's final decision in such case within 110 days after the date of the administrative law judge's determination, such benefits shall be currently paid for the months during the period beginning with the month in which such 110-day period expires and ending with the month in which such final decision is issued.

(B) For purposes of subparagraph (A), in determining whether the 110-day period referred to in subparagraph (A) has elapsed, any period of time for which the action or inaction of such individual or such individual's representative without good cause results in the delay in the issuance of the Commissioner's final decision shall not be taken into account to the extent that such period of time exceeds 20 calendar days.

(C) Any benefits currently paid under this title pursuant to this paragraph (for the months described in subparagraph (A)) shall not be considered overpayments for any purposes of this title, unless payment of such benefits was fraudulently obtained.

(9) Benefits under this title shall not be denied to any individual solely by reason of the refusal of the individual to accept an amount offered as compensation for a crime of which the individual was a victim.

(10) (A) If an individual is eligible for past-due monthly benefits under this title in an amount that (after any withholding for reimbursement to a State for interim assistance under subsection (g)) equals or exceeds the product of —

(i) 12, and

(ii) the maximum monthly benefit payable under this title to an eligible individual (or, if appropriate, to an eligible individual and eligible spouse),

then the payment of such past-due benefits (after any such reimbursement to a State) shall be made in installments as provided in subparagraph (B).

(B) (i) The payment of past-due benefits subject to this subparagraph shall be made in not to exceed 3 installments that are made at 6-month intervals.

(ii) Except as provided in clause (iii), the amount of each of the first and second installments may not exceed an amount equal to the product of clauses (i) and (ii) of subparagraph (A).

(iii) In the case of an individual who has —

(I) outstanding debt attributable to —

(aa) food,

(bb) clothing,

(cc) shelter, or

(dd) medically necessary services, supplies or equipment, or medicine; or

(II) current expenses or expenses anticipated in the near term attributable to —

(aa) medically necessary services, supplies or equipment, or medicine, or

(bb) the purchase of a home, and

such debt or expenses are not subject to reimbursement by a public assistance program, the Secretary under title XVIII, a State plan approved under title XIX, or any private entity legally liable to provide payment pursuant to an insurance policy, pre-paid plan, or other arrangement, the limitation specified in clause (ii) may be exceeded by an amount equal to the total of such debt and expenses.

(C) This paragraph shall not apply to any individual who, at the time of the Commissioner's determination that such individual is eligible for the payment of past-due monthly benefits under this title —

(i) is afflicted with a medically determinable impairment that is expected to result in death within 12 months; or

(ii) is ineligible for benefits under this title and the Commissioner determines that such individual is likely to remain ineligible for the next 12 months.

(D) For purposes of this paragraph, the term "benefits under this title" includes supplementary payments pursuant to an agreement for Federal administration under section 1616(a), and payments pursuant to an agreement entered into under section 212(b) of Public Law 93-66.

(b) *Overpayments and underpayments; adjustment, recovery, or payment of amounts by Commissioner of Social Security*

(1)   (A) Whenever the Commissioner of Social Security finds that more or less than the correct amount of benefits has been paid with respect to any individual, proper adjustment or recovery shall, subject to the succeeding provisions of this subsection, be made by appropriate adjustments in future payments to such individual or by recovery from such individual or his eligible spouse (or from the estate of either) or by payment to such individual or his eligible spouse, or, if such individual is deceased, by payment —

(i) to any surviving spouse of such individual, whether or not the individual's eligible spouse, if (within the meaning of the first sentence of section 202(i)) such surviving husband or wife was living in the same household with the individual at the time of his death or within the 6 months immediately preceding the month of such death, or

(ii) if such individual was a disabled or blind child who was living with his parent or parents at the time of his death or within the 6 months immediately preceding the month of such death, to such parent or parents.

(B) The Commissioner of Social Security

(i) shall make such provision as the Commissioner finds appropriate in the case of payment of more than the correct amount of benefits with respect to an individual with a view to avoiding penalizing such individual or his eligible spouse who was without fault in connection with the overpayment, if adjustment or recovery on account of such overpayment in such case would defeat the purposes of this title, or be against equity and good conscience, or (because of the small amount involved) impede efficient or effective administration of this title, and

(ii) shall in any event make the adjustment or recovery (in the case of payment of more than the correct amount of benefits), in the case of an individual or eligible spouse receiving monthly benefit payments under this title (including supplementary payments of the type described in section 1616(a) and payments pursuant to an agreement entered into under section 212(a) of Public Law 93-66), in amounts which in the aggregate do not exceed (for any month) the lesser of

(I) the amount of his or their benefit under this title for that month or

(II) an amount equal to 10 percent of his or their income for that month (including such benefit but excluding any other income excluded pursuant to section 1612(b)), and in the case of an individual or eligible spouse to whom a lump sum is payable under this title (including under section 1616(a) of this Act or under an agreement entered into under section 212(a) of Public Law 93-66) shall, as at least one means of recovering such overpayment, make the adjustment or recovery from the lump sum payment in an amount equal to not less than the lesser of the amount of the overpayment or 50 percent of the lump sum payment, unless fraud, willful misrepresentation, or concealment of material information was involved on the part of the individual or spouse in connection with the overpayment, or unless the individual requests that such adjustment or recovery be made at a higher or lower rate and the Commissioner of Social Security determines that adjustment or recovery at such rate is justified and appropriate. The availability (in the case of an individual who has been paid more than the correct amount of benefits) of procedures for adjustment or recovery at a limited rate under clause (ii) of the preceding sentence shall not, in and of itself, prevent or restrict the provision (in such case) of more substantial relief under clause (i) of such sentence.

(2) Notwithstanding any other provision of this section, when any payment of more than the correct amount is made to or on behalf of an individual who has died, and such payment —

(A) is made by direct deposit to a financial institution;

(B) is credited by the financial institution to a joint account of the deceased individual and another person; and

(C) such other person is the surviving spouse of the deceased individual, and was eligible for a payment under this title (including any State supplementation payment paid by the Commissioner of Social Security) as an eligible spouse (or as either member of an eligible couple) for the month in which the deceased individual died, the amount of such payment in excess of the correct amount shall be treated as a payment of more than the correct amount to such other person.

If any payment of more than the correct amount is made to a representative payee on behalf of an individual after the individual's death, the representative payee shall be liable for the repayment of the overpayment, and the Commissioner of Social Security shall establish an overpayment control record under the social security account number of the representative payee.

(3) If any overpayment with respect to an individual (or an individual and his or her spouse) is attributable solely to the ownership or possession by such individual (and spouse if any) of resources having a value which exceeds the applicable dollar figure specified in paragraph (1)(B) or (2)(B) of section 1611(a) by $50 or less, such individual (and spouse if any) shall be deemed for purposes of the second sentence of paragraph (1) to have been without fault in connection with the overpayment, and no adjustment or recovery shall be made under the first sentence of such paragraph, unless the Commissioner of Social Security finds that the failure of such individual (and spouse if any) to report such value correctly and in a timely manner was knowing and willful.

(4)   (A) With respect to any delinquent amount, the Commissioner of Social Security may use the collection practices described in sections 3711(f), 3716, 3717, and 3718 of title 31, United States Code, and in section 5514 of title 5, United States Code, all as in effect immediately after the enactment of the Debt Collection Improvement Act of 1996 [enacted April 26, 1996].

(B) For purposes of subparagraph (A), the term "delinquent amount" means an amount —

(i) in excess of the correct amount of payment under this title;

(ii) paid to a person after such person has attained 18 years of age; and

(iii) determined by the Commissioner of Social Security, under regulations, to be otherwise unrecoverable under this section after such person ceases to be a beneficiary under this title.

(5) For payments for which adjustments are made by reason of a retroactive payment of benefits under title II, see section 1127.

(6) For provisions relating to the recovery of benefits incorrectly paid under this title from benefits payable under title II, see section 1147.

(c) *Hearing to determine eligibility or amount of benefits; time within which to request hearing; time for determinations of Commissioner of Social Security pursuant to hearing; judicial review*

(1)   (A) The Commissioner of Social Security is directed to make findings of fact, and decisions as to the rights of any individual applying for payment under this title.  Any such decision by the Commissioner of Social Security which involves a determination of disability and which is in whole or in part unfavorable to such individual shall contain a statement of the case, in understandable language, setting forth a discussion of the evidence, and stating the Commissioner's determination and the reason or reasons upon which it is based.  The Commissioner of Social Security shall provide reasonable notice and opportunity for a hearing to any individual who is or claims to be an eligible individual or eligible spouse and is in disagreement with any determination under this title with respect to eligibility of such individual for benefits, or the amount of such individual's benefits, if such individual requests a hearing on the matter in disagreement within sixty days after notice of such determination is received, and, if a hearing is held, shall, on the basis of evidence adduced at the hearing affirm, modify, or reverse the Commissioner's findings of fact and such decision.  The Commissioner of Social Security is further authorized, on the Commissioner's own motion, to hold such hearings and to conduct such investigations and other proceedings as the Commissioner may deem necessary or proper for the administration of this title.  In the course of any hearing, investigation, or other proceeding, the Commissioner may administer oaths and affirmations, examine witnesses, and receive evidence.  Evidence may be received at any hearing before the Commissioner of Social Security even though inadmissible under the rules of evidence applicable to court procedure.  The Commissioner of Social Security shall specifically take into account any physical, mental, educational, or linguistic limitation of such individual (including any lack of facility with the English language) in determining, with respect to the eligibility of such individual for benefits under this title, whether such individual acted in good faith or was at fault, and in determining fraud, deception, or intent.

(B)   (i) A failure to timely request review of an initial adverse determination with respect to an application for any payment under this title or an adverse determination on reconsideration of such an initial determination shall not serve as a basis for denial of a subsequent application for any payment under this title if the applicant demonstrates that the applicant, or any other individual referred to in subparagraph A, failed to so request such a review acting in good faith reliance upon incorrect, incomplete, or misleading information, relating to the consequences of reapplying for payments in lieu of seeking review of an adverse determination, provided by any officer or employee of the Social Security Administration or any State agency acting under section 221.

(ii) In any notice of an adverse determination with respect to which a review may be requested under subparagraph A, the Commissioner of Social Security shall describe in clear and specific language the effect on possible eligibility to receive payments under this title of choosing to reapply in lieu of requesting review of the determination.

(2) Determination on the basis of such hearing, except to the extent that the matter in disagreement involves a disability (within the meaning of section 1614(a)(3)), shall be made within ninety days after the individual requests the hearing as provided in paragraph (1).

(3) The final determination of the Commissioner of Social Security after a hearing under paragraph (1) shall be subject to judicial review as provided in section 205(g) to the same extent as the Commissioner's final determinations under section 205.

(d) *Procedures applicable; prohibition on assignment of payments; representation of claimants; maximum fees; penalties for violations*

(1) The provisions of section 207 and subsections (a), (d), and (e) of section 205 shall apply with respect to this part to the same extent as they apply in the case of title II.

(2)   (A) The provisions of section 206(a) (other than paragraph (4) thereof) shall apply to this part to the same extent as they apply in the case of title II, except that paragraph (2) thereof shall be applied —

(i) by substituting, in subparagraphs (A)(ii)(I) and (C)(i), the phrase "(as determined before any applicable reduction under section 1631(g) [subsec. (g) of this section], and reduced by the amount of any reduction in benefits under this title or title II made pursuant to section 1127(a))" for the parenthetical phrase contained therein; and

(ii) by substituting "section 1631(a)(7)(A) [subsec. (a)(7)(A) of this section] or the requirements of due process of law" for "subsection (g) or (h) of section 223."

(B) The Commissioner of Social Security shall notify each claimant in writing, together with the notice to such claimant of an adverse determination, of the options for obtaining attorneys to represent individuals in presenting their cases before the Commissioner of Social Security. Such notification shall also advise the claimant of the availability to qualifying claimants of legal services organizations which provide legal services free of charge.

(e) *Administrative requirements prescribed by Commissioner of Social Security; criteria; reduction of benefits to individual for noncompliance with requirements; payment to homeless*

(1)  (A) The Commissioner of Social Security shall, subject to subparagraph (B) and subsection (j), prescribe such requirements with respect to the filing of applications, the suspension or termination of assistance, the furnishing of other data and material, and the reporting of events and changes in circumstances, as may be necessary for the effective and efficient administration of this title.

(B)  (i) The requirements prescribed by the Commissioner of Social Security pursuant to subparagraph (A) shall require that eligibility for benefits under this title will not be determined solely on the basis of declarations by the applicant concerning eligibility factors or other relevant facts, and that relevant information will be verified from independent or collateral sources and additional information obtained as necessary in order to assure that such benefits are only provided to eligible individuals (or eligible spouses) and that the amounts of such benefits are correct. For this purpose and for purposes of federally administered supplementary payments of the type described in section 1616(a) of this Act (including payments pursuant to an agreement entered into under section 212(a) of Public Law 93-66), the Commissioner of Social Security shall, as may be necessary, request and utilize information available pursuant to section 6103(l)(7) of the Internal Revenue Code of 1954, and any information which may be available from State systems under section 1137 of this Act, and shall comply with the requirements applicable to States (with respect to information available pursuant to section 6103(l)(7)(B) of such Code) under subsections (a)(6) and (c) of such section 1137.

(ii)  (I) The Commissioner of Social Security may require each applicant for, or recipient of, benefits under this title to provide authorization by the applicant or recipient (or by any other person whose income or resources are material to the determination of the eligibility of the applicant or recipient for such benefits) for the Commissioner to obtain (subject to the cost reimbursement requirements of section 1115(a) of the Right to Financial Privacy Act) from any financial institution (within the meaning of section 1101(1) of such Act) any financial record (within the meaning of section 1101(2) of such Act) held by the institution with respect to the applicant or recipient (or any such other person) whenever the Commissioner determines the record is needed in connection with a determination with respect to such eligibility or the amount of such benefits.

(II) Notwithstanding section 1104(a)(1) of the Right to Financial Privacy Act, an authorization provided by an applicant or recipient (or any other person whose income or resources are material to the determination of the eligibility of the applicant or recipient) pursuant to subclause (I) of this clause shall remain effective until the earliest of —

(aa) the rendering of a final adverse decision on the applicant's application for eligibility for benefits under this title;

(bb) the cessation of the recipient's eligibility for benefits under this title; or

(cc) the express revocation by the applicant or recipient (or such other person referred to in subclause (I)) of the authorization, in a written notification to the Commissioner.

(III) (aa) An authorization obtained by the Commissioner of Social Security pursuant to this clause shall be considered to meet the requirements of the Right to Financial Privacy Act for purposes of section 1103(a) of such Act, and need not be furnished to the financial institution, notwithstanding section 1104(a) of such Act .

(bb) The certification requirements of section 1103(b) of the Right to Financial Privacy Act shall not apply to requests by the Commissioner of Social Security pursuant to an authorization provided under this clause.

(cc) A request by the Commissioner pursuant to an authorization provided under this clause is deemed to meet the requirements of section 1104(a)(3) of the Right to Financial Privacy Act and the flush language of section 1102 of such Act.

(IV) The Commissioner shall inform any person who provides authorization pursuant to this clause of the duration and scope of the authorization.

(V) If an applicant for, or recipient of, benefits under this title (or any such other person referred to in subclause (I)) refuses to provide, or revokes, any authorization made by the applicant or recipient for the Commissioner of Social Security to obtain from any financial institution any financial record, the Commissioner may, on that basis, determine that the applicant or recipient is ineligible for benefits under this title.

(C) For purposes of making determinations under section 1611(e), the requirements prescribed by the Commissioner of Social Security pursuant to subparagraph (A) of this paragraph shall require each administrator of a nursing home, extended care facility, or intermediate care facility, within 2 weeks after the admission of any eligible individual or eligible spouse receiving benefits under this title, to transmit to the Commissioner a report of the admission.

(2) In case of the failure by any individual to submit a report of events and changes in circumstances relevant to eligibility for or amount of benefits under this title as required by the Commissioner of Social Security under paragraph (1), or delay by any individual in submitting a report as so required, the Commissioner of Social Security (in addition to taking any other action the Commissioner may consider appropriate under paragraph (1)) shall reduce any benefits which may subsequently become payable to such individual under this title by —

(A) $25 in the case of the first such failure or delay,

(B) $50 in the case of the second such failure or delay, and

(C) $100 in the case of the third or a subsequent such failure or delay,

except where the individual was without fault or good cause for such failure or delay existed.

(3) The Commissioner of Social Security shall provide a method of making payments under this title to an eligible individual who does not

reside in a permanent dwelling or does not have a fixed home or mailing address.

(4) A translation into English by a third party of a statement made in a foreign language by an applicant for or recipient of benefits under this title shall not be regarded as reliable for any purpose under this title unless the third party, under penalty of perjury —

(A) certifies that the translation is accurate; and

(B) discloses the nature and scope of the relationship between the third party and the applicant or recipient, as the case may be.

(5) In any case in which it is determined to the satisfaction of the Commissioner of Social Security that an individual failed as of any date to apply for benefits under this title by reason of misinformation provided to such individual by any officer or employee of the Social Security Administration relating to such individual's eligibility for benefits under this title, such individual shall be deemed to have applied for such benefits on the later of —

(A) the date on which such misinformation was provided to such individual, or

(B) the date on which such individual met all requirements for entitlement to such benefits (other than application therefor).

(6) In any case in which an individual visits a field office of the Social Security Administration and represents during the visit to an officer or employee of the Social Security Administration in the office that the individual's visit is occasioned by —

(A) the receipt of a notice from the Social Security Administration indicating a time limit for response by the individual, or

(B) the theft, loss, or nonreceipt of a benefit payment under this title,

the Commissioner of Social Security shall ensure that the individual is granted a face-to-face interview at the office with an officer or employee of the Social Security Administration before the close of business on the day of the visit.

(7) (A) (i) The Commissioner of Social Security shall immediately redetermine the eligibility of an individual for benefits under this title if there is reason to believe that fraud or similar fault was involved in the application of the individual for such benefits, unless a United States attorney, or equivalent State prosecutor, with jurisdiction over potential or actual related criminal cases, certifies, in writing, that there is a substantial risk that such action by the Commissioner of Social Security with regard

to recipients in a particular investigation would jeopardize the criminal prosecution of a person involved in a suspected fraud.

(ii) When redetermining the eligibility, or making an initial determination of eligibility, of an individual for benefits under this title, the Commissioner of Social Security shall disregard any evidence if there is reason to believe that fraud or similar fault was involved in the providing of such evidence.

(B) For purposes of subparagraph (A), similar fault is involved with respect to a determination if —

(i) an incorrect or incomplete statement that is material to the determination is knowingly made; or

(ii) information that is material to the determination is knowingly concealed.

(C) If, after redetermining the eligibility of an individual for benefits under this title, the Commissioner of Social Security determines that there is insufficient evidence to support such eligibility, the Commissioner of Social Security may terminate such eligibility and may treat benefits paid on the basis of such insufficient evidence as overpayments.

(8) (A) The Commissioner of Social Security shall request the Immigration and Naturalization Service or the Centers for Disease Control to provide the Commissioner of Social Security with whatever medical information, identification information, and employment history either such entity has with respect to any alien who has applied for benefits under title XVI to the extent that the information is relevant to any determination relating to eligibility for such benefits under title XVI.

(B) Subparagraph (A) shall not be construed to prevent the Commissioner of Social Security from adjudicating the case before receiving such information.

(9) Notwithstanding any other provision of law, the Commissioner shall, at least 4 times annually and upon request of the Immigration and Naturalization Service (hereafter in this paragraph referred to as the "Service"), furnish the Service with the name and address of, and other identifying information on, any individual who the Commissioner knows is not lawfully present in the United States, and shall ensure that each agreement entered into under section 1616(a) with a State provides that the State shall furnish such information at such times with respect to any individual who the State knows is not lawfully present in the United States.

**(f)** *Furnishing of information by Federal agencies*

The head of any Federal agency shall provide such information as the Commissioner of Social Security needs for purposes of determining eligibility for or amount of benefits, or verifying other information with respect thereto.

. . . .

**(g)** *Notice requirements*

The Commissioner of Social Security shall take such actions as are necessary to ensure that any notice to one or more individuals issued pursuant to this title by the Commissioner of Social Security or by a State agency —

(1) is written in simple and clear language, and

(2) includes the address and telephone number of the local office of the Social Security Administration which serves the recipient.

In the case of any such notice which is not generated by a local servicing office, the requirements of paragraph (2) shall be treated as satisfied if such notice includes the address of the local office of the Social Security Administration which services the recipient of the notice and a telephone number through which such office can be reached.

## § 1383a. Fraudulent acts; penalties; restitution

(a) Whoever —

(1) knowingly and willfully makes or causes to be made any false statement or representation of a material fact in any application for any benefit under this title,

(2) at any time knowingly and willfully makes or causes to be made any false statement or representation of a material fact for use in determining rights to any such benefit,

(3) having knowledge of the occurrence of any event affecting (A) his initial or continued right to any such benefit, or (B) the initial or continued right to any such benefit of any other individual in whose behalf he has applied for or is receiving such benefit, conceals or fails to disclose such event with an intent fraudulently to secure such benefit either in a greater amount or quantity than is due or when no such benefit is authorized, or

(4) having made application to receive any such benefit for the use and benefit of another and having received it, knowingly and

willfully converts such benefit or any part thereof to a use other than for the use and benefit of such other person,

shall be fined under title 18, United States Code, imprisoned not more than 5 years, or both.

(b)    (1) If a person or entity violates subsection (a) in the person's or entity's role as, or in applying to become, a representative payee under section 1631(a)(2) on behalf of another individual (other than the person's eligible spouse), and the violation includes a willful misuse of funds by the person or entity, the court may also require that full or partial restitution of funds be made to such other individual.

(2) Any person or entity convicted of a violation of subsection (a) of this section or of section 208 may not be certified as a representative payee under section 1631(a)(2).

## § 1383c. Eligibility for medical assistance of aged, blind or disabled individuals under State's medical assistance plan

(a)   *Determination by Commissioner of Social Security pursuant to agreement between Commissioner of Social Security and State; costs*

The Commissioner of Social Security may enter into an agreement with any State which wishes to do so under which the Commissioner will determine eligibility for medical assistance in the case of aged, blind, or disabled individuals under such State's plan approved under title XIX. Any such agreement shall provide for payments by the State, for use by the Commissioner of Social Security in carrying out the agreement, of an amount equal to one-half of the cost of carrying out the agreement, but in computing such cost with respect to individuals eligible for benefits under this title, the Commissioner of Social Security shall include only those costs which are additional to the costs incurred in carrying out this title.

(b)   *Preservation of benefit status for certain disabled widows and widowers*

(1) An eligible disabled widow or widower (described in paragraph (2)) who is entitled to a widow's or widower's insurance benefit based on a disability for any month under section 202(e) or (f) but is not eligible for benefits under this title in that month, and who applies for the protection of this subsection under paragraph (3), shall be deemed for purposes of title XIX to be an individual with respect to whom benefits under this title are paid in that month if he or she —

(A) has been continuously entitled to such widow's or widower's insurance benefits from the first month for which the increase described in paragraph (2)(C) was reflected in such benefits through the month involved, and

(B) would be eligible for benefits under this title in the month involved if the amount of the increase described in paragraph (2)(C) in his or her widow's or widower's insurance benefits, and any subsequent cost-of-living adjustments in such benefits under section 215(i), were disregarded.

(2) For purposes of paragraph (1), the term "eligible disabled widow or widower" means an individual who —

(A) was entitled to a monthly insurance benefit under title II for December 1983,

(B) was entitled to a widow's or widower's insurance benefit based on a disability under section 202(e) or (f) for January 1984 and with respect to whom a benefit under this title was paid in that month, and

(C) because of the increase in the amount of his or her widow's or widower's insurance benefits which resulted from the amendments made by section 134 of the Social Security Amendments of 1983 (Public Law 98-21), (q), and note] (eliminating the additional reduction factor for disabled widows and widowers under age 60), was ineligible for benefits under this title in the first month in which such increase was paid to him or her (and in which a retroactive payment of such increase for prior months was not made).

(3) This subsection shall only apply to an individual who files a written application for protection under this subsection, in such manner and form as the Commissioner of Social Security may prescribe, no later than July 1, 1988.

(4) For purposes of this subsection, the term "benefits under this title" includes payments of the type described in section 1616(a) or of the type described in section 212(a) of Public Law 93-66.

(c) Loss of benefits upon entitlement to child's insurance benefits based on disability. If any individual who has attained the age of 18 and is receiving benefits under this title on the basis of blindness or a disability which began before he or she attained the age of 22 —

(1) becomes entitled, on or after the effective date of this subsection [July 1, 1987], to child's insurance benefits which are payable under section 202(d) on the basis of such disability or to an increase in the amount of the child's insurance benefits which are so payable, and

(2) ceases to be eligible for benefits under this title because of such child's insurance benefits or because of the increase in such child's insurance benefits,

such individual shall be treated for purposes of title XIX as receiving benefits under this title so long as he or she would be eligible for benefits under this title in the absence of such child's insurance benefits or such increase.

(d) *Retention of Medicaid when SSI benefits are lost upon entitlement to early widow's or widower's insurance benefits*

(1) This subsection applies with respect to any person who —

(A) applies for and obtains benefits under subsection (e) or (f) of section 202 (or under any other subsection of section 202 if such person is also eligible for benefits under such subsection (e) or (f)) being then not entitled to hospital insurance benefits under part A of title XVIII, and

(B) is determined to be ineligible (by reason of the receipt of such benefits under section 202) for supplemental security income benefits under this title or for State supplementary payments of the type described in section 1616(a) (or payments of the type described in section 212(a) of Public Law 93-66).

(2) For purposes of title XIX, each person with respect to whom this subsection applies —

(A) shall be deemed to be a recipient of supplemental security income benefits under this title if such person received such a benefit for the month before the month in which such person began to receive a benefit described in paragraph (1)(A), and

(B) shall be deemed to be a recipient of State supplementary payments of the type referred to in section 1616(a) of this Act (or payments of the type described in section 212(a) of Public Law 93-66) if such person received such a payment for the month before the month in which such person began to receive a benefit described in paragraph (1)(A),

for so long as such person (i) would be eligible for such supplemental security income benefits, or such State supplementary payments (or payments of the type described in section 212(a) of Public Law 93-66), in the absence of benefits described in paragraph (1)(A), and (ii) is not entitled to hospital insurance benefits under part A of title XVIII.

# Medicare Act (Excerpts)
## 42 U.S.C. §1395 et seq.

## SUBCHAPTER XVIII — HEALTH INSURANCE FOR AGED AND DISABLED

### § 1395. Prohibition against any Federal interference

Nothing in this subchapter shall be construed to authorize any Federal officer or employee to exercise any supervision or control over the practice of medicine or the manner in which medical services are provided, or over the selection, tenure, or compensation of any officer or employee of any institution, agency, or person providing health services; or to exercise any supervision or control over the administration or operation of any such institution, agency, or person.

### § 1395a. Free choice by patient guaranteed

(a) *Basic freedom of choice*

Any individual entitled to insurance benefits under this subchapter may obtain health services from any institution, agency, or person qualified to participate under this subchapter if such institution, agency, or person undertakes to provide him such services.

(b) *Use of private contracts by medicare beneficiaries*

(1) *In general*

Subject to the provisions of this subsection, nothing in this subchapter shall prohibit a physician or practitioner from entering into a private contract with a medicare beneficiary for any item or service —

(A) for which no claim for payment is to be submitted under this subchapter, and

(B) for which the physician or practitioner receives —

(i) no reimbursement under this subchapter directly or on a capitated basis, and

(ii) receives no amount for such item or service from an organization which receives reimbursement for such item or service under this subchapter directly or on a capitated basis.

(2) *Beneficiary protections*

(A) *In general*

Paragraph (1) shall not apply to any contract unless —

(i) the contract is in writing and is signed by the medicare beneficiary before any item or service is provided pursuant to the contract;

(ii)   the contract contains the items described in subparagraph (B); and

(iii) the contract is not entered into at a time when the medicare beneficiary is facing an emergency or urgent health care situation.

(B) *Items required to be included in contract*

Any contract to provide items and services to which paragraph (1) applies shall clearly indicate to the medicare beneficiary that by signing such contract the beneficiary —

(i)   agrees not to submit a claim (or to request that the physician or practitioner submit a claim) under this subchapter for such items or services even if such items or services are otherwise covered by this subchapter;

(ii)  agrees to be responsible, whether through insurance or otherwise, for payment of such items or services and understands that no reimbursement will be provided under this subchapter for such items or services;

(iii) acknowledges that no limits under this subchapter (including the limits under section 1395w-4(g) of this title) apply to amounts that may be charged for such items or services;

(iv)  acknowledges that Medigap plans under section 1395ss of this title do not, and other supplemental insurance plans may elect not to, make payments for such items and services because payment is not made under this subchapter; and

(v)   acknowledges that the medicare beneficiary has the right to have such items or services provided by other physicians or practitioners for whom payment would be made under this subchapter.

Such contract shall also clearly indicate whether the physician or practitioner is excluded from participation under the medicare program under section 1320a-7 of this title.

(3) *Physician or practitioner requirements*

(A) *In general*

Paragraph (1) shall not apply to any contract entered into by a physician or practitioner unless an affidavit described in subparagraph (B) is in effect during the period any item or service is to be provided pursuant to the contract.

(B) *Affidavit*

An affidavit is described in this subparagraph if —

 (i) the affidavit identifies the physician or practitioner and is in writing and is signed by the physician or practitioner;

 (ii) the affidavit provides that the physician or practitioner will not submit any claim under this subchapter for any item or service provided to any medicare beneficiary (and will not receive any reimbursement or amount described in paragraph (1)(B) for any such item or service) during the 2-year period beginning on the date the affidavit is signed; and

 (iii) a copy of the affidavit is filed with the Secretary no later than 10 days after the first contract to which such affidavit applies is entered into.

(C) *Enforcement*

If a physician or practitioner signing an affidavit under subparagraph (B) knowingly and willfully submits a claim under this subchapter for any item or service provided during the 2-year period described in subparagraph (B)(ii) (or receives any reimbursement or amount described in paragraph (1)(B) for any such item or service) with respect to such affidavit —

 (i) this subsection shall not apply with respect to any items and services provided by the physician or practitioner pursuant to any contract on and after the date of such submission and before the end of such period; and

 (ii) no payment shall be made under this subchapter for any item or service furnished by the physician or practitioner during the period described in clause (i) (and no reimbursement or payment of any amount described in paragraph (1)(B) shall be made for any such item or service).

(4) *Limitation on actual charge and claim submission requirement not applicable*

Section 1395w-4(g) of this title shall not apply with respect to any item or service provided to a medicare beneficiary under a contract described in paragraph (1).

(5) *Definitions*

In this subsection:

(A) *Medicare beneficiary*

The term "medicare beneficiary" means an individual who is entitled to benefits under part A of this subchapter or enrolled under part B of this subchapter.

(B) *Physician*

The term "physician" has the meaning given such term by paragraphs (1), (2), (3), and (4) of section 1395x(r) of this title.

(C) *Practitioner*

The term "practitioner" has the meaning given such term by section 1395u(b)(18)(C) of this title.

## § 1395b. Option to individuals to obtain other health insurance protection

Nothing contained in this subchapter shall be construed to preclude any State from providing, or any individual from purchasing or otherwise securing, protection against the cost of any health services.

## § 1395b-2. Notice of medicare benefits; medicare and medigap information

(a) The Secretary shall prepare (in consultation with groups representing the elderly and with health insurers) and provide for distribution of a notice containing —

(1) a clear, simple explanation of the benefits available under this subchapter and the major categories of health care for which benefits are not available under this subchapter,

(2) the limitations on payment (including deductibles and coinsurance amounts) that are imposed under this subchapter, and

(3) a description of the limited benefits for long-term care services available under this subchapter and generally available under State plans approved under subchapter XIX of this chapter. Such notice shall be mailed annually to individuals entitled to benefits under part A or part B of this subchapter and when an individual applies for benefits under part A of this subchapter or enrolls under part B of this subchapter.

(b) The Secretary shall provide information via a toll-free telephone number on the programs under this subchapter. The Secretary shall provide, through the toll-free telephone number 1-800-MEDICARE, for a means by which individuals seeking information about, or assistance with, such programs who phone such toll-free number are transferred (without charge) to appropriate entities for the provision of such information or assistance. Such toll-free number shall be the toll-free number listed for general information and assistance in the annual notice under subsection (a) of this section instead of the listing of numbers of individual contractors.

(c) The notice provided under subsection (a) of this section shall include —

(1) a statement which indicates that because errors do occur and because medicare fraud, waste, and abuse is a significant problem, beneficiaries should carefully check any explanation of benefits or itemized statement furnished pursuant to section 1395b-7 of this title for accuracy and report any errors or questionable charges by calling the toll-free phone number described in paragraph (4);

(2) a statement of the beneficiary's right to request an itemized statement for medicare items and services (as provided in section 1395b-7(b) of this title);

(3) a description of the program to collect information on medicare fraud and abuse established under section 1395b-5(b) of this title; and

(4) a toll-free telephone number maintained by the Inspector General in the Department of Health and Human Services for the receipt of complaints and information about waste, fraud, and abuse in the provision or billing of services under this subchapter.

## § 1395b-3. Health insurance advisory service for medicare beneficiaries

(a) *In general*

The Secretary of Health and Human Services shall establish a health insurance advisory service program (in this section referred to as the "beneficiary assistance program") to assist medicare-eligible individuals with the receipt of services under the medicare and medicaid programs and other health insurance programs.

(b) *Outreach elements*

The beneficiary assistance program shall provide assistance —

(1) through operation using local Federal offices that provide information on the medicare program,

(2) using community outreach programs, and

(3) using a toll-free telephone information service.

(c) *Assistance provided*

The beneficiary assistance program shall provide for information, counseling, and assistance for medicare-eligible individuals with respect to at least the following:

    (1)  With respect to the medicare program —

        (A)  eligibility,

        (B)  benefits (both covered and not covered),

        (C)  the process of payment for services,

        (D)  rights and process for appeals of determinations,

        (E)  other medicare-related entities (such as peer review organizations, fiscal intermediaries, and carriers), and

        (F)  recent legislative and administrative changes in the medicare program.

    (2)  With respect to the medicaid program —

        (A)  eligibility, benefits, and the application process,

        (B)  linkages between the medicaid and medicare programs, and

        (C)  referral to appropriate State and local agencies involved in the medicaid program.

    (3)  With respect to medicare supplemental policies —

        (A)  the program under section 1395ss of this title and standards required under such program,

        (B)  how to make informed decisions on whether to purchase such policies and on what criteria to use in evaluating different policies,

        (C)  appropriate Federal, State, and private agencies that provide information and assistance in obtaining benefits under such policies, and

        (D)  other issues deemed appropriate by the Secretary.

The beneficiary assistance program also shall provide such other services as the Secretary deems appropriate to increase beneficiary understanding of, and confidence in, the medicare program and to improve the relationship between beneficiaries and the program.

(d) *Educational material*

The Secretary, through the Administrator of the Centers for Medicare & Medicaid Services, shall develop appropriate educational materials and other appropriate techniques to assist employees in carrying out this section.

(e) *Notice to beneficiaries*

The Secretary shall take such steps as are necessary to assure that medicare-eligible beneficiaries and the general public are made aware of the beneficiary assistance program.

(f) *Report*

The Secretary shall include, in an annual report transmitted to the Congress, a report on the beneficiary assistance program and on other health insurance informational and counseling services made available to medicare-eligible individuals. The Secretary shall include in the report recommendations for such changes as may be desirable to improve the relationship between the medicare program and medicare-eligible individuals.

PART A — HOSPITAL INSURANCE BENEFITS FOR AGED AND DISABLED

## § 1395c.  Description of program

The insurance program for which entitlement is established by sections 226 and 226A provides basic protection against the costs of hospital, related post-hospital, home health services, and hospice care in accordance with this part for (1) individuals who are age 65 or over and are eligible for retirement benefits under title II of this Act (or would be eligible for such benefits if certain government employment were covered employment under such title) or under the railroad retirement system, (2) individuals under age 65 who have been entitled for not less than 24 months to benefits under title II of this Act (or would have been so entitled to such benefits if certain government employment were covered employment under such title) or under the railroad retirement system on the basis of a disability, and (3) certain individuals who do not meet the conditions specified in either clause (1) or (2) but who are medically determined to have end stage renal disease.

## § 1395d.  Scope of benefits

(a) *Entitlement to payment for inpatient hospital services, post-hospital extended care services, home health services, and hospice care*

The benefits provided to an individual by the insurance program under this part shall consist of entitlement to have payment made on his behalf or, in the case of payments referred to in section 1814(d)(2) to him (subject to the provisions of this part) for —

(1) inpatient hospital services or inpatient critical access hospital services for up to 150 days during any spell of illness minus 1 day for each day of such services in excess of 90 received during any preceding spell of illness (if such individual was entitled to have payment for such services made under this part unless he specifies in accordance with regulations of the Secretary that he does not desire to have such payment made);

(2) (A) post-hospital extended care services for up to 100 days during any spell of illness, and (B) to the extent provided in subsection (f), extended care services that are not post-hospital extended care services;

(3) for individuals not enrolled in part B, home health services, and for individuals so enrolled, post-institutional home health services furnished during a home health spell of illness for up to 100 visits during such spell of illness; and

(4) in lieu of certain other benefits, hospice care with respect to the individual during up to two periods of 90 days each and an unlimited number of subsequent periods of 60 days each with respect to which the individual makes an election under subsection (d)(1).

(b) *Services not covered*

Payment under this part for services furnished an individual during a spell of illness may not (subject to subsection (c)) be made for —

(1) inpatient hospital services furnished to him during such spell after such services have been furnished to him for 150 days during such spell minus 1 day for each day of inpatient hospital services in excess of 90 received during any preceding spell of illness (if such individual was entitled to have payment for such services made under this part unless he specifies in accordance with regulations of the Secretary that he does not desire to have such payment made);

(2) post-hospital extended care services furnished to him during such spell after such services have been furnished to him for 100 days during such spell; or

(3) inpatient psychiatric hospital services furnished to him after such services have been furnished to him for a total of 190 days during his lifetime.

Payment under this part for post-institutional home health services furnished an individual during a home health spell of illness may not be made for such services beginning after such services have been furnished for a total of 100 visits during such spell.

(c) *Inpatients of psychiatric hospitals*

If an individual is an inpatient of a psychiatric hospital on the first day of the first month for which he is entitled to benefits under this part, the days on which he was an inpatient of such a hospital in the 150-day period immediately before such first day shall be included in determining the number of days limit under subsection (b)(1) insofar as such limit applies to (1) inpatient psychiatric hospital services, or (2) inpatient hospital services for an individual who is an inpatient primarily for the diagnosis or treatment of mental illness (but shall not be included in determining such number of days limit insofar as it applies to other inpatient hospital services or in determining the 190-day limit under subsection (b)(3)).

(d) *Hospice care; election; waiver of rights; revocation; change of election*

(1) Payment under this part may be made for hospice care provided with respect to an individual only during two periods of 90 days each, a subsequent period of 30 days and an unlimited number of subsequent periods of 60 days each, if the individual makes an election under this paragraph to receive hospice care under this part provided by, or under arrangements made by, a particular hospice program instead of certain other benefits under this title.

(2) (A) Except as provided in subparagraphs (B) and (C) and except in such exceptional and unusual circumstances as the Secretary may provide, if an individual makes such an election for a period with respect to a particular hospice program, the individual shall be deemed to have waived all rights to have payment made under this title with respect to —

> (i) hospice care provided by another hospice program (other than under arrangements made by the particular hospice program) during the period, and
> (ii) services furnished during the period that are determined (in accordance with guidelines of the Secretary) to be —
>> (I) related to the treatment of the individual's condition with respect to which a diagnosis of terminal illness has been made or
>> (II) equivalent to (or duplicative of) hospice care;

except that clause (ii) shall not apply to physicians' services furnished by the individual's attending physician (if not an employee of the hospice program) or to services provided by (or under arrangements made by) the hospice program.

(B) After an individual makes such an election with respect to a 90-day period or a subsequent 60-day period, the individual may revoke the election during the period, in which case —

(i) the revocation shall act as a waiver of the right to have payment made under this part for any hospice care benefits for the remaining time in such period and (for purposes of subsection (a)(4) and subparagraph (A)) the individual shall be deemed to have been provided such benefits during such entire period, and

(ii) the individual may at any time after the revocation execute a new election for a subsequent period, if the individual otherwise is entitled to hospice care benefits with respect to such a period.

(C) An individual may, once in each such period, change the hospice program with respect to which the election is made and such change shall not be considered a revocation of an election under subparagraph (B).

(D) For purposes of this title, an individual's election with respect to a hospice program shall no longer be considered to be in effect with respect to that hospice program after the date the individual's revocation or change of election with respect to that election takes effect.

(e) *Services taken into account*

For purposes of subsections (b) and (c), inpatient hospital services, inpatient psychiatric hospital services, and post-hospital extended care services shall be taken into account only if payment is or would be, except for this section or the failure to comply with the request and certification requirements of or under section 1814(a), made with respect to such services under this part.

(f) *Coverage of extended care services without regard to three-day prior hospitalization requirement*

(1) The Secretary shall provide for coverage, under clause (B) of subsection (a)(2), of extended care services which are not post-hospital extended care services at such time and for so long as the Secretary determines, and under such terms and conditions (described in paragraph (2)) as the Secretary finds appropriate, that the inclusion of such services

will not result in any increase in the total of payments made under this title and will not alter the acute care nature of the benefit described in subsection (a)(2).

(2) The Secretary may provide —

(A) for such limitations on the scope and extent of services described in subsection (a)(2)(B) and on the categories of individuals who may be eligible to receive such services, and

(B) notwithstanding sections 1814, 1861(v), and 1866, for such restrictions and alternatives on the amounts and methods of payment for services described in such subsection,

as may be necessary to carry out paragraph (1).

(g) *"Spell of illness" defined*

For definition of "spell of illness", and for definitions of other terms used in this part, see section 1861.

## § 1395e. Deductibles and coinsurance

(a) *Inpatient hospital services or inpatient critical access hospital services; outpatient hospital diagnostic services; blood; post-hospital extended care services*

(1) The amount payable for inpatient hospital services or inpatient critical access hospital services furnished an individual during any spell of illness shall be reduced by a deduction equal to the inpatient hospital deductible or, if less, the charges imposed with respect to such individual for such services, except that, if the customary charges for such services are greater than the charges so imposed, such customary charges shall be considered to be the charges so imposed. Such amount shall be further reduced by a coinsurance amount equal to —

(A) one-fourth of the inpatient hospital deductible for each day (before the 91st day) on which such individual is furnished such services during such spell of illness after such services have been furnished to him for 60 days during such spell; and

(B) one-half of the inpatient hospital deductible for each day (before the day following the last day for which such individual is entitled under section 1812(a)(1) to have payment made on his behalf for inpatient hospital services or inpatient critical access hospital services during such spell of illness) on which such individual is furnished such services during such spell of illness after such services have been furnished to him for 90 days during such spell;

except that the reduction under this sentence for any day shall not exceed the charges imposed for that day with respect to such individual for such services (and for this purpose, if the customary charges for such services are greater than the charges so imposed, such customary charges shall be considered to be the charges so imposed).

(2) (A) The amount payable to any provider of services under this part for services furnished an individual shall be further reduced by a deduction equal to the expenses incurred for the first three pints of whole blood (or equivalent quantities of packed red blood cells, as defined under regulations) furnished to the individual during each calendar year, except that such deductible for such blood shall in accordance with regulations be appropriately reduced to the extent that there has been a replacement of such blood (or equivalent quantities of packed red blood cells, as so defined); and for such purposes blood (or equivalent quantities of packed red blood cells, as so defined) furnished such individual shall be deemed replaced when the institution or other person furnishing such blood (or such equivalent quantities of packed red blood cells, as so defined) is given one pint of blood for each pint of blood (or equivalent quantities of packed red blood cells, as so defined) furnished such individual with respect to which a deduction is made under this sentence.

(B) The deductible under subparagraph (A) for blood or blood cells furnished an individual in a year shall be reduced to the extent that a deductible has been imposed under section 1833(b) to blood or blood cells furnished the individual in the year.

(3) The amount payable for post-hospital extended care services furnished an individual during any spell of illness shall be reduced by a coinsurance amount equal to one-eighth of the inpatient hospital deductible for each day (before the 101st day) on which he is furnished such services after such services have been furnished to him for 20 days during such spell.

(4) (A) The amount payable for hospice care shall be reduced —

(i) in the case of drugs and biologicals provided on an outpatient basis by (or under arrangements made by) the hospice program, by a coinsurance amount equal to an amount (not to exceed $5 per prescription) determined in accordance with a drug copayment schedule (established by the hospice program) which is related to, and approximates 5 percent of, the cost of the drug or biological to the program, and

(ii) in the case of respite care provided by (or under arrangements made by) the hospice program, by a coinsurance amount equal to 5 percent of the amount estimated by the hospice program (in accordance with regulations of the Secretary) to be equal to the amount of payment under section 1814(i) to that program for respite care;

except that the total of the coinsurance required under clause (ii) for an individual may not exceed for a hospice coinsurance period the inpatient hospital deductible applicable for the year in which the period began. For purposes of this subparagraph, the term "hospice coinsurance period" means, for an individual, a period of consecutive days beginning with the first day for which an election under section 1812(d) is in effect for the individual and ending with the close of the first period of 14 consecutive days on each of which such an election is not in effect for the individual.

(B) During the period of an election by an individual under section 1812(d)(1), no copayments or deductibles other than those under subparagraph (A) shall apply with respect to services furnished to such individual which constitute hospice care, regardless of the setting in which such services are furnished.

(b) *Inpatient hospital deductible; application*

(1) The inpatient hospital deductible for 1987 shall be $520. The inpatient hospital deductible for any succeeding year shall be an amount equal to the inpatient hospital deductible for the preceding calendar year, changed by the Secretary's best estimate of the payment-weighted average of the applicable percentage increases (as defined in section 1886(b)(3)(B)) which are applied under section 1886(d)(3)(A) for discharges in the fiscal year that begins on October 1 of such preceding calendar year, and adjusted to reflect changes in real case mix (determined on the basis of the most recent case mix data available). Any amount determined under the preceding sentence which is not a multiple of $4 shall be rounded to the nearest multiple of $4 (or, if it is midway between two multiples of $4, to the next higher multiple of $4).

(2) The Secretary shall promulgate the inpatient hospital deductible and all coinsurance amounts under this section between September 1 and September 15 of the year preceding the year to which they will apply.

(3) The inpatient hospital deductible for a year shall apply to —

(A) the deduction under the first sentence of subsection (a)(1) for the year in which the first day of inpatient hospital services or inpatient critical access hospital services occurs in a spell of illness, and

(B) to the coinsurance amounts under subsection (a) for inpatient hospital services, inpatient critical access hospital services and post-hospital extended care services furnished in that year.

## § 1395h.  Use of public or private agencies or organizations to facilitate payment to providers of services

(a) *Authorization for agreement by Secretary for implementation; scope of agreement*

If any group or association of providers of services wishes to have payments under this part to such providers made through a national, State, or other public or private agency or organization and nominates such agency or organization for this purpose, the Secretary is authorized to enter into an agreement with such agency or organization providing for the determination by such agency or organization (subject to the provisions of section 1878 and to such review by the Secretary as may be provided for by the agreement) of the amount of the payments required pursuant to this part to be made to such providers (and to providers assigned to such agency or organization under subsection (e)), and for the making of such payments by such agency or organization to such providers (and to providers assigned to such agency or organization under subsection (e)). Such agreement may also include provision for the agency or organization to do all or any part of the following: (1) to provide consultative services to institutions or agencies to enable them to establish and maintain fiscal records necessary for purposes of this part and otherwise to qualify as hospitals, extended care facilities, or home health agencies, and (2) with respect to the providers of services which are to receive payments through it (A) to serve as a center for, and communicate to providers, any information or instructions furnished to it by the Secretary, and serve as a channel of communication from providers to the Secretary; (B) to make such audits of the records of providers as may be necessary to insure that proper payments are made under this part; and (C) to perform such other functions as are necessary to carry out this subsection. As used in this title and part B of title XI, the term "fiscal intermediary" means an agency or organization with a contract under this section.

. . . .

## § 1395i-3. Requirements for, and assuring quality of care in, skilled nursing facilities

(a) *"Skilled nursing facility" defined*

In this title, the term "skilled nursing facility" means an institution (or a distinct part of an institution) which —

(1) is primarily engaged in providing to residents —

(A) skilled nursing care and related services for residents who require medical or nursing care, or

(B) rehabilitation services for the rehabilitation of injured, disabled, or sick persons,

and is not primarily for the care and treatment of mental diseases;

(2) has in effect a transfer agreement (meeting the requirements of section 1861(l)) with one or more hospitals having agreements in effect under section 1866; and

(3) meets the requirements for a skilled nursing facility described in subsections (b), (c), and (d) of this section.

(b) *Requirements relating to provision of services*

(1) *Quality of life*

(A) *In general*

A skilled nursing facility must care for its residents in such a manner and in such an environment as will promote maintenance or enhancement of the quality of life of each resident.

(B) *Quality assessment and assurance*

A skilled nursing facility must maintain a quality assessment and assurance committee, consisting of the director of nursing services, a physician designated by the facility, and at least 3 other members of the facility's staff, which (i) meets at least quarterly to identify issues with respect to which quality assessment and assurance activities are necessary and (ii) develops and implements appropriate plans of action to correct identified quality deficiencies. A State or the Secretary may not require disclosure of the records of such committee except insofar as such disclosure is related to the compliance of such committee with the requirements of this subparagraph.

(2) *Scope of services and activities under plan of care*

A skilled nursing facility must provide services to attain or maintain the highest practicable physical, mental, and psychosocial well-being of each resident, in accordance with a written plan of care which —

(A) describes the medical, nursing, and psychosocial needs of the resident and how such needs will be met;

(B) is initially prepared, with the participation to the extent practicable of the resident or the resident's family or legal representative, by a team which includes the resident's attending physician and a registered professional nurse with responsibility for the resident; and

(C) is periodically reviewed and revised by such team after each assessment under paragraph (3).

(3) *Residents' assessment*

(A) *Requirement*

A skilled nursing facility must conduct a comprehensive, accurate, standardized, reproducible assessment of each resident's functional capacity, which assessment —

(i) describes the resident's capability to perform daily life functions and significant impairments in functional capacity;

(ii) is based on a uniform minimum data set specified by the Secretary under subsection (f)(6)(A);

(iii) uses an instrument which is specified by the State under subsection (e)(5); and

(iv) includes the identification of medical problems.

(B) *Certification*

(i) *In general*

Each such assessment must be conducted or coordinated (with the appropriate participation of health professionals) by a registered professional nurse who signs and certifies the completion of the assessment. Each individual who completes a portion of such an assessment shall sign and certify as to the accuracy of that portion of the assessment.

(ii) *Penalty for falsification*

(I) An individual who willfully and knowingly certifies under clause (i) a material and false statement in a resident assessment is subject to a civil money penalty of not more than $1,000 with respect to each assessment.

(II) An individual who willfully and knowingly causes another individual to certify under clause (i) a material and false statement in a resident assessment is subject to a civil money penalty of not more than $5,000 with respect to each assessment.

(III) The provisions of section 1128A (other than subsections (a) and (b)) shall apply to a civil money penalty under this clause in the same manner as such provisions apply to a penalty or proceeding under section 1128A(a).

(iii) *Use of independent assessors*

If a State determines, under a survey under subsection (g) or otherwise, that there has been a knowing and willful certification of false assessments under this paragraph, the State may require (for a period specified by the State) that resident assessments under this paragraph be conducted and certified by individuals who are independent of the facility and who are approved by the State.

(C) *Frequency*

(i) *In general*

Subject to timeframes prescribed by the Secretary under section 1888(e)(6), such an assessment must be conducted —

(I) promptly upon (but no later than 14 days after the date of) admission for each individual admitted on or after October 1, 1990, and by not later than January 1, 1991, for each resident of the facility on that date;

(II) promptly after a significant change in the resident's physical or mental condition; and

(III) in no case less often than once every 12 months.

(ii) *Resident review*

The skilled nursing facility must examine each resident no less frequently than once every 3 months and, as appropriate, revise the resident's assessment to assure the continuing accuracy of the assessment.

(D) *Use*

The results of such an assessment shall be used in developing, reviewing, and revising the resident's plan of care under paragraph (2).

(E) *Coordination*

Such assessments shall be coordinated with any State-required preadmission screening program to the maximum extent practicable in order to avoid duplicative testing and effort.

(4) *Provision of services and activities*

(A) *In general*

To the extent needed to fulfill all plans of care described in paragraph (2), a skilled nursing facility must provide, directly or under arrangements (or, with respect to dental services, under agreements) with others for the provision of —

(i) nursing services and specialized rehabilitative services to attain or maintain the highest practicable physical, mental, and psychosocial well-being of each resident;

(ii) medically-related social services to attain or maintain the highest practicable physical, mental, and psychosocial well-being of each resident;

(iii) pharmaceutical services (including procedures that assure the accurate acquiring, receiving, dispensing, and administering of all drugs and biologicals) to meet the needs of each resident;

(iv) dietary services that assure that the meals meet the daily nutritional and special dietary needs of each resident;

(v) an on-going program, directed by a qualified professional, of activities designed to meet the interests and the physical, mental, and psychosocial well-being of each resident;

(vi) routine and emergency dental services to meet the needs of each resident; and

(vii) treatment and services required by mentally ill and mentally retarded residents not otherwise provided or arranged for (or required to be provided or arranged for) by the State.

The services provided or arranged by the facility must meet professional standards of quality. Nothing in clause (vi) shall be construed as requiring a facility to provide or arrange for dental services described in that clause without additional charge.

(B) *Qualified persons providing services*

Services described in clauses (i), (ii), (iii), (iv), and (vi) of subparagraph (A) must be provided by qualified persons in accordance with each resident's written plan of care.

(C) *Required nursing care*

(i) *In general*

Except as provided in clause (ii), a skilled nursing facility must provide 24-hour licensed nursing service which is sufficient to meet nursing needs of its residents and must use the services of a registered professional nurse [at least] at least 8 consecutive hours a day, 7 days a week.

(ii) *Exception*

To the extent that clause (i) may be deemed to require that a skilled nursing facility engage the services of a registered professional nurse for more than 40 hours a week, the Secretary is authorized to waive such requirement if the Secretary finds that —

(I) the facility is located in a rural area and the supply of skilled nursing facility services in such area is not sufficient to meet the needs of individuals residing therein,

(II) the facility has one full-time registered professional nurse who is regularly on duty at such facility 40 hours a week,

(III) the facility either has only patients whose physicians have indicated (through physicians' orders or admission notes) that each such patient does not require the services of a registered nurse or a physician for a 48-hour period, or has made arrangements for a registered professional nurse or a physician to spend such time at such facility as may be indicated as necessary by the physician to provide necessary skilled nursing services on days when the regular full-time registered professional nurse is not on duty,

(IV) the Secretary provides notice of the waiver to the State long-term care ombudsman (established under section 307(a)(12) of the Older Americans Act of 1965) and the protection and advocacy system in the State for the mentally ill and the mentally retarded, and

(V) the facility that is granted such a waiver notifies residents of the facility (or, where appropriate, the guardians or legal representatives of such residents) and members of their immediate families of the waiver.

A waiver under this subparagraph shall be subject to annual renewal.

(5) *Required training of nurse aides*

(A) *In general*

(i) Except as provided in clause (ii), a skilled nursing facility must not use on a full-time basis any individual as a nurse aide in the facility on or after October 1, 1990 for more than 4 months unless the individual —

(I) has completed a training and competency evaluation program, or a competency evaluation program, approved by the State under subsection (e)(1)(A), and

(II) is competent to provide nursing or nursing-related services.

(ii) A skilled nursing facility must not use on a temporary, per diem, leased, or on any basis other than as a permanent employee any individual as a nurse aide in the facility on or after January 1, 1991, unless the individual meets the requirements described in clause (i).

(B) *Offering competency evaluation programs for current employees*

A skilled nursing facility must provide, for individuals used as a nurse aide [nurse aides] by the facility as of January 1, 1990, for a competency evaluation program approved by the State under subsection (e)(1) and such preparation as may be necessary for the individual to complete such a program by October 1, 1990.

(C) *Competency*

The skilled nursing facility must not permit an individual, other than in a training and competency evaluation program approved by the State, to serve as a nurse aide or provide services of a type for which the individual has not demonstrated competency and must not use such an individual as a nurse aide unless the facility has inquired of any State registry established under subsection (e)(2)(A) that the facility believes will include information concerning the individual.

(D) *Re-training required*

For purposes of subparagraph (A), if, since an individual's most recent completion of a training and competency evaluation program, there has been a continuous period of 24 consecutive months during none of which the individual performed nursing or nursing-related services for monetary compensation, such individual shall complete a new training and competency evaluation program or a new competency evaluation program.

(E) *Regular in-service education*

The skilled nursing facility must provide such regular performance review and regular in-service education as assures that individuals used as nurse aides are competent to perform services as nurse aides, including training for individuals providing nursing and nursing-related services to residents with cognitive impairments.

(F) *Nurse aide defined*

In this paragraph, the term "nurse aide" means any individual providing nursing or nursing-related services to residents in a skilled nursing facility, but does not include an individual —

(i) who is a licensed health professional (as defined in subparagraph (G)) or a registered dietician, or

(ii) who volunteers to provide such services without monetary compensation.

(G) *Licensed health professional defined*

In this paragraph, the term "licensed health professional" means a physician, physician assistant, nurse practitioner, physical, speech, or occupational therapist, physical or occupational therapy assistant, registered professional nurse, licensed practical nurse, licensed or certified social worker, registered respiratory therapist, or certified respiratory therapy technician.

(6) *Physician supervision and clinical records*

A skilled nursing facility must —

(A) require that the medical care of every resident be provided under the supervision of a physician;

(B) provide for having a physician available to furnish necessary medical care in case of emergency; and

(C) maintain clinical records on all residents, which records include the plans of care (described in paragraph (2)) and the residents' assessments (described in paragraph (3)).

(7) *Required social services*

In the case of a skilled nursing facility with more than 120 beds, the facility must have at least one social worker (with at least a bachelor's degree in social work or similar professional qualifications) employed full-time to provide or assure the provision of social services.

(8) *Information on nurse staffing*

(A) *In general*

A skilled nursing facility shall post daily for each shift the current number of licensed and unlicensed nursing staff directly responsible for resident care in the facility. The information shall be displayed in a uniform manner (as specified by the Secretary) and in a clearly visible place.

(B) *Publication of data*

A skilled nursing facility shall, upon request, make available to the public the nursing staff data described in subparagraph (A).

(c) *Requirements relating to residents' rights*

(1) *General rights*

(A) *Specified rights*

A skilled nursing facility must protect and promote the rights of each resident, including each of the following rights:

(i) *Free choice*

The right to choose a personal attending physician, to be fully informed in advance about care and treatment, to be fully informed in advance of any changes in care or treatment that may affect the resident's well-being, and (except with respect to a resident adjudged incompetent) to participate in planning care and treatment or changes in care and treatment.

(ii) *Free from restraints*

The right to be free from physical or mental abuse, corporal punishment, involuntary seclusion, and any physical or chemical restraints imposed for purposes of discipline or convenience and not required to treat the resident's medical symptoms. Restraints may only be imposed —

(I) to ensure the physical safety of the resident or other residents, and

(II) only upon the written order of a physician that specifies the duration and circumstances under which the restraints are to be used (except in emergency circumstances specified by the Secretary until such an order could reasonably be obtained).

(iii)  *Privacy*

The right to privacy with regard to accommodations, medical treatment, written and telephonic communications, visits, and meetings of family and of resident groups.

(iv)  *Confidentiality*

The right to confidentiality of personal and clinical records and to access to current clinical records of the resident upon request by the resident or the resident's legal representative, within 24 hours (excluding hours occurring during a weekend or holiday) after making such a request.

(v)  *Accommodation of needs*

The right —

(I) to reside and receive services with reasonable accommodation of individual needs and preferences, except where the health or safety of the individual or other residents would be endangered, and

(II) to receive notice before the room or roommate of the resident in the facility is changed.

(vi)  *Grievances*

The right to voice grievances with respect to treatment or care that is (or fails to be) furnished, without discrimination or reprisal for voicing the grievances and the right to prompt efforts by the facility to resolve grievances the resident may have, including those with respect to the behavior of other residents.

(vii)  *Participation in resident and family groups*

The right of the resident to organize and participate in resident groups in the facility and the right of the resident's family to meet in the facility with the families of other residents in the facility.

(viii)  *Participation in other activities*

The right of the resident to participate in social, religious, and community activities that do not interfere with the rights of other residents in the facility.

(ix)  *Examination of survey results*

The right to examine, upon reasonable request, the results of the most recent survey of the facility conducted by the Secretary or a State with respect to the facility and any plan of correction in effect with respect to the facility.

(x) *Refusal of certain transfers*

The right to refuse a transfer to another room within the facility, if a purpose of the transfer is to relocate the resident from a portion of the facility that is a skilled nursing facility (for purposes of this title) to a portion of the facility that is not such a skilled nursing facility.

(xi) *Other rights*

Any other right established by the Secretary.

Clause (iii) shall not be construed as requiring the provision of a private room. A resident's exercise of a right to refuse transfer under clause (x) shall not affect the resident's eligibility or entitlement to benefits under this title or to medical assistance under title XIX of this Act.

(B) *Notice of rights and services*

A skilled nursing facility must —

(i) inform each resident, orally and in writing at the time of admission to the facility, of the resident's legal rights during the stay at the facility;

(ii) make available to each resident, upon reasonable request, a written statement of such rights (which statement is updated upon changes in such rights) including the notice (if any) of the State developed under section 1919(e)(6); and

(iii) inform each other resident, in writing before or at the time of admission and periodically during the resident's stay, of services available in the facility and of related charges for such services, including any charges for services not covered under this title or by the facility's basic per diem charge.

The written description of legal rights under this subparagraph shall include a description of the protection of personal funds under paragraph (6) and a statement that a resident may file a complaint with a State survey and certification agency respecting resident abuse and neglect and misappropriation of resident property in the facility.

(C) *Rights of incompetent residents*

In the case of a resident adjudged incompetent under the laws of a State, the rights of the resident under this title shall devolve upon, and, to the extent judged necessary by a court of competent jurisdiction, be exercised by, the person appointed under State law to act on the resident's behalf.

(D) *Use of psychopharmacologic drugs*

Psychopharmacologic drugs may be administered only on the orders of a physician and only as part of a plan (included in the written plan of care described in paragraph (2)) designed to eliminate or modify the symptoms for which the drugs are prescribed and only if, at least annually, an independent, external consultant reviews the appropriateness of the drug plan of each resident receiving such drugs. In determining whether such a consultant is qualified to conduct reviews under the preceding sentence, the Secretary shall take into account the needs of nursing facilities under this title to have access to the services of such a consultant on a timely basis.

(E) *Information respecting advance directives*

A skilled nursing facility must comply with the requirement of section 1866(f) (relating to maintaining written policies and procedures respecting advance directives).

(2) *Transfer and discharge rights*

(A) *In general*

A skilled nursing facility must permit each resident to remain in the facility and must not transfer or discharge the resident from the facility unless —

(i) the transfer or discharge is necessary to meet the resident's welfare and the resident's welfare cannot be met in the facility;

(ii) the transfer or discharge is appropriate because the resident's health has improved sufficiently so the resident no longer needs the services provided by the facility;

(iii) the safety of individuals in the facility is endangered;

(iv) the health of individuals in the facility would otherwise be endangered;

(v) the resident has failed, after reasonable and appropriate notice, to pay (or to have paid under this title or title XIX on the resident's behalf) for a stay at the facility; or

(vi) the facility ceases to operate.

In each of the cases described in clauses (i) through (v), the basis for the transfer or discharge must be documented in the resident's clinical record. In the cases described in clauses (i) and (ii), the documentation must be made by the resident's physician, and in the cases described in clauses (iii) and (iv) the documentation must be made by a physician.

(B) *Pre-transfer and pre-discharge notice*

(i) *In general*

Before effecting a transfer or discharge of a resident, a skilled nursing facility must —

(I) notify the resident (and, if known, a family member of the resident or legal representative) of the transfer or discharge and the reasons therefor,

(II) record the reasons in the resident's clinical record (including any documentation required under subparagraph (A)), and

(III) include in the notice the items described in clause (iii).

(ii) *Timing of notice*

The notice under clause (i)(I) must be made at least 30 days in advance of the resident's transfer or discharge except—

(I) in a case described in clause (iii) or (iv) of subparagraph (A);

(II) in a case described in clause (ii) of subparagraph (A), where the resident's health improves sufficiently to allow a more immediate transfer or discharge;

(III) in a case described in clause (i) of subparagraph (A), where a more immediate transfer or discharge is necessitated by the resident's urgent medical needs; or

(IV) in a case where a resident has not resided in the facility for 30 days.

In the case of such exceptions, notice must be given as many days before the date of the transfer or discharge as is practicable.

(iii) *Items included in notice*

Each notice under clause (i) must include —

(I) for transfers or discharges effected on or after October 1, 1990, notice of the resident's right to appeal the transfer or discharge under the State process established under subsection (e)(3); and

(II) the name, mailing address, and telephone number of the State long-term care ombudsman ( established under title III or VII of the Older Americans Act of 1965 in accordance with section 712 of the Act).

(C) *Orientation*

A skilled nursing facility must provide sufficient preparation and orientation to residents to ensure safe and orderly transfer or discharge from the facility.

(3) *Access and visitation rights*

A skilled nursing facility must —

(A) permit immediate access to any resident by any representative of the Secretary, by any representative of the State, by an ombudsman described in paragraph (2)(B)(iii)(II), or by the resident's individual physician;

(B) permit immediate access to a resident, subject to the resident's right to deny or withdraw consent at any time, by immediate family or other relatives of the resident;

(C) permit immediate access to a resident, subject to reasonable restrictions and the resident's right to deny or withdraw consent at any time, by others who are visiting with the consent of the resident;

(D) permit reasonable access to a resident by any entity or individual that provides health, social, legal, or other services to the resident, subject to the resident's right to deny or withdraw consent at any time; and

(E) permit representatives of the State ombudsman (described in paragraph (2)(B)(iii)(II)), with the permission of the resident (or the resident's legal representative) and consistent with State law, to examine a resident's clinical records.

(4) *Equal access to quality care*

A skilled nursing facility must establish and maintain identical policies and practices regarding transfer, discharge, and covered services under this title for all individuals regardless of source of payment.

(5) *Admissions policy*

(A) *Admissions*

With respect to admissions practices, a skilled nursing facility must —

(i) (I) not require individuals applying to reside or residing in the facility to waive their rights to benefits under this title or under a State plan under title XIX, (II) not require oral or written assurance that such individuals are not eligible for, or will not apply for, benefits under this title or such a State plan, and (III) prominently display in the facility and provide to such individuals written information about how to apply for and use such benefits and how to receive refunds for previous payments covered by such benefits; and

(ii) not require a third party guarantee of payment to the facility as a condition of admission (or expedited admission) to, or continued stay in, the facility.

(B) *Construction*

(i) *No preemption of stricter standards*

Subparagraph (A) shall not be construed as preventing States or political subdivisions therein from prohibiting, under State or local law, the discrimination against individuals who are entitled to medical assistance under this title with respect to admissions practices of skilled nursing facilities.

(ii) *Contracts with legal representatives*

Subparagraph (A)(ii) shall not be construed as preventing a facility from requiring an individual, who has legal access to a resident's income or resources available to pay for care in the facility, to sign a contract (without incurring personal financial liability) to provide payment from the resident's income or resources for such care.

(6) *Protection of resident funds*

(A) *In general*

The skilled nursing facility —

(i) may not require residents to deposit their personal funds with the facility, and

(ii) hold, safeguard, and account for such personal funds under a system established and maintained by the facility in accordance with this paragraph.

(B) *Management of personal funds*

Upon written authorization of a resident under subparagraph (A)(ii), the facility must manage and account for the personal funds of the resident deposited with the facility as follows:

(i) *Deposit*

The facility must deposit any amount of personal funds in excess of $100 with respect to a resident in an interest bearing account (or accounts) that is separate from any of the facility's operating accounts and credits [credit] all interest earned on such separate account to such account. With respect to any other personal funds, the facility must maintain such funds in a non-interest bearing account or petty cash fund.

(ii) *Accounting and records*

The facility must assure a full and complete separate accounting of each such resident's personal funds, maintain a written record of all financial transactions involving the personal funds of a resident deposited with the facility, and afford the resident (or a legal representative of the resident) reasonable access to such record.

(iii) *Conveyance upon death*

Upon the death of a resident with such an account, the facility must convey promptly the resident's personal funds (and a final accounting of such funds) to the individual administering the resident's estate.

(C) *Assurance of financial security*

The facility must purchase a surety bond, or otherwise provide assurance satisfactory to the Secretary, to assure the security of all personal funds of residents deposited with the facility.

(D) *Limitation on charges to personal funds*

The facility may not impose a charge against the personal funds of a resident for any item or service for which payment is made under this title or title XIX

(d) *Requirements relating to administration and other matters*

(1) *Administration*

(A) *In general*

A skilled nursing facility must be administered in a manner that enables it to use its resources effectively and efficiently to attain or maintain the highest practicable physical mental, and psychosocial well-being of each resident (consistent with requirements established under subsection (f)(5)).

(B) *Required notices*

If a change occurs in —

(i) the persons with an ownership or control interest (as defined in section 1124(a)(3)) in the facility,

(ii) the persons who are officers, directors, agents, or managing employees (as defined in section 1126(b)) of the facility,

(iii) the corporation, association, or other company responsible for the management of the facility, or

> (iv) the individual who is the administrator or director of nursing of the facility,

the skilled nursing facility must provide notice to the State agency responsible for the licensing of the facility, at the time of the change, of the change and of the identity of each new person, company, or individual described in the respective clause.

> (C) *Skilled nursing facility administrator*
> The administrator of a skilled nursing facility must meet standards established by the Secretary under subsection (f)(4).

(2) *Licensing and Life Safety Code*

> (A) *Licensing*
> A skilled nursing facility must be licensed under applicable State and local law.

> (B) *Life Safety Code*
> A skilled nursing facility must meet such provisions of such edition (as specified by the Secretary in regulation) of the Life Safety Code of the National Fire Protection Association as are applicable to nursing homes; except that —

>> (i) the Secretary may waive, for such periods as he deems appropriate, specific provisions of such Code which if rigidly applied would result in unreasonable hardship upon a facility, but only if such waiver would not adversely affect the health and safety of residents or personnel, and

>> (ii) the provisions of such Code shall not apply in any State if the Secretary finds that in such State there is in effect a fire and safety code, imposed by State law, which adequately protects residents of and personnel in skilled nursing facilities.

(3) *Sanitary and infection control and physical environment*

A skilled nursing facility must —

> (A) establish and maintain an infection control program designed to provide a safe, sanitary, and comfortable environment in which residents reside and to help prevent the development and transmission of disease and infection, and

> (B) be designed, constructed, equipped, and maintained in a manner to protect the health and safety of residents, personnel, and the general public.

(4) *Miscellaneous*

(A) Compliance with Federal, State, and local laws and professional standards. A skilled nursing facility must operate and provide services in compliance with all applicable Federal, State, and local laws and regulations (including the requirements of section 1124) and with accepted professional standards and principles which apply to professionals providing services in such a facility.

(B) *Other*

A skilled nursing facility must meet such other requirements relating to the health, safety, and well-being of residents or relating to the physical facilities thereof as the Secretary may find necessary.

(e) *State requirements relating to skilled nursing facility requirements*

The requirements, referred to in section 1864(d), with respect to a State are as follows:

(1) *Specification and review of nurse aide training and competency evaluation programs and of nurse aide competency evaluation programs*

The State must —

(A) by not later than January 1, 1989, specify those training and competency evaluation programs, and those competency evaluation programs, that the State approves for purposes of subsection (b)(5) and that meet the requirements established under subsection (f)(2), and

(B) by not later than January 1, 1990, provide for the review and reapproval of such programs, at a frequency and using a methodology consistent with the requirements established under subsection (f)(2)(A)(iii).

The failure of the Secretary to establish requirements under subsection (f)(2) shall not relieve any State of its responsibility under this paragraph.

(2) *Nurse aide registry*

(A) *In general*

By not later than January 1, 1989, the State shall establish and maintain a registry of all individuals who have satisfactorily completed a nurse aide training and competency evaluation program, or a nurse aide competency evaluation program, approved under paragraph (1) in the State, or any individual described in subsection (f)(2)(B)(ii) or in subparagraph (B), (C), or (D) of section 6901(b)(4) of the Omnibus Budget Reconciliation Act of 1989 [note to this section].

(B) *Information in registry*

The registry under subparagraph (A) shall provide (in accordance with regulations of the Secretary) for the inclusion of specific documented findings by a State under subsection (g)(1)(C) of resident neglect or abuse or misappropriation of resident property involving an individual listed in the registry, as well as any brief statement of the individual disputing the findings, but shall not include any allegations of resident abuse or neglect or misappropriation of resident property that are not specifically documented by the State under such subsection. The State shall make available to the public information in the registry. In the case of inquiries to the registry concerning an individual listed in the registry, any information disclosed concerning such a finding shall also include disclosure of any such statement in the registry relating to the finding or a clear and accurate summary of such a statement.

(C) *Prohibition against charges*

A State may not impose any charges on a nurse aide relating to the registry established and maintained under subparagraph (A).

(3) *State appeals process for transfers and discharges*

The State, for transfers and discharges from skilled nursing facilities effected on or after October 1, 1989, must provide for a fair mechanism for hearing appeals on transfers of residents of such facilities. Such mechanism must meet the guidelines established by the Secretary under subsection (f)(3); but the failure of the Secretary to establish such guidelines shall not relieve any State of its responsibility to provide for such a fair mechanism.

(4) *Skilled nursing facility administrator standards*

By not later than January 1, 1990, the State must have implemented and enforced the skilled nursing facility administrator standards developed under subsection (f)(4) respecting the qualification of administrators of skilled nursing facilities.

(5) *Specification of resident assessment instrument*

Effective July 1, 1990, the State shall specify the instrument to be used by nursing facilities in the State in complying with the requirement of subsection (b)(3)(A)(iii). Such instrument shall be —

(A) one of the instruments designated under subsection (f)(6)(B), or

(B) an instrument which the Secretary has approved as being consistent with the minimum data set of core elements, common definitions, and utilization guidelines specified by the Secretary under subsection (f)(6)(A).

(f) *Responsibilities of Secretary relating to skilled nursing facility requirements*

(1) *General responsibility*

It is the duty and responsibility of the Secretary to assure that requirements which govern the provision of care in skilled nursing facilities under this title, and the enforcement of such requirements, are adequate to protect the health, safety, welfare, and rights of residents and to promote the effective and efficient use of public moneys.

(2) *Requirements for nurse aide training and competency evaluation programs and for nurse aide competency evaluation of programs*

(A) *In general*

For purposes of subsections (b)(5) and (e)(1)(A), the Secretary shall establish, by not later than September 1, 1988 —

(i) requirements for the approval of nurse aide training and competency evaluation programs, including requirements relating to (I) the areas to be covered in such a program (including at least basic nursing skills, personal care skills, recognition of mental health and social service needs, care of cognitively impaired residents, basic restorative services, and residents' rights) and content of the curriculum, (II) minimum hours of initial and ongoing training and retraining (including not less than 75 hours in the case of initial training), (III) qualifications of instructors, and (IV) procedures for determination of competency;

(ii) requirements for the approval of nurse aide competency evaluation programs, including requirement relating to the areas to be covered in such a program, including at least basic nursing skills, personal care skills, recognition of mental health and social service needs, care of cognitively impaired residents, basic restorative services, residents' rights, and procedures for determination of competency;

(iii) requirements respecting the minimum frequency and methodology to be used by a State in reviewing such programs compliance with the requirements for such programs; and

(iv) requirements, under both such programs, that —

(I) provide procedures for determining competency that permit a nurse aide, at the nurse aide's option, to establish competency through procedures or methods other than the passing of a written examination and to have the competency evaluation conducted at the nursing facility at which the aide is (or will be) employed (unless the facility is described in subparagraph (B)(iii)(I)),

(II) prohibit the imposition on a nurse aide who is employed by (or who has received an offer of employment from) a facility on the date on which the aide begins either such program of any charges (including any charges for textbooks and other required course materials and any charges for the competency evaluation) for either such program, and

(III) in the case of a nurse aide not described in subclause (II) who is employed by (or who has received an offer of employment from) a facility not later than 12 months after completing either such program, the State shall provide for the reimbursement of costs incurred in completing such program on a prorata [pro rata] basis during the period in which the nurse aide is so employed.

(B) *Approval of certain programs*

Such requirements —

(i) may permit approval of programs offered by or in facilities (subject to clause (iii)), as well as outside facilities (including employee organizations), and of programs in effect on the date of the enactment of this section [enacted Dec. 22, 1987];

(ii) shall permit a State to find that an individual who has completed (before July 1, 1989) a nurse aide training and competency evaluation program shall be deemed to have completed such a program approved under subsection (b)(5) if the State determines that, at the time the program was offered, the program met the requirements for approval under such paragraph; and

(iii) subject to subparagraph (C), shall prohibit approval of such a program —

(I) offered by or in a skilled nursing facility which, within the previous 2 years —

(a) has operated under a waiver under subsection (b)(4)(C)(ii)(II);

(b) has been subject to an extended (or partial extended) survey under subsection (g)(2)(B)(i) or section 1919(g)(2)(B)(i), unless the survey shows that the facility is in compliance with the requirements of subsections (b), (c), and (d) of this section; or

(c) has been assessed a civil money penalty described in subsection (h)(2)(B)(ii) or section 1919(h)(2)(A)(ii) of not less than $5,000, or has been subject to a remedy described in clause (i) or (iii) of subsection (h)(2)(B), subsection (h)(4), section 1919(h)(1)(B)(i), or in clause (i), (iii), or (iv) of section 1919(h)(2)(A), or

(II) offered by or in a skilled nursing facility unless the State makes the determination, upon an individual's completion of the program, that the individual is competent to provide nursing and nursing-related services in skilled nursing facilities.

A State may not delegate (through subcontract or otherwise) its responsibility under clause (iii)(II) to the skilled nursing facility.

(C) *Waiver authorized*

Clause (iii)(I) of subparagraph (B) shall not apply to a program offered in (but not by) a nursing facility (or skilled nursing facility for purposes of title XVIII) in a State if the State —

(i) determines that there is no other such program offered within a reasonable distance of the facility,

(ii) assures, through an oversight effort, that an adequate environment exists for operating the program in the facility, and

(iii) provides notice of such determination and assurances to the State long-term care ombudsman.

(3) *Federal guidelines for State appeals process for transfers and discharges*

For purposes of subsections (c)(2)(B)(iii)(I) and (e)(3), by not later than October 1, 1988, the Secretary shall establish guidelines for minimum standards which State appeals processes under subsection (e)(3) must meet to provide a fair mechanism for hearing appeals on transfers and discharges of residents from skilled nursing facilities.

(4) *Secretarial standards for qualification of administrators*

For purposes of subsections (d)(1)(C) and (e)(4), the Secretary shall develop, by not later than March 1, 1989, standards to be applied in assuring the qualifications of administrators of skilled nursing facilities.

(5) *Criteria for administration*

The Secretary shall establish criteria for assessing a skilled nursing facility's compliance with the requirement of subsection (d)(1) with respect to —

(A) its governing body and management,

(B) agreements with hospitals regarding transfers of residents to and from the hospitals and to and from other skilled nursing facilities,

(C) disaster preparedness,

(D) direction of medical care by a physician,

(E) laboratory and radiological services,

(F) clinical records, and

(G) resident and advocate participation.

(6) *Specification of resident assessment data set and instruments*

The Secretary shall —

(A) not later than January 1, 1989, specify a minimum data set of core elements and common definitions for use by nursing facilities in conducting the assessments required under subsection (b)(3), and establish guidelines for utilization of the data set; and

(B) by not later than April 1, 1990, designate one or more instruments which are consistent with the specification made under subparagraph (A) and which a State may specify under subsection (e)(5)(A) for use by nursing facilities in complying with the requirements of subsection (b)(3)(A)(iii).

(7) *List of items and services furnished in skilled nursing facilities not chargeable to the personal funds of a resident*

(A) *Regulations required*

Pursuant to the requirement of section 21(b) of the Medicare-Medicaid Anti-Fraud and Abuse Amendments of 1977, the Secretary shall issue regulations, on or before the first day of the seventh month to begin after the date of enactment of this section [enacted Dec. 22, 1987], that define those costs which may be charged to the personal funds of residents in skilled nursing facilities who are individuals receiving benefits under this part and those costs which are to be included in the reasonable cost (or other payment amount) under this title for extended care services.

(B) *Rule if failure to publish regulations*

If the Secretary does not issue the regulations under subparagraph (A) on or before the date required in such subparagraph, in the case of a resident of a skilled nursing facility who is eligible to receive benefits under this part, the costs which may not be charged to the personal funds of such resident (and for which payment is considered to be made under this title) shall include, at a minimum, the costs for routine personal hygiene items and services furnished by the facility.

(g) *Survey and certification process*

(1) *State and Federal responsibility*

(A) *In general*

Pursuant to an agreement under section 1864, each State shall be responsible for certifying, in accordance with surveys conducted under paragraph (2), the compliance of skilled nursing facilities (other than facilities of the State) with the requirements of subsections (b), (c), and (d). The Secretary shall be responsible for certifying, in accordance with surveys conducted under paragraph (2), the compliance of State skilled nursing facilities with the requirements of such subsections.

(B) *Educational program*

Each State shall conduct periodic educational programs for the staff and residents (and their representatives) of skilled nursing facilities in order to present current regulations, procedures, and policies under this section.

(C) *Investigation of allegations of resident neglect and abuse and misappropriation of resident property*

The State shall provide, through the agency responsible for surveys and certification of nursing facilities under this subsection, for a process for the receipt and timely review and investigation of allegations of neglect and abuse and misappropriation of resident property by a nurse aide of a resident in a nursing facility of by another individual used by the facility in providing services to such a resident. The State shall, after providing the individual involved with a written notice of the allegations (including a statement of the availability of a hearing for the individual to rebut the allegations) and the opportunity for a hearing on the record, make a written finding as to the accuracy of the allegations. If the State finds that a nurse aide has neglected or abused a resident or misappropriated resident property in a facility, the State shall notify the nurse aide and the registry of such finding. If the State finds that any other individual used by the facility has neglected or abused a resident or misappropriated resident property in a facility, the State shall notify the appropriate licensure authority. A State shall not make a finding that an individual has neglected a resident if the individual demonstrates that such neglect was caused by factors beyond the control of the individual.

(D) *Removal of name from nurse aide registry*

(i) *In general*

In the case of a finding of neglect under subparagraph (C), the State shall establish a procedure to permit a nurse aide to petition the State to have his or her name removed from the registry upon a determination by the State that —

(I) the employment and personal history of the nurse aide does not reflect a pattern of abusive behavior or neglect; and

(II) the neglect involved in the original finding was a singular occurrence.

(ii) *Timing of determination*

In no case shall a determination on a petition submitted under clause (i) be made prior to the expiration of the 1-year period beginning on the date on which the name of the petitioner was added to the registry under subparagraph (C).

(E) *Construction*

The failure of the Secretary to issue regulations to carry out this subsection shall not relieve a State of its responsibility under this subsection.

(2) *Surveys*

    (A) *Standard survey*

        (i) *In general*

Each skilled nursing facility shall be subject to a standard survey, to be conducted without any prior notice to the facility. Any individual who notifies (or causes to be notified) a skilled nursing facility of the time or date on which such a survey is scheduled to be conducted is subject to a civil money penalty of not to exceed $2,000. The provisions of section 1128A (other than subsections (a) and (b)) shall apply to a civil money penalty under the previous sentence in the same manner as such provisions apply to a penalty or proceeding under section 1128A(a). The Secretary shall review each State's procedures for the scheduling and conduct of standard surveys to assure that the State has taken all reasonable steps to avoid giving notice of such a survey through the scheduling procedures and the conduct of the surveys themselves.

        (ii) *Contents*

Each standard survey shall include, for a case-mix stratified sample of residents —

            (I) a survey of the quality of care furnished, as measured by indicators of medical, nursing, and rehabilitative care, dietary and nutrition services, activities and social participation, and sanitation, infection control, and the physical environment,

            (II) written plans of care provided under subsection (b)(2) and an audit of the residents' assessments under subsection (b)(3) to determine the accuracy of such assessments and the adequacy of such plans of care, and

            (III) a review of compliance with residents' rights under subsection (c).

        (iii) *Frequency*

            (I) *In general*

Each skilled nursing facility shall be subject to a standard survey not later than 15 months after the date of the previous standard survey conducted under this subparagraph. The Statewide average interval between standard surveys of skilled nursing facilities under this subsection shall not exceed 12 months.

(II) *Special surveys*

If not otherwise conducted under subclause (I), a standard survey (or an abbreviated standard survey) may be conducted within 2 months of any change of ownership, administration, management of a skilled nursing facility, or the director of nursing in order to determine whether the change has resulted in any decline in the quality of care furnished in the facility.

(B) *Extended surveys*

(i) *In general*

Each skilled nursing facility which is found, under a standard survey, to have provided substandard quality of care shall be subject to an extended survey. Any other facility may, at the Secretary's or State's discretion, be subject to such an extended survey (or a partial extended survey).

(ii) *Timing*

The extended survey shall be conducted immediately after the standard survey (or, if not practicable, not later than 2 weeks after the date of completion of the standard survey).

(iii) *Contents*

In such an extended survey, the survey team shall review and identify the policies and procedures which produced such substandard quality of care and shall determine whether the facility has complied with all the requirements described in subsections (b), (c), and (d). Such review shall include an expansion of the size of the sample of residents' assessments reviewed and a review of the staffing, of in-service training, and, if appropriate, of contracts with consultants.

(iv) *Construction*

Nothing in this paragraph shall be construed as requiring an extended or partial extended survey as a prerequisite to imposing a sanction against a facility under subsection (h) on the basis of findings in a standard survey.

(C) *Survey protocol*

Standard and extended surveys shall be conducted —

(i) based upon a protocol which the Secretary has developed, tested, and validated by not later than January 1, 1990, and

(ii) by individuals, of a survey team, who meet such minimum qualifications as the Secretary establishes by not later than such date.

The failure of the Secretary to develop, test, or validate such protocols or to establish such minimum qualifications shall not relieve any State of its responsibility (or the Secretary of the Secretary's responsibility) to conduct surveys under this subsection.

(D) *Consistency of surveys*

Each State and the Secretary shall implement programs to measure and reduce inconsistency in the application of survey results among surveyors.

(E) *Survey teams*

(i) *In general*

Surveys under this subsection shall be conducted by a multidisciplinary team of professionals (including a registered professional nurse).

(ii) *Prohibition of conflicts of interest*

A State may not use as a member of a survey team under this subsection an individual who is serving (or has served within the previous 2 years) as a member of the staff of, or as a consultant to, the facility surveyed respecting compliance with the requirements of subsections (b), (c), and (d), or who has a personal or familial financial interest in the facility being surveyed.

(iii) *Training*

The Secretary shall provide for the comprehensive training of State and Federal surveyors in the conduct of standard and extended surveys under this subsection, including the auditing of resident assessments and plans of care. No individual shall serve as a member of a survey team unless the individual has successfully completed a training and testing program in survey and certification techniques that has been approved by the Secretary.

(3) *Validation surveys*

(A) *In general*

The Secretary shall conduct onsite surveys of a representative sample of skilled nursing facilities in each State, within 2 months of the date of surveys conducted under paragraph (2) by the State, in a sufficient number to allow inferences about the adequacies of each State's surveys conducted under paragraph (2). In conducting such surveys, the Secretary shall use the same survey protocols as the State is required to use under paragraph (2). If the State has determined that an individual skilled nursing facility meets the requirements of subsections (b), (c), and (d), but the Secretary determines that the facility does not meet such requirements, the Secretary's determination as to the facility's noncompliance with such requirements is binding and supersedes that of the State survey.

(B) *Scope*

With respect to each State, the Secretary shall conduct surveys under subparagraph (A) each year with respect to at least 5 percent of the number of skilled nursing facilities surveyed by the State in the year, but in no case less than 5 skilled nursing facilities in the State.

(C) *Remedies for substandard performance.*

If the Secretary finds, on the basis of such surveys, that a State has failed to perform surveys as required under paragraph (2) or that a State's survey and certification performance otherwise is not adequate, the Secretary shall provide for an appropriate remedy, which may include the training of survey teams in the State.

(D) *Special surveys of compliance*

Where the Secretary has reason to question the compliance of a skilled nursing facility with any of the requirements of subsections (b), (c), and (d), the Secretary may conduct a survey of the facility and, on the basis of that survey, make independent and binding determinations concerning the extent to which the skilled nursing facility meets such requirements.

(4) *Investigation of complaints and monitoring compliance*

Each State shall maintain procedures and adequate staff to —

(A) investigate complaints of violations of requirements by skilled nursing facilities, and

(B) monitor, on-site, on a regular, as needed basis, a skilled nursing facility's compliance with the requirements of subsections (b), (c), and (d), if —

(i) the facility has been found not to be in compliance with such requirements and is in the process of correcting deficiencies to achieve such compliance;

(ii) the facility was previously found not to be in compliance with such requirements, has corrected deficiencies to achieve such compliance, and verification of continued compliance is indicated; or

(iii) the State has reason to question the compliance of the facility with such requirements.

A State may maintain and utilize a specialized team (including an attorney, an auditor, and appropriate health care professionals) for the purpose of identifying, surveying, gathering and preserving evidence, and carrying out appropriate enforcement actions against substandard skilled nursing facilities.

(5) *Disclosure of results of inspections and activities*

(A) *Public information*

Each State, and the Secretary, shall make available to the public —

(i) information respecting all surveys and certifications made respecting skilled nursing facilities, including statements of deficiencies, within 14 calendar days after such information is made available to those facilities, and approved plans of correction,

(ii) copies of cost reports of such facilities filed under this title or title XIX,

(iii) copies of statements of ownership under section 1124, and

(iv) information disclosed under section 1126.

(B) *Notice to ombudsman*

Each State shall notify the State long-term care ombudsman (established under title III or VII of the Older Americans Act of 1965 in accordance with section 712 of the Act) of the State's findings of noncompliance with any of the requirements of subsections (b), (c), and (d), or of any adverse action taken against a skilled nursing facility under paragraph (1), (2), or (4) of subsection (h), with respect to a skilled nursing facility in the State.

(C) *Notice to physicians and skilled nursing facility administrator licensing board*

If a State finds that a skilled nursing facility has provided substandard quality of care, the State shall notify —

(i) the attending physician of each resident with respect to which such finding is made, and

(ii) the State board responsible for the licensing of the skilled nursing facility administrator at the facility.

(D) *Access to fraud control units*

Each State shall provide its State medicaid fraud and abuse control unit (established under section 1903(q)) with access to all information of the State agency responsible for surveys and certifications under this subsection.

(h) *Enforcement process*

(1) *In general*

If a State finds, on the basis of a standard, extended, or partial extended survey under subsection (g)(2) or otherwise, that a skilled nursing facility no longer meets a requirement of subsection (b), (c), or (d), and further finds that the facility's deficiencies —

(A) immediately jeopardize the health or safety of its residents, the State shall recommend to the Secretary that the Secretary take such action as described in paragraph (2)(A)(i); or

(B) do not immediately jeopardize the health or safety of its residents, the State may recommend to the Secretary that the Secretary take such action as described in paragraph (2)(A)(ii).

If a State finds that a skilled nursing facility meets the requirements of subsections (b), (c), and (d), but, as of a previous period, did not meet such requirements, the State may recommend a civil money penalty under paragraph (2)(B)(ii) for the days in which it finds that the facility was not in compliance with such requirements.

(2) *Secretarial authority*

(A) *In general*

With respect to any skilled nursing facility in a State, if the Secretary finds, or pursuant to a recommendation of the State under paragraph (1) finds, that a skilled nursing facility no longer meets a requirement of subsection (b), (c), (d), or (e), and further finds that the facility's deficiencies —

(i) immediately jeopardize the health or safety of its residents, the Secretary shall take immediate action to remove the jeopardy and correct the deficiencies through the remedy specified in subparagraph (B)(iii), or terminate the facility's participation under this title and may provide, in addition, for one or more of the other remedies described in subparagraph (B); or

(ii) do not immediately jeopardize the health or safety of its residents, the Secretary may impose any of the remedies described in subparagraph (B).

Nothing in this subparagraph shall be construed as restricting the remedies available to the Secretary to remedy a skilled nursing facility's deficiencies. If the Secretary finds, or pursuant to the recommendation of the State under paragraph (1) finds, that a skilled nursing facility meets such requirements but, as of a previous period, did not meet such requirements, the Secretary may provide for a civil money penalty under subparagraph (B)(ii) for the days on which he finds that the facility was not in compliance with such requirements.

(B) *Specified remedies*

The Secretary may take the following actions with respect to a finding that a facility has not met an applicable requirement:

(i) *Denial of payment*

The Secretary may deny any further payments under this title with respect to all individuals entitled to benefits under this title in the facility or with respect to such individuals admitted to the facility after the effective date of the finding.

(ii) *Authority with respect to civil money penalties*

The Secretary may impose a civil money penalty in an amount not to exceed $10,000 for each day of noncompliance. The provisions of section 1128A (other than subsections (a) and (b)) shall apply to a civil money penalty under the previous sentence in the same manner as such provisions apply to a penalty or proceeding under section 1128A(a).

(iii) *Appointment of temporary management*

In consultation with the State, the Secretary may appoint temporary management to oversee the operation of the facility and to assure the health and safety of the facility's residents, where there is a need for temporary management while —

(I) there is an orderly closure of the facility, or

(II) improvements are made in order to bring the facility into compliance with all the requirements of subsections (b), (c), and (d).

The temporary management under this clause shall not be terminated under subclause (II) until the Secretary has determined that the facility has the management capability to ensure continued compliance with all the requirements of subsections (b), (c), and (d). The Secretary shall specify criteria, as to when and how each of such remedies is to be applied, the amounts of any fines, and the severity of each of these remedies, to be used in the imposition of such remedies. Such criteria shall be designed so as to minimize the time between the identification of violations and final imposition of the remedies and shall provide for the imposition of incrementally more severe fines for repeated or uncorrected deficiencies. In addition, the Secretary may provide for other specified remedies, such as directed plans of correction.

(C) *Continuation of payments pending remediation*

The Secretary may continue payments, over a period of not longer than 6 months after the effective date of the findings, under this title with respect to a skilled nursing facility not in compliance with a requirement of subsection (b), (c), or (d), if —

(i) the State survey agency finds that it is more appropriate to take alternative action to assure compliance of the facility with the requirements than to terminate the certification of the facility,

(ii) the State has submitted a plan and timetable for corrective action to the Secretary for approval and the Secretary approves the plan of corrective action, and

(iii) the facility agrees to repay to the Federal Government payments received under this subparagraph if the corrective action is not taken in accordance with the approved plan and timetable.

The Secretary shall establish guidelines for approval of corrective actions requested by States under this subparagraph.

(D) *Assuring prompt compliance*

If a skilled nursing facility has not complied with any of the requirements of subsections (b), (c), and (d), within 3 months after the date the facility is found to be out of compliance with such requirements, the Secretary shall impose the remedy described in subparagraph (B)(i) for all individuals who are admitted to the facility after such date.

(E) *Repeated noncompliance*

In the case of a skilled nursing facility which, on 3 consecutive standard surveys conducted under subsection (g)(2), has been found to have provided substandard quality of care, the Secretary shall (regardless of what other remedies are provided) —

(i) impose the remedy described in subparagraph (B)(i), and

(ii) monitor the facility under subsection (g)(4)(B),

until the facility has demonstrated, to the satisfaction of the Secretary, that it is in compliance with the requirements of subsections (b), (c), and (d), and that it will remain in compliance with such requirements.

(3) *Effective period of denial of payment*

A finding to deny payment under this subsection shall terminate when the Secretary finds that the facility is in substantial compliance with all the requirements of subsections (b), (c), and (d).

(4)   *Immediate termination of participation for facility where Secretary finds noncompliance and immediate jeopardy*

If the Secretary finds that a skilled nursing facility has not met a requirement of subsection (b), (c), or (d), and finds that the failure immediately jeopardizes the health or safety of its residents, the Secretary shall take immediate action to remove the jeopardy and correct the deficiencies through the remedy specified in paragraph (2)(B)(iii), or the Secretary shall terminate the facility's participation under this title. If the facility's participation under this title is terminated, the State shall provide for the safe and orderly transfer of the residents eligible under this title consistent with the requirements of subsection (c)(2).

(5) *Construction*

The remedies provided under this subsection are in addition to those otherwise available under State or Federal law and shall not be construed as limiting such other remedies, including any remedy available to an individual at common law. The remedies described in clauses (i), and (iii) of paragraph (2)(B) may be imposed during the pendency of any hearing. (6) Sharing of information. Notwithstanding any other provision of law, all information concerning skilled nursing facilities required by this section to be filed with the Secretary or a State agency shall be made available by such facilities to Federal or State employees for purposes consistent with the effective administration of programs established under this title and title XIX, including investigations by State medicaid fraud control units.

## (i) *Construction*

Where requirements or obligations under this section are identical to those provided under section 1919 of this Act, the fulfillment of those requirements or obligations under section 1919 shall be considered to be the fulfillment of the corresponding requirements or obligations under this section.

## § 1395j. Establishment of supplementary medical insurance program for the aged and disabled

There is hereby established a voluntary insurance program to provide medical insurance benefits in accordance with the provisions of this part for aged and disabled individuals who elect to enroll under such program, to be financed from premium payments by enrollees together with contributions from funds appropriated by the Federal Government.

## § 1395k. Scope of benefits; definitions

### (a) *Scope of benefits*

The benefits provided to an individual by the insurance program established by this part shall consist of —

(1) entitlement to have payment made to him or on his behalf (subject to the provisions of this part) for medical and other health services, except those described in subparagraphs (B) and (D) of paragraph (2) and subparagraphs (E) and (F) of section 1842(b)(6); and

(2) entitlement to have payment made on his behalf (subject to the provisions of this part) for —

(A) home health services (other than items described in subparagraph (G) or subparagraph (I));

(B) medical and other health services (other than items described in subparagraph (G) or subparagraph (I)) furnished by a provider of services or by others under arrangement with them made by a provider of services, excluding —

(i) physician services except where furnished by —

(I) a resident or intern of a hospital, or

(II) a physician to a patient in a hospital which has a teaching program approved as specified in paragraph (6) of section 1861(b) (including services in conjunction with the teaching programs of such hospital whether or not such patient is an inpatient of such hospital) where the conditions specified in paragraph (7) of such section are met,

(ii) services for which payment may be made pursuant to section 1835(b)(2),

(iii) services described by section 1861(s)(2)(K)(i), certified nurse-midwife services, qualified psychologist services, and services of a certified registered nurse anesthetist; [,]

(iv) services of a nurse practitioner or clinical nurse specialist but only if no facility or other provider charges or is paid any amounts with respect to the furnishing of such services; [and]

(C) outpatient physical therapy services (other than services to which the second sentence of section 1861(p) applies) and outpatient occupational therapy services (other than services to which such sentence applies through the operation of section 1861(g));

(D) (i) rural health clinic services and (ii) Federally qualified health center services;

(E) comprehensive outpatient rehabilitation facility services;

(F) facility services furnished in connection with surgical procedures specified by the Secretary —

(i) pursuant to section 1833(i)(1)(A) and performed in an ambulatory surgical center (which meets health, safety, and other standards specified by the Secretary in regulations) if the center has an agreement in effect with the Secretary by which the center agrees to accept the standard overhead amount determined under section 1833(i)(2)(A) as full payment for such services (including intraocular lens in cases described in section 1833(i)(2)(A)(iii)) and to accept an assignment described in section 1842(b)(3)(B)(ii) with respect to payment for all such services (including intraocular lens in cases described in section 1833(i)(2)(A)(iii), or

(ii) pursuant to section 1833(i)(1)(B) and performed by a physician, described in paragraph (1), (2), or (3) of section 1861(r), in his office, if the Secretary has determined that —

(I) a quality control and peer review organization (having a contract with the Secretary under part B of title XI of this Act) is willing, able, and has agreed to carry out a review (on a sample or other reasonable basis) of the physician's performing such procedures in the physician's office,

(II) the particular physician involved has agreed to make available to such organization such records as the Secretary determines to be necessary to carry out the review, and

(III) the physician is authorized to perform the procedure in a hospital located in the area in which the office is located,

and if the physician agrees to accept the standard overhead amount determined under section 1833(i)(2)(B) as full payment for such services and to accept payment on an assignment-related basis with respect to payment for all services (including all pre- and post-operative services) described in paragraphs (1) and (2)(A) of section 1861(s) and furnished in connection with such surgical procedure to individuals enrolled under this part;

(G) covered items (described in section 1834(a)(13)) furnished by a provider of services or by others under arrangements with them made by a provider of services;

(H) outpatient critical access hospital services (as defined in section 1861(mm)(3));

(I) prosthetic devices and orthotics and prosthetics (described in section 1834(h)(4)) furnished by a provider of services or by others under arrangements with them made by a provider of services; and

(J) partial hospitalization services provided by a community mental health center (as described in section 1861(ff)(2)(B)).

(b) *Definitions*

For definitions of "spell of illness", "medical and other health services", and other terms used in this part, see section 1861.

PART B — SUPPLEMENTARY MEDICAL INSURANCE
BENEFITS FOR AGED AND DISABLED

## § 1395l. Payment of benefits

(a) *Amounts*

Except as provided in section 1876, and subject to the succeeding provisions of this section, there shall be paid from the Federal Supplementary Medical Insurance Trust Fund, in the case of each individual who is covered under the insurance program established by this part and incurs expenses for services with respect to which benefits are payable under this part, amounts equal to —

(1) in the case of services described in section 1832(a)(1) — 80 percent of the reasonable charges for the services; except that (A) an organization which provides medical and other health services (or arranges for their availability) on a prepayment basis (and either is sponsored by a union or employer, or does not provide, or arrange for the provision of, any inpatient hospital services) may elect to be paid 80 percent of the reasonable cost of services for which payment may be made under this part on behalf of individuals enrolled in such organization in lieu of 80 percent of the reasonable charges for such services if the organization undertakes to charge such individuals no more than 20 percent of such reasonable cost plus any amounts payable by them as a result of subsection (b), (B) with respect to items and services described in section 1861(s)(10)(A), the amounts paid shall be 100 percent of the reasonable charges for such items and services, (C) with respect to expenses incurred for those physicians' services for which payment may be made under this part that are described in section 1862(a)(4), the amounts paid shall be subject to such limitations as may be prescribed by regulations, (D) with respect to clinical diagnostic laboratory tests for which payment is made under this part (i) on the basis of a fee schedule under subsection (h)(1) or section 1834(d)(1), the amount paid shall be equal to 80 percent (or 100 percent, in the case of such tests for which payment is made on an assignment-related basis) of the lesser of the amount determined under such fee schedule, the limitation amount for that test determined under subsection (h)(4)(B), or the amount of the charges billed for the tests, or (ii) on the basis of a negotiated rate established under subsection (h)(6), the amount paid shall be equal to 100 percent of such negotiated rate, (E) with respect

to services furnished to individuals who have been determined to have end stage renal disease, the amounts paid shall be determined subject to the provisions of section 1881, (F) with respect to clinical social worker services under section 1861(s)(2)(N), the amounts paid shall be 80 percent of the lesser of (i) the actual charge for the services or (ii) 75 percent of the amount determined for payment of a psychologist under clause (L), (G) [Deleted] (H) with respect to services of a certified registered nurse anesthetist under section 1861(s)(11), the amounts paid shall be 80 percent of the least of the actual charge, the prevailing charge that would be recognized (or, for services furnished on or after January 1, 1992, the fee schedule amount provided under section 1848) if the services had been performed by an anesthesiologist, or the fee schedule for such services established by the Secretary in accordance with subsection (1), (I) with respect to covered items (described in section 1834(a)(13)), the amounts paid shall be the amounts described in section 1834(a)(1), [and] (J) with respect to expenses incurred for radiologist services (as defined in section 1834(b)(6)), subject to section 1848, the amounts paid shall be 80 percent of the lesser of the actual charge for the services or the amount provided under the fee schedule established under section 1834(b), (K) with respect to certified nurse-midwife services under section 1861(s)(2)(L), the amounts paid shall be 80 percent of the lesser of the actual charge for the services or the amount determined by a fee schedule established by the Secretary for the purposes of this subparagraph (but in no event shall such fee schedule exceed 65 percent of the prevailing charge that would be allowed for the same service performed by a physician, or, for services furnished on or after January 1, 1992, 65 percent of the fee schedule amount provided under section 1848 for the same service performed by a physician), (L) with respect to qualified psychologist services under section 1861(s)(2)(M), the amounts paid shall be 80 percent of the lesser of the actual charge for the services or the amount determined by a fee schedule established by the Secretary for the purposes of this subparagraph, (M) with respect to prosthetic devices and orthotics and prosthetics (as defined in section 1834(h)(4)), the amounts paid shall be the amounts described in section 1834(h)(1), (N) with respect to expenses incurred for physicians' services (as defined in section 1848(j)(3)), the amounts paid shall be 80 percent of the payment basis determined under section 1848(a)(1), (O) with respect to services described in

1861(s)(2)(K) (relating to services furnished by physician assistants, nurse practitioners, or clinic nurse specialists), the amounts paid shall be equal to 80 percent of (i) the lesser of the actual charge or 85 percent of the fee schedule amount provided under section 1848, or (ii) in the case of services as an assistant at surgery, the lesser of the actual charge or 85 percent of the amount that would otherwise be recognized if performed by a physician who is serving as an assistant at surgery, (P) with respect to surgical dressings, the amounts paid shall be the amounts determined under section 1834(i), (Q) with respect to items or services for which fee schedules are established pursuant to section 1842(s), the amounts paid shall be 80 percent of the lesser of the actual charge or the fee schedule established in such section, (R) with respect to ambulance services, (i) the amounts paid shall be 80 percent of the lesser of the actual charge for the services or the amount determined by a fee schedule established by the Secretary under section 1834(l) and (ii) with respect to ambulance services described in section 1834(l)(8), the amounts paid shall be the amounts determined under section 1834(g) for outpatient critical access hospital services, (S) with respect to drugs and biologicals not paid on a cost or prospective payment basis as otherwise provided in this part (other than items and services described in subparagraph (B)), the amounts paid shall be 80 percent of the lesser of the actual charge or the payment amount established in section 1842(o), (T) with respect to medical nutrition therapy services (as defined in section 1861(vv)), the amount paid shall be 80 percent of the lesser of the actual charge for the services or 85 percent of the amount determined under the fee schedule established under section 1848(b) for the same services if furnished by a physician, and (U) with respect to facility fees described in section 1834(m)(2)(B), the amounts paid shall be 80 percent of the lesser of the actual charge or the amounts specified in such section;

(2) in the case of services described in section 1832(a)(2) (except those services described in subparagraphs (C), (D), (E), (F), (G), (H), and (I) of such section and unless otherwise specified in section 1881) —

    (A) with respect to home health services (other than a covered osteoporosis drug) (as defined in section 1861(kk)), the amount determined under the prospective payment system under section 1895;

(B) with respect to other items and services (except those described in subparagraph (C), (D), or (E) of this paragraph and except as may be provided in section 1886 or section 1888(e)(9)) —

(i) furnished before January 1, 1999, the lessor of —

(I) the reasonable cost of such services, as determined under section 1861(v), or

(II) the customary charges with respect to such services,

less the amount a provider may charge as described in clause (ii) of section 1866(a)(2)(A), but in no case may the payment for such other services exceed 80 percent of such reasonable cost, or

(ii) if such services are furnished before January 1, 1999, by a public provider of services, or by another provider which demonstrates to the satisfaction of the Secretary that a significant portion of its patients are low-income (and requests that payment be made under this clause), free of charge or at nominal charges to the public, 80 percent of the amount determined in accordance with section 1814(b)(2), or

(iii) if such services are furnished on or after January 1, 1999, the amount determined under subsection (t), or

(iv) if (and for so long as) the conditions described in section 1814(b)(3) are met, the amounts determined under the reimbursement system described in such section;

(C) with respect to services described in the second sentence of section 1861(p), 80 percent of the reasonable charges for such services;

(D) with respect to clinical diagnostic laboratory tests for which payment is made under this part (i) on the basis of a fee schedule determined under subsection (h)(1) or section 1834(d)(1), the amount paid shall be equal to 80 percent (or 100 percent, in the case of such tests for which payment is made on an assignment-related basis or to a provider having an agreement under section 1866) of the lesser of the amount determined under such fee schedule or the amount of the charges billed for the tests, or (ii) on the basis of a negotiated rate established under subsection (h)(6), the amount paid shall be equal to 100 percent of such negotiated rate for such tests;

(E) with respect to —

(i) outpatient hospital radiology services (including diagnostic and therapeutic radiology, nuclear medicine and

CAT scan procedures, magnetic resonance imaging, and ultrasound and other imaging services, but excluding screening mammography), and

(ii) effective for procedures performed on or after October 1, 1989, diagnostic procedures (as defined by the Secretary) described in section 1861(s)(3) (other than diagnostic x-ray tests and diagnostic laboratory tests),

the amount determined under subsection (n) or, for services or procedures performed on or after January 1, 1999, subsection (t);

(F) respect to a covered osteoporosis drug (as defined in section 1861(kk)) furnished by a home health agency, 80 percent of the reasonable cost of such service, as determined under section 1861(v); and

(G) with respect to items and services described in section 1861(s)(10)(A), the lesser of —

(i) the reasonable cost of such services, as determined under section 1861(v), or

(ii) the customary charges with respect to such services,

or, if such services are furnished by a public provider of services, or by another provider which demonstrates to the satisfaction of the Secretary that a significant portion of its patients are low-income (and requests that payment be made under this provision), free of charge or at nominal charges to the public, the amount determined in accordance with section 1814(b)(2);

(3) in the case of services described in section 1832(a)(2)(D), the costs which are reasonable and related to the cost of furnishing such services or which are based on such other tests of reasonableness as the Secretary may prescribe in regulations, including those authorized under section 1861(v)(1)(A), less the amount a provider may charge as described in clause (ii) of section 1866(a)(2)(A), but in no case may the payment for such services (other than for items and services described in section 1861(s)(10)(A)) exceed 80 percent of such costs;

(4) in the case of facility services described in section 1832(a)(2)(F), and outpatient hospital facility services furnished in connection with surgical procedures specified by the Secretary pursuant to section 1833(i)(1)(A) [subsec. (i)(1)(A) of this section], the applicable amount as determined under paragraph (2) or (3) of subsection (i) or subsection (t);

(5) in the case of covered items (described in section 1834(a)(13)) the amounts described in section 1834(a)(1);

(6) in the case of outpatient critical access hospital services, the amounts described in section 1834(g);

(7) in the case of prosthetic devices and orthotics and prosthetics (as described in section 1834(h)(4)), the amounts described in section 1834(h);

(8) in the case of —

(A) outpatient physical therapy services (which includes outpatient speech-language pathology services) and outpatient occupational therapy services furnished —

(i) by a rehabilitation agency, public health agency, clinic, comprehensive outpatient rehabilitation facility, or skilled nursing facility,

(ii) by a home health agency to an individual who is not homebound, or

(iii) by another entity under an arrangement with an entity described in clause (i) or (ii); and

(B) outpatient physical therapy services (which includes outpatient speech-language pathology services) and outpatient occupational therapy services furnished —

(i) by a hospital to an outpatient or to a hospital inpatient who is entitled to benefits under part A but has exhausted benefits for inpatient hospital services during a spell of illness or is not so entitled to benefits under part A, or

(ii) by another entity under an arrangement with a hospital described in clause (i),

the amounts described in section 1834(k); and

(9) in the case of services described in section 1832(a)(2)(E) that are not described in paragraph (8), the amounts described in section 1834(k).

(b) *Deductible provision*

Before applying subsection (a) with respect to expenses incurred by an individual during any calendar year, the total amount of the expenses incurred by such individual during such year (which would, except for this subsection, constitute incurred expenses from which benefits payable under subsection (a) are determinable) shall be reduced by a deductible of $75 for calendar years before 1991 and $100 for 1991 and subsequent years; except that (1) such total amount shall not include expenses incurred for items and services described in section 1861(s)(10)(A), (2) such deductible shall not apply with respect to home health services (other than a covered osteoporosis drug (as defined in section 1861(kk))),

(3) such deductible shall not apply with respect to clinical diagnostic laboratory tests for which payment is made under this part (A) under subsection (a)(1)(D)(i) or (a)(2)(D)(i) on an assignment-related basis, or to a provider having an agreement under section 1866, or (B) on the basis of a negotiated rate determined under subsection (h)(6), (4) such deductible shall not apply to Federally qualified health center services. The total amount of the expenses incurred by an individual as determined under the preceding sentence shall, after the reduction specified in such sentence, be further reduced by an amount equal to the expenses incurred for the first three pints of whole blood (or equivalent quantities of packed red blood cells, as defined under regulations) furnished to the individual during the calendar year, except that such deductible for such blood shall in accordance with regulations be appropriately reduced to the extent that there has been a replacement of such blood (or equivalent quantities of packed red blood cells, as so defined); and for such purposes blood (or equivalent quantities of packed red blood cells, as so defined) furnished such individual shall be deemed replaced when the institution or other person furnishing such blood (or such equivalent quantities of packed red blood cells, as so defined) is given one pint of blood for each pint of blood (or equivalent quantities of packed red blood cells, as so defined) furnished such individual with respect to which a deduction is made under this sentence. The deductible under the previous sentence for blood or blood cells furnished an individual in a year shall be reduced to the extent that a deductible has been imposed under section 1813(a)(2) to blood or blood cells furnished the individual in the year. The deductible under the previous sentence for blood or blood cells furnished an individual in a year shall be reduced to the extent that a deductible has been imposed under section 1813(a)(2) to blood or blood cells furnished the individual in the year, (5) such deductible shall not apply with respect to screening mammography (as described in section 1861(jj)), and (6) such deductible shall not apply with respect to screening pap smear and screening pelvic exam (as described in section 1861(nn)).

## (c) *Mental disorders*

Notwithstanding any other provision of this part, with respect to expenses incurred in any calendar year in connection with the treatment of mental, psychoneurotic, and personality disorders of an individual who is not an inpatient of a hospital at the time such expenses are incurred, there shall be considered as incurred expenses for purposes of subsections (a) and (b) only 62½ percent of such expenses. For purposes of this subsection, the term "treatment" does not include brief office visits (as defined by the Secretary) for the sole purpose of monitoring or changing drug prescriptions used in the treatment of such disorders or partial hospitalization services that are not directly provided by a physician.

(d) *Nonduplication of payments*

No payment may be made under this part with respect to any services furnished an individual to the extent that such individual is entitled (or would be entitled except for section 1813) to have payment made with respect to such services under part A.

(e) *Information for determination of amounts due*

No payment shall be made to any provider of services or other person under this part unless there has been furnished such information as may be necessary in order to determine the amounts due such provider or other person under this part for the period with respect to which the amounts are being paid or for any prior period.

(f) *Updating maximum rate of payment per visit for independent rural health clinics*

In establishing limits under subsection (a) on payment for rural health clinic services provided by rural health clinics (other than such clinics in hospitals with less than 50 beds), the Secretary shall establish such limit, for services provided —

(1) in 1988, after March 31, at $46 per visit, and

(2) in a subsequent year, at the limit established under this subsection for the previous year increased by the percentage increase in the MEI (as defined in section 1842(i)(3)) applicable to primary care services (as defined in section 1842(i)(4)) furnished as of the first day of that year.

(g) *Physical therapy services*

(1) Subject to paragraph (4), in the case of physical therapy services of the type described in section 1861(p), but not described in section 1833(a)(8)(B) [subsec. (a)(8)(B) of this section], and physical therapy services of such type which are furnished by a physician or as incident to physicians' services, with respect to expenses incurred in any calendar year, no more than the amount specified in paragraph (2) for the year shall be considered as incurred expenses for purposes of subsections (a) and (b).

(2) The amount specified in this paragraph —

(A) for 1999, 2000, and 2001, is $1,500, and

(B) for a subsequent year is the amount specified in this paragraph for the preceding year increased by the percentage increase in the MEI (as defined in section 1842(i)(3)) for such subsequent year;except that if an increase under subparagraph (B) for a year is not a multiple of $10, it shall be rounded to the nearest multiple of $10.

(3) Subject to paragraph (4), in the case of occupational therapy services (of the type that are described in section 1861(p) (but not described in section 1833(a)(8)(B) [subsec. (a)(8)(B) of this section]) through the operation of section 1861(g) and of such type which are furnished by a physician or as incident to physicians' services), with respect to expenses incurred in any calendar year, no more than the amount specified in paragraph (2) for the year shall be considered as incurred expenses for purposes of subsections (a) and (b).

(4) This subsection shall not apply to expenses incurred with respect to services furnished during 2000, 2001, and 2002.

. . . .

(o) *Limitation on benefit for payment for therapeutic shoes for individuals with severe diabetic foot disease*

(1) In the case of shoes described in section 1395x(s)(12) of this title —

(A) no payment may be made under this part, with respect to any individual for any year, for the furnishing of —

(i) more than one pair of custom molded shoes (including inserts provided with such shoes) and 2 additional pairs of inserts for such shoes, or

(ii) more than one pair of extra-depth shoes (not including inserts provided with such shoes) and 3 pairs of inserts for such shoes, and

(B) with respect to expenses incurred in any calendar year, no more than the amount of payment applicable under paragraph (2) shall be considered as incurred expenses for purposes of subsections (a) and (b) of this section.

Payment for shoes (or inserts) under this part shall be considered to include payment for any expenses for the fitting of such shoes (or inserts).

(2) (A) Except as provided by the Secretary under subparagraphs (B) and (C), the amount of payment under this paragraph for custom molded shoes, extra-depth shoes, and inserts shall be the amount

determined for such items by the Secretary under section 1395m(h) of this title.

(B) The Secretary may establish payment amounts for shoes and inserts that are lower than the amount established under section 1395m(h) of this title if the Secretary finds that shoes and inserts of an appropriate quality are readily available at or below the amount established under such section.

(C) In accordance with procedures established by the Secretary, an individual entitled to benefits with respect to shoes described in section 1395x(s)(12) of this title may substitute modification of such shoes instead of obtaining one (or more, as specified by the Secretary) pair of inserts (other than the original pair of inserts with respect to such shoes). In such case, the Secretary shall substitute, for the payment amount established under section 1395m(h) of this title, a payment amount that the Secretary estimates will assure that there is no net increase in expenditures under this subsection as a result of this subparagraph.

(3) In this subchapter, the term "shoes" includes, except for purposes of subparagraphs (A)(ii) and (B) of paragraph (2), inserts for extra-depth shoes.

## § 1395m. Special payment rules for particular items and services

(a) *Payment for durable medical equipment*

(1) *General rule for payment*

(A) *In general*

With respect to a covered item (as defined in paragraph (13)) for which payment is determined under this subsection, payment shall be made in the frequency specified in paragraphs (2) through (7) and in an amount equal to 80 percent of the payment basis described in subparagraph (B).

(B) *Payment basis*

Subject to subparagraph (F)(i), the payment basis described in this subparagraph is the lesser of —

(i) the actual charge for the item, or

(ii) the payment amount recognized under paragraphs (2) through (7) of this subsection for the item;

except that clause (i) shall not apply if the covered item is furnished by a public home health agency (or by another home health agency which demonstrates to the satisfaction of the Secretary that a significant portion of its patients are low income) free of charge or at nominal charges to the public.

(C) *Exclusive payment rule*

Subject to subparagraph (F)(ii), this subsection shall constitute the exclusive provision of this subchapter for payment for covered items under this part or under part A of this subchapter to a home health agency.

(D) *Reduction in fee schedules for certain items*

With respect to a seat-lift chair or transcutaneous electrical nerve stimulator furnished on or after April 1, 1990, the Secretary shall reduce the payment amount applied under subparagraph (B)(ii) for such an item by 15 percent, and, in the case of a transcutaneous electrical nerve stimulator furnished on or after January 1, 1991, the Secretary shall further reduce such payment amount (as previously reduced) by 45 percent.

(E) *Clinical conditions for coverage*

(i) In general

The Secretary shall establish standards for clinical conditions for payment for covered items under this subsection.

(ii) Requirements

The standards established under clause (i) shall include the specification of types or classes of covered items that require, as a condition of payment under this subsection, a face-to-face examination of the individual by a physician (as defined in section 1395x(r)(1) of this title, a physician assistant, nurse practitioner, or a clinical nurse specialist (as those terms are defined in section 1395x(aa)(5)) of this title and a prescription for the item.

(iii) Priority of establishment of standards

In establishing the standards under this subparagraph, the Secretary shall first establish standards for those covered items for which the Secretary determines there has been a proliferation of use, consistent findings of charges for covered items that are not delivered, or consistent findings of falsification of documentation to provide for payment of such covered items under this part.

(iv) Standards for power wheelchairs

Effective on the date of the enactment of this subparagraph, in the case of a covered item consisting of a motorized or power wheelchair for an individual, payment may not be made for such covered item unless a physician (as defined in section 1395x(r)(1)), a physician assistant, nurse practitioner, or a clinical nurse specialist (as those terms are defined in section 1395x(aa)(5)) has conducted a face-to-face examination of the individual and written a prescription for the item.

(v)  Limitation on payment for covered items

Payment may not be made for a covered item under this subsection unless the item meets any standards established under this subparagraph for clinical condition of coverage.

(F)  *Application of competitive acquisition; limitation of inherent reasonableness authority*

In the case of covered items furnished on or after January 1, 2009, that are included in a competitive acquisition program in a competitive acquisition area under section 1395w-3(a) of this title —

(i)  the payment basis under this subsection for such items and services furnished in such area shall be the payment basis determined under such competitive acquisition program; and

(ii)  the Secretary may use information on the payment determined under such competitive acquisition programs to adjust the payment amount otherwise recognized under subparagraph (B)(ii) for an area that is not a competitive acquisition area under section 1395w-3 of this title and in the case of such adjustment, paragraph (10)(B) shall not be applied.

(2)  *Payment for inexpensive and other routinely purchased durable medical equipment*

(A)  *In general*

Payment for an item of durable medical equipment (as defined in paragraph (13)) —

(i)  the purchase price of which does not exceed $150,

(ii)  which the Secretary determines is acquired at least 75 percent of the time by purchase, or

(iii)  which is an accessory used in conjunction with a nebulizer, aspirator, or a ventilator excluded under paragraph (3)(A),

shall be made on a rental basis or in a lump-sum amount for the purchase of the item. The payment amount recognized for purchase or rental of such equipment is the amount specified in subparagraph (B) for purchase or rental, except that the total amount of payments with respect to an item may not exceed the payment amount specified in subparagraph (B) with respect to the purchase of the item.

## § 1395o.  Eligible individuals

Every individual who —

(1) is entitled to hospital insurance benefits under part A, or

(2) has attained age 65 and is a resident of the United States,

and is either (A) a citizen or (B) an alien lawfully admitted for permanent residence who has resided in the United States continuously during the 5 years immediately preceding the month in which he applies for enrollment under this part, is eligible to enroll in the insurance program established by this part.

## § 1395p.  Enrollment periods

(a) *Generally; regulations*

An individual may enroll in the insurance program established by this part only in such manner and form as may be prescribed by regulations, and only during an enrollment period prescribed in or under this section.
. . . .

(f) *Individuals deemed enrolled in the medical insurance program*

Any individual —

(1) who is eligible under section 1836 to enroll in the medical insurance program by reason of entitlement to hospital insurance benefits as described in paragraph (1) of such section, and

(2) whose initial enrollment period under subsection (d) begins after March 31, 1973, and

(3) who is residing in the United States, exclusive of Puerto Rico, shall be deemed to have enrolled in the medical insurance program established by this part.
. . . .

## § 1395r.  Amount of premiums for individuals enrolled under this part

(a) *Determination of monthly actuarial rates and premiums*

(1) The Secretary shall, during September of 1983 and of each year thereafter, determine the monthly actuarial rate for enrollees age 65 and over which shall be applicable for the succeeding calendar year.  Such actuarial rate shall be the amount the Secretary estimates to be necessary so that the aggregate amount for such calendar year with respect to those enrollees age 65 and older will equal one-half of the total of the benefits

and administrative costs which he estimates will be payable from the Federal Supplementary Medical Insurance Trust Fund for services performed and related administrative costs incurred in such calendar year with respect to such enrollees. In calculating the monthly actuarial rate, the Secretary shall include an appropriate amount for a contingency margin.

(2) The monthly premium of each individual enrolled under this part for each month after December 1983 shall be the amount determined under paragraph (3), adjusted as required in accordance with subsections (b), (c), (f), and (i) of this section and to reflect any credit provided under section 1395w-24(b)(1)(C)(ii)(III) of this title.

(3) The Secretary, during September of each year, shall determine and promulgate a monthly premium rate for the succeeding calendar year that (except as provided in subsection (g) is equal to 50 percent of the monthly actuarial rate for enrollees age 65 and over, determined according to paragraph (1), for that succeeding calendar year.

Whenever the Secretary promulgates the dollar amount which shall be applicable as the monthly premium rate for any period, he shall, at the time such promulgation is announced, issue a public statement setting forth the actuarial assumptions and bases employed by him in arriving at the amount of an adequate actuarial rate for enrollees age 65 and older as provided in paragraph (1).

(4) The Secretary shall also, during September of 1983 and of each year thereafter, determine the monthly actuarial rate for disabled enrollees under age 65 which shall be applicable for the succeeding calendar year. Such actuarial rate shall be the amount the Secretary estimates to be necessary so that the aggregate amount for such calendar year with respect to disabled enrollees under age 65 will equal one-half of the total of the benefits and administrative costs which he estimates will be payable from the Federal Supplementary Medical Insurance Trust Fund for services performed and related administrative costs incurred in such calendar year with respect to such enrollees. In calculating the monthly actuarial rate under this paragraph, the Secretary shall include an appropriate amount for a contingency margin.

(b) *Increase in monthly premium*

In the case of an individual whose coverage period began pursuant to an enrollment after his initial enrollment period (determined pursuant to subsection (c) or (d) of section 1395p of this title) and not pursuant to a special enrollment period under section 1395p(4) of this title, the monthly premium determined under subsection (a) of this section (without regard to any adjustment under subsection (i) of this section) shall be increased by 10 percent of the monthly premium so determined for each full 12 months (in the same continuous period of eligibility) in which he could have been but was not enrolled. For purposes of the preceding sentence, there shall be taken into account (1) the months which elapsed between the close of his initial enrollment period and the close of the enrollment period in which he enrolled, plus (in the case of an individual who reenrolls) (2) the months which elapsed between the date of termination of a previous coverage period and the close of the enrollment period in which he reenrolled, but there shall not be taken into account months for which the individual can demonstrate that the individual was enrolled in a group health plan described in section 1395y(b)(1)(A)(v) of this title by reason of the individual's (or the individual's spouse's) current employment status or months during which the individual has not attained the age of 65 and for which the individual can demonstrate that the individual was enrolled in a large group health plan (as that term is defined in section 1395y(b)(1)(B)(iii) of this title) by reason of the individual's current employment status (or the current employment status of a family member of the individual). Any increase in an individual's monthly premium under the first sentence of this subsection with respect to a particular continuous period of eligibility shall not be applicable with respect to any other continuous period of eligibility which such individual may have. No increase in the premium shall be effected for a month in the case of an individual who enrolls under this part during 2001, 2002, 2003, or 2004 and who demonstrates to the Secretary before December 31, 2004, that the individual is a covered beneficiary (as defined in section 1072(5) of Title 10). The Secretary of Health and Human Services shall consult with the Secretary of Defense in identifying individuals described in the previous sentence.

(c) *Premiums rounded to nearest multiple of ten cents*

If any monthly premium determined under the foregoing provisions of this section is not a multiple of 10 cents, such premium shall be rounded to the nearest multiple of 10 cents.

(d) *"Continuous period of eligibility" defined*

For purposes of subsection (b) of this section (and section 1395p(g)(1) of this title), an individual's "continuous period of eligibility" is the period beginning with the first day on which he is eligible to enroll under section 1395o of this title and ending with his death; except that any period during all of which an individual satisfied paragraph (1) of section 1395o of this title and which terminated in or before the month preceding the month in which he attained age 65 shall be a separate "continuous period of eligibility" with respect to such individual (and each such period which terminates shall be deemed not to have existed for purposes of subsequently applying this section).

(e) *State payment of part B late enrollment premium increases*

(1)  Upon the request of a State (or any appropriate State or local government entity specified by the Secretary), the Secretary may enter into an agreement with the State (or such entity) under which the State (or such entity) agrees to pay on a quarterly or other periodic basis to the Secretary (to be deposited in the Treasury to the credit of the Federal Supplementary Medical Insurance Trust Fund) an amount equal to the amount of the part B late enrollment premium increases with respect to the premiums for eligible individuals (as defined in paragraph (3)(A)).

(2)  No part B late enrollment premium increase shall apply to an eligible individual for premiums for months for which the amount of such an increase is payable under an agreement under paragraph (1).

(3)  In this subsection:

(A) The term "eligible individual" means an individual who is enrolled under this part B of this subchapter and who is within a class of individuals specified in the agreement under paragraph (1).

(B) The term "part B late enrollment premium increase" means any increase in a premium as a result of the application of subsection (b) of this section.

(f) *Limitation on increase in monthly premium*

For any calendar year after 1988, if an individual is entitled to monthly benefits under section 402 or 423 of this title or to a monthly annuity under section 3(a), 4(a), or 4(f) of the Railroad Retirement Act of 1974 [ed. 45 U.S.C.A. § 231b(a), 231c(a), or 231c(f)] for November and December of the preceding year, if the monthly premium of the individual under this section for December and for January is deducted from those benefits under section 1395s(a)(1) or section 1395s(b)(1) of this title, and if the amount of the individual's premium is not adjusted for such January under subsection (i) of this section, the monthly premium otherwise determined under this section for an individual for that year shall not be increased, pursuant to this subsection, to the extent that such increase would reduce the amount of benefits payable to that individual for that December below the amount of benefits payable to that individual for that November (after the deduction of the premium under this section). For purposes of this subsection, retroactive adjustments or payments and deductions on account of work shall not be taken into account in determining the monthly benefits to which an individual is entitled under section 402 or 423 of this title or under the Railroad Retirement Act of 1974 [ed. 45 U.S.C.A. § 231 *et seq.*].

### § 1395w-4. Payment for physicians' services

(a) *Payment based on fee schedule*

(1) *In general*

Effective for all physicians' services (as defined in subsection (j)(3) of this section) furnished under this part during a year (beginning with 1992) for which payment is otherwise made on the basis of a reasonable charge or on the basis of a fee schedule under section 1395m(b) of this title, payment under this part shall instead be based on the lesser of —

(A) the actual charge for the service, or

(B) subject to the succeeding provisions of this subsection, the amount determined under the fee schedule established under subsection (b) of this section for services furnished during that year (in this subsection referred to as the "fee schedule amount").

PART C — MEDICARE+CHOICE PROGRAM

### § 1395w-21. Eligibility, election, and enrollment

(a) *Choice of medicare benefits through Medicare+Choice plans*

(1) *In general*

Subject to the provisions of this section, each Medicare+Choice eligible individual (as defined in paragraph (3)) is entitled to elect to receive benefits (other than qualified prescription drug benefits) under this title —

(A) through the original medicare fee-for-service program under parts A and B of this subchapter, or

(B) through enrollment in a Medicare+Choice plan under this part,

and may elect qualified prescription drug coverage in accordance with section 1395w-101 of this section.

(2) *Types of Medicare+Choice plans that may be available*

A Medicare+Choice plan may be any of the following types of plans of health insurance:

(A) Coordinated care plans (including regional plans)

(i) In general

Coordinated care plans which provide health care services, including but not limited to health maintenance organization plans (with or without point of service options), plans offered by provider-sponsored organizations (as defined in section 1395w-25(d) of this title), and regional or local preferred provider organization plans (including MA regional plans).

(ii) Specialized MA plans for special needs individuals

Specialized MA plans for special needs individuals (as defined in section 1395w-28(b)(6) of this title) may be any type of coordinated care plan.

(B) Combination of MSA plan and contributions to Medicare+Choice MSA

An MSA plan, as defined in section 1395w-28(b)(3) of this title, and a contribution into a Medicare+Choice medical savings account (MSA).

(C) Private fee-for-service plans

A Medicare+Choice private fee-for-service plan, as defined in section 1395w-28(b)(2) of this title.

(3) *Medicare+Choice eligible individual*

(A) In general

In this title, subject to subparagraph (B), the term "Medicare+Choice eligible individual" means an individual who is entitled to benefits under part A of this subchapter and enrolled under part B of this subchapter.

(B) Special rule for end-stage renal disease

Such term shall not include an individual medically determined to have end-stage renal disease, except that —

(i) an individual who develops end-stage renal disease while enrolled in a Medicare+Choice plan may continue to be enrolled in that plan; and

(ii) in the case of such an individual who is enrolled in a Medicare+Choice plan under clause (i) (or subsequently under this clause), if the enrollment is discontinued under circumstances described in subsection (e)(4)(A) of this section, then the individual will be treated as a "Medicare+Choice eligible individual" for purposes of electing to continue enrollment in another Medicare+Choice plan.

. . . .

(c) *Process for exercising choice*

(1) *In general*

The Secretary shall establish a process through which elections described in subsection (a) of this section are made and changed, including the form and manner in which such elections are made and changed. Such elections shall be made or changed only during coverage election periods specified under subsection (e) of this section and shall become effective as provided in subsection (f) of this section.

(2) *Coordination through Medicare+Choice organizations*

(A) Enrollment

Such process shall permit an individual who wishes to elect a Medicare+Choice plan offered by a Medicare+Choice organization to make such election through the filing of an appropriate election form with the organization.

(B) Disenrollment

Such process shall permit an individual, who has elected a Medicare+Choice plan offered by a Medicare+Choice organization and who wishes to terminate such election, to terminate such election through the filing of an appropriate election form with the organization.

(3) *Default*

(A) Initial election

(i) In general

Subject to clause (ii), an individual who fails to make an election during an initial election period under subsection (e)(1) of this section is deemed to have chosen the original medicare fee-for-service program option.

(ii) Seamless continuation of coverage

The Secretary may establish procedures under which an individual who is enrolled in a health plan (other than Medicare+Choice plan) offered by a Medicare+Choice organization at the time of the initial election period and who fails to elect to receive coverage other than through the organization is deemed to have elected the Medicare+Choice plan offered by the organization (or, if the organization offers more than one such plan, such plan or plans as the Secretary identifies under such procedures).

(B) Continuing periods

An individual who has made (or is deemed to have made) an election under this section is considered to have continued to make such election until such time as —

(i) the individual changes the election under this section, or

(ii) the Medicare+Choice plan with respect to which such election is in effect is discontinued or, subject to subsection (b)(1)(B) of this section, no longer serves the area in which the individual resides.

(d) *Providing information to promote informed choice*

(1) *In general*

The Secretary shall provide for activities under this subsection to broadly disseminate information to medicare beneficiaries (and prospective medicare beneficiaries) on the coverage options provided under this section in order to promote an active, informed selection among such options.

(2) *Provision of notice*

(A) Open season notification

At least 15 days before the beginning of each annual, coordinated election period (as defined in subsection (e)(3)(B) of this section), the Secretary shall mail to each Medicare+Choice eligible individual residing in an area the following:

(i) General information

The general information described in paragraph (3).

(ii) List of plans and comparison of plan options

A list identifying the Medicare+Choice plans that are (or will be) available to residents of the area and information described in paragraph (4) concerning such plans. Such information shall be presented in a comparative form.

(iii) Additional information

Any other information that the Secretary determines will assist the individual in making the election under this section.

The mailing of such information shall be coordinated, to the extent practicable, with the mailing of any annual notice under section 1395b-2 of this title.

(B) Notification to newly eligible Medicare+Choice eligible individuals

To the extent practicable, the Secretary shall, not later than 30 days before the beginning of the initial Medicare+Choice enrollment period for an individual described in subsection (e)(1) of this section, mail to the individual the information described in subparagraph (A).

(C) Form

The information disseminated under this paragraph shall be written and formatted using language that is easily understandable by medicare beneficiaries.

(D) Periodic updating

The information described in subparagraph (A) shall be updated on at least an annual basis to reflect changes in the availability of Medicare+Choice plans and the benefits and Medicare+Choice monthly basic and supplemental beneficiary premiums for such plans.

(3) *General information*

General information under this paragraph, with respect to coverage under this part during a year, shall include the following:

(A) Benefits under original medicare fee-for-service program option

A general description of the benefits covered under the original medicare fee-for-service program under parts A and B of this subchapter, including —

(i) covered items and services,

(ii) beneficiary cost sharing, such as deductibles, coinsurance, and copayment amounts, and

(iii) any beneficiary liability for balance billing.

(B) Election procedures

Information and instructions on how to exercise election options under this section.

(C) Rights

A general description of procedural rights (including grievance and appeals procedures) of beneficiaries under the original medicare fee-for-service program and the Medicare+Choice program and the right to be protected against discrimination based on health status-related factors under section 1395w-22(b) of this title.

(D) Information on medigap and medicare select

A general description of the benefits, enrollment rights, and other requirements applicable to medicare supplemental policies under section 1395ss of this title and provisions relating to medicare select policies described in section 1395ss(t) of this title.

(E) Potential for contract termination

The fact that a Medicare+Choice organization may terminate its contract, refuse to renew its contract, or reduce the service area included in its contract, under this part, and the effect of such a termination, nonrenewal, or service area reduction may have on individuals enrolled with the Medicare+Choice plan under this part.

(F) Catastrophic coverage and single deductible

In the case of an MA regional plan, a description of the catastrophic coverage and single deductible applicable under the plan.

(4) *Information comparing plan options*

Information under this paragraph, with respect to a Medicare+Choice plan for a year, shall include the following:

(A) Benefits

The benefits covered under the plan, including the following:

(i) Covered items and services beyond those provided under the original medicare fee-for-service program.

(ii) Any beneficiary cost sharing, including information on the single deductible (if applicable) under section 1395w-27a(b)(1) of this title.

(iii) Any maximum limitations on out-of-pocket expenses.

(iv) In the case of an MSA plan, differences in cost sharing, premiums, and balance billing under such a plan compared to under other Medicare+Choice plans.

(v) In the case of a Medicare+Choice private fee-for-service plan, differences in cost sharing, premiums, and balance billing under such a plan compared to under other Medicare+Choice plans.

(vi) The extent to which an enrollee may obtain benefits through out-of-network health care providers.

(vii) The extent to which an enrollee may select among in-network providers and the types of providers participating in the plan's network.

(viii) The organization's coverage of emergency and urgently needed care.

(B) Premiums

(i) In general

The monthly amount of the premium charged to an individual.

(ii) Reductions

The reduction in part B premiums, if any.

(C) Service area

The service area of the plan.

(D) Quality and performance

To the extent available, plan quality and performance indicators for the benefits under the plan (and how they compare to such indicators under the original medicare fee-for-service program under parts A and B of this subchapter in the area involved), including —

(i) disenrollment rates for medicare enrollees electing to receive benefits through the plan for the previous 2 years (excluding disenrollment due to death or moving outside the plan's service area),

(ii) information on medicare enrollee satisfaction,

(iii) information on health outcomes, and

(iv) the recent record regarding compliance of the plan with requirements of this part (as determined by the Secretary).

(E) Supplemental benefits

Supplemental health care benefits, including any reductions in cost-sharing under section 1395w-22(a)(3) of this title and the terms and conditions (including premiums) for such benefits.

(5) *Maintaining a toll-free number and Internet site*

The Secretary shall maintain a toll-free number for inquiries regarding Medicare+Choice options and the operation of this part in all areas in which Medicare+Choice plans are offered and an Internet site through which individuals may electronically obtain information on such options and Medicare+Choice plans.

(6) *Use of non-Federal entities*

The Secretary may enter into contracts with non-Federal entities to carry out activities under this subsection.

(7) *Provision of information*

A Medicare+Choice organization shall provide the Secretary with such information on the organization and each Medicare+Choice plan it offers as may be required for the preparation of the information referred to in paragraph (2)(A).

(e) *Coverage election periods*

. . . .

(2) *Open enrollment and disenrollment opportunities*

Subject to paragraph (5) —

. . . .

(C) Continuous open enrollment and disenrollment for first 3 months in subsequent years

(i) In general

Subject to clauses (ii) and (iii) and subparagraph (D), at any time during the first 3 months of a year after 2005, or, if the individual first becomes a Medicare+Choice eligible individual during a year after 2006, during the first 3 months of such year in which the individual is a Medicare+Choice eligible individual, a Medicare+Choice eligible individual may change the election under subsection (a)(1) of this section if this section.

(ii) Limitation of one change during open enrollment period each year

An individual may exercise the right under clause (i) only once during the applicable 3-month period described in such clause in each year. The limitation under this clause shall not apply to changes in elections effected during an annual, coordinated election period under paragraph (3) or during a special enrollment period under paragraph (4).

(iii) Limitation on exercise of right with respect to prescription drug coverage

Effective for plan years beginning on or after January 1, 2006, in applying clause (i) (and clause (i) of subparagraph (B)) in the case of an individual who —

(I)   is enrolled in an MA plan that does provide qualified prescription drug coverage, the individual may exercise the right under such clause only with respect to coverage under the original fee-for-service plan or coverage under another MA plan that does not provide such coverage and may not exercise such right to obtain coverage under an MA-PD plan or under a prescription drug plan under part D of this subchapter; or

(II)  is enrolled in an MA-PD plan, the individual may exercise the right under such clause only with respect to coverage under another MA-PD plan (and not an MA plan that does not provide qualified prescription drug coverage) or under the original fee-for-service plan and coverage under a prescription drug plan under part D of this subchapter.

. . . .

(3)  *Annual, coordinated election period*

(A)  In general

Subject to paragraph (5), each individual who is eligible to make an election under this section may change such election during an annual, coordinated election period.

(B)  Annual, coordinated election period

For purposes of this section, the term "annual, coordinated election period" means —

(i)   with respect to a year before 2002, the month of November before such year;

(ii)  with respect to 2002, 2003, 2004, and 2005, the period beginning on November 15 and ending on December 31 of the year before such year;

(iii)  with respect to 2006, the period beginning on November 15, 2005, and ending on May 15, 2006; and

(iv) with respect to 2007 and succeeding years, the period beginning on November 15 and ending on December 31 of the year before such year.

(C)  Medicare+Choice health information fairs

During the fall season of each year (beginning with 1999) and during the period described in subparagraph (B)(iii), in conjunction with the annual coordinated election period defined in subparagraph (B), the Secretary shall provide for a nationally coordinated educational and publicity campaign to inform Medicare+Choice eligible individuals about Medicare+Choice plans and the election process provided under this section.

(D) Special information campaigns

During November 1998 the Secretary shall provide for an educational and publicity campaign to inform Medicare+Choice eligible individuals about the availability of Medicare+Choice plans, and eligible organizations with risk-sharing contracts under section 1395mm of this title, offered in different areas and the election process provided under this section. During the period described in subparagraph (B)(iii), the Secretary shall provide for an educational and publicity campaign to inform MA eligible individuals about the availability of MA plans (including MA-PD plans) offered in different areas and the election process provided under this section.

. . . .

## § 1395w-22. Benefits and beneficiary protections

(a) *Basic benefits*

(1) *Requirement*

(A) In general

Except as provided in section 1395w-28(b)(3) of this title for MSA plans and except as provided in paragraph (6) for MA regional plans, each Medicare+Choice plan shall provide to members enrolled under this part, through providers and other persons that meet the applicable requirements of this subchapter and part A of subchapter XI benefits under the original medicare fee-for-service program option (and, for plan years before 2006, additional benefits required under section 1395w-24(f)(1)(A) of this title).

. . . .

(2) *Satisfaction of requirement*

(A) In general

A Medicare+Choice plan (other than an MSA plan) offered by a Medicare+Choice organization satisfies paragraph (1)(A), with respect to benefits for items and services furnished other than through a provider or other person that has a contract with the organization offering the plan, if the plan provides payment in an amount so that —

(i) the sum of such payment amount and any cost sharing provided for under the plan, is equal to at least

(ii) the total dollar amount of payment for such items and services as would otherwise be authorized under parts A and B (including any balance billing permitted under such parts).

. . . .

(3) *Supplemental benefits*

(A) Benefits included subject to Secretary's approval

Each Medicare+Choice organization may provide to individuals enrolled under this part, other than under an MSA plan (without affording those individuals an option to decline the coverage), supplemental health care benefits that the Secretary may approve. The Secretary shall approve any such supplemental benefits unless the Secretary determines that including such supplemental benefits would substantially discourage enrollment by Medicare+Choice eligible individuals with the organization.

. . . .

(b) *Antidiscrimination*

(1) *Beneficiaries*

(A) In general

A Medicare+Choice organization may not deny, limit, or condition the coverage or provision of benefits under this part, for individuals permitted to be enrolled with the organization under this part, based on any health status-related factor described in section 300gg-1(a)(1) of this title. The Secretary shall not approve a plan of an organization if the Secretary determines that the design of the plan and its benefits are likely to substantially discourage enrollment by certain MA eligible individuals with the organization.

. . . .

(c) *Disclosure requirements*

(1) *Detailed description of plan provisions*

A Medicare+Choice organization shall disclose, in clear, accurate, and standardized form to each enrollee with a Medicare+Choice plan offered by the organization under this part at the time of enrollment and at least annually thereafter, the following information regarding such plan:

(A) Service area

The plan's service area.

(B) Benefits

Benefits offered under the plan, including information described in section 1395w-21(d)(3)(A) of this title and exclusions from coverage and, if it is an MSA plan, a comparison of benefits under such a plan with benefits under other Medicare+Choice plans.

(C) Access

The number, mix, and distribution of plan providers, out-of-network coverage (if any) provided by the plan, and any point-of-service option (including the supplemental premium for such option).

(D) Out-of-area coverage

Out-of-area coverage provided by the plan.

(E) Emergency coverage

Coverage of emergency services, including —

(i) the appropriate use of emergency services, including use of the 911 telephone system or its local equivalent in emergency situations and an explanation of what constitutes an emergency situation;

(ii) the process and procedures of the plan for obtaining emergency services; and

(iii) the locations of (I) emergency departments, and (II) other settings, in which plan physicians and hospitals provide emergency services and post-stabilization care.

(F) Supplemental benefits

Supplemental benefits available from the organization offering the plan, including —

(i) whether the supplemental benefits are optional,

(ii) the supplemental benefits covered, and

(iii) the Medicare+Choice monthly supplemental beneficiary premium for the supplemental benefits.

(G) Prior authorization rules

Rules regarding prior authorization or other review requirements that could result in nonpayment.

(H) Plan grievance and appeals procedures

All plan appeal or grievance rights and procedures.

(I) Quality improvement program

A description of the organization's quality improvement program under subsection (e) of this section.

(2) *Disclosure upon request*

Upon request of a Medicare+Choice eligible individual, a Medicare+Choice organization must provide the following information to such individual:

    (A) The general coverage information and general comparative plan information made available under clauses (i) and (ii) of section 1395w-21(d)(2)(A) of this title.

    (B) Information on procedures used by the organization to control utilization of services and expenditures.

    (C) Information on the number of grievances, redeterminations, and appeals and on the disposition in the aggregate of such matters.

    (D) An overall summary description as to the method of compensation of participating physicians.

. . . .

(f) *Grievance mechanism*

Each Medicare+Choice organization must provide meaningful procedures for hearing and resolving grievances between the organization (including any entity or individual through which the organization provides health care services) and enrollees with Medicare+Choice plans of the organization under this part.

. . . .

PART D — VOLUNTARY PRESCRIPTION DRUG BENEFIT PROGRAM

## § 1395w-101. Eligibility, enrollment, and information

(a) *Provision of qualified prescription drug coverage through enrollment in plans* —

(1) *In general*

Subject to the succeeding provisions of this part, each part D eligible individual (as defined in paragraph (3)(A)) is entitled to obtain qualified prescription drug coverage (described in section 1395w-102(a) of this title) as follows:

    (A) Fee-for-service enrollees may receive coverage through a prescription drug plan

    A part D eligible individual who is not enrolled in an MA plan may obtain qualified prescription drug coverage through enrollment in a prescription drug plan (as defined in section 1395w-151(a)(14) of this title).

    (B) Medicare advantage enrollees

        (i) Enrollees in a plan providing qualified prescription drug coverage receive coverage through the plan

    A part D eligible individual who is enrolled in an MA-PD plan obtains such coverage through such plan.

        (ii) Limitation on enrollment of MA plan enrollees in prescription drug plans

    Except as provided in clauses (iii) and (iv), a part D eligible individual who is enrolled in an MA plan may not enroll in a prescription drug plan under this part.

        (iii) Private fee-for-service enrollees in MA plans not providing qualified prescription drug coverage permitted to enroll in a prescription drug plan

    A part D eligible individual who is enrolled in an MA private fee-for-service plan (as defined in section 1395w-28(b)(2) of this title that does not provide qualified prescription drug coverage may obtain qualified prescription drug coverage through enrollment in a prescription drug plan.

        (iv) Enrollees in MSA plans permitted to enroll in a prescription drug plan

    A part D eligible individual who is enrolled in an MSA plan (as defined in section 1395w-28(b)(3) of this title) may obtain qualified prescription drug coverage through enrollment in a prescription drug plan.

(2) *Coverage first effective January 1, 2006*

Coverage under prescription drug plans and MA-PD plans shall first be effective on January 1, 2006.

(3) *Definitions*

For purposes of this part:

    (A) Part D eligible individual

    The term "part D eligible individual" means an individual who is entitled to benefits under part A of this subchapter or enrolled under part B of this subchapter.

    (B) MA plan

    The term "MA plan" has the meaning given such term in section 1395w-28(b)(1) of this title.

(C) MA-PD plan

The term "MA-PD plan" means an MA plan that provides qualified prescription drug coverage.

(b) *Enrollment process for prescription drug plans*

(1) *Establishment of process*

(A) In general

The Secretary shall establish a process for the enrollment, disenrollment, termination, and change of enrollment of part D eligible individuals in prescription drug plans consistent with this subsection.

(B) Application of MA rules

In establishing such process, the Secretary shall use rules similar to (and coordinated with) the rules for enrollment, disenrollment, termination, and change of enrollment with an MA-PD plan under the following provisions of section 1395w-21 of this title:

(i) Residence requirements

Section 1395w-21(b)(1)(A) of this title, relating to residence requirements.

(ii) Exercise of choice

Section 1395w-21(c) of this title (other than paragraph (3)(A) of such section), relating to exercise of choice.

(iii) Coverage election periods

Subject to paragraphs (2) and (3) of this subsection, section 1395w-21(e) of this title (other than subparagraphs (B), (C), and (E) of paragraph (2) and the second sentence of paragraph (4) of such section), relating to coverage election periods, including initial periods, annual coordinated election periods, special election periods, and election periods for exceptional circumstances.

(iv) Coverage periods

Section 1395w-21(f) of this title, relating to effectiveness of elections and changes of elections.

(v) Guaranteed issue and renewal

Section 1395w-21(g) of this title (other than paragraph (2) of such section and clause (i) and the second sentence of clause (ii) of paragraph (3)(C) of such section), relating to guaranteed issue and renewal.

(vi)  Marketing material and application forms

Section 1395w-21(h) of this title, relating to approval of marketing material and application forms.

In applying clauses (ii), (iv), and (v) of this subparagraph, any reference to  section 1395w-21(e) of this title shall be treated as a reference to such section as applied pursuant to clause (iii) of this subparagraph.

(C)  Special rule

The process established under subparagraph (A) shall include, in the case of a part D eligible individual who is a full-benefit dual eligible individual (as defined in section 1396u-5(c)(6) of this title) who has failed to enroll in a prescription drug plan or an MA-PD plan, for the enrollment in a prescription drug plan that has a monthly beneficiary premium that does not exceed the premium assistance available under section 1395w-114(a)(1)(A) of this title).  If there is more than one such plan available, the Secretary shall enroll such an individual on a random basis among all such plans in the PDP region.  Nothing in the previous sentence shall prevent such an individual from declining or changing such enrollment.

(2)  *Initial enrollment period*

(A)  Program initiation

In the case of an individual who is a part D eligible individual as of November 15, 2005, there shall be an initial enrollment period that shall be the same as the annual, coordinated open election period described in section 1395w-21(e)(3)(B)(iii) of this title, as applied under paragraph (1)(B)(iii).

(B)  Continuing periods

In the case of an individual who becomes a part D eligible individual after November 15, 2005, there shall be an initial enrollment period which is the period under section 1395w-21(e)(1) of this title, as applied under paragraph (1)(B)(iii) of this section, as if "entitled to benefits under part A of this subchapter or enrolled under part B of this subchapter" were substituted for "entitled to benefits under part A of this subchapter and enrolled under part B of this subchapter", but in no case shall such period end before the period described in subparagraph (A).

(3) *Additional special enrollment periods*

The Secretary shall establish special enrollment periods, including the following:

(A)  Involuntary loss of creditable prescription drug coverage

(i)  In general

In the case of a part D eligible individual who involuntarily loses creditable prescription drug coverage (as defined in section 1395w-113(b)(4) of this title).

(ii)  Notice

In establishing special enrollment periods under clause (i), the Secretary shall take into account when the part D eligible individuals are provided notice of the loss of creditable prescription drug coverage.

(iii)  Failure to pay premium

For purposes of clause (i), a loss of coverage shall be treated as voluntary if the coverage is terminated because of failure to pay a required beneficiary premium.

(iv)  Reduction in coverage

For purposes of clause (i), a reduction in coverage so that the coverage no longer meets the requirements under section 1395w-113(b)(5) of this title (relating to actuarial equivalence) shall be treated as an involuntary loss of coverage.

(B)  Errors in enrollment

In the case described in section 1395p(h) of this title (relating to errors in enrollment), in the same manner as such section applies to part B of this subchapter.

(C)  Exceptional circumstances

In the case of part D eligible individuals who meet such exceptional conditions (in addition to those conditions applied under paragraph (1)(B)(iii)) as the Secretary may provide.

(D)  Medicaid coverage

In the case of an individual (as determined by the Secretary) who is a full-benefit dual eligible individual (as defined in section 1396v(c)(6) of this title).

(E)  Discontinuance of MA-PD election during first year of eligibility

In the case of a part D eligible individual who discontinues enrollment in an MA-PD plan under the second sentence of section 1395w-21(e)(4) of this title at the time of the election of coverage under such sentence under the original medicare fee-for-service program.

(4) *Information to facilitate enrollment*

(A) In general

Notwithstanding any other provision of law but subject to subparagraph (B), the Secretary may provide to each PDP sponsor and MA organization such identifying information about part D eligible individuals as the Secretary determines to be necessary to facilitate efficient marketing of prescription drug plans and MA-PD plans to such individuals and enrollment of such individuals in such plans.

(B) Limitation

(i) Provision of information

The Secretary may provide the information under subparagraph (A) only to the extent necessary to carry out such subparagraph.

(ii) Use of information

Such information provided by the Secretary to a PDP sponsor or an MA organization may be used by such sponsor or organization only to facilitate marketing of, and enrollment of part D eligible individuals in, prescription drug plans and MA-PD plans.

(5) *Reference to enrollment procedures for MA-PD plans*

For rules applicable to enrollment, disenrollment, termination, and change of enrollment of part D eligible individuals in MA-PD plans, see section 1395w-21 of this title.

(6) *Reference to penalties for late enrollment*

Section 1395w-113(b) of this title imposes a late enrollment penalty for part D eligible individuals who —

(A) enroll in a prescription drug plan or an MA-PD plan after the initial enrollment period described in paragraph (2); and

(B) fail to maintain continuous creditable prescription drug coverage during the period of non-enrollment.

(c) *Providing information to beneficiaries*

(1) *Activities*

The Secretary shall conduct activities that are designed to broadly disseminate information to part D eligible individuals (and prospective part D eligible individuals) regarding the coverage provided under this part. Such activities shall ensure that such information is first made available at least 30 days prior to the initial enrollment period described in subsection (b)(2)(A) of this section.

(2) *Requirements*

The activities described in paragraph (1) shall —

(A)  be similar to the activities performed by the Secretary under section 1395w-21(d) of this title, including dissemination (including through the toll-free telephone number 1-800-MEDICARE) of comparative information for prescription drug plans and MA-PD plans; and

(B)  be coordinated with the activities performed by the Secretary under such section and under section 1395b-2 of this title.

(3) *Comparative information*

(A) In general

Subject to subparagraph (B), the comparative information referred to in paragraph (2)(A) shall include a comparison of the following with respect to qualified prescription drug coverage:

(i) Benefits

The benefits provided under the plan.

(ii) Monthly beneficiary premium

The monthly beneficiary premium under the plan.

(iii) Quality and performance

The quality and performance under the plan.

(iv) Beneficiary cost-sharing

The cost-sharing required of part D eligible individuals under the plan.

(v) Consumer satisfaction surveys

The results of consumer satisfaction surveys regarding the plan conducted pursuant to section 1395w-104(d) of this title.

(B) Exception for unavailability of information

The Secretary is not required to provide comparative information under clauses (iii) and (v) of subparagraph (A) with respect to a plan —

(i) for the first plan year in which it is offered; and

(ii) for the next plan year if it is impracticable or the information is otherwise unavailable.

(4) *Information on late enrollment penalty*

The information disseminated under paragraph (1) shall include information concerning the methodology for determining the late enrollment penalty under section 1395w-113(b) of this title.

## § 1395w-102. Prescription drug benefits

(a) *Requirements —*

(1) *In general*

For purposes of this part and part C of this subchapter, the term "qualified prescription drug coverage" means either of the following:

(A) Standard prescription drug coverage with access to negotiated prices

Standard prescription drug coverage (as defined in subsection (b) of this section) and access to negotiated prices under subsection (d) of this section.

(B) Alternative prescription drug coverage with at least actuarially equivalent benefits and access to negotiated prices

Coverage of covered part D drugs which meets the alternative prescription drug coverage requirements of subsection (c) of this section and access to negotiated prices under subsection (d) of this section, but only if the benefit design of such coverage is approved by the Secretary, as provided under subsection (c) of this section.

(2) *Permitting supplemental prescription drug coverage*

(A) In general

Subject to subparagraph (B), qualified prescription drug coverage may include supplemental prescription drug coverage consisting of either or both of the following:

(i) Certain reductions in cost-sharing

(I) In general

A reduction in the annual deductible, a reduction in the coinsurance percentage, or an increase in the initial coverage limit with respect to covered part D drugs, or any combination thereof, insofar as such a reduction or increase increases the actuarial value of benefits above the actuarial value of basic prescription drug coverage.

(II) Construction

Nothing in this paragraph shall be construed as affecting the application of subsection (c)(3) of this section.

(ii) Optional drugs

Coverage of any product that would be a covered part D drug but for the application of subsection (e)(2)(A) of this section.

(B) Requirement

A PDP sponsor may not offer a prescription drug plan that provides supplemental prescription drug coverage pursuant to subparagraph (A) in an area unless the sponsor also offers a prescription drug plan in the area that only provides basic prescription drug coverage.

(3) *Basic prescription drug coverage*

For purposes of this part and part C of this subchapter, the term "basic prescription drug coverage" means either of the following:

(A) Coverage that meets the requirements of paragraph (1)(A).

(B) Coverage that meets the requirements of paragraph (1)(B) but does not have any supplemental prescription drug coverage described in paragraph (2)(A).

(4) *Application of secondary payor provisions*

The provisions of section 1395w-22(a)(4) of this title shall apply under this part in the same manner as they apply under part C of this subchapter.

(5) *Construction*

Nothing in this subsection shall be construed as changing the computation of incurred costs under subsection (b)(4) of this section.

. . . .

## § 1395w-103. Access to a choice of qualified prescription drug coverage

### (a) *Assuring access to a choice of coverage*

#### (1) *Choice of at least two plans in each area*

The Secretary shall ensure that each part D eligible individual has available, consistent with paragraph (2), a choice of enrollment in at least 2 qualifying plans (as defined in paragraph (3)) in the area in which the individual resides, at least one of which is a prescription drug plan. In any such case in which such plans are not available, the part D eligible individual shall be given the opportunity to enroll in a fallback prescription drug plan.

#### (2) *Requirement for different plan sponsors*

The requirement in paragraph (1) is not satisfied with respect to an area if only one entity offers all the qualifying plans in the area.

#### (3) *Qualifying plan defined*

For purposes of this section, the term "qualifying plan" means —

    (A) a prescription drug plan; or

    (B) an MA-PD plan described in section 1395w-21(a)(2)(A)(i) of this title that provides —

        (i) basic prescription drug coverage; or

        (ii) qualified prescription drug coverage that provides supplemental prescription drug coverage so long as there is no MA monthly supplemental beneficiary premium applied under the plan, due to the application of a credit against such premium of a rebate under section 1395w-24(b)(1)(C) of this title.

### (b) *Flexibility in risk assumed and application of fallback plan*

In order to ensure access pursuant to subsection (a) of this section in an area —

    (1) the Secretary may approve limited risk plans under section 1395w-111(f) of this title for the area; and

    (2) only if such access is still not provided in the area after applying paragraph (1), the Secretary shall provide for the offering of a fallback prescription drug plan for that area under section 1395w-111(g) of this title.

## § 1395w-104. Beneficiary protections for qualified prescription drug coverage

(a) *Dissemination of information* —

(1) *General information*

(A) Application of MA information

A PDP sponsor shall disclose, in a clear, accurate, and standardized form to each enrollee with a prescription drug plan offered by the sponsor under this part at the time of enrollment and at least annually thereafter, the information described in section 1395w-22(c)(1) of this title relating to such plan, insofar as the Secretary determines appropriate with respect to benefits provided under this part, and including the information described in subparagraph (B).

(B) Drug specific information

The information described in this subparagraph is information concerning the following:

(i) Access to specific covered part D drugs, including access through pharmacy networks.

(ii) How any formulary (including any tiered formulary structure) used by the sponsor functions, including a description of how a part D eligible individual may obtain information on the formulary consistent with paragraph (3).

(iii) Beneficiary cost-sharing requirements and how a part D eligible individual may obtain information on such requirements, including tiered or other copayment level applicable to each drug (or class of drugs), consistent with paragraph (3).

(iv) The medication therapy management program required under subsection (c) of this section.

(2) *Disclosure upon request of general coverage, utilization, and grievance information*

Upon request of a part D eligible individual who is eligible to enroll in a prescription drug plan, the PDP sponsor offering such plan shall provide information similar (as determined by the Secretary) to the information described in subparagraphs (A), (B), and (C) of section 1395w-22(c)(2) of this title to such individual.

(3) *Provision of specific information*

(A)  Response to beneficiary questions

Each PDP sponsor offering a prescription drug plan shall have a mechanism for providing specific information on a timely basis to enrollees upon request. Such mechanism shall include access to information through the use of a toll-free telephone number and, upon request, the provision of such information in writing.

(B)  Availability of information on changes in formulary through the Internet

A PDP sponsor offering a prescription drug plan shall make available on a timely basis through an Internet website information on specific changes in the formulary under the plan (including changes to tiered or preferred status of covered part D drugs).

(4) *Claims information*

A PDP sponsor offering a prescription drug plan must furnish to each enrollee in a form easily understandable to such enrollees —

(A)  an explanation of benefits (in accordance with section 1395b-7(a) of this title or in a comparable manner); and

(B)  when prescription drug benefits are provided under this part, a notice of the benefits in relation to —

(i)  the initial coverage limit for the current year; and

(ii)  the annual out-of-pocket threshold for the current year.

Notices under subparagraph (B) need not be provided more often than as specified by the Secretary and notices under subparagraph (B)(ii) shall take into account the application of section 1395w-102(b)(4)(C) of this title to the extent practicable, as specified by the Secretary.

(b) *Access to covered part D drugs*

(1) *Assuring pharmacy access*

(A)  Participation of any willing pharmacy

A prescription drug plan shall permit the participation of any pharmacy that meets the terms and conditions under the plan.

. . . .

(D)  Level playing field

Such a sponsor shall permit enrollees to receive benefits (which may include a 90-day supply of drugs or biologicals) through a pharmacy (other than a mail order pharmacy), with any differential in charge paid by such enrollees.

. . . .

(3) *Requirements on development and application of formularies*

If a PDP sponsor of a prescription drug plan uses a formulary (including the use of tiered cost-sharing), the following requirements must be met:

. . . .

(C) Inclusion of drugs in all therapeutic categories and classes
(i) In general
The formulary must include drugs within each therapeutic category and class of covered part D drugs, although not necessarily all drugs within such categories and classes.
(ii) Model guidelines
The Secretary shall request the United States Pharmacopeia to develop, in consultation with pharmaceutical benefit managers and other interested parties, a list of categories and classes that may be used by prescription drug plans under this paragraph and to revise such classification from time to time to reflect changes in therapeutic uses of covered part D drugs and the additions of new covered part D drugs.
(iii) Limitation on changes in therapeutic classification
The PDP sponsor of a prescription drug plan may not change the therapeutic categories and classes in a formulary other than at the beginning of each plan year except as the Secretary may permit to take into account new therapeutic uses and newly approved covered part D drugs.
(D) Provider and patient education
The PDP sponsor shall establish policies and procedures to educate and inform health care providers and enrollees concerning the formulary.

. . . .

# § 1395w-113. Premiums; late enrollment penalty

(a) *Monthly beneficiary premium* —

   (1) *Computation*

      (A) In general

      The monthly beneficiary premium for a prescription drug plan is the base beneficiary premium computed under paragraph (2) as adjusted under this paragraph.

      (B) Adjustment to reflect difference between bid and national average bid

         (i) Above average bid

         If for a month the amount of the standardized bid amount (as defined in paragraph (5)) exceeds the amount of the adjusted national average monthly bid amount (as defined in clause (iii)), the base beneficiary premium for the month shall be increased by the amount of such excess.

         (ii) Below average bid

         If for a month the amount of the adjusted national average monthly bid amount for the month exceeds the standardized bid amount, the base beneficiary premium for the month shall be decreased by the amount of such excess.

         (iii) Adjusted national average monthly bid amount defined

         For purposes of this subparagraph, the term "adjusted national average monthly bid amount" means the national average monthly bid amount computed under paragraph (4), as adjusted under section 1395w-115(c)(2) of this title.

      (C) Increase for supplemental prescription drug benefits

      The base beneficiary premium shall be increased by the portion of the PDP approved bid that is attributable to supplemental prescription drug benefits.

      (D) Increase for late enrollment penalty

      The base beneficiary premium shall be increased by the amount of any late enrollment penalty under subsection (b) of this section.

      (E) Decrease for low-income assistance

      The monthly beneficiary premium is subject to decrease in the case of a subsidy eligible individual under section 1395w-114 of this title.

(F) Uniform premium

Except as provided in subparagraphs (D) and (E), the monthly beneficiary premium for a prescription drug plan in a PDP region is the same for all part D eligible individuals enrolled in the plan.

. . . .

(3) *Beneficiary premium percentage*

For purposes of this subsection, the beneficiary premium percentage for any year is the percentage equal to a fraction —

(A) the numerator of which is 25.5 percent; and

(B) the denominator of which is 100 percent minus a percentage equal to —

(i) the total reinsurance payments which the Secretary estimates are payable under section 1395w-115(b) of this title with respect to the coverage year; divided by

(ii) the sum of —

(I) the amount estimated under clause (i) for the year; and

(II) the total payments which the Secretary estimates will be paid to prescription drug plans and MA-PD plans that are attributable to the standardized bid amount during the year, taking into account amounts paid by the Secretary and enrollees.

. . . .

(b) *Late enrollment penalty*

(1) *In general*

Subject to the succeeding provisions of this subsection, in the case of a part D eligible individual described in paragraph (2) with respect to a continuous period of eligibility, there shall be an increase in the monthly beneficiary premium established under subsection (a) of this section in an amount determined under paragraph (3).

(2) *Individuals subject to penalty*

A part D eligible individual described in this paragraph is, with respect to a continuous period of eligibility, an individual for whom there is a continuous period of 63 days or longer (all of which in such continuous period of eligibility) beginning on the day after the last date of the individual's initial enrollment period under section 1395w-101(b)(2) of this title and ending on the date of enrollment under a prescription drug plan or MA-PD plan during all of which the individual was not covered under any creditable prescription drug coverage.

(3) *Amount of penalty*

    (A) In general

The amount determined under this paragraph for a part D eligible individual for a continuous period of eligibility is the greater of —

        (i) an amount that the Secretary determines is actuarially sound for each uncovered month (as defined in subparagraph (B)) in the same continuous period of eligibility; or

        (ii) 1 percent of the base beneficiary premium (computed under subsection (a)(2) of this section) for each such uncovered month in such period.

    (B) Uncovered month defined

For purposes of this subsection, the term "uncovered month" means, with respect to a part D eligible individual, any month beginning after the end of the initial enrollment period under section 1395w-101(b)(2) of this title unless the individual can demonstrate that the individual had creditable prescription drug coverage (as defined in paragraph (4)) for any portion of such month.

(4) *Creditable prescription drug coverage defined*

For purposes of this part, the term "creditable prescription drug coverage" means any of the following coverage, but only if the coverage meets the requirement of paragraph (5):

    (A) Coverage under prescription drug plan or MA-PD plan

Coverage under a prescription drug plan or under an MA-PD plan.

    (B) Medicaid

Coverage under a medicaid plan under subchapter XIX or under a waiver under section 1315 of this title.

    (C) Group health plan

Coverage under a group health plan, including a health benefits plan under chapter 89 of Title 5, (commonly known as the Federal employees health benefits program), and a qualified retiree prescription drug plan (as defined in section 1395w-132(a)(2) of this title).

(D) State pharmaceutical assistance program

Coverage under a State pharmaceutical assistance program described in section 1395w-133(b)(1) of this title.

(E) Veterans' coverage of prescription drugs

Coverage for veterans, and survivors and dependents of veterans, under chapter 17 of Title 38.

(F) Prescription drug coverage under medigap policies

Coverage under a medicare supplemental policy under section 1395ss of this title that provides benefits for prescription drugs (whether or not such coverage conforms to the standards for packages of benefits under section 1395ss(p)(1) of this title).

(G) Military coverage (including TRICARE)

Coverage under chapter 55 of Title 10.

(H) Other coverage

Such other coverage as the Secretary determines appropriate.

## § 1395w-114. Premium and cost-sharing subsidies for low-income individuals

(a) *Income-related subsidies for individuals with income up to 150 percent of poverty line —*

(1) *Individuals with income below 135 percent of poverty line*

In the case of a subsidy eligible individual (as defined in paragraph (3)) who is determined to have income that is below 135 percent of the poverty line applicable to a family of the size involved and who meets the resources requirement described in paragraph (3)(D) or who is covered under this paragraph under paragraph (3)(B)(i), the individual is entitled under this section to the following:

(A) Full premium subsidy

An income-related premium subsidy equal to —

(i) 100 percent of the amount described in subsection (b)(1) of this section, but not to exceed the premium amount specified in subsection (b)(2)(B) of this section; plus

(ii) 80 percent of any late enrollment penalties imposed under section 1395w-113(b) of this title for the first 60 months in which such penalties are imposed for that individual, and 100 percent of any such penalties for any subsequent month.

(B) Elimination of deductible

A reduction in the annual deductible applicable under section 1395w-102(b)(1) of this title to $0.

(C)  Continuation of coverage above the initial coverage limit

The continuation of coverage from the initial coverage limit (under  paragraph (3) of section 1395w-102(b) of this title) for expenditures incurred through the total amount of expenditures at which benefits are available under paragraph (4) of such section, subject to the reduced cost-sharing described in subparagraph (D).

(D)  Reduction in cost-sharing below out-of-pocket threshold

(i)  Institutionalized individuals

In the case of an individual who is a full-benefit dual eligible individual and who is an institutionalized individual or couple (as defined in section 1396a(q)(1)(B) of this title), the elimination of any beneficiary coinsurance described in section 1395w-102(b)(2) of this title (for all amounts through the total amount of expenditures at which benefits are available under section 1395w-102(b)(4) of this title).

(ii)  Lowest income dual eligible individuals

In the case of an individual not described in clause (i) who is a full-benefit dual eligible individual and whose income does not exceed 100 percent of the poverty line applicable to a family of the size involved, the substitution for the beneficiary coinsurance described in section 1395w-102(b)(2) of this title (for all amounts through the total amount of expenditures at which benefits are available under section 1395w-102(b)(4) of this title) of a copayment amount that does not exceed $1 for a generic drug or a preferred drug that is a multiple source drug (as defined in section 1396r-8(k)(7)(A)(i) of this title) and $3 for any other drug, or, if less, the copayment amount applicable to an individual under clause (iii).

(iii)  Other individuals

In the case of an individual not described in clause (i) or (ii), the substitution for the beneficiary coinsurance described in section 1395w-102(b)(2) of this title (for all amounts through the total amount of expenditures at which benefits are available under section 1395w-1022(b)(4) of this title) of a copayment amount that does not exceed the copayment amount specified under section 1395w-102(b)(4)(A)(i)(I) of this title for the drug and year involved.

(E) Elimination of cost-sharing above annual out-of-pocket threshold

The elimination of any cost-sharing imposed under section 1395w-102(b)(4)(A) of this title.

(2) *Other individuals with income below 150 percent of poverty line*

In the case of a subsidy eligible individual who is not described in paragraph (1), the individual is entitled under this section to the following:

(A) Sliding scale premium subsidy

An income-related premium subsidy determined on a linear sliding scale ranging from 100 percent of the amount described in paragraph (1)(A) for individuals with incomes at or below 135 percent of such level to 0 percent of such amount for individuals with incomes at 150 percent of such level.

(B) Reduction of deductible

A reduction in the annual deductible applicable under section 1395w-102(b)(1) of this title to $50.

(C) Continuation of coverage above the initial coverage limit

The continuation of coverage from the initial coverage limit (under paragraph (3) of section 1395w-102(b) of this title) for expenditures incurred through the total amount of expenditures at which benefits are available under paragraph (4) of such section, subject to the reduced coinsurance described in subparagraph (D).

(D) Reduction in cost-sharing below out-of-pocket threshold

The substitution for the beneficiary coinsurance described in section 1395w-102(b)(2) of this title (for all amounts above the deductible under subparagraph (B) through the total amount of expenditures at which benefits are available under section 1395w-102(b)(4) of this title) of coinsurance of "15 percent" instead of coinsurance of "25 percent' in section 1395w-102(b)(2) of this title.

(E) Reduction of cost-sharing above annual out-of-pocket threshold

Subject to subsection (c) of this section, the substitution for the cost-sharing imposed under section 1395w-102(b)(4)(A) of this title of a copayment or coinsurance not to exceed the copayment or coinsurance amount specified under section 1395w-102(b)(4)(A)(i)(I) of this title for the drug and year involved.

(3)  *Determination of eligibility*

(A)  Subsidy eligible individual defined

For purposes of this part, subject to subparagraph (F), the term "subsidy eligible individual" means a part D eligible individual who —

(i)  is enrolled in a prescription drug plan or MA-PD plan;

(ii)  has income below 150 percent of the poverty line applicable to a family of the size involved; and

(iii)  meets the resources requirement described in subparagraph (D) or (E).

. . . .

(C)  Income determinations

For purposes of applying this section —

(i)  in the case of a part D eligible individual who is not treated as a subsidy eligible individual under subparagraph (B)(v), income shall be determined in the manner described in section 1396d(p)(1)(B) of this title, without regard to the application of section 1396a(r)(2) of this title; and

(ii)  the term "poverty line" has the meaning given such term in 9902(2) of this title, including any revision required by such section.

Nothing in clause (i) shall be construed to affect the application of  section 1396a(r)(2) of this title for the determination of eligibility for medical assistance under subchapter XIX of this chapter.

(D) Resource standard applied to full low-income subsidy to be based on three times SSI resource standard

The resources requirement of this subparagraph is that an individual's resources (as determined under section 1382b of this title for purposes of the supplemental security income program) do not exceed —

(i)  for 2006 three times the maximum amount of resources that an individual may have and obtain benefits under that program; and

(ii)  for a subsequent year the resource limitation established under this clause for the previous year increased by the annual percentage increase in the consumer price index (all items; U.S. city average) as of September of such previous year.

Any resource limitation established under clause (ii) that is not a multiple of $10 shall be rounded to the nearest multiple of $10.

(E)  Alternative resource standard

(i)  In general

The resources requirement of this subparagraph is that an individual's resources (as determined under section 1382b of this title for purposes of the supplemental security income program) do not exceed —

(I)  for 2006, $10,000 (or $20,000 in the case of the combined value of the individual's assets or resources and the assets or resources of the individual's spouse); and

(II)  for a subsequent year the dollar amounts specified in this subclause (or subclause (I)) for the previous year increased by the annual percentage increase in the consumer price index (all items; U.S. city average) as of September of such previous year.

Any dollar amount established under subclause (II) that is not a multiple of $10 shall be rounded to the nearest multiple of $10.

. . . .

## § 1395x.  Definitions

For purpose of this title —

(a)  *Spell of illness*

The term "spell of illness" with respect to any individual means a period of consecutive days —

(1) beginning with the first day (not included in a previous spell of illness) (A) on which such individual is furnished inpatient hospital services, inpatient critical access hospital services or extended care services, and (B) which occurs in a month for which he is entitled to benefits under part A, and

(2) ending with the close of the first period of 60 consecutive days thereafter on each of which he is neither an inpatient of a hospital or critical access hospital nor an inpatient of a facility described in section 1819(a)(2) or subsection (y)(1).

(b) *Inpatient hospital services*

The term "inpatient hospital services" means the following items and services furnished to an inpatient of a hospital and (except as provided in paragraph (3)) by the hospital —

    (1) bed and board;

    (2) such nursing services and other related services, such use of hospital facilities, and such medical social services as are ordinarily furnished by the hospital for the care and treatment of inpatients, and such drugs, biologicals, supplies, appliances, and equipment, for use in the hospital, as are ordinarily furnished by such hospital for the care and treatment of inpatients; and

    (3) such other diagnostic or therapeutic items or services, furnished by the hospital or by others under arrangements with them made by the hospital, as are ordinarily furnished to inpatients either by such hospital or by others under such arrangements;

excluding, however —

    (4) medical or surgical services provided by a physician, resident, or, services described by subsection (s)(2)(K), certified nurse-midwife services, qualified psychologist services, and services of a certified registered nurse anesthetist; and

    (5) the services of a private-duty nurse or other private-duty attendant.

Paragraph (4) shall not apply to services provided in a hospital by —

    (6) an intern or a resident-in-training under a teaching program approved by the Council on Medical Education of the American Medical Association or, in the case of an osteopathic hospital, approved by the Committee on Hospitals of the Bureau of Professional Education of the American Osteopathic Association, or, in the case of services in a hospital or osteopathic hospital by an intern or resident-in-training in the field of dentistry, approved by the Council on Dental Education of the American Dental Association, or in the case of services in a hospital or osteopathic hospital by an intern or resident-in-training in the field of podiatry, approved by the Council on Podiatric Medical Education of the American Podiatric Medical Association; or

    (7) a physician where the hospital has a teaching program approved as specified in paragraph (6), if (A) the hospital elects to receive any payment due under this title for reasonable costs of such services, and (B) all physicians in such hospital agree not to bill

charges for professional services rendered in such hospital to individuals covered under the insurance program established by this title.

(c) *Inpatient psychiatric hospital services*

The term "inpatient psychiatric hospital services" means inpatient hospital services furnished to an inpatient of a psychiatric hospital.

. . . .

(e) *Hospital*

The term "hospital" (except for purposes of sections 1814(d), 1814(f), and 1835(b), subsection (a)(2) of this section, paragraph (7) of this subsection, and subsection (i) of this section) means an institution which —

(1) is primarily engaged in providing, by or under the supervision of physicians, to inpatients (A) diagnostic services and therapeutic services for medical diagnosis, treatment, and care of injured, disabled, or sick persons, or (B) rehabilitation services for the rehabilitation of injured, disabled, or sick persons;

(2) maintains clinical records on all patients;

(3) has bylaws in effect with respect to its staff of physicians;

(4) has a requirement that every patient with respect to whom payment may be made under this title must be under the care of a physician, except that a patient receiving qualified psychologist services (as defined in subsection (ii)) may be under the care of a clinical psychologist with respect to such services to the extent permitted under State law;

(5) provides 24-hour nursing service rendered or supervised by a registered professional nurse, and has a licensed practical nurse or registered professional nurse on duty at all times; except that until January 1, 1979, the Secretary is authorized to waive the requirement of this paragraph for any one-year period with respect to any institution, insofar as such requirement relates to the provision of twenty-four-hour nursing service rendered or supervised by a registered professional nurse (except that in any event a registered professional nurse must be present on the premises to render or supervise the nursing service provided, during at least the regular daytime shift), where immediately preceding such one-year period he finds that —

(A) such institution is located in a rural area and the supply of hospital services in such area is not sufficient to meet the needs of individuals residing therein,

(B) the failure of such institution to qualify as a hospital would seriously reduce the availability of such services to such individuals, and

(C) such institution has made and continues to make a good faith effort to comply with this paragraph, but such compliance is impeded by the lack of qualified nursing personnel in such area;

. . . .

(f) *Psychiatric hospital*

The term "psychiatric hospital" means an institution which —

(1) is primarily engaged in providing, by or under the supervision of a physician, psychiatric services for the diagnosis and treatment of mentally ill persons;

(2) satisfies the requirements of paragraphs (3) through (9) of subsection (e);

(3) maintains clinical records on all patients and maintains such records as the Secretary finds to be necessary to determine the degree and intensity of the treatment provided to individuals entitled to hospital insurance benefits under part A and

(4) meets such staffing requirements as the Secretary finds necessary for the institution to carry out an active program of treatment for individuals who are furnished services in the institution.

In the case of an institution which satisfies paragraphs (1) and (2) of the preceding sentence and which contains a distinct part which also satisfies paragraphs (3) and (4) of such sentence, such distinct part shall be considered to be a "psychiatric hospital."

(g) *Outpatient occupational therapy services*

The term "outpatient occupational therapy services" has the meaning given the term "outpatient physical therapy services" in subsection (p), except that "occupational" shall be substituted for "physical" each place it appears therein.

## (h) *Extended care services*

The term "extended care services" means the following items and services furnished to an inpatient of a skilled nursing facility and (except as provided in paragraphs (3), (6), and (7)) by such skilled nursing facility —

>　　(1) nursing care provided by or under the supervision of a registered professional nurse;

>　　(2) bed and board in connection with the furnishing of such nursing care;

>　　(3) physical or occupational therapy or speech-language pathology services furnished by the skilled nursing facility or by others under arrangements with them made by the facility;

>　　(4) medical social services;

>　　(5) such drugs, biologicals, supplies, appliances, and equipment, furnished for use in the skilled nursing facility, as are ordinarily furnished by such facility for the care and treatment of inpatients;

>　　(6) medical services provided by an intern or resident-in-training of a hospital with which the facility has in effect a transfer agreement (meeting the requirements of subsection (l)), under a teaching program of such hospital approved as provided in the last sentence of subsection (b), and other diagnostic or therapeutic services provided by a hospital with which the facility has such an agreement in effect; and

>　　(7) such other services necessary to the health of the patients as are generally provided by skilled nursing facilities, or by others under arrangements with them made by the facility;

excluding, however, any item or service if it would not be included under subsection (b) if furnished to an inpatient of a hospital.

## (i) *Post-hospital extended care services*

The term "post-hospital extended care services" means extended care services furnished an individual after transfer from a hospital in which he was an inpatient for not less than 3 consecutive days before his discharge from the hospital in connection with such transfer. For purposes of the preceding sentence, items and services shall be deemed to have been furnished to an individual after transfer from a hospital, and he shall be deemed to have been an inpatient in the hospital immediately before transfer therefrom, if he is admitted to the skilled nursing facility

(A) within 30 days after discharge from such hospital, or (B) within such time as it would be medically appropriate to begin an active course of treatment, in the case of an individual whose condition is such that skilled nursing facility care would not be medically appropriate within 30 days after discharge from a hospital; and an individual shall be deemed not to have been discharged from a skilled nursing facility if, within 30 days after discharge therefrom, he is admitted to such facility or any other skilled nursing facility.

. . . .

## (m)  *Home health services*

The term "home health services" means the following items and services furnished to an individual, who is under the care of a physician, by a home health agency or by others under arrangements with them made by such agency, under a plan (for furnishing such items and services to such individual) established and periodically reviewed by a physician, which items and services are, except as provided in paragraph (7), provided on a visiting basis in a place of residence used as such individual's home —

(1) part-time or intermittent nursing care provided by or under the supervision of a registered professional nurse;

(2) physical or occupational therapy or speech-language pathology services;

(3) medical social services under the direction of a physician;

(4) to the extent permitted in regulations, part-time or intermittent services of a home health aide who has successfully completed a training program approved by the Secretary;

(5) medical supplies (including catheters, catheter supplies, ostomy bags, and supplies related to ostomy care, and a covered osteoporosis drug (as defined in subsection (kk)), but excluding other drugs and biologicals) and durable medical equipment while under such a plan;

(6) in the case of a home health agency which is affiliated or under common control with a hospital, medical services provided by an intern or resident-in-training of such hospital, under a teaching program of such hospital approved as provided in the last sentence of subsection (b); and

(7) any of the foregoing items and services which are provided on an out-patient basis, under arrangements made by the home health agency, at a hospital or skilled nursing facility, or at a rehabilitation

center which meets such standards as may be prescribed in regulations, and —

> (A) the furnishing of which involves the use of equipment of such a nature that the items and services cannot readily be made available to the individual in such place of residence, or
>
> (B) which are furnished at such facility while he is there to receive any such item or service described in clause (A),

but not including transportation of the individual in connection with any such item or service;

excluding, however, any item or service if it would not be included under subsection (b) if furnished to an inpatient of a hospital. For purposes of paragraphs (1) and (4), the term "part-time or intermittent services" means skilled nursing and home health aide services furnished any number of days per week as long as they are furnished (combined) less than 8 hours each day and 28 or fewer hours each week (or, subject to review on a case-by-case basis as to the need for care, less than 8 hours each day and 35 or fewer hours per week). For purposes of sections 1814(a)(2)(C) and 1835(a)(2)(A), "intermittent" means skilled nursing care that is either provided or needed on fewer than 7 days each week, or less than 8 hours of each day for periods of 21 days or less (with extensions in exceptional circumstances when the need for additional care is finite and predictable).

(n) *Durable medical equipment*

The term "durable medical equipment" includes iron lungs, oxygen tents, hospital beds, and wheelchairs (which may include a power-operated vehicle that may be appropriately used as a wheelchair, but only where the use of such a vehicle is determined to be necessary on the basis of the individual's medical and physical condition and the vehicle meets such safety requirements as the Secretary may prescribe) used in the patient's home (including an institution used as his home other than an institution that meets the requirements of subsection (e)(1) of this section or of section 1819(a)(1)), whether furnished on a rental basis or purchased, and includes blood-testing strips and blood glucose monitors for individuals with diabetes without regard to whether the individual has Type I or Type II diabetes or to the individual's use of insulin (as determined under standards established by the Secretary in consultation with the appropriate organizations); except that such term does not include such equipment furnished by a supplier who has used, for the demonstration and use of specific equipment, an individual who has not met such minimum training standards as the Secretary may establish with respect to the demonstration and use of such specific equipment. With respect to a seat-lift chair, such term includes only the seat-lift mechanism and does not include the chair.

(o) *Home health agency*

The term "home health agency" means a public agency or private organization, or a subdivision of such an agency or organization, which —

(1) is primarily engaged in providing skilled nursing services and other therapeutic services;

(2) has policies, established by a group of professional personnel (associated with the agency or organization), including one or more physicians and one or more registered professional nurses, to govern the services (referred to in paragraph (1)) which it provides, and provides for supervision of such services by a physician or registered professional nurse;

(3) maintains clinical records on all patients;

(4) in the case of an agency or organization in any State in which State or applicable local law provides for the licensing of agencies or organizations of this nature, (A) is licensed pursuant to such law, or (B) is approved, by the agency of such State or locality responsible for licensing agencies or organizations of this nature, as meeting the standards established for such licensing;

(5) has in effect an overall plan and budget that meets the requirements of subsection (z);

(6) meets the conditions of participation specified in section 1891(a) such other conditions of participation as the Secretary may find necessary in the interest of the health and safety of individuals who are furnished services by such agency or organization;

(7) provides the Secretary with a surety bond —

(A) effective for a period of 4 years (as specified by the Secretary) or in the case of a change in the ownership or control of the agency (as determined by the Secretary) during or after such 4-year period, an additional period of time that the Secretary determines appropriate, such additional period not to exceed 4 years from the date of such change in ownership or control;

(B) in a form specified by the Secretary; and

(C) for a year in the period described in subparagraph (A) in an amount that is equal to the lesser of $50,000 or 10 percent of the aggregate amount of payments to the agency under this title and title XIX for that year, as estimated by the Secretary; and

(8) meets such additional requirements (including conditions relating to bonding or establishing of escrow accounts as the Secretary finds necessary for the financial security of the program) as the Secretary finds necessary for the effective and efficient operation of the program;

except that for purposes of part A such term shall not include any agency or organization which is primarily for the care and treatment of mental diseases. The Secretary may waive the requirement of a surety bond under paragraph (7) in the case of an agency or organization that provides a comparable surety bond under State law.

(p) *Outpatient physical therapy services*

The term "outpatient physical therapy services" means physical therapy services furnished by a provider of services, a clinic, rehabilitation agency, or a public health agency, or by others under an arrangement with, and under the supervision of, such provider, clinic, rehabilitation agency, or public health agency to an individual as an outpatient —

(1) who is under the care of a physician (as defined in paragraph (1), (3), or (4) of section 1861(r) [subsec. (r) of this section]), and

(2) with respect to whom a plan prescribing the type, amount, and duration of physical therapy services that are to be furnished such individual has been established by a physician (as so defined) or by a qualified physical therapist and is periodically reviewed by a physician (as so defined);

excluding, however —

(3) any item or service if it would not be included under subsection (b) if furnished to an inpatient of a hospital; and

(4) any such service —

(A) if furnished by a clinic or rehabilitation agency, or by others under arrangements with such clinic or agency, unless such clinic or rehabilitation agency —

(i) provides an adequate program of physical therapy services for outpatients and has the facilities and personnel required for such program or required for the supervision of such a program, in accordance with such requirements as the Secretary may specify,

(ii) has policies, established by a group of professional personnel, including one or more physicians (associated with the clinic or rehabilitation agency) and one or more qualified physical therapists, to govern the services (referred to in clause (i)) it provides,

(iii) maintains clinical records on all patients,

(iv) if such clinic or agency is situated in a State in which State or applicable local law provides for the licensing of institutions of this nature, (I) is licensed pursuant to such law, or (II) is approved by the agency of such State or locality responsible for licensing institutions of this nature, as meeting the standards established for such licensing; and

(v) meets such other conditions relating to the health and safety of individuals who are furnished services by such clinic or agency on an outpatient basis, as the Secretary may find necessary, and provides the Secretary on a continuing basis with a surety bond in a form specified by the Secretary and in an amount that is not less than $50,000,or

(B) if furnished by a public health agency, unless such agency meets such other conditions relating to health and safety of individuals who are furnished services by such agency on an outpatient basis, as the Secretary may find necessary.

The term "outpatient physical therapy services" also includes physical therapy services furnished an individual by a physical therapist (in his office or in such individual's home) who meets licensing and other standards prescribed by the Secretary in regulations, otherwise than under an arrangement with and under the supervision of a provider of services, clinic, rehabilitation agency, or public health agency, if the furnishing of such services meets such conditions relating to health and safety as the Secretary may find necessary. In addition, such term includes physical therapy services which meet the requirements of the first sentence of this subsection except that they are furnished to an individual as an inpatient of a hospital or extended care facility. The term "outpatient physical therapy services" also includes speech-language pathology services furnished by a provider of services, a clinic, rehabilitation agency, or by a public health agency, or by others under an arrangement with, and under the supervision of, such provider, clinic, rehabilitation agency, or public health agency to an individual as an outpatient, subject to the conditions prescribed in this subsection. Nothing in this subsection shall be construed as requiring, with respect to outpatients who are not entitled to benefits under this title, a physical therapist to provide outpatient physical therapy services only to outpatients who are under the care of a physician or pursuant to a plan of care established by a physician. The Secretary may waive the requirement of a surety bond under paragraph (4)(A)(v) in the case of a clinic or agency that provides a comparable surety bond under State law.

(q) *Physicians' services*

The term "physicians' services" means professional services performed by physicians, including surgery, consultation, and home, office, and institutional calls (but not including services described in subsection (b)(6)).

(r) *Physician*

The term "physician", when used in connection with the performance of any function or action, means (1) a doctor of medicine or osteopathy legally authorized to practice medicine and surgery by the State in which he performs such function or action (including a physician within the meaning of section 1101(a)(7)), (2) a doctor of dental surgery or of dental medicine who is legally authorized to practice dentistry by the State in which he performs such function and who is acting within the scope of his license when he performs such functions, (3) a doctor of podiatric medicine for the purposes of subsections (k), (m), (p)(1), and (s) of this section and sections 1814(a), 1832(a)(2)(F)(ii), and 1835 but only with respect to functions which he is legally authorized to perform as such by the State in which he performs them, (4) a doctor of optometry, but only for purposes of subsection (p)(1) and with respect to the provision of items or services described in subsection (s) which he is legally authorized to perform as a doctor of optometry by the State in which he performs them, or (5) a chiropractor who is licensed as such by the State (or in a State which does not license chiropractors as such, is legally authorized to perform the services of a chiropractor in the jurisdiction in which he performs such services), and who meets uniform minimum standards promulgated by the Secretary, but only for the purpose of sections 1861(s)(1) and 1861(s)(2)(A) [subsecs. (s)(1) and (s)(2)(A) of this section] and only with respect to treatment by means of manual manipulation of the spine (to correct a subluxation which he is legally authorized to perform by the State or jurisdiction in which such treatment is provided. For the purposes of section 1862(a)(4) and subject to the limitations and conditions provided in the previous sentence, such term includes a doctor of one of the arts, specified in such previous sentence, legally authorized to practice such art in the country in which the inpatient hospital services (referred to in such section 1862(a)(4) are furnished.

. . . .

## § 1395y. Exclusions from coverage and medicare as secondary payer

(a) *Items or services specifically excluded*

Notwithstanding any other provision of this title, no payment may be made under part A or part B for any expenses incurred for items or services —

    (1)  (A) which, except for items and services described in a succeeding subparagraph, are not reasonable and necessary for the diagnosis or treatment of illness or injury or to improve the functioning of a malformed body member,

    (B) in the case of items and services described in section 1861(s)(10), which are not reasonable and necessary for the prevention of illness,

    (C) in the case of hospice care, which are not reasonable and necessary for the palliation or management of terminal illness,

    (D) in the case of clinical care items and services provided with the concurrence of the Secretary and with respect to research and experimentation conducted by, or under contract with, the Medicare Payment Advisory Commission or the Secretary, which are not reasonable and necessary to carry out the purposes of section 1886(e)(6),

    (E) in the case of research conducted pursuant to section 1142, which is not reasonable and necessary to carry out the purposes of that section,

    (F) in the case of screening mammography, which is performed more frequently than is covered under section 1834(c)(2) or which is not conducted by a facility described in section 1834(c)(1)(B), in the case of screening pap smear and screening pelvic exam, which is performed more frequently than is provided under section 1861(nn), and, in the case of screening for glaucoma, which is performed more frequently than is provided under section 1861(uu),

(G) in the case of prostate cancer screening tests (as defined in section 1861(oo)), which are performed more frequently than is covered under such section,

(H) in the case of colorectal cancer screening tests, which are performed more frequently than is covered under section 1834(d), and

(I) the frequency and duration of home health services which are in excess of normative guidelines that the Secretary shall establish by regulation;

. . . .

## § 1395ss. Certification of Medicare supplemental health insurance policies

(a) *Submission of policy by insurer*

(1) The Secretary shall establish a procedure whereby medicare supplemental policies (as defined in subsection (g)(1)) may be certified by the Secretary as meeting minimum standards and requirements set forth in subsection (c). Such procedure shall provide an opportunity for any insurer to submit any such policy, and such additional data as the Secretary finds necessary, to the Secretary for his examination and for his certification thereof as meeting the standards and requirements set forth in subsection (c). Subject to subsections (k)(3), (m), and (n), such certification shall remain in effect if the insurer files a notarized statement with the Secretary no later than June 30 of each year stating that the policy continues to meet such standards and requirements and if the insurer submits such additional data as the Secretary finds necessary to independently verify the accuracy of such notarized statement. Where the Secretary determines such a policy meets (or continues to meet) such standards and requirements, he shall authorize the insurer to have printed on such policy (but only in accordance with such requirements and conditions as the Secretary may prescribe) an emblem which the Secretary shall cause to be designed for use as an indication that a policy has received the Secretary's certification. The Secretary shall provide each State commissioner or superintendent of insurance with a list of all the policies which have received his certification.

(2) No medicare supplemental policy may be issued in a State on or after the date specified in subsection (p)(1)(c) unless —

(A) the State's regulatory program under subsection (b)(1) provides for the application and enforcement of the standards and requirements set forth in such subsection (including the 1991 NAIC Model Regulation or 1991 Federal Regulation (as the case may be)) by the date specified in subsection (p)(1)(c); or

(B) if the State's program does not provide for the application and enforcement of such standards and requirements, the policy has been certified by the Secretary under paragraph (1) as meeting the standards and requirements set forth in subsection (c) (including such applicable standards) by such date.

Any person who issues a medicare supplemental policy, on and after the effective date specified in subsection (p)(1)(C), in violation of this paragraph is subject to a civil money penalty of not to exceed $25,000 for each such violation. The provisions of section 1128A (other than the first sentence of subsection (a) and other than subsection (b)) shall apply to a civil money penalty under the previous sentence in the same manner as such provisions apply to a penalty or proceeding under section 1128A(a).

(b) *Standards and requirements; periodic review by Secretary*

(1) [Caution: For application and termination of Nov. 5, 1990 amendment of this section, see § 4358(c) of Act Nov. 5, 1990, P.L. 101-508, which appears as a note to this section.] Any medicare supplemental policy issued in any State which the Secretary determines has established under State law a regulatory program that —

(A) [Caution: For application and termination of 1990 amendment, see § 4358(c) of Act Nov. 4, 1990, P.L. 101-508, which appears as a note to this section.] provides for the application and enforcement of standards with respect to such policies equal to or more stringent than the NAIC Model Standards (as defined in subsection (g)(2)(A)), except as otherwise provided by subparagraph (H);

(B) includes requirements equal to or more stringent than the requirements described in paragraphs (2) through (5) of subsection (c);

(C) provides that —

(i) information with respect to the actual ratio of benefits provided to premiums collected under such policies will be reported to the State on forms conforming to those developed by the National Association of Insurance Commissioners for such purpose, or

(ii) such ratios will be monitored under the program in an alternative manner approved by the Secretary, and that a copy of each such policy, the most recent premium for each such policy, and a listing of the ratio of benefits provided to premiums collected for the most recent 3-year period for each such policy issued or sold in the State is maintained and made available to interested persons;

(D) provides for application and enforcement of the standards and requirements described in subparagraphs (A), (B), and (C) to all medicare supplemental policies (as defined in subsection (g)(1)) issued in such State,

(E) provides the Secretary periodically (but at least annually) with a list containing the name and address of the issuer of each such policy and the name and number of each such policy (including an indication of policies that have been previously approved, newly approved, or withdrawn from approval since the previous list was provided),

(F) reports to the Secretary on the implementation and enforcement of standards and requirements of this paragraph at intervals established by the Secretary,

(G) provides for a process for approving or disapproving proposed premium increases with respect to such policies, and establishes a policy for the holding of public hearings prior to approval of a premium increase, and

(H) [Caution: For application and termination of this subparagraph, see § 4358(c) of Act Nov. 4, 1990, P.L. 101-508, which appears as a note to this section.] in the case of a policy that meets the standards under subparagraph (A) except that benefits under the policy are limited to items and services furnished by certain entities (or reduced benefits are provided when items or services are furnished by other entities), provides for the application of requirements equal to or more stringent than the requirements under subsection (t),

shall be deemed (subject to subsections (k)(3), (m), and (n), for so long as the Secretary finds that such State regulatory program continues to meet the standards and requirements of this paragraph) to meet the standards and requirements set forth in subsection (c). Each report required under subparagraph (F) shall include information on loss ratios of policies sold in the State, frequency and types of instances in which policies approved by the State fail to meet the standards and requirements of this paragraph, actions taken by the State to bring such policies into compliance, information regarding State programs implementing consumer protection provisions, and such further information as the Secretary in consultation with the National Association of Insurance Commissioners may specify.

(2) The Secretary periodically shall review State regulatory programs to determine if they continue to meet the standards and requirements specified in paragraph (1). If the Secretary finds that a State regulatory program no longer meets the standards and requirements, before making a final determination, the Secretary shall provide the State an opportunity to adopt such a plan of correction as would permit the State regulatory program to continue to meet such standards and requirements. If the Secretary makes a final determination that the State regulatory program, after such an opportunity, fails to meet such standards and requirements, the program shall no longer be considered to have in operation a program meeting such standards and requirements.

(3) Notwithstanding paragraph (1), a medicare supplemental policy offered in a State shall not be deemed to meet the standards and requirements set forth in subsection (c), with respect to an advertisement (whether through written, radio, or television medium) used (or, at a State's option, to be used) for the policy in the State, unless the entity issuing the policy provides a copy of each advertisement to the Commissioner of Insurance (or comparable officer identified by the Secretary) of that State for review or approval to the extent it may be required under State law.

(c) *Requisite findings*

The Secretary shall certify under this section any medicare supplemental policy, or continue certification of such a policy, only if he finds that such policy (or, with respect to paragraph (3) or the requirement described in subsection (s), the issuer of the policy) —

> (1) [Caution: For application and termination of Nov. 5, 1990 amendment of this section, see § 4358(c) of Act Nov. 5, 1990, P.L. 101-508, which appears as a note to this section.] meets or exceeds (either in a single policy or, in the case of nonprofit hospital and medical service associations, in one or more policies issued in conjunction with one another) the NAIC Model Standards (except as otherwise provided by subsection (t));
>
> (2) meets the requirements of subsection (r);
>
> (3) (A) accepts a notice under section 1842(h)(3)(B) as a claim form for benefits under such policy in lieu of any claim form otherwise required and agrees to make a payment determination on the basis of the information contained in such notice;

(B) where such a notice is received —

(i) provides notice to such physician or supplier and the beneficiary of the payment determination under the policy, and

(ii) provides any payment covered by such policy directly to the participating physician or supplier involved;

(C) provides each enrollee at the time of enrollment a card listing the policy name and number and a single mailing address to which notices under section 1842(h)(3)(B) respecting the policy are to be sent;

(D) agrees to pay any user fees established under section 1842(h)(3)(B) with respect to information transmitted to the issuer of the policy; and

(E) provides to the Secretary at least annually, for transmittal to carriers, a single mailing address to which notices under section 1842(h)(3)(B) respecting the policy are to be sent;

(4) may, during a period of not less than 30 days after the policy is issued, be returned for a full refund of any premiums paid (without regard to the manner in which the purchase of the policy was solicited); and

(5) meets the applicable requirements of subsections (o) through (t).

(d) *Criminal penalties; civil penalties for certain violations*

(1) Whoever knowingly and willfully makes or causes to be made or induces or seeks to induce the making of any false statement or representation of a material fact with respect to the compliance of any policy with the standards and requirements set forth in subsection (c) or in regulations promulgated pursuant to such subsection, or with respect to the use of the emblem designed by the Secretary under subsection (a), shall be fined under title 18, United States Code, or imprisoned not more than 5 years, or both, and, in addition to or in lieu of such a criminal penalty, is subject to a civil money penalty of not to exceed $5,000 for each such prohibited act.

(2) Whoever falsely assumes or pretends to be acting, or misrepresents in any way that he is acting, under the authority of or in association with, the program of health insurance established by this title, or any Federal agency, for the purpose of selling or attempting to sell insurance, or in such pretended character demands, or obtains money, paper, documents, or anything of value, shall be fined under title 18,

United States Code, or imprisoned not more than 5 years, or both, and, in addition to or in lieu of such a criminal penalty, is subject to a civil money penalty of not to exceed $5,000 for each such prohibited act.

(3) (A) (i) It is unlawful for a person to sell or issue to an individual entitled to benefits under part A or enrolled under part B of this title (including an individual electing a Medicare + Choice plan under section 1851) —

> (I) a health insurance policy with knowledge that the policy duplicates health benefits to which the individual is otherwise entitled under this title or title XIX,

> (II) in the case of an individual not electing a Medicare + Choice plan[,] a medicare supplemental policy with knowledge that the individual is entitled to benefits under another medicare supplemental policy or in the case of an individual electing a Medicare + Choice plan, a medicare supplemental policy with knowledge that the policy duplicates health benefits to which the individual is otherwise entitled under the Medicare + Choice plan or under another medicare supplemental policy, or

> (III) a health insurance policy (other than a medicare supplemental policy) with knowledge that the policy duplicates health benefits to which the individual is otherwise entitled, other than benefits to which the individual is entitled under a requirement of State or Federal law.

> (ii) Whoever violates clause (i) shall be fined under title 18, United States Code, or imprisoned not more than 5 years, or both, and, in addition to or in lieu of such a criminal penalty, is subject to a civil money penalty of not to exceed $25,000 (or $15,000 in the case of a person other than the issuer of the policy) for each such prohibited act.

> (iii) A seller (who is not the issuer of a health insurance policy) shall not be considered to violate clause (i)(II) with respect to the sale of a medicare supplemental policy if the policy is sold in compliance with subparagraph (B).

> (iv) For purposes of this subparagraph, a health insurance policy (other than a Medicare supplemental policy) providing for benefits which are payable to or on behalf of an individual without regard to other health benefit coverage of such individual is not considered to "duplicate" any health benefits

under this title, under title XIX, or under a health insurance policy, and subclauses (I) and (III) of clause (i) do not apply to such a policy.

(v) For purposes of this subparagraph, a health insurance policy (or a rider to an insurance contract which is not a health insurance policy) is not considered to "duplicate" health benefits under this title or under another health insurance policy if it —

(I) provides health care benefits only for long-term care, nursing home care, home health care, or community-based care, or any combination thereof,

(II) coordinates against or excludes items and services available or paid for under this title or under another health insurance policy, and

(III) for policies sold or issued on or after the end of the 90-day period beginning on the date of enactment of the Health Insurance Portability and Accountability Act of 1996 [enacted Aug. 21, 1996] discloses such coordination or exclusion in the policy's outline of coverage.

For purposes of this clause, the terms "coordinates" and "coordination" mean, with respect to a policy in relation to health benefits under this title or under another health insurance policy, that the policy under its terms is secondary to, or excludes from payment, items and services to the extent available or paid for under this title or under another health insurance policy.

(vi) (I) An individual entitled to benefits under part A or enrolled under part B of this title who is applying for a health insurance policy (other than a policy described in subclause (III)) shall be furnished a disclosure statement described in clause (vii) for the type of policy being applied for. Such statement shall be furnished as a part of (or together with) the application for such policy.

(II) Whoever issues or sells a health insurance policy (other than a policy described in subclause (III)) to an individual described in subclause (I) and fails to furnish the appropriate disclosure statement as required under such subclause shall be fined under title 18, United States Code, or imprisoned not more than 5 years, or both, and, in addition to or in lieu of such a criminal penalty, is subject to a civil money penalty of not to exceed $25,000 (or $15,000 in the case of a person other than the issuer of the policy) for each such violation.

(III) A policy described in this subclause (to which subclauses (I) and (II) do not apply) is a Medicare supplemental policy, a policy described in clause (v), or a health insurance policy identified under 60 Federal Register 30880 (June 12, 1995) as a policy not required to have a disclosure statement.

(IV) Any reference in this section to the revised NAIC model regulation (referred to in subsection (m)(1)(A)) is deemed a reference to such regulation as revised by section 171(m)(2) of the Social Security Act Amendments of 1994 (Public Law 103-432) and as modified by substituting, for the disclosure required under section 16D(2), disclosure under subclause (I) of an appropriate disclosure statement under clause (vii).

(vii) The disclosure statement described in this clause for a type of policy is the statement specified under subparagraph (D) of this paragraph (as in effect before the date of the enactment of the Health Insurance Portability and Accountability Act of 1996 [enacted Aug. 21, 1996]) for that type of policy, as revised as follows:

(I) In each statement, amend the second line to read as follows:

"THIS IS NOT MEDICARE SUPPLEMENT INSURANCE."

(II) In each statement, strike the third line and insert the following: "Some health care services paid for by Medicare may also trigger the payment of benefits under this policy."

(III) In each statement not described in subclause (V), strike the boldface matter that begins "This insurance" and all that follows up to the next paragraph that begins "Medicare."

(IV) In each statement not described in subclause (V), insert before the boxed matter (that states "Before You Buy This Insurance") the following: "This policy must pay benefits without regard to other health benefit coverage to which you may be entitled under Medicare or other insurance."

(V) In a statement relating to policies providing both nursing home and non-institutional coverage, to policies providing nursing home benefits only, or policies providing home care benefits only, amend the sentence that begins "Federal law" to read as follows: "Federal law requires us to inform you that in certain situations this insurance may pay for some care also covered by Medicare."

(viii)          (I) Subject to subclause (II), nothing in this subparagraph shall restrict or preclude a State's ability to regulate health insurance policies, including any health insurance policy that is described in clause (iv), (v), or (vi)(III).

(II) A State may not declare or specify, in statute, regulation, or otherwise, that a health insurance policy (other than a Medicare supplemental policy) or rider to an insurance contract which is not a health insurance policy, that is described in clause (iv), (v), or (vi)(III) and that is sold, issued, or renewed to an individual entitled to benefits under part A or enrolled under part B "duplicates" health benefits under this title or under a Medicare supplemental policy.

(B)    (i) It is unlawful for a person to issue or sell a medicare supplemental policy to an individual entitled to benefits under part A or enrolled under part B, whether directly, through the mail, or otherwise, unless —

(I) the person obtains from the individual, as part of the application for the issuance or purchase and on a form described in clause ii, a written statement signed by the individual stating, to the best of the individual's knowledge, what health insurance policies (including any Medicare + Choice plan) the individual has, from what source, and whether the individual is entitled to any medical assistance under title XIX, whether as a qualified medicare beneficiary or otherwise, and

(II) the written statement is accompanied by a written acknowledgment, signed by the seller of the policy, of the request for and receipt of such statement.

(ii) The statement required by clause (i) shall be made on a form that —

(I) states in substance that a medicare-eligible individual does not need more than one medicare supplemental policy,

(II) states in substance that individuals may be eligible for benefits under the State medicaid program under title XIX and that such individuals who are entitled to benefits under that program usually do not need a medicare supplemental policy and that benefits and premiums under any such policy shall be suspended upon request of the policyholder during the period (of not longer than 24 months) of entitlement to benefits under such title and may be reinstituted upon loss of such entitlement, and

(III) states that counseling services may be available in the State to provide advice concerning the purchase of medicare supplemental policies and enrollment under the medicaid program and may provide the telephone number for such services.

(iii)  (I) Except as provided in subclauses (II) and (III), if the statement required by clause (i) is not obtained or indicates that the individual has a medicare supplemental policy or indicates that the individual is entitled to any medical assistance under title XIX, the sale of a medicare supplemental policy shall be considered to be a violation of subparagraph (A).

(II) Subclause (I) shall not apply in the case of an individual who has a medicare supplemental policy, if the individual indicates in writing, as part of the application for purchase, that the policy being purchased replaces such other policy and indicates an intent to terminate the policy being replaced when the new policy becomes effective and the issuer or seller certifies in writing that such policy will not, to the best of the issuer [issuer's] or seller's knowledge, duplicate coverage (taking into account any such replacement).

(III) If the statement required by clause (i) is obtained and indicates that the individual is entitled to any medical assistance under title XIX, the sale of the policy is not in violation of clause (i) (insofar as such clause relates to such medical assistance), if (aa) a State medicaid plan under such title pays the premiums for the policy, (bb) in the case of a qualified medicare beneficiary described in section 1905(p)(1), the policy provides for coverage of outpatient prescription drugs, or (cc) the only medical assistance to which the individual is entitled under the State plan is medicare cost sharing described in section 1905(p)(3)(A)(ii).

(iv) Whoever issues or sells a medicare supplemental policy in violation of this subparagraph shall be fined under title 18, United States Code, or imprisoned not more than 5 years, or both, and, in addition to or in lieu of such a criminal penalty, is subject to a civil money penalty of not to exceed $25,000 (or $15,000 in the case of a seller who is not the issuer of a policy) for each such violation.

(C) Subparagraph (A) shall not apply with respect to the sale or issuance of a group policy or plan of one or more employers or labor organizations, or of the trustees of a fund established by one or more employers or labor organizations (or combination thereof), for employees or former employees (or combination thereof) or for members or former members (or combination thereof) of the labor organizations.

(4) (A) Whoever knowingly, directly or through his agent, mails or causes to be mailed any matter for a prohibited purpose (as determined under subparagraph (B)) shall be fined under title 18, United States Code, or imprisoned not more than 5 years, or both, and, in addition to or in lieu of such a criminal penalty, is subject to a civil money penalty of not to exceed $5,000 for each such prohibited act.

(B) For purposes of subparagraph (A), a prohibited purpose means the advertising, solicitation, or offer for sale of a medicare supplemental policy, or the delivery of such a policy, in or into any State in which such policy has not been approved by the State commissioner or superintendent of insurance.

(C) Subparagraph (A) shall not apply in the case of a person who mails or causes to be mailed a medicare supplemental policy into a State if such person has ascertained that the party insured under such policy to whom (or on whose behalf) such policy is mailed is located in such State on a temporary basis.

(D) Subparagraph (A) shall not apply in the case of a person who mails or causes to be mailed a duplicate copy of a medicare supplemental policy previously issued to the party to whom (or on whose behalf) such duplicate copy is mailed.

(E) Subparagraph (A) shall not apply in the case of an issuer who mails or causes to be mailed a policy, certificate, or other matter solely to comply with the requirements of subsection (q).

(5) The provisions of section 1128A (other than subsections (a) and (b)) shall apply to civil money penalties under paragraphs (1), (2), (3)(A), and (4)(A) in the same manner as such provisions apply to penalties and proceedings under section 1128A(a).

. . . .

(g) *Definitions*

(1) For purposes of this section, a medicare supplemental policy is a health insurance policy or other health benefit plan offered by a private entity to individuals who are entitled to have payment made under this title, which provides reimbursement for expenses incurred for services and items for which payment may be made under this title but which are not reimbursable by reason of the applicability of deductibles, coinsurance amounts, or other limitations imposed pursuant to this title; but does not include a Medicare + Choice plan or any such policy or plan of one or more employers or labor organizations, or of the trustees of a fund established by one or more employers or labor organizations (or combination thereof), for employees or former employees (or combination thereof) or for members or former members (or combination thereof) of the labor organizations and does not include a policy or plan of an eligible organization (as defined in section 1876(b)) if the policy or plan provides benefits pursuant to a contract under section 1876 or an approved demonstration project described in section 603(c) of the Social Security Amendments of 1983 [unclassified], section 2355 of the Deficit Reduction Act of 1984 [unclassified], or section 9412(b) of the Omnibus Budget Reconciliation Act of 1986 [unclassified], or a policy or plan of an organization if the policy or plan provides benefits pursuant to an agreement under section 1833(a)(1)(A). For purposes of this section, the term "policy" includes a certificate issued under such policy.

(2) For purposes of this section:

(A) The term "NAIC Model Standards" means the "NAIC Model Regulation to Implement the Individual Accident and Sickness Insurance Minimum Standards Act", adopted by the National Association of Insurance Commissioners on June 6, 1979, as it applies to medicare supplement [supplemental] policies.

(B) The term "State with an approved regulatory program" means a State for which the Secretary has made a determination under subsection (b)(1).

(C) The State in which a policy is issued means —

(i) in the case of an individual policy, the State in which the policyholder resides; and

(ii) in the case of a group policy, the State in which the holder of the master policy resides.

. . . .

(q) *Requirements*

The requirements of this subsection are as follows:

(1) Each medicare supplemental policy shall be guaranteed renewable and —

(A) the issuer may not cancel or nonrenew the policy solely on the ground of health status of the individual; and

(B) the issuer shall not cancel or nonrenew the policy for any reason other than nonpayment of premium or material misrepresentation.

(2) If the medicare supplemental policy is terminated by the group policyholder and is not replaced as provided under paragraph (4), the issuer shall offer certificateholders an individual medicare supplemental policy which (at the option of the certificateholder) —

(A) provides for continuation of the benefits contained in the group policy, or

(B) provides for such benefits as otherwise meets [meet] the requirements of this section.

(3) If an individual is a certificateholder in a group medicare supplemental policy and the individual terminates membership in the group, the issuer shall —

(A) offer the certificateholder the conversion opportunity described in paragraph (2), or

(B) at the option of the group policyholder, offer the certificateholder continuation of coverage under the group policy.

(4) If a group medicare supplemental policy is replaced by another group medicare supplemental policy purchased by the same policyholder, [the] issuer of the replacement policy shall offer coverage to all persons covered under the old group policy on its date of termination. Coverage under the new group policy shall not result

in any exclusion for preexisting conditions that would have been covered under the group policy being replaced.

(5) (A) Each medicare supplemental policy shall provide that benefits and premiums under the policy shall be suspended at the request of the policyholder for the period (not to exceed 24 months) in which the policyholder has applied for and is determined to be entitled to medical assistance under title XIX, but only if the policyholder notifies the issuer of such policy within 90 days after the date the individual becomes entitled to such assistance. If such suspension occurs and if the policyholder or certificate holder loses entitlement to such medical assistance, such policy shall be automatically reinstituted (effective as of the date of termination of such entitlement) under terms described in subsection (n)(6)(A)(ii) as of the termination of such entitlement if the policyholder provides notice of loss of such entitlement within 90 days after the date of such loss.

(B) Nothing in this section shall be construed as affecting the authority of a State, under title XIX, to purchase a medicare supplemental policy for an individual otherwise entitled to assistance under such title.

(C) Any person who issues a medicare supplemental policy and fails to comply with the requirements of this paragraph or paragraph (6) is subject to a civil money penalty of not to exceed $25,000 for each such violation. The provisions of section 1128A (other than the first sentence of subsection (a) and other than subsection (b)) shall apply to a civil money penalty under the previous sentence in the same manner as such provisions apply to a penalty or proceeding under section 1128A(a).

(6) Each medicare supplemental policy shall provide that benefits and premiums under the policy shall be suspended at the request of the policyholder if the policyholder is entitled to benefits under section 226(b) and is covered under a group health plan (as defined in section 1862(b)(1)(A)(v)). If such suspension occurs and if the policyholder or certificate holder loses coverage under the group health plan, such policy shall be automatically reinstituted (effective as of the date of such loss of coverage) under terms described in subsection (n)(6)(A)(ii) as of the loss of such coverage if the policyholder provides notice of loss of such coverage within 90 days after the date of such loss.

. . . .

## § 1395yy.  Payment to skilled nursing facilities for routine service costs

(a) *Per diem limitations*

The Secretary, in determining the amount of the payments which may be made under this title with respect to routine service costs of extended care services shall not recognize as reasonable (in the efficient delivery of health services) per diem costs of such services to the extent that such per diem costs exceed the following per diem limits, except as otherwise provided in this section:

(1) With respect to freestanding skilled nursing facilities located in urban areas, the limit shall be equal to 112 percent of the mean per diem routine service costs for freestanding skilled nursing facilities located in urban areas.

(2) With respect to freestanding skilled nursing facilities located in rural areas, the limit shall be equal to 112 percent of the mean per diem routine service costs for freestanding skilled nursing facilities located in rural areas.

(3) With respect to hospital-based skilled nursing facilities located in urban areas, the limit shall be equal to the sum of the limit for freestanding skilled nursing facilities located in urban areas, plus 50 percent of the amount by which 112 percent of the mean per diem routine service costs for hospital-based skilled nursing facilities located in urban areas exceeds the limit for freestanding skilled nursing facilities located in urban areas.

(4) With respect to hospital-based skilled nursing facilities located in rural areas, the limit shall be equal to the sum of the limit for freestanding skilled nursing facilities located in rural areas, plus 50 percent of the amount by which 112 percent of the mean per diem routine service costs for hospital-based skilled nursing facilities located in rural areas exceeds the limit for freestanding skilled nursing facilities located in rural areas.

In applying this subsection the Secretary shall make appropriate adjustments to the labor related portion of the costs based upon an appropriate wage index, and shall, for cost reporting periods beginning on or after October 1, 1992, on or after October 1, 1995, and every 2 years thereafter, provide for an update to the per diem cost limits described in this subsection, except that the limits effective for cost reporting periods

beginning on or after October 1, 1997, shall be based on the limits effective for cost reporting periods beginning on or after October 1, 1996.
. . . .

## § 1395bbb. Conditions of participation for home health agencies; home health quality

(a) *Conditions of participation; protection of individual rights; notification of State entities; use of home health aides; medical equipment; individual's plan of care compliance with Federal State, and local laws and regulations*

The conditions of participation that a home health agency is required to meet under this subsection are as follows:

(1) The agency protects and promotes the rights of each individual under its care, including each of the following rights:

(A) The right to be fully informed in advance about the care and treatment to be provided by the agency, to be fully informed in advance of any changes in the care or treatment to be provided by the agency that may affect the individual's well-being, and (except with respect to an individual adjudged incompetent) to participate in planning care and treatment or changes in care or treatment.

(B) The right to voice grievances with respect to treatment or care that is (or fails to be) furnished without discrimination or reprisal for voicing grievances.

(C) The right to confidentiality of the clinical records described in section 1861(o)(3).

(D) The right to have one's property treated with respect.

(E) The right to be fully informed orally and in writing (in advance of coming under the care of the agency) of —

(i) all items and services furnished by (or under arrangements with) the agency for which payment may be made under this title,

(ii) the coverage available for such items and services under this title, title XIX, and any other Federal program of which the agency is reasonably aware,

(iii) any charges for items and services not covered under this title and any charges the individual may have to pay with respect to items and services furnished by (or under arrangements with) the agency, and

(iv) any changes in the charges or items and services described in clause (i), (ii), or (iii).

(F) The right to be fully informed in writing (in advance of coming under the care of the agency) of the individual's rights and obligations under this title.

(G) The right to be informed of the availability of the State home health agency hot-line established under section 1864(a).

(2) The agency notifies the State entity responsible for the licensing or certification of the agency of a change in —

(A) the persons with an ownership or control interest (as defined in section 1124(a)(3)) in the agency,

(B) the persons who are officers, directors, agents, or managing employees (as defined in section 1126(b)) of the agency, and

(C) the corporation, association, or other company responsible for the management of the agency.

Such notice shall be given at the time of the change and shall include the identity of each new person or company described in the previous sentence.

(3)  (A) The agency must not use as a home health aide (on a full-time, temporary, per diem, or other basis), any individual to provide items or services described in section 1861(m)] on or after January 1, 1990, unless the individual —

(i) has completed a training and competency evaluation program, or a competency evaluation program, that meets the minimum standards established by the Secretary under subparagraph (D), and

(ii) is competent to provide such items and services.

For purposes of clause (i), an individual is not considered to have completed a training and competency evaluation program, or a competency evaluation program if, since the individual's most recent completion of such a program, there has been a continuous period of 24 consecutive months during none of which the individual provided items and services described in section 1861(m) for compensation.

(B) (i) The agency must provide, with respect to individuals used as a home health aide by the agency as of July 1, 1989, for a competency evaluation program (as described in subparagraph (A)(i)) and such preparation as may be necessary for the individual to complete such a program by January 1, 1990.

(ii) The agency must provide such regular performance review and regular in-service education as assures that individuals used to provide items and services described in section 1861(m) are competent to provide those items and services.

(C) The agency must not permit an individual, other than in a training and competency evaluation program that meets the minimum standards established by the Secretary under subparagraph (D), to provide items or services of a type for which the individual has not demonstrated competency.

(D) (i) The Secretary shall establish minimum standards for the programs described in subparagraph (A) by not later than October 1, 1988.

(ii) Such standards shall include the content of the curriculum, minimum hours of training, qualification of instructors, and procedures for determination of competency.

(iii) Such standards may permit approval of programs offered by or in home health agencies, as well as outside agencies (including employee organizations), and of programs in effect on the date of the enactment of this section [enacted Dec. 22, 1987]; except that they may not provide for the approval of a program offered by or in a home health agency which, within the previous 2 years —

(I) has been determined to be out of compliance with subparagraph (A), (B), or (C);

(II) has been subject to an extended (or partial extended) survey under subsection (c)(2)(D);

(III) has been assessed a civil money penalty described in subsection (f)(2)(A)(i) of not less than $5,000; or

(IV) has been subject to the remedies described in subsection (e)(1) or in clauses (ii) or (iii) of subsection (f)(2)(A).

(iv) Such standards shall permit a determination that an individual who has completed (before July 1, 1989) a training and competency evaluation program or a competency evaluation program shall be deemed for purposes of subparagraph (A) to have completed a program that is approved by the Secretary under the standards established under this subparagraph if the Secretary determines that, at the time the program was offered, the program met such standards.

(E) In this paragraph, the term "home health aide" means any individual who provides the items and services described in section 1861(m), but does not include an individual —

(i) who is a licensed health professional (as defined in subparagraph (F)), or

(ii) who volunteers to provide such services without monetary compensation.

(F) In this paragraph, the term "licensed health professional" means a physician, physician assistant, nurse practitioner, physical, speech, or occupational therapist, physical or occupational therapy assistant, registered professional nurse, licensed practical nurse, or licensed or certified social worker.

(4) The agency includes an individual's plan of care required under section 1861(m) as part of the clinical records described in section 1861(o)(3).

(5) The agency operates and provides services in compliance with all applicable Federal, State, and local laws and regulations (including the requirements of section 1124) and with accepted professional standards and principles which apply to professionals providing items and services in such an agency.

(6) The agency complies with the requirement of section 1866(f) (relating to maintaining written policies and procedures respecting advance directives).

# Medicaid Act (Excerpts)

42 U.S.C. § 1396 et seq.

## SUBCHAPTER XIX – GRANTS TO STATES FOR MEDICAL ASSISTANCE PROGRAMS

## § 1396a. State plans for medical assistance

(a) *Contents*

A State plan for medical assistance must —

(1) provide that it shall be in effect in all political subdivisions of the State, and, if administered by them, be mandatory upon them;

(2) provide for financial participation by the State equal to not less than 40 per centum of the non-Federal share of the expenditures under the plan with respect to which payments under section 1903 are authorized by this title; and, effective July 1, 1969, provide for financial participation by the State equal to all of such non-Federal share or provide for distribution of funds from Federal or State sources, for carrying out the State plan, on an equalization or other basis which will assure that the lack of adequate funds from local sources will not result in lowering the amount, duration, scope, or quality of care and services available under the plan;

(3) provide for granting an opportunity for a fair hearing before the State agency to any individual whose claim for medical assistance under the plan is denied or is not acted upon with reasonable promptness;

(4) provide (A) such methods of administration (including methods relating to the establishment and maintenance of personnel standards on a merit basis, except that the Secretary shall exercise no authority with respect to the selection, tenure of office, and compensation of any individual employed in accordance with such methods, and including provision for utilization of professional

369

medical personnel in the administration and, where administered locally, supervision of administration of the plan) as are found by the Secretary to be necessary for the proper and efficient operation of the plan, (B) for the training and effective use of paid subprofessional staff, with particular emphasis on the full-time or part-time employment of recipients and other persons of low income, as community service aides, in the administration of the plan and for the use of nonpaid or partially paid volunteers in a social service volunteer program in providing services to applicants and recipients and in assisting any advisory committees established by the State agency, (C) that each State or local officer, employee, or independent contractor who is responsible for the expenditure of substantial amounts of funds under the State plan, each individual who formerly was such an officer, employee, or contractor, and each partner of such an officer, employee, or contractor shall be prohibited from committing any act, in relation to any activity under the plan, the commission of which, in connection with any activity concerning the United States Government, by an officer or employee of the United States Government, an individual who was such an officer or employee, or a partner of such an officer or employee is prohibited by section 207 or 208 of title 18, United States Code, and (D) that each State or local officer, employee, or independent contractor who is responsible for selecting, awarding, or otherwise obtaining items and services under the State plan shall be subject to safeguards against conflicts of interest that are at least as stringent as the safeguards that apply under section 27 of the Office of Federal Procurement Policy Act (41 U.S.C. 423) to persons described in subsection (a)(2) of such section of that Act;

(5) either provide for the establishment or designation of a single State agency to administer or to supervise the administration of the plan; or provide for the establishment or designation of a single State agency to administer or to supervise the administration of the plan, except that the determination of eligibility for medical assistance under the plan shall be made by the State or local agency administering the State plan approved under title I or XVI (insofar as it relates to the aged) if the State is eligible to participate in the State plan program established under title XVI, or by the agency or agencies administering the supplemental security income program established under title XVI or the State Plan approved under part A

of title IV if the State is not eligible to participate in the State plan program established under title XVI;

(6) provide that the State agency will make such reports, in such form and containing such information, as the Secretary may from time to time require, and comply with such provisions as the Secretary may from time to time find necessary to assure the correctness and verification of such reports;

(7) provide safeguards which restrict the use or disclosure of information concerning applicants and recipients to purposes directly connected with the administration of the plan;

(8) provide that all individuals wishing to make application for medical assistance under the plan shall have opportunity to do so, and that such assistance shall be furnished with reasonable promptness to all eligible individuals;

. . . .

(10) provide —

(A) for making medical assistance available, including at least the care and services listed in paragraphs (1) through (5), (17) and (21) of section 1905(a), to —

(i) all individuals —

(I) who are receiving aid or assistance under any plan of the State approved under title I, X, XIV, or XVI, or part A or part E of title IV (including individuals eligible under this title by reason of section 402(a)(37), 406(h), or 473(b), or considered by the State to be receiving such aid as authorized under section 482(e)(6)),

(II) with respect to whom supplemental security income benefits are being paid under title XVI(or were being paid as of the date of the enactment of section 211(a) of the Personal Responsibility and Work Opportunity Reconciliation Act of 1996 (P.L. 104-193) [enacted Aug. 22, 1996]) and would continue to be paid but for the enactment of that section or who are qualified severely impaired individuals (as defined in section 1905(q)),

(III) who are qualified pregnant women or children as defined in section 1905(n),

(IV) who are described in subparagraph (A) or (B) of subsection (l)(1) and whose family income does not exceed the minimum income level the State is required to establish under subsection (l)(2)(A) for such a family;[,] or

(V) who are qualified family members as defined in section 1905(m)(1),

(VI) who are described in subparagraph (C) of subsection (l)(1) and whose family income does not exceed the income level the State is required to establish under subsection (l)(2)(B) for such a family, or

(VII) who are described in subparagraph (D) of subsection (l)(1) and whose family income does not exceed the income level the State is required to establish under subsection (l)(2)(C) for such a family; [and]

(ii) at the option of the State, to any group or groups of individuals described in section 1905(a) (or, in the case of individuals described in section 1905(a)(i), to any reasonable categories of such individuals) who are not individuals described in clause (i) of this subparagraph but —

(I) who meet the income and resources requirements of the appropriate State plan described in clause (i) or the supplemental security income program (as the case may be),

(II) who would meet the income and resources requirements of the appropriate State plan described in clause (i) if their work-related child care costs were paid from their earnings rather than by a State agency as a service expenditure,

(III) who would be eligible to receive aid under the appropriate State plan described in clause (i) if coverage under such plan was as broad as allowed under Federal law,

(IV) with respect to whom there is being paid, or who are eligible, or would be eligible if they were not in a medical institution, to have paid with respect to them, aid or assistance under the appropriate State plan described in clause (i), supplemental security income benefits under title XVI, or a State supplementary payment;[,]

(V) who are in a medical institution for a period of not less than 30 consecutive days (with eligibility by reason of this subclause beginning on the first day of such period), who meet the resource requirements of the appropriate State plan described in clause (i) or the supplemental security income program, and whose income does not exceed a separate income standard established by the State which is consistent with the limit established under section 1903(f)(4)(C),

(VI) who would be eligible under the State plan under this title if they were in a medical institution, with respect to whom there has been a determination that but for the provision of home or community-based services described in subsection (c), (d), or (e) of section 1915 they would require the level of care provided in a hospital, nursing facility or intermediate care facility for the mentally retarded the cost of which could be reimbursed under the State plan, and who will receive home or community-based services pursuant to a waiver granted by the Secretary under subsection (c), (d), or (e) of section 1915,

(VII) who would be eligible under the State plan under this title if they were in a medical institution, who are terminally ill, and who will receive hospice care pursuant to a voluntary election described in section 1905(o);[,]

(VIII) who is a child described in section 1905(a)(i) —

(aa) for whom there is in effect an adoption assistance agreement (other than an agreement under part E of title IV) between the State and an adoptive parent or parents,

(bb) who the State agency responsible for adoption assistance has determined cannot be placed with adoptive parents without medical assistance because such child has special needs for medical or rehabilitative care, and

(cc) who was eligible for medical assistance under the State plan prior to the adoption assistance agreement being entered into, or who would have been eligible for medical assistance at such time if the eligibility standards and methodologies of the State's foster care program under part E of title IV were applied rather than the eligibility standards and methodologies of the State's aid to families with dependent children program under part A of title IV;[,]

(IX) who are described in subsection (l)(1) and are not described in clause (i)(IV), clause (i)(VI), or clause (i)(VII);[,]

(X) who are described in subsection (m)(1);[,]

(XI) who receive only an optional State supplementary payment based on need and paid on a regular basis, equal to the difference between the individual's countable income and the income standard used to determine eligibility for such supplementary payment (with countable income being the income remaining after deductions as established by the State pursuant to standards that may be more restrictive than the standards for supplementary security income benefits under title XVI), which are available to all individuals in the State (but which may be based on different income standards by political subdivision according to cost of living differences), and which are paid by a State that does not have an agreement with the Commissioner of Social Security under section 1616 or 1634;

(XII) who are described in subsection (z)(1) (relating to certain TB-infected individuals);

(XIII) who are in families whose income is less than 250 percent of the income official poverty line (as defined by the Office of Management and Budget, and revised annually in accordance with section 673(2) of the Omnibus Budget Reconciliation Act of 1981) applicable to a family of the size involved, and who but for earnings in excess of the limit established under section 1905(q)(2)(B), would be considered to be receiving supplemental security income (subject, notwithstanding section 1916, to payment of premiums or other cost-sharing charges (set on a sliding scale based on income) that the State may determine);

(XIV) who are optional targeted low-income children described in section 1905(u)(2)(B);

(XV) who, but for earnings in excess of the limit established under section 1905(q)(2)(B), would be considered to be receiving supplemental security income, who is at least 16, but less than 65, years of age, and whose assets, resources, and earned or unearned income (or both) do not exceed such limitations (if any) as the State may establish;

(XVI) who are employed individuals with a medically improved disability described in section 1905(v)(1) and whose assets, resources, and earned or unearned income (or both) do not exceed such limitations (if any) as the State may establish, but only if the State provides medical assistance to individuals described in subclause (XV);

(XVII) who are independent foster care adolescents (as defined in section 1905(w)(1)), or who are within any reasonable categories of such adolescents specified by the State; or

(XVIII) who are described in subsection (aa) (relating to certain breast or cervical cancer patients);

. . . .

(q) *Minimum monthly personal needs allowance deduction; "institutionalized individual or couple" defined*

(1) (A) In order to meet the requirement of subsection (a)(50), the State plan must provide that, in the case of an institutionalized individual or couple described in subparagraph (B), in determining the amount of the individual's or couple's income to be applied monthly to payment for the

cost of care in an institution, there shall be deducted from the monthly income (in addition to other allowances otherwise provided under the State plan) a monthly personal needs allowance —

        (i) which is reasonable in amount for clothing and other personal needs of the individual (or couple) while in an institution, and

        (ii) which is not less (and may be greater) than the minimum monthly personal needs allowance described in paragraph (2).

    (B) In this subsection, the term "institutionalized individual or couple" means an individual or married couple —

        (i) who is an inpatient (or who are inpatients) in a medical institution or nursing facility for which payments are made under this title throughout a month, and

        (ii) who is or are determined to be eligible for medical assistance under the State plan.

    (2) The minimum monthly personal needs allowance described in this paragraph [subsection] is $30 for an institutionalized individual and $60 for an institutionalized couple (if both are aged, blind, or disabled, and their incomes are considered available to each other in determining eligibility).

. . . .

## § 1396d. Definitions

    For purposes of this title —

(a) *Medical assistance*

    The term "medical assistance" means payment of part or all of the cost of the following care and services (if provided in or after the third month before the month in which the recipient makes application for assistance or, in the case of medicare cost-sharing with respect to a qualified medicare beneficiary described in subsection (p)(1), if provided after the month in which the individual becomes such a beneficiary) for individuals, and, with respect to physicians' or dentists' services, at the option of the State, to individuals (other than individuals with respect to whom there is being paid, or who are eligible, or would be eligible if they were not in a medical institution, to have paid with respect to them a State supplementary payment and are eligible for medical assistance equal in amount, duration, and scope to the medical assistance made available to individuals described in section 1902(a)(10)(A)) not receiving aid or assistance under any plan of the State approved under title I, X, XIV, or XVI, or part A of title IV, and with respect to whom supplemental security income benefits are not being paid under title XVI, who are —

(i) under the age of 21, or, at the option of the State, under the age of 20, 19, or 18 as the State may choose,

(ii) relatives specified in section 406(b)(1) with whom a child is living if such child is (or would, if needy, be) a dependent child under part A of title IV,

(iii) 65 years of age or older,

(iv) blind, with respect to States eligible to participate in the State plan program established under title XVI,

(v) 18 years of age or older and permanently and totally disabled, with respect to States eligible to participate in the State plan program established under title XVI,

(vi) persons essential (as described in the second sentence of this subsection) to individuals receiving aid or assistance under State plans approved under title I, X, XIV, or XVI,

(vii) blind or disabled as defined in section 1614, with respect to States not eligible to participate in the State plan program established under title XVI,

(viii) pregnant women,

(ix) individuals provided extended benefits under section 1925,

(x) individuals described in section 1902(u)(1),

(xi) individuals described in section 1902(z)(1),

(xii) employed individuals with a medically improved disability (as defined in subsection (v)), or

(xiii) individuals described in section 1902(aa),

but whose income and resources are insufficient to meet all of such cost —

(1) inpatient hospital services (other than services in an institution for mental diseases);

(2) (A) outpatient hospital services, (B) consistent with State law permitting such services, rural health clinic services (as defined in subsection (l)(1)) and any other ambulatory services which are offered by a rural health clinic (as defined in subsection (l)(1)) and which are otherwise included in the plan, and (C) Federally-qualified health center services (as defined in subsection (l)(2)) and any other ambulatory services offered by a Federally-qualified health center and which are otherwise included in the plan;

(3) other laboratory and X-ray services;

(4) (A) nursing facility services (other than services in an institution for mental diseases) for individuals 21 years of age or older; (B) early and periodic screening, diagnostic, and treatment services (as defined in subsection (r)) for individuals who are eligible under the plan and are under the age of 21; and (C) family planning services and supplies furnished (directly or under arrangements with others) to individuals of childbearing age (including minors who can be considered to be sexually active) who are eligible under the State plan and who desire such services and supplies;

(5) (A) physicians' services furnished by a physician (as defined in section 1861(r)(1)), whether furnished in the office, the patient's home, a hospital, or a nursing facility, or elsewhere, and (B) medical and surgical services furnished by a dentist (described in section 1861(r)(2)) to the extent such services may be performed under State law either by a doctor of medicine or by a doctor of dental surgery or dental medicine and would be described in clause (A) if furnished by a physician (as defined in section 1861(r)(1));

(6) medical care, or any other type of remedial care recognized under State law, furnished by licensed practitioners within the scope of their practice as defined by State law;

(7) home health care services;

(8) private duty nursing services;

(9) clinic services furnished by or under the direction of a physician, without regard to whether the clinic itself is administered by a physician, including such services furnished outside the clinic by clinic personnel to an eligible individual who does not reside in a permanent dwelling or does not have a fixed home or mailing address;

(10) dental services;

(11) physical therapy and related services;

(12) prescribed drugs, dentures, and prosthetic devices; and eyeglasses prescribed by a physician skilled in diseases of the eye or by an optometrist, whichever the individual may select;

(13) other diagnostic, screening, preventive, and rehabilitative services, including any medical or remedial services (provided in a facility, a home, or other setting) recommended by a physician or other licensed practitioner of the healing arts within the scope of their practice under State law, for the maximum reduction of physical or

mental disability and restoration of an individual to the best possible functional level;

(14) inpatient hospital services and nursing facility services for individuals 65 years of age or over in an institution for mental diseases;

(15) services in an intermediate care facility for the mentally retarded (other than in an institution for mental diseases) for individuals who are determined, in accordance with section 1902(a)(31), to be in need of such care;

(16) effective January 1, 1973, inpatient psychiatric hospital services for individuals under age 21, as defined in subsection (h);

(17) services furnished by a nurse-midwife (as defined in section 1861(gg)) which the nurse-midwife is legally authorized to perform under State law (or the State regulatory mechanism provided by State law), whether or not the nurse-midwife is under the supervision of, or associated with, a physician or other health care provider, and without regard to whether or not the services are performed in the area of management of the care of mothers and babies throughout the maternity cycle;

(18) hospice care (as defined in subsection (o));

(19) case management services (as defined in section 1915(g)(2)) and TB-related services described in section 1902(z)(2)(F);

(20) respiratory care services (as defined in section 1902(e)(9)(C));

(21) services furnished by a certified pediatric nurse practitioner or certified family nurse practitioner (as defined by the Secretary) which the certified pediatric nurse practitioner or certified family nurse practitioner is legally authorized to perform under State law (or the State regulatory mechanism provided by State law), whether or not the certified pediatric nurse practitioner or certified family nurse practitioner is under the supervision of, or associated with, a physician or other health care provider;

(22) home and community care (to the extent allowed and as defined in section 1929) for functionally disabled elderly individuals;

(23) community supported living arrangements services (to the extent allowed and as defined in section 1930;

(24) personal care services furnished to an individual who is not an inpatient or resident of a hospital, nursing facility, intermediate care facility for the mentally retarded, or institution for mental

disease that are (A) authorized for the individual by a physician in accordance with a plan of treatment or (at the option of the State) otherwise authorized for the individual in accordance with a service plan approved by the State, (B) provided by an individual who is qualified to provide such services and who is not a member of the individual's family, and (C) furnished in a home or other location;

(25) primary care case management services (as defined in subsection (t));

(26) services furnished under a PACE program under section 1934 to PACE program eligible individuals enrolled under the program under such section; and

(27) any other medical care, and any other type of remedial care recognized under State law, specified by the Secretary,

except as otherwise provided in paragraph (16), such term does not include —

(A) any such payments with respect to care or services for any individual who is an inmate of a public institution (except as a patient in a medical institution); or

(B) any such payments with respect to care or services for any individual who has not attained 65 years of age and who is a patient in an institution for mental diseases.

For purposes of clause (vi) of the preceding sentence, a person shall be considered essential to another individual if such person is the spouse of and is living with such individual, the needs of such person are taken into account in determining the amount of aid or assistance furnished to such individual (under a State Plan approved under title I, X, XIV, or XVI), and such person is determined, under such a State plan, to be essential to the well-being of such individual. The payment described in the first sentence may include expenditures for medicare cost-sharing and for premiums under part B of title XVIII for individuals who are eligible for medical assistance under the plan and (A) are receiving aid or assistance under any plan of the State approved under title I, X, XIV, or XVI, or part A of title IV, or with respect to whom supplemental security income benefits are being paid under title XVI, or (B) with respect to whom there is being paid a State supplementary payment and are eligible for medical assistance equal in amount, duration, and scope to the medical assistance made available to individuals described in section 1902(a)(10)(A), and, except in the case of individuals 65 years of age or older and disabled individuals entitled to health insurance benefits under title XVIII who are not enrolled under part B of title XVIII, other insurance premiums for medical or any other type of remedial care or the cost thereof. No service (including counseling) shall be excluded from the definition of "medical assistance" solely because it is provided as a treatment service for alcoholism or drug dependency.

. . . .

## § 1396g.  State programs for licensing of administrators of nursing homes

(a) *Nature of State program*

For purposes of section 1902(a)(29), a "State program for the licensing of administrators of nursing homes" is a program which provides that no nursing home within the State may operate except under the supervision of an administrator licensed in the manner provided in this section.

(b) *Licensing by State agency or board representative of concerned professions and institutions*

Licensing of nursing home administrators shall be carried out by the agency of the State responsible for licensing under the healing arts licensing act of the State, or, in the absence of such act or such an agency, a board representative of the professions and institutions concerned with care of chronically ill and infirm aged patients and established to carry out the purposes of this section.

(c) *Functions and duties of State agency or board*

It shall be the function and duty of such agency or board to —

(1) develop, impose, and enforce standards which must be met by individuals in order to receive a license as a nursing home administrator, which standards shall be designed to insure that nursing home administrators will be individuals who are of good character and are otherwise suitable, and who, by training or experience in the field of institutional administration, are qualified to serve as nursing home administrators;

(2) develop and apply appropriate techniques, including examinations and investigations, for determining whether an individual meets such standards;

(3) issue licenses to individuals determined, after the application of such techniques, to meet such standards, and revoke or suspend licenses previously issued by the board in any case where

the individual holding any such license is determined substantially to have failed to conform to the requirements of such standards;

(4) establish and carry out procedures designed to insure that individuals licensed as nursing home administrators will, during any period that they serve as such, comply with the requirements of such standards;

(5) receive, investigate, and take appropriate action with respect to, any charge or complaint filed with the board to the effect that any individual licensed as a nursing home administrator has failed to comply with the requirements of such standards; and

(6) conduct a continuing study and investigation of nursing homes and administrators of nursing homes within the State with a view to the improvement of the standards imposed for the licensing of such administrators and of procedures and methods for the enforcement of such standards with respect to administrators of nursing homes who have been licensed as such.

(d) *Waiver of standards other than good character or suitability standards*

No State shall be considered to have failed to comply with the provisions of section 1902(a)(29) because the agency or board of such State (established pursuant to subsection (b) of this section) shall have granted any waiver, with respect to any individual who, during all of the three calendar years immediately preceding the calendar year in which the requirements prescribed in section 1902(a)(29) are first met by the State, has served as a nursing home administrator, of any of the standards developed, imposed, and enforced by such agency or board pursuant to subsection (c).

(e) *"Nursing home" and "nursing home administrator" defined*

As used in this section, the term —

(1) "nursing home" means any institution or facility defined as such for licensing purposes under State law, or, if State law does not employ the term nursing home, the equivalent term or terms as determined by the Secretary, but does not include a religious nonmedical health care institution (as defined in section 1861(ss)(1)).

(2) "nursing home administrator" means any individual who is charged with the general administration of a nursing home whether or not such individual has an ownership interest in such home and

whether or not his functions and duties are shared with one or more other individuals.

### § 1396p.  Liens, adjustments and recoveries, and transfers of assets

(a) *Imposition of lien against the property of an individual on account of medical assistance rendered to him under a State plan.*

(1) No lien may be imposed against the property of any individual prior to his death on account of medical assistance paid or to be paid on his behalf under the State plan, except —

(A) pursuant to the judgment of a court on account of benefits incorrectly paid on behalf of such individual, or

(B) in the case of the real property of an individual —

(i) who is an inpatient in a nursing facility, intermediate care facility for the mentally retarded, or other medical institution, if such individual is required, as a condition of receiving services in such institution under the State plan, to spend for costs of medical care all but a minimal amount of his income required for personal needs, and

(ii) with respect to whom the State determines, after notice and opportunity for a hearing (in accordance with procedures established by the State), that he cannot reasonably be expected to be discharged from the medical institution and to return home,

except as provided in paragraph (2).

(2) No lien may be imposed under paragraph (1)(B) on such individual's home if —

(A) the spouse of such individual,

(B) such individual's child who is under age 21, or (with respect to States eligible to participate in the State program established under title XVI) is blind or permanently and totally disabled, or (with respect to States which are not eligible to participate in such program) is blind or disabled as defined in section 1614, or

(C) a sibling of such individual (who has an equity interest in such home and who was residing in such individual's home for a period of at least one year immediately before the date of the individual's admission to the medical institution),

is lawfully residing in such home.

(3) Any lien imposed with respect to an individual pursuant to paragraph (1)(B) shall dissolve upon that individual's discharge from the medical institution and return home.

(b) *Adjustment or recovery of medical assistance correctly paid under a State plan*

(1) No adjustment or recovery of any medical assistance correctly paid on behalf of an individual under the State plan may be made, except that the State shall seek adjustment or recovery of any medical assistance correctly paid on behalf of an individual under the State plan in the case of the following individuals:

(A) In the case of an individual described in subsection (a)(1)(B), the State shall seek adjustment or recovery from the individual's estate or upon sale of the property subject to a lien imposed on account of medical assistance paid on behalf of the individual.

(B) In the case of an individual who was 55 years of age or older when the individual received such medical assistance, the State shall seek adjustment or recovery from the individual's estate, but only for medical assistance consisting of —

(i) nursing facility services, home and community-based services, and related hospital and prescription drug services, or

(ii) at the option of the State, any items or services under the State plan.

(C) (i) In the case of an individual who has received (or is entitled to receive) benefits under a long-term care insurance policy in connection with which assets or resources are disregarded in the manner described in clause (ii), except as provided in such clause, the State shall seek adjustment or recovery from the individual's estate on account of medical assistance paid on behalf of the individual for nursing facility and other long-term care services.

(ii) Clause (i) shall not apply in the case of an individual who received medical assistance under a State plan of a State which had a State plan amendment approved as of May 14, 1993, which provided for the disregard of any assets or resources —

(I) to the extent that payments are made under a long-term care insurance policy; or

(II) because an individual has received (or is entitled to receive) benefits under a long-term care insurance policy.

(2) Any adjustment or recovery under paragraph (1) may be made only after the death of the individual's surviving spouse, if any, and only at a time —

(A) when he has no surviving child who is under age 21, or (with respect to States eligible to participate in the State program established under title XVI) is blind or permanently and totally disabled, or (with respect to States which are not eligible to participate in such program) is blind or disabled as defined in section 1614; and

(B) in the case of a lien on an individual's home under subsection (a)(1)(B), when —

(i) no sibling of the individual (who was residing in the individual's home for a period of at least one year immediately before the date of the individual's admission to the medical institution), and

(ii) no son or daughter of the individual (who was residing in the individual's home for a period of at least two years immediately before the date of the individual's admission to the medical institution, and who establishes to the satisfaction of the State that he or she provided care to such individual which permitted such individual to reside at home rather than in an institution),

is lawfully residing in such home who has lawfully resided in such home on a continuous basis since the date of the individual's admission to the medical institution.

(3) The State agency shall establish procedures (in accordance with standards specified by the Secretary) under which the agency shall waive the application of this subsection (other than paragraph (1)(C)) if such application would work an undue hardship as determined on the basis of criteria established by the Secretary.

(4) For purposes of this subsection, the term "estate", with respect to a deceased individual —

(A) shall include all real and personal property and other assets included within the individual's estate, as defined for purposes of State probate law; and

(B) may include, at the option of the State (and shall include, in the case of an individual to whom paragraph (1)(C)(i) applies), any other real and personal property and other assets in which the individual had any legal title or interest at the time of death (to the extent of such interest), including such assets conveyed to a survivor, heir, or assign of the deceased individual through joint tenancy, tenancy in common, survivorship, life estate, living trust, or other arrangement.

(c) *Taking into account certain transfers of assets*

(1)   (A) In order to meet the requirements of this subsection for purposes of section 1902(a)(18), the State plan must provide that if an institutionalized individual or the spouse of such an individual (or, at the option of a State, a noninstitutionalized individual or the spouse of such an individual) disposes of assets for less than fair market value on or after the look-back date specified in subparagraph (B)(i), the individual is ineligible for medical assistance for services described in subparagraph (C)(i) (or, in the case of a noninstitutionalized individual, for the services described in subparagraph (C)(ii)) during the period beginning on the date specified in subparagraph (D) and equal to the number of months specified in subparagraph (E).

(B)   (i) The look-back date specified in this subparagraph is a date that is 36 months (or, in the case of payments from a trust or portions of a trust that are treated as assets disposed of by the individual pursuant to paragraph (3)(A)(iii) or (3)(B)(ii) of subsection (d), 60 months) before the date specified in clause (ii).

(ii) The date specified in this clause, with respect to —

(I) an institutionalized individual is the first date as of which the individual both is an institutionalized individual and has applied for medical assistance under the State plan, or

(II) a noninstitutionalized individual is the date on which the individual applies for medical assistance under the State plan or, if later, the date on which the individual disposes of assets for less than fair market value.

(C)   (i) The services described in this subparagraph with respect to an institutionalized individual are the following:

(I) Nursing facility services.

(II) A level of care in any institution equivalent to that of nursing facility services.

(III) Home or community-based services furnished under a waiver granted under subsection (c) or (d) of section 1915.

(ii) The services described in this subparagraph with respect to a noninstitutionalized individual are services (not including any services described in clause (i)) that are described in paragraph (7), (22), or (24) of section 1905(a), and, at the option of a State, other long-term care services for which medical assistance is otherwise available under the State plan to individuals requiring long-term care.

(D) The date specified in this subparagraph is the first day of the first month during or after which assets have been transferred for less than fair market value and which does not occur in any other periods of ineligibility under this subsection.

(E) (i) With respect to an institutionalized individual, the number of months of ineligibility under this subparagraph for an individual shall be equal to —

(I) the total, cumulative uncompensated value of all assets transferred by the individual (or individual's spouse) on or after the look-back date specified in subparagraph (B)(i), divided by

(II) the average monthly cost to a private patient of nursing facility services in the State (or, at the option of the State, in the community in which the individual is institutionalized) at the time of application.

(ii) With respect to a noninstitutionalized individual, the number of months of ineligibility under this subparagraph for an individual shall not be greater than a number equal to —

(I) the total, cumulative uncompensated value of all assets transferred by the individual (or individual's spouse) on or after the look-back date specified in subparagraph (B)(i), divided by

(II) the average monthly cost to a private patient of nursing facility services in the State (or, at the option of the State, in the community in which the individual is institutionalized) at the time of application.

(iii) The number of months of ineligibility otherwise determined under clause (i) or (ii) with respect to the disposal of an asset shall be reduced —

(I) in the case of periods of ineligibility determined under clause (i), by the number of months of ineligibility applicable to the individual under clause (ii) as a result of such disposal, and

(II) in the case of periods of ineligibility determined under clause (ii), by the number of months of ineligibility applicable to the individual under clause (i) as a result of such disposal.

(2) An individual shall not be ineligible for medical assistance by reason of paragraph (1) to the extent that —

(A) the assets transferred were a home and title to the home was transferred to —

(i) the spouse of such individual;

(ii) a child of such individual who (I) is under age 21, or (II) (with respect to States eligible to participate in the State program established under title XVI) is blind or permanently and totally disabled, or (with respect to States which are not eligible to participate in such program) is blind or disabled as defined in section 1614;

(iii) a sibling of such individual who has an equity interest in such home and who was residing in such individual's home for a period of at least one year immediately before the date the individual becomes an institutionalized individual; or

(iv) a son or daughter of such individual (other than a child described in clause (ii)) who was residing in such individual's home for a period of at least two years immediately before the date the individual becomes an institutionalized individual, and who (as determined by the State) provided care to such individual which permitted such individual to reside at home rather than in such an institution or facility;

(B) the assets —

(i) were transferred to the individual's spouse or to another for the sole benefit of the individual's spouse,

(ii) were transferred from the individual's spouse to another for the sole benefit of the individual's spouse,

(iii) were transferred to, or to a trust (including a trust described in subsection (d)(4)) established solely for the benefit of, the individual's child described in subparagraph (A)(ii)(II), or

(iv) were transferred to a trust (including a trust described in subsection (d)(4)) established solely for the benefit of an individual under 65 years of age who is disabled (as defined in section 1614(a)(3));

(C) a satisfactory showing is made to the State (in accordance with regulations promulgated by the Secretary) that (i) the individual intended to dispose of the assets either at fair market value, or for other valuable consideration, (ii) the assets were transferred exclusively for a purpose other than to qualify for medical assistance, or (iii) all assets transferred for less than fair market value have been returned to the individual; or

(D) the State determines, under procedures established by the State (in accordance with standards specified by the Secretary), that the denial of eligibility would work an undue hardship as determined on the basis of criteria established by the Secretary;[.]

(3) For purposes of this subsection, in the case of an asset held by an individual in common with another person or persons in a joint tenancy, tenancy in common, or similar arrangement, the asset (or the affected portion of such asset) shall be considered to be transferred by such individual when any action is taken, either by such individual or by any other person, that reduces or eliminates such individual's ownership or control of such asset.

(4) A State (including a State which has elected treatment under section 1902(f)) may not provide for any period of ineligibility for an individual due to transfer of resources for less than fair market value except in accordance with this subsection. In the case of a transfer by the spouse of an individual which results in a period of ineligibility for medical assistance under a State plan for such individual, a State shall, using a reasonable methodology (as specified by the Secretary), apportion such period of ineligibility (or any portion of such period) among the individual and the individual's spouse if the spouse otherwise becomes eligible for medical assistance under the State plan.

(5) In this subsection, the term "resources" has the meaning given such term in section 1613, without regard to the exclusion described in subsection (a)(1) thereof.

## (d) *Treatment of trust amounts*

(1) For purposes of determining an individual's eligibility for, or amount of, benefits under a State plan under this title, subject to paragraph

(4), the rules specified in paragraph (3) shall apply to a trust established by such individual.

(2) (A) For purposes of this subsection, an individual shall be considered to have established a trust if assets of the individual were used to form all or part of the corpus of the trust and if any of the following individuals established such trust other than by will:

(i) The individual.

(ii) The individual's spouse.

(iii) A person, including a court or administrative body, with legal authority to act in place of or on behalf of the individual or the individual's spouse.

(iv) A person, including any court or administrative body, acting at the direction or upon the request of the individual or the individual's spouse.

(B) In the case of a trust the corpus of which includes assets of an individual (as determined under subparagraph (A)) and assets of any other person or persons, the provisions of this subsection shall apply to the portion of the trust attributable to the assets of the individual.

(C) Subject to paragraph (4), this subsection shall apply without regard to —

(i) the purposes for which a trust is established,

(ii) whether the trustees have or exercise any discretion under the trust,

(iii) any restrictions on when or whether distributions may be made from the trust, or

(iv) any restrictions on the use of distributions from the trust.

(3) (A) In the case of a revocable trust —

(i) the corpus of the trust shall be considered resources available to the individual,

(ii) payments from the trust to or for the benefit of the individual shall be considered income of the individual, and

(iii) any other payments from the trust shall be considered assets disposed of by the individual for purposes of subsection (c).

(B) In the case of an irrevocable trust —

(i) if there are any circumstances under which payment from the trust could be made to or for the benefit of the individual, the portion of the corpus from which, or the income on the corpus from which, payment to the individual could be made shall be considered resources available to the individual, and payments from that portion of the corpus or income —

        (I) to or for the benefit of the individual, shall be considered income of the individual, and

        (II) for any other purpose, shall be considered a transfer of assets by the individual subject to subsection (c); and

        (ii) any portion of the trust from which, or any income on the corpus from which, no payment could under any circumstances be made to the individual shall be considered, as of the date of establishment of the trust (or, if later, the date on which payment to the individual was foreclosed) to be assets disposed by the individual for purposes of subsection (c), and the value of the trust shall be determined for purposes of such subsection by including the amount of any payments made from such portion of the trust after such date.

(4) This subsection shall not apply to any of the following trusts:

(A) A trust containing the assets of an individual under age 65 who is disabled (as defined in section 1614(a)(3)) and which is established for the benefit of such individual by a parent, grandparent, legal guardian of the individual, or a court if the State will receive all amounts remaining in the trust upon the death of such individual up to an amount equal to the total medical assistance paid on behalf of the individual under a State plan under this title.

(B) A trust established in a State for the benefit of an individual if —

        (i) the trust is composed only of pension, Social Security, and other income to the individual (and accumulated income in the trust),

        (ii) the State will receive all amounts remaining in the trust upon the death of such individual up to an amount equal to the total medical assistance paid on behalf of the individual under a State plan under this title, and

        (iii) the State makes medical assistance available to individuals described in section 1902(a)(10)(A)(ii)(V), but does not make such assistance available to individuals for nursing facility services under section 1902(a)(10)(C).

(C) A trust containing the assets of an individual who is disabled (as defined in section 1614(a)(3)) that meets the following conditions:

(i) The trust is established and managed by a non-profit association.

(ii) A separate account is maintained for each beneficiary of the trust, but, for purposes of investment and management of funds, the trust pools these accounts.

(iii) Accounts in the trust are established solely for the benefit of individuals who are disabled (as defined in section 1614(a)(3)) by the parent, grandparent, or legal guardian of such individuals, by such individuals, or by a court.

(iv) To the extent that amounts remaining in the beneficiary's account upon the death of the beneficiary are not retained by the trust, the trust pays to the State from such remaining amounts in the account an amount equal to the total amount of medical assistance paid on behalf of the beneficiary under the State plan under this title.

(5) The State agency shall establish procedures (in accordance with standards specified by the Secretary) under which the agency waives the application of this subsection with respect to an individual if the individual establishes that such application would work an undue hardship on the individual as determined on the basis of criteria established by the Secretary.

(6) The term "trust" includes any legal instrument or device that is similar to a trust but includes an annuity only to such extent and in such manner as the Secretary specifies.

(e) *Definitions*

In this section, the following definitions shall apply:

(1) The term "assets", with respect to an individual, includes all income and resources of the individual and of the individual's spouse, including any income or resources which the individual or such individual's spouse is entitled to but does not receive because of action —

(A) by the individual or such individual's spouse,

(B) by a person, including a court or administrative body, with legal authority to act in place of or on behalf of the individual or such individual's spouse, or

(C) by any person, including any court or administrative body, acting at the direction or upon the request of the individual or such individual's spouse.

(2) The term "income" has the meaning given such term in section 1612.

(3) The term "institutionalized individual" means an individual who is an inpatient in a nursing facility, who is an inpatient in a medical institution and with respect to whom payment is made based on a level of care provided in a nursing facility, or who is described in section 1902(a)(10)(A)(ii)(VI).

(4) The term "noninstitutionalized individual" means an individual receiving any of the services specified in subsection (c)(1)(C)(ii).

(5) The term "resources" has the meaning given such term in section 1613, without regard (in the case of an institutionalized individual) to the exclusion described in subsection (a)(1) of such section.

## § 1396r. Requirements for nursing facilities

(a) *"Nursing facility" defined*

In this title, the term "nursing facility" means an institution (or a distinct part of an institution) which —

(1) is primarily engaged in providing to residents —

(A) skilled nursing care and related services for residents who require medical or nursing care,

(B) rehabilitation services for the rehabilitation of injured, disabled, or sick persons, or

(C) on a regular basis, health-related care and services to individuals who because of their mental or physical condition require care and services (above the level of room and board) which can be made available to them only through institutional facilities,

and is not primarily for the care and treatment of mental diseases;

(2) has in effect a transfer agreement (meeting the requirements of section 1861(1)) with one or more hospitals having agreements in effect under section 1866; and

(3) meets the requirements for a nursing facility described in subsections (b), (c), and (d) of this section.

## § 1396r-5.  Treatment of income and resources for certain institutionalized spouses

(a) *Special treatment for institutionalized spouses*

(1) Supersedes other provisions.  In determining the eligibility for medical assistance of an institutionalized spouse (as defined in subsection (h)(1)), the provisions of this section supersede any other provision of this title (including sections 1902(a)(17) and 1902(f)) which is inconsistent with them.

(2) No comparable treatment required.  Any different treatment provided under this section for institutionalized spouses shall not, by reason of paragraph (10) or (17) of section 1902(a), require such treatment for other individuals.

(3) Does not affect certain determinations.  Except as this section specifically provides, this section does not apply to —

(A) the determination of what constitutes income or resources, or

(B) the methodology and standards for determining and evaluating income and resources.

(4) Application in certain States and territories.

(A) Application in States operating under demonstration projects.  In the case of any State which is providing medical assistance to its residents under a waiver granted under section 1115, the Secretary shall require the State to meet the requirements of this section in the same manner as the State would be required to meet such requirement if the State had in effect a plan approved under this title.

(B) No application in commonwealths and territories.  This section shall only apply to a State that is one of the 50 States or the District of Columbia.

(5) Application to individuals receiving services under PACE programs.  This section applies to individuals receiving institutional or noninstitutional services under a PACE demonstration waiver program (as defined in section 1934(a)(7)) or under a PACE program under section 1934 or 1894.

(b) *Rules for treatment of income*

(1)  Separate treatment of income

During any month in which an institutionalized spouse is in the institution, except as provided in paragraph (2), no income of the community spouse shall be deemed available to the institutionalized spouse.

(2) Attribution of income

In determining the income of an institutionalized spouse or community spouse for purposes of the post-eligibility income determination described in subsection (d), except as otherwise provided in this section and regardless of any State laws relating to community property or the division of marital property, the following rules apply:

(A) Non-trust property.  Subject to subparagraphs (C) and (D), in the case of income not from a trust, unless the instrument providing the income otherwise specifically provides —

(i) if payment of income is made solely in the name of the institutionalized spouse or the community spouse, the income shall be considered available only to that respective spouse;

(ii) if payment of income is made in the names of the institutionalized spouse and the community spouse, one-half of the income shall be considered available to each of them; and

(iii) if payment of income is made in the names of the institutionalized spouse or the community spouse, or both, and to another person or persons, the income shall be considered available to each spouse in proportion to the spouse's interest (or, if payment is made with respect to both spouses and no such interest is specified, one-half of the joint interest shall be considered available to each spouse).

(B) Trust property.  In the case of a trust —

(i) except as provided in clause (ii), income shall be attributed in accordance with the provisions of this title(including sections 1902(a)(17) and 1917(d)), and

(ii) income shall be considered available to each spouse as provided in the trust, or, in the absence of a specific provision in the trust —

(I) if payment of income is made solely to the institutionalized spouse or the community spouse, the income shall be considered available only to that respective spouse;

(II) if payment of income is made to both the institutionalized spouse and the community spouse, one-half of the income shall be considered available to each of them; and

(III) if payment of income is made to the institutionalized spouse or the community spouse, or both, and to another person or persons, the income shall be considered available to each spouse in proportion to the spouse's interest (or, if payment is made with respect to both spouses and no such interest is specified, one-half of the joint interest shall be considered available to each spouse).

(C) Property with no instrument.  In the case of income not from a trust in which there is no instrument establishing ownership, subject to subparagraph (D), one-half of the income shall be considered to be available to the institutionalized spouse and one-half to the community spouse.

(D) Rebutting ownership.  The rules of subparagraphs (A) and (C) are superseded to the extent that an institutionalized spouse can establish, by a preponderance of the evidence, that the ownership interests in income are other than as provided under such subparagraphs.

(c)  *Rules for treatment of resources*

(1)  Computation of spousal share at time of institutionalization

(A) Total joint resources.  There shall be computed (as of the beginning of the first continuous period of institutionalization (beginning on or after September 30, 1989) of the institutionalized spouse) —

(i) the total value of the resources to the extent either the institutionalized spouse or the community spouse has an ownership interest, and

(ii) a spousal share which is equal to 1/2 of such total value.

(B) Assessment.  At the request of an institutionalized spouse or community spouse, at the beginning of the first continuous period of institutionalization (beginning on or after September 30, 1989) of the institutionalized spouse and upon the receipt of relevant documentation of resources, the State shall promptly assess and document the total value described in subparagraph (A)(i) and shall provide a copy of such assessment and documentation to each spouse and shall retain a copy of the assessment for use under this section. If the request is not part of an application for medical assistance under this title, the State may, at its option as a condition of providing the assessment, require payment of a fee not exceeding the reasonable expenses of providing and documenting the assessment. At the time of providing the copy of the assessment, the State shall include a notice indicating that the spouse will have a right to a fair hearing under subsection (e)(2).

(2) Attribution of resources at time of initial eligibility determination

In determining the resources of an institutionalized spouse at the time of application for benefits under this title, regardless of any State laws relating to community property or the division of marital property —

(A) except as provided in subparagraph (B), all the resources held by either the institutionalized spouse, community spouse, or both, shall be considered to be available to the institutionalized spouse, and

(B) resources shall be considered to be available to an institutionalized spouse, but only to the extent that the amount of such resources exceeds the amount computed under subsection (f)(2)(A) (as of the time of application for benefits).

(3) Assignment of support rights. The institutionalized spouse shall not be ineligible by reason of resources determined under paragraph (2) to be available for the cost of care where —

(A) the institutionalized spouse has assigned to the State any rights to support from the community spouse;

(B) the institutionalized spouse lacks the ability to execute an assignment due to physical or mental impairment but the State has the right to bring a support proceeding against a community spouse without such assignment; or

(C) the State determines that denial of eligibility would work an undue hardship.

(4) Separate treatment of resources after eligibility for benefits established. During the continuous period in which an institutionalized spouse is in an institution and after the month in which an institutionalized spouse is determined to be eligible for benefits under this title, no

resources of the community spouse shall be deemed available to the institutionalized spouse.

(5) Resources defined. In this section, the term "resources" does not include —

(A) resources excluded under subsection (a) or (d) of section 1613, and

(B) resources that would be excluded under section 1613(a)(2)(A) but for the limitation on total value described in such section.

(d) *Protecting income for community spouse*

(1) Allowances to be offset from income of institutionalized spouse. After an institutionalized spouse is determined or redetermined to be eligible for medical assistance, in determining the amount of the spouse's income that is to be applied monthly to payment for the costs of care in the institution, there shall be deducted from the spouse's monthly income the following amounts in the following order:

(A) A personal needs allowance (described in section 1902(q)(1)), in an amount not less than the amount specified in section 1902(q)(2).

(B) A community spouse monthly income allowance (as defined in paragraph (2)), but only to the extent income of the institutionalized spouse is made available to (or for the benefit of) the community spouse.

(C) A family allowance, for each family member, equal to at least 1/3 of the amount by which the amount described in paragraph (3)(A)(i) exceeds the amount of the monthly income of that family member.

(D) Amounts for incurred expenses for medical or remedial care for the institutionalized spouse (as provided under section 1902(r) ). In subparagraph (C), the term "family member" only includes minor or dependent children, dependent parents, or dependent siblings of the institutionalized or community spouse who are residing with the community spouse.

(2) Community spouse monthly income allowance defined

In this section (except as provided in paragraph (5)), the "community spouse monthly income allowance" for a community spouse is an amount by which —

(A) except as provided in subsection (e), the minimum monthly maintenance needs allowance (established under and in accordance with paragraph (3)) for the spouse, exceeds

(B) the amount of monthly income otherwise available to the community spouse (determined without regard to such an allowance).

(3) Establishment of minimum monthly maintenance needs allowance.

(A) In general. Each State shall establish a minimum monthly maintenance needs allowance for each community spouse which, subject to subparagraph (C), is equal to or exceeds —

(i) the applicable percent (described in subparagraph (B)) of 1/12 of the income official poverty line (defined by the Office of Management and Budget and revised annually in accordance with section 673(2) of the Omnibus Budget Reconciliation Act of 1981) for a family unit of 2 members; plus

(ii) an excess shelter allowance (as defined in paragraph (4)).

A revision of the official poverty line referred to in clause (i) shall apply to medical assistance furnished during and after the second calendar quarter that begins after the date of publication of the revision.

(B) Applicable percent. For purposes of subparagraph (A)(i), the "applicable percent" described in this paragraph, effective as of —

(i) September 30, 1989, is 122 percent,

(ii) July 1, 1991, is 133 percent, and

(iii) July 1, 1992, is 150 percent.

(C) Cap on minimum monthly maintenance needs allowance. The minimum monthly maintenance needs allowance established under subparagraph (A) may not exceed $1,500 (subject to adjustment under subsections (e) and (g)).

(4) Excess shelter allowance defined. In paragraph (3)(A)(ii), the term "excess shelter allowance" means, for a community spouse, the amount by which the sum of —

(A) the spouse's expenses for rent or mortgage payment (including principal and interest), taxes and insurance and, in the case of a condominium or cooperative, required maintenance charge, for the community spouse's principal residence, and

(B) the standard utility allowance (used by the State under section 5(e) of the Food Stamp Act of 1977) or, if the State does not use such an allowance, the spouse's actual utility expenses,

exceeds 30 percent of the amount described in paragraph (3)(A)(i), except that, in the case of a condominium or cooperative, for which a maintenance charge is included under subparagraph (A), any allowance under subparagraph (B) shall be reduced to the extent the maintenance charge includes utility expenses.

(5) Court ordered support. If a court has entered an order against an institutionalized spouse for monthly income for the support of the community spouse, the community spouse monthly income allowance for the spouse shall be not less than the amount of the monthly income so ordered.

(e) *Notice and fair hearing*

(1) Notice. Upon —

(A) a determination of eligibility for medical assistance of an institutionalized spouse, or

(B) a request by either the institutionalized spouse, or the community spouse, or a representative acting on behalf of either spouse,

each State shall notify both spouses (in the case described in subparagraph (A)) or the spouse making the request (in the case described in subparagraph (B)) of the amount of the community spouse monthly income allowance (described in subsection (d)(1)(B)), of the amount of any family allowances (described in subsection (d)(1)(C)), of the method for computing the amount of the community spouse resources allowance permitted under subsection (f), and of the spouse's right to a fair hearing under this subsection respecting ownership or availability of income or resources, and the determination of the community spouse monthly income or resource allowance.

(2) Fair hearing

(A) In general

If either the institutionalized spouse or the community spouse is dissatisfied with a determination of —

(i) the community spouse monthly income allowance;

(ii) the amount of monthly income otherwise available to the community spouse (as applied under subsection (d)(2)(B));

     (iii) the computation of the spousal share of resources under subsection (c)(1);

     (iv) the attribution of resources under subsection (c)(2); or

     (v) the determination of the community spouse resource allowance (as defined in subsection (f)(2));

such spouse is entitled to a fair hearing described in section 1902(a)(3) with respect to such determination if an application for benefits under this title has been made on behalf of the institutionalized spouse. Any such hearing respecting the determination of the community spouse resource allowance shall be held within 30 days of the date of the request for the hearing.

    (B) Revision of minimum monthly maintenance needs allowance. If either such spouse establishes that the community spouse needs income, above the level otherwise provided by the minimum monthly maintenance needs allowance, due to exceptional circumstances resulting in significant financial duress, there shall be substituted, for the minimum monthly maintenance needs allowance in subsection (d)(2)(A), an amount adequate to provide such additional income as is necessary.

    (C) Revision of community spouse resource allowance. If either such spouse establishes that the community spouse resource allowance (in relation to the amount of income generated by such an allowance) is inadequate to raise the community spouse's income to the minimum monthly maintenance needs allowance, there shall be substituted, for the community spouse resource allowance under subsection (f)(2), an amount adequate to provide such a minimum monthly maintenance needs allowance.

## (f) *Permitting transfer of resources to community spouse*

### (1) In general

  An institutionalized spouse may, without regard to section 1917(c)(1), transfer an amount equal to the community spouse resource allowance (as defined in paragraph (2)), but only to the extent the resources of the institutionalized spouse are transferred to (or for the sole benefit of) the community spouse. The transfer under the preceding sentence shall be made as soon as practicable after the date of the initial determination of eligibility, taking into account such time as may be necessary to obtain a court order under paragraph (3).

(2) Community spouse resource allowance defined

In paragraph (1), the "community spouse resource allowance" for a community spouse is an amount (if any) by which —

(A) the greatest of —

(i) $12,000 (subject to adjustment under subsection (g)), or, if greater (but not to exceed the amount specified in clause (ii)(II)) an amount specified under the State plan,

(ii) the lesser of (I) the spousal share computed under subsection (c)(1), or (II) $60,000 (subject to adjustment under subsection (g)),

(iii) the amount established under subsection (e)(2); or

(iv) the amount transferred under a court order under paragraph (3);

exceeds

(B) the amount of the resources otherwise available to the community spouse (determined without regard to such an allowance).

(3) Transfers under court orders. If a court has entered an order against an institutionalized spouse for the support of the community spouse, section 1917 shall not apply to amounts of resources transferred pursuant to such order for the support of the spouse or a family member (as defined in subsection (d)(1)).

(g) *Indexing dollar amounts*

For services furnished during a calendar year after 1989, the dollar amounts specified in subsections (d)(3)(C), (f)(2)(A)(i), and (f)(2)(A)(ii)(II) shall be increased by the same percentage as the percentage increase in the consumer price index for all urban consumers (all items; U.S. city average) between September 1988 and the September before the calendar year involved.

(h) *Definitions. In this section:*

(1) The term "institutionalized spouse" means an individual who —

(A) is in a medical institution or nursing facility or who (at the option of the State) is described in section 1902(a)(10)(A)(ii)(VI), and

(B) is married to a spouse who is not in a medical institution or nursing facility;

but does not include any such individual who is not likely to meet the requirements of subparagraph (A) for at least 30 consecutive days.

(2) The term "community spouse" means the spouse of an institutionalized spouse.

## § 1396t. Home and community care for functionally disabled elderly individuals

(a) *"Home and community care" defined*

In this title, the term "home and community care" means one or more of the following services furnished to an individual who has been determined, after an assessment under subsection (c), to be a functionally disabled elderly individual, furnished in accordance with an individual community care plan (established and periodically reviewed and revised by a qualified community care case manager under subsection (d)):

(1) Homemaker/home health aide services.

(2) Chore services.

(3) Personal care services.

(4) Nursing care services provided by, or under the supervision of, a registered nurse.

(5) Respite care.

(6) Training for family members in managing the individual.

(7) Adult day care.

(8) In the case of an individual with chronic mental illness, day treatment or other partial hospitalization, psychosocial rehabilitation services, and clinic services (whether or not furnished in a facility).

(9) Such other home and community-based services (other than room and board) as the Secretary may approve.

(b) *"Functionally disabled elderly individual" defined*

(1) In general. In this title, the term "functionally disabled elderly individual" means an individual who —

(A) is 65 years of age or older,

(B) is determined to be a functionally disabled individual under subsection (c), and

(C) subject to section 1902(f) (as applied consistent with section 1902(r)(2)), is receiving supplemental security income benefits under title XVI(or under a State plan approved under title XVI) or, at the option of the State, is described in section 1902(a)(10)(C).

(2) Treatment of certain individuals previously covered under a waiver.

(A) In the case of a State which —

(i) at the time of its election to provide coverage for home and community care under this section has a waiver approved under section 1915(c) or 1915(d) with respect to individuals 65 years of age or older, and

(ii) subsequently discontinues such waiver, individuals who were eligible for benefits under the waiver as of the date of its discontinuance and who would, but for income or resources, be eligible for medical assistance for home and community care under the plan shall, notwithstanding any other provision of this title, be deemed a functionally disabled elderly individual for so long as the individual would have remained eligible for medical assistance under such waiver.

(B) In the case of a State which used a health insuring organization before January 1, 1986, and which, as of December 31, 1990, had in effect a waiver under section 1115 that provides under the State plan under this title for personal care services for functionally disabled individuals, the term "functionally disabled elderly individual" may include, at the option of the State, an individual who-

(i) is 65 years of age or older or is disabled (as determined under the supplemental security income program under title XVI);

(ii) is determined to meet the test of functional disability applied under the waiver as of such date; and

(iii) meets the resource requirement and income standard that apply in the State to individuals described in section 1902(a)(10)(A)(ii)(V).

(3) Use of projected income.  In applying section 1903(f)(1) in determining the eligibility of an individual (described in section 1902(a)(10)(C)) for medical assistance for home and community care, a State may, at its option, provide for the determination of the individual's anticipated medical expenses (to be deducted from income) over a period of up to 6 months.

(c)  *Determinations of functional disability*

(1) In general

In this section, an individual is "functionally disabled" if the individual —

(A) is unable to perform without substantial assistance from another individual at least 2 of the following 3 activities of daily living: toileting, transferring, and eating; or

(B) has a primary or secondary diagnosis of Alzheimer's disease and is (i) unable to perform without substantial human assistance (including verbal reminding or physical cueing) or supervision at least 2 of the following 5 activities of daily living: bathing, dressing, toileting, transferring, and eating; or (ii) cognitively impaired so as to require substantial supervision from another individual because he or she engages in inappropriate behaviors that pose serious health or safety hazards to himself or herself or others.

(2) Assessments of functional disability.

(A) Requests for assessments. If a State has elected to provide home and community care under this section, upon the request of an individual who is 65 years of age or older and who meets the requirements of subsection (b)(1)(C) (or another person on such individual's behalf), the State shall provide for a comprehensive functional assessment under this subparagraph which —

(i) is used to determine whether or not the individual is functionally disabled,

(ii) is based on a uniform minimum data set specified by the Secretary under subparagraph (C)(i), and

(iii) uses an instrument which has been specified by the State under subparagraph (B). No fee may be charged for such an assessment.

(B) Specification of assessment instrument. The State shall specify the instrument to be used in the State in complying with the requirement of subparagraph (A)(iii) which instrument shall be —

(i) one of the instruments designated under subparagraph (C)(ii); or

(ii) an instrument which the Secretary has approved as being consistent with the minimum data set of core elements, common definitions, and utilization guidelines specified by the Secretary in subparagraph (C)(i).

(C) Specification of assessment data set and instruments. The Secretary shall —

(i) not later than July 1, 1991 —

(I) specify a minimum data set of core elements and common definitions for use in conducting the assessments required under subparagraph (A); and

(II) establish guidelines for use of the data set; and

(ii) by not later than July 1, 1991, designate one or more instruments which are consistent with the specification made under subparagraph (A) and which a State may specify under subparagraph (B) for use in complying with the requirements of subparagraph (A).

(D) Periodic review. Each individual who qualifies as a functionally disabled elderly individual shall have the individual's assessment periodically reviewed and revised not less often than once every 12 months.

(E) Conduct of assessment by interdisciplinary teams. An assessment under subparagraph (A) and a review under subparagraph (D) must be conducted by an interdisciplinary team designated by the State. The Secretary shall permit a State to provide for assessments and reviews through teams under contracts —

(i) with public organizations; or

(ii) with nonpublic organizations which do not provide home and community care or nursing facility services and do not have a direct or indirect ownership or control interest in, or direct or indirect affiliation or relationship with, an entity that provides, community care or nursing facility services.

(F) Contents of assessment. The interdisciplinary team must —

(i) identify in each such assessment or review each individual's functional disabilities and need for home and community care, including information about the individual's health status, home and community environment, and informal support system; and

(ii) based on such assessment or review, determine whether the individual is (or continues to be) functionally disabled.

The results of such an assessment or review shall be used in establishing, reviewing, and revising the individual's ICCP under subsection (d)(1).

(G) Appeal procedures. Each State which elects to provide home and community care under this section must have in effect an appeals process for individuals adversely affected by determinations under subparagraph (F).

(d)  *Individual community care plan (ICCP)*

(1) Individual community care plan defined.  In this section, the terms "individual community care plan" and "ICCP" mean, with respect to a functionally disabled elderly individual, a written plan which —

(A) is established, and is periodically reviewed and revised, by a qualified case manager after a face-to-face interview with the individual or primary caregiver and based upon the most recent comprehensive functional assessment of such individual conducted under subsection (c)(2);

(B) specifies, within any amount, duration, and scope limitations imposed on home and community care provided under the State plan, the home and community care to be provided to such individual under the plan, and indicates the individual's preferences for the types and providers of services; and

(C) may specify other services required by such individual. An ICCP may also designate the specific providers (qualified to provide home and community care under the State plan) which will provide the home and community care described in subparagraph (B). Nothing in this section shall be construed as authorizing an ICCP or the State to restrict the specific persons or individuals (who are competent to provide home and community care under the State plan) who will provide the home and community care described in subparagraph (B).

(2) Qualified community care case manager defined. In this section, the term "qualified community care case manager" means a nonprofit or public agency or organization which —

(A) has experience or has been trained in establishing, and in periodically reviewing and revising, individual community care plans and in the provision of case management services to the elderly;

(B) is responsible for (i) assuring that home and community care covered under the State plan and specified in the ICCP is being provided, (ii) visiting each individual's home or community setting where care is being provided not less often than once every 90 days, and (iii) informing the elderly individual or primary caregiver on how to contact the case manager if service providers fail to properly provide services or other similar problems occur;

(C) in the case of a nonpublic agency, does not provide home and community care or nursing facility services and does not have a direct or indirect ownership or control interest in, or direct or indirect affiliation or relationship with, an entity that provides, home and community care or nursing facility services;

(D) has procedures for assuring the quality of case management services that includes a peer review process;

(E) completes the ICCP in a timely manner and reviews and discusses new and revised ICCPs with elderly individuals or primary caregivers; and

(F) meets such other standards, established by the Secretary, as to assure that —

(i) such a manager is competent to perform case management functions;

(ii) individuals whose home and community care they manage are not at risk of financial exploitation due to such a manager; and

(iii) meets such other standards as the State may establish.

The Secretary may waive the requirement of subparagraph (C) in the case of a nonprofit agency located in a rural area.

(3) Appeals process. Each State which elects to provide home and community care under this section must have in effect an appeals process for individuals who disagree with the ICCP established.

# Long Term Care Facilities and Home Health Agencies
### 42 CFR Parts 483 & 484

## PART 483 — CONDITIONS OF PARTICIPATION AND REQUIREMENTS FOR LONG TERM CARE FACILITIES

### Subpart A – [Reserved]

### Subpart B – Requirements for Long Term Care Facilities

### Subpart C – [Reserved]

### Subpart D – Requirements That Must Be Met by States and State Agencies: Nurse Aide Training and Competency Evaluation

Subparts E-H – [Reserved]

## Subpart I – Conditions of Participation for Intermediate Care Facilities for the Mentally Retarded

## Subpart A – [Reserved]

## Subpart B – Requirements for Long Term Care Facilities

## § 483.1.  Basis and scope

(a) *Statutory basis*

(1) Sections 1819 (a), (b), (c), and (d) of the Act provide that —

(i) Skilled nursing facilities participating in Medicare must meet certain specified requirements; and

(ii) The Secretary may impose additional requirements (see section 1819(d)(4)(B)) if they are necessary for the health and safety of individuals to whom services are furnished in the facilities.

(2) Section 1861(l) of the Act requires the facility to have in effect a transfer agreement with a hospital.

(3) Sections 1919 (a), (b), (c), and (d) of the Act provide that nursing facilities participating in Medicaid must meet certain specific requirements.

(b) *Scope*

The provisions of this part contain the requirements that an institution must meet in order to qualify to participate as a SNF in the Medicare program, and as a nursing facility in the Medicaid program. They serve as the basis for survey activities for the purpose of determining whether a facility meets the requirements for participation in Medicare and Medicaid.

## § 483.5.  Definitions

For purposes of this subpart —

Facility means, a skilled nursing facility (SNF) or a nursing facility (NF) which meets the requirements of sections 1819 or 1919 (a), (b), (c), and (d) of the Act. "Facility" may include a distinct part of an institution specified in § 440.40 of this chapter, but does not include an institution for the mentally retarded or persons with related conditions described in § 440.150 of this chapter. For Medicare and Medicaid purposes (including eligibility, coverage, certification, and payment), the "facility" is always the entity which participates in the program, whether that entity is comprised of all of, or a distinct part of a larger institution. For Medicare, a SNF (see section 1819(a)(1)), and for Medicaid, a NF (see section 1919(a)(1)) may not be an institution for mental diseases as defined in § 435.1009.

## § 483.10.  Resident rights

The resident has a right to a dignified existence, self-determination, and communication with and access to persons and services inside and outside the facility. A facility must protect and promote the rights of each resident, including each of the following rights:

(a)  *Exercise of rights*

(1) The resident has the right to exercise his or her rights as a resident of the facility and as a citizen or resident of the United States.

(2) The resident has the right to be free of interference, coercion, discrimination, and reprisal from the facility in exercising his or her rights.

(3) In the case of a resident adjudged incompetent under the laws of a State by a court of competent jurisdiction, the rights of the resident are exercised by the person appointed under State law to act on the resident's behalf.

(4) In the case of a resident who has not been adjudged incompetent by the State court, any legal-surrogate designated in accordance with State law may exercise the resident's rights to the extent provided by State law.

(b)  *Notice of rights and services*

(1) The facility must inform the resident both orally and in writing in a language that the resident understands of his or her rights and all rules and regulations governing resident conduct and responsibilities during the

stay in the facility. The facility must also provide the resident with the notice (if any) of the State developed under section 1919(e)(6) of the Act. Such notification must be made prior to or upon admission and during the resident's stay. Receipt of such information, and any amendments to it, must be acknowledged in writing;

(2) The resident or his or her legal representative has the right —

(i) Upon an oral or written request, to access all records pertaining to himself or herself including current clinical records within 24 hours (excluding weekends and holidays); and

(ii) After receipt of his or her records for inspection, to purchase at a cost not to exceed the community standard photocopies of the records or any portions of them upon request and 2 working days advance notice to the facility.

(3) The resident has the right to be fully informed in language that he or she can understand of his or her total health status, including but not limited to, his or her medical condition;

(4) The resident has the right to refuse treatment, to refuse to participate in experimental research, and to formulate an advance directive as specified in paragraph (8) of this section; and

(5) The facility must —

(i) Inform each resident who is entitled to Medicaid benefits, in writing, at the time of admission to the nursing facility or, when the resident becomes eligible for Medicaid of —

(A) The items and services that are included in nursing facility services under the State plan and for which the resident may not be charged;

(B) Those other items and services that the facility offers and for which the resident may be charged, and the amount of charges for those services; and

(ii) Inform each resident when changes are made to the items and services specified in paragraphs (5)(i) (A) and (B) of this section.

(6) The facility must inform each resident before, or at the time of admission, and periodically during the resident's stay, of services available in the facility and of charges for those services, including any charges for services not covered under Medicare or by the facility's per diem rate.

(7) The facility must furnish a written description of legal rights that includes —

(i) A description of the manner of protecting personal funds, under paragraph (c) of this section;

(ii) A description of the requirements and procedures for establishing eligibility for Medicaid, including the right to request an assessment under section 1924(c) which determines the extent of a couple's non-exempt resources at the time of institutionalization and attributes to the community spouse an equitable share of resources which cannot be considered available for payment toward the cost of the institutionalized spouse's medical care in his or her process of spending down to Medicaid eligibility levels;

(iii) A posting of names, addresses, and telephone numbers of all pertinent State client advocacy groups such as the State survey and certification agency, the State licensure office, the State ombudsman program, the protection and advocacy network, and the Medicaid fraud control unit; and

(iv) A statement that the resident may file a complaint with the State survey and certification agency concerning resident abuse, neglect, misappropriation of resident property in the facility, and non-compliance with the advance directives requirements.

(8) The facility must comply with the requirements specified in subpart I of part 489 of this chapter relating to maintaining written policies and procedures regarding advance directives. These requirements include provisions to inform and provide written information to all adult residents concerning the right to accept or refuse medical or surgical treatment and, at the individual's option, formulate an advance directive. This includes a written description of the facility's policies to implement advance directives and applicable State law. Facilities are permitted to contract with other entities to furnish this information but are still legally responsible for ensuring that the requirements of this section are met. If an adult individual is incapacitated at the time of admission and is unable to receive information (due to the incapacitating condition or a mental disorder) or articulate whether or not he or she has executed an advance directive, the facility may give advance directive information to the individual's family or surrogate in the same manner that it issues other materials about policies and procedures to the family of the incapacitated individual or to a surrogate or other concerned persons in accordance with State law. The facility is not relieved of its obligation to provide this information to the individual once he or she is no longer incapacitated or unable to receive such information. Follow-up procedures must be in place to provide the information to the individual directly at the appropriate time.

(9) The facility must inform each resident of the name, specialty, and way of contacting the physician responsible for his or her care.

(10) The facility must prominently display in the facility written information, and provide to residents and applicants for admission oral and written information about how to apply for and use Medicare and Medicaid benefits, and how to receive refunds for previous payments covered by such benefits.

(11) Notification of changes.

(i) A facility must immediately inform the resident; consult with the resident's physician; and if known, notify the resident's legal representative or an interested family member when there is —

(A) An accident involving the resident which results in injury and has the potential for requiring physician intervention;

(B) A significant change in the resident's physical, mental, or psychosocial status (i.e., a deterioration in health, mental, or psychosocial status in either life-threatening conditions or clinical complications);

(C) A need to alter treatment significantly (i.e., a need to discontinue an existing form of treatment due to adverse consequences, or to commence a new form of treatment); or

(D) A decision to transfer or discharge the resident from the facility as specified in § 483.12(a).

(ii) The facility must also promptly notify the resident and, if known, the resident's legal representative or interested family member when there is —

(A) A change in room or roommate assignment as specified in § 483.15(e)(2); or

(B) A change in resident rights under Federal or State law or regulations as specified in paragraph (b)(1) of this section.

(iii) The facility must record and periodically update the address and phone number of the resident's legal representative or interested family member.

(c) *Protection of Resident Funds*

(1) The resident has the right to manage his or her financial affairs, and the facility may not require residents to deposit their personal funds with the facility.

(2) Management of personal funds. Upon written authorization of a resident, the facility must hold, safeguard, manage, and account for the

personal funds of the resident deposited with the facility, as specified in paragraphs (c)(3)-(8) of this section.

(3) Deposit of funds.

(i) Funds in excess of $50. The facility must deposit any residents' personal funds in excess of $50 in an interest bearing account (or accounts) that is separate from any of the facility's operating accounts, and that credits all interest earned on resident's funds to that account. (In pooled accounts, there must be a separate accounting for each resident's share.)

(ii) Funds less than $50. The facility must maintain a resident's personal funds that do not exceed $50 in a non-interest bearing account, interest-bearing account, or petty cash fund.

(4) Accounting and records. The facility must establish and maintain a system that assures a full and complete and separate accounting, according to generally accepted accounting principles, of each resident's personal funds entrusted to the facility on the resident's behalf.

(i) The system must preclude any commingling of resident funds with facility funds or with the funds of any person other than another resident.

(ii) The individual financial record must be available through quarterly statements and on request to the resident or his or her legal representative.

(5) Notice of certain balances. The facility must notify each resident that receives Medicaid benefits —

(i) When the amount in the resident's account reaches $200 less than the SSI resource limit for one person, specified in section 1611(a)(3)(B) of the Act; and

(ii) That, if the amount in the account, in addition to the value of the resident's other nonexempt resources, reaches the SSI resource limit for one person, the resident may lose eligibility for Medicaid or SSI.

(6) Conveyance upon death. Upon the death of a resident with a personal fund deposited with the facility, the facility must convey within 30 days the resident's funds, and a final accounting of those funds, to the individual or probate jurisdiction administering the resident's estate.

(7) Assurance of financial security. The facility must purchase a surety bond, or otherwise provide assurance satisfactory to the Secretary, to assure the security of all personal funds of residents deposited with the facility.

(8) Limitation on charges to personal funds. The facility may not impose a charge against the personal funds of a resident for any item or service for which payment is made under Medicaid or Medicare (except for applicable deductible and coinsurance amounts). The facility may charge the resident for requested services that are more expensive than or in excess of covered services in accordance with § 489.32 of this chapter. (This does not affect the prohibition on facility charges for items and services for which Medicaid has paid. See § 447.15, which limits participation in the Medicaid program to providers who accept, as payment in full, Medicaid payment plus any deductible, coinsurance, or copayment required by the plan to be paid by the individual.)

(i) Services included in Medicare or Medicaid payment. During the course of a covered Medicare or Medicaid stay, facilities may not charge a resident for the following categories of items and services:

(A) Nursing services as required at § 483.30 of this subpart.

(B) Dietary services as required at § 483.35 of this subpart.

(C) An activities program as required at § 483.15(f) of this subpart.

(D) Room/bed maintenance services.

(E) Routine personal hygiene items and services as required to meet the needs of residents, including, but not limited to, hair hygiene supplies, comb, brush, bath soap, disinfecting soaps or specialized cleansing agents when indicated to treat special skin problems or to fight infection, razor, shaving cream, toothbrush, toothpaste, denture adhesive, denture cleaner, dental floss, moisturizing lotion, tissues, cotton balls, cotton swabs, deodorant, incontinence care and supplies, sanitary napkins and related supplies, towels, washcloths, hospital gowns, over the counter drugs, hair and nail hygiene services, bathing, and basic personal laundry.

(F) Medically-related social services as required at § 483.15(g) of this subpart.

(ii) Items and services that may be charged to residents' funds. Listed below are general categories and examples of items and services that the facility may charge to residents' funds if they are requested by a resident, if the facility informs the resident that there will be a charge, and if payment is not made by Medicare or Medicaid:

(A) Telephone.

(B) Television/radio for personal use.

(C) Personal comfort items, including smoking materials, notions and novelties, and confections.

(D) Cosmetic and grooming items and services in excess of those for which payment is made under Medicaid or Medicare.

(E) Personal clothing.

(F) Personal reading matter.

(G) Gifts purchased on behalf of a resident.

(H) Flowers and plants.

(I) Social events and entertainment offered outside the scope of the activities program, provided under § 483.15(f) of this subpart.

(J) Noncovered special care services such as privately hired nurses or aides.

(K) Private room, except when therapeutically required (for example, isolation for infection control).

(L) Specially prepared or alternative food requested instead of the food generally prepared by the facility, as required by § 483.35 of this subpart.

(iii) Requests for items and services. (A) The facility must not charge a resident (or his or her representative) for any item or service not requested by the resident.

(B) The facility must not require a resident (or his or her representative) to request any item or service as a condition of admission or continued stay.

(C) The facility must inform the resident (or his or her representative) requesting an item or service for which a charge will be made that there will be a charge for the item or service and what the charge will be.

(d) *Free choice*

The resident has the right to —

(1) Choose a personal attending physician;

(2) Be fully informed in advance about care and treatment and of any changes in that care or treatment that may affect the resident's well-being; and

(3) Unless adjudged incompetent or otherwise found to be incapacitated under the laws of the State, participate in planning care and treatment or changes in care and treatment.

(e) *Privacy and confidentiality*

The resident has the right to personal privacy and confidentiality of his or her personal and clinical records.

(1) Personal privacy includes accommodations, medical treatment, written and telephone communications, personal care, visits, and meetings of family and resident groups, but this does not require the facility to provide a private room for each resident;

(2) Except as provided in paragraph (e)(3) of this section, the resident may approve or refuse the release of personal and clinical records to any individual outside the facility;

(3) The resident's right to refuse release of personal and clinical records does not apply when —

> (i) The resident is transferred to another health care institution; or

> (ii) Record release is required by law.

(f) *Grievances*

A resident has the right to —

(1) Voice grievances without discrimination or reprisal. Such grievances include those with respect to treatment which has been furnished as well as that which has not been furnished; and

(2) Prompt efforts by the facility to resolve grievances the resident may have, including those with respect to the behavior of other residents.

(g) *Examination of survey results*

A resident has the right to —

(1) Examine the results of the most recent survey of the facility conducted by Federal or State surveyors and any plan of correction in effect with respect to the facility. The facility must make the results available for examination in a place readily accessible to residents, and must post a notice of their availability; and

(2) Receive information from agencies acting as client advocates, and be afforded the opportunity to contact these agencies.

(h) *Work*

The resident has the right to —

(1) Refuse to perform services for the facility;

(2) Perform services for the facility, if he or she chooses, when —

(i) The facility has documented the need or desire for work in the plan of care;

(ii) The plan specifies the nature of the services performed and whether the services are voluntary or paid;

(iii) Compensation for paid services is at or above prevailing rates; and

(iv) The resident agrees to the work arrangement described in the plan of care.

(i) *Mail*

The resident has the right to privacy in written communications, including the right to —

(1) Send and promptly receive mail that is unopened; and

(2) Have access to stationery, postage, and writing implements at the resident's own expense.

(j) *Access and visitation rights*

(1) The resident has the right and the facility must provide immediate access to any resident by the following:

(i) Any representative of the Secretary;

(ii) Any representative of the State:

(iii) The resident's individual physician;

(iv) The State long term care ombudsman (established under section 307(a)(12) of the Older Americans Act of 1965);

(v) The agency responsible for the protection and advocacy system for developmentally disabled individuals (established under part C of the Developmental Disabilities Assistance and Bill of Rights Act);

(vi) The agency responsible for the protection and advocacy system for mentally ill individuals (established under the Protection and Advocacy for Mentally Ill Individuals Act);

(vii) Subject to the resident's right to deny or withdraw consent at any time, immediate family or other relatives of the resident; and

(viii) Subject to reasonable restrictions and the resident's right to deny or withdraw consent at any time, others who are visiting with the consent of the resident.

(2) The facility must provide reasonable access to any resident by any entity or individual that provides health, social, legal, or other services to the resident, subject to the resident's right to deny or withdraw consent at any time.

(3) The facility must allow representatives of the State Ombudsman, described in paragraph (j)(1)(iv) of this section, to examine a resident's clinical records with the permission of the resident or the resident's legal representative, and consistent with State law.

(k) *Telephone*

The resident has the right to have reasonable access to the use of a telephone where calls can be made without being overheard.

(l) *Personal property*

The resident has the right to retain and use personal possessions, including some furnishings, and appropriate clothing, as space permits, unless to do so would infringe upon the rights or health and safety of other residents.

(m) *Married couples*

The resident has the right to share a room with his or her spouse when married residents live in the same facility and both spouses consent to the arrangement.

(n) *Self-Administration of Drugs*

An individual resident may self-administer drugs if the interdisciplinary team, as defined by § 483.20(d)(2)(ii), has determined that this practice is safe.

(o) *Refusal of certain transfers*

(1) An individual has the right to refuse a transfer to another room within the institution, if the purpose of the transfer is to relocate —

(i) A resident of a SNF from the distinct part of the institution that is a SNF to a part of the institution that is not a SNF, or

(ii) A resident of a NF from the distinct part of the institution that is a NF to a distinct part of the institution that is a SNF.

(2) A resident's exercise of the right to refuse transfer under paragraph (o)(1) of this section does not affect the individual's eligibility or entitlement to Medicare or Medicaid benefits.

## § 483.12. Admission, transfer and discharge rights

(a) *Transfer and discharge* —

(1) *Definition*: Transfer and discharge includes movement of a resident to a bed outside of the certified facility whether that bed is in the same physical plant or not. Transfer and discharge does not refer to movement of a resident to a bed within the same certified facility.

(2) *Transfer and discharge requirements*. The facility must permit each resident to remain in the facility, and not transfer or discharge the resident from the facility unless —

(i) The transfer or discharge is necessary for the resident's welfare and the resident's needs cannot be met in the facility;

(ii) The transfer or discharge is appropriate because the resident's health has improved sufficiently so the resident no longer needs the services provided by the facility;

(iii) The safety of individuals in the facility is endangered;

(iv) The health of individuals in the facility would otherwise be endangered;

(v) The resident has failed, after reasonable and appropriate notice, to pay for (or to have paid under Medicare or Medicaid) a stay at the facility. For a resident who becomes eligible for Medicaid after admission to a facility, the facility may charge a resident only allowable charges under Medicaid; or

(vi) The facility ceases to operate.

(3) Documentation. When the facility transfers or discharges a resident under any of the circumstances specified in paragraphs (a)(2)(i) through (v) of this section, the resident's clinical record must be documented. The documentation must be made by —

(i) The resident's physician when transfer or discharge is necessary under paragraph (a)(2)(i) or paragraph (a)(2)(ii) of this section; and

(ii) A physician when transfer or discharge is necessary under paragraph (a)(2)(iv) of this section.

(4) Notice before transfer. Before a facility transfers or discharges a resident, the facility must —

(i) Notify the resident and, if known, a family member or legal representative of the resident of the transfer or discharge and the reasons for the move in writing and in a language and manner they understand.

(ii) Record the reasons in the resident's clinical record; and

(iii) Include in the notice the items described in paragraph (a)(6) of this section.

(5) Timing of the notice.

(i) Except when specified in paragraph (a)(5)(ii) of this section, the notice of transfer or discharge required under paragraph (a)(4) of this section must be made by the facility at least 30 days before the resident is transferred or discharged.

(ii) Notice may be made as soon as practicable before transfer or discharge when —

(A) the safety of individuals in the facility would be endangered under paragraph (a)(2)(iii) of this section;

(B) The health of individuals in the facility would be endangered, under paragraph (a)(2)(iv) of this section;

(C) The resident's health improves sufficiently to allow a more immediate transfer or discharge, under paragraph (a)(2)(ii) of this section;

(D) An immediate transfer or discharge is required by the resident's urgent medical needs, under paragraph (a)(2)(i) of this section; or

(E) A resident has not resided in the facility for 30 days.

(6) Contents of the notice. The written notice specified in paragraph (a)(4) of this section must include the following:

(i) The reason for transfer or discharge;

(ii) The effective date of transfer or discharge;

(iii) The location to which the resident is transferred or discharged;

(iv) A statement that the resident has the right to appeal the action to the State;

(v) The name, address and telephone number of the State long term care ombudsman;

(vi) For nursing facility residents with developmental disabilities, the mailing address and telephone number of the agency responsible for the protection and advocacy of developmentally disabled individuals established under Part C of the Developmental Disabilities Assistance and Bill of Rights Act; and

(vii) For nursing facility residents who are mentally ill, the mailing address and telephone number of the agency responsible for the protection and advocacy of mentally ill individuals established under the Protection and Advocacy for Mentally Ill Individuals Act.

(7) Orientation for transfer or discharge. A facility must provide sufficient preparation and orientation to residents to ensure safe and orderly transfer or discharge from the facility.

(b) *Notice of bed-hold policy and readmission* —

(1) Notice before transfer. Before a nursing facility transfers a resident to a hospital or allows a resident to go on therapeutic leave, the nursing facility must provide written information to the resident and a family member or legal representative that specifies —

(i) The duration of the bed-hold policy under the State plan, if any, during which the resident is permitted to return and resume residence in the nursing facility; and

(ii) The nursing facility's policies regarding bed-hold periods, which must be consistent with paragraph (b)(3) of this section, permitting a resident to return.

(2) Bed-hold notice upon transfer. At the time of transfer of a resident for hospitalization or therapeutic leave, a nursing facility must provide to the resident and a family member or legal representative written notice which specifies the duration of the bed-hold policy described in paragraph (b)(1) of this section.

(3) Permitting resident to return to facility. A nursing facility must establish and follow a written policy under which a resident, whose hospitalization or therapeutic leave exceeds the bed-hold period under the State plan, is readmitted to the facility immediately upon the first availability of a bed in a semi-private room if the resident —

(i) Requires the services provided by the facility; and

(ii) Is eligible for Medicaid nursing facility services.

(c) *Equal access to quality care*

(1) A facility must establish and maintain identical policies and practices regarding transfer, discharge, and the provision of services under the State plan for all individuals regardless of source of payment;

(2) The facility may charge any amount for services furnished to non-Medicaid residents consistent with the notice requirement in § 483.10(b)(5)(i) and (b)(6) describing the charges; and

(3) The State is not required to offer additional services on behalf of a resident other than services provided in the State plan.

(d) *Admissions policy*

(1) The facility must —

(i) Not require residents or potential residents to waive their rights to Medicare or Medicaid; and

(ii) Not require oral or written assurance that residents or potential residents are not eligible for, or will not apply for, Medicare or Medicaid benefits.

(2) The facility must not require a third party guarantee of payment to the facility as a condition of admission or expedited admission, or continued stay in the facility. However, the facility may require an individual who has legal access to a resident's income or resources available to pay for facility care to sign a contract, without incurring personal financial liability, to provide facility payment from the resident's income or resources.

(3) In the case of a person eligible for Medicaid, a nursing facility must not charge, solicit, accept, or receive, in addition to any amount otherwise required to be paid under the State plan, any gift, money, donation, or other consideration as a precondition of admission, expedited admission or continued stay in the facility. However, —

(i) A nursing facility may charge a resident who is eligible for Medicaid for items and services the resident has requested and received, and that are not specified in the State plan as included in the term "nursing facility services" so long as the facility gives proper notice of the availability and cost of these services to residents and does not condition the resident's admission or continued stay on the request for and receipt of such additional services; and

(ii) A nursing facility may solicit, accept, or receive a charitable, religious, or philanthropic contribution from an organization or from a person unrelated to a Medicaid eligible resident or potential resident, but only to the extent that the contribution is not a condition of admission, expedited admission, or continued stay in the facility for a Medicaid eligible resident.

(4) States or political subdivisions may apply stricter admissions standards under State or local laws than are specified in this section, to prohibit discrimination against individuals entitled to Medicaid.

## § 483.13.  Resident behavior and facility practices

(a) *Restraints*

The resident has the right to be free from any physical or chemical restraints imposed for purposes of discipline or convenience, and not required to treat the resident's medical symptoms.

(b) *Abuse*

The resident has the right to be free from verbal, sexual, physical, and mental abuse, corporal punishment, and involuntary seclusion.

(c) *Staff treatment of residents*

The facility must develop and implement written policies and procedures that prohibit mistreatment, neglect, and abuse of residents and misappropriation of resident property.

(1) The facility must —

(i) Not use verbal, mental, sexual, or physical abuse, corporal punishment, or involuntary seclusion;

(ii) Not employ individuals who have been —

(A) Found guilty of abusing, neglecting, or mistreating residents by a court of law; or

(B) Have had a finding entered into the State nurse aide registry concerning abuse, neglect, mistreatment of residents or misappropriation of their property; and

(iii) Report any knowledge it has of actions by a court of law against an employee, which would indicate unfitness for service as a nurse aide or other facility staff to the State nurse aide registry or licensing authorities.

(2) The facility must ensure that all alleged violations involving mistreatment, neglect, or abuse, including injuries of unknown source, and misappropriation of resident property are reported immediately to the administrator of the facility and to other officials in accordance with State law through established procedures (including to the State survey and certification agency).

(3) The facility must have evidence that all alleged violations are thoroughly investigated, and must prevent further potential abuse while the investigation is in progress.

(4) The results of all investigations must be reported to the administrator or his designated representative and to other officials in accordance with State law (including to the State survey and certification

agency) within 5 working days of the incident, and if the alleged violation is verified appropriate corrective action must be taken.

## § 483.15.  Quality of life

A facility must care for its residents in a manner and in an environment that promotes maintenance or enhancement of each resident's quality of life.

(a)  *Dignity*

The facility must promote care for residents in a manner and in an environment that maintains or enhances each resident's dignity and respect in full recognition of his or her individuality.

(b)  *Self-determination and participation*

The resident has the right to —

(1) Choose activities, schedules, and health care consistent with his or her interests, assessments, and plans of care;

(2) Interact with members of the community both inside and outside the facility; and

(3) Make choices about aspects of his or her life in the facility that are significant to the resident.

(c)  *Participation in resident and family groups*

(1) A resident has the right to organize and participate in resident groups in the facility;

(2) A resident's family has the right to meet in the facility with the families of other residents in the facility;

(3) The facility must provide a resident or family group, if one exists, with private space;

(4) Staff or visitors may attend meetings at the group's invitation;

(5) The facility must provide a designated staff person responsible for providing assistance and responding to written requests that result from group meetings;

(6) When a resident or family group exists, the facility must listen to the views and act upon the grievances and recommendations of residents and families concerning proposed policy and operational decisions affecting resident care and life in the facility.

(d) *Participation in other activities*

A resident has the right to participate in social, religious, and community activities that do not interfere with the rights of other residents in the facility.

(e) *Accommodation of needs*

A resident has the right to —

(1) Reside and receive services in the facility with reasonable accommodation of individual needs and preferences, except when the health or safety of the individual or other residents would be endangered; and

(2) Receive notice before the resident's room or roommate in the facility is changed.

(f) *Activities*

(1) The facility must provide for an ongoing program of activities designed to meet, in accordance with the comprehensive assessment, the interests and the physical, mental, and psychosocial well-being of each resident.

(2) The activities program must be directed by a qualified professional who —

(i) Is a qualified therapeutic recreation specialist or an activities professional who —

(A) Is licensed or registered, if applicable, by the State in which practicing; and

(B) Is eligible for certification as a therapeutic recreation specialist or as an activities professional by a recognized accrediting body on or after October 1, 1990; or

(ii) Has 2 years of experience in a social or recreational program within the last 5 years, 1 of which was full-time in a patient activities program in a health care setting; or

(iii) Is a qualified occupational therapist or occupational therapy assistant; or

(iv) Has completed a training course approved by the State.

(g) *Social Services*

(1) The facility must provide medically-related social services to attain or maintain the highest practicable physical, mental, and psychosocial well-being of each resident.

(2) A facility with more than 120 beds must employ a qualified social worker on a full-time basis.

(3) Qualifications of social worker. A qualified social worker is an individual with —

(i) A bachelor's degree in social work or a bachelor's degree in a human services field including but not limited to sociology, special education, rehabilitation counseling, and psychology; and

(ii) One year of supervised social work experience in a health care setting working directly with individuals.

(h) *Environment*

The facility must provide —

(1) A safe, clean, comfortable, and homelike environment, allowing the resident to use his or her personal belongings to the extent possible;

(2) Housekeeping and maintenance services necessary to maintain a sanitary, orderly, and comfortable interior;

(3) Clean bed and bath linens that are in good condition;

(4) Private closet space in each resident room, as specified in § 483.70(d)(2)(iv) of this part;

(5) Adequate and comfortable lighting levels in all areas;

(6) Comfortable and safe temperature levels. Facilities initially certified after October 1, 1990 must maintain a temperature range of 71-81[degrees]F; and

(7) For the maintenance of comfortable sound levels.

## § 483.20. Resident assessment

The facility must conduct initially and periodically a comprehensive, accurate, standardized, reproducible assessment of each resident's functional capacity.

(a) *Admission orders*

At the time each resident is admitted, the facility must have physician orders for the resident's immediate care.

(b) *Comprehensive assessments*

(1) Resident assessment instrument. A facility must make a comprehensive assessment of a resident's needs, using the resident assessment instrument (RAI) specified by the State. The assessment must include at least the following:

(i) Identification and demographic information.

(ii) Customary routine.

(iii) Cognitive patterns.

(iv) Communication.

(v) Vision.

(vi) Mood and behavior patterns.

(vii) Psychosocial well-being.

(viii) Physical functioning and structural problems.

(ix) Continence.

(x) Disease diagnoses and health conditions.

(xi) Dental and nutritional status.

(xii) Skin condition.

(xiii) Activity pursuit.

(xiv) Medications.

(xv) Special treatments and procedures.

(xvi) Discharge potential.

(xvii) Documentation of summary information regarding the additional assessment performed through the resident assessment protocols.

(xviii) Documentation of participation in assessment.

The assessment process must include direct observation and communication with the resident, as well as communication with licensed and nonlicensed direct care staff members on all shifts.

(2) When required. Subject to the timeframes prescribed in § 413.343(b) of this chapter, a facility must conduct a comprehensive assessment of a resident in accordance with the timeframes specified in paragraphs (b)(2) (i) through (iii) of this section. The timeframes prescribed in § 413.343(b) of this chapter do not apply to CAHs.

(i) Within 14 calendar days after admission, excluding readmissions in which there is no significant change in the resident's physical or mental condition. (For purposes of this section, "readmission" means a return to the facility following a temporary absence for hospitalization or for therapeutic leave.)

(ii) Within 14 calendar days after the facility determines, or should have determined, that there has been a significant change in the resident's physical or mental condition. (For purposes of this section, a "significant change" means a major decline or improvement in the resident's status that will not normally resolve itself without further intervention by staff or by implementing standard disease-related clinical interventions, that has an impact on more than one area of the resident's health status, and requires interdisciplinary review or revision of the care plan, or both.)

(iii) Not less often than once every 12 months.

(c) *Quarterly review assessment*

A facility must assess a resident using the quarterly review instrument specified by the State and approved by CMS not less frequently than once every 3 months.

(d) *Use*

A facility must maintain all resident assessments completed within the previous 15 months in the resident's active record and use the results of the assessments to develop, review, and revise the resident's comprehensive plan of care.

(e) *Coordination*

A facility must coordinate assessments with the preadmission screening and resident review program under Medicaid in part 483, subpart C to the maximum extent practicable to avoid duplicative testing and effort.

(f) *Automated data processing requirement*

(1) Encoding data.  Within 7 days after a facility completes a resident's assessment, a facility must encode the following information for each resident in the facility:

(i) Admission assessment.

(ii) Annual assessment updates.

(iii) Significant change in status assessments.

(iv) Quarterly review assessments.

(v) A subset of items upon a resident's transfer, reentry, discharge, and death.

(vi) Background (face-sheet) information, if there is no admission assessment.

(2) Transmitting data.  Within 7 days after a facility completes a resident's assessment, a facility must be capable of transmitting to the State information for each resident contained in the MDS in a format that conforms to standard record layouts and data dictionaries, and that passes standardized edits defined by CMS and the State.

(3) Monthly transmittal requirements.  A facility must electronically transmit, at least monthly, encoded, accurate, complete MDS data to the State for all assessments conducted during the previous month, including the following:

(i) Admission assessment.

(ii) Annual assessment.

(iii) Significant change in status assessment.

(iv) Significant correction of prior full assessment.

(v) Significant correction of prior quarterly assessment.

(vi) Quarterly review.

(vii) A subset of items upon a resident's transfer, reentry, discharge, and death.

(viii) Background (face-sheet) information, for an initial transmission of MDS data on a resident that does not have an admission assessment.

(4) Data format. The facility must transmit data in the format specified by CMS or, for a State which has an alternate RAI approved by CMS, in the format specified by the State and approved by CMS.

(5) Resident-identifiable information.

(i) A facility may not release information that is resident-identifiable to the public.

(ii) The facility may release information that is resident-identifiable to an agent only in accordance with a contract under which the agent agrees not to use or disclose the information except to the extent the facility itself is permitted to do so.

(g) *Accuracy of assessments*

The assessment must accurately reflect the resident's status.

(h) *Coordination*

A registered nurse must conduct or coordinate each assessment with the appropriate participation of health professionals.

(i) *Certification*

(1) A registered nurse must sign and certify that the assessment is completed.

(2) Each individual who completes a portion of the assessment must sign and certify the accuracy of that portion of the assessment.

(j) *Penalty for falsification*

(1) Under Medicare and Medicaid, an individual who willfully and knowingly —

(i) Certifies a material and false statement in a resident assessment is subject to a civil money penalty of not more than $1,000 for each assessment; or

(ii) Causes another individual to certify a material and false statement in a resident assessment is subject to a civil money penalty of not more than $5,000 for each assessment.

(2) Clinical disagreement does not constitute a material and false statement.

(k) *Comprehensive care plans*

(1) The facility must develop a comprehensive care plan for each resident that includes measurable objectives and timetables to meet a resident's medical, nursing, and mental and psychosocial needs that are identified in the comprehensive assessment. The care plan must describe the following —

(i) The services that are to be furnished to attain or maintain the resident's highest practicable physical, mental, and psychosocial well-being as required under § 483.25; and

(ii) Any services that would otherwise be required under § 483.25 but are not provided due to the resident's exercise of rights under § 483.10, including the right to refuse treatment under § 483.10(b)(4).

(2) A comprehensive care plan must be —

(i) Developed within 7 days after completion of the comprehensive assessment;

(ii) Prepared by an interdisciplinary team, that includes the attending physician, a registered nurse with responsibility for the resident, and other appropriate staff in disciplines as determined by the resident's needs, and, to the extent practicable, the participation of the resident, the resident's family or the resident's legal representative; and

(iii) Periodically reviewed and revised by a team of qualified persons after each assessment.

(3) The services provided or arranged by the facility must —

(i) Meet professional standards of quality; and

(ii) Be provided by qualified persons in accordance with each resident's written plan of care.

(l) *Discharge summary*

When the facility anticipates discharge a resident must have a discharge summary that includes —

(1) A recapitulation of the resident's stay;

(2) A final summary of the resident's status to include items in paragraph (b)(2) of this section, at the time of the discharge that is available for release to authorized persons and agencies, with the consent of the resident or legal representative; and

(3) A post-discharge plan of care that is developed with the participation of the resident and his or her family, which will assist the resident to adjust to his or her new living environment.

(m) *Preadmission screening for mentally ill individuals and individuals with mental retardation*

(1) A nursing facility must not admit, on or after January 1, 1989, any new resident with —

(i) Mental illness as defined in paragraph (f)(2)(i) of this section, unless the State mental health authority has determined, based on an independent physical and mental evaluation performed by a person or entity other than the State mental health authority, prior to admission,

(A) That, because of the physical and mental condition of the individual, the individual requires the level of services provided by a nursing facility; and

(B) If the individual requires such level of services, whether the individual requires specialized services; or

(ii) Mental retardation, as defined in paragraph (f)(2)(ii) of this section, unless the State mental retardation or developmental disability authority has determined prior to admission —

(A) That, because of the physical and mental condition of the individual, the individual requires the level of services provided by a nursing facility; and

(B) If the individual requires such level of services, whether the individual requires specialized services for mental retardation.

(2) Definition. For purposes of this section —

(i) An individual is considered to have mental illness if the individual has a serious mental illness as defined in § 483.102(b)(1).

(ii) An individual is considered to be mentally retarded if the individual is mentally retarded as defined in § 483.102(b)(3) or is a person with a related condition as described in 42 CFR 435.1009.

## § 483.25. Quality of care

Each resident must receive and the facility must provide the necessary care and services to attain or maintain the highest practicable physical, mental, and psychosocial well-being, in accordance with the comprehensive assessment and plan of care.

(a) *Activities of daily living*

Based on the comprehensive assessment of a resident, the facility must ensure that —

(1) A resident's abilities in activities of daily living do not diminish unless circumstances of the individual's clinical condition demonstrate that diminution was unavoidable. This includes the resident's ability to —

    (i) Bathe, dress, and groom;

    (ii) Transfer and ambulate;

    (iii) Toilet;

    (iv) Eat; and

    (v) Use speech, language, or other functional communication systems.

(2) A resident is given the appropriate treatment and services to maintain or improve his or her abilities specified in paragraph (a)(1) of this section; and

(3) A resident who is unable to carry out activities of daily living receives the necessary services to maintain good nutrition, grooming, and personal and oral hygiene.

(b) *Vision and hearing*

To ensure that residents receive proper treatment and assistive devices to maintain vision and hearing abilities, the facility must, if necessary, assist the resident —

(1) In making appointments, and

(2) By arranging for transportation to and from the office of a practitioner specializing in the treatment of vision or hearing impairment or the office of a professional specializing in the provision of vision or hearing assistive devices.

(c) *Pressure sores*

Based on the comprehensive assessment of a resident, the facility must ensure that —

(1) A resident who enters the facility without pressure sores does not develop pressure sores unless the individual's clinical condition demonstrates that they were unavoidable; and

(2) A resident having pressure sores receives necessary treatment and services to promote healing, prevent infection and prevent new sores from developing.

(d) *Urinary Incontinence*

Based on the resident's comprehensive assessment, the facility must ensure that —

(1) A resident who enters the facility without an indwelling catheter is not catheterized unless the resident's clinical condition demonstrates that catheterization was necessary; and

(2) A resident who is incontinent of bladder receives appropriate treatment and services to prevent urinary tract infections and to restore as much normal bladder function as possible.

(e) *Range of motion*

Based on the comprehensive assessment of a resident, the facility must ensure that —

(1) A resident who enters the facility without a limited range of motion does not experience reduction in range of motion unless the resident's clinical condition demonstrates that a reduction in range of motion is unavoidable; and

(2) A resident with a limited range of motion receives appropriate treatment and services to increase range of motion and/or to prevent further decrease in range of motion.

(f) *Mental and Psychosocial functioning*

Based on the comprehensive assessment of a resident, the facility must ensure that —

(1) A resident who displays mental or psychosocial adjustment difficulty, receives appropriate treatment and services to correct the assessed problem, and

(2) A resident whose assessment did not reveal a mental or psychosocial adjustment difficulty does not display a pattern of decreased social interaction and/or increased withdrawn, angry, or depressive behaviors, unless the resident's clinical condition demonstrates that such a pattern was unavoidable.

(g)  *Naso-gastric tubes*

Based on the comprehensive assessment of a resident, the facility must ensure that —

(1) A resident who has been able to eat enough alone or with assistance is not fed by naso-gastric tube unless the resident's clinical condition demonstrates that use of a naso-gastric tube was unavoidable; and

(2) A resident who is fed by a naso-gastric or gastrostomy tube receives the appropriate treatment and services to prevent aspiration pneumonia, diarrhea, vomiting, dehydration, metabolic abnormalities, and nasal-pharyngeal ulcers and to restore, if possible, normal eating skills.

(h)  *Accidents*

The facility must ensure that —

(1) The resident environment remains as free of accident hazards as is possible; and

(2) Each resident receives adequate supervision and assistance devices to prevent accidents.

(i)  *Nutrition*

Based on a resident's comprehensive assessment, the facility must ensure that a resident —

(1) Maintains acceptable parameters of nutritional status, such as body weight and protein levels, unless the resident's clinical condition demonstrates that this is not possible; and

(2) Receives a therapeutic diet when there is a nutritional problem.

(j)  *Hydration*

The facility must provide each resident with sufficient fluid intake to maintain proper hydration and health.

(k)  *Special needs*

The facility must ensure that residents receive proper treatment and care for the following special services:

(1) Injections;

(2) Parenteral and enteral fluids;

(3) Colostomy, ureterostomy, or ileostomy care;

(4) Tracheostomy care;

(5) Tracheal suctioning;

(6) Respiratory care;

(7) Foot care; and

(8) Prostheses.

(l)  *Unnecessary drugs* —

(1) General.  Each resident's drug regimen must be free from unnecessary drugs.  An unnecessary drug is any drug when used:

(i) In excessive dose (including duplicate drug therapy); or

(ii) For excessive duration; or

(iii) Without adequate monitoring; or

(iv) Without adequate indications for its use; or

(v) In the presence of adverse consequences which indicate the dose should be reduced or discontinued; or

(vi) Any combinations of the reasons above.

(2) Antipsychotic Drugs.  Based on a comprehensive assessment of a resident, the facility must ensure that —

(i) Residents who have not used antipsychotic drugs are not given these drugs unless antipsychotic drug therapy is necessary to treat a specific condition as diagnosed and documented in the clinical record; and

(ii) Residents who use antipsychotic drugs receive gradual dose reductions, and behavioral interventions, unless clinically contraindicated, in an effort to discontinue these drugs.

(m)  *Medication Errors* —

The facility must ensure that —

(1) It is free of medication error rates of five percent or greater; and

(2) Residents are free of any significant medication errors.

### § 483.30.  Nursing services

The facility must have sufficient nursing staff to provide nursing and related services to attain or maintain the highest practicable physical, mental, and psychosocial well-being of each resident, as determined by resident assessments and individual plans of care.

(a)  *Sufficient staff*

(1) The facility must provide services by sufficient numbers of each of the following types of personnel on a 24-hour basis to provide nursing care to all residents in accordance with resident care plans:

(i) Except when waived under paragraph (c) of this section, licensed nurses; and

(ii) Other nursing personnel.

(2) Except when waived under paragraph (c) of this section, the facility must designate a licensed nurse to serve as a charge nurse on each tour of duty.

(b) *Registered nurse*

(1) Except when waived under paragraph (c) or (d) of this section, the facility must use the services of a registered nurse for at least 8 consecutive hours a day, 7 days a week.

(2) Except when waived under paragraph (c) or (d) of this section, the facility must designate a registered nurse to serve as the director of nursing on a full time basis.

(3) The director of nursing may serve as a charge nurse only when the facility has an average daily occupancy of 60 or fewer residents.

(c) *Nursing facilities*:

Waiver of requirement to provide licensed nurses on a 24-hour basis. To the extent that a facility is unable to meet the requirements of paragraphs (a)(2) and (b)(1) of this section, a State may waive such requirements with respect to the facility if —

(1) The facility demonstrates to the satisfaction of the State that the facility has been unable, despite diligent efforts (including offering wages at the community prevailing rate for nursing facilities), to recruit appropriate personnel;

(2) The State determines that a waiver of the requirement will not endanger the health or safety of individuals staying in the facility;

(3) The State finds that, for any periods in which licensed nursing services are not available, a registered nurse or a physician is obligated to respond immediately to telephone calls from the facility;

(4) A waiver granted under the conditions listed in paragraph (c) of this section is subject to annual State review;

(5) In granting or renewing a waiver, a facility may be required by the State to use other qualified, licensed personnel;

(6) The State agency granting a waiver of such requirements provides notice of the waiver to the State long term care ombudsman (established under section 307(a)(12) of the Older Americans Act of 1965) and the protection and advocacy system in the State for the mentally ill and mentally retarded; and

(7) The nursing facility that is granted such a waiver by a State notifies residents of the facility (or, where appropriate, the guardians or

legal representatives of such residents) and members of their immediate families of the waiver.

(d) *SNFs*:

Waiver of the requirement to provide services of a registered nurse for more than 40 hours a week.

(1) The Secretary may waive the requirement that a SNF provide the services of a registered nurse for more than 40 hours a week, including a director of nursing specified in paragraph (b) of this section, if the Secretary finds that —

(i) The facility is located in a rural area and the supply of skilled nursing facility services in the area is not sufficient to meet the needs of individuals residing in the area;

(ii) The facility has one full-time registered nurse who is regularly on duty at the facility 40 hours a week; and

(iii) The facility either —

(A) Has only patients whose physicians have indicated (through physicians' orders or admission notes) that they do not require the services of a registered nurse or a physician for a 48-hours period, or

(B) Has made arrangements for a registered nurse or a physician to spend time at the facility, as determined necessary by the physician, to provide necessary skilled nursing services on days when the regular full-time registered nurse is not on duty;

(iv) The Secretary provides notice of the waiver to the State long term care ombudsman (established under section 307(a)(12) of the Older Americans Act of 1965) and the protection and advocacy system in the State for the mentally ill and mentally retarded; and

(v) The facility that is granted such a waiver notifies residents of the facility (or, where appropriate, the guardians or legal representatives of such residents) and members of their immediate families of the waiver.

(2) A waiver of the registered nurse requirement under paragraph (d)(1) of this section is subject to annual renewal by the Secretary.

## § 483.35.  Dietary services

The facility must provide each resident with a nourishing, palatable, well-balanced diet that meets the daily nutritional and special dietary needs of each resident.

## (a) *Staffing*

The facility must employ a qualified dietitian either full-time, part-time, or on a consultant basis.

(1) If a qualified dietitian is not employed full-time, the facility must designate a person to serve as the director of food service who receives frequently scheduled consultation from a qualified dietitian.

(2) A qualified dietitian is one who is qualified based upon either registration by the Commission on Dietetic Registration of the American Dietetic Association, or on the basis of education, training, or experience in identification of dietary needs, planning, and implementation of dietary programs.

## (b) *Sufficient staff*

The facility must employ sufficient support personnel competent to carry out the functions of the dietary service.

## (c) *Menus and nutritional adequacy*

Menus must —

(1) Meet the nutritional needs of residents in accordance with the recommended dietary allowances of the Food and Nutrition Board of the National Research Council, National Academy of Sciences;

(2) Be prepared in advance; and

(3) Be followed.

## (d) *Food*

Each resident receives and the facility provides —

(1) Food prepared by methods that conserve nutritive value, flavor, and appearance;

(2) Food that is palatable, attractive, and at the proper temperature;

(3) Food prepared in a form designed to meet individual needs; and

(4) Substitutes offered of similar nutritive value to residents who refuse food served.

## (e) *Therapeutic diets*

Therapeutic diets must be prescribed by the attending physician.

## (f) *Frequency of meals*

(1) Each resident receives and the facility provides at least three meals daily, at regular times comparable to normal mealtimes in the community.

(2) There must be no more than 14 hours between a substantial evening meal and breakfast the following day, except as provided in (4) below.

(3) The facility must offer snacks at bedtime daily.

(4) When a nourishing snack is provided at bedtime, up to 16 hours may elapse between a substantial evening meal and breakfast the following day if a resident group agrees to this meal span, and a nourishing snack is served.

(g) *Assistive devices*

The facility must provide special eating equipment and utensils for residents who need them.

(h) *Sanitary conditions*

The facility must —

(1) Procure food from sources approved or considered satisfactory by Federal, State, or local authorities;

(2) Store, prepare, distribute, and serve food under sanitary conditions; and

(3) Dispose of garbage and refuse properly.

## § 483.40. Physician services

A physician must personally approve in writing a recommendation that an individual be admitted to a facility. Each resident must remain under the care of a physician.

(a) *Physician supervision*

The facility must ensure that —

(1) The medical care of each resident is supervised by a physician; and

(2) Another physician supervises the medical care of residents when their attending physician is unavailable.

(b) *Physician visits*

The physician must —

(1) Review the resident's total program of care, including medications and treatments, at each visit required by paragraph (c) of this section;

(2) Write, sign, and date progress notes at each visit; and

(3) Sign and date all orders with the exception of influenza and pneumococcal polysaccharide vaccines, which may be administered per

physician-approved facility policy after an assessment for contraindications.

(c) *Frequency of physician visits*

(1) The resident must be seen by a physician at least once every 30 days for the first 90 days after admission, and at least once every 60 days thereafter.

(2) A physician visit is considered timely if it occurs not later than 10 days after the date the visit was required.

(3) Except as provided in paragraphs (c)(4) and (f) of this section, all required physician visits must be made by the physician personally.

(4) At the option of the physician, required visits in SNFs after the initial visit may alternate between personal visits by the physician and visits by a physician assistant, nurse practitioner, or clinical nurse specialist in accordance with paragraph (e) of this section.

(d) *Availability of physicians for emergency care*

The facility must provide or arrange for the provision of physician services 24 hours a day, in case of an emergency.

(e) *Physician delegation of tasks in SNFs*

(1) Except as specified in paragraph (e)(2) of this section, a physician may delegate tasks to a physician assistant, nurse practitioner, or clinical nurse specialist who —

(i) Meets the applicable definition in § 491.2 of this chapter or, in the case of a clinical nurse specialist, is licensed as such by the State;

(ii) Is acting within the scope of practice as defined by State law; and

(iii) Is under the supervision of the physician.

(2) A physician may not delegate a task when the regulations specify that the physician must perform it personally, or when the delegation is prohibited under State law or by the facility's own policies.

(f) *Performance of physician tasks in NFs*

At the option of the State, any required physician task in a NF (including tasks which the regulations specify must be performed personally by the physician) may also be satisfied when performed by a nurse practitioner, clinical specialist, or physician assistant who is not an employee of the facility but who is working in collaboration with a physician.

## § 483.45.  Specialized rehabilitative services

(a) *Provision of services*

If specialized rehabilitative services such as but not limited to physical therapy, speech-language pathology, occupational therapy, and mental health rehabilitative services for mental illness and mental retardation, are required in the resident's comprehensive plan of care, the facility must —

(1) Provide the required services; or

(2) Obtain the required services from an outside resource (in accordance with § 483.75(h) of this part) from a provider of specialized rehabilitative services.

(b) *Qualifications*

Specialized rehabilitative services must be provided under the written order of a physician by qualified personnel.

## § 483.55.  Dental services

The facility must assist residents in obtaining routine and 24-hour emergency dental care.

(a) *Skilled nursing facilities*

A facility

(1) Must provide or obtain from an outside resource, in accordance with § 483.75(h) of this part, routine and emergency dental services to meet the needs of each resident;

(2) May charge a Medicare resident an additional amount for routine and emergency dental services;

(3) Must if necessary, assist the resident —

(i) In making appointments; and

(ii) By arranging for transportation to and from the dentist's office; and

(4) Promptly refer residents with lost or damaged dentures to a dentist.

(b) *Nursing facilities*

The facility

(1) Must provide or obtain from an outside resource, in accordance with § 483.75(h) of this part, the following dental services to meet the needs of each resident:

(i) Routine dental services (to the extent covered under the State plan); and

(ii) Emergency dental services;

(2) Must, if necessary, assist the resident —

(i) In making appointments; and

(ii) By arranging for transportation to and from the dentist's office; and

(3) Must promptly refer residents with lost or damaged dentures to a dentist.

## § 483.60.  Pharmacy services.

The facility must provide routine and emergency drugs and biologicals to its residents, or obtain them under an agreement described in § 483.75(h) of this part. The facility may permit unlicensed personnel to administer drugs if State law permits, but only under the general supervision of a licensed nurse.

(a) *Procedures*

A facility must provide pharmaceutical services (including procedures that assure the accurate acquiring, receiving, dispensing, and administering of all drugs and biologicals) to meet the needs of each resident.

(b) *Service consultation*

The facility must employ or obtain the services of a licensed pharmacist who —

(1) Provides consultation on all aspects of the provision of pharmacy services in the facility;

(2) Establishes a system of records of receipt and disposition of all controlled drugs in sufficient detail to enable an accurate reconciliation; and

(3) Determines that drug records are in order and that an account of all controlled drugs is maintained and periodically reconciled.

(c) *Drug regimen review*

(1) The drug regimen of each resident must be reviewed at least once a month by a licensed pharmacist.

(2) The pharmacist must report any irregularities to the attending physician and the director of nursing, and these reports must be acted upon.

(d)  *Labeling of drugs and biologicals*

Drugs and biologicals used in the facility must be labeled in accordance with currently accepted professional principles, and include the appropriate accessory and cautionary instructions, and the expiration date when applicable.

(e)  *Storage of drugs and biologicals*

(1) In accordance with State and Federal laws, the facility must store all drugs and biologicals in locked compartments under proper temperature controls, and permit only authorized personnel to have access to the keys.

(2) The facility must provide separately locked, permanently affixed compartments for storage of controlled drugs listed in Schedule II of the Comprehensive Drug Abuse Prevention and Control Act of 1976 and other drugs subject to abuse, except when the facility uses single unit package drug distribution systems in which the quantity stored is minimal and a missing dose can be readily detected.

## § 483.65.  Infection control

The facility must establish and maintain an infection control program designed to provide a safe, sanitary, and comfortable environment and to help prevent the development and transmission of disease and infection.

(a)  *Infection control program*

The facility must establish an infection control program under which it —

(1) Investigates, controls, and prevents infections in the facility;

(2) Decides what procedures, such as isolation, should be applied to an individual resident; and

(3) Maintains a record of incidents and corrective actions related to infections.

(b)  *Preventing spread of infection*

(1) When the infection control program determines that a resident needs isolation to prevent the spread of infection, the facility must isolate the resident.

(2) The facility must prohibit employees with a communicable disease or infected skin lesions from direct contact with residents or their food, if direct contact will transmit the disease.

(3) The facility must require staff to wash their hands after each direct resident contact for which handwashing is indicated by accepted professional practice.

(c) *Linens*

Personnel must handle, store, process, and transport linens so as to prevent the spread of infection.

## § 483.70. Physical environment

The facility must be designed, constructed, equipped, and maintained to protect the health and safety of residents, personnel and the public.

(a) *Life safety from fire*

Except as otherwise provided in this section, the facility must meet the applicable provisions of the 2000 edition of the Life Safety Code of the National Fire Protection Association. The Director of the Office of the Federal Register has approved the NFPA 101 [registered trademark] 2000 edition of the Life Safety Code, issued January 14, 2000, for incorporation by reference in accordance with 5 U.S.C. 552(a) and 1 CFR part 51. A copy of the Code is available for inspection at the CMS Information Resource Center, 7500 Security Boulevard, Baltimore, MD and at the Office of the Federal Register, 800 North Capitol Street NW., Suite 700, Washington, DC. Copies may be obtained from the National Fire Protection Association, 1 Batterymarch Park, Quincy, MA 02269. If any changes in this edition of the Code are incorporated by reference, CMS will publish notice in the Federal Register to announce the changes. Chapter 19.3.6.3.2, exception number 2 of the adopted edition of the LSC does not apply to long-term care facilities.

(1) A facility is considered to be in compliance with this requirement as long as the facility —

(i) On November 26, 1982, complied with or without waivers, with the requirements of the 1967 or 1973 editions of the Life Safety Code and continues to remain in compliance with those editions of the Code; or

(ii) On May 9, 1988, complied, with or without waivers, with the 1981 edition of the Life Safety Code and continues to remain in compliance with that edition of the Code.

(2) After consideration of State survey agency findings, CMS may waive specific provisions of the Life Safety Code which, if rigidly applied would result in unreasonable hardship upon the facility, but only if the

waiver does not adversely affect the health and safety of residents or personnel.

(3) The provisions of the Life Safety Code do not apply in a State where CMS finds, in accordance with applicable provisions of sections 1819(d)(2)(B)(ii) and 1919(d)(2)(B)(ii) of the Act, that a fire and safety code imposed by State law adequately protects patients, residents and personnel in long term care facilities.

(4) A long-term care facility must be in compliance with the following provisions beginning on March 13, 2006:

(i) Chapter 19.3.6.3.2, exception number 2.

(ii) Chapter 19.2.9, Emergency Lighting.

(b) *Emergency power*

(1) An emergency electrical power system must supply power adequate at least for lighting all entrances and exits; equipment to maintain the fire detection, alarm, and extinguishing systems; and life support systems in the event the normal electrical supply is interrupted.

(2) When life support systems are used, the facility must provide emergency electrical power with an emergency generator (as defined in NFPA 99, Health Care Facilities) that is located on the premises.

(c) *Space and equipment*

The facility must —

(1) Provide sufficient space and equipment in dining, health services, recreation, and program areas to enable staff to provide residents with needed services as required by these standards and as identified in each resident's plan of care; and

(2) Maintain all essential mechanical, electrical, and patient care equipment in safe operating condition.

(d) *Resident rooms*

Resident rooms must be designed and equipped for adequate nursing care, comfort, and privacy of residents.

(1) Bedrooms must —

(i) Accommodate no more than four residents;

(ii) Measure at least 80 square feet per resident in multiple resident bedrooms, and at least 100 square feet in single resident rooms;

(iii) Have direct access to an exit corridor;

(iv) Be designed or equipped to assure full visual privacy for each resident;

(v) In facilities initially certified after March 31, 1992, except in private rooms, each bed must have ceiling suspended curtains, which extend around the bed to provide total visual privacy in combination with adjacent walls and curtains;

(vi) Have at least one window to the outside; and

(vii) Have a floor at or above grade level.

(2) The facility must provide each resident with —

(i) A separate bed of proper size and height for the convenience of the resident;

(ii) A clean, comfortable mattress;

(iii) Bedding appropriate to the weather and climate; and

(iv) Functional furniture appropriate to the resident's needs, and individual closet space in the resident's bedroom with clothes racks and shelves accessible to the resident.

(3) CMS, or in the case of a nursing facility the survey agency, may permit variations in requirements specified in paragraphs (d)(1) (i) and (ii) of this section relating to rooms in individual cases when the facility demonstrates in writing that the variations —

(i) Are in accordance with the special needs of the residents; and

(ii) Will not adversely affect residents' health and safety.

(e) *Toilet facilities*

Each resident room must be equipped with or located near toilet and bathing facilities.

(f) *Resident call system*

The nurse's station must be equipped to receive resident calls through a communication system from —

(1) Resident rooms; and

(2) Toilet and bathing facilities.

(g) *Dining and resident activities*

The facility must provide one or more rooms designated for resident dining and activities. These rooms must —

(1) Be well lighted;

(2) Be well ventilated, with nonsmoking areas identified;

(3) Be adequately furnished; and

(4) Have sufficient space to accommodate all activities.

(h) *Other environmental conditions*

The facility must provide a safe, functional, sanitary, and comfortable environment for the residents, staff and the public. The facility must —

(1) Establish procedures to ensure that water is available to essential areas when there is a loss of normal water supply;

(2) Have adequate outside ventilation by means of windows, or mechanical ventilation, or a combination of the two;

(3) Equip corridors with firmly secured handrails on each side; and

(4) Maintain an effective pest control program so that the facility is free of pests and rodents.

## § 483.75. Administration

A facility must be administered in a manner that enables it to use its resources effectively and efficiently to attain or maintain the highest practicable physical, mental, and psychosocial well-being of each resident.

(a) *Licensure*

A facility must be licensed under applicable State and local law.

(b) *Compliance with Federal, State, and local laws and professional standards*

The facility must operate and provide services in compliance with all applicable Federal, State, and local laws, regulations, and codes, and with accepted professional standards and principles that apply to professionals providing services in such a facility.

(c) *Relationship to other HHS regulations*

In addition to compliance with the regulations set forth in this subpart, facilities are obliged to meet the applicable provisions of other HHS regulations, including but not limited to those pertaining to nondiscrimination on the basis of race, color, or national origin (45 CFR part 80); nondiscrimination on the basis of handicap (45 CFR part 84); nondiscrimination on the basis of age (45 CFR part 91); protection of human subjects of research (45 CFR part 46); and fraud and abuse (42 CFR part 455). Although these regulations are not in themselves considered requirements under this part, their violation may result in the termination or suspension of, or the refusal to grant or continue payment with Federal funds.

(d) *Governing body*

(1) The facility must have a governing body, or designated persons functioning as a governing body, that is legally responsible for establishing and implementing policies regarding the management and operation of the facility; and

(2) The governing body appoints the administrator who is —

(i) Licensed by the State where licensing is required; and

(ii) Responsible for management of the facility.

(e) *Required training of nursing aides* —

(1) Definitions.

Licensed health professional means a physician; physician assistant; nurse practitioner; physical, speech, or occupational therapist; physical or occupational therapy assistant; registered professional nurse; licensed practical nurse; or licensed or certified social worker.

Nurse aide means any individual providing nursing or nursing-related services to residents in a facility who is not a licensed health professional, a registered dietitian, or someone who volunteers to provide such services without pay.

(2) General rule.  A facility must not use any individual working in the facility as a nurse aide for more than 4 months, on a full-time basis, unless:

(i) That individual is competent to provide nursing and nursing related services; and

(ii) (A) That individual has completed a training and competency evaluation program, or a competency evaluation program approved by the State as meeting the requirements of §§ 483.151-483.154 of this part; or (B) That individual has been deemed or determined competent as provided in § 483.150 (a) and (b).

(3) Non-permanent employees.  A facility must not use on a temporary, per diem, leased, or any basis other than a permanent employee any individual who does not meet the requirements in paragraphs (e)(2) (i) and (ii) of this section.

(4) Competency.  A facility must not use any individual who has worked less than 4 months as a nurse aide in that facility unless the individual —

(i) Is a full-time employee in a State-approved training and competency evaluation program;

(ii) Has demonstrated competence through satisfactory participation in a State-approved nurse aide training and competency evaluation program or competency evaluation program; or

(iii) Has been deemed or determined competent as provided in § 483.150 (a) and (b).

(5) Registry verification. Before allowing an individual to serve as a nurse aide, a facility must receive registry verification that the individual has met competency evaluation requirements unless —

(i) The individual is a full-time employee in a training and competency evaluation program approved by the State; or

(ii) The individual can prove that he or she has recently successfully completed a training and competency evaluation program or competency evaluation program approved by the State and has not yet been included in the registry. Facilities must follow up to ensure that such an individual actually becomes registered.

(6) Multi-State registry verification. Before allowing an individual to serve as a nurse aide, a facility must seek information from every State registry established under sections 1819(e)(2)(A) or 1919(e)(2)(A) of the Act the facility believes will include information on the individual.

(7) Required retraining. If, since an individual's most recent completion of a training and competency evaluation program, there has been a continuous period of 24 consecutive months during none of which the individual provided nursing or nursing-related services for monetary compensation, the individual must complete a new training and competency evaluation program or a new competency evaluation program.

(8) Regular in-service education. The facility must complete a performance review of every nurse aide at least once every 12 months, and must provide regular in-service education based on the outcome of these reviews. The in-service training must —

(i) Be sufficient to ensure the continuing competence of nurse aides, but must be no less than 12 hours per year;

(ii) Address areas of weakness as determined in nurse aides' performance reviews and may address the special needs of residents as determined by the facility staff; and

(iii) For nurse aides providing services to individuals with cognitive impairments, also address the care of the cognitively impaired.

(f) *Proficiency of Nurse aides*

The facility must ensure that nurse aides are able to demonstrate competency in skills and techniques necessary to care for residents' needs, as identified through resident assessments, and described in the plan of care.

(g) *Staff qualifications*

(1) The facility must employ on a full-time, part-time or consultant basis those professionals necessary to carry out the provisions of these requirements.

(2) Professional staff must be licensed, certified, or registered in accordance with applicable State laws.

(h) *Use of outside resources*

(1) If the facility does not employ a qualified professional person to furnish a specific service to be provided by the facility, the facility must have that service furnished to residents by a person or agency outside the facility under an arrangement described in section 1861(w) of the Act or (with respect to services furnished to NF residents and dental services furnished to SNF residents) an agreement described in paragraph (h)(2) of this section.

(2) Arrangements as described in section 1861(w) of the Act or agreements pertaining to services furnished by outside resources must specify in writing that the facility assumes responsibility for —

(i) Obtaining services that meet professional standards and principles that apply to professionals providing services in such a facility; and

(ii) The timeliness of the services.

(i) *Medical director*

(1) The facility must designate a physician to serve as medical director.

(2) The medical director is responsible for —

(i) Implementation of resident care policies; and

(ii) The coordination of medical care in the facility.

(j) *Level B requirement*:

Laboratory services.

(1) The facility must provide or obtain laboratory services to meet the needs of its residents. The facility is responsible for the quality and timeliness of the services.

    (i) If the facility provides its own laboratory services, the services must meet the applicable requirements for laboratories specified in part 493 of this chapter.

    (ii) If the facility provides blood bank and transfusion services, it must meet the applicable requirements for laboratories specified in part 493 of this chapter.

    (iii) If the laboratory chooses to refer specimens for testing to another laboratory, the referral laboratory must be certified in the appropriate specialties and subspecialties of services in accordance with the requirements of part 493 of this chapter.

    (iv) If the facility does not provide laboratory services on site, it must have an agreement to obtain these services from a laboratory that meets the applicable requirements of part 493 of this chapter.

(2) The facility must —

    (i) Provide or obtain laboratory services only when ordered by the attending physician;

    (ii) Promptly notify the attending physican of the findings;

    (iii) Assist the resident in making transportation arrangements to and from the source of service, if the resident needs assistance; and

    (iv) File in the resident's clinical record laboratory reports that are dated and contain the name and address of the testing laboratory.

(k) *Radiology and other diagnostic services*

(1) The facility must provide or obtain radiology and other diagnostic services to meet the needs of its residents. The facility is responsible for the quality and timeliness of the services.

    (i) If the facility provides its own diagnostic services, the services must meet the applicable conditions of participation for hospitals contained in § 482.26 of this subchapter.

    (ii) If the facility does not provide its own diagnostic services, it must have an agreement to obtain these services from a provider or supplier that is approved to provide these services under Medicare.

(2) The facility must —

(i) Provide or obtain radiology and other diagnostic services only when ordered by the attending physician;

(ii) Promptly notify the attending physician of the findings;

(iii) Assist the resident in making transportation arrangements to and from the source of service, if the resident needs assistance; and

(iv) File in the resident's clinical record signed and dated reports of x-ray and other diagnostic services.

(l) *Clinical records*

(1) The facility must maintain clinical records on each resident in accordance with accepted professional standards and practices that are —

(i) Complete;

(ii) Accurately documented;

(iii) Readily accessible; and

(iv) Systematically organized.

(2) Clinical records must be retained for —

(i) The period of time required by State law; or

(ii) Five years from the date of discharge when there is no requirement in State law; or

(iii) For a minor, three years after a resident reaches legal age under State law.

(3) The facility must safeguard clinical record information against loss, destruction, or unauthorized use;

(4) The facility must keep confidential all information contained in the resident's records, regardless of the form or storage method of the records, except when release is required by —

(i) Transfer to another health care institution;

(ii) Law;

(iii) Third party payment contract; or

(iv) The resident.

(5) The clinical record must contain —

(i) Sufficient information to identify the resident;

(ii) A record of the resident's assessments;

(iii) The plan of care and services provided;

(iv) The results of any preadmission screening conducted by the State; and

(v) Progress notes.

(m) *Disaster and emergency preparedness*

(1) The facility must have detailed written plans and procedures to meet all potential emergencies and disasters, such as fire, severe weather, and missing residents.

(2) The facility must train all employees in emergency procedures when they begin to work in the facility, periodically review the procedures with existing staff, and carry out unannounced staff drills using those procedures.

(n) *Transfer agreement*

(1) In accordance with section 1861(l) of the Act, the facility (other than a nursing facility which is located in a State on an Indian reservation) must have in effect a written transfer agreement with one or more hospitals approved for participation under the Medicare and Medicaid programs that reasonably assures that —

    (i) Residents will be transferred from the facility to the hospital, and ensured of timely admission to the hospital when transfer is medically appropriate as determined by the attending physician; and

    (ii) Medical and other information needed for care and treatment of residents, and, when the transferring facility deems it appropriate, for determining whether such residents can be adequately cared for in a less expensive setting than either the facility or the hospital, will be exchanged between the institutions.

(2) The facility is considered to have a transfer agreement in effect if the facility has attempted in good faith to enter into an agreement with a hospital sufficiently close to the facility to make transfer feasible.

(o) *Quality assessment and assurance*

(1) A facility must maintain a quality assessment and assurance committee consisting of —

    (i) The director of nursing services;

    (ii) A physician designated by the facility; and

    (iii) At least 3 other members of the facility's staff.

(2) The quality assessment and assurance committee —

    (i) Meets at least quarterly to identify issues with respect to which quality assessment and assurance activities are necessary; and

    (ii) Develops and implements appropriate plans of action to correct identified quality deficiencies.

(3) A State or the Secretary may not require disclosure of the records of such committee except in so far as such disclosure is related to the compliance of such committee with the requirements of this section.

(4) Good faith attempts by the committee to identify and correct quality deficiencies will not be used as a basis for sanctions.

(p) *Disclosure of ownership*

(1) The facility must comply with the disclosure requirements of §§ 420.206 and 455.104 of this chapter.

(2) The facility must provide written notice to the State agency responsible for licensing the facility at the time of change, if a change occurs in —

(i) Persons with an ownership or control interest, as defined in §§ 420.201 and 455.101 of this chapter;

(ii) The officers, directors, agents, or managing employees;

(iii) The corporation, association, or other company responsible for the management of the facility; or

(iv) The facility's administrator or director of nursing.

(3) The notice specified in paragraph (p)(2) of this section must include the identity of each new individual or company.

Subpart C – [Reserved]

Subpart D – Requirements That Must Be Met by States and State Agencies: Nurse Aide Training and Competency Evaluation

## § 483.150. Statutory basis; Deemed meeting or waiver of requirements

(a) *Statutory basis*

This subpart is based on sections 1819(b)(5) and 1919(b)(5) of the Act, which establish standards for training nurse-aides and for evaluating their competency.

(b) *Deemed meeting of requirements*

A nurse aide is deemed to satisfy the requirement of completing a training and competency evaluation approved by the State if he or she successfully completed a training and competency evaluation program before July 1, 1989 if —

(1) The aide would have satisfied this requirement if —

(i) At least 60 hours were substituted for 75 hours in sections 1819(f)(2) and 1919(f)(2) of the Act, and

(ii) The individual has made up at least the difference in the number of hours in the program he or she completed and 75 hours in supervised practical nurse aide training or in regular in-service nurse aide education; or

(2) The individual was found to be competent (whether or not by the State) after the completion of nurse aide training of at least 100 hours duration.

(c) *Waiver of requirements*

A State may —

(1) Waive the requirement for an individual to complete a competency evaluation program approved by the State for any individual who can demonstrate to the satisfaction of the State that he or she has served as a nurse aide at one or more facilities of the same employer in the state for at least 24 consecutive months before December 19, 1989; or

(2) Deem an individual to have completed a nurse aide training and competency evaluation program approved by the State if the individual completed, before July 1, 1989, such a program that the State determines would have met the requirements for approval at the time it was offered.

## § 483.151. State review and approval of nurse aide training and competency evaluation programs and competency evaluation programs

(a) *State review and administration*

(1) The State —

(i) Must specify any nurse aide training and competency evaluation programs that the State approves as meeting the requirements of § 483.152 and/or competency evaluations programs that the State approves as meeting the requirements of § 483.154; and

(ii) May choose to offer a nurse aide training and competency evaluation program that meets the requirements of § 483.152 and/or a competency evaluation program that meets the requirements of § 483.154.

(2) If the State does not choose to offer a nurse aide training and competency evaluation program or competency evaluation program, the State must review and approve or disapprove nurse aide training and

competency evaluation programs and nurse aide competency evaluation programs upon request.

(3) The State survey agency must in the course of all surveys, determine whether the nurse aide training and competency evaluation requirements of § 483.75(e) are met.

(b) *Requirements for approval of programs*

(1) Before the State approves a nurse aide training and competency evaluation program or competency evaluation program, the State must —

(i) Determine whether the nurse aide training and competency evaluation program meets the course requirements of §§ 483.152:

(ii) Determine whether the nurse aide competency evaluation program meets the requirements of § 483.154; and

(iii) In all reviews other than the initial review, visit the entity providing the program.

(2) The State may not approve a nurse aide training and competency evaluation program or competency evaluation program offered by or in a facility which, in the previous two years —

(i) In the case of a skilled nursing facility, has operated under a waiver under section 1819(b)(4)(C)(ii)(II) of the Act;

(ii) In the case of a nursing facility, has operated under a waiver under section 1919(b)(4)(C)(ii) of the Act that was granted on the basis of a demonstration that the facility is unable to provide nursing care required under section 1919(b)(4)(C)(i) of the Act for a period in excess of 48 hours per week;

(iii) Has been subject to an extended (or partial extended) survey under sections 1819(g)(2)(B)(i) or 1919(g)(2)(B)(i) of the Act;

(iv) Has been assessed a civil money penalty described in section 1819(h)(2)(B)(ii) of 1919(h)(2)(A)(ii) of the Act of not less than $5,000; or

(v) Has been subject to a remedy described in sections 1819(h)(2)(B) (i) or (iii), 1819(h)(4), 1919(h)(1)(B)(i), or 1919(h)(2)(A) (i), (iii) or (iv) of the Act.

(3) A State may not, until two years since the assessment of the penalty (or penalties) has elapsed, approve a nurse aide training and competency evaluation program or competency evaluation program offered by or in a facility that, within the two-year period beginning October 1, 1988 —

(i) Had its participation terminated under title XVIII of the Act or under the State plan under title XIX of the Act;

(ii) Was subject to a denial of payment under title XVIII or title XIX;

(iii) Was assessed a civil money penalty of not less than $5,000 for deficiencies in nursing facility standards;

(iv) Operated under temporary management appointed to oversee the operation of the facility and to ensure the health and safety of its residents; or

(v) Pursuant to State action, was closed or had its residents transferred.

(c) *Time frame for acting on a request for approval*

The State must, within 90 days of the date of a request under paragraph (a)(3) of this section or receipt of additional information from the requester —

(1) Advise the requester whether or not the program has been approved; or

(2) Request additional information form the requesting entity.

(d) *Duration of approval*

The State may not grant approval of a nurse aide training and competency evaluation program for a period longer than 2 years. A program must notify the State and the State must review that program when there are substantive changes made to that program within the 2-year period.

(e) *Withdrawal of approval*

(1) The State must withdraw approval of a nurse aide training and competency evaluation program or nurse aide competency evaluation program offered by or in a facility described in paragraph (b)(2) of this section.

(2) The State may withdraw approval of a nurse aide training and competency evaluation program or nurse aide competency evaluation program if the State determines that any of the applicable requirements of §§ 483.152 or 483.154 are not met by the program.

(3) The State must withdraw approval of a nurse aide training and competency evaluation program or a nurse aide competency evaluation program if the entity providing the program refuses to permit unannounced visits by the State.

(4) If a State withdraws approval of a nurse aide training and competency evaluation program or competency evaluation program —

(i) The State must notify the program in writing, indicating the reason(s) for withdrawal of approval of the program.

(ii) Students who have started a training and competency evaluation program from which approval has been withdrawn must be allowed to complete the course.

### § 483.152. Requirements for approval of a nurse aide training and competency evaluation program

(a) *For a nurse aide training and competency evaluation program to be approved by the State, it must, at a minimum —*

(1) Consist of no less than 75 clock hours of training;

(2) Include at least the subjects specified in paragraph (b) of this section;

(3) Include at least 16 hours of supervised practical training. Supervised practical training means training in a laboratory or other setting in which the trainee demonstrates knowledge while performing tasks on an individual under the direct supervision of a registered nurse or a licensed practical nurse;

(4) Ensure that —

(i) Students do not perform any services for which they have not trained and been found proficient by the instructor; and

(ii) Students who are providing services to residents are under the general supervision of a licensed nurse or a registered nurse;

(5) Meet the following requirements for instructors who train nurse aides;

(i) The training of nurse aides must be performed by or under the general supervision of a registered nurse who possesses a minimum of 2 years of nursing experience, at least 1 year of which must be in the provision of long term care facility services;

(ii) Instructors must have completed a course in teaching adults or have experience in teaching adults or supervising nurse aides;

(iii) In a facility-based program, the training of nurse aides may be performed under the general supervision of the director of nursing for the facility who is prohibited from performing the actual training; and

(iv) Other personnel from the health professions may supplement the instructor, including, but not limited to, registered nurses, licensed practical/vocational nurses, pharmacists, dietitians, social workers, sanitarians, fire safety experts, nursing home administrators, gerontologists, psychologists, physical and occupational therapists, activities specialists, speech/language/hearing therapists, and resident rights experts. Supplemental personnel must have at least 1 year of experience in their fields;

(6) Contain competency evaluation procedures specified in § 483.154.

(b) *The curriculum of the nurse aide training program must include —*

(1) At least a total of 16 hours of training in the following areas prior to any direct contact with a resident:

(i) Communication and interpersonal skills;

(ii) Infection control;

(iii) Safety/emergency procedures, including the Heimlich maneuver;

(iv) Promoting residents' independence; and

(v) Respecting residents' rights.

(2) Basic nursing skills;

(i) Taking and recording vital signs;

(ii) Measuring and recording height and weight;

(iii) Caring for the residents' environment;

(iv) Recognizing abnormal changes in body functioning and the importance of reporting such changes to a supervisor; and

(v) Caring for residents when death is imminent.

(3) Personal care skills, including, but not limited to —

(i) Bathing;

(ii) Grooming, including mouth care;

(iii) Dressing;

(iv) Toileting;

(v) Assisting with eating and hydration;

(vi) Proper feeding techniques;

(vii) Skin care; and

(viii) Transfers, positioning, and turning.

(4) Mental health and social service needs:

(i) Modifying aide's behavior in response to residents' behavior;

(ii) Awareness of developmental tasks associated with the aging process;

(iii) How to respond to resident behavior;

(iv) Allowing the resident to make personal choices, providing and reinforcing other behavior consistent with the resident's dignity; and

(v) Using the resident's family as a source of emotional support.

(5) Care of cognitively impaired residents:

(i) Techniques for addressing the unique needs and behaviors of individual with dementia (Alzheimer's and others);

(ii) Communicating with cognitively impaired residents;

(iii) Understanding the behavior of cognitively impaired residents;

(iv) Appropriate responses to the behavior of cognitively impaired residents; and

(v) Methods of reducing the effects of cognitive impairments.

(6) Basic restorative services:

(i) Training the resident in self care according to the resident's abilities;

(ii) Use of assistive devices in transferring, ambulation, eating, and dressing;

(iii) Maintenance of range of motion;

(iv) Proper turning and positioning in bed and chair;

(v) Bowel and bladder training; and

(vi) Care and use of prosthetic and orthotic devices.

(7) Residents' Rights.

(i) Providing privacy and maintenance of confidentiality;

(ii) Promoting the residents' right to make personal choices to accommodate their needs;

(iii) Giving assistance in resolving grievances and disputes;

(iv) Providing needed assistance in getting to and participating in resident and family groups and other activities;

(v) Maintaining care and security of residents' personal possessions;

(vi) Promoting the resident's right to be free from abuse, mistreatment, and neglect and the need to report any instances of such treatment to appropriate facility staff;

(vii) Avoiding the need for restraints in accordance with current professional standards.

(c) *Prohibition of charges*

(1) No nurse aide who is employed by, or who has received an offer of employment from, a facility on the date on which the aide begins a nurse aide training and competency evaluation program may be charged for any portion of the program (including any fees for textbooks or other required course materials).

(2) If an individual who is not employed, or does not have an offer to be employed, as a nurse aide becomes employed by, or receives an offer of employment from, a facility not later than 12 months after completing a nurse aide training and competency evaluation program, the State must provide for the reimbursement of costs incurred in completing the program on a pro rata basis during the period in which the individual is employed as a nurse aide.

## § 483.154. Nurse aide competency evaluation

(a) *Notification to Individual*

The State must advise in advance any individual who takes the competency evaluation that a record of the successful completion of the evaluation will be included in the State's nurse aid registry.

(b) *Content of the competency evaluation program —*

(1) Written or oral examinations. The competency evaluation must —

(i) Allow an aide to choose between a written and an oral examination;

(ii) Address each course requirement specified in § 483.152(b);

(iii) Be developed from a pool of test questions, only a portion of which is used in any one examination;

(iv) Use a system that prevents disclosure of both the pool of questions and the individual competency evaluations; and

(v) If oral, must be read from a prepared text in a neutral manner.

(2) Demonstration of skills. The skills demonstration must consist of a demonstration of randomly selected items drawn from a pool consisting of the tasks generally performed by nurse aides. This pool of skills must include all of the personal care skills listed in § 483.152(b)(3).

(c) *Administration of the competency evaluation*

(1) The competency examination must be administered and evaluated only by —

(i) The State directly; or

(ii) A State approved entity which is neither a skilled nursing facility that participates in Medicare nor a nursing facility that participates in Medicaid.

(2) No nurse aide who is employed by, or who has received an offer of employment from, a facility on the date on which the aide begins a nurse aide competency evaluation program may be charged for any portion of the program.

(3) If an individual who is not employed, or does not have an offer to be employed, as a nurse aide becomes employed by, or receives an offer of employment from, a facility not later than 12 months after completing a nurse aide competency evaluation program, the State must provide for the reimbursement of costs incurred in completing the program on a pro rata basis during the period in which the individual is employed as a nurse aide.

(4) The skills demonstration part of the evaluation must be —

(i) Performed in a facility or laboratory setting comparable to the setting in which the individual will function as a nurse aide; and

(ii) Administered and evaluated by a registered nurse with at least one year's experience in providing care for the elderly or the chronically ill of any age.

(d) *Facility proctoring of the competency evaluation*

(1) The competency evaluation may, at the nurse aide's option, be conducted at the facility in which the nurse aide is or will be employed unless the facility is described in § 483.151(b)(2).

(2) The State may permit the competency evaluation to be proctored by facility personnel if the State finds that the procedure adopted by the facility assures that the competency evaluation program —

(i) Is secure from tampering;

(ii) Is standardized and scored by a testing, educational, or other organization approved by the State; and

(iii) Requires no scoring by facility personnel.

(3) The State must retract the right to proctor nurse aide competency evaluations from facilities in which the State finds any evidence of impropriety, including evidence of tampering by facility staff.

(e) *Successful completion of the competency evaluation program*

(1) The State must establish a standard for satisfactory completion of the competency evaluation.  To complete the competency evaluation successfully an individual must pass both the written or oral examination and the skills demonstration.

(2) A record of successful completion of the competency evaluation must be included in the nurse aide registry provided in § 483.156 within 30 days of the date if the individual is found to be competent.

(f) *Unsuccessful completion of the competency evaluation program*

(1) If the individual does not complete the evaluation satisfactorily, the individual must be advised —

    (i) Of the areas which he or she; did not pass; and

    (ii) That he or she has at least three opportunities to take the evaluation.

(2) The State may impose a maximum upon the number of times an individual upon the number of times an individual may attempt to complete the competency evaluation successfully, but the maximum may be no less than three.

### § 483.156.  Registry of nurse aides

(a) *Establishment of registry*

The State must establish and maintain a registry of nurse aides that meets the requirement of this section.  The registry —

(1) Must include as a minimum the information contained in paragraph (c) of this section:

(2) Must be sufficiently accessible to meet the needs of the public and health care providers promptly;

(3) May include home health aides who have successfully completed a home health aide competency evaluation program approved by the State if home health aides are differentiated from nurse aides; and

(4) Must provide that any response to an inquiry that includes a finding of abuse, neglect, or misappropriation of property also include any statement disputing the finding made by the nurse aide, as provided under paragraph (c)(1)(ix) of this section.

(b) *Registry operation*

(1) The State may contract the daily operation and maintenance of the registry to a non-State entity. However, the State must maintain accountability for overall operation of the registry and compliance with these regulations.

(2) Only the State survey and certification agency may place on the registry findings of abuse, neglect, or misappropriation of property.

(3) The State must determine which individuals who (i) have successfully completed a nurse aide training and competency evaluation program or nurse aide competency evaluation program; (ii) have been deemed as meeting these requirements; or (iii) have had these requirements waived by the State do not qualify to remain on the registry because they have performed no nursing or nursing-related services for a period of 24 consecutive months.

(4) The State may not impose any charges related to registration on individuals listed in the registry.

(5) The State must provide information on the registry promptly.

(c) *Registry Content*

(1) The registry must contain at least the following information on each individual who has successfully completed a nurse aide training and competency evaluation program which meets the requirements of § 483.152 or a competency evaluation which meets the requirements of § 483.154 and has been found by the State to be competent to function as a nurse aide or who may function as a nurse aide because of meeting criteria in § 483.150:

(i) The individual's full name.

(ii) Information necessary to identify each individual;

(iii) The date the individual became eligible for placement in the registry through successfully completing a nurse aide training and competency evaluation program or competency evaluation program or by meeting the requirements of § 483.150; and

(iv) The following information on any finding by the State survey agency of abuse, neglect, or misappropriation of property by the individual:

(A) Documentation of the State's investigation, including the nature of the allegation and the evidence that led the State to conclude that the allegation was valid;

(B) The date of the hearing, if the individual chose to have one, and its outcome; and

(C) A statement by the individual disputing the allegation, if he or she chooses to make one; and

(D) This information must be included in the registry within 10 working days of the finding and must remain in the registry permanently, unless the finding was made in error, the individual was found not guilty in a court of law, or the State is notified of the individual's death.

(2) The registry must remove entries for individuals who have performed no nursing or nursing-related services for a period of 24 consecutive months, unless the individual's registry entry includes documented findings of abuse, neglect, or misappropriation of property.

(d) *Disclosure of information. The State must —*

(1) Disclose all of the information in § 483.156(c)(1) (iii) and (iv) to all requesters and may disclose additional information it deems necessary; and

(2) Promptly provide individuals with all information contained in the registry on them when adverse findings are placed on the registry and upon request. Individuals on the registry must have sufficient opportunity to correct any misstatements or inaccuracies contained in the registry.

## § 483.158.  FFP for nurse aide training and competency evaluation

(a) State expenditures for nurse aide training and competency evaluation programs and competency evaluation programs are administrative costs They are matched as indicated in § 433.15(b)(8) of this chapter.

(b) FFP is available for State expenditures associated with nurse aide training and competency evaluation programs and competency evaluation programs only for —

(1) Nurse aides employed by a facility;

(2) Nurse aides who have an offer of employment from a facility;

(3) Nurse aides who become employed by a facility not later than 12 months after completing a nurse aide training and competency evaluation program or competency evaluation program; or

(4) Nurse aides who receive an offer of employment from a facility not later than 12 months after completing a nurse aide training and competency evaluation program or competency evaluation program.

Subparts E–H – [Reversed]

Subpart I – Conditions of Participation for Intermediate Care Facilities for the Mentally Retarded

## § 483.400. Basis and purpose

This subpart implements section 1905 (c) and (d) of the Act which gives the Secretary authority to prescribe regulations for intermediate care facility services in facilities for the mentally retarded or persons with related conditions.

## § 483.405. Relationship to other HHS regulations

In addition to compliance with the regulations set forth in this subpart, facilities are obliged to meet the applicable provisions of other HHS regulations, including but not limited to those pertaining to nondiscrimination on the basis of race, color, or national origin (45 CFR Part 80), nondiscrimination on the basis of handicap (45 CFR Part 84), nondiscrimination on the basis of age (45 CFR Part 91), protection of human subjects of research (45 CFR Part 46), and fraud and abuse (42 CFR Part 455). Although those regulations are not in themselves considered conditions of participation under this Part, their violation may result in the termination or suspension of, or the refusal to grant or continue, Federal financial assistance.

## § 483.410. Condition of participation: Governing body and management

(a) *Standard: Governing body*

The facility must identify an individual or individuals to constitute the governing body of the facility. The governing body must —

(1) Exercise general policy, budget, and operating direction over the facility;

(2) Set the qualifications (in addition to those already set by State law, if any) for the administrator of the facility; and

(3) Appoint the administrator of the facility.

(b) *Standard: Compliance with Federal, State, and local laws*

The facility must be in compliance with all applicable provisions of Federal, State and local laws, regulations and codes pertaining to health, safety, and sanitation.

(c) *Standard: Client records*

(1) The facility must develop and maintain a recordkeeping system that includes a separate record for each client and that documents the client's health care, active treatment, social information, and protection of the client's rights.

(2) The facility must keep confidential all information contained in the clients' records, regardless of the form or storage method of the records.

(3) The facility must develop and implement policies and procedures governing the release of any client information, including consents necessary from the client, or parents (if the client is a minor) or legal guardian.

(4) Any individual who makes an entry in a client's record must make it legibly, date it, and sign it.

(5) The facility must provide a legend to explain any symbol or abbreviation used in a client's record.

(6) The facility must provide each identified residential living unit with appropriate aspects of each client's record.

(d) *Standard: Services provided under agreements with outside sources*

(1) If a service required under this subpart is not provided directly, the facility must have a written agreement with an outside program, resource, or service to furnish the necessary service, including emergency and other health care.

(2) The agreement must —

(i) Contain the responsibilities, functions, objectives, and other terms agreed to by both parties; and

(ii) Provide that the facility is responsible for assuring that the outside services meet the standards for quality of services contained in this subpart.

(3) The facility must assure that outside services meet the needs of each client.

(4) If living quarters are not provided in a facility owned by the ICF/MR, the ICF/MR remains directly responsible for the standards relating to physical environment that are specified in § 483.470 (a) through (g), (j) and (k).

(e) *Standard: Licensure*

The facility must be licensed under applicable State and local law.

## § 483.420.  Condition of participation:  Client protections

(a) *Standard: Protection of clients' rights. The facility must ensure the rights of all clients. Therefore, the facility must —*

(1) Inform each client, parent (if the client is a minor), or legal guardian, of the client's rights and the rules of the facility;

(2) Inform each client, parent (if the client is a minor), or legal guardian, of the client's medical condition, developmental and behavioral status, attendant risks of treatment, and of the right to refuse treatment;

(3) Allow and encourage individual clients to exercise their rights as clients of the facility, and as citizens of the United States, including the right to file complaints, and the right to due process;

(4) Allow individual clients to manage their financial affairs and teach them to do so to the extent of their capabilities;

(5) Ensure that clients are not subjected to physical, verbal, sexual or psychological abuse or punishment;

(6) Ensure that clients are free from unnecessary drugs and physical restraints and are provided active treatment to reduce dependency on drugs and physical restraints;

(7) Provide each client with the opportunity for personal privacy and ensure privacy during treatment and care of personal needs;

(8) Ensure that clients are not compelled to perform services for the facility and ensure that clients who do work for the facility are compensated for their efforts at prevailing wages and commensurate with their abilities;

(9) Ensure clients the opportunity to communicate, associate and meet privately with individuals of their choice, and to send and receive unopened mail;

(10) Ensure that clients have access to telephones with privacy for incoming and outgoing local and long distance calls except as contraindicated by factors identified within their individual program plans;

(11) Ensure clients the opportunity to participate in social, religious, and community group activities;

(12) Ensure that clients have the right to retain and use appropriate personal possessions and clothing, and ensure that each client is dressed in his or her own clothing each day; and

(13) Permit a husband and wife who both reside in the facility to share a room.

(b) *Standard: Client finances*

(1) The facility must establish and maintain a system that —

(i) Assures a full and complete accounting of clients' personal funds entrusted to the facility on behalf of clients; and

(ii) Precludes any commingling of client funds with facility funds or with the funds of any person other than another client.

(2) The client's financial record must be available on request to the client, parents (if the client is a minor) or legal guardian.

(c) *Standard: Communication with clients, parents, and guardians*

The facility must —

(1) Promote participation of parents (if the client is a minor) and legal guardians in the process of providing active treatment to a client unless their participation is unobtainable or inappropriate;

(2) Answer communications from clients' families and friends promptly and appropriately;

(3) Promote visits by individuals with a relationship to the client (such as family, close friends, legal guardians and advocates) at any reasonable hour, without prior notice, consistent with the right of that client's and other clients' privacy, unless the interdisciplinary team determines that the visit would not be appropriate;

(4) Promote visits by parents or guardians to any area of the facility that provides direct client care services to the client, consistent with the right of that client's and other clients' privacy;

(5) Promote frequent and informal leaves from the facility for visits, trips, or vacations; and

(6) Notify promptly the client's parents or guardian of any significant incidents, or changes in the client's condition including, but not limited to, serious illness, accident, death, abuse, or unauthorized absence.

(d) *Standard: Staff treatment of clients*

(1) The facility must develop and implement written policies and procedures that prohibit mistreatment, neglect or abuse of the client.

(i) Staff of the facility must not use physical, verbal, sexual or psychological abuse or punishment.

(ii) Staff must not punish a client by withholding food or hydration that contributes to a nutritionally adequate diet.

(iii) The facility must prohibit the employment of individuals with a conviction or prior employment history of child or client abuse, neglect or mistreatment.

(2) The facility must ensure that all allegations of mistreatment, neglect or abuse, as well as injuries of unknown source, are reported immediately to the administrator or to other officials in accordance with State law through established procedures.

(3) The facility must have evidence that all alleged violations are thoroughly investigated and must prevent further potential abuse while the investigation is in progress.

(4) The results of all investigations must be reported to the administrator or designated representative or to other officials in accordance with State law within five working days of the incident and, if the alleged violation is verified, appropriate corrective action must be taken.

### § 483.430. Condition of participation: Facility staffing

(a) *Standard: Qualified mental retardation professional*

Each client's active treatment program must be integrated, coordinated and monitored by a qualified mental retardation professional who —

(1) Has at least one year of experience working directly with persons with mental retardation or other developmental disabilities; and

(2) Is one of the following:

(i) A doctor of medicine or osteopathy.

(ii) A registered nurse.

(iii) An individual who holds at least a bachelor's degree in a professional category specified in paragraph (b)(5) of this section.

(b) *Standard: Professional program services*

(1) Each client must receive the professional program services needed to implement the active treatment program defined by each client's individual program plan. Professional program staff must work directly with clients and with paraprofessional, nonprofessional and other professional program staff who work with clients.

(2) The facility must have available enough qualified professional staff to carry out and monitor the various professional interventions in accordance with the stated goals and objectives of every individual program plan.

(3) Professional program staff must participate as members of the interdisciplinary team in relevant aspects of the active treatment process.

(4) Professional program staff must participate in on-going staff development and training in both formal and informal settings with other professional, paraprofessional, and nonprofessional staff members.

(5) Professional program staff must be licensed, certified, or registered, as applicable, to provide professional services by the State in which he or she practices. Those professional program staff who do not fall under the jurisdiction of State licensure, certification, or registration requirements, specified in § 483.410(b), must meet the following qualifications:

(i) To be designated as an occupational therapist, an individual must be eligible for certification as an occupational therapist by the American Occupational Therapy Association or another comparable body.

(ii) To be designated as an occupational therapy assistant, an individual must be eligible for certification as a certified occupational therapy assistant by the American Occupational Therapy Association or another comparable body.

(iii) To be designated as a physical therapist, an individual must be eligible for certification as a physical therapist by the American Physical Therapy Association or another comparable body.

(iv) To be designated as a physical therapy assistant, an individual must be eligible for registration by the American Physical Therapy Association or be a graduate of a two year college-level program approved by the American Physical Therapy Association or another comparable body.

(v) To be designated as a psychologist, an individual must have at least a master's degree in psychology from an accredited school.

(vi) To be designated as a social worker, an individual must —

(A) Hold a graduate degree from a school of social work accredited or approved by the Council on Social Work Education or another comparable body; or

(B) Hold a Bachelor of Social Work degree from a college or university accredited or approved by the Council on Social Work Education or another comparable body.

(vii) To be designated as a speech-language pathologist or audiologist, an individual must —

(A) Be eligible for a Certificate of Clinical Competence in Speech-Language Pathology or Audiology granted by the

American Speech-Language-Hearing Association or another comparable body; or

(B) Meet the educational requirements for certification and be in the process of accumulating the supervised experience required for certification.

(viii) To be designated as a professional recreation staff member, an individual must have a bachelor's degree in recreation or in a specialty area such as art, dance, music or physical education.

(ix) To be designated as a professional dietitian, an individual must be eligible for registration by the American Dietetics Association.

(x) To be designated as a human services professional an individual must have at least a bachelor's degree in a human services field (including, but not limited to: sociology, special education, rehabilitation counseling, and psychology).

(xi) If the client's individual program plan is being successfully implemented by facility staff, professional program staff meeting the qualifications of paragraph (b)(5) (i) through (x) of this section are not required —

(A) Except for qualified mental retardation professionals;

(B) Except for the requirements of paragraph (b)(2) of this section concerning the facility's provision of enough qualified professional program staff; and

(C) Unless otherwise specified by State licensure and certification requirements.

(c) *Standard: Facility staffing*

(1) The facility must not depend upon clients or volunteers to perform direct care services for the facility.

(2) There must be responsible direct care staff on duty and awake on a 24-hour basis, when clients are present, to take prompt, appropriate action in case of injury, illness, fire or other emergency, in each defined residential living unit housing —

(i) Clients for whom a physician has ordered a medical care plan;

(ii) Clients who are aggressive, assaultive or security risks;

(iii) More than 16 clients; or

(iv) Fewer than 16 clients within a multi-unit building.

(3) There must be a responsible direct care staff person on duty on a 24 hour basis (when clients are present) to respond to injuries and

symptoms of illness, and to handle emergencies, in each defined residential living unit housing —

      (i) Clients for whom a physician has not ordered a medical care plan;

      (ii) Clients who are not aggressive, assaultive or security risks; and

      (iii) Sixteen or fewer clients,

(4) The facility must provide sufficient support staff so that direct care staff are not required to perform support services to the extent that these duties interfere with the exercise of their primary direct client care duties.

(d) *Standard: Direct care (residential living unit) staff*

(1) The facility must provide sufficient direct care staff to manage and supervise clients in accordance with their individual program plans.

(2) Direct care staff are defined as the present on-duty staff calculated over all shifts in a 24-hour period for each defined residential living unit.

(3) Direct care staff must be provided by the facility in the following minimum ratios of direct care staff to clients:

      (i) For each defined residential living unit serving children under the age of 12, severely and profoundly retarded clients, clients with severe physical disabilities, or clients who are aggressive, assaultive, or security risks, or who manifest severely hyperactive or psychotic-like behavior, the staff to client ratio is 1 to 3.2.

      (ii) For each defined residential living unit serving moderately retarded clients, the staff to client ratio is 1 to 4.

      (iii) For each defined residential living unit serving clients who function within the range of mild retardation, the staff to client ratio is 1 to 6.4.

(4) When there are no clients present in the living unit, a responsible staff member must be available by telephone.

(e) *Standard: Staff training program*

(1) The facility must provide each employee with initial and continuing training that enables the employee to perform his or her duties effectively, efficiently, and competently.

(2) For employees who work with clients, training must focus on skills and competencies directed toward clients' developmental, behavioral, and health needs.

(3) Staff must be able to demonstrate the skills and techniques necessary to administer interventions to manage the inappropriate behavior of clients.

(4) Staff must be able to demonstrate the skills and techniques necessary to implement the individual program plans for each client for whom they are responsible.

## § 483.440. Condition of participation: Active treatment services

(a) *Standard: Active treatment*

(1) Each client must receive a continuous active treatment program, which includes aggressive, consistent implementation of a program of specialized and generic training, treatment, health services and related services described in this subpart, that is directed toward —

(i) The acquisition of the behaviors necessary for the client to function with as much self determination and independence as possible; and

(ii) The prevention or deceleration of regression or loss of current optimal functional status.

(2) Active treatment does not include services to maintain generally independent clients who are able to function with little supervision or in the absence of a continuous active treatment program.

(b) *Standard: Admissions, transfers, and discharge*

(1) Clients who are admitted by the facility must be in need of and receiving active treatment services.

(2) Admission decisions must be based on a preliminary evaluation of the client that is conducted or updated by the facility or by outside sources.

(3) A preliminary evaluation must contain background information as well as currently valid assessments of functional developmental, behavioral, social, health and nutritional status to determine if the facility can provide for the client's needs and if the client is likely to benefit from placement in the facility.

(4) If a client is to be either transferred or discharged, the facility must —

(i) Have documentation in the client's record that the client was transferred or discharged for good cause; and

(ii) Provide a reasonable time to prepare the client and his or her parents or guardian for the transfer or discharge (except in emergencies).

(5) At the time of the discharge, the facility must —

(i) Develop a final summary of the client's developmental, behavioral, social, health and nutritional status and, with the consent of the client, parents (if the client is a minor) or legal guardian, provide a copy to authorized persons and agencies; and

(ii) Provide a post-discharge plan of care that will assist the client to adjust to the new living environment.

(c) *Standard: Individual program plan*

(1) Each client must have an individual program plan developed by an interdisciplinary team that represents the professions, disciplines or service areas that are relevant to —

(i) Identifying the client's needs, as described by the comprehensive functional assessments required in paragraph (c)(3) of this section; and

(ii) Designing programs that meet the client's needs.

(2) Appropriate facility staff must participate in interdisciplinary team meetings. Participation by other agencies serving the client is encouraged. Participation by the client, his or her parent (if the client is a minor), or the client's legal guardian is required unless that participation is unobtainable or inappropriate.

(3) Within 30 days after admission, the interdisciplinary team must perform accurate assessments or reassessments as needed to supplement the preliminary evaluation conducted prior to admission. The comprehensive functional assessment must take into consideration the client's age (for example, child, young adult, elderly person) and the implications for active treatment at each stage, as applicable, and must —

(i) Identify the presenting problems and disabilities and where possible, their causes;

(ii) Identify the client's specific developmental strengths;

(iii) Identify the client's specific developmental and behavioral management needs;

(iv) Identify the client's need for services without regard to the actual availability of the services needed; and

(v) Include physical development and health, nutritional status, sensorimotor development, affective development, speech and language development and auditory functioning, cognitive development, social development, adaptive behaviors or independent living skills necessary for the client to be able to function in the community, and as applicable, vocational skills.

(4) Within 30 days after admission, the interdisciplinary team must prepare for each client an individual program plan that states the specific objectives necessary to meet the client's needs, as identified by the comprehensive assessment required by paragraph (c)(3) of this section, and the planned sequence for dealing with those objectives. These objectives must —

(i) Be stated separately, in terms of a single behavioral outcome;

(ii) Be assigned projected completion dates;

(iii) Be expressed in behavioral terms that provide measurable indices of performance;

(iv) Be organized to reflect a developmental progression appropriate to the individual; and

(v) Be assigned priorities.

(5) Each written training program designed to implement the objectives in the individual program plan must specify:

(i) The methods to be used;

(ii) The schedule for use of the method;

(iii) The person responsible for the program;

(iv) The type of data and frequency of data collection necessary to be able to assess progress toward the desired objectives;

(v) The inappropriate client behavior(s), if applicable; and

(vi) Provision for the appropriate expression of behavior and the replacement of inappropriate behavior, if applicable, with behavior that is adaptive or appropriate.

(6) The individual program plan must also:

(i) Describe relevant interventions to support the individual toward independence.

(ii) Identify the location where program strategy information (which must be accessible to any person responsible for implementation) can be found.

(iii) Include, for those clients who lack them, training in personal skills essential for privacy and independence (including, but not limited to, toilet training, personal hygiene, dental hygiene, self-feeding, bathing, dressing, grooming, and communication of basic needs), until it has been demonstrated that the client is developmentally incapable of acquiring them.

(iv) Identify mechanical supports, if needed, to achieve proper body position, balance, or alignment. The plan must specify the reason for each support, the situations in which each is to be applied, and a schedule for the use of each support.

(v) Provide that clients who have multiple disabling conditions spend a major portion of each waking day out of bed and outside the bedroom area, moving about by various methods and devices whenever possible.

(iv) Include opportunities for client choice and self-management.

(7) A copy of each client's individual program plan must be made available to all relevant staff, including staff of other agencies who work with the client, and to the client, parents (if the client is a minor) or legal guardian.

(d) *Standard: Program implementation*

(1) As soon as the interdisciplinary team has formulated a client's individual program plan, each client must receive a continuous active treatment program consisting of needed interventions and services in sufficient number and frequency to support the achievement of the objectives identified in the individual program plan.

(2) The facility must develop an active treatment schedule that outlines the current active treatment program and that is readily available for review by relevant staff.

(3) Except for those facets of the individual program plan that must be implemented only by licensed personnel, each client's individual program plan must be implemented by all staff who work with the client, including professional, paraprofessional and nonprofessional staff.

(e) *Standard: Program documentation*

(1) Data relative to accomplishment of the criteria specified in client individual program plan objectives must be documented in measurable terms.

(2) The facility must document significant events that are related to the client's individual program plan and assessments and that contribute to an overall understanding of the client's ongoing level and quality of functioning.

(f) *Standard: Program monitoring and change*

(1) The individual program plan must be reviewed at least by the qualified mental retardation professional and revised as necessary, including, but not limited to situations in which the client —

(i) Has successfully completed an objective or objectives identified in the individual program plan;

(ii) Is regressing or losing skills already gained;

(iii) Is failing to progress toward identified objectives after reasonable efforts have been made; or

(iv) Is being considered for training towards new objectives.

(2) At least annually, the comprehensive functional assessment of each client must be reviewed by the interdisciplinary team for relevancy and updated as needed, and the individual program plan must be revised, as appropriate, repeating the process set forth in paragraph (c) of this section.

(3) The facility must designate and use a specially constituted committee or committees consisting of members of facility staff, parents, legal guardians, clients (as appropriate), qualified persons who have either experience or training in contemporary practices to change inappropriate client behavior, and persons with no ownership or controlling interest in the facility to —

(i) Review, approve, and monitor individual programs designed to manage inappropriate behavior and other programs that, in the opinion of the committee, involve risks to client protection and rights;

(ii) Insure that these programs are conducted only with the written informed consent of the client, parent (if the client is a minor), or legal guardian; and

(iii) Review, monitor and make suggestions to the facility about its practices and programs as they relate to drug usage, physical restraints, time-out rooms, application of painful or noxious stimuli, control of inappropriate behavior, protection of client rights and funds, and any other area that the committee believes need to be addressed.

(4) The provisions of paragraph (f)(3) of this section may be modified only if, in the judgment of the State survey agency, Court decrees, State law or regulations provide for equivalent client protection and consultation.

## § 483.450.  Condition of participation:  Client behavior and facility practices

(a) *Standard:  Facility practices — Conduct toward clients*

(1) The facility must develop and implement written policies and procedures for the management of conduct between staff and clients. These policies and procedures must —

(i) Promote the growth, development and independence of the client;

(ii) Address the extent to which client choice will be accommodated in daily decision-making, emphasizing self-determination and self-management, to the extent possible;

(iii) Specify client conduct to be allowed or not allowed; and

(iv) Be available to all staff, clients, parents of minor children, and legal guardians.

(2) To the extent possible, clients must participate in the formulation of these policies and procedures.

(3) Clients must not discipline other clients, except as part of an organized system of self-government, as set forth in facility policy.

(b) *Standard: Management of inappropriate client behavior*

(1) The facility must develop and implement written policies and procedures that govern the management of inappropriate client behavior. These policies and procedures must be consistent with the provisions of paragraph (a) of this section. These procedures must —

(i) Specify all facility approved interventions to manage inappropriate client behavior;

(ii) Designate these interventions on a hierarchy to be implemented, ranging from most positive or least intrusive, to least positive or most intrusive;

(iii) Insure, prior to the use of more restrictive techniques, that the client's record documents that programs incorporating the use of less intrusive or more positive techniques have been tried systematically and demonstrated to be ineffective; and

(iv) Address the following:

(A) The use of time-out rooms.

(B) The use of physical restraints.

(C) The use of drugs to manage inappropriate behavior.

(D) The application of painful or noxious stimuli.

(E) The staff members who may authorize the use of specified interventions.

(F) A mechanism for monitoring and controlling the use of such interventions.

(2) Interventions to manage inappropriate client behavior must be employed with sufficient safeguards and supervision to ensure that the safety, welfare and civil and human rights of clients are adequately protected.

(3) Techniques to manage inappropriate client behavior must never be used for disciplinary purposes, for the convenience of staff or as a substitute for an active treatment program.

(4) The use of systematic interventions to manage inappropriate client behavior must be incorporated into the client's individual program plan, in accordance with § 483.440(c) (4) and (5) of this subpart.

(5) Standing or as needed programs to control inappropriate behavior are not permitted.

(c) *Standard: Time-out rooms*

(1) A client may be placed in a room from which egress is prevented only if the following conditions are met:

(i) The placement is a part of an approved systematic time-out program as required by paragraph (b) of this section. (Thus, emergency placement of a client into a time-out room is not allowed.)

(ii) The client is under the direct constant visual supervision of designated staff.

(iii) The door to the room is held shut by staff or by a mechanism requiring constant physical pressure from a staff member to keep the mechanism engaged.

(2) Placement of a client in a time-out room must not exceed one hour.

(3) Clients placed in time-out rooms must be protected from hazardous conditions including, but not limited to, presence of sharp corners and objects, uncovered light fixtures, unprotected electrical outlets.

(4) A record of time-out activities must be kept.

(d) *Standard: Physical restraints*

(1) The facility may employ physical restraint only —

(i) As an integral part of an individual program plan that is intended to lead to less restrictive means of managing and eliminating the behavior for which the restraint is applied;

(ii) As an emergency measure, but only if absolutely necessary to protect the client or others from injury; or

(iii) As a health-related protection prescribed by a physician, but only if absolutely necessary during the conduct of a specific medical or surgical procedure, or only if absolutely necessary for client protection during the time that a medical condition exists.

(2) Authorizations to use or extend restraints as an emergency must be:

(i) In effect no longer than 12 consecutive hours; and

(ii) Obtained as soon as the client is restrained or stable.

(3) The facility must not issue orders for restraint on a standing or as needed basis.

(4) A client placed in restraint must be checked at least every 30 minutes by staff trained in the use of restraints, released from the restraint as quickly as possible, and a record of these checks and usage must be kept.

(5) Restraints must be designed and used so as not to cause physical injury to the client and so as to cause the least possible discomfort.

(6) Opportunity for motion and exercise must be provided for a period of not less than 10 minutes during each two hour period in which restraint is employed, and a record of such activity must be kept.

(7) Barred enclosures must not be more than three feet in height and must not have tops.

(e) *Standard: Drug usage*

(1) The facility must not use drugs in doses that interfere with the individual client's daily living activities.

(2) Drugs used for control of inappropriate behavior must be approved by the interdisciplinary team and be used only as an integral part of the client's individual program plan that is directed specifically towards the reduction of and eventual elimination of the behaviors for which the drugs are employed.

(3) Drugs used for control of inappropriate behavior must not be used until it can be justified that the harmful effects of the behavior clearly outweigh the potentially harmful effects of the drugs.

(4) Drugs used for control of inappropriate behavior must be —

(i) Monitored closely, in conjunction with the physician and the drug regimen review requirement at § 483.460(j), for desired responses and adverse consequences by facility staff; and

(ii) Gradually withdrawn at least annually in a carefully monitored program conducted in conjunction with the interdisciplinary team, unless clinical evidence justifies that this is contraindicated.

## § 483.460. Condition of participation: Health care services

(a) *Standard: Physician services*

(1) The facility must ensure the availability of physician services 24 hours a day.

(2) The physician must develop, in coordination with licensed nursing personnel, a medical care plan of treatment for a client if the physician determines that an individual client requires 24-hour licensed nursing care. This plan must be integrated in the individual program plan.

(3) The facility must provide or obtain preventive and general medical care as well as annual physical examinations of each client that at a minimum include the following:

(i) Evaluation of vision and hearing.

(ii) Immunizations, using as a guide the recommendations of the Public Health Service Advisory Commitee on Immunization Practices or of the Committee on the Control of Infectious Diseases of the American Academy of Pediatrics.

(iii) Routine screening laboratory examinations as determined necessary by the physician, and special studies when needed.

(iv) Tuberculosis control, appropriate to the facility's population, and in accordance with the recommendations of the American College of Chest Physicians or the section of diseases of the chest of the American Academy of Pediatrics, or both.

(4) To the extent permitted by State law, the facility may utilize physician assistants and nurse practitioners to provide physician services as described in this section.

(b) *Standard: Physician participation in the individual program plan*

A physician must participate in —

(1) The establishment of each newly admitted client's initial individual program plan as required by § 456.380 of this chapter that specified plan of care requirements for ICFs; and

(2) If appropriate, physicians must participate in the review and update of an individual program plan as part of the interdisciplinary team process either in person or through written report to the interdisciplinary team.

(c) *Standard: Nursing services*

The facility must provide clients with nursing services in accordance with their needs. These services must include —

(1) Participation as appropriate in the development, review, and update of an individual program plan as part of the interdisciplinary team process;

(2) The development, with a physician, of a medical care plan of treatment for a client when the physician has determined that an individual client requires such a plan;

(3) For those clients certified as not needing a medical care plan, a review of their health status which must —

(i) Be by a direct physical examination;

(ii) Be by a licensed nurse;

(iii) Be on a quarterly or more frequent basis depending on client need;

(iv) Be recorded in the client's record; and

(v) Result in any necessary action (including referral to a physician to address client health problems).

(4) Other nursing care as prescribed by the physician or as identified by client needs; and

(5) Implementing, with other members of the interdisciplinary team, appropriate protective and preventive health measures that include, but are not limited to —

(i) Training clients and staff as needed in appropriate health and hygiene methods;

(ii) Control of communicable diseases and infections, including the instruction of other personnel in methods of infection control; and

(iii) Training direct care staff in detecting signs and symptoms of illness or dysfunction, first aid for accidents or illness, and basic skills required to meet the health needs of the clients.

(d) *Standard: Nursing staff*

(1) Nurses providing services in the facility must have a current license to practice in the State.

(2) The facility must employ or arrange for licensed nursing services sufficient to care for clients health needs including those clients with medical care plans.

(3) The facility must utilize registered nurses as appropriate and required by State law to perform the health services specified in this section.

(4) If the facility utilizes only licensed practical or vocational nurses to provide health services, it must have a formal arrangement with a registered nurse to be available for verbal or onsite consultation to the licensed practical or vocational nurse.

(5) Non-licensed nursing personnel who work with clients under a medical care plan must do so under the supervision of licensed persons.

(e) *Standard: Dental services*

(1) The facility must provide or make arrangements for comprehensive diagnostic and treatment services for each client from qualified personnel, including licensed dentists and dental hygienists either through organized dental services in-house or through arrangement.

(2) If appropriate, dental professionals must participate, in the development, review and update of an individual program plan as part of the interdisciplinary process either in person or through written report to the interdisciplinary team.

(3) The facility must provide education and training in the maintenance of oral health.

(f) *Standard: Comprehensive dental diagnostic services*

Comprehensive dental diagnostic services include —

(1) A complete extraoral and intraoral examination, using all diagnostic aids necessary to properly evaluate the client's oral condition, not later than one month after admission to the facility (unless the examination was completed within twelve months before admission);

(2) Periodic examination and diagnosis performed at least annually, including radiographs when indicated and detection of manifestations of systemic disease; and

(3) A review of the results of examination and entry of the results in the client's dental record.

(g) *Standard: Comprehensive dental treatment*

The facility must ensure comprehensive dental treatment services that include —

(1) The availability for emergency dental treatment on a 24-hour-a-day basis by a licensed dentist; and

(2) Dental care needed for relief of pain and infections, restoration of teeth, and maintenance of dental health.

(h) *Standard: Documentation of dental services*

(1) If the facility maintains an in-house dental service, the facility must keep a permanent dental record for each client, with a dental summary maintained in the client's living unit.

(2) If the facility does not maintain an in-house dental service, the facility must obtain a dental summary of the results of dental visits and maintain the summary in the client's living unit.

(i) *Standard: Pharmacy services*

The facility must provide or make arrangements for the provision of routine and emergency drugs and biologicals to its clients. Drugs and biologicals may be obtained from community or contract pharmacists or the facility may maintain a licensed pharmacy.

(j) *Standard: Drug regimen review*

(1) A pharmacist with input from the interdisciplinary team must review the drug regimen of each client at least quarterly.

(2) The pharmacist must report any irregularities in clients' drug regimens to the prescribing physician and interdisciplinary team.

(3) The pharmacist must prepare a record of each client's drug regimen reviews and the facility must maintain that record.

(4) An individual medication administration record must be maintained for each client.

(5) As appropriate the pharmacist must participate in the development, implementation, and review of each client's individual program plan either in person or through written report to the interdisciplinary team.

(k) *Standard: Drug administration*

The facility must have an organized system for drug administration that identifies each drug up to the point of administration. The system must assure that —

(1) All drugs are administered in compliance with the physician's orders;

(2) All drugs, including those that are self-administered, are administered without error;

(3) Unlicensed personnel are allowed to administer drugs only if State law permits;

(4) Clients are taught how to administer their own medications if the interdisciplinary team determines that self administration of medications is an appropriate objective, and if the physician does not specify otherwise;

(5) The client's physician is informed of the interdisciplinary team's decision that self-administration of medications is an objective for the client;

(6) No client self-administers medications until he or she demonstrates the competency to do so;

(7) Drugs used by clients while not under the direct care of the facility are packaged and labeled in accordance with State law; and

(8) Drug administration errors and adverse drug reactions are recorded and reported immediately to a physician.

(l) *Standard: Drug storage and recordkeeping*

(1) The facility must store drugs under proper conditions of sanitation, temperature, light, humidity, and security.

(2) The facility must keep all drugs and biologicals locked except when being prepared for administration. Only authorized persons may have access to the keys to the drug storage area. Clients who have been trained to self administer drugs in accordance with § 483.460(k)(4) may have access to keys to their individual drug supply.

(3) The facility must maintain records of the receipt and disposition of all controlled drugs.

(4) The facility must, on a sample basis, periodically reconcile the receipt and disposition of all controlled drugs in schedules II through IV (drugs subject to the Comprehensive Drug Abuse Prevention and Control Act of 1970, 21 U.S.C. 801 et seq., as implemented by 21 CFR part 308).

(5) If the facility maintains a licensed pharmacy, the facility must comply with the regulations for controlled drugs.

(m) *Standard: Drug labeling*

(1) Labeling of drugs and biologicals must —

(i) Be based on currently accepted professional principles and practices; and

(ii) Include the appropriate accessory and cautionary instructions, as well as the expiration date, if applicable.

(2) The facility must remove from use —

(i) Outdated drugs; and

(ii) Drug containers with worn, illegible, or missing labels.

(3) Drugs and biologicals packaged in containers designated for a particular client must be immediately removed from the client's current medication supply if discontinued by the physician.

(n) *Standard: Laboratory services*

(1) If a facility chooses to provide laboratory services, the laboratory must meet the requirements specified in part 493 of this chapter.

(2) If the laboratory chooses to refer specimens for testing to another laboratory, the referral laboratory must be certified in the appropriate specialties and subspecialities of service in accordance with the requirements of part 493 of this chapter.

## § 483.470. Condition of participation: Physical environment

(a) *Standard: Client living environment*

(1) The facility must not house clients of grossly different ages, developmental levels, and social needs in close physical or social proximity unless the housing is planned to promote the growth and development of all those housed together.

(2) The facility must not segregate clients solely on the basis of their physical disabilities. It must integrate clients who have ambulation deficits or who are deaf, blind, or have seizure disorders, etc., with others of comparable social and intellectual development.

(b) *Standard: Client bedrooms*

(1) Bedrooms must —

(i) Be rooms that have at least one outside wall;

(ii) Be equipped with or located near toilet and bathing facilities;

(iii) Accommodate no more than four clients unless granted a variance under paragraph (b)(3) of this section;

(iv) Measure at least 60 square feet per client in multiple client bedrooms and at least 80 square feet in single client bedrooms; and

(v) In all facilities initially certified, or in buildings constructed or with major renovations or conversions on or after October 3, 1988, have walls that extend from floor to ceiling.

(2) If a bedroom is below grade level, it must have a window that —

(i) Is usable as a second means of escape by the client(s) occupying the room; and

(ii) Is no more than 44 inches (measured to the window sill) above the floor unless the facility is surveyed under the Health Care

Occupancy Chapter of the Life Safety Code, in which case the window must be no more than 36 inches (measured to the window sill) above the floor.

(3) The survey agency may grant a variance from the limit of four clients per room only if a physician who is a member of the interdisciplinary team and who is a qualified mental retardation professional —

(i) Certifies that each client to be placed in a bedroom housing more than four persons is so severely medically impaired as to require direct and continuous monitoring during sleeping hours; and

(ii) Documents the reasons why housing in a room of only four or fewer persons would not be medically feasible.

(4) The facility must provide each client with —

(i) A separate bed of proper size and height for the convenience of the client;

(ii) A clean, comfortable, mattress;

(iii) Bedding appropriate to the weather and climate; and

(iv) Functional furniture appropriate to the client's needs, and individual closet space in the client's bedroom with clothes racks and shelves accessible to the client.

(c) *Standard: Storage space in bedroom*

The facility must provide —

(1) Space and equipment for daily out-of-bed activity for all clients who are not yet mobile, except those who have a short-term illness or those few clients for whom out-of-bed activity is a threat to health and safety; and

(2) Suitable storage space, accessible to clients, for personal possessions, such as TVs, radios, prosthetic equipment and clothing.

(d) *Standard: Client bathrooms*

The facility must —

(1) Provide toilet and bathing facilities appropriate in number, size, and design to meet the needs of the clients;

(2) Provide for individual privacy in toilets, bathtubs, and showers; and

(3) In areas of the facility where clients who have not been trained to regulate water temperature are exposed to hot water, ensure that the temperature of the water does not exceed 110[degrees] Fahrenheit.

(e) *Standard: Heating and ventilation*

 (1) Each client bedroom in the facility must have —

  (i) At least one window to the outside; and

  (ii) Direct outside ventilation by means of windows, air conditioning, or mechanical ventilation.

 (2) The facility must —

  (i) Maintain the temperature and humidity within a normal comfort range by heating, air conditioning or other means; and

  (ii) Ensure that the heating apparatus does not constitute a burn or smoke hazard to clients.

(f) *Standard: Floors*

 The facility must have —

 (1) Floors that have a resilient, nonabrasive, and slip-resistant surface;

 (2) Nonabrasive carpeting, if the area used by clients is carpeted and serves clients who lie on the floor or ambulate with parts of their bodies, other than feet, touching the floor; and

 (3) Exposed floor surfaces and floor coverings that promote mobility in areas used by clients, and promote maintenance of sanitary conditions.

(g) *Standard: Space and equipment*

 The facility must —

 (1) Provide sufficient space and equipment in dining, living, health services, recreation, and program areas (including adequately equipped and sound treated areas for hearing and other evaluations if they are conducted in the facility) to enable staff to provide clients with needed services as required by this subpart and as identified in each client's individual program plan.

 (2) Furnish, maintain in good repair, and teach clients to use and to make informed choices about the use of dentures, eyeglasses, hearing and other communications aids, braces, and other devices identified by the interdisciplinary team as needed by the client.

 (3) Provide adequate clean linen and dirty linen storage areas.

(h) *Standard: Emergency plan and procedures*

 (1) The facility must develop and implement detailed written plans and procedures to meet all potential emergencies and disasters such as fire, severe weather, and missing clients.

(2) The facility must communicate, periodically review, make the plan available, and provide training to the staff.

(i) *Standard:  Evacuation drills*

(1) The facility must hold evacuation drills at least quarterly for each shift of personnel and under varied conditions to —

(i) Ensure that all personnel on all shifts are trained to perform assigned tasks;

(ii) Ensure that all personnel on all shifts are familiar with the use of the facility's fire protection features; and

(iii) Evaluate the effectiveness of emergency and disaster plans and procedures.

(2) The facility must —

(i) Actually evacuate clients during at least one drill each year on each shift;

(ii) Make special provisions for the evacuation of clients with physical disabilities;

(iii) File a report and evaluation on each evacuation drill;

(iv) Investigate all problems with evacuation drills, including accidents, and take corrective action; and

(v) During fire drills, clients may be evacuated to a safe area in facilities certified under the Health Care Occupancies Chapter of the Life Safety Code.

(3) Facilities must meet the requirements of paragraphs (i)(1) and (2) of this section for any live-in and relief staff they utilize.

(j) *Standard:  Fire protection* —

(1) General.

(i) Except as otherwise provided in this section, the facility must meet the applicable provisions of either the Health Care Occupancies Chapters or the Residential Board and Care Occupancies Chapter of the 2000 edition of the Life Safety Code of the National Fire Protection Association.  The Director of the Office of the Federal Register has approved the NFPA 101 [registered trademark] 2000 edition of the Life Safety Code, issued January 14, 2000, for incorporation by reference in accordance with 5 U.S.C. 552(a) and 1 CFR part 51.  A copy of the Code is available for inspection at the CMS Information Resource Center, 7500 Security Boulevard, Baltimore, MD and at the Office of the Federal Register, 800 North Capitol Street NW., Suite 700, Washington, DC.  Copies may be obtained from the National Fire Protection Association, 1 Batterymarch Park, Quincy, MA 02269. If any changes in this edition of the Code are incorporated by reference, CMS will publish notice in the Federal Register to announce the changes.

(ii) The State survey agency may apply a single chapter of the LSC to the entire facility or may apply different chapters to different buildings or parts of buildings as permitted by the LSC.

(iii) A facility that meets the LSC definition of a residential board and care occupancy must have its evacuation capability evaluated in accordance with the Evacuation Difficulty Index of the Fire Safety Evaluation System for Board and Care facilities (FSES/BC).

(2) Exceptions for all facilities.

(i) Chapter 19.3.6.3.2, exception number 2 of the adopted LSC does not apply to a facility.

(ii) If CMS finds that the State has a fire and safety code imposed by State law that adequately protects a facility's clients, CMS may allow the State survey agency to apply the State's fire and safety code instead of the LSC.

(iii) The facility must be in compliance with the following provisions beginning on March 13, 2006:

(A) Chapter 19.3.6.3.2, exception number 2.

(B) Chapter 19.2.9, Emergency Lighting.

(3) Facilities that meet the LSC definition of a health care occupancy.

(i) After consideration of State survey agency recommendations, CMS may waive, for appropriate periods, specific provisions of the Life Safety Code if the following requirements are met:

(A) The waiver would not adversely affect the health and safety of the clients.

(B) Rigid application of specific provisions would result in an unreasonable hardship for the facility.

(ii) [Reserved]

(k) *Standard: Paint*

The facility must —

(1) Use lead-free paint inside the facility; and

(2) Remove or cover interior paint or plaster containing lead so that it is not accessible to clients.

(l) *Standard: Infection control*

(1) The facility must provide a sanitary environment to avoid sources and transmission of infections. There must be an active program for the prevention, control, and investigation of infection and communicable diseases.

(2) The facility must implement successful corrective action in affected problem areas.

(3) The facility must maintain a record of incidents and corrective actions related to infections.

(4) The facility must prohibit employees with symptoms or signs of a communicable disease from direct contact with clients and their food.

## § 483.480.  Condition of participation:  Dietetic services

(a) *Standard: Food and nutrition services*

(1) Each client must receive a nourishing, well-balanced diet including modified and specially-prescribed diets.

(2) A qualified dietitian must be employed either full-time, part-time, or on a consultant basis at the facility's discretion.

(3) If a qualified dietitian is not employed full-time, the facility must designate a person to serve as the director of food services.

(4) The client's interdisciplinary team, including a qualified dietitian and physician, must prescribe all modified and special diets including those used as a part of a program to manage inappropriate client behavior.

(5) Foods proposed for use as a primary reinforcement of adaptive behavior are evaluated in light of the client's nutritional status and needs.

(6) Unless otherwise specified by medical needs, the diet must be prepared at least in accordance with the latest edition of the recommended dietary allowances of the Food and Nutrition Board of the National Research Council, National Academy of Sciences, adjusted for age, sex, disability and activity.

(b) *Standard: Meal services*

(1) Each client must receive at least three meals daily, at regular times comparable to normal mealtimes in the community with —

(i) Not more than 14 hours between a substantial evening meal and breakfast of the following day, except on weekends and holidays when a nourishing snack is provided at bedtime, 16 hours may elapse between a substantial evening meal and breakfast; and

(ii) Not less than 10 hours between breakfast and the evening meal of the same day, except as provided under paragraph (b)(1)(i) of this section.

(2) Food must be served —

(i) In appropriate quantity;

(ii) At appropriate temperature;

(iii) In a form consistent with the developmental level of the client; and

(iv) With appropriate utensils.

(3) Food served to clients individually and uneaten must be discarded.

(c) *Standard: Menus*

(1) Menus must —

(i) Be prepared in advance;

(ii) Provide a variety of foods at each meal;

(iii) Be different for the same days of each week and adjusted for seasonal changes; and

(iv) Include the average portion sizes for menu items.

(2) Menus for food actually served must be kept on file for 30 days.

(d) *Standard: Dining areas and service*

The facility must —

(1) Serve meals for all clients, including persons with ambulation deficits, in dining areas, unless otherwise specified by the interdisciplinary team or a physician;

(2) Provide table service for all clients who can and will eat at a table, including clients in wheelchairs;

(3) Equip areas with tables, chairs, eating utensils, and dishes designed to meet the developmental needs of each client;

(4) Supervise and staff dining rooms adequately to direct self-help dining procedure, to assure that each client receives enough food and to assure that each client eats in a manner consistent with his or her developmental level: and

(5) Ensure that each client eats in an upright position, unless otherwise specified by the interdisciplinary team or a physician.

## PART 484 – CONDITIONS OF PARTICIPATION: HOME HEALTH AGENCIES

### Subpart A – General Provisions

### Subpart B – Administration

### Subpart C – Furnishing of Services

## § 484.1. Basis and scope.

(a) *Basis and scope.* This part is based on the indicated provisions of the following sections of the Act:

(1) Sections 1861(o) and 1891 establish the conditions that an HHA must meet in order to participate in Medicare.

(2) Section 1861(z) specifies the Institutional planning standards that HHAs must meet.

(3) Section 1895 provides for the establishment of a prospective payment system for home health services covered under Medicare.

(b) This part also sets forth additional requirements that are considered necessary to ensure the health and safety of patients.

## § 484.2. Definitions.

As used in this part, unless the context indicates otherwise — Bylaws or equivalent means a set of rules adopted by an HHA for governing the agency's operation.

Branch office means a location or site from which a home health agency provides services within a portion of the total geographic area served by the parent agency. The branch office is part of the home health agency and is located sufficiently close to share administration, supervision, and services in a manner that renders it unnecessary for the branch independently to meet the conditions of participation as a home health agency.

Clinical note means a notation of a contact with a patient that is written and dated by a member of the health team, and that describes signs and symptoms, treatment and drugs administered and the patient's reaction, and any changes in physical or emotional condition.

HHA stands for home health agency.

Nonprofit agency means an agency exempt from Federal income taxation under section 501 of the Internal Revenue Code of 1954.

Parent home health agency means the agency that develops and maintains administrative controls of subunits and/or branch offices.

Primary home health agency means the agency that is responsible for the services furnished to patients and for implementation of the plan of care.

Progress note means a written notation, dated and signed by a member of the health team, that summarizes facts about care furnished and the patient's response during a given period of time.

Proprietary agency means a private profit-making agency licensed by the State.

Public agency means an agency operated by a State or local government.

Subdivision means a component of a multi-function health agency, such as the home care department of a hospital or the nursing division of a health department, which independently meets the conditions of participation for HHAs. A subdivision that has subunits or branch offices is considered a parent agency.

Subunit means a semi-autonomous organization that —

(1) Serves patients in a geographic area different from that of the parent agency; and

(2) Must independently meet the conditions of participation for HHAs because it is too far from the parent agency to share administration, supervision, and services on a daily basis.

Summary report means the compilation of the pertinent factors of a patient's clinical notes and progress notes that is submitted to the patient's physician.

Supervision means authoritative procedural guidance by a qualified person for the accomplishment of a function or activity. Unless otherwise specified in this part, the supervisor must be on the premises to supervise an individual who does not meet the qualifications specified in § 484.4.

## § 484.4.  Personnel qualifications

Staff required to meet the conditions set forth in this part are staff who meet the qualifications specified in this section.

*Administrator, home health agency.* A person who:

(a) Is a licensed physician; or

(b) Is a registered nurse; or

(c) Has training and experience in health service administration and at least 1 year of supervisory or administrative experience in home health care or related health programs.

*Audiologist.* A person who:

(a) Meets the education and experience requirements for a Certificate of Clinical Competence in audiology granted by the American Speech-Language-Hearing Association; or

(b) Meets the educational requirements for certification and is in the process of accumulating the supervised experience required for certification

*Home health aide.* Effective for services furnished after August 14, 1990, a person who has successfully completed a State-established or other training program that meets the requirements of § 484.36(a) and a competency evaluation program or State licensure program that meets the requirements of § 484.36 (b) or (e), or a competency evaluation program or State licensure program that meets the requirements of § 484.36 (b) or (e). An individual is not considered to have completed a training and competency evaluation program, or a competency evaluation program if, since the individual's most recent completion of this program(s), there has been a continuous period of 24 consecutive months during none of which the individual furnished services described in § 409.40 of this chapter for compensation.

*Occupational therapist.* A person who:

(a) Is a graduate of an occupational therapy curriculum accredited jointly by the Committee on Allied Health Education and Accreditation of the American Medical Association and the American Occupational Therapy Association; or

(b) Is eligible for the National Registration Examination of the American Occupational Therapy Association; or

(c) Has 2 years of appropriate experience as an occupational therapist, and has achieved a satisfactory grade on a proficiency examination conducted, approved, or sponsored by the U.S. Public Health Service, except that such determinations of proficiency do not apply with respect to persons initially licensed by a State or seeking initial qualification as an occupational therapist after December 31, 1977.

*Occupational therapy assistant.* A person who:

(a) Meets the requirements for certification as an occupational therapy assistant established by the American Occupational Therapy Association; or

(b) Has 2 years of appropriate experience as an occupational therapy assistant, and has achieved a satisfactory grade on a proficiency examination conducted, approved, or sponsored by the U.S. Public Health Service, except that such determinations of proficiency do not apply with respect to persons initially licensed by a State or seeking initial qualification as an occupational therapy assistant after December 31, 1977.

*Physical therapist.* A person who is licensed as a physical therapist by the State in which practicing, and

(a) Has graduated from a physical therapy curriculum approved by:

(1) The American Physical Therapy Association, or

(2) The Committee on Allied Health Education and Accreditation of the American Medical Association, or

(3) The Council on Medical Education of the American Medical Association and the American Physical Therapy Association; or

(b) Prior to January 1, 1966,

(1) Was admitted to membership by the American Physical Therapy Association, or

(2) Was admitted to registration by the American Registry of Physical Therapist, or

(3) Has graduated from a physical therapy curriculum in a 4-year college or university approved by a State department of education; or

(c)  Has 2 years of appropriate experience as a physical therapist, and has achieved a satisfactory grade on a proficiency examination conducted, approved, or sponsored by the U.S.  Public Health Service except that such determinations of proficiency do not apply with respect to persons initially licensed by a State or seeking qualification as a physical therapist after December 31, 1977; or

(d)  Was licensed or registered prior to January 1, 1966, and prior to January 1, 1970, had 15 years of full-time experience in the treatment of illness or injury through the practice of physical therapy in which services were rendered under the order and direction of attending and referring doctors of medicine or osteopathy; or

(e)  If trained outside the United States,

(1) Was graduated since 1928 from a physical therapy curriculum approved in the country in which the curriculum was located and in which there is a member organization of the World Confederation for Physical Therapy.

(2) Meets the requirements for membership in a member organization of the World Confederation for Physical Therapy,

*Physical therapy assistant.*  A person who is licensed as a physical therapy assistant, if applicable, by the State in which practicing, and

(1)  Has graduated from a 2-year college-level program approved by the American Physical Therapy Association; or

(2) Has 2 years of appropriate experience as a physical therapy assistant, and has achieved a satisfactory grade on a proficiency examination conducted, approved, or sponsored by the U.S.  Public Health Service, except that these determinations of proficiency do not apply with respect to persons initially licensed by a State or seeking initial qualification as a physical therapy assistant after December 31, 1977.

*Physician.*  A doctor of medicine, osteophathy or podiatry legally authorized to practice medicine and surgery by the State in which such function or action is performed.

*Practical (vocational) nurse.*  A person who is licensed as a practical (vocational) nurse by the State in which practicing.

*Public health nurse.*  A registered nurse who has completed a baccalaureate degree program approved by the National League for Nursing for public health nursing preparation or postregistered nurse study that includes content approved by the National League for Nursing for public health nursing preparation.

*Registered nurse (RN).* A graduate of an approved school of professional nursing, who is licensed as a registered nurse by the State in which practicing.

*Social work assistant.* A person who:

(1) Has a baccalaureate degree in social work, psychology, sociology, or other field related to social work, and has had at least 1 year of social work experience in a health care setting; or

(2) Has 2 years of appropriate experience as a social work assistant, and has achieved a satisfactory grade on a proficiency examination conducted, approved, or sponsored by the U.S. Public Health Service, except that these determinations of proficiency do not apply with respect to persons initially licensed by a State or seeking initial qualification as a social work assistant after December 31, 1977.

*Social worker.* A person who has a master's degree from a school of social work accredited by the Council on Social Work Education, and has 1 year of social work experience in a health care setting.

*Speech-language pathologist.* A person who:

(1) Meets the education and experience requirements for a Certificate of Clinical Competence in (speech pathology or audiology) granted by the American Speech-Language-Hearing Association; or

(2) Meets the educational requirements for certification and is in the process of accumulating the supervised experience required for certification.

## Subpart B – Administration

### § 484.10. Condition of participation: Patient rights

The patient has the right to be informed of his or her rights. The HHA must protect and promote the exercise of these rights.

(a) *Standard: Notice of rights*

(1) The HHA must provide the patient with a written notice of the patient's rights in advance of furnishing care to the patient or during the initial evaluation visit before the initiation of treatment.

(2) The HHA must maintain documentation showing that it has complied with the requirements of this section.

(b) *Standard: Exercise of rights and respect for property and person*

(1) The patient has the right to exercise his or her rights as a patient of the HHA.

(2) The patient's family or guardian may exercise the patient's rights when the patient has been judged incompetent.

(3) The patient has the right to have his or her property treated with respect.

(4) The patient has the right to voice grievances regarding treatment or care that is (or fails to be) furnished, or regarding the lack of respect for property by anyone who is furnishing services on behalf of the HHA and must not be subjected to discrimination or reprisal for doing so.

(5) The HHA must investigate complaints made by a patient or the patient's family or guardian regarding treatment or care that is (or fails to be) furnished, or regarding the lack of respect for the patient's property by anyone furnishing services on behalf of the HHA, and must document both the existence of the complaint and the resolution of the complaint.

(c) *Standard: Right to be informed and to participate in planning care and treatment*

(1) The patient has the right to be informed, in advance about the care to be furnished, and of any changes in the care to be furnished.

(i) The HHA must advise the patient in advance of the disciplines that will furnish care, and the frequency of visits proposed to be furnished.

(ii) The HHA must advise the patient in advance of any change in the plan of care before the change is made.

(2) The patient has the right to participate in the planning of the care.

(i) The HHA must advise the patient in advance of the right to participate in planning the care or treatment and in planning changes in the care or treatment.

(ii) The HHA complies with the requirements of subpart I of part 489 of this chapter relating to maintaining written policies and procedures regarding advance directives. The HHA must inform and distribute written information to the patient, in advance, concerning its policies on advance directives, including a description of applicable State law. The HHA may furnish advance directives information to a patient at the time of the first home visit, as long as the information is furnished before care is provided.

(d) *Standard: Confidentiality of medical records*

The patient has the right to confidentiality of the clinical records maintained by the HHA. The HHA must advise the patient of the agency's policies and procedures regarding disclosure of clinical records.

(e) *Standard: Patient liability for payment*

(1) The patient has the right to be advised, before care is initiated, of the extent to which payment for the HHA services may be expected from Medicare or other sources, and the extent to which payment may be required from the patient. Before the care is initiated, the HHA must inform the patient, orally and in writing, of —

(i) The extent to which payment may be expected from Medicare, Medicaid, or any other Federally funded or aided program known to the HHA;

(ii) The charges for services that will not be covered by Medicare; and

(iii) The charges that the individual may have to pay.

(2) The patient has the right to be advised orally and in writing of any changes in the information provided in accordance with paragraph (e)(1) of this section when they occur. The HHA must advise the patient of these changes orally and in writing as soon as possible, but no later than 30 calendar days from the date that the HHA becomes aware of a change.

(f) *Standard: Home health hotline*

The patient has the right to be advised of the availability of the toll-free HHA hotline in the State. When the agency accepts the patient for treatment or care, the HHA must advise the patient in writing of the telephone number of the home health hotline established by the State, the hours of its operation, and that the purpose of the hotline is to receive complaints or questions about local HHAs. The patient also has the right to use this hotline to lodge complaints concerning the implementation of the advance directives requirements.

## § 484.12. Condition of participation: Compliance with Federal, State, and local laws, disclosure and ownership information, and accepted professional standards and principles

(a) *Standard: Compliance with Federal, State, and local laws and regulations*

The HHA and its staff must operate and furnish services in compliance with all applicable Federal, State, and local laws and regulations. If State or applicable local law provides for the licensure of HHAs, an agency not subject to licensure is approved by the licensing authority as meeting the standards established for licensure.

(b) *Standard: Disclosure of ownership and management information*

The HHA must comply with the requirements of Part 420, Subpart C of this chapter. The HHA also must disclose the following information to the State survey agency at the time of the HHA's initial request for certification, for each survey, and at the time of any change in ownership or management:

(1) The name and address of all persons with an ownership or control interest in the HHA as defined in §§ 420.201, 420.202, and 420.206 of this chapter.

(2) The name and address of each person who is an officer, a director, an agent or a managing employee of the HHA as defined in §§ 420.201, 420.202, and 420.206 of this chapter.

(3) The name and address of the corporation, association, or other company that is responsible for the management of the HHA, and the name and address of the chief executive officer and the chairman of the board of directors of that corporation, association, or other company responsible for the management of the HHA.

(c) *Standard: Compliance with accepted professional standards and principles*

The HHA and its staff must comply with accepted professional standards and principles that apply to professionals furnishing services in an HHA.

## § 484.14. Condition of participation: Organization, services, and administration

Organization, services furnished, administrative control, and lines of authority for the delegation of responsibility down to the patient care level are clearly set forth in writing and are readily identifiable. Administrative and supervisory functions are not delegated to another agency or organization and all services not furnished directly, including services provided through subunits are monitored and controlled by the parent agency. If an agency has subunits, appropriate administrative records are maintained for each subunit.

(a) *Standard: Services furnished*

Part-time or intermittent skilled nursing services and at least one other therapeutic service (physical, speech, or occupational therapy; medical social services; or home health aide services) are made available on a visiting basis, in a place of residence used as a patient's home. An HHA must provide at least one of the qualifying services directly through agency employees, but may provide the second qualifying service and additional services under arrangements with another agency or organization.

(b) *Standard: Governing body*

A governing body (or designated persons so functioning) assumes full legal authority and responsibility for the operation of the agency. The governing body appoints a qualified administrator, arranges for professional advice as required under § 484.16, adopts and periodically reviews written bylaws or an acceptable equivalent, and oversees the management and fiscal affairs of the agency.

(c) *Standard: Administrator*

The administrator, who may also be the supervising physician or registered nurse required under paragraph (d) of this section, organizes and directs the agency's ongoing functions; maintains ongoing liaison among the governing body, the group of professional personnel, and the staff; employs qualified personnel and ensures adequate staff education and evaluations; ensures the accuracy of public information materials and activities; and implements an effective budgeting and accounting system. A qualified person is authorized in writing to act in the absence of the administrator.

(d) *Standard: Supervising physician or registered nurse*

The skilled nursing and other therapeutic services furnished are under the supervision and direction of a physician or a registered nurse (who preferably has at least 1 year of nursing experience and is a public health nurse). This person, or similarly qualified alternate, is available at all times during operating hours and participates in all activities relevant to the professional services furnished, including the development of qualifications and the assignment of personnel.

(e) *Standard: Personnel policies*

Personnel practices and patient care are supported by appropriate, written personnel policies. Personnel records include qualifications and licensure that are kept current.

(f) *Standard: Personnel under hourly or per visit contracts*

If personnel under hourly or per visit contracts are used by the HHA, there is a written contract between those personnel and the agency that specifies the following:

(1) Patients are accepted for care only by the primary HHA.

(2) The services to be furnished.

(3) The necessity to conform to all applicable agency policies, including personnel qualifications.

(4) The responsibility for participating in developing plans of care.

(5) The manner in which services will be controlled, coordinated, and evaluated by the primary HHA.

(6) The procedures for submitting clinical and progress notes, scheduling of visits, periodic patient evaluation.

(7) The procedures for payment for services furnished under the contract.

(g) *Standard: Coordination of patient services*

All personnel furnishing services maintain liaison to ensure that their efforts are coordinated effectively and support the objectives outlined in the plan of care. The clinical record or minutes of case conferences establish that effective interchange, reporting, and coordination of patient care does occur. A written summary report for each patient is sent to the attending physician at least every 60 days.

(h) *Standard: Services under arrangements*

Services furnished under arrangements are subject to a written contract conforming with the requirements specified in paragraph (f) of this section and with the requirements of section 1861(w) of the Act (42 U.S.C. 1495x(w)).

(i) *Standard: Institutional planning*

The HHA, under the direction of the governing body, prepares an overall plan and a budget that includes an annual operating budget and capital expenditure plan.

(1) Annual operating budget. There is an annual operating budget that includes all anticipated income and expenses related to items that would, under generally accepted accounting principles, be considered income and expense items. However, it is not required that there be prepared, in connection with any budget, an item by item identification of the components of each type of anticipated income or expense.

(2) Capital expenditure plan. (i) There is a capital expenditure plan for at least a 3-year period, including the operating budget year. The plan includes and identifies in detail the anticipated sources of financing for, and the objectives of, each anticipated expenditure of more than $600,000 for items that would under generally accepted accounting principles, be considered capital items. In determining if a single capital expenditure exceeds $600,000, the cost of studies, surveys, designs, plans, working drawings, specifications, and other activities essential to the acquisition, improvement, modernization, expansion, or replacement of land, plant, building, and equipment are included. Expenditures directly or indirectly related to capital expenditures, such as grading, paving, broker commissions, taxes assessed during the construction period, and costs involved in demolishing or razing structures on land are also included. Transactions that are separated in time, but are components of an overall plan or patient care objective, are viewed in their entirety without regard to their timing. Other costs related to capital expenditures include title fees, permit and license fees, broker commissions, architect, legal, accounting, and appraisal fees; interest, finance, or carrying charges on bonds, notes and other costs incurred for borrowing funds.

(ii) If the anticipated source of financing is, in any part, the anticipated payment from title V (Maternal and Child Health and Crippled Children's Services) or title XVIII (Medicare) or title XIX (Medicaid) of the Social Security Act, the plan specifies the following:

(A) Whether the proposed capital expenditure is required to conform, or is likely to be required to conform, to current standards, criteria, or plans developed in accordance with the Public Health Service Act or the Mental Retardation Facilities and Community Mental Health Centers Construction Act of 1963.

(B) Whether a capital expenditure proposal has been submitted to the designated planning agency for approval in accordance with section 1122 of the Act (42 U.S.C. 1320a-1) and implementing regulations.

(C) Whether the designated planning agency has approved or disapproved the proposed capital expenditure if it was presented to that agency.

(3) Preparation of plan and budget. The overall plan and budget is prepared under the direction of the governing body of the HHA by a committee consisting of representatives of the governing body, the administrative staff, and the medical staff (if any) of the HHA.

(4) Annual review of plan and budget. The overall plan and budget is reviewed and updated at least annually by the committee referred to in paragraph (i)(3) of this section under the direction of the governing body of the HHA.

(j) *Standard: Laboratory services*

(1) If the HHA engages in laboratory testing outside of the context of assisting an individual in self-administering a test with an appliance that has been cleared for that purpose by the FDA, such testing must be in compliance with all applicable requirements of part 493 of this chapter.

(2) If the HHA chooses to refer specimens for laboratory testing to another laboratory, the referral laboratory must be certified in the appropriate specialties and subspecialties of services in accordance with the applicable requirements of part 493 of this chapter.

## § 484.16.  Condition of participation:  Group of professional personnel

A group of professional personnel, which includes at least one physician and one registered nurse (preferably a public health nurse), and with appropriate representation from other professional disciplines, establishes and annually reviews the agency's policies governing scope of services offered, admission and discharge policies, medical supervision and plans of care, emergency care, clinical records, personnel qualifications, and program evaluation. At least one member of the group is neither an owner nor an employee of the agency.

(a) *Standard: Advisory and evaluation function*

The group of professional personnel meets frequently to advise the agency on professional issues, to participate in the evaluation of the agency's program, and to assist the agency in maintaining liaison with other health care providers in the community and in the agency's community information program. The meetings are documented by dated minutes.

## § 484.18. Condition of participation: Acceptance of patients, plan of care, and medical supervision

Patients are accepted for treatment on the basis of a reasonable expectation that the patient's medical, nursing, and social needs can be met adequately by the agency in the patient's place of residence. Care follows a written plan of care established and periodically reviewed by a doctor of medicine, osteopathy, or podiatric medicine.

(a) *Standard: Plan of care*

The plan of care developed in consultation with the agency staff covers all pertinent diagnoses, including mental status, types of services and equipment required, frequency of visits, prognosis, rehabilitation potential, functional limitations, activities permitted, nutritional requirements, medications and treatments, any safety measures to protect against injury, instructions for timely discharge or referral, and any other appropriate items. If a physician refers a patient under a plan of care that cannot be completed until after an evaluation visit, the physician is consulted to approve additions or modifications to the original plan. Orders for therapy services include the specific procedures and modalities to be used and the amount, frequency, and duration. The therapist and other agency personnel participate in developing the plan of care.

(b) *Standard: Periodic review of plan of care*

The total plan of care is reviewed by the attending physician and HHA personnel as often as the severity of the patient's condition requires, but at least once every 60 days or more frequently when there is a beneficiary elected transfer; a significant change in condition resulting in a change in the case-mix assignment; or a discharge and return to the same HHA during the 60-day episode. Agency professional staff promptly alert the physician to any changes that suggest a need to alter the plan of care.

(c) *Standard: Conformance with physician orders*

Drugs and treatments are administered by agency staff only as ordered by the physician with the exception of influenza and pneumococcal polysaccharide vaccines, which may be administered per agency policy developed in consultation with a physician, and after an assessment for contraindications. Verbal orders are put in writing and signed and dated with the date of receipt by the registered nurse or qualified therapist (as defined in § 484.4 of this chapter) responsible for furnishing or supervising the ordered services. Verbal orders are only accepted by personnel authorized to do so by applicable State and Federal laws and regulations as well as by the HHA's internal policies.

## Subpart C – Furnishing of Services

## § 484.30. Condition of participation: Skilled nursing services

The HHA furnishes skilled nursing services by or under the supervision of a registered nurse and in accordance with the plan of care.

(a) *Standard: Duties of the registered nurse*

The registered nurse makes the initial evaluation visit, regularly reevaluates the patient's nursing needs, initiates the plan of care and necessary revisions, furnishes those services requiring substantial and specialized nursing skill, initiates appropriate preventive and rehabilitative nursing procedures, prepares clinical and progress notes, coordinates services, informs the physician and other personnel of changes in the patient's condition and needs, counsels the patient and family in meeting nursing and related needs, participates in in-service programs, and supervises and teaches other nursing personnel.

(b) *Standard: Duties of the licensed practical nurse*

The licensed practical nurse furnishes services in accordance with agency policies, prepares clinical and progress notes, assists the physician and registered nurse in performing specialized procedures, prepares equipment and materials for treatments observing aseptic technique as required, and assists the patient in learning appropriate self-care techniques.

## § 484.32. Condition of participation: Therapy services

Any therapy services offered by the HHA directly or under arrangement are given by a qualified therapist or by a qualified therapy assistant under the supervision of a qualified therapist and in accordance with the plan of care. The qualified therapist assists the physician in evaluating level of function, helps develop the plan of care (revising it as necessary), prepares clinical and progress notes, advises and consults with the family and other agency personnel, and participates in in-service programs.

(a) *Standard: Supervision of physical therapy assistant and occupational therapy assistant*

Services furnished by a qualified physical therapy assistant or qualified occupational therapy assistant may be furnished under the supervision of a qualified physical or occupational therapist. A physical therapy assistant or occupational therapy assistant performs services planned, delegated, and supervised by the therapist, assists in preparing clinical notes and progress reports, and participates in educating the patient and family, and in in-service programs.

(b) *Standard: Supervision of speech therapy services*

Speech therapy services are furnished only by or under supervision of a qualified speech pathologist or audiologist.

## § 484.34. Condition of participation: Medical social services

If the agency furnishes medical social services, those services are given by a qualified social worker or by a qualified social work assistant under the supervision of a qualified social worker, and in accordance with the plan of care. The social worker assists the physician and other team members in understanding the significant social and emotional factors related to the health problems, participates in the development of the plan of care, prepares clinical and progress notes, works with the family, uses appropriate community resources, participates in discharge planning and in-service programs, and acts as a consultant to other agency personnel.

## § 484.36. Condition of participation: Home health aide services

Home health aides are selected on the basis of such factors as a sympathetic attitude toward the care of the sick, ability to read, write, and carry out directions, and maturity and ability to deal effectively with the demands of the job. They are closely supervised to ensure their competence in providing care. For home health services furnished (either directly or through arrangements with other organizations) after August 14, 1990, the HHA must use individuals who meet the personnel qualifications specified in § 484.4 for "home health aide."

(a) *Standard: Home health aide training* —

(1) Content and duration of training

The aide training program must address each of the following subject areas through classroom and supervised practical training totaling at least 75 hours, with at least 16 hours devoted to supervised practical training. The individual being trained must complete at least 16 hours of classroom training before beginning the supervised practical training.

(i) Communications skills.

(ii) Observation, reporting and documentation of patient status and the care or service furnished.

(iii) Reading and recording temperature, pulse, and respiration.

(iv) Basic infection control procedures.

(v) Basic elements of body functioning and changes in body function that must be reported to an aide's supervisor.

(vi) Maintenance of a clean, safe, and healthy environment.

(vii) Recognizing emergencies and knowledge of emergency procedures.

(viii) The physical, emotional, and developmental needs of and ways to work with the populations served by the HHA, including the need for respect for the patient, his or her privacy and his or her property.

(ix) Appropriate and safe techniques in personal hygiene and grooming that include —

(A) Bed bath.

(B) Sponge, tub, or shower bath.

(C) Shampoo, sink, tub, or bed.

(D) Nail and skin care.

(E) Oral hygiene.

(F) Toileting and elimination.

(x) Safe transfer techniques and ambulation.

(xi) Normal range of motion and positioning.

(xii) Adequate nutrition and fluid intake.

(xiii) Any other task that the HHA may choose to have the home health aide perform.

"Supervised practical training" means training in a laboratory or other setting in which the trainee demonstrates knowledge while performing tasks on an individual under the direct supervision of a registered nurse or licensed practical nurse.

(2) Conduct of training —

(i) Organizations

A home health aide training program may be offered by any organization except an HHA that, within the previous 2 years has been found —

(A) Out of compliance with requirements of this paragraph (a) or paragraph (b) of this section;

(B) To permit an individual that does not meet the definition of "home health aide" as specified in § 484.4 to furnish home health aide services (with the exception of licensed health professionals and volunteers);

(C) Has been subject to an extended (or partial extended) survey as a result of having been found to have furnished substandard care (or for other reasons at the discretion of the CMS or the State);

(D) Has been assessed a civil monetary penalty of not less than $5,000 as an intermediate sanction;

(E) Has been found to have compliance deficiencies that endanger the health and safety of the HHA's patients and has had a temporary management appointed to oversee the management of the HHA;

(F) Has had all or part of its Medicare payments suspended; or

(G) Under any Federal or State law within the 2-year period beginning on October 1, 1988 —

(1) Has had its participation in the Medicare program terminated;

(2) Has been assessed a penalty of not less than $5,000 for deficiencies in Federal or State standards for HHAs;

(3) Was subject to a suspension of Medicare payments to which it otherwise would have been entitled;

(4) Had operated under a temporary management that was appointed to oversee the operation of the HHA and to ensure the health and safety of the HHA's patients; or

(5) Was closed or had it's residents transferred by the State.

(ii) Qualifications for instructors. The training of home health aides and the supervision of home health aides during the supervised practical portion of the training must be performed by or under the general supervision of a registered nurse who possesses a minimum of 2 years of nursing experience, at least 1 year of which must be in the provision of home health care. Other individuals may be used to provide instruction under the supervision of a qualified registered nurse.

(3) Documentation of training

The HHA must maintain sufficient documentation to demonstrate that the requirements of this standard are met.

(b) *Standard: Competency evaluation and in-service training —*

(1) Applicability

An individual may furnish home health aide services on behalf of an HHA only after that individual has successfully completed a competency evaluation program as described in this paragraph. The HHA is responsible for ensuring that the individuals who furnish home health aide services on its behaif meet the competency evaluation requirements of this section.

(2) Content and frequency of evaluations and amount of in-service training

(i) The competency evaluation must address each of the subjects listed in paragraph (a)(1) (ii) through (xiii) of this section.

(ii) The HHA must complete a performance review of each home health aide no less frequently than every 12 months.

(iii) The home health aide must receive at least 12 hours of in-service training during each 12-month period. The in-service training may be furnished while the aide is furnishing care to the patient.

(3) Conduct of evaluation and training —

(i) Organizations. A home health aide competency evaluation program may be offered by any organization except as specified in paragraph (a)(2)(i) of this section.
The in-service training may be offered by any organization.

(ii) Evaluators and instructors. The competency evaluation must be performed by a registered nurse. The in-service training generally must be supervised by a registered nurse who possesses a minimum of 2 years of nursing experience at least 1 year of which must be in the provision of home health care.

(iii) Subject areas. The subject areas listed at paragraphs (a)(1) (iii), (ix), (x), and (xi) of this section must be evaluated after observation of the aide's performance of the tasks with a patient. The other subject areas in paragraph (a)(1) of this section may be evaluated through written examination, oral examination, or after observation of a home health aide with a patient.

(4) Competency determination.  (i) A home health aide is not considered competent in any task for which he or she is evaluated as "unsatisfactory." The aide must not perform that task without direct supervision by a licensed nurse until after he or she receives training in the task for which he or she was evaluated as "unsatisfactory" and passes a subsequent evaluation with "satisfactory."

(ii) A home health aide is not considered to have successfully passed a competency evaluation if the aide has an "unsatisfactory" rating in more than one of the required areas.

(5) Documentation of competency evaluation. The HHA must maintain documentation which demonstrates that the requirements of this standard are met.

(6) Effective date. The HHA must implement a competency evaluation program that meets the requirements of this paragraph before February 14, 1990. The HHA must provide the preparation necessary for the individual to successfully complete the competency evaluation program. After August 14, 1990, the HHA may use only those aides that have been found to be competent in accordance with § 484.36(b).

(c) *Standard: Assignment and duties of the home health aide —*

(1) Assignment. The home health aide is assigned to a specific patient by the registered nurse. Written patient care instructions for the home health aide must be prepared by the registered nurse or other appropriate professional who is responsible for the supervision of the home health aide under paragraph (d) of this section.

(2) Duties. The home health aide provides services that are ordered by the physician in the plan of care and that the aide is permitted to perform under State law. The duties of a home health aide include the provision of hands-on personal care, performance of simple procedures as an extension of therapy or nursing services, assistance in ambulation or exercises, and assistance in administering medications that are ordinarily

self-administered. Any home health aide services offered by an HHA must be provided by a qualified home health aide.

(d) *Standard: Supervision*

(1) If the patient receives skilled nursing care, the registered nurse must perform the supervisory visit required by paragraph (d)(2) of this section. If the patient is not receiving skilled nursing care, but is receiving another skilled service (that is, physical therapy, occupational therapy, or speech-language pathology services), supervision may be provided by the appropriate therapist.

(2) The registered nurse (or another professional described in paragraph (d)(1) of this section) must make an on-site visit to the patient's home no less frequently than every 2 weeks.

(3) If home health aide services are provided to a patient who is not receiving skilled nursing care, physical or occupational therapy or speech-language pathology services, the registered nurse must make a supervisory visit to the patient's home no less frequently than every 60 days. In these cases, to ensure that the aide is properly caring for the patient, each supervisory visit must occur while the home health aide is providing patient care.

(4) If home health aide services are provided by an individual who is not employed directly by the HHA (or hospice), the services of the home health aide must be provided under arrangements, as defined in section 1861(w)(1) of the Act. If the HHA (or hospice) chooses to provide home health aide services under arrangements with another organization, the HHA's (or hospice's) responsibilities include, but are not limited to —

    (i) Ensuring the overall quality of the care provided by the aide;

    (ii) Supervision of the aide's services as described in paragraphs (d)(1) and (d)(2) of this section; and

    (iii) Ensuring that home health aides providing services under arrangements have met the training requirements of paragraphs (a) and (b) of this section.

(e) *Personal care attendant: Evaluation requirements* —

(1) Applicability. This paragraph applies to individuals who are employed by HHAs exclusively to furnish personal care attendant services under a Medicaid personal care benefit.

(2) Rule. An individual may furnish personal care services, as defined in § 440.170 of this chapter, on behalf of an HHA after the individual has been found competent by the State to furnish those services

for which a competency evaluation is required by paragraph (b) of this section and which the individual is required to perform. The individual need not be determined competent in those services listed in paragraph (a) of this section that the individual is not required to furnish.

## § 484.38. Condition of participation: Qualifying to furnish outpatient physical therapy or speech pathology services

An HHA that wishes to furnish outpatient physical therapy or speech pathology services must meet all the pertinent conditions of this part and also meet the additional health and safety requirements set forth in §§ 485.711, 485.713, 485.715, 485.719, 485.723, and 485.727 of this chapter to implement section 1861(p) of the Act.

## § 484.48. Condition of participation: Clinical records

A clinical record containing pertinent past and current findings in accordance with accepted professional standards is maintained for every patient receiving home health services. In addition to the plan of care, the record contains appropriate identifying information; name of physician; drug, dietary, treatment, and activity orders; signed and dated clinical and progress notes; copies of summary reports sent to the attending physician; and a discharge summary. The HHA must inform the attending physician of the availability of a discharge summary. The discharge summary must be sent to the attending physician upon request and must include the patient's medical and health status at discharge.

(a) *Standards: Retention of records*

Clinical records are retained for 5 years after the month the cost report to which the records apply is filed with the intermediary, unless State law stipulates a longer period of time. Policies provide for retention even if the HHA discontinues operations. If a patient is transferred to another health facility, a copy of the record or abstract is sent with the patient.

(b) *Standards: Protection of records*

Clinical record information is safe-guarded against loss or unauthorized use. Written procedures govern use and removal of records and the conditions for release of information. Patient's written consent is required for release of information not authorized by law.

**§ 484.52.  Condition of participation:  Evaluation of the agency's program**

The HHA has written policies requiring an overall evaluation of the agency's total program at least once a year by the group of professional personnel (or a committee of this group), HHA staff, and consumers, or by professional people outside the agency working in conjunction with consumers.  The evaluation consists of an overall policy and administrative review and a clinical record review.  The evaluation assesses the extent to which the agency's program is appropriate, adequate, effective, and efficient. Results of the evaluation are reported to and acted upon by those responsible for the operation of the agency and are maintained separately as administrative records.

(a) *Standard:  Policy and administrative review*

As a part of the evaluation process the policies and administrative practices of the agency are reviewed to determine the extent to which they promote patient care that is appropriate, adequate, effective, and efficient. Mechanisms are established in writing for the collection of pertinent data to assist in evaluation.

(b) *Standard:  Clinical record review*

At least quarterly, appropriate health professionals, representing at least the scope of the program, review a sample of both active and closed clinical records to determine whether established policies are followed in furnishing services directly or under arrangement.  There is a continuing review of clinical records for each 60-day period that a patient receives home health services to determine adequacy of the plan of care and appropriateness of continuation of care.

# Health Care Quality Improvement Act of 1986 (Excerpts)

## 42 U.S.C. § 11101 et seq.

## § 11101. Findings

The Congress finds the following:

(1) The increasing occurrence of medical malpractice and the need to improve the quality of medical care have become nationwide problems that warrant greater efforts than those that can be undertaken by any individual State.

(2) There is a national need to restrict the ability of incompetent physicians to move from State to State without disclosure or discovery of the physician's previous damaging or incompetent performance.

(3) This nationwide problem can be remedied through effective professional peer review.

(4) The threat of private money damage liability under Federal laws, including treble damage liability under Federal antitrust law, unreasonably discourages physicians from participating in effective professional peer review.

(5) There is an overriding national need to provide incentive and protection for physicians engaging in effective professional peer review.

## SUBCHAPTER I – PROMOTION OF PROFESSIONAL REVIEW ACTIVITIES

## § 11111. Professional review

(a) *In general*

(1) Limitation on damages for professional review actions. If a professional review action (as defined in section 431(9) of a professional review body meets all the standards specified in section 412(a), except as provided in subsection (b) —

    (A) the professional review body,

    (B) any person acting as a member or staff to the body,

(C) any person under a contract or other formal agreement with the body, and

(D) any person who participates with or assists the body with respect to the action, shall not be liable in damages under any law of the United States or of any State (or political subdivision thereof) with respect to the action. The preceding sentence shall not apply to damages under any law of the United States or any State relating to the civil rights of any person or persons, including the Civil Rights Act of 1964, 42 U.S.C. 2000e, et seq. and the Civil Rights Acts, 42 U.S.C. 1981, et seq. Nothing in this paragraph shall prevent the United States or any Attorney General of a State from bringing an action, including an action under section 4C of the Clayton Act, 15 U.S.C. 15C, where such an action is otherwise authorized.

(2) Protection for those providing information to professional review bodies. Notwithstanding any other provision of law, no person (whether as a witness or otherwise) providing information to a professional review body regarding the competence or professional conduct of a physician shall be held, by reason of having provided such information, to be liable in damages under any law of the United States or of any State (or political subdivision thereof) unless such information is false and the person providing it knew that such information was false.

(b) *Exception*

If the Secretary has reason to believe that a health care entity has failed to report information in accordance with section 423(a), the Secretary shall conduct an investigation. If, after providing notice of noncompliance, an opportunity to correct the noncompliance, and an opportunity for a hearing, the Secretary determines that a health care entity has failed substantially to report information in accordance with section 423(a), the Secretary shall publish the name of the entity in the Federal Register. The protections of subsection (a)(1) shall not apply to an entity the name of which is published in the Federal Register under the previous sentence with respect to professional review actions of the entity commenced during the 3-year period beginning 30 days after the date of publication of the name.

(c) *Treatment under State laws*

(1) Professional review actions taken on or after October 14, 1989

Except as provided in paragraph (2), subsection (a) shall apply to State laws in a State only for professional review actions commenced on or after October 14, 1989.

(2) Exceptions

(A) State early opt-in. Subsection (a) shall apply to State laws in a State for actions commenced before October 14, 1989, if the State by legislation elects such treatment.

(B) Effective date of election. An election under State law is not effective, for purposes of [subparagraph (A)], for actions commenced before the effective date of the State law, which may not be earlier than the date of the enactment of that law.

## § 11112. Standards for professional review actions

(a) *In general*

For purposes of the protection set forth in section 411(a), a professional review action must be taken —

(1) in the reasonable belief that the action was in the furtherance of quality health care,

(2) after a reasonable effort to obtain the facts of the matter,

(3) after adequate notice and hearing procedures are afforded to the physician involved or after such other procedures as are fair to the physician under the circumstances, and

(4) in the reasonable belief that the action was warranted by the facts known after such reasonable effort to obtain facts and after meeting the requirement of paragraph (3). A professional review action shall be presumed to have met the preceding standards necessary for the protection set out in section 411(a) unless the presumption is rebutted by a preponderance of the evidence.

(b) *Adequate notice and hearing*

A health care entity is deemed to have met the adequate notice and hearing requirement of subsection (a)(3) with respect to a physician if the following conditions are met (or are waived voluntarily by the physician):

(1)  Notice of proposed action

The physician has been given notice stating —

(A)   (i) that a professional review action has been proposed to be taken against the physician,

(ii) reasons for the proposed action,

(B)   (i) that the physician has the right to request a hearing on the proposed action,

(ii) any time limit (of not less than 30 days) within which to request such a hearing, and

(C) a summary of the rights in the hearing under paragraph (3).

(2) Notice of hearing.  If a hearing is requested on a timely basis under paragraph (1)(B), the physician involved must be given notice stating —

(A) the place, time, and date, of the hearing, which date shall not be less than 30 days after the date of the notice, and

(B) a list of the witnesses (if any) expected to testify at the hearing on behalf of the professional review body.

(3) Conduct of hearing and notice.  If a hearing is requested on a timely basis under paragraph (1)(b) —

(A) subject to subparagraph (B), the hearing shall be held (as determined by the health care entity) —

(i) before an arbitrator mutually acceptable to the physician and the health care entity,

(ii) before a hearing officer who is appointed by the entity and who is not in direct economic competition with the physician involved, or

(iii) before a panel of individuals who are appointed by the entity and are not in direct economic competition with the physician involved;

(B) the right to the hearing may be forfeited if the physician fails, without good cause, to appear;

(C) in the hearing the physician involved has the right —

(i) to representation by an attorney or other person of the physician's choice,

(ii) to have a record made of the proceedings, copies of which may be obtained by the physician upon payment of any reasonable charges associated with the preparation thereof,

(iii) to call, examine, and cross-examine witnesses,

(iv) to present evidence determined to be relevant by the hearing officer, regardless of its admissibility in a court of law, and

(v) to submit a written statement at the close of the hearing; and

(D) upon completion of the hearing, the physician involved has the right —

(i) to receive the written recommendation of the arbitrator, officer, or panel, including a statement of the basis for the recommendations, and

(ii) to receive a written decision of the health care entity, including a statement of the basis for the decision.

A professional review body's failure to meet the conditions described in this subsection shall not, in itself, constitute failure to meet the standards of subsection (a)(3).

(c) *Adequate procedures in investigations or health emergencies*

For purposes of section 411(a), nothing in this section shall be construed as —

(1) requiring the procedures referred to in subsection (a)(3) —

(A) where there is no adverse professional review action taken, or

(B) in the case of a suspension or restriction of clinical privileges, for a period of not longer than 14 days, during which an investigation is being conducted to determine the need for a professional review action; or

(2) precluding an immediate suspension or restriction of clinical privileges, subject to subsequent notice and hearing or other adequate procedures, where the failure to take such an action may result in an imminent danger to the health of any individual.

## SUBCHAPTER II – REPORTING OF INFORMATION

### § 11131. Requiring reports on medical malpractice payments

(a) *In general*

Each entity (including an insurance company) which makes payment under a policy of insurance, self-insurance, or otherwise in settlement (or partial settlement) of, or in satisfaction of a judgment in, a medical malpractice action or claim shall report, in accordance with section 424, information respecting the payment and circumstances thereof.

(b) *Information to be reported*

The information to be reported under subsection (a) includes —

(1) the name of any physician or licensed health care practitioner for whose benefit the payment is made,

(2) the amount of the payment,

(3) the name (if known) of any hospital with which the physician or practitioner is affiliated or associated,

(4) a description of the acts or omissions and injuries or illnesses upon which the action or claim was based, and

(5) such other information as the Secretary determines is required for appropriate interpretation of information reported under this section.

(c) *Sanctions for failure to report*

Any entity that fails to report information on a payment required to be reported under this section shall be subject to a civil money penalty of not more than $10,000 for each such payment involved. Such penalty shall be imposed and collected in the same manner as civil money penalties under subsection (a) of section 1128A of the Social Security Act are imposed and collected under that section.

(d) *Report on treatment of small payments*

The Secretary shall study and report to Congress, not later than two years after the date of the enactment of this Act [enacted Nov. 14, 1986], on whether information respecting small payments should continue to be required to be reported under subsection (a) and whether information respecting all claims made concerning a medical malpractice action should be required to be reported under such subsection.

## § 11132. Reporting of sanctions taken by Boards of Medical Examiners

(a) *In general*

(1) Actions subject to reporting. Each Board of Medical Examiners —

(A) which revokes or suspends (or otherwise restricts) a physician's license or censures, reprimands, or places on probation a physician, for reasons relating to the physician's professional competence or professional conduct, or

(B) to which a physician's license is surrendered, shall report, in accordance with section 424, the information described in paragraph (2).

(2) Information to be reported. The information to be reported under paragraph (1) is —

(A) the name of the physician involved,

(B) a description of the acts or omissions or other reasons (if known) for the revocation, suspension, or surrender of license, and

(C) such other information respecting the circumstances of the action or surrender as the Secretary deems appropriate.

(b) *Failure to report*

If, after notice of noncompliance and providing opportunity to correct noncompliance, the Secretary determines that a Board of Medical Examiners has failed to report information in accordance with subsection (a), the Secretary shall designate another qualified entity for the reporting of information under section 423.

## § 11133. Reporting of certain professional review actions taken by health care entities

(a) *Reporting by health care entities*

(1) On physicians. Each health care entity which —

(A) takes a professional review action that adversely affects the clinical privileges of a physician for a period longer than 30 days;

(B) accepts the surrender of clinical privileges of a physician —

(i) while the physician is under an investigation by the entity relating to possible incompetence or improper professional conduct, or

(ii) in return for not conducting such an investigation or proceeding; or

(C) in the case of such an entity which is a professional society, takes a professional review action which adversely affects the membership of a physician in the society, shall report to the Board of Medical Examiners, in accordance with section 424(a), the information described in paragraph (3).

(2) Permissive reporting on other licensed health care practitioners. A health care entity may report to the Board of Medical Examiners, in accordance with section 424(a), the information described in paragraph (3) in the case of a licensed health care practitioner who is not a physician, if

the entity would be required to report such information under paragraph (1) with respect to the practitioner if the practitioner were a physician.

(3) Information to be reported. The information to be reported under this subsection is —

(A) the name of the physician or practitioner involved,

(B) a description of the acts or omissions or other reasons for the action or, if known, for the surrender, and

(C) such other information respecting the circumstances of the action or surrender as the Secretary deems appropriate.

(b) *Reporting by Board of Medical Examiners*

Each Board of Medical Examiners shall report, in accordance with section 424, the information reported to it under subsection (a) and known instances of a health care entity's failure to report information under subsection (a)(1).

(c) *Sanctions*

(1) Health care entities. A health care entity that fails substantially to meet the requirement of subsection (a)(1) shall lose the protections of section 411(a)(1) if the Secretary publishes the name of the entity under section 411(b).

(2) Board of Medical Examiners. If, after notice of noncompliance and providing an opportunity to correct noncompliance, the Secretary determines that a Board of Medical Examiners has failed to report information in accordance with subsection (b), the Secretary shall designate another qualified entity for the reporting of information under subsection (b).

(d) *References to Board of Medical Examiners*

Any reference in this part to a Board of Medical Examiners includes, in the case of a Board in a State that fails to meet the reporting requirements of section 422(a) or subsection (b), a reference to such other qualified entity as the Secretary designates.

## § 10225.101. Short title

This act shall be known and may be cited as the Older Adults Protective Services Act.

## § 10225.102. Legislative policy

It is declared the policy of the Commonwealth of Pennsylvania that older adults who lack the capacity to protect themselves and are at imminent risk of abuse, neglect, exploitation or abandonment shall have access to and be provided with services necessary to protect their health, safety and welfare. It is not the purpose of this act to place restrictions upon the personal liberty of incapacitated older adults, but this act should be liberally construed to assure the availability of protective services to all older adults in need of them. Such services shall safeguard the rights of incapacitated older adults while protecting them from abuse, neglect, exploitation and abandonment. It is the intent of the General Assembly to provide for the detection and reduction, correction or elimination of abuse, neglect, exploitation and abandonment, and to establish a program of protective services for older adults in need of them.

## § 10225.103. Definitions

The following words and phrases when used in this act shall have the meanings given to them in this section unless the context clearly indicates otherwise:

"Abandonment." The desertion of an older adult by a caretaker.

"Abuse." The occurrence of one or more of the following acts:

(1) The infliction of injury, unreasonable confinement, intimidation or punishment with resulting physical harm, pain or mental anguish.

(2) The willful deprivation by a caretaker of goods or services which are necessary to maintain physical or mental health.

(3) Sexual harassment, rape or abuse, as defined in the act of October 7, 1976 (P.L. 1090, No. 218), known as the Protection From Abuse Act. No older adult shall be found to be abused solely on the grounds of environmental factors which are beyond the control of the older adult or the caretaker, such

527

as inadequate housing, furnishings, income, clothing or medical care.

"Administrator." The person responsible for the administration of a facility. The term includes a person responsible for employment decisions or an independent contractor.

"Agency." The local provider of protective services, which is the area agency on aging or the agency designated by the area agency on aging to provide protective services in the area agency's planning and service area.

"Care." Services provided to meet a person's need for personal care or health care. Services may include homemaker services, assistance with activities of daily living, physical therapy, occupational therapy, speech therapy, medical social services, home-care aide services, companion-care services, private duty nursing services, respiratory therapy, intravenous therapy, in-home dialysis and durable medical equipment services, which are routinely provided unsupervised and which require interaction with the care-dependent person. The term does not include durable medical equipment delivery.

"Care-dependent individual." An adult who, due to physical or cognitive disability or impairment, requires assistance to meet needs for food, shelter, clothing, personal care or health care.

"Caretaker." An individual or institution that has assumed the responsibility for the provision of care needed to maintain the physical or mental health of an older adult. This responsibility may arise voluntarily, by contract, by receipt of payment for care, as a result of family relationship, or by order of a court of competent jurisdiction. It is not the intent of this act to impose responsibility on any individual if such responsibility would not otherwise exist in law.

"Client assessment." Social, physical and psychological findings along with a description of the person's current resources and needs.

"Court." A court of common pleas or a district magistrate court, where applicable.

"Department." The Department of Aging of the Commonwealth.

"Employee." An individual who is employed by a facility. The term includes contract employees who have direct contact with residents or unsupervised access to their personal living quarters.

The term includes any person who is employed or who enters into a contractual relationship to provide care to a care-dependent individual for monetary consideration in the individual's place of residence.

"Exploitation." An act or course of conduct by a caretaker or other person against an older adult or an older adult's resources, without the informed consent of the older adult or with consent obtained through misrepresentation, coercion or threats of force, that results in monetary, personal or other benefit, gain or profit for the perpetrator or monetary or personal loss to the older adult.

"Facility." Any of the following:

(1) A domiciliary care home as defined in section 2202-A of the act of April 9, 1929 (P.L. 177, No. 175), known as The Administrative Code of 1929.

(2) A home health care agency.

(3) A long-term care nursing facility as defined in section 802.1 of the act of July 19, 1979 (P.L. 130, No. 48), known as the Health Care Facilities Act.

(4) An older adult daily living center as defined in section 2 of the act of July 11, 1990 (P.L. 499, No. 118), known as the Older Adult Daily Living Centers Licensing Act.

(5) A personal care home as defined in section 1001 of the act of June 13, 1967 (P.L. 31, No. 21), known as the Public Welfare Code.

"Home health care agency." Any of the following:

(1) A home health care organization or agency licensed by the Department of Health.

(2) A public or private agency or organization, or part of an agency or organization, which provides care to a care-dependent individual in the individual's place of residence.

"Intimidation." An act or omission by any person or entity toward another person which is intended to, or with knowledge that the act or omission will, obstruct, impede, impair, prevent or interfere with the administration of this act or any law intended to protect older adults from mistreatment.

"Law enforcement official." Any of the following:

(1) A police officer of a municipality.

(2) A district attorney.

(3) The Pennsylvania State Police.

"Neglect." The failure to provide for oneself or the failure of a caretaker to provide goods or services essential to avoid a clear and serious threat to physical or mental health. No older adult who does not consent to the provision of protective services shall be found to be neglected solely on the grounds of environmental factors which are beyond the control of the older adult or the caretaker, such as inadequate housing, furnishings, income, clothing or medical care.

"Older adult." A person within the jurisdiction of the Commonwealth who is 60 years of age or older.

"Older adult in need of protective services." An incapacitated older adult who is unable to perform or obtain services that are necessary to maintain physical or mental health, for whom there is no responsible caretaker and who is at imminent risk of danger to his person or property.

"Protective services." Those activities, resources and supports provided to older adults under this act to detect, prevent, reduce or eliminate abuse, neglect, exploitation and abandonment.

"Protective setting." A setting chosen by the agency where services can be provided in the least restrictive environment to protect the physical and mental well-being of the older adult.

"Recipient." An individual who receives care, services or treatment in or from a facility.

"Secretary." The Secretary of Aging of the Commonwealth.

"Serious bodily injury." Injury which creates a substantial risk of death or which causes serious permanent disfigurement or protracted loss or impairment of the function of a body member or organ.

"Serious physical injury." An injury that:

(1) causes a person severe pain; or

(2) significantly impairs a person's physical functioning, either temporarily or permanently.

"Service plan." A written plan developed by the agency on the basis of comprehensive assessment of a client's need which describes identified needs, goals to be achieved and specific services to support goal attainment, with regular follow-up and predetermined reassessment of client progress. Specific services to support goal attainment may include, but is not limited to, homemaker services, home-delivered meals, attendant care, other in-home services, emergency shelter or food, legal aid services, transportation and other such services.

Service plans are cooperatively developed by the agency staff, the client or the client's appointed guardian, and other family members when appropriate. The plan shall also address, where applicable, special needs of other members of the household unit as they may affect the older adult's need for protective services.

"Sexual abuse." Intentionally, knowingly or recklessly causing or attempting to cause rape, involuntary deviate sexual intercourse, sexual assault, statutory sexual assault, aggravated indecent assault, indecent assault or incest.

## § 10225.301. Duties of department and area agencies on aging

(a) *Public information and interdepartmental consultation*

The department shall conduct an ongoing campaign designed to inform and educate older adults, professionals and the general public about the need for an availability of protective services under this chapter. The department shall consult with other departments of the commonwealth on the design and implementation of the ongoing public awareness campaign. The department shall also consider the concerns of area agencies on aging and the entities identified by them under subsection (c).

(b) *Staff training*

The department shall establish minimum standards of training and experience which protective services providers funded by the department shall be required to follow in the selection and assignment of staff for the provision of protective services.

(c) *Protective services plans*

Each area agency on aging shall include a protective services plan as part of its annual plan. The plan shall describe the local implementation of this chapter, including the organization, staffing, mode of operations and financing of protective services, as well as the provisions made for purchase of services, interagency relations, interagency agreements, service referral mechanisms and locus of responsibility for cases with multiservice agency needs. The description of the methods that will be used by the agency, its designees and its service providers to assure the privacy of older adults receiving services and the confidentiality of all records shall be established by the department. The department shall establish a schedule for the submission and approval of the plans. The plan shall include a list of all entities, whether public or private, that have been identified by the area agency on aging as having substantial contact with potential victims or perpetrators of abuse, neglect, exploitation and abandonment. This list shall be submitted to the department for purposes of the public information campaign under subsection (a).

## § 10225.302. Reporting; protection from retaliation; immunity

(a) *Reporting*

Any person having reasonable cause to believe that an older adult is in need of protective services may report such information to the agency which is the local provider of protective services. Where applicable, reports shall comply with the provisions of chapter 7.

(b) *Receiving reports*

The agency shall be capable of receiving reports of older adults in need of protective services 24 hours a day, seven days a week (including holidays). This capability may include the use of a local emergency response system or a crisis intervention agency, provided that access can be made to a protective services caseworker in appropriate emergency situations as set forth in regulations promulgated by the department. All reports received orally under this section shall be reduced to writing immediately by the person who receives the report.

(c) *Retaliatory action; Penalty*

Any person making a report or cooperating with the agency, including providing testimony in any administrative or judicial proceeding, and the victim shall be free from any discriminatory, retaliatory or disciplinary action by an employer or by any other person or entity. Any person who violates this subsection is subject to a civil lawsuit by the reporter or the victim wherein the reporter or victim shall recover treble compensatory damages, compensatory and punitive damages or $5,000, whichever is greater.

(C.1) Intimidation; Penalty.–Any person, including the victim, with knowledge sufficient to justify making a report or cooperating with the agency, including possibly providing testimony in any administrative or judicial proceeding, shall be free from any intimidation by an employer or by any other person or entity. Any person who violates this subsection is subject to civil lawsuit by the person intimidated or the victim wherein the person intimidated or the victim shall recover treble compensatory damages, compensatory and punitive damages or $5,000, whichever is greater.

(d) *Immunity*

Any person participating in the making of a report or who provides testimony in any administrative or judicial proceeding arising out of a report shall be immune from any civil or criminal liability on account of the report or testimony unless the person acted in bad faith or with malicious purpose. This immunity shall not extend to liability for acts of abuse, neglect, exploitation or abandonment, even if such acts are the subject of the report or testimony.

## § 10225.303. Investigations of reports of need for protective services

(a) *Investigation*

It shall be the agency's responsibility to provide for an investigation of each report made under section 302. The investigation shall be initiated within 72 hours after the receipt of the report and shall be carried out under regulations issued by the department. These regulations shall provide for the methods of conducting investigations under this section and shall assure that steps are taken to avoid any conflict of interest between the investigator and service delivery functions. Reports and investigations under this section shall comply with chapter 7, where applicable.

(b) *Investigation involving licensed facilities*

Any report concerning older adults residing in a state-licensed facility shall be investigated under procedures developed by the department in consultation with the state agency licensing such facility. If the report concerns a resident of a state-licensed facility for whom the area agency on aging provides ombudsman services, the ombudsman of the area agency on aging must be notified.

(c) *Unsubstantiated reports*

If, after investigation by the agency, the report is unsubstantiated, the case shall be closed and all information identifying the reporter and the alleged abuser shall be immediately deleted from all records. For purposes of substantiating a pattern of abuse, neglect, exploitation or abandonment, the name of the alleged victim and any information describing the alleged act of abuse, neglect, exploitation or abandonment may be maintained for a period of six months under procedures established by the department.

(d) *Substantiated reports*

If the report is substantiated by the agency, or if the client assessment is necessary in order to determine whether or not the report is substantiated, the agency shall provide for a timely client assessment if the older adult consents to an assessment.    Upon completion of the assessment, written findings shall be prepared which shall include recommended action.    This service plan shall provide for the least restrictive alternative, encouraging client self-determination and continuity of care.    The service plan shall be in writing and shall include a recommended course of action, which may include the pursuit of civil or criminal remedies.    If an older adult found to be in need of protective services does not consent to a client assessment or the development of a service plan, the agency may apply to the case the provisions of section 307.

### § 10225.304.  Provision of services; access to records and persons

(a) *Availability of protective services* — the agency shall offer protective services under any of the following conditions:

(1) An older adult requests such services.

(2) Another interested person requests such services on behalf of an older adult.

(3) If, after investigation of a report, the agency determines the older adult is in need of such services.

(b) *Consent by request* — Except as provided in section 307, an individual shall receive protective services voluntarily.  In no event may protective services be provided under this chapter to any person who does not consent to such services or who, having consented, withdraws such consent, unless such services are ordered by a court, requested by a guardian of the older adult or provided under section 307.  Nothing in this chapter shall prevent the agency from petitioning for the appointment of a guardian pursuant to title 20 of the Pennsylvania consolidated statutes (relating to decedents, estates and fiduciaries).

(c) *Interference with services* — If any person interferes with the provision of services or interferes with the right of an older adult to consent to provision of services, the agency may petition the court for an order enjoining such interference.

(d) *Access to records* — the agency shall have access to all records relevant to:

(1) Investigations of reports under section 303.

(2) Assessment of client need.

(3) Service planning when an older adult's need for protective services has been or is being established.

(4) The delivery of services arranged for under the service plan developed by the agency to respond to an older adult's assessed need for specific services.

(e) *Access to persons* — The agency shall have access to older persons who have been reported to be in need of protective services in order to:

(1) Investigate reports under section 303 and Chapter 7.

(2) Assess client need and develop a service plan for addressing needs determined.

(3) Provide for the delivery of services by the agency or other service provider arranged for under the service plan developed by the agency.

(f) *Denial of access to persons* — If the agency is denied access to an older adult reported to be in need of protective services and access is necessary to complete the investigation or the client assessment and service plan, or the delivery of needed services in order to prevent further abuse, neglect, exploitation or abandonment of the older adult reported to be in need of protective services, the agency may petition the court for an order to require the appropriate access when either of the following conditions apply:

(1) The caretaker or a third party has interfered with the completion of the investigation or the client assessment and service plan or the delivery of services.

(2) The agency can demonstrate that the older adult reported to be in need of protective services is denying access because of coercion, extortion or justifiable fear of future abuse, neglect, or exploitation or abandonment.

(g) *Access by consent* — The agency's access to confidential records held by other agencies or individuals and the agency's access to an older adult reported to be in need of protective services shall require the consent of the older adult or a court-appointed guardian except as provided for under this section or section 307.

(h) *Denial of access to records* — If the agency is denied access to records necessary for the completion of a proper investigation of a report or a client assessment and service plan, or the delivery of needed services in order to prevent further abuse, neglect, exploitation or abandonment of the older adult reported to be in need of protective services, the agency may petition the court of common pleas for an order requiring the appropriate access when either of the following conditions apply:

(1) The older adult has provided written consent for any confidential records to be disclosed and the keeper of the records denies access.

(2) The agency can demonstrate that the older adult is denying access to records because of incompetence, coercion, extortion or justifiable fear of future abuse, neglect, exploitation or abandonment.

## § 10225.305. Immunity from civil and criminal liability

In the absence of willful misconduct or gross negligence, the agency, the director, employees of the agency, protective services workers or employees of the department shall not be civilly or criminally liable for any decision or action or resulting consequence of decisions or action when acting under and according to the provisions of this chapter.

## § 10225.306. Confidentiality of records

(a) *General rule* — Information contained in reports, records of investigation, client assessment and service plans shall be considered confidential and shall be maintained under regulations promulgated by the department to safeguard confidentiality. Except as provided below, this information shall not be disclosed to anyone outside the agency other than to a court of competent jurisdiction or pursuant to a court order.

(b) *limited access to the agency's protective services records* —

(1) In the event that an investigation by the agency results in a report of criminal conduct, law enforcement officials shall have access to all relevant records maintained by the agency or the department.

(2) In arranging specific services to carry out service plans, the agency may disclose to appropriate service providers such information as may be necessary to initiate the delivery of services.

(3) A subject of a report made under section 302 may receive, upon written request, all information contained in the report except that prohibited from being disclosed by paragraph (4).

(4) The release of information that would identify the person who made a report of suspected abuse, neglect, exploitation or abandonment or person who cooperated in a subsequent

investigation, is hereby prohibited unless the secretary can determine that such a release will not be detrimental to the safety of such person.

### § 10225.307. Involuntary intervention by emergency court order

(a) *Emergency petition* — Where there was clear and convincing evidence that if protective services are not provided, the person to be protected is at imminent risk of death or serious physical harm, the agency may petition the court for an emergency order to provide the necessary services. The courts of common pleas of each judicial district shall ensure that a judge or district justice is available on a 24-hour-a-day, 365-day-a-year basis to accept and decide on petitions for an emergency court order under this section whenever the agency determines that a delay until normal court hours would significantly increase the danger the older adult faces.

(b) *Limited order* — The court, after finding clear and convincing evidence of the need for an emergency order, shall order only such services as are necessary to remove the conditions creating the established need.

(c) *Right to counsel* — In order to protect the rights of an older adult for whom protective services are being ordered, an emergency court order under this section shall provide that the older adult has the right to legal counsel. If the older adult is unable to provide for counsel, such counsel shall be appointed by the court.

(d) *Forcible entry* — Where it is necessary to forcibly enter premises after obtaining a court order, a peace officer may do so, accompanied by a representative of the agency.

(e) *Health and safety requirements* — The agency shall take reasonable steps to assure that while the person is receiving services under an emergency court order, the health and safety needs of any of the person's dependents are met and that personal property and the dwelling the person occupies are secure.

(f) *Exclusion of remedy* — Nothing in this chapter shall be interpreted to deny any older adult access to the emergency medical services or police protection that would be provided to anyone, regardless of age, in similar circumstances.

(5) When the department is involved in the hearing of an appeal by a subject of a report made under section 302, the appropriate department staff shall have access to all information in the report record relevant to the appeal.

(6) For the purposes of monitoring agency performance, appropriate staff of the department may access agency protective services records.

## § 10225.308. Individual rights

(a) *Rights of protective services clients* — The agency shall observe the following minimum requirements to safeguard the rights of an older adult who is reported to be in need of protective services:

(1) The agency shall discreetly notify the older person during the investigation that a report has been made and shall provide the person with a brief summary of the nature of the report.

(2) As provided under section 306(b)(3), the older adult may request, and the agency shall provide, additional information contained in the report.

(3) Any denial of services by the department or an authorized agency under this chapter may be appealed according to the provisions of the rules and regulations issued by the department under Article XXII-A of the act of April 9, 1929 (P.L. 177, No. 175), known as The Administrative Code of 1929.

(4) Nothing in this act shall limit the right of any older person to file a petition pursuant to the act of October 7, 1976 (P.L. 1090, No. 218), known as the Protection from Abuse Act.

(b) *Rights of alleged abusers* — An individual who is alleged in a protective services report to be a perpetrator of the abuse, neglect, exploitation or abandonment of an older adult shall be entitled to the following if the report is substantiated by the agency:

(1) Such an individual shall be notified by the agency at the conclusion of the investigation of the report that allegations have been made and shall be given a brief summary of the allegations.

(2) As provided under section 306(b)(3), the alleged perpetrator may request, and the agency shall provide, additional information contained in the report.

(3) An alleged perpetrator is entitled to file an appeal with the department under 1 Pa. Code Part II (relating to general rules of administrative practice and procedure) to challenge the agency's finding resulting from the investigation of a report made under section 303.

## § 10225.309.  Financial obligations; liabilities and payments

All individuals receiving services and all agencies providing services under this chapter shall comply with the following provisions regarding liability for the payment of services:

(1) Funding to provide or make available protective services under this chapter shall not supplant any public and private entitlements or resources for which persons receiving protective services under this chapter are or may be eligible, and shall not be available until such persons have exhausted their eligibility and receipt of benefits under said public and private entitlements or resources.

(2) Funding available to local protective services agencies under this chapter may be used to cover the costs of activities including, but not limited to, the following:

(i) Administering protective services plans required under section 301(c).

(ii) Receiving and maintaining records of reports of abuse under section 302.

(iii) Conducting investigations of reported abuse under section 303.

(iv) Carrying out client assessments and developing service plans under section 303.

(v) Petitioning the court under sections 304 and 307.

(vi) Providing emergency involuntary intervention under section 307.

(vii) Arranging for available services needed to carry out service plans, which may include, as appropriate, arranging for services for other household members in order to reduce, correct or eliminate abuse, neglect, exploitation or abandonment of an older adult.

(viii) Purchasing, on a temporary basis, services determined by a service plan to be necessary to reduce, correct or eliminate abuse, neglect, exploitation or abandonment of an older adult when such services are not available within the existing resources of the agency or other appropriate provider. Purchase of services under this provision is limited to a 30-day period which may be renewed with adequate justification under regulations promulgated by the department.

(3) The obligation of the Commonwealth and the counties to provide funds to the department or any agency for services provided pursuant to this chapter shall be entirely discharged by the appropriations made to the department or an agency. Provided that the agency has met its responsibility under the law, no action at law or equity shall be instituted in any court to require the department, any agency, county or the Commonwealth to provide benefits or services under this chapter for which appropriations from the Commonwealth or counties are not available.

(4) Protective services clients receiving the same services provided to others under an agency service plan shall not be required to pay a fee for any services not subject to cost sharing for other older adults.

## § 10225.310. Regulations; enforcement

(a) *Promulgation of regulations* — The department shall promulgate the rules and regulations to carry out this chapter and shall be responsible for presenting to the general assembly annually a report on the program and services performed.

(b) *Enforcement* — This chapter shall be enforced only after promulgation of regulations by the department, which shall occur no later than 12 months following passage of this chapter, except that section 301 shall apply when the area agency on aging certifies to the department that it is prepared to fulfill its responsibilities. The certification shall be made within 90 days following promulgation of regulations.

## § 10225.312. Funds for payment of administration of chapter

Funds necessary to administer this chapter shall be provided by annual appropriation by the General Assembly.

# Florida Durable Power of Attorney Statute
Fla. Stat. § 709.08 (2002)

## § 709.08. Durable power of attorney

(1) *CREATION OF DURABLE POWER OF ATTORNEY.* — A durable power of attorney is a written power of attorney by which a principal designates another as the principal's attorney in fact. The durable power of attorney must be in writing, must be executed with the same formalities required for the conveyance of real property by Florida law, and must contain the words: "This durable power of attorney is not affected by subsequent incapacity of the principal except as provided in § 709.08, Florida Statutes"; or similar words that show the principal's intent that the authority conferred is exercisable notwithstanding the principal's subsequent incapacity, except as otherwise provided by this section. The durable power of attorney is exercisable as of the date of execution; however, if the durable power of attorney is conditioned upon the principal's lack of capacity to manage property as defined in § 744.102(10)(a), the durable power of attorney is exercisable upon the delivery of affidavits in paragraphs (4)(c) and (d) to the third party.

(2) *WHO MAY SERVE AS ATTORNEY IN FACT.* — The attorney in fact must be a natural person who is 18 years of age or older and is of sound mind, or a financial institution, as defined in chapter 655, with trust powers, having a place of business in this state and authorized to conduct trust business in this state. A not-for-profit corporation, organized for charitable or religious purposes in this state, which has qualified as a court-appointed guardian prior to January 1, 1996, and which is a tax-exempt organization under 26 U.S.C. § 501(c)(3), may also act as an attorney in fact. Notwithstanding any contrary clause in the written power of attorney, no assets of the principal may be used for the benefit of the corporate attorney in fact, or its officers or directors.

(3) *EFFECT OF DELEGATION, REVOCATION, OR FILING OF PETITION TO DETERMINE INCAPACITY.*

(a) A durable power of attorney is nondelegable except as permitted in subparagraph (7)(a)1.

(b) The attorney in fact may exercise the authority granted under a durable power of attorney until the principal dies, revokes the power, or is adjudicated totally or partially incapacitated by a court of competent jurisdiction, unless the court determines that certain authority granted by the durable power of attorney is to remain exercisable by the attorney in fact.

(c)   1. If any person or entity initiates proceedings in any court of competent jurisdiction to determine the principal's incapacity, the authority granted under the durable power of attorney is suspended until the petition is dismissed or withdrawn. Notice of the petition must be served upon all attorneys in fact named in any power of attorney which is known to the petitioner.

2. If an emergency arises after initiation of proceedings to determine incapacity and before adjudication regarding the principal's capacity, the attorney in fact may petition the court in which the proceeding is pending for authorization to exercise a power granted under the durable power of attorney. The petition must set forth the nature of the emergency, the property or matter involved, and the power to be exercised by the attorney in fact.

3. Notwithstanding the provisions of this section, a proceeding to determine incapacity must not affect any authority of the attorney in fact to make health care decisions for the principal, including, but not limited to, those defined in chapter 765, unless otherwise ordered by the court. If the principal has executed a health care advance directive designating a health care surrogate pursuant to chapter 765, the terms of the directive will control if the two documents are in conflict unless the durable power of attorney is later executed and expressly states otherwise.

(4) *PROTECTION WITHOUT NOTICE; GOOD FAITH ACTS; AFFIDAVITS.*

(a) Any third party may rely upon the authority granted in a durable power of attorney that is not conditioned on the principal's lack of capacity to manage property until the third party has received notice as provided in subsection (5). A third party may, but need not, require the attorney in fact to execute an affidavit pursuant to paragraph (c).

(b) Any third party may rely upon the authority granted in a durable power of attorney that is conditioned on the principal's lack of capacity to manage property as defined in § 744.102(10)(a) only after receiving the affidavits provided in paragraphs (c) and (d), and such reliance shall end when the third party has received notice as provided in subsection (5).

(c) An affidavit executed by the attorney in fact must state where the principal is domiciled, that the principal is not deceased, and that there has been no revocation, partial or complete termination by adjudication of incapacity or by the occurrence of an event referenced in the durable power of attorney, or suspension by initiation of proceedings to determine incapacity or to appoint a guardian of the durable power of attorney at the time the power of attorney is exercised. A written affidavit executed by the attorney in fact under this paragraph may, but need not, be in the following form:

STATE OF

COUNTY OF

Before me, the undersigned authority, personally appeared (attorney in fact) ("Affiant"), who swore or affirmed that:

1. Affiant is the attorney in fact named in the Durable Power of Attorney executed by (principal) ("Principal") on (date).

2. This Durable Power of Attorney is currently exercisable by Affiant. The principal is domiciled in (insert name of state, territory, or foreign country).

3. To the best of the Affiant's knowledge after diligent search and inquiry:

a. The Principal is not deceased; and

b. There has been no revocation, partial or complete termination by adjudication of incapacity or by the occurrence of an event referenced in the durable power of attorney, or suspension by initiation of proceedings to determine incapacity or to appoint a guardian.

4. Affiant agrees not to exercise any powers granted by the Durable Power of Attorney if Affiant attains knowledge that it has been revoked, partially or completely terminated, suspended, or is no longer valid because of the death or adjudication of incapacity of the Principal.

(Affiant)

Sworn to (or affirmed) and subscribed before me this day of (month), (year), by (name of person making statement)

(Signature of Notary Public-State of Florida)

(Print, Type, or Stamp Commissioned Name of Notary Public)

Personally Known OR Produced Identification

(Type of Identification Produced)

(d) A determination that a principal lacks the capacity to manage property as defined in § 744.102(10)(a) must be made and evidenced by the affidavit of a physician licensed to practice medicine pursuant to chapters 458 and 459 as of the date of the affidavit.  A judicial determination that the principal lacks the capacity to manage property pursuant to chapter 744 is not required prior to the determination by the physician and the execution of the affidavit.  For purposes of this section, the physician executing the affidavit must be the primary physician who has responsibility for the treatment and care of the principal.  The affidavit executed by a physician must state where the physician is licensed to practice medicine, that the physician is the primary physician who has responsibility for the treatment and care of the principal, and that the physician believes that the principal lacks the capacity to manage property as defined in § 744.102(10)(a).  The affidavit may, but need not, be in the following form:

STATE OF

COUNTY OF

Before me, the undersigned authority, personally appeared (name of physician), Affiant, who swore or affirmed that:

1. Affiant is a physician licensed to practice medicine in (name of state, territory, or foreign country).

2. Affiant is the primary physician who has responsibility for the treatment and care of (principal's name).

3. To the best of Affiant's knowledge after reasonable inquiry, Affiant believes that the principal lacks the capacity to manage property, including taking those actions necessary to obtain, administer, and dispose of real and personal property, intangible property, business property, benefits, and income.

(Affiant)

Sworn to (or affirmed) and subscribed before me this (day of) (month), (year), by (name of person making statement)

(Signature of Notary Public-State of Florida)

(Print, Type, or Stamp Commissioned Name of Notary Public)

Personally Known OR Produced Identification

(Type of Identification Produced)

(e) A physician who makes a determination of incapacity to manage property under paragraph (d) is not subject to criminal prosecution or civil liability and is not considered to have engaged in unprofessional conduct as a result of making such determination, unless it is shown by a preponderance of the evidence that the physician making the determination did not comply in good faith with the provisions of this section.

(f) A third party may not rely on the authority granted in a durable power of attorney conditioned on the principal's lack of capacity to manage property as defined in § 744.102(10)(a) when any affidavit presented has been executed more than 6 months prior to the first presentation of the durable power of attorney to the third party.

(g) Third parties who act in reliance upon the authority granted to the attorney in fact under the durable power of attorney and in accordance with the instructions of the attorney in fact must be held harmless by the principal from any loss suffered or liability incurred as a result of actions taken prior to receipt of written notice pursuant to subsection (5). A person who acts in good faith upon any representation, direction, decision, or act of the attorney in fact is not liable to the principal or the principal's estate, beneficiaries, or joint owners for those acts.

(h) A durable power of attorney may provide that the attorney in fact is not liable for any acts or decisions made by the attorney in fact in good faith and under the terms of the durable power of attorney.

(5) *NOTICE.*

(a) A notice, including, but not limited to, a notice of revocation, notice of partial or complete termination by adjudication of incapacity or by the occurrence of an event referenced in the durable power of attorney, notice of death of the principal, notice of suspension by initiation of proceedings to determine incapacity or to appoint a guardian, or other notice, is not effective until written notice is served upon the attorney in fact or any third persons relying upon a durable power of attorney.

(b) Notice must be in writing and served on the person or entity to be bound by the notice. Service may be by any form of mail that requires a signed receipt or by personal delivery as provided for service of process. Service is complete when received by interested persons or entities specified in this section and in chapter 48, where applicable. In the case of a financial institution as defined in chapter 655, notice, when not mailed, must be served during regular business hours upon an officer or manager of the financial institution at the financial institution's principal place of business in Florida and its office where the power of attorney or account was presented, handled, or administered. Notice by mail to a financial institution must be mailed to the financial institution's principal place of business in this state and its office where the power of attorney or account was presented, handled, or administered. Except for service of court orders, a third party served with notice must be given 14 calendar days after service to act upon that notice. In the case of a financial institution, notice must be served before the occurrence of any of the events described in § 674.303.

(6) *PROPERTY SUBJECT TO DURABLE POWER OF ATTORNEY.* — Unless otherwise stated in the durable power of attorney, the durable power of attorney applies to any interest in property owned by the principal, including, without limitation, the principal's interest in all real property, including homestead real property; all personal property, tangible or intangible; all property held in any type of joint tenancy, including a tenancy in common, joint tenancy with right of survivorship, or a tenancy by the entirety; all property over which the principal holds a general, limited, or special power of appointment; choses in action; and all other contractual or statutory rights or elections, including, but not limited to, any rights or elections in any probate or similar proceeding to which the principal is or may become entitled.

(7) *POWERS OF THE ATTORNEY IN FACT AND LIMITATIONS.*

(a) Except as otherwise limited by this section, by other applicable law, or by the durable power of attorney, the attorney in fact has full authority to perform, without prior court approval, every act authorized and specifically enumerated in the durable power of attorney. Such authorization may include, except as otherwise limited in this section:

1. The authority to execute stock powers or similar documents on behalf of the principal and delegate to a transfer agent or similar person the authority to register any stocks, bonds, or other securities either into or out of the principal's or nominee's name.

2. The authority to convey or mortgage homestead property. If the principal is married, the attorney in fact may

not mortgage or convey homestead property without joinder of the spouse of the principal or the spouse's legal guardian. Joinder by a spouse may be accomplished by the exercise of authority in a durable power of attorney executed by the joining spouse, and either spouse may appoint the other as his or her attorney in fact.

(b) Notwithstanding the provisions of this section, an attorney in fact may not:

1. Perform duties under a contract that requires the exercise of personal services of the principal;

2. Make any affidavit as to the personal knowledge of the principal;

3. Vote in any public election on behalf of the principal;

4. Execute or revoke any will or codicil for the principal;

5. Create, amend, modify, or revoke any document or other disposition effective at the principal's death or transfer assets to an existing trust created by the principal unless expressly authorized by the power of attorney; or

6. Exercise powers and authority granted to the principal as trustee or as court-appointed fiduciary.

(c) If such authority is specifically granted in the durable power of attorney, the attorney in fact may make all health care decisions on behalf of the principal, including, but not limited to, those set forth in chapter 765.

(8) *STANDARD OF CARE.* — Except as otherwise provided in paragraph (4)(e), an attorney in fact is a fiduciary who must observe the standards of care applicable to trustees as described in § 737.302. The attorney in fact is not liable to third parties for any act pursuant to the durable power of attorney if the act was authorized at the time. If the exercise of the power is improper, the attorney in fact is liable to interested persons as described in § 731.201 for damage or loss resulting from a breach of fiduciary duty by the attorney in fact to the same extent as the trustee of an express trust.

(9) *MULTIPLE ATTORNEYS IN FACT; WHEN JOINT ACTION REQUIRED.* — Unless the durable power of attorney provides otherwise:

(a) If a durable power of attorney is vested jointly in two attorneys in fact by the same instrument, concurrence of both is required on all acts in the exercise of the power.

(b) If a durable power of attorney is vested jointly in three or more attorneys in fact by the same instrument, concurrence of a majority is required in all acts in the exercise of the power.

(c) An attorney in fact who has not concurred in the exercise of authority is not liable to the principal or any other person for the consequences of the exercise. A dissenting attorney in fact is not liable for the consequences of an act in which the attorney in fact joins at the direction of the majority of the joint attorneys in fact if the attorney in fact expresses such dissent in writing to any of the other joint attorneys in fact at or before the time of the joinder.

(d) If the attorney in fact has accepted appointment either expressly in writing or by acting under the power, this section does not excuse the attorney in fact from liability for failure either to participate in the administration of assets subject to the power or for failure to attempt to prevent a breach of fiduciary obligations thereunder.

(10) *POWERS OF REMAINING ATTORNEY IN FACT.* — Unless the durable power of attorney provides otherwise, all authority vested in multiple attorneys in fact may be exercised by the one or more that remain after the death, resignation, or incapacity of one or more of the multiple attorneys in fact.

(11) *DAMAGES AND COSTS.* — In any judicial action under this section, including, but not limited to, the unreasonable refusal of a third party to allow an attorney in fact to act pursuant to the power, and challenges to the proper exercise of authority by the attorney in fact, the prevailing party is entitled to damages and costs, including reasonable attorney's fees.

(12) *APPLICATION.* — This section applies to only those durable powers of attorney executed on or after October 1, 1995.

(13) *PARTIAL INVALIDITY.* — If any provision of this section or its application to any person or circumstance is held invalid, the invalidity does not affect other provisions or applications of this section which can be given effect without the invalid provision or application and to this end the provisions of this section are severable.

# New Mexico Health Care Decisions Act (Uniform Health-Care Decisions Act)

N.M. Stat. Ann. § 24-7A-1 to 24-7A-18

## § 24-7A-1. Definitions

As used in the Uniform Health-Care Decisions Act:

A. "advance health-care directive" means an individual instruction or a power of attorney for health care made, in either case, while the individual has capacity;

B. "agent" means an individual designated in a power of attorney for health care to make a health-care decision for the individual granting the power;

C. "capacity" means an individual's ability to understand and appreciate the nature and consequences of proposed health care, including its significant benefits, risks and alternatives to proposed health care and to make and communicate an informed health-care decision. A determination of lack of capacity shall be made only according to the provisions of Section 24-7A-11 NMSA 1978;

D. "emancipated minor" means a person between the ages of sixteen and eighteen who has been married, who is on active duty in the armed forces or who has been declared by court order to be emancipated;

E. "guardian" means a judicially appointed guardian or conservator having authority to make a health-care decision for an individual;

F. "health care" means any care, treatment, service or procedure to maintain, diagnose or otherwise affect an individual's physical or mental condition;

G. "health-care decision" means a decision made by an individual or the individual's agent, guardian or surrogate, regarding the individual's health care, including:

(1) selection and discharge of health-care providers and institutions;

(2) approval or disapproval of diagnostic tests, surgical procedures, programs of medication and orders not to resuscitate;

(3) directions relating to life-sustaining treatment, including withholding or withdrawing life-sustaining treatment and the termination of life support; and

(4) directions to provide, withhold or withdraw artificial nutrition and hydration and all other forms of health care;

H. "health-care institution" means an institution, facility or agency licensed, certified or otherwise authorized or permitted by law to provide health care in the ordinary course of business;

I. "health-care provider" means an individual licensed, certified or otherwise authorized or permitted by law to provide health care in the ordinary course of business or practice of a profession;

J. "individual instruction" means an individual's direction concerning a health-care decision for the individual, made while the individual has capacity;

K. "life-sustaining treatment" means any medical treatment or procedure without which the individual is likely to die within a relatively short time, as determined to a reasonable degree of medical certainty by the primary physician;

L. "person" means an individual, corporation, business trust, estate, trust, partnership, association, joint venture, government, governmental subdivision, agency or instrumentality or any other legal or commercial entity;

M. "physician" means an individual authorized to practice medicine or osteopathy;

N. "power of attorney for health care" means the designation of an agent to make health-care decisions for the individual granting the power, made while the individual has capacity;

O. "primary physician" means a physician designated by an individual or the individual's agent, guardian or surrogate to have primary responsibility for the individual's health care or, in the absence of a designation or if the designated physician is not reasonably available, a physician who undertakes the responsibility;

P. "principal" means an adult or emancipated minor who, while having capacity, has made a power of attorney for health care by which he delegates his right to make health-care decisions for himself to an agent;

Q. "qualified health-care professional" means a health-care provider who is a physician, physician assistant, nurse practitioner, nurse, psychologist or social worker;

R. "reasonably available" means readily able to be contacted without undue effort and willing and able to act in a timely manner considering the urgency of the patient's health-care needs;

S. "state" means a state of the United States, the District of Columbia, the commonwealth of Puerto Rico or a territory or insular possession subject to the jurisdiction of the United States;

T. "supervising health-care provider" means the primary physician or, if there is no primary physician or the primary physician is not reasonably available, the health-care provider who has undertaken primary responsibility for an individual's health care;

U. "surrogate" means an individual, other than a patient's agent or guardian, authorized under the Uniform Health-Care Decisions Act to make a health-care decision for the patient; and

V. "ward" means an adult or emancipated minor for whom a guardian has been appointed.

## § 24-7A-2. Advance health-care directives

A. An adult or emancipated minor, while having capacity, has the right to make his or her own health-care decisions and may give an individual instruction. The instruction may be oral or written; if oral, it must be made by personally informing a health-care provider. The instruction may be limited to take effect only if a specified condition arises.

B. An adult or emancipated minor, while having capacity, may execute a power of attorney for health care, which may authorize the agent to make any health-care decision the principal could have made while having capacity. The power must be in writing and signed by the principal. The power remains in effect notwithstanding the principal's later incapacity under the Uniform Health-Care Decisions Act or Article 5 of the Uniform Probate Code. The power may include individual instructions. Unless related to the principal by blood, marriage or adoption, an agent may not be an owner, operator or employee of a health-care institution at which the principal is receiving care.

C. Unless otherwise specified in a power of attorney for health care, the authority of an agent becomes effective only upon a determination that the principal lacks capacity, and ceases to be effective upon a determination that the principal has recovered capacity.

D. Unless otherwise specified in a written advance health-care directive, a determination that an individual lacks or has recovered capacity or that another condition exists that affects an individual instruction or the authority of an agent, shall be made according to the provisions of Section 11 of the Uniform Health-Care Decisions Act.

E. An agent shall make a health-care decision in accordance with the principal's individual instructions, if any, and other wishes to the extent known to the agent. Otherwise, the agent shall make the decision in accordance with the agent's determination of the principal's best interest.

In determining the principal's best interest, the agent shall consider the principal's personal values to the extent known to the agent.

F. A health-care decision made by an agent for a principal is effective without judicial approval.

G. A written advance health-care directive may include the individual's nomination of a guardian of the person.

## § 24-7A-3.  Revocation of advance health-care directive

A. An individual, while having capacity, may revoke the designation of an agent either by a signed writing or by personally informing the supervising health-care provider.  If the individual cannot sign, a written revocation must be signed for the individual and be witnessed by two witnesses, each of whom has signed at the direction and in the presence of the individual and of each other.

B. An individual, while having capacity, may revoke all or part of an advance health-care directive, other than the designation of an agent, at any time and in any manner that communicates an intent to revoke.

C. A health-care provider, agent, guardian or surrogate who is informed of a revocation shall promptly communicate the fact of the revocation to the supervising health-care provider and to any health-care institution at which the patient is receiving care.

D. The filing of a petition for or a decree of annulment, divorce, dissolution of marriage or legal separation revokes a previous designation of a spouse as agent unless otherwise specified in the decree or in a power of attorney for health care.  A designation revoked solely by this subsection is revived by the individual's remarriage to the former spouse, by a nullification of the divorce, annulment or legal separation or by the dismissal or withdrawal, with the individual's consent, of a petition seeking annulment, divorce, dissolution of marriage or legal separation.

E. An advance health-care directive that conflicts with an earlier advance health-care directive revokes the earlier directive to the extent of the conflict.

## § 24-7A-4.  Optional form

The following form may, but need not, be used to create an advance health-care directive.  The other sections of the Uniform Health-Care Decisions Act govern the effect of this or any other writing used to create an advance health-care directive.  An individual may complete or modify all or any part of the following form:

"OPTIONAL ADVANCE HEALTH-CARE DIRECTIVE

Explanation

You have the right to give instructions about your own health care. You also have the right to name someone else to make health-care decisions for you. This form lets you do either or both of these things. It also lets you express your wishes regarding the designation of your primary physician.

THIS FORM IS OPTIONAL. Each paragraph and word of this form is also optional. If you use this form, you may cross out, complete or modify all or any part of it. You are free to use a different form. If you use this form, be sure to sign it and date it.

PART 1 of this form is a power of attorney for health care. PART 1 lets you name another individual as agent to make health-care decisions for you if you become incapable of making your own decisions or if you want someone else to make those decisions for you now even though you are still capable. You may also name an alternate agent to act for you if your first choice is not willing, able or reasonably available to make decisions for you. Unless related to you, your agent may not be an owner, operator or employee of a health-care institution at which you are receiving care.

Unless the form you sign limits the authority of your agent, your agent may make all health-care decisions for you. This form has a place for you to limit the authority of your agent. You need not limit the authority of your agent if you wish to rely on your agent for all health-care decisions that may have to be made. If you choose not to limit the authority of your agent, your agent will have the right to:

(a) consent or refuse consent to any care, treatment, service or procedure to maintain, diagnose or otherwise affect a physical or mental condition;

(b) select or discharge health-care providers and institutions;

(c) approve or disapprove diagnostic tests, surgical procedures, programs of medication and orders not to resuscitate; and

(d) direct the provision, withholding or withdrawal of artificial nutrition and hydration and all other forms of health care.

PART 2 of this form lets you give specific instructions about any aspect of your health care. Choices are provided for you to express your wishes regarding life-sustaining treatment, including the provision of artificial nutrition and hydration, as well as the provision of pain relief. In addition, you may express your wishes regarding whether you want to make an anatomical gift of some or all of your organs and tissue. Space is also provided for you to add to the choices you have made or for you to write out any additional wishes.

PART 3 of this form lets you designate a physician to have primary responsibility for your health care. After completing this form, sign and date the form at the end. It is recommended but not required that you request two other individuals to sign as witnesses. Give a copy of the signed and completed form to your physician, to any other health-care providers you may have, to any health-care institution at which you are receiving care and to any health-care agents you have named. You should talk to the person you have named as agent to make sure that he or she understands your wishes and is willing to take the responsibility.

You have the right to revoke this advance health-care directive or replace this form at any time.

\* \* \* \* \* \* \* \* \* \* \* \* \* \* \* \* \* \* \* \* \* \*

## PART 1
## POWER OF ATTORNEY FOR HEALTH CARE

(1) DESIGNATION OF AGENT: I designate the following individual as my agent to make health-care decisions for me:
(name of individual you choose as agent)
(address) (city)
(state) (zip code)
(home phone)
(work phone)
If I revoke my agent's authority or if my agent is not willing, able or reasonably available to make a health-care decision for me, I designate as my first alternate agent:
(name of individual you choose as first alternate agent)
(address) (city)
(state) (zip code)
(home phone)
(work phone)
If I revoke the authority of my agent and first alternate agent or if neither is willing, able or reasonably available to make a health-care decision for me, I designate as my second alternate agent:

(name of individual you choose as second alternate agent)
(address) (city)
(state) (zip code)
(home phone)
(work phone)

(2) AGENT'S AUTHORITY: My agent is authorized to obtain and review medical records, reports and information about me and to make all health-care decisions for me, including decisions to provide, withhold or withdraw artificial nutrition, hydration and all other forms of health care to keep me alive, except as I state here:

(Add additional sheets if needed.)

(3) WHEN AGENT'S AUTHORITY BECOMES EFFECTIVE: My agent's authority becomes effective when my primary physician and one other qualified health-care professional determine that I am unable to make my own health-care decisions. If I initial this box [ ], my agent's authority to make health-care decisions for me takes effect immediately.

(4) AGENT'S OBLIGATION: My agent shall make health-care decisions for me in accordance with this power of attorney for health care, any instructions I give in Part 2 of this form and my other wishes to the extent known to my agent. To the extent my wishes are unknown, my agent shall make health-care decisions for me in accordance with what my agent determines to be in my best interest. In determining my best interest, my agent shall consider my personal values to the extent known to my agent.

(5) NOMINATION OF GUARDIAN: If a guardian of my person needs to be appointed for me by a court, I nominate the agent designated in this form. If that agent is not willing, able or reasonably available to act as guardian, I nominate the alternate agents whom I have named, in the order designated.

## PART 2
## INSTRUCTIONS FOR HEALTH CARE

If you are satisfied to allow your agent to determine what is best for you in making end-of-life decisions, you need not fill out this part of the form. If you do fill out this part of the form, you may cross out any wording you do not want.

(6) END-OF-LIFE DECISIONS: If I am unable to make or communicate decisions regarding my health care, and IF (i) I have an incurable or irreversible condition that will result in my death within a

relatively short time, OR (ii) I become unconscious and, to a reasonable degree of medical certainty, I will not regain consciousness, OR (iii) the likely risks and burdens of treatment would outweigh the expected benefits, THEN I direct that my health-care providers and others involved in my care provide, withhold or withdraw treatment in accordance with the choice I have initialed below in one of the following three boxes:

[ ] I CHOOSE NOT To Prolong Life

I do not want my life to be prolonged.

[ ] I CHOOSE To Prolong Life

I want my life to be prolonged as long as possible within the limits of generally accepted health-care standards.

[ ] I CHOOSE To Let My Agent Decide

My agent under my power of attorney for health care may make life-sustaining treatment decisions for me.

(7) ARTIFICIAL NUTRITION AND HYDRATION: If I have chosen above NOT to prolong life, I also specify by marking my initials below:

[ ] I DO NOT want artificial nutrition OR

[ ] I DO want artificial nutrition.

[ ] I DO NOT want artificial hydration unless required for my comfort OR

[ ] I DO want artificial hydration.

(8) RELIEF FROM PAIN: Regardless of the choices I have made in this form and except as I state in the following space, I direct that the best medical care possible to keep me clean, comfortable and free of pain or discomfort be provided at all times so that my dignity is maintained, even if this care hastens my death:

(9) ANATOMICAL GIFT DESIGNATION: Upon my death I specify as marked below whether I choose to make an anatomical gift of all or some of my organs or tissue:

[ ] I CHOOSE to make an anatomical gift of all of my organs or tissue to be determined by medical suitability at the time of death, and artificial support may be maintained long enough for organs to be removed.

[ ] I CHOOSE to make a partial anatomical gift of some of my organs and tissue as specified below, and artificial support may be maintained long enough for organs to be removed.

[ ] I REFUSE to make an anatomical gift of any of my organs or tissue.

[ ] I CHOOSE to let my agent decide.

(10) OTHER WISHES: (If you wish to write your own instructions, or if you wish to add to the instructions you have given above, you may do so here.)

I direct that:

(Add additional sheets if needed.)

## PART 3

## PRIMARY PHYSICIAN

(11) I designate the following physician as my primary physician:

(name of physician)

(address) (city)

(state) (zip code)

(phone)

If the physician I have designated above is not willing, able or reasonably available to act as my primary physician, I designate the following physician as my primary physician:

(name of physician)

(address) (city)

(state) (zip code)

(phone)

* * * * * * * * * * * * * * * * * * * *

(12) EFFECT OF COPY: A copy of this form has the same effect as the original.

(13) REVOCATION:  I understand that I may revoke this OPTIONAL ADVANCE HEALTH-CARE DIRECTIVE at any time, and that if I revoke it, I should promptly notify my supervising health-care provider and any health-care institution where I am receiving care and any others to whom I have given copies of this power of attorney. I understand that I may revoke the designation of an agent either by a signed writing or by personally informing the supervising health-care provider.

(14) SIGNATURES:  Sign and date the form here:

(date)

(sign your name)

(address)

(print your name)

(city) (state)

(your social security number)
(Optional) SIGNATURES OF WITNESSES:
First witness
Second witness
(print name)
(print name)
(address)
(address)
(city) (state)
(city) (state)
(signature of witness)
(signature of witness)
(date)
(date)."

## § 24-7A-5. Decisions by surrogate

A. A surrogate may make a health-care decision for a patient who is an adult or emancipated minor if the patient has been determined according to the provisions of Section 24-7A-11 NMSA 1978 to lack capacity and no agent or guardian has been appointed or the agent or guardian is not reasonably available.

B. An adult or emancipated minor, while having capacity, may designate any individual to act as surrogate by personally informing the supervising health-care provider. In the absence of a designation or if the designee is not reasonably available, any member of the following classes of the patient's family who is reasonably available, in descending order of priority, may act as surrogate:

    (1) the spouse, unless legally separated or unless there is a pending petition for annulment, divorce, dissolution of marriage or legal separation;

    (2) an individual in a long-term relationship of indefinite duration with the patient in which the individual has demonstrated an actual commitment to the patient similar to the commitment of a spouse and in which the individual and the patient consider themselves to be responsible for each other's well-being;

    (3) an adult child;

    (4) a parent;

    (5) an adult brother or sister; or

    (6) a grandparent.

C. If none of the individuals eligible to act as surrogate under Subsection B of this section is reasonably available, an adult who has exhibited special care and concern for the patient, who is familiar with the patient's personal values and who is reasonably available may act as surrogate.

D. A surrogate shall communicate his assumption of authority as promptly as practicable to the patient, to members of the patient's family specified in Subsection B of this section who can be readily contacted and to the supervising health-care provider.

E. If more than one member of a class assumes authority to act as surrogate and they do not agree on a health-care decision and the supervising health-care provider is so informed, the supervising health-care provider shall comply with the decision of a majority of the members of that class who have communicated their views to the provider. If the class is evenly divided concerning the health-care decision and the supervising health-care provider is so informed, that class and all individuals having lower priority are disqualified from making the decision.

F. A surrogate shall make a health-care decision in accordance with the patient's individual instructions, if any, and other wishes to the extent known to the surrogate. Otherwise, the surrogate shall make the decision in accordance with the surrogate's determination of the patient's best interest. In determining the patient's best interest, the surrogate shall consider the patient's personal values to the extent known to the surrogate.

G. A health-care decision made by a surrogate for a patient shall not be made solely on the basis of the patient's pre-existing physical or medical condition or pre-existing or projected disability.

H. A health-care decision made by a surrogate for a patient is effective without judicial approval.

I. A patient, at any time, may disqualify any person, including a member of the patient's family, from acting as the patient's surrogate by a signed writing or by personally informing a health-care provider of the disqualification. A health-care provider who is informed by the patient of a disqualification shall promptly communicate the fact of disqualification to the supervising health-care provider and to any health-care institution at which the patient is receiving care.

J. Unless related to the patient by blood, marriage or adoption, a surrogate may not be an owner, operator or employee of a health-care institution at which the patient is receiving care.

K. A supervising health-care provider may require an individual claiming the right to act as surrogate for a patient to provide a written declaration under penalty of perjury stating facts and circumstances reasonably sufficient to establish the claimed authority.

## § 24-7A-6. Decisions by guardian

A. A guardian shall comply with the ward's individual instructions and may not revoke the ward's advance health-care directive unless the appointing court expressly so authorizes after notice to the agent and the ward.

B. A health-care decision of an agent appointed by an individual having capacity takes precedence over that of a guardian, unless the appointing court expressly directs otherwise after notice to the agent and the ward.

C. Subject to the provisions of Subsections A and B of this section, a health-care decision made by a guardian for the ward is effective without judicial approval, if the appointing court has expressly authorized the guardian to make health-care decisions for the ward, in accordance with the provisions of Section 45-5-312 NMSA 1978, after notice to the ward and any agent.

## § 24-7A-7. Obligations of health-care provider

A. Before implementing a health-care decision made for a patient, a supervising health-care provider shall promptly communicate to the patient the decision made and the identity of the person making the decision.

B. A supervising health-care provider who knows of the existence of an advance health-care directive, a revocation of an advance health-care directive, a challenge to a determination of lack of capacity or a designation or disqualification of a surrogate shall promptly record its existence in the patient's health-care record and, if it is in writing, shall request a copy and, if one is furnished, shall arrange for its maintenance in the health-care record.

C. A supervising health-care provider who makes or is informed of a determination that a patient lacks or has recovered capacity or that another condition exists that affects an individual instruction or the authority of an agent, guardian or surrogate shall promptly record the determination in the patient's health-care record and communicate the determination to the patient and to any person then authorized to make health-care decisions for the patient.

D. Except as provided in Subsections E and F of this section, a health-care provider or health-care institution providing care to a patient shall comply:

(1) before and after the patient is determined to lack capacity, with an individual instruction of the patient made while the patient had capacity;

(2) with a reasonable interpretation of that instruction made by a person then authorized to make health-care decisions for the patient; and

(3) with a health-care decision for the patient that is not contrary to an individual instruction of the patient and is made by a person then authorized to make health-care decisions for the patient, to the same extent as if the decision had been made by the patient while having capacity.

E. A health-care provider may decline to comply with an individual instruction or health-care decision for reasons of conscience. A health-care institution may decline to comply with an individual instruction or health-care decision if the instruction or decision is contrary to a policy of the health-care institution that is expressly based on reasons of conscience and if the policy was timely communicated to the patient or to a person then authorized to make health-care decisions for the patient.

F. A health-care provider or health-care institution may decline to comply with an individual instruction or health-care decision that requires medically ineffective health care or health care contrary to generally accepted health-care standards applicable to the health-care provider or health-care institution. "Medically ineffective health care" means treatment that would not offer the patient any significant benefit, as determined by a physician.

G. A health-care provider or health-care institution that declines to comply with an individual instruction or health-care decision shall:

(1) promptly so inform the patient, if possible, and any person then authorized to make health-care decisions for the patient;

(2) provide continuing care to the patient until a transfer can be effected; and

(3) unless the patient or person then authorized to make health-care decisions for the patient refuses assistance, immediately make all reasonable efforts to assist in the transfer of the patient to another health-care provider or health-care institution that is willing to comply with the instruction or decision.

H. A health-care provider or health-care institution may not require or prohibit the execution or revocation of an advance health-care directive as a condition for providing health care.

I. The Uniform Health-Care Decisions Act does not require or permit a health-care institution or health-care provider to provide any type of health care for which the health-care institution or health-care provider is not licensed, certified or otherwise authorized or permitted by law to provide.

## § 24-7A-8. Health-care information

Unless otherwise specified in an advance health-care directive, a person then authorized to make health-care decisions for a patient has the same rights as the patient to request, receive, examine, copy and consent to the disclosure of medical or any other health-care information.

## § 24-7A-9. Immunities

A. A health-care provider or health-care institution acting in good faith and in accordance with generally accepted health-care standards applicable to the health-care provider or health-care institution is not subject to civil or criminal liability or to discipline for unprofessional conduct for:

(1) complying or attempting to comply with a health-care decision of a person apparently having authority to make a health-care decision for a patient, including a decision to withhold or withdraw health care or make an anatomical gift;

(2) declining to comply with a health-care decision of a person based on a belief that the person then lacked authority;

(3) complying or attempting to comply with an advance health-care directive and assuming that the directive was valid when made and has not been revoked or terminated;

(4) declining to comply with a health-care directive as permitted by Subsection E or F of Section 24-7A-7 NMSA 1978; or

(5) complying or attempting to comply with any other provision of the Uniform Health-Care Decisions Act.

B. An individual acting as agent, guardian or surrogate under the Uniform Health-Care Decisions Act is not subject to civil or criminal liability or to discipline for unprofessional conduct for health-care decisions made in good faith.

## § 24-7A-10. Statutory damages

A. A health-care provider or health-care institution that intentionally violates the Uniform Health-Care Decisions Act is subject to liability to the aggrieved individual for damages of five thousand dollars ($5,000) or actual damages resulting from the violation, whichever is greater, plus reasonable attorney fees.

B. A person who intentionally falsifies, forges, conceals, defaces or obliterates an individual's advance health-care directive or a revocation of an advance health-care directive without the individual's consent or a person who coerces or fraudulently induces an individual to give, revoke or not give or revoke an advance health-care directive is subject to liability to that individual for damages of five thousand dollars ($5,000) or actual damages resulting from the action, whichever is greater, plus reasonable attorney fees.

C. The damages provided in this section are in addition to other types of relief available under other law, including civil and criminal law and law providing for disciplinary procedures.

## § 24-7A-11. Capacity

A. The Uniform Health-Care Decisions Act does not affect the right of an individual to make health-care decisions while having capacity to do so.

B. An individual is presumed to have capacity to make a health-care decision, to give or revoke an advance health-care directive and to designate a surrogate.

C. Unless otherwise specified in a written advance health- care directive, a determination that an individual lacks or has recovered capacity or that another condition exists that affects an individual instruction or the authority of an agent shall be made by two qualified health-care professionals, one of whom shall be the primary physician. If the lack of capacity is determined to exist because of mental illness or developmental disability, one of the qualified health-care professionals shall be a person whose training and expertise aid in the assessment of functional impairment.

D. An individual shall not be determined to lack capacity solely on the basis that the individual chooses not to accept the treatment recommended by a health-care provider.

E. An individual, at any time, may challenge a determination that the individual lacks capacity by a signed writing or by personally informing a health-care provider of the challenge. A health-care provider who is informed by the individual of a challenge shall promptly communicate the fact of the challenge to the supervising health-care provider and to any health-care institution at which the individual is receiving care. Such a challenge shall prevail unless otherwise ordered by the court in a proceeding brought pursuant to the provisions of Section 24-7A-14 NMSA 1978.

F. A determination of lack of capacity under the Uniform Health-Care Decisions Act shall not be evidence of incapacity under the provisions of Article 5 of the Uniform Probate Code.

## § 24-7A-12. Effect of copy

A copy of a written advance health-care directive, revocation of an advance health-care directive or designation or disqualification of a surrogate has the same effect as the original.

## § 24-7A-13. Effect of the Uniform Health-Care Decisions Act

A. The Uniform Health-Care Decisions Act does not create a presumption concerning the intention of an individual who has not made or who has revoked an advance health-care directive.

B. Death resulting from the withholding or withdrawal of health care in accordance with the Uniform Health-Care Decisions Act does not for any purpose:

(1) constitute a suicide, a homicide or other crime; or

(2) legally impair or invalidate a governing instrument, notwithstanding any term of the governing instrument to the contrary. "Governing instrument" means a deed, will, trust, insurance or annuity policy, account with POD (payment on death designation), security registered in beneficiary form (TOD), pension, profit-sharing, retirement, employment or similar benefit plan, instrument creating or exercising a power of appointment or a dispositive, appointive or nominative instrument of any similar type.

C. The Uniform Health-Care Decisions Act does not authorize mercy killing, assisted suicide, euthanasia or the provision, withholding or withdrawal of health care, to the extent prohibited by other statutes of this state.

D. The Uniform Health-Care Decisions Act does not authorize or require a health-care provider or health-care institution to provide health care contrary to generally accepted health-care standards applicable to the health-care provider or health-care institution.

E. The Uniform Health-Care Decisions Act does not authorize an agent or surrogate to consent to the admission of an individual to a mental health-care facility. If the individual's written advance health-care directive expressly permits treatment in a mental health-care facility, the agent or surrogate may present the individual to a facility for evaluation for admission.

F. The Uniform Health-Care Decisions Act does not affect other statutes of this state governing treatment for mental illness of an individual admitted to a mental health-care institution.

## § 24-7A-14. Judicial relief

On petition of a patient, the patient's agent, guardian or surrogate, a health-care provider or health-care institution involved with the patient's care, an individual described in Subsection B or C of Section 24-7A-5 NMSA 1978, the district court may enjoin or direct a health-care decision or order other equitable relief. A proceeding under this section is governed by the Rules of Civil Procedure for the District Courts.

## § 24-7A-15. Uniformity of application and construction

The Uniform Health-Care Decisions Act shall be applied and construed to effectuate its general purpose to make uniform the law with respect to the subject matter of that act among states enacting it.

## § 24-7A-16. Transitional provisions

A. An advance health-care directive is valid for purposes of the Uniform Health-Care Decisions Act if it complies with the provisions of that act, regardless of when or where executed or communicated.

B. The Uniform Health-Care Decisions Act does not impair a guardianship, living will, durable power of attorney, right-to-die statement or declaration or other advance directive for health-care decisions that is in effect before July 1, 1995.

C. Any advance directive, durable power of attorney for heath care decisions, living will, right-to-die statement or declaration or similar document that is executed in another state or jurisdiction in compliance with the laws of that state or jurisdiction shall be deemed valid and enforceable in this state to the same extent as if it were properly made in this state.

## § 24-7A-17. Short title

Sections 1 through 17 of this act may be cited as the "Uniform Health-Care Decisions Act."

## § 24-7A-18. Severability

If any provision of the Uniform Health-Care Decisions Act or its application to any person or circumstance is held invalid, the invalidity does not affect other provisions or applications of that act which can be given effect without the invalid provision or application, and to this end the provisions of that act are severable.